MCSA

Microsoft Windows

Complete Study Guide

MCSA
Microsoft® Windows® 8.1
Complete Study Guide

Jeffrey R. Shapiro

Darril Gibson

Senior Acquisitions Editor: Kenyon Brown
Development Editor: Amy Breguet
Technical Editors: Ed Tittle and Troy McMillan
Production Editor: Christine O'Connor
Copy Editor: Elizabeth Welch
Editorial Manager: Mary Beth Wakefield
Production Manager: Kathleen Wisor
Associate Publisher: Jim Minatel
Media Supervisor: Richard Graves
Book Designers: Judy Fung and Bill Gibson
Proofreader: Nancy Bell
Indexer: Ted Laux
Project Coordinator, Cover: Brent Savage
Cover Designer: Wiley
Cover Image: Wiley

To my wife Esther, who reminds me how much better life is when you share it with someone you love. God willing, we will spend another 20 years together in love and in learning.

Acknowledgments

Books of this size and depth succeed because of the hard work of a full team of professionals. I'm grateful for all the hard work put in by several people at Sybex on this project. I would like to first thank Jeff Kellum and Kenyon Brown, my acquisitions editors, for believing I could write this book for Sybex, and also for their support and for making sense of the complicated business of book publishing. Amy Breguet was a great developmental editor; she helped keep things on track and provided excellent editorial guidance. A big thanks goes to Elizabeth Welch, who copyedited the book, and Christine O'Connor, who guided the book through production. The technical editors, Ed Tittell, Andrew Bettany, and Troy McMillan provided insightful input throughout the book.

About the Authors

Jeffrey R. Shapiro, MSCD, MCT, MCSE, MCITP, has been involved with Microsoft in infrastructure — servers, desktops and networks — and software for more than 20 years. He has taught many courses on MCSE (NT 4.0, Windows Server 2000–2012), MCITP (Windows XP, Windows 8 and 8.1, SQL Server, IIS, Active Directory and more), MCSD (Visual Basic, C#, ASP, ASP.NET and the .NET Framework), networking fundamentals, and network security. Jeffrey has authored, coauthored, or contributed on more than 20 IT books.

Darril Gibson is a veteran trainer who holds Microsoft, CompTIA, and (ISC)2 certifications. He has authored or coauthored more than 30 books.

Contents at a Glance

Contents

Table of Exercises

Introduction

Windows is the number-one desktop operating system worldwide. Microsoft has created two major exams for Windows 8.1:

- 70-687: Microsoft Certified Technology Specialist (MCSA): Windows 8.1, Configuration

- 70-688: Microsoft Certified Professional (Pro): Windows 8.1, Enterprise Desktop Administrator

 You can view the objectives for each of these exams with the following links: troyhttps://www.microsoft.com/learning/en-us/exam-70-687.aspx and https://www.microsoft.com/learning/en-us/exam-70-687.aspx

The exams are designed to measure your skill and ability to implement, administer, and troubleshoot computers running all editions of Windows 8.1. Microsoft not only tests you on your knowledge of the desktop operating system, but also has developed questions on the exams to force you to apply your knowledge to work out solutions in the same way you would when presented with real-life problems. Passing these exams demonstrates your competency in administration and support. In these challenging economic times, keeping ahead of the competition—standing out among your colleagues—can make a big difference in whether you gain a promotion or possibly keep your job instead of being the one who gets laid off. Or maybe this is your first attempt at certification because you've decided to venture into a new career in IT. You've realized that getting into the IT sector is smart because the demand for knowledgeable professionals in this dynamic field will only intensify dramatically.

This book covers all the objectives to help you develop the specific core competencies that you need to master as a desktop support specialist. You should be able to pass the exam by learning the material in this book without taking a class.

Who Should Read This Book

This book was written for two primary audiences:

Administrators on the Job This book is primarily written for administrators who need to install, deploy, and support Windows 8.1. It's intended to be an on-the-job reference book to help real-world administrators support Windows 8.1 from a desktop administrator or desktop support technician perspective.

Exam Takers   This book covers all of the objectives for the core 70-687 and 70-688 exams as well as the upgrade exam 70-689. If you're studying for either of the two core exams, this book is an excellent supplement to other exam materials. It can help you master the objectives so that you will pass either of these exams the first time you take it.

What You Need

This book leads you through the paces of managing and supporting Windows 8.1. It includes many exercises that require you to have Windows 8.1 installed on your system.

What Is Covered in This Book

MCSA Windows 8.1 Complete Study Guide: Exams 70-687, 70-688, and 70-689 is organized to provide the knowledge you'll need to support Windows 8.1. It includes the following chapters:

Chapter 1: Introducing Windows 8.1   This chapter provides an overview of important new user interface elements first introduced in Windows 8, including the Start screen and its tiles and charms. You'll learn how a Windows Live account is used to streamline the use of Microsoft cloud-based services. You'll also learn about picture passwords and other forms of user authentication. Finally, you'll find out about two important administrator tools: the command prompt and Windows PowerShell. Many of the questions covered by the exam are related to commands executed with these tools.

Chapter 2: Planning the Windows 8.1 Installation   This chapter covers the features and capabilities of the versions of Windows 8.1 as well as the specific hardware requirements for each version. You'll learn how to perform a clean installation of Windows 8.1 and upgrade from a Windows 7 or Windows 8 installation. Windows 8.1 deployment strategies for larger enterprises are also covered, as well as issues related to Windows To Go, virtualization, booting from a virtual hard disk (VHD) file, and multiboot systems.

Chapter 3: Installing Windows 8.1   This chapter provides more details on Windows 8.1 installation topics, including using Windows To Go to install the operating system on an external USB drive and creating a virtual hard disk for a Windows 8.1 installation. You'll learn about managing user settings and data with local, remote, and mandatory profiles and how Windows Easy Transfer can be used to streamline setting and data migration for single users. You'll also find out how the User State Migration Tool's loadstate and scanstate commands can simplify installations and upgrades for multiple users by automatically migrating user settings and data to the new operating system.

Chapter 4: Using Virtualization Technologies   This chapter covers virtualization capabilities that allow you to run one or more virtual machines (VMs) on a single physical host computer. You'll review the requirements for Hyper-V and work through several exercises related to virtual network creation. These exercises will provide you with a virtual environment where you can experiment with Windows 8.1 without modifying your primary installation. This chapter also covers the design basics for a virtual application strategy, including using an App-V server to stream virtual applications or using Remote Desktop Services to host virtual desktops or RemoteApp applications.

Chapter 5: Networking   This chapter explains the basics of networking with Windows 8.1 clients. You'll learn about IPv4 and IPv6 addresses and how DNS resolves computer names to IP addresses. Then you'll move on to troubleshooting DNS and other networking issues with ipconfig, nslookup, and ping. You'll also learn about private, public, and domain network profiles; wireless network settings and security; and how to configure HomeGroups. Lastly, you'll find out about built-in diagnostics and command-line tools that can be used to troubleshoot connectivity issues.

Chapter 6: Windows Firewall and Remote Access   This chapter begins by describing how the Windows 8.1 Firewall can be used to protect a computer from network attacks. You'll learn how to configure firewall settings and how to set up Windows Firewall with Advanced Security. Next, you'll learn about Windows 8.1 remote management tools, including Remote Assistance, Remote Desktop, VPN connections, DirectAccess, Windows PowerShell, and BranchCache. You'll also find out about synchronizing mobile devices with a computer via Sync Center.

Chapter 7: Managing Windows 8.1 in a Domain   This chapter covers the management of devices in a domain. It describes the difference between workgroups and domains, explains how to manage Windows 8.1 in a domain, and provides instruction on how to set up domain authentication and authorization. You'll learn how to use Group Policies to manage users and computers within a domain and how to use the Group Policy Management Console (GPMC) to configure Group Policy settings.

Chapter 8: Users and Groups   This chapter covers some of the most critical network management tasks performed by Windows 8.1 administrators. You'll read about the different types of Windows 8.1 users and accounts and then learn how to set up users to log on locally or through Active Directory; how to create and manage new users and groups; and how to apply security using local and Group Policy objects. You'll also learn how to use policies to manage user accounts, user rights, and security options.

Chapter 9: Managing Security   This chapter continues with the topic of user and group account management and also covers the important topic of security. You'll learn how to use policies to manage user accounts, user rights, and security options. This chapter describes the Group Policy Results Tool, which helps determine which Group Polices will be applied to a computer or user, and the Action Center, which allows you to monitor and configure critical security settings from a central location. Other Windows 8.1 security options, including SmartScreen, SecureBoot, multifactor authentication, smart cards, and BitLocker Drive Encryption, are covered. This chapter also discusses the relationship between NTFS security and shared permissions on folders.

Chapter 10: Managing Files and Disks on Windows 8.1   This chapter covers file and folder management using the Windows 8.1 filesystem. You'll learn how to configure and customize folder sharing; then you'll learn out how to configure OneDrive cloud storage and find out more about how it has been integrated into the operating system. This chapter also covers the benefits of HomeGroups for home networks and explains how to set one up. Finally, you'll learn how to implement best practices for folder security using folder options and NTFS permissions.

Chapter 11: Managing Windows 8.1 Hardware and Printers   This chapter focuses on the management of hardware resources such as printers, keyboards, monitors, and pointing devices for Windows 8.1 computers. You'll learn how to install, manage, and troubleshoot hardware device drivers. This chapter also provides details on setting up printers for both stand-alone systems and networks and on configuring and managing printer drivers for network environments.

Chapter 12: Monitoring System Performance and Recovery   This chapter covers system monitoring and troubleshooting tools that are available in Windows 8.1. The first of these tools is Task Manager, which has been enhanced to be more accessible in Windows 8/8.1. You'll learn how to configure and use Task Manager for performance monitoring and to terminate unresponsive applications. You'll also learn about Event Viewer, a tool that allows you to view Windows 8.1 event logs. Another important tool covered in this chapter is Performance Monitor, which allows you to access information about computer and hardware resource performance. This chapter also explains how System Recovery can help return Windows 8.1 to a stable configuration following system crashes.

Chapter 13: Recovery and Backup Options   This chapter builds on the System Recovery information provided in the previous chapter. You'll learn about System Protection and find out how to create restore points for System Restore. You'll also learn about refreshing and resetting Windows 8.1 and how to use File History to back up and restore data.

Chapter 14: Installing and Configuring Applications   With the arrival of Windows 8.1, all the various types of apps and applications are easy to use and very efficient. The operating system is designed to use so-called "live" tiles on the phone or tablet Start screen. These tiles are also part and parcel of the desktop operating system running on workstations and laptops. The Windows Store is a place online where you can search for, download, and install all Windows 8.1 apps. You can search for an app in a variety of ways, and once you find the app you want, it's easy to install it on the computer so you can start using it immediately. Windows Intune can also be used to sideload and manage applications.

Appendix A includes the answers to the Review Questions at the end of chapters.

What's Included in the Book

I've included several study learning tools throughout the book, which will help you prepare for the exams:

Assessment Test   At the end of this introduction is an Assessment Test that you can use to check your readiness for the exam. Take this test before you start reading the book; it will help you determine the areas you might need to brush up on. The answers to these questions appear on a separate page after the last question of the test. Each answer includes an explanation and a note telling you the chapter in which the material appears.

Objective Map and Opening List of Objectives   A detailed exam objective map shows you where each of the exam objectives is covered in this book. In addition, each chapter opens with a list of the exam objectives it covers. Use these to see exactly where each of the exam topics is covered.

Exam Essentials   Each chapter, just after the summary, includes a number of Exam Essentials. These are the key topics from the chapter that you should focus on when preparing for the exam.

Review Questions   To test your knowledge as you progress through the book, review questions appear at the end of each chapter. As you finish each chapter, answer the review questions and then check your answers—the correct answers and explanations are in Appendix A. You can go back to reread the section that deals with any questions you got wrong to ensure that you answer correctly the next time you're tested on the material.

Interactive Online Learning Environment and Test Bank

The interactive online learning environment that accompanies *MCSA Windows 8.1 Complete Study Guide: Exams 70-687, 70-688, and 70-689* provides a test bank with study tools to help you prepare for the certification exam—and increase your chances of passing it the first time! The test bank includes the following:

Sample Tests   All of the questions in this book are provided, including the Assessment Test, which you'll find at the end of this introduction, and the Review Questions at the end of each chapter. In addition, there are two Practice Exams. Use these questions to test your knowledge of the study guide material. The online test bank runs on multiple devices.

Flashcards   Questions are provided in digital flashcard format (a question followed by a single correct answer). You can use the flashcards to reinforce your learning and provide last-minute test prep before the exam.

Other Study Tools   A glossary of key terms from this book and their definitions are available as a fully searchable PDF.

Go to http://sybextestbanks.wiley.com to register and gain access to this interactive online learning environment and test bank with study tools.

How to Use This Book

If you want a solid foundation for the purpose of preparing for the MCSA Windows 8.1 exams, this book is loaded with valuable information. You will get the most out of your study time if you understand how I put the book together. Here's a list that describes how to approach studying:

1. Take the Assessment Test immediately following this introduction. (The answers are at the end of the test, but no peeking!) It's okay if you don't know any of the answers— that's what this book is for. Carefully read over the explanations for any question you get wrong, and make note of the chapters where that material is covered.

2. Study each chapter carefully, making sure you fully understand the information and the exam objectives listed at the beginning of each one. Again, pay extra-close attention to any chapter that includes material covered in questions you missed on the Assessment Test.

3. Answer all the Review Questions related to each chapter. Specifically note any questions that confuse you, and study the corresponding sections of the book again. And don't just skim these questions—make sure you understand each answer completely.

4. Try your hand at the Practice Exams. Review the answers to the questions you missed to help focus your study.

5. Test yourself using all the electronic flashcards. This is a brand-new and updated flashcard program to help you prepare for the latest MCSA Windows 8.1 exams, and it is a really great study tool.

Learning the material in this book is going to require applying yourself with a good measure of discipline. So try to set aside the same time period every day to study, and select a comfortable and quiet place to do so. If you work hard, you will be surprised at how quickly you learn this material.

How to Contact the Author

I welcome feedback from you about this book or about books you'd like to see from me in the future. You can reach me by writing to jshapiro@codetimes.com. For more information about my work, please visit my website at misiq.com or search "Jeffrey Shapiro" on Amazon.com.

Exams 70-687, 70-688, and 70-689 Objectives Map

Objective	Chapter
Exam 70-687: Configuring Windows 8.1	
1. Install and upgrade to Windows 8.1	
Evaluate hardware readiness and compatibility	Chapter 2
Choose between an upgrade and a clean installation	
Determine which SKU to use, including Windows RT	
Determine requirements for particular features, including Hyper-V, Miracast display, pervasive device encryption, virtual smart cards, and Secure Boot	
Install Windows 8.1	Chapters 2, 3
Install as Windows To Go	
Migrate from previous versions of Windows to Windows 8.1	
Upgrade from Windows 7 or Windows 8 to Windows 8.1	
Install to VHD	
Install additional Windows features	
Configure Windows for additional languages	
Migrate and configure user data	Chapters 3, 8
Migrate user profiles	
Configure folder location	
Configure profiles, including profile version, local, roaming, and mandatory	
2. Configure hardware and applications	
Configure devices and device drivers	Chapter 11
Install, update, disable, and roll back drivers	
Resolve driver issues	
Configure driver settings, including signed and unsigned drivers	
Manage driver packages	
Install and configure desktop apps and Windows Store apps	Chapter 14
Install and repair applications by using Windows Installer	
Configure default program settings	
Modify file associations	
Manage access to Windows Store	

Objective	Chapter
Control access to local hardware and applications	Chapter 14
Configure application restrictions, including Software Restriction Policies and AppLocker; Manage installation of and access to removable devices	
Configure Assigned Access	
Configure Internet Explorer 11 and Internet Explorer for the desktop	Chapter 9
Configure compatibility view	
Configure Internet Explorer 11 settings, including add-ons, downloads, security, and privacy	
Configure Hyper-V	Chapter 4
Create and configure virtual machines, including integration services;	
Create and manage checkpoints	
Create and configure virtual switches	
Create and configure virtual disks	
Move a virtual machine's storage	

3. Configure network connectivity

Configure IP settings	Chapter 5
Configure name resolution	
Connect to a network	
Configure network locations	
Configure networking settings	Chapter 5, 11
Connect to a wireless network	
Manage preferred wireless networks	
Configure network adapters	
Configure location-aware printing	
Configure and maintain network security	Chapter 5
Configure Windows Firewall	
Configure Windows Firewall with Advanced Security	
Configure connection security rules (IPsec)	
Configure authenticated exceptions	
Configure network discovery	

Objective	Chapter
Configure remote management	Chapter 3
Choose the appropriate remote management tools	
Configure remote management settings	
Modify settings remotely by using MMCs or Windows PowerShell	
Configure Remote Assistance, including Easy Connect	

4. Configure access to resources

Configure shared resources	Chapter 5, 10, 11
Configure shared folder permissions	
Configure HomeGroup settings	
Configure libraries	
Configure shared printers	
Set up and configure OneDrive	
Configure file and folder access	Chapter 10
Encrypt files and folders by using Encrypting File System (EFS)	
Configure NTFS permissions	
Configure disk quotas	
Configure file access auditing	
Configure authentication and authorization	Chapters
Configure user rights	1, 7, 8
Manage credentials, manage certificates	
Configure biometrics	
Configure picture password	
Configure PIN	
Set up and configure Microsoft account	
Configure virtual smart cards	
Configure authentication in workgroups or domains	
Configure User Account Control (UAC) behavior	

5. Configure remote access and mobility

Configure remote connections	Chapter 6
Configure remote authentication	
Configure Remote Desktop settings	
Configure virtual private network (VPN) connections and authentication	
Enable VPN reconnect	
Configure broadband tethering	

Objective	Chapter
Perform a driver rollback	
Perform a refresh or recycle	
Configure restore points	
Configure file recovery options	Chapter 13
Restore previous versions of files and folders	
Configure file history	
Recover files from OneDrive	

Exam 70-688: Supporting Windows 8.1

1. Support operating system and application installation

Support operating system installation	Chapter 2
Support Windows To Go	
Manage boot settings, including native virtual hard disk (VHD) and multiboot	
Manage desktop images	
Customize a Windows installation by using Windows Preinstallation Environment (PE)	
Support desktop apps	Chapter 4
Desktop app compatibility using Application Compatibility Toolkit (ACT), including shims and compatibility database	
Desktop application co-existence using Hyper-V, RemoteApp, and App-V	
Installation and configuration of User Experience Virtualization (UE-V)	
Deploy desktop apps by using Windows Intune	
Support Windows Store and cloud apps	Chapter 14
Install and manage software by using Office 365 and Windows Store apps	
Sideload apps by using Windows Intune	
Sideload apps into online and offline images	
Deep link apps by using Windows Intune	
Integrate Microsoft account, including personalization settings and Trusted PC	

Objective	Chapter
2. Support resource access	

Support network connectivity — Chapters 5, 6

IPv4 and IPv6, including transition technologies; names resolution, including Peer Name Resolution Protocol (PNRP) and Domain Name System Security Extensions (DNSSECs)

Wireless networks and connections

Network security, including Windows Firewall and IP security

Support remote access — Chapter 6

Virtual private network (VPN), including Connection Manager Administration Kit (CMAK)

Remote Desktop Protocol (RDP), including Remote Desktop Services Gateway access

DirectAccess

Remote administration

Network Access Protection (NAP)

Support authentication and authorization — Chapters 6, 7, 9

Multi-factor authentication, including certificates, virtual smart cards, picture passwords, and biometrics

Workgroup versus domain

Homegroup

Computer and user authentication, including secure channel

Account policies

Credential caching, and Credential Manager

Local account versus Microsoft account

Workplace Join

Support data storage — Chapter 10

Distributed File System (DFS) client, including caching settings

Storage spaces, including capacity and fault tolerance

Optimizing data access by using BranchCache

OneDrive

Support data security — Chapter 10

Permissions, including share, NTFS, and Dynamic Access Control (DAC)

Encrypting File System (EFS), including Data Recovery Agent

Access to removable media

BitLocker and BitLocker To Go, including Data Recovery Agent and Microsoft BitLocker Administration and Monitoring (MBAM)

Objective	Chapter
3. Support Windows clients and devices	
Support operating system and hardware	Chapters 6, 11
Resolve hardware and device issues, including STOP errors and Reliability Monitor	
Optimize performance by using Windows Performance Toolkit (WPT), including Xperf.exe, Xbootmgr.exe, XperfView.exe, and Windows Performance Recorder (WPR)	
Monitor performance by using Data Collector Sets, Task Manager, and Resource Monitor	
Monitor and manage printers, including NFC Tap-to-Pair and printer sharing	
Remediate startup issues by using the Diagnostics and Recovery Toolkit (DaRT)	
Support mobile devices	Chapters 6, 11
Support mobile device policies, including security policies, remote access, and remote wipe	
Support mobile access and data synchronization, including Work Folders and Sync Center	
Support broadband connectivity, including broadband tethering and metered networks	
Support Mobile Device Management by using Windows Intune, including Windows RT, Windows Phone 8, iOS, and Android	
Support client compliance	Chapter 9
Manage updates by using Windows Update and Windows Intune, including non-Microsoft updates	
Manage client security by using Windows Defender, Windows Intune Endpoint Protection, or Microsoft System Center 2012 Endpoint Protection	
Manage Internet Explorer 11 security	
Support Group Policy application, including Resultant Set of Policy (RSoP), policy processing, and Group Policy caching	
Manage clients by using Windows Intune	Chapters 8, 14
Manage user and computer groups	
Configure monitoring and alerts	
Manage policies	
Manage remote computers	

Assessment Test

1. What charm can be used to add Administrative Tools items to the Start screen?
    A. Devices
    B. Search
    C. Share
    D. Settings

2. A Windows 8.1 user is pressing Windows logo key+. (period) to snap an app to the screen location, but this is not working. What is the most likely reason?
    A. Apps are snapped to the screen with Windows logo key+S.
    B. Apps are snapped to the screen with Windows logo key+I.
    C. The screen resolution isn't at least 1024×768.
    D. Apps are snapped to the screen with the Windows logo key+. / and then by using the arrow keys to snap the application to a screen location.

3. Of the following choices, what accurately describes the differences between authentication and authorization? (Choose all that apply.)
    A. Users prove an identity with authentication.
    B. Users prove an identity with authorization.
    C. Authorization methods are used to grant users access to resources.
    D. Authentication methods are used to grant users access to resources.

4. A home user plans on purchasing a Windows 8.1 computer. He wants to use it to create a virtual network using Client Hyper-V. Which Windows version should he choose?
    A. Windows 8.1 Pro 32-bit
    B. Windows 8.1 Pro 64-bit
    C. Windows 8.1 Enterprise 32-bit
    D. Windows 8.1 Enterprise 64-bit

5. A home user wants to be able to join a new Windows 8.1 computer to a domain. What version of Windows is needed?
    A. Windows 8.1
    B. Windows 8.1 Pro
    C. Windows 8.1 Enterprise
    D. Windows 8.1 RT

6. What is the maximum amount of RAM that can be recognized by Windows 8.1 Pro? (Choose all that apply.)
    A. 4 GB on 32-bit systems
    B. 128 GB on 32-bit systems

  C. 128 GB on 64-bit systems

  D. 512 GB on 64-bit systems

7. You need to install a 64-bit edition of Windows 8.1 on a computer currently running a 32-bit edition of Windows 7. You do not want the Windows 7 files on the computer when you complete the installation. What should you do?

  A. Perform an upgrade to Windows 8.1 and do not modify existing partitions.

  B. Perform a custom installation of Windows 8.1 and do not modify existing partitions.

  C. Perform an upgrade to Windows 8.1 and delete existing partitions during the installation.

  D. Perform a custom installation of Windows 8.1 and delete existing partitions during the installation.

8. A computer is currently running Windows 7 Professional. The user wants to upgrade it to Windows 8.1 Pro. Which of the following methods can be used? (Choose all that apply.)

  A. Start the computer from the Windows 8.1 installation DVD.

  B. Start the computer normally, and run the startup program from the installation DVD.

  C. Copy the files on the installation DVD to a network share and run the startup program from the share.

  D. Use the startup program to partition the disk and install Windows 8.1 on the new partition.

9. A user has a Windows To Go workspace on a portable USB system. It automatically boots to Windows To Go on her work computer. Her home computer runs Windows 7 by default but does not boot to Windows To Go. What is the most likely solution?

  A. Modify the Windows To Go boot settings in Windows 7.

  B. Modify the Windows To Go boot settings in Windows 8.1.

  C. Modify the BIOS settings on her home computer.

  D. Install Windows 8.1 on her home computer.

10. You are running a 32-bit edition of Windows 8.1 Pro and decide to enable Hyper-V to add some virtual machines. However, you are not able to enable it. What is the most likely reason?

  A. Your computer doesn't have enough RAM.

  B. Hyper-V is not supported on 32-bit systems.

  C. Hyper-V is only supported on server products.

  D. Hyper-V is not supported on Windows 8.1 Pro.

11. You are running a 64-bit edition of Windows 8.1 Pro with 3 GB of RAM and decide to enable Hyper-V to add some virtual machines. What will you need to do first?

  A. Start the Programs and Features applet.

  B. Upgrade to Windows 8.1 Enterprise.

  C. Create a virtual switch.

  D. Add more RAM.

12. A user needs to run an application that isn't compatible with Windows 8.1 and the application needs to access a server on the network. You install the application within a Hyper-V VM, but the application fails when it tries to connect to the server. Of the following choices, what is the most likely problem?

   A. The application is not compatible with Windows 8.1.

   B. The application is not compatible with Hyper-V.

   C. The virtual switch is not set to Network.

   D. The virtual switch is not set to External.

13. You are troubleshooting a computer that is having connectivity issues. You use `ipconfig` and determine that it has an address of 169.254.4.7. What is the problem?

   A. DNS is not working.

   B. DHCP is not working.

   C. The network location is set to private.

   D. The network location is set to public.

14. Your network uses IPv6 addresses. Of the following choices, what is a valid IPv6 address?

   A. 2000 : 0021 : 4137 : 0000 : 006C : 0000 : 01E5

   B. 2000 : 0021 : 0 : 4137 : 0 : 6C : 0 : 0 : 1E5

   C. 2000 : 21 : 4137 : 0 : 6C :: 1E5

   D. 2000 : 21 : 4137 :: 6C :: 1E5

15. Your organization includes over 100 computers configured in a domain. What would these computers use for name resolution?

   A. DHCP

   B. DNS

   C. Domain controller

   D. WINS

16. You suspect that the DNS resolver cache has incorrect entries. What can you use to remove the entries?

   A. Use `ipconfig`.

   B. Use `nslookup`.

   C. Use `ping`.

   D. Disable DHCP.

17. You have Windows Firewall set to restrict all incoming traffic except for web traffic. You would like to set up a rule to allow a specific type of network service, such as FTP transfers. Which of the following rules would be recommended for this situation?

   A. Protocol

   B. Program

   C. Port

   D. IPsec

18. You are researching to see if Windows Firewall is adequate to protect your computer from attacks. Which of the following are the types of packet information analyzed by Windows Firewall?

A. Source IP address of the packet

B. Destination IP address

C. TCP/UDP port number

D. All of the above

19. Your company wants to allow remote users to access the company's internal network in a secure way. Which of the following would allow users to connect to the internal network?

A. Remote Assistance

B. AppLocker

C. PowerShell

D. VPN

20. You install Windows 8.1 on a stand-alone computer. You then connect that computer to a network. What is the default network configuration for the new computer on the network?

A. Domain

B. Workgroup

C. Both A and B

D. Neither A nor B

21. You are assigned as the network administrator for your company and you have multiple servers and 100+ client computers running Microsoft Windows 8.1. You want to make a change so that you turn off the Windows Store feature on all client computers. What is the most efficient method for doing so?

A. Registry Editor

B. Group Policy Management Console

C. Domain Control Security Policy

D. Terminal Servers Configuration tool

22. Which of the following Group Policy nodes lets you deploy applications to clients?

A. Administrative Settings

B. Windows Settings

C. Configuration Settings

D. Software Settings

23. After choosing a naming convention for user accounts that works, based on First Name + Last Name, the executive officers decide they want to change the naming convention to Last Name + First Name. Do you have to delete all the user accounts and start again?

A. Yes, once the accounts are created the name cannot be changed because it is associated with a security identifier (SID).

B. Yes, usernames are remembered by network resources.

C. No, but you need to change the security identifier.

D. No, when you change the username it affects nothing on the network because only the SID is associated with network resources.

24. Rick has been added to the Administrators group, but you suspect that he is abusing his administrative privileges. He only really needs permission to view event information and schedule logging of performance counters. To which group or groups should you add Rick so that he can do his job but will have the minimum level of administrative rights? (Choose all that apply.)

A. Administrators

B. Power Users

C. Event Log Readers

D. Performance Log Users

E. Performance Monitor Users

25. You are logged on as a member of the Administrators group on a Windows 8.1 computer. You are adding a new user account to the computer. You want to create a temporary password that the user must change, and you want to ensure that the account is enabled. Which of the following options should you configure? (Choose all that apply.)

A. User Must Change Password At Next Logon

B. User Cannot Change Password

C. Password Never Expires

D. Account Is Disabled

26. You have a user who has access to the applications folder on your network server. This user belongs to the following groups:

NTFS

Sales	Read only
Marketing	Full Control

Shared Permissions

Sales	Read only
Marketing	Change

When this user logs into the applications folder from their Windows 8.1 machine, what are their effective permissions?

A. Full Control

B. Read only

C. Change

D. Read and Write

27. You are setting up a machine for a home user who does not know much about computers. You do not want to make the user a local administrator, but you do want to give this user the right to change Windows Update manually. How can you configure this?

A. Modify the LGPO for Windows Update to allow the user to make changes manually.

B. Explain to the user how to log on as the Administrator account.

C. Set Windows Update modifications to anyone.

D. This can't be done. Only administrators can change Windows Update.

28. You are the administrator for a large organization with multiple Windows Server 2012 R2 domain controllers and multiple domains. You have a Windows 8.1 machine that is set up for all users to access. You have an application called StellApp.exe that everyone on this Windows 8.1 computer can use except for the sales group. How do you stop the sales group from accessing this one application?

A. Deny the Everyone group the rights to the application.

B. Create an executable rule from the Application Control Policy.

C. Create a security role from the Application Control Policy.

D. Give the Everyone group full control to the application.

29. You have a Windows 8.1 machine that multiple users access. All users have the rights to use USB removable devices but you need to deny one user from using USB removable devices. How do you accomplish this?

A. Deny the one user from using the machine.

B. Set a USB rule on Hardware Manager.

C. Deny all users from using USB devices.

D. Create a removable storage access policy through an LGPO.

30. Which of the following describes the purpose of a driver signature?

A. To identify the driver in the driver folder

B. To verify the integrity of the driver

C. To verify the identity of the device

D. To prevent software piracy

31. You installed a new video driver on a user's laptop, but when the user docks his laptop to an external monitor, the laptop display is duplicated on the external monitor. What should you do to make both the laptop screen and the external monitor behave like one monitor?

A. Press the F+M button on the laptop.

B. Install a second video card in the laptop.

C. Open the Charms bar, click/tap on Devices, click Project, and then click Extend.

D. Run the DisplayExtend /switch command.

32. Which of the following approaches cannot be used to add a driver package to an image?

    A. On an offline Windows image by using DISM

    B. During an automated deployment by using Windows Setup and an answer file

    C. After deployment on a running operating system by using PnPUtil

    D. On an online Windows image by using DISM

33. Your computer's application has stopped responding. What should you do?

    A. Run Event Viewer.

    B. Start backing up like crazy.

    C. Press Ctrl+Alt+Del and then click Task Manager.

    D. Restart the computer.

34. Your user tells you that an application is working but the label printer he is using is not working when the application attempts to print labels. What is the first thing you should do to find the problem?

    A. Restart the label printer.

    B. Restart the application.

    C. Buy a new label printer.

    D. Look in the event log for an error.

35. You manage to get Task Manager started but every time you click on an application Task Manager disappears and you waste time trying to find it under the many applications running. What is the best way to make sure you always have Task Manager in easy reach?

    A. Start a second computer and run Task Manager from it, connecting remotely.

    B. Pin Task Manager to the status bar.

    C. Right-click in any area of Task Manager and select Always On Top.

    D. Simply restart Task Manager.

36. You are tasked with getting a machine up and running as quickly as possible, but it's taking too long for Task Manager to update information and you need instant data after each time you tweak something on the machine. How would you configure Task Manager to give you instant information?

    A. Task Manager updates every 4 seconds and you can't change that.

    B. Click on the View tab and select Update Now.

    C. Grab a beer and wait a few more seconds.

    D. On the View tab, choose Manual Update.

37. You are asked to set up System Protection on users' computers. What are your first steps?

    A. Open Control Panel and select System Protection.

    B. Press Ctrl+Alt+Del and select System Protection.

    C. Invoke the Charms bar, select Search, enter **System Protection**, and then click Settings.

    D. Restart the computer and press F8 until System Protection appears.

38. How much space should you reserve on your computer for System Protection to do its work?

   A. Nothing. System Protection saves to network locations.

   B. You need at least a gigabyte on the local hard disk

   C. System Protection should have 500 MB on a USB hard drive.

   D. You need at least 300 MB for each volume.

39. If the restore point failed to make any difference, what is your next step?

   A. Use the Refresh PC option.

   B. Reinstall Windows 8.1 from installation media.

   C. Use the Undo The Restore Operation feature.

   D. Try a few more times and then call technical support.

40. Your company has decided to migrate to Windows 8.1 from Windows 7. You are asked to ensure that all applications needed by the users are migrated to the new operating system. What are your first steps to migrate the applications?

   A. Have every user list the applications they need.

   B. Connect to Microsoft and run the Application Migration Utility (AMU).

   C. Remove all the applications before upgrading the machines.

   D. Use Microsoft Application Compatibility Toolkit (ACT) to check for application compatibility.

Answers to Assessment Test

1. D. You can add the Administrative Tools items from the Settings charm (after pressing Windows logo key+C). You cannot add these tools from the Devices, Search, or Share charms.

2. D. The shortcut to snap apps is Windows logo key+. / (period), not Windows logo key+S / or Windows logo key+I. Then you can use an arrow key or your mouse to snap the app.

3. A, C. Users claim an identity with a user account and prove the identity by providing credentials such as a password. If the username credential is accurate, the user is authenticated. Authenticated users are given authorized access to resources by granting them permissions.

4. B. Client Hyper-V will work only on 64-bit editions of Windows 8.1 and is supported only on Windows 8.1 Pro and Windows 8.1 Enterprise. It will not work on 32-bit editions, and home users cannot purchase Windows 8.1 Enterprise.

5. B. Windows 8.1 Pro and Windows 8.1 Enterprise both support joining the computer to a domain, but only Windows 8.1 Pro is available to home users. The basic versions of Windows 8.1 and Windows 8.1 RT do not support joining a computer to a domain.

6. A, D. Windows 8.1 Pro supports 4 GB on 32-bit systems and 512 GB on 64-bit systems. This is the same for Windows 8.1 Enterprise. None of the 32-bit versions support more than 4 GB. The basic edition of Windows 8.1 supports a maximum of 128 GB on 64-bit systems.

7. D. You should perform a custom installation, which installs Windows 8.1 by itself, and delete the existing partitions during the installation. You cannot upgrade a 32-bit edition of Windows 7 to a 64-bit edition of Windows 8.1. If you do not modify the existing partitions, the Windows 7 files will remain on the system in a `Windows.old` folder.

8. A, B, C. Starting the computer from the installation DVD and selecting Upgrade: Install Windows and Keep Files, Settings, And Applications will upgrade Windows 7 Professional to Windows 8.1 Pro. It's also possible to start the startup program from within Windows 7 (either from the installation DVD or a network share) and select Upgrade. If the partitions are modified during the installation, it will delete the data on the disk and only a clean installation is possible.

9. C. The BIOS on the user's home computer should be modified to boot to the USB drive when it is inserted. Windows 7 doesn't have the option of modifying the Windows To Go boot settings. Modifying the boot settings in the Windows To Go workspace only affects the computer where it is installed and so cannot be done on the home computer until it can boot into the Windows To Go workspace. It is not necessary to install Windows 8.1 on the home computer.

10. B. Hyper-V is not supported on 32-bit systems but is supported on 64-bit systems. You need a minimum of 4 GB of RAM, but it's not clear how much RAM the computer in the scenario is using. Client Hyper-V can be installed on 64-bit Windows 8.1 Pro and Windows 8.1 Enterprise editions.

11. D. Hyper-V requires a minimum of 4 GB of RAM, so you'll need to add RAM first. Hyper-V is enabled through the Programs and Features applet, but you won't be able to enable it with only 3 GB of RAM. It is not necessary to upgrade to Windows 8.1 Enterprise because Hyper-V is supported on Windows 8.1 Pro. You can create a virtual switch only after Hyper-V is enabled on a system.

12. D. The most likely problem is that the virtual switch for the VM is not set to External. If it is set to Internal or Private, it will not have access to the network and won't be able to connect to the server. An application running within a VM doesn't have to be compatible with Windows 8.1. It only needs to be compatible with the operating system running in the VM. If the operating system is compatible with Hyper-V, the application within the operating system is also compatible with Hyper-V. Virtual switches do not have a Network setting.

13. B. An address starting with 169.254 is an APIPA address, and a DHCP client assigns itself an APIPA address when it doesn't receive a response from a DHCP server. DNS is used for name resolution and does not assign APIPA addresses. The network location is unrelated to how IP addresses are assigned.

14. C. An IPv6 address includes eight groups of four hexadecimal characters but can be shortened by eliminating leading zeroes and using zero compression with a single set of double colons. Only seven sets of hexadecimal characters without double colons are not valid. Nine sets of characters are not valid. An IPv6 address cannot use two double colons.

15. Answer: B. DNS is used for hostname resolution in a domain. DHCP is used to assign IP addresses. Domain controllers are needed in a domain and DNS is required within a domain, but domain controllers do not provide name resolution. WINS is used for NetBIOS name resolution, but NetBIOS names are used less and less, so a WINS server might not be needed.

16. A. The `ipconfig /flushdns` command can be used to remove entries from the DNS resolver cache. NSlookup can be used to verify if DNS has the correct entries, but it doesn't affect the DNS resolver cache on the local computer. Ping is used to check connectivity. Disabling DHCP won't affect the DNS resolver cache.

17. C. A port rule would enable you to specify the port number (such as port 20 and port 21 for FTP transfers). To set up the port rule, you use Windows Firewall with Advanced Security and specify that you want to create a new inbound rule.

18. D. Windows Firewall analyzes the source IP of the packet, destination IP address, TCP/UDP port number, and other items.

19. D. VPNs, or virtual private networks, allow users to access private networks while connecting from an outside network, such as the Internet. Remote Assistance is used to allow a user to connect to one client computer. AppLocker is used to restrict which applications can run on different computers and isn't useful here. PowerShell is a Windows scripting language.

20. B. When you first install Windows 8.1 on a computer, it automatically belongs to a workgroup. If you want it to connect to a domain, you must specify the domain name.

21. B. Group Policy settings can be configured using the Group Policy Management Console in a domain.

22. D. The Software Settings node can be used to deploy software to clients.

23. D. Windows 8.1 uses the SID as the user object. All security settings get associated with the SID and not the user account.

24. C, D. The members of the Event Log Readers group have the ability to read event logs on the local machine. Members of the Performance Log Users group have the ability to schedule logging of performance counters and to enable trace providers.

25. A. To configure a temporary password that the user must change, you can select the User Must Change Password At Next Logon option in the New User dialog box. By configuring this option, users will be required to change their password when they first log on to the computer.

26. C. To figure out a user's rights, you must first add up what their effective NTFS rights are and their effective Shared permissions. Then the most restrictive set takes precedence. So in this example, the user's NTFS rights were Full Control and the Shared permissions were Change, so Change would be the effective permission.

27. A. You do not want this user to have any administrator rights. To allow this user to change Windows Update manually, you must set this in an LGPO.

28. B. Application Control Policy (AppLocker) allows you to configure a Denied list and an Accepted list for applications or users. Applications that are configured on the Denied list will not run on the system or by specific groups, and applications on the Accepted list will operate properly.

29. D. LGPOs are policies that you can set on a local Windows 8.1 machine to limit hardware and user usage. You also have the ability to control individual users within the Local Group Policy.

30. B. A driver that is digitally signed is one that attaches an identifier called a digital signature used to verify the integrity of the driver and to verify the identity of the vendor (software publisher) who provides the driver.

31. C. You can configure an external and a local screen on a laptop to behave as one screen.

32. D. DISM is used to service offline, not online, images.

33. C. When a computer stops responding, the only thing you might still be able to do is start Task Manager. This can best be achieved by pressing Ctrl+Alt+Del to launch the menu option that will allow you to start Task Manager.

34. D. All applications that conform to best practices report errors to the event log. This should be the first place you look to find a reason the device is not working. The event may tell you something bad is wrong, or it could be something simple such as "printer out of paper."

35. C. You can configure Task Manager to always stay on top. That way, if you are busy troubleshooting or managing the computer, Task Manager will not get lost behind other windows. Option D would also work but it would be a hassle if the machine is slow.

36. B. You have several options to change the speed with which Task Manager updates information. To get the latest information, Click on the View tab and select Update Now.

37. C. System Protection is best accessed from the Search feature of the Charms bar.

38. D. Note that you will need at least 300 MB of free space on each volume for restore points. System Protection does not need a lot of space for future multiple restore points and in fact overwrites the old ones that you don't need.

39. C. Your next step is to use the Undo The Restore Operation feature.

40. D. When you run the ACT, it makes an inventory of all the applications on the current system and logs all the information into a local database for you to access.

MCSA

Microsoft Windows™ 8.1
Complete Study Guide

Chapter

1

Introducing Windows 8.1

70-687 MICROSOFT EXAM OBJECTIVES COVERED IN THIS CHAPTER:

✓ **Configure access to resources**

- Configure user rights

- Manage credentials

- Manage certificates

- Configure biometrics

- Configure picture password

- Configure PIN

- Set up and configure Microsoft account

- Configure virtual smart cards

- Configure authentication in workgroups or domains

- Configure User Account Control (UAC) behavior

Windows 8.1 has a significantly different interface than previous Windows versions. New users might take to it quite easily, but for many experienced Windows users it presents some challenges—and frustrations. It includes a Start screen with tiles and charms, but the Desktop is just a keystroke or a mouse click away. In this chapter, you'll learn about the new interface, including some ways to navigate it and reach tools you'll need to do common tasks.

Users prove who they are by authenticating, so it's important to understand the various account types available in Windows 8.1. This chapter includes exercises for creating different account types, including the new Microsoft Live account type. You'll also learn about new picture passwords and the new login PIN feature.

The command prompt and Windows PowerShell are both available in Windows 8.1, and they are required to do many of the tasks covered by the Windows 8.1 exams. PowerShell is much richer than the command prompt, but if you understand how PowerShell commands use the verb-noun format and how to get help, you'll be able to use it for common tasks. In this chapter, you'll learn how to start these tools and execute basic commands.

Navigating Windows 8.1

The Windows 8.1 interface can be a little confusing if you're not used to it. However, once you grasp a few simple concepts it becomes much easier to navigate.

Figure 1.1 shows the Windows 8.1 Start screen with some items highlighted. The username is displayed at the top right, the default tiles and apps are in the center, and some additional tiles and apps are on the right. If you scroll to the right, you'll reveal more apps. At the bottom right, you can see the negative symbol (–), which is the *semantic zoom* icon. This feature is useful when you have tiles that span multiple pages and allows you to quickly select, and move to, another area. You can also access this feature by pressing Ctrl+– (minus key), or by holding the Ctrl key and spinning the mouse wheel.

In addition to what you can see, several features aren't displayed. If you move the mouse to each of the four corners, the additional features appear:

Top Left   When you move your mouse to this corner, Windows displays an icon of a recently used app and also displays one or more tabs on the left edge of the screen. If you move your mouse to one of the tabs, Windows displays a list of icons for other recently opened apps. If other apps are currently open, it displays icons you can select to switch apps.

Bottom Left   This shows the Start button. Clicking it toggles between the traditional desktop and the Start screen. If you right-click the Start button you get the Start button menu, which gives you access to a number of applications and features, usually a list of programs commonly used by technicians. You can also use the Windows logo key on the keyboard to toggle between the Start screen and the Desktop, or between the Start screen and a running app. If you right-click over this display, it shows a preview menu.

FIGURE 1.1   Windows Start screen

 The Windows logo key is between the Ctrl (or FN) and Alt keys on the left of the spacebar on most keyboards. This key is combined with other keys to invoke Windows 8.1 shortcuts.

Top Right   Moving your mouse to this corner displays the Charms bar, allowing you to pick from one of the five charms. You can also display the Charms bar by pressing Windows logo key+C, which also brings up the Time display.

Bottom Right   If you hover over this area, it will also display the Charms bar, similar to hovering over the top-right area. This area also includes the semantic zoom icon.

Using Gestures

Windows 8.1 is designed so that it can work on a tablet, with a touch screen, or with a mouse. If you have a smartphone or tablet device, you are probably familiar with many gestures used on a touch screen. However, if you're not familiar with these gestures, read on. The following list shows common gestures used with Windows 8.1 and how they can be simulated with a mouse and keyboard:

 Two-fingered gestures are commonly done with a finger and a thumb. However, you can also use two fingers if desired.

Tap   You can tap an item by touching it once with your finger. This is similar to a single mouse click.

Press and Hold   This is similar to a tap, but you don't remove your finger. After a moment, a context menu or information box will appear, depending on the item. This is similar to right-clicking with a mouse.

Pinch   You can touch the screen with a finger and thumb and bring them closer together as if you're pinching something between them. This causes the display to zoom in. This works similar to holding down the Ctrl key while spinning the mouse wheel in one direction. If the Start screen is displayed, this action invokes semantic zoom.

Stretch   This is the opposite of pinch. You can zoom out by touching the display with your finger and thumb and spreading them apart. You can also mimic this with the Ctrl key and the mouse wheel by spinning the wheel in the opposite direction.

Rotate   If an item can be rotated, you can place your finger and thumb on the screen and twist your hand either clockwise or counterclockwise. This only works with certain items in certain apps, such as when rotating an image or graphic in a photo-editing app.

Slide to Scroll   If you touch and drag your finger across the screen, it allows you to scroll through the screen. This technique is the same as scrolling with a mouse and can be used to scroll horizontally and/or vertically, depending on what is currently displayed.

Slide to Move   If you touch a movable item, you can keep your finger on the item and move it around the screen. This is similar to dragging an item with the mouse by selecting and holding it with the mouse button. For example, you can rearrange items on the Start screen by using the slide-to-move gesture (or by dragging an item with the mouse button held down).

Swipe to Select   Some items allow you to quickly slide them a short distance and they will bring up different commands. This isn't repeatable with the mouse.

Swipe from Edge   If you swipe your finger from the right edge, it brings up the Charms bar. If you swipe your finger from the left edge, it either shows open apps or allows you to manipulate how the apps are displayed. If you swipe from the top or bottom, it shows additional commands for the current app. You can also close an app by swiping it down to the bottom of the screen.

Using Charms

A significant difference in Windows 8.1 is the use of charms. Instead of the traditional Start menu, Windows 8.1 starts with the Start screen (also called the Start charm). Apps, tools, and utilities are accessed through the Start screen or other charms. The easiest way to bring up the Charms bar is by pressing Windows logo key+C. There are five primary charms:

Start This is the primary display showing the default apps. You can also press the Windows logo key to toggle back and forth between the Start screen and the Desktop or between the Start screen and a running app. As mentioned earlier, clicking the Start button on the bottom left of the screen lets you toggle between Start and Desktop.

Search Selecting this brings up a Search text box. As you type, Windows looks for and displays apps, settings, or files that match the text. If the Start screen is displayed, you can just start typing and the Search charm automatically appears. You can press Windows logo key+F to search for files, Windows logo key+Q to search for apps, or Windows logo key+W for specific settings.

Share The Share charm lets you send links and photos to friends from within certain apps. You can also access the Share charm with Windows logo key+H.

Devices You can use this charm to send files and stream movies to TV, printers, and other devices connected on a network. This is not related to devices managed with the Device Manager. You can also access Devices with Windows logo key+K.

Settings This charm is used to do many basic tasks such as configure the network interface card (NIC), adjust the sound volume or brightness, configure notifications, and turn off or restart the computer. You can select Change PC Settings from here to modify many basic computer settings. You can also open Settings with Windows logo key+I.

It's worth your time to learn how the Search charm works. Using this charm makes it easy to find what you need, and you can start by simply typing from the Start screen. Additionally, the Settings charm is important for Windows 8.1 administrators. It includes a link to the PC Settings tool, which is used in Exercises 1.2 and 1.4, and elsewhere in this book.

Using Tiles

The Start screen includes several icons called *tiles* in Windows 8.1. Tiles can be dynamic and display live information based on the purpose of the underlying app. For example, the Weather tile shows weather for a specific location.

You can drag tiles around the screen to rearrange them. You can also create new groups and organize them in a new group. Exercise 1.1 (later in this chapter) shows how to manipulate some of these tiles.

Using Alt Menus

In traditional Windows applications, you can right-click an item and an alt menu appears. If you do this with items in the Start screen, you'll see menu selections appear on the bottom of the screen. For example, Figure 1.2 shows the alt menu that appears for the Weather tile.

FIGURE 1.2   Alt menu

For this selection, you have the following choices:

Unpin From Start   Select this option to remove the app from the Start screen. You can pin items that are not already pinned to the Start screen by right-clicking over an empty area of the Start screen, selecting All Apps, right-clicking over an app, and selecting Pin To Start.

Uninstall   For some apps, this option will uninstall the app after prompting you to confirm it. For other apps, it launches the Programs And Features Control Panel applet and you can uninstall it from there.

Resize   This option reduces or enlarges the size of the tile on the Start screen. When you click this option, you get a submenu with Large, Wide, Medium, and Small as the tile size choices.

Turn Live Tile Off   This option stops the animation for the tile. The app is still accessible but the icon returns to the default icon.

Using the Start Menu

The Start menu is available by right-clicking the Start icon at the bottom left of the screen. You can see the preview icon by dragging your mouse to the bottom left. When you right-click it, you'll see a display similar to Figure 1.3. These tools are valuable to administrators, and this menu is likely to be popular among many administrators.

You can also access the Start menu by pressing Windows logo key+X.

FIGURE 1.3   Start menu

Showing Administrative Tools

Many administrators will likely want to add the Administrative tools menu to the Start screen. Exercise 1.1 shows how to do this. You'll also learn how to create a tile group and how to organize tiles in the group. This exercise assumes you're logged in and the Start screen is showing.

EXERCISE 1.1

Adding Administrative Tools to the Start Screen

1. Access the Settings charm by pressing Windows logo key+I.

2. Select Tiles. Note that the Tiles selection is not available if you access the Settings charm from the Desktop.

3. The Show Administrative Tools selection appears. Click the icon next to No to change it to Yes.

4. Click a blank area on the Start screen. There is a slight delay before the tools appear. Keep in mind that Windows includes 22 administrative tools and will take up a substantial part of the Start screen when all tools are added.

5. There might be some administrative tools that you don't use. You can follow these steps to remove and add items to the Start screen:

    a. Right-click over ODBC Data Sources. You'll see a check mark indicating this item is selected and the alt menu appears along the bottom of the screen. Select Unpin From Start. Doing so removes the item from the Start screen. You can use this method to remove any items from the Start screen.

    b. Right-click in a blank area of the Start screen. Select All Apps from the lower-right corner.

    c. Right-click over ODBC Data Sources. You'll see a check mark indicating this item is selected and the alt menu appears along the bottom of the screen. Select Pin To Start from the alt menu.

6. The following steps will create a group for Administrative Tools items:

    a. Pin the Performance Monitor, or any other Administrative app, to Start. Click and hold the app's tile, and drag it up but don't release it. Once it's away from the other tiles, drag it to the right. When a white horizontal bar appears, release it. This puts the Performance Monitor in a separate group.

    b. Right-click the tile. It will immediately be checked as selected and allow you to customize the tile and its group.

    c. Select Name Group, which appears above the tile groups, and type **My Tools** in the text box. Your display will look similar to this:

d. Click a blank area of the Start screen to expand it to regular size. You can then drag and drop the tools that have been pinned to Start into the new group by dragging and dropping the tile onto the name of the group. You can right-click and select Unpin From Start for any tools that you don't want to keep in this group.

Snapping Apps

Windows 8.1 allows you to share your screen between different apps by snapping an app to the screen edge. With an app open, hold down the Windows logo key, toggle the period (.), and press an arrow button to position the application. You can also drag the app and snap it to the right or left edge. To return to full screen, simply pull it away from the edge and expand it as usual.

Snapping apps works best if the resolution is set to 1366×768 or higher. A default installation of Windows 8.1 starts with a minimum resolution of 1024×768, so this feature won't make sense unless the resolution is much higher. You can access the Screen Resolution page by right-clicking the Desktop and selecting Screen Resolution.

Using Windows 8.1 Shortcuts

Just as with most other Windows operating systems, you'll find that there are many shortcuts you can use to get to a desired app or tool. One of the most important tools is the Search charm, which starts as soon as you begin typing from the Start screen. In Figure 1.4 the Search charm is displaying the Control Panel tile after a user types **control**. You can use the Search charm to find many familiar tools if you know the name.

FIGURE 1.4   Using the Search charm to search apps

Table 1.1 shows shortcuts for accessing many common tools, and Table 1.2 shows the shortcuts you can use to access Windows 8.1 charms.

TABLE 1.1   Windows 8.1 shortcuts

Feature	Key combination
Toggle between Start and the Desktop.	Windows logo key
Show the Desktop when an app is running.	Windows logo key+D

Feature	Key combination
Cycle through apps (except Desktop apps).	Windows logo key+Tab (shows a taskbar on the left side of the screen)
Cycle through apps in reverse order (except Desktop apps).	Windows logo key+Shift+Tab (shows a taskbar on the left side of the screen)
Cycle through Desktop apps.	Alt+Tab
Cycle through Desktop apps in reverse order.	Alt+Shift+Tab
Open the App Switcher from the Start screen.	Alt+Tab
Show the preview menu (Programs And Features, Power Options, Event Viewer, and more).	Windows logo key+X
Lock display.	Windows logo key+L
Peek at the Desktop.	Windows logo key+, (comma)
Start File Explorer.	Windows logo key+E
Open the App Switcher.	Alt+Tab (toggle Alt to select different apps)
Zoom in.	Windows logo key ++ (plus key)
Zoom out.	Windows logo key + − (minus key)
Move Start screen and open apps to monitor on the left.	Windows logo key+Page Up
Move Start screen and open apps to monitor on the right.	Windows logo key+Page Down
Show Shut Down Windows menu (from the Desktop).	Alt+F4
Shut Down Windows (from Start screen).	Windows logo key+I, select Power

TABLE 1.2   Windows 8.1 charms

Charm	Key combination
Open the Charms bar.	Windows logo key+C
Open the Settings charm.	Windows logo key+I
Open the Search charm to search files.	Windows logo key+F
Open the Search charm to search everywhere.	Windows logo key+Q
Open the Search charm to search settings.	Windows logo key+W
Open the Devices charm.	Windows logo key+K
Open the Share charm.	Windows logo key+H

Understanding Authentication and Authorization

As with all recent Windows operating systems, you need an account to use Windows 8.1. This is a core requirement for basic *authentication* and *authorization*. Here's the difference between these two terms:

Authentication   A user claims an identity with a user account and proves this is the user's identity by authenticating with a password or other authentication method. Authentication methods supported in Windows 8.1 are text passwords, picture passwords, personal identification numbers (PINs), smart cards, and biometric methods.

Authorization   After users are authenticated, they are granted access to resources based on their proven identity.

Account Types

There are multiple types of accounts you can use in Windows 8.1. Many of these are the same types of accounts you could use in previous versions, but the Microsoft Live account is new.

Local User Account   When a computer is in a workgroup or HomeGroup, users have a local user account stored on the computer. They are able to log on to the local computer only with this account. If users need to log on to other computers, they need an account on each of these computers.

Domain Account   When the computer is in a domain, users have an account within the domain. Their account information is stored on a domain controller and managed by Active Directory Domain Services (AD DS). By default, users can use this account to log on to any computer in the domain except for domain controllers.

Microsoft Live Account   This is an email address that users can use to access multiple Microsoft services, including Windows Phone and Xbox LIVE. Microsoft hosts hotmail.com, outlook.com, and live.com email services, and you can use an account from one of these services. You can also use any email address after registering it with Microsoft.

Microsoft domain accounts can be used as a Microsoft Live account. Microsoft domain accounts support the use of user principal names (UPNs), which takes the format of *username@domain.extension*. For example, a user named Darril in the GetCertifiedGetAhead.com domain can have a UPN of Darril@GetCertifiedGetAhead.com and use it to log on and for email. This same account name can be used as a Microsoft Live account after registering it with Microsoft.

There are several benefits to using a Microsoft Live account. The primary benefit is that it provides single sign-on (SSO) capabilities for many Microsoft services. You need to sign in only once to Windows and you can then access other Microsoft services without signing in again. However, users might be prompted to provide a password again when starting certain transactions, such as purchasing an app from the Windows Store.

There are four types of local user accounts:

Administrator Account   An administrator account is a member of the Administrators group and has full control over the computer. The first user account that is created when Windows 8.1 is installed is an administrator account by default. This is in addition to the built-in Administrator account, which is disabled by default.

Standard Account   This is the default account designed for basic use and created as needed. Users have the ability to run applications but not make significant changes to the system. Standard accounts but can be changed to administrator accounts by adding them to the Administrators group.

Guest Account   This account is used as a temporary account. It is disabled by default but can be enabled temporarily for a user instead of creating a new account. When the guest account is no longer needed, it should be disabled again.

HomeGroupUser Account   This is a built-in account used to connect from one device in a HomeGroup to another device in the same HomeGroup.

Exercise 1.2 shows how to create a local user account. This account is created as a standard account by default. This exercise assumes you're logged in with an administrator account and the Start screen is showing.

EXERCISE 1.2

Creating a Local User Account

1. Access the Settings charm by pressing Windows logo key+I.

2. Select Change PC Settings from the bottom of the display.

3. Click Accounts.

4. Click Other Accounts.

5. Click Add An Account.

6. Click Sign In Without A Microsoft Account (at the bottom of the screen). Ignore the "Not Recommended." warning.

7. Select Local Account at the bottom of the page.

8. Enter the user's name, the user's password (twice), and a password hint. The hint is displayed if the user forgets the password. Click Next.

9. Click Finish.

Exercise 1.3 shows how you can change a standard user account to an administrator account. This exercise assumes you're logged in with an administrator account and the Start screen is showing.

EXERCISE 1.3

Changing a Standard Account to an Administrator Account

1. Type **computer**. Select Computer Management. You can also access the Computer Management applet by right-clicking on the Start button.

2. Expand Computer Management ➤ System Tools ➤ Local Users And Groups, and select Users.

3. Right-click the user you want to modify and select Properties.

4. Select the Member Of tab and click Add.

5. Type **administrators** and click Check Names. This should change the computer name to a backslash (\) followed by the word Administrators, as shown in the following graphic. Click OK twice.

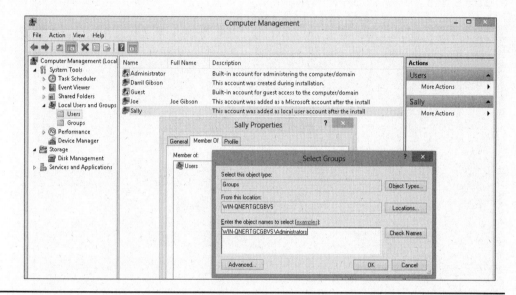

CERT
OBJECTIVE PIN and Picture Passwords

A new feature available with Windows 8.1 is the ability to use a personal identification number (PIN) or a picture password instead of a standard password. A PIN is a four-digit code similar to a code you might use with an automated teller machine (ATM).

Picture passwords are useful on touch screens. Instead of a user typing a PIN or a password, it's possible for the user to use gestures on the screen as a password. The user picks an image and then enters three gestures as their password. Supported gestures are taps, straight lines, and circles. Picture passwords aren't restricted to only touch screens. The gestures can also be drawn with a mouse.

For example, we've created a picture password with a graphic from the Administrative Tools tiles. For the first gesture, we tapped Performance Monitor. For the second gesture, we drew a circle around Resource Monitor. Figure 1.5 shows the third gesture, where we're drawing a straight line from the Defragment and Optimize Drives tool to the Disk Cleanup tool.

FIGURE 1.5 Using a picture password

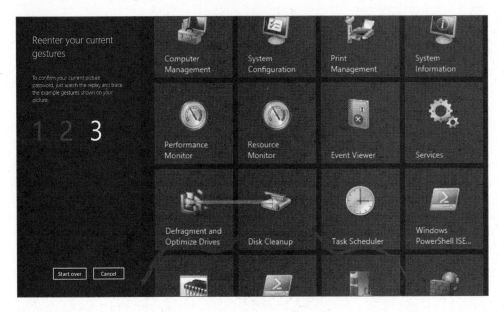

When the picture password is configured, users have the choice of logging on with the picture password or with a regular password.

Exercise 1.5 shows how to set up a picture password. This exercise assumes you're logged in with an administrator account and the Account screen is showing.

EXERCISE 1.5

Creating a Picture Password

1. Select Sign-in options from the left side of the screen.

2. Click the Add button under Picture Password.

3. Verify your account information and enter your password on the next screen.

4. On the Welcome Picture Password screen, click Choose Picture.

5. On the Files screen, select a picture. Click Open.

6. If necessary, move the picture until it is in the position you want for your picture password. Click Use This Picture.

7. Draw three gestures to indicate the gestures you want to use for your picture password. You can use any combination of straight lines, taps, or circles. Be sure to remember where you drew the shapes.

8. Redraw all three shapes to confirm your password.

9. Click Finish.

Using the Windows Command Prompt

The *command prompt* is used to type commands from a prompt rather than using the Windows graphical user interface (GUI). Although Windows and other operating systems depend heavily on the GUI for ease of use, the command prompt is extremely important for administrators.

The command prompt may look out of fashion to some, but it is indeed an integral tool needed to accomplish many basic and advanced administrative tasks. In short, the command prompt is not going away. It's stronger than ever. One of the biggest reasons is that anything that can be executed at the command prompt can be scripted and anything that can be scripted can be scheduled or programmed to respond to specific events.

In this section, you'll learn some basics related to the command prompt and perform some exercises to start and use it. The next section covers Windows PowerShell basics, and it's important to realize that many of the same concepts that apply to the command prompt also apply to PowerShell.

Launching the Command Prompt

This is a participative sport. You can't just read about it—you need to get your hands on the keyboard and execute these commands to see how they work. Start by launching the command prompt. In Windows 8.1, you can launch it using one of these two methods:

Typing method

1. Type **cmd.** As soon as you start typing, the Search Apps text box appears.

2. Click on Command Prompt to start it.

Keyboard shortcut method

1. Press Windows logo key+X to open the Start/preview menu.

2. Click on Command Prompt to start it.

The command prompt starts with white text on a black screen, though you can modify it if you desire. After launching the command prompt, right-click the title bar, select Properties, and then select the Colors tab, as shown in Figure 1.6.

You can select different colors for the background and the text. For example, when showing commands to an audience we often change the background to white and the text to black so that it is easier for participants to see it. Similarly, you can modify the fonts from the Font tab, and we often increase the font size when doing demonstrations so that everyone can easily see the commands—even from the cheap seats.

FIGURE 1.6   Modifying the display of the command prompt

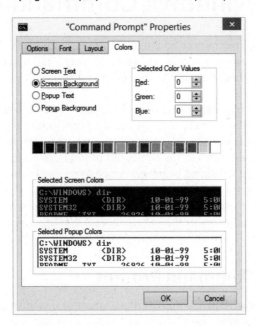

Launching with Administrator Privileges

The command prompt will launch without administrative permissions by default. However, some commands require administrative permissions to execute, so you need to start the command prompt with administrative permissions. Exercise 1.6 shows how. This exercise assumes you're logged in and the Start screen is showing.

EXERCISE 1.6

Launching the Command Prompt with Administrative Privileges

1. Locate the Command Prompt app on the Start page.

2. Right-click over it.

3. The context menu will appear next to the app.

4. Click Run As Administrator.

5. If prompted by User Account Control, click Yes to continue. If you are logged in with a nonadministrative account, you'll be prompted to provide the credentials for an administrative account.

When you start the command prompt normally, it will start in the *\users\username* folder by default, where *username* is the name of the currently logged-on user. When you start it with administrative privileges, the prompt starts in the \windows\system32 folder by default. Also, the title bar changes from Command Prompt to Administrator: Command Prompt.

Command Prompt Basics

There are many basics related to the command prompt that are important to understand. These apply if you're using basic commands, advanced commands, or commands in scripts. Additionally, many of these same basics apply to PowerShell commands.

Commands Are Modified with Switches

A switch is identified with either a / symbol or a – symbol. The / symbol was used often in older DOS commands, and the – symbol was common in Unix and Unix derivatives. However, at this point most commands will accept either switch.

As a simple example, you can use the dir command to view the contents of the current directory (by typing **dir** and pressing Enter). If you want to find a specific file named file.txt that might be in any subdirectory, you can use the /s switch like this: **dir file.txt /s**.

You can view a full listing of switches for any command by entering the command and the /? switch.

Help Is Always Available

You can find help for just about any command by typing the command with the help switch (/?). In other words, to get help on the manage-bde command, you can enter **manage-bde /?** at the command prompt.

Also, for many commands you can access help by typing **help** and then the command. For example, if you know you can restart the computer into the Windows Recovery Environment (RE) with the shutdown command but you don't remember how, you can enter **help shutdown**. (In case you're interested, the actual command to reboot and start in the Windows RE is shutdown /r /o.)

You can also access help available from the TechNet Command-Line Reference page:

http://technet.microsoft.com/library/cc754340.aspx

The manage-bde command is a BitLocker Drive Encryption tool. For example, you can type **manage-bde -status** to list drives that have Bit-Locker enabled. A new switch (-WipeFreeSpace or -w) will erase all data fragments in a volume's free space. BitLocker is explored in more depth in Chapter 9, "Managing Files and Disks on Windows 8.1."

Spelling Counts

At some point in the future, computers will do what we want them to do, not what we ask them to do. For now, they interpret our commands literally. For example, if you want to extend the display to a second monitor you can do so with this command:

displayswitch /extend

However, if you accidentally enter the following command instead (displaywitch instead of displayswitch), the command prompt gives a syntax error:

displaywitch /extend

'displaywitch' is not recognized as an internal or external command, operable program or batch file.

The error indicates the command is not recognized because it is trying to execute a command called displaywitch (which doesn't exist). When things don't work, it's worth your time to read the error message. It will often point you in the right direction.

Commands Are Not Case Sensitive

Most command prompt commands are not case sensitive. In other words, a command is interpreted the same if it's entered as all upper case, all lower case, or a mixture of both upper case and lower case. For example, the `msiexec` (Windows Installer) command allows you to install, modify, and perform other Windows Installer actions from the command line. You would see the same result if you entered it as `MSIEXEC`, `MsiExec`, or even `mSiExEc`.

It's rare, but occasionally you'll run across a parameter used within a command prompt command that needs to be a specific case. When this true, it will be stressed.

 For consistency, commands will be listed in lower case within this book. If the command must be entered using a specific case, it will be accompanied by a comment saying so.

Commands Can Use Wildcards

A *wildcard* is a character that can take the place of other characters. They are often used for search and copy operations. The command prompt includes two wildcard characters: the asterisk (*) and the question mark (?).

The * symbol will look for any instance of zero or more characters in the place of the * symbol. For example, if you want to know if you have any text files (with the `.txt` extension) in the current directory, you can use the following command:

`dir *.txt`

Similarly, if you want a listing of all files that start with `app` and end with `.exe`, you can use this command:

`dir app*.exe`

Note that it will include a file named `app.exe`, if it exists, in addition to any files that that have letters after `app`.

The ? wildcard will take the place of a single character. It isn't used as often, but you can use it if you're looking for something more specific. For example, if you were looking for any files that had an extension of `.ex` and any third character, you could use this command:

`dir *.ex?`

It would not include any files that ended with `.ex` without a third character in the extension. In other words, the ? wildcard specifies that a single character must exist for a match to occur. This is different from the * symbol, which will match for zero or more characters.

Strings with Spaces Need Quotes

Many commands will accept parameters, and when the parameters include spaces, the parameter usually needs to be enclosed in quotes.

For example, imagine you were using the `msiexec` command to install an application named `success for me.msi`. The filename includes spaces, so you need to include the entire filename with quotes like this:

```
msiexec /i "success for me.msi" /qb
```

In this example, the `/i` switch indicates that the MSI file should be installed. The `/qb` switch specifies a basic user interface level that will display a progress bar and progress messages if the MSI file includes them. Notice the name of the MSI file is included in quotes because it has spaces.

However, the following command (without the quotes) would be interpreted quite differently:

```
msiexec /i success for me.msi /qb
```

In this second example, `success` will be interpreted as the name of the file to install. Even if a file exists named `success` without an extension of `.msi`, the `msiexec` command won't know how to interpret the word `for`, which comes right after the space. This causes an error.

You can occasionally get away without using the quotes. For example, if you're at the root of C (C:\) and want to change to the `Program Files` folder (which has a space), the following command will work:

```
cd program files
```

This is only because the `CD` command has been programmed to accept it, but that wasn't always the case. You could also enter this command like this:

```
cd "program files"
```

Doskey Saves Typing

Doskey is a utility that is constantly running in the background of the command prompt and can be very valuable—if you know how to use it. Every time you enter a command in a command prompt session, it is recorded by Doskey and can be recalled.

For example, suppose you're testing connectivity with a server using the following `ping` command:

```
ping dc1.training.getcertifiedgetahead.com
```

You could execute the command and then realize the NIC wasn't configured correctly, or the host cache needed to be cleared with `ipconfig /flushdns`, or something else needed to be done. After resolving the issue, you want to execute the `ping` command again. Instead of typing it in from scratch, you can simply use the up arrow to recall it and press Enter, and you've executed it again (without retyping it).

The up arrow can be used to retrieve any previous command that you've entered in the current command prompt session (up to the limit of the buffer, which is rather large). This can be valuable when you're entering very long commands or even short commands if you use the hunt-and-peck method of typing.

Typos are also common at the command line. However, you don't have to retype the entire command. If you get an error, you can use the up arrow to recall the command, and then use the left and right arrows to position the cursor where you want to modify the text. Make your corrections and press Enter, and the corrected command executes.

You can also use the F7 key to display a pop-up window that shows a history listing. It includes all of the commands you've entered in the current session. You can then use the up or down arrows to select the desired command or press the Esc key to dismiss the window.

Doskey is a command prompt utility itself and includes some commands you can use. For example, if you want to view all the commands that have been entered in the current session, enter **doskey /history**.

By default, the system includes a buffer size of 50 commands. If you need more, you can modify the buffer size. For example, the following command changes the buffer to 99:

```
doskey /listsize=99
```

Using *runas*

You can also start a separate instance of the command prompt with the runas command. This allows you to start it in the context of a specific user account. The basic syntax is as follows:

```
runas /user:domain\username [/profile or /noprofile] application
```

Table 1.3 shows some common switches used with the runas command.

TABLE 1.3   runas switches

Feature	Key combination
/profile	Specifies that the user's profile should be loaded. This is the default. It cannot be used with /netonly.
/noprofile	Specifies that the user's profile should not be loaded. This causes the application to load more quickly, but can cause some applications to malfunction.
/env	Specifies that the current environment will be used instead of the specified user's environment.
/netonly	Use if the credentials specified are for remote access only. This cannot be used with /profile.
/savecred	Use credentials previously saved by the user.
/smartcard	Use if the credentials are to be supplied from a smart card.

Say you are logged on as a regular user but have an account named JoeAdmin with administrator privileges within a domain named GetCertifiedGetAhead.com. You can use the runas command to run the command with the administrator account with this command:

```
runas /user:getcertifiedgetahead\joeadmin /profile yourapp.exe
```

System Variables

Many *system variables* are available within Windows 8.1, and you'll see these often when using the command prompt and Windows PowerShell. System variables are settings that are global to all users, not just the currently logged-in user (the latter are commonly referred to as *environment variables*). System variables are useful in identifying specific values about the environment. As a simple example, every computer has a computer name, but the computer names are different. The system variable %computername% holds the value of the local computer's computer name.

System variables are easy to identify in text. They always start and end with a percent symbol (%). An easy way to view the value of any variable is by using the echo command in the following format:

```
echo %variablename%
```

Table 1.4 shows many of the commonly used system variables and their value. You use the echo command with each to see its value.

TABLE 1.4 Commonly used system variables

Variable	Value
%windir% %systemroot%	Both %windir% and %systemroot% identify the folder where Windows was installed, typically C:\Windows.
%systemdrive%	The folder where the system boot files are located, typically C:\.
%computername%	The name of the local computer.
%username%	The name of the user logged on to this session.
%date%	Holds the value of the current date in the format ddd mm/dd/yyyy. The first three letters are an abbreviation of the day of the week, such as Mon, Tue, Wed, and so on. The remaining format is all numbers with mm for the month, dd for the day, and yyyy for the year.

`%time%`	Holds the value of the current time in a 24-hour format as `hh.mm.ss.ms`.
`%errorlevel%`	Indicates whether the previous command resulted in an error. If it didn't result in an error, the value is 0.
`%ProgramFiles%`	Points to the location of the `Program Files` folder, which is normally `C:\Program Files`.
`%Public%`	The location of the `Public` folder, typically `C:\Users\Public`.

Commands and Paths

When you execute commands from the command prompt, the system needs to know where to find the command. It first tries to execute it in the current path and then looks for it in predefined paths. A path identifies a location on the hard drive.

For example, when you first launch the command prompt, it will start in the `c:\users\%username%` path by default, where `%username%` will be replaced with the username you're logged on with. If you launch it with administrator privileges, it will start in the `c:\%windir%\system32` folder.

If you execute a command (such as `ipconfig`), it will look for the command in the current folder first. If it isn't located in the current folder, the system will search the folders identified in the predefined paths. If the command isn't located in any of the known paths, you'll see an error. For example, if you type **xyz** and press Enter, you'll see this error:

```
'xyz' is not recognized as an internal or external command,
operable program or batch file.
```

 Documentation commonly uses the terms *folders* and *directories* interchangeably. In the early DOS days, they were almost always called directories. When the Windows GUI came out, they were referred to as folders because the icon looks like a folder. It matches a metaphor users could easily understand; that is, files are placed in folders in the real world and they are placed in folders in Windows. However, there is no difference between a folder and a directory; both terms mean the same thing.

If the system didn't have predefined paths, it would search only the current folder, and commands would be a lot harder to enter and execute. However, the system starts with several predefined paths. On a new installation, this path includes all of these directories:

- `C:\Windows\system32`
- `C:\Windows`

- `C:\Windows\System32\Wbem`
- `C:\Windows\System32\WindowsPowerShell\v1.0\`

You can execute the `path` or the `set path` command to view the predefined path for your system. Some applications will modify the path, and you can also modify the path yourself.

Identifying Executables

When you execute the `set path` statement, you also see something else valuable: a list of file types that are known to be executables. Some files can be executed or run, whereas others are simply data files used by executable programs.

So what is an executable? It is any file that can be run. For example, you can run the `ipconfig.exe` file because it's an executable. If a file named `ipconfig.txt` existed, it could not be executed. The extension `.exe` identifies the first file as an executable, whereas the extension `.txt` identifies the second file as a text file.

Known executable files are defined by the system variable `pathext` (path extension). The following are the path extensions, or file extensions, known to be executables. They are listed as they appear on this author's system:

- `.com` (executable file)
- `.exe` (command file or executable file)
- `.bat` (batch file)
- `.cmd` (command file)
- `.vbs` (Visual Basic Script file)
- `.vbe` (Visual Basic executable file)
- `.js` (JavaScript file)
- `.jse` (JavaScript executable file)
- `.wsf` (Windows Script file), `.wsh` (Windows Script Host file)
- `.msc` (Microsoft Management Console file)

So when you execute the `ipconfig` command, it searches for a file that starts with `ipconfig` and ends with one of the identified known executable extensions. Since the `ipconfig` program ends with `.exe`, the `ipconfig.exe` command is located and executed.

Modifying the Path to Executables

If you need to modify the known paths of the system, you can do so with either the `set path` statement or via the GUI. For example, you may have an executable in the `c:\app` path, and you may want this path included in the path variable. You can use one of these methods.

Set Path Command

Before modifying the path, take a look at what it currently is with the command set path.

You can use the set path statement to modify the path to include the c:\app folder with the following command:

```
set path = c:\app
```

After you modify the path, view the current path by executing set path again. You'll notice that there are two paths currently set—the original default path and another path = c:\app path that you just created, as shown in Listing 1.1 and Listing 1.2. Listing 1.1 is what appears before you execute the set path = c:\app statement. Listing 1.2 shows what appears after you execute the statement, with the next path highlighted.

Listing 1.1: Output of the set path statement

```
Path=C:\Windows\system32;C:\Windows;C:\Windows\System32\Wbem;
C:\Windows\System32\WindowsPowerShell\v1.0\
PATHEXT=.COM;.EXE;.BAT;.CMD;.VBS;.VBE;.JS;.JSE;.WSF;.WSH;.MSC
```

Listing 1.2: Output of the set path statement after appending the path

```
Path=C:\Windows\system32;C:\Windows;C:\Windows\System32\Wbem;
C:\Windows\System32\WindowsPowerShell\v1.0\
path = c:\app
PATHEXT=.COM;.EXE;.BAT;.CMD;.VBS;.VBE;.JS;.JSE;.WSF;.WSH;.MSC
```

This behavior of the set path statement is different in Windows 7 and Windows 8.1 than it was in previous versions of Windows. In previous versions, if you used the set path = c:\app statement, it would overwrite the previous path and only c:\app would be included in the path. However, when you execute the set path statement in Windows 7 and Windows 8.1, it appends, not replaces, the current path.

This modified path will be modified for only the current session. In other words, if you exit the command prompt window, launch it again, and enter **set path**, you'll see only the original system default path.

Modifying the Path with the GUI

The path can also be modified by modifying the system variables in the GUI, as shown in Exercise 1.7.

EXERCISE 1.7

Modifying the Path System Variable

1. Drag your mouse to the lower-left corner of the screen and right-click on the Start button.

2. When the Start menu appears, select System.

3. Select Advanced System Settings. Ensure the Advanced tab is selected.

4. Click the Environment Variables button.

5. Scroll to Path in the System Variables pane. Select Path and click Edit.

6. Scroll to the end of the text (or press Ctrl+End) in the Variable Value text box.

    Warning: Make sure you separate each path with a semicolon. If the semicolon is omitted, the path will be interpreted as a part of the previous path and the previous path will no longer be accessible.

7. Enter a semicolon (;) and then the path you want added, as shown here:

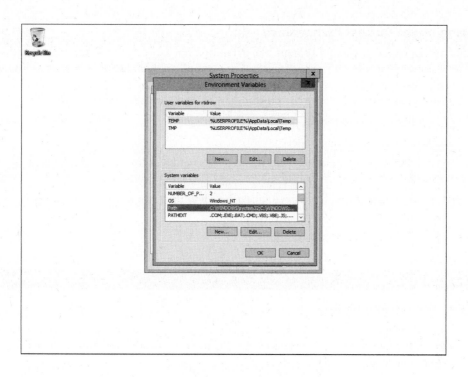

8. Click OK three times to dismiss all of the windows. If you launch the command prompt, you'll see that the new path has been appended to the system path.

Changing the Current Path with *cd*

When you open the command prompt, the default path is c:\users\%username%, with %username% replaced with your username. For example, if you logged on with a username of Darril, the default path would be c:\users\darril.

 You can change the path with the cd command (short for change directory):

- cd \ will take you to the root of the current drive.

- cd .. will take you up one folder.

- cd *foldername* will take you into the folder specified as long as the folder is in the current folder.

- cd \1st *folder*\2nd *folder*\3rd *folder* will take you to the third folder, as long as the full path is valid.

 Use Exercise 1.8 to see this in action.

EXERCISE 1.8

Using the *cd* Command

1. Launch a command prompt and note the current path. Unless you launched it with administrative privileges, it will point to a directory with your username in the c:\ users directory.

2. Type **cd ..** and press Enter. This will take you up one folder to the c:\users folder.

3. Type **cd ** and press Enter. This will take to you the root of c:\.

4. Type **dir** and press Enter to view the contents of the root.

5. Type the following command to change the directory to the windows\system32 folder:

   cd \windows\system32

   Note that the backslash (\) before windows causes the path to start from the root of the C drive.

6. Type **dir** and press Enter to view the contents of this folder.

7. Press the up arrow twice to recall the cd \ command, and press Enter. You'll be returned to the root.

8. Enter the following command to change to the system32 folder using the windows variable:

   cd %windir%\system32

Changing the Current Path with File Explorer

A neat feature that's available with the command prompt is the ability to use drag and drop from File Explorer to copy the path. This technique doesn't change the directory, but you can use it to make things a lot easier.

This feature is not available when you run the command prompt with administrator privileges. Exercise 1.9 shows how this technique can be useful.

EXERCISE 1.9

Using Drag and Drop with the Command Prompt

1. If a command prompt is not already open, launch a command prompt.

2. Launch File Explorer and browse to the Desktop\Libraries\Documents\My Documents folder.

3. Position File Explorer and the command prompt window side by side.

4. Click My Documents in File Explorer, drag it to the command prompt window, and release it. You'll notice that the path is now displayed in the window. Your display will be similar to this:

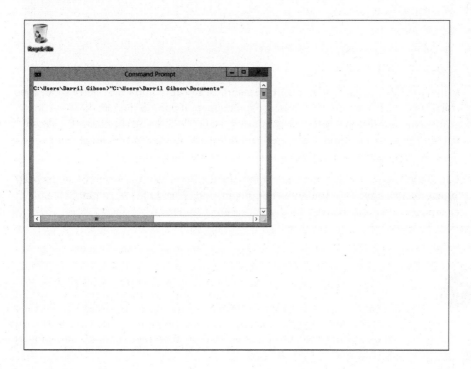

EXERCISE 1.9 *(continued)*

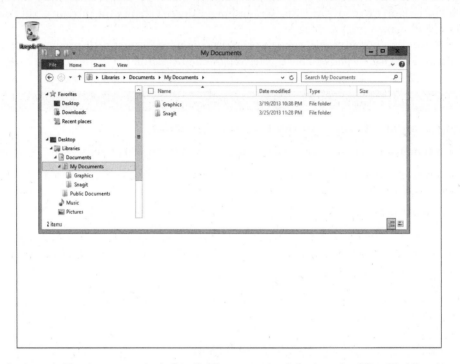

5. In the graphic, the username is Darril Gibson, so the default path of Darril's Libraries starts as `C:\Users\Darril Gibson` and the actual path to the `Libraries\Documents\My Documents` folder is `C:\Users\Darril Gibson\Documents`. When the My Documents folder is dragged and dropped into the command prompt window, the path is typed out. However, you're not finished yet.

6. Use the left arrow (or the Home key) to position your cursor to the left of all the text. Type **cd** and a space to modify the command, and press Enter. Your path will be changed to the equivalent of the My Documents folder.

The previous exercise showed how you can easily change the path using File Explorer, but you can also launch the command prompt to any folder's location from File Explorer. With File Explorer open, press the Shift key, right-click the folder, and select Open Command Window Here. The command prompt will be launched with the directory set at the same folder as File Explorer.

Using Copy and Paste with the Command Prompt

At first glance it looks like you can't copy and paste to or from the command prompt. It doesn't work exactly as it does in Windows, causing a lot of people to assume you can't, but doing so is possible.

You can actually copy and paste by default, but enabling the QuickEdit mode makes it a little easier. This can be valuable when you are testing commands that you want to paste into a script file. Exercise 1.10 shows how copy and paste works from the command prompt, how to enable QuickEdit mode, and its benefits.

EXERCISE 1.10

Using Copy and Paste from the Command Prompt

1. Open a command prompt window, type **notepad**, and press Enter. This will launch an instance of Notepad that you'll use to copy and paste text to and from the command prompt window.

2. Type **ping localhost** in the Notepad window. Press Ctrl+A to select the text and Ctrl+C to copy it.

3. Click in the command prompt window. Right-click and select Paste. You'll see the command pasted into the command prompt window. Press Enter and the command will execute.

4. Right-click the command prompt title bar and select Edit ➢ Mark.

5. Use your mouse to highlight the output from the ping command. When the text has been highlighted, press Enter to copy it to the Clipboard.

6. Click in Notepad and press Ctrl+V to paste the output into the text file.

7. Enable QuickEdit mode with these steps:

   a. Right-click the title bar and select Properties. If necessary, select the Options tab.

   b. Select the check box next to QuickEdit Mode, as shown in the following graphic. Click OK.

EXERCISE 1.10 *(continued)*

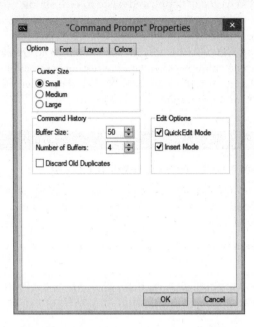

8. Now you can select text within the command prompt window without selecting Mark. Simply use the mouse to select the text and press Enter. The following graphic shows how text can be selected by highlighting it and using the menu to select Edit ➤ Copy, you can simply press the Enter key.

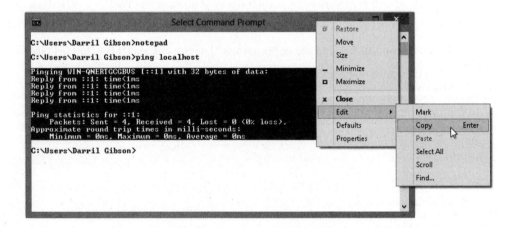

Capturing the Output

It's common to need to capture the output of commands executed at the command prompt. This can easily be done by redirecting the output to a text file using the > symbol.

For example, you may want to document the current status of all of the services in a text file so that you can review them later. The following command will list all of the services on the system, including the current state, such as running or stopped:

```
sc query state= all
```

 The state= all option must be entered without a space after state and with a space after the equals (=) symbol. Other combinations result in an error.

If you execute this command at the command prompt, you'll see that output quickly scrolls off the screen. However, you can redirect the output to a text file by modifying the command like this:

```
sc query state= all > servicestatus.txt
```

You can then view the file in Notepad with the following command:

```
notepad servicestatus.txt
```

Of course, you can also redirect the file to any location by including the path in the filename. The following command creates and stores the file in the c:\data folder:

```
sc query state= all > c:\data\ servicestatus.txt
```

Creating a Batch File

A *batch file* is a listing of one or more command prompt commands within a text file. When the batch file is called or executed, the commands are executed. The best way to understand this is to do it. Although there are sophisticated text editors you can use, Notepad will work.

Exercise 1.11 shows the steps used to create a simple batch file, and then it builds on the simple batch file to add extra capabilities. Ultimately, you'll end up with a batch file you can use to create a list of all services on a computer and their current state. The batch file can then copy the file to a share on another computer.

EXERCISE 1.11

Creating a Batch File

1. Launch the command prompt.

2. Type **notepad servicestatus.bat** and press Enter. Notepad will launch, and since a file named servicestatus.bat doesn't exist, you'll be prompted to create it. Click Yes.

   Note that the file will be created in the same directory in which the command prompt window was launched.

3. Type in the following text in Notepad:

   ```
   @echo off
   echo Hello %username%. Today is %date%.
   ```

   Press Ctrl+S to save the file, but don't close it.

4. Return to the command prompt, type **servicestatus**, and press Enter. Notice that because the batch file is considered one of the executable types, it is automatically located and executed. You'll see a greeting with today's date. This is okay but not very useful.

5. Open Notepad and type the following text after your first two lines:

   ```
   sc query state= all > %computername%servicestatus.txt
   ```

   This command will create a list of updates currently installed on this system and store the updates in the file named *computername*servicestatus.txt (the computer name will be different for each computer where it is executed). Press Ctrl+S to save the file.

6. Return to the command prompt, press the up arrow, and press Enter to execute the batch file again. Notice that it almost seems as though it's the same as before. A greeting appears, it pauses for a second or two, and then the command prompt returns.

7. Provide some user feedback by adding the following line to the batch file:

   ```
   echo A list of services is stored in the
   %computername%servicestatus.txt file.
   ```

   Press Ctrl+S to save the file.

8. Access the command prompt, press the up arrow to retrieve the last command, and press Enter to view the difference. Notice that instead of %computername%, your actual computer name is used.

9. You could also open the file for the user by adding this command to the batch file:

   ```
   %SystemDrive%\Users\%Username%\Documents\%computername%servicestatus.
   txt
   ```

   If you add this to the batch file to test it, make sure you remove it before moving on.

10. If you want to copy the file to a network share (such as a central computer that will hold files from multiple computers), you can use the net use command. For this set of commands, we're assuming you have a share named services on a server named srv1 that you can access in the network and that you have permissions to copy the file. You're accessing it using the \\srv1\services UNC path. You can use any server (or another Windows 8.1 computer) and any share that has appropriate permissions.

    ```
    net use z:  /delete
    net use z:  \\srv1\services
    copy %computername%servicestatus.txt z:
    net use Z: /delete
    ```

    The first command ensures that the Z drive isn't already mapped to something else. The next command maps the Z drive to the UNC path using the \\serverName\shareName format. The third line copies the file to the Z drive using the copy command, and the fourth line returns the environment to normal.

The UNC path always uses the format of *servername**sharename*. The *servername* is the name of any computer that can share folders and can be another Windows 8.1 system.

Now that the file is created, it can be configured to execute automatically based on a schedule. Windows 8.1 includes the built-in *Task Scheduler* that can be used to schedule tasks.

Real World Scenario

Preparing a Classroom

As a trainer, this author (Darril) teaches many technical courses and the courses require different student materials. Since I'm never sure what previous students might have done, I often refresh the files on computer systems before a class.

Walking around the room with my USB and touching as many as 18 student computers could easily take an hour or so. However, I've created scripts to load these materials onto the systems for the different courses. I simply turn on the student computers and launch my script from the instructor computer. A few minutes later, I verify that the script ran successfully and I'm done.

The script ensures that the process is always exactly the same for each student. Additionally, it saves me a lot of time and effort.

Using Windows PowerShell and the PowerShell ISE

Windows PowerShell is an extensible version of the command prompt. It is integrated with the Microsoft .NET Framework, which gives it extensive capabilities well beyond the command prompt. Windows 8.1 comes with both Windows PowerShell and the *Windows PowerShell Integrated Scripting Environment (ISE)*.

The PowerShell commands can be used to perform and automate many administrative tasks, such as managing services, managing event logs, modifying the Registry, and interacting with Windows Management Instrumentation (WMI). PowerShell was designed with scripting in mind so you'll find that you can create elegant scripts that can automate many of your administrative tasks.

One of the challenges with PowerShell is that it is so rich in capabilities and features that it can be intimidating. However, you can start using it without understanding everything about it. You can learn as you go.

 You'll get the most out of this section if you're able to launch PowerShell, execute the commands, and see them in action. You can launch PowerShell normally or with administrative permissions. However, we strongly recommend that you launch it normally unless you specifically need to use administrative permissions (such as when you need to change the execution policy as shown later in this chapter).

Just as the command prompt has its own environment, PowerShell too has its own environment. It also has a distinctive look and feel. Launch it and see for yourself by following these steps from the Start screen:

1. Type **powershell**. As soon as you start typing, the Search Everywhere text box appears.

2. Click on Windows PowerShell to start it.

In addition to seeing Windows PowerShell in the search results, you'll see the *Windows PowerShell ISE*, which is the integrated scripting environment (ISE). If you're running a 64-bit system, you'll see the following four choices:

- Windows PowerShell (x86) (32-bit version)

- Windows PowerShell ISE (x86) (32-bit version)

- Windows PowerShell (64-bit version)

- Windows PowerShell ISE (64-bit version)

We haven't run across any issues using the 64-bit Windows PowerShell and ISE for any scripts, but if you need to step down to the 32-bit version, you can.

> You can also launch PowerShell from the command prompt with the following command: **powershell_ise.exe**. If you add the -noprofile switch (**powershell_ise.exe -noprofile**), the command will not run the default profile script and PowerShell will start quicker.

If you need to run PowerShell with administrative permissions, right-click the app when it appears and select Run As Administrator from the alt context menu.

Although the look and feel of PowerShell is different from the command prompt, you can right-click over the title bar and you'll see you have access to the same menu as the command prompt. You can also copy and paste to and from the PowerShell window and enable QuickEdit mode, so this is a little easier. Copy and paste works exactly the same as shown with the command prompt earlier in this chapter.

Windows PowerShell ISE

The Windows PowerShell Integrating Scripting Environment can be used just as easily as the Windows PowerShell prompt, but it gives you a lot more capabilities. Figure 1.7 shows the PowerShell ISE.

You can see that it has a familiar menu across the top just like any other Windows application. Below the menu are several icons. As with other applications, you can hover over the icon to see the name. If you're working with scripts, the most common icons you'll use are Save, Run Script (green arrow), and Run Selection. The Run Script icon is the right arrow icon, and if you highlight any text, the icon next to it will be enabled so that you execute the selected text.

FIGURE 1.7 Windows PowerShell ISE

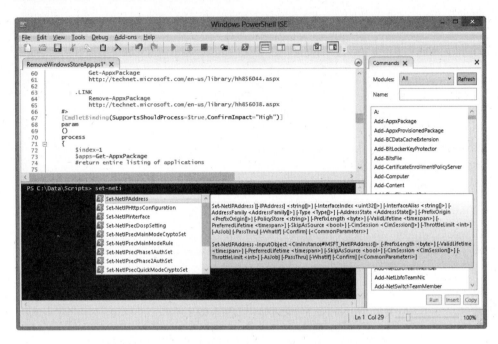

In Figure 1.7, we've opened a script and opened the script pane by clicking the down arrow labeled Script. The icon changes to an up arrow and clicking it will hide the script.

The bottom pane is the PowerShell prompt. Any commands you can enter at the PowerShell prompt can also be entered at this prompt in the ISE. You can even save the script you're writing and execute it using the full path and name from this prompt.

An extremely useful feature is IntelliSense. In Figure 1.7, we've typed **set-neti** and IntelliSense is displaying a list of cmdlets that start with set-neti. Additionally, IntelliSense is showing the specific syntax required for the Set-NetIPAddress cmdlet.

At the right is a listing of PowerShell commands. It defaults to show all PowerShell modules (all commands), but you can filter it to show only specific commands based on the module name. For example, you can select NetAdapter and it will show only the commands related to network adapters. You can also type the name of a command in the Name text box and get details on a specific command.

At the bottom right, you'll notice some status information that can be useful if you're working on scripts. Right now, we have the cursor at the beginning of line 5, and the status shows it at "Ln 1 Col 29." Sometimes, an error message will indicate there's an error at a specific line and column and you can use this information to determine the exact location of the error.

Last, you can easily zoom in to make the text bigger or smaller. Currently, it's set at 100 percent, but the pointer can be moved to the right to increase the size or to the left to decrease the size.

Getting Help on PowerShell

You'll find a rich set of help available to you within PowerShell. Many people are uneasy about using the help provided from the command prompt or PowerShell. However, this help has become much richer in recent years. If you overlook it, you'll be missing a lot. Here are some of the commands you can use to get help:

Help or **Get-Help**   Either will display generic help information on how to execute help commands and their results. Both Help and Get-Help will work.

Get-Help *commandName*   You can request help on any PowerShell command by simply typing **Help** followed by the command name. The command can be a cmdlet, a function, or an alias. When you request help for an alias, it provides help on the associated cmdlets. For example, if you type **Get-Help dir** it will return help on the Get-Children cmdlet since dir is an alias for Get-Children.

Get-Help *commandName* **-Examples**   Examples are only a few keystrokes away just by adding the -examples switch to your Get-Help request. For example, you can use the following command to see examples with descriptions of the Get-Service command. There are several pages, so the More command will allow you to view a page at a time. Press the spacebar to scroll to the next page.

```
Get-Help Get-Service -Examples | More
```

Get-Help *commandName* **-detailed**   The -detailed switch can be used to provide more detailed help than the basic Help command. It will include examples.

Get-Help *commandName* **-full**   The -full switch provides all of the available help on the topic. This will often provide more information on parameters used within the command.

Updating Help

Some of the newer advanced PowerShell cmdlets have only basic help by default. For example, if you use the following command you will only get basic help by default:

```
Get-Help Set-NetIPAddress
```

The output will include a Remarks section that indicates the Get-Help cmdlet cannot find advanced help. However, you can update the basic help with the Update-Help cmdlet. You can use Exercise 1.12 to update the help topics. This exercise assumes you're logged in, the Start screen is showing, and you have access to the Internet.

EXERCISE 1.12

Updating Help

1. Type **powershell**. Right-click Windows PowerShell and select Run As Administrator. If prompted by User Account Control, click Yes.

2. Enter the following command to start the process:

    Update-Help

3. This process will take some time but you'll see progress indicators showing that the help files are being updated. When it completes, close PowerShell.

 Many help files are available within PowerShell that provide more information about specific topics (after updating help). They are referred to as "about" topics. For example, if you want information on the pipelines command, you can enter **Help about_pipelines**. To see a full listing of all of these "about" topics, enter **help about**.

PowerShell Command Overview

PowerShell includes three types of commands that can be executed or scripted:

Cmdlets PowerShell *cmdlets* are built-in commands that come with PowerShell. They are different from command prompt commands in that they are tightly integrated with Microsoft's .NET Framework and thus provide a much richer set of capabilities. You can think of them as mini-programs. Many cmdlets can accept parameters and return values. Values can be displayed, assigned to variables, or passed to other cmdlets or functions.

For example, the Get-Command cmdlet will retrieve a list of all PowerShell commands. You can modify the command with parameters to modify the results. The following three commands can be used to retrieve a list of only the cmdlets, only the aliases, and only the functions. In these examples, the Get-Command cmdlet is being used with the -CommandType switch and cmdlet, alias, and function are the parameters passed to the Get-Command cmdlet.

```
Get-Command -CommandType cmdlet
Get-Command -CommandType alias
Get-Command -CommandType function
```

PowerShell commands can be entered with any case. However, they are commonly displayed with camel case (capping the first letter of a word) to make them easier to read. You'll see them displayed this way in this chapter and elsewhere in the book when they are used.

Aliases An *alias* is another name for a cmdlet. Many command prompt commands have been rewritten as PowerShell commands. Although the actual PowerShell command is different from the command prompt command, many aliases have been created so that you enter the command prompt command and it will launch the PowerShell command. For example, the cd command prompt command is used to change the current directory. The PowerShell cmdlet is Set-Location, but cd is recognized as an alias for Set-Location.

Try it. These two commands will achieve the same result of changing the current path to the root of the C drive.

```
CD \
Set-Location \
```

All command prompt commands have not been rewritten. If you enter a command such as path that works at the command prompt, you'll see it doesn't work here. You can enter the Get-Alias command to get a list of all the aliases supported within PowerShell. Additionally, some longer cmdlets have been rewritten as aliases. For example, the Get-WMIObject cmdlet has an alias of gwmi.

Functions A *function* is a type of command that you can run within PowerShell or PowerShell scripts. They are very similar to cmdlets. They can accept parameters and return values that are displayed, assigned to variables, or passed to other functions or cmdlets.

A commonly used function is Help, which provides help on PowerShell topics and concepts. When executed without a parameter, it provides one set of information. When a valid PowerShell command is added as a parameter (such as Help Get-Command), it provides specific help on the command. Another function that is commonly used is the drive letter (such as C:, D:, and so on). It will change the current PowerShell prompt location to the named drive. You can also create your own functions.

Any of these commands can be executed from the PowerShell prompt or embedded into PowerShell scripts. Additionally, many server applications (such as Internet Information Services [IIS], used to serve web pages, or Exchange Server 2013, used for email) are heavily intertwined with PowerShell commands. In other words, what you learn here for Windows 8.1 will be useful when you're managing servers as well.

Verbs and Nouns

PowerShell cmdlets are composed of verbs and nouns in the format of verb-noun, with the dash (-) separating the two. You may remember from your English classes that verbs denote action and nouns are things. Common PowerShell verbs are Get, Set, and Test. You can combine them with nouns to get information on objects or to set properties on objects.

Earlier, you saw the Set-Location cmdlet, which is similar to the command prompt change directory command (cd). Set is the verb and Location is the noun. Similarly, Get-Service uses the verb Get to retrieve information on services, and Out-File uses the verb Out to send information to a file.

If you can remember Get, Set, and Test, you're halfway there because PowerShell will give you a lot of clues. Try this. Type **Get-** and then press the Tab key. PowerShell will display each of the legal commands that can be executed starting with Get- (from Get-ACL to Get-WSManInstance).

You can do the same thing with the Set and Test verbs. Type **Set-** and press Tab to see all of the objects (nouns) that can have properties set: Set-ACL to Set-WSManQuickConfig. If you type **Test-** you'll be able to tab through the choices, from Test-AppLockerPolicy to Test-WSMan.

Functions don't necessarily follow the verb-noun format but instead are just commands. For example, the E: function will set the current drive to E: by calling the Set-Location cmdlet using the parameter E:. However, the Clear-Host function does use a verb-noun format to indicate the host screen (the noun) is being cleared (the verb).

Sending Output to a Text File

Many times you'll want the output of the PowerShell command to be written to a file instead of the screen. This can be especially useful when you're creating documentation. While learning, you may want to send the output of some of these commands so you can read them later. There are two ways this can be done.

The first is the same method used with the command prompt using the redirection symbol (>). For example, if you want to send a listing of all aliases to a text file named PSAlias.txt and then open the text file, you could use these commands:

```
Get-Alias > PSAlias.txt
Notepad PSAlias.txt
```

PowerShell also uses the Out-File cmdlet to send the output to a file. If you want to send a listing of services and their current status to a file, you can use the Get-Service cmdlet and the Out-File cmdlet in the same line.

Just as pipelining can be used at the command line, it can be used in PowerShell. When you want the output of one PowerShell command to be used as the input to another command on the same line, you separate the commands with the pipe symbol (|), which is Shift+Backslash (\) on most keyboards. The following shows how this is done:

```
Get-Service | Out-File Service.txt
Notepad Service.txt
```

Of course, if you wanted to save the file to a different location, you could include the full path. For example, you can save the file in the `Data` folder on the C drive with this command:

```
Get-Service | Out-File C:\Data\Service.txt
```

PowerShell Syntax

Many of the rules that apply to the command prompt also apply to PowerShell. As a reminder, here are some of these rules:

- Spelling counts.
- Commands are not case sensitive.
- Commands are modified with switches.
- Spaces usually need to be enclosed in quotes.
- Help is always available.
- Doskey saves typing.

There are a few other items you should know about PowerShell. These include variables, comparison operators, and command separators (such as parentheses, brackets, and braces), which are all covered in the following sections.

Variables Created with a $ Symbol

Many times, you'll need to create a variable that will be used to store information and later retrieve it. This can be as simple as loading a number (such as 5) into a variable like this:

```
$num = 5
```

and then retrieving the value with the variable like this:

```
$num
```

You can also use variables to hold collections of information. Collections can hold several similar items. For example, the following command will load a list of all the event logs into the variable named `$Log` and store them as a collection:

```
$Log = Get-EventLog -list
```

Once the collection is created, data about any of the items stored in the collection can be retrieved.

Comparison Operators

There are many comparison operators you can use to specify or identify a condition. Comparison operators will compare two values to determine whether a condition exists. Most comparison operators will return True if the condition exists and False if it doesn't exist.

Let's look at a simple example. Suppose a variable called $num has a value of 5. The comparison $num -eq 5 evaluates as True, whereas $num -eq 100 evaluates as False.

Comparisons can also compare text. However, when comparing text data, the text string needs to be enclosed in quotes. For example, if you wanted to know if a variable named $str has a value of "Success," you'd use this comparison:

```
$str -eq "Success"
```

String comparisons are case insensitive by default. In other words, both of these evaluate to True:

```
$str -eq "success"
$str -eq "SUCCESS"
```

However, if you want the comparison to be case sensitive, you can add the letter c to the operator switch, like this:

```
$str -ceq "Success"
```

Table 1.5 shows a listing of some of the commonly used comparison operators. You can enter these at the command line to see the result. For example, to see how the -eq command works, you could populate the variable $num with 5 and then use the variable in a comparison like this:

```
$num = 5
$num -eq 100
```

PowerShell will return False.

TABLE 1.5 Comparison operators

Operator	Description
-eq	Equals, as in $x -eq 100, or $x -eq "y"
-ne	Not equal, as in $x -ne 100 or $x -ne "y"
-gt	Greater than, as in $x -gt 100
-ge	Greater than or equal to, as in $x -ge 100
-lt	Less than, as in $x -lt 100
-le	Less than or equal to, as in $x -le 100

-like   Compares strings using the wildcard character * and returns True if a match
              is found. The wildcard character can be used at the beginning, middle, or
              end to look for specific matches. If a variable named $str holds the string
              "MCSA Windows 8.," then all of the following comparisons will return True:

              $str -like "MCSA*"

              $str -like "*Win*"

              $str -like "*8"

-notlike   Compares strings using the wildcard character * and returns True if the
              match is not found.

You'll see comparison operators used in many different ways. For example, they are used in cmdlet switches when a comparison is needed and in IF statements when you're scripting.

Parentheses, Brackets, and Braces

PowerShell commands can include parentheses (), brackets [ ], and braces { }. Braces are also referred to as "curly brackets" and even "funky brackets" by some. Each is interpreted differently within PowerShell.

Parentheses ( )   Parentheses are commonly used to provide arguments. For example, when a script needs to accept a parameter, you can use Param($input). Here $input is identified as an argument for the Param command.

The terms *parameters* and *arguments* are often used interchangeably. On one level, they are the same thing, but there is a subtle difference between the two. A parameter is provided as input to a piece of code, and an argument is what is provided. The value is the same, but the perspective is different. Parameters are passed in, and the value of this parameter is used as an argument within the code.

Brackets [ ]   Brackets are used for various purposes. You'll see them used when accessing arrays when using -like comparisons and with some parameters. For example, the following command uses brackets to indicate the output should only include names that start with the letters a through g:

```
Get-wmiObject Win32_ComputerSystem | Format-List [a-g]*
```

Braces { }   Braces are used to enclose a portion of code within a statement that is interpreted as a block of code. You'll see them in condition statements (like ForEach). The following example shows how braces are used to separate the block in the Where clause in a single line of code:

```
Get-service | Select * | Where {$_.name -like "Win*"}
```

The point here is not that you need to memorize when these characters need to be used. Instead, the goal is to let you know that all three could be used and, when you're executing code and writing scripts, to recognize each. If you replace curly braces with parentheses when you type your own code, you'll find things simply don't work.

Running PowerShell Commands

Exercise 1.13 gives you some practice running PowerShell commands. This exercise assumes you're logged on and the Start screen is showing.

EXERCISE 1.13

Running PowerShell Commands

1. Type **powershell**. Right-click Windows PowerShell and select Run As Administrator. If prompted by User Account Control, click Yes. Note that you don't always have to run PowerShell with administrative permissions, but some of the commands in this exercise require administrative permissions.

2. Enter the following command to retrieve help information on the Get-NetIPAddress cmdlet and store it in a text file:

    ```
    Get-Help Get-NetIPAddress -Full > netIP.txt
    ```

3. Use the following command to open the text file you just created. You can browse this file while entering commands.

    ```
    Notepad netIP.txt
    ```

4. Enter the following command to retrieve information on network adapters in the system:

    ```
    Get-NetIPAddress
    ```

    This command displays information on all of the network adapters. The wired Ethernet adapter (assigned an InterfaceAlias of Ethernet) is typically the first one in the list and assigned an InterfaceIndex of 12. Note the InterfaceIndex for your Ethernet adapter.

5. Enter the following command to create a table of information on the adapters showing only the index, alias, and IP address:

    ```
    Get-NetIPAddress | format-table interfaceindex, interfacealias,
    ipaddress
    ```

You'll see a display similar to the following output:

```
InterfaceIndex InterfaceAlias                      IPAddress
-------------- --------------                      ---------
12             Ethernet                            fe80::4973:2314:eca0:8dfc%12
1              Loopback Pseudo-Interface 1         ::1
12             Ethernet                            192.168.59.100
1              Loopback Pseudo-Interface 1         127.0.0.1
```

6. Enter the following command to get information on the Ethernet adapter:

   ```
   Get-NetIPAddress -InterfaceIndex 12
   ```

   You will normally see both IPv6 and IPv4 data listed.

7. Enter the following command to set a new IPv4 address of 192.168.59.121 with a subnet mask of 255.255.255.0 for the adapter with an InterfaceIndex of 12:

   ```
   New-NetIPAddress -IPAddress 192.168.59.121 -PrefixLength 24
   -InterfaceIndex 12
   ```

8. If the adapter doesn't currently have an IP address assigned, you can assign the address with the Set-NetIPAddress command:

   ```
   Set-NetIPAddress -IPAddress 192.168.59.121 -PrefixLength 24
   -InterfaceIndex 12
   ```

Running PowerShell Scripts

Creating and running PowerShell scripts has a couple of hurdles that can stop you in your tracks if you don't know what they are. These hurdles aren't hard to overcome, though. They are:

- PowerShell Execution Policy
- Path usage in PowerShell

Both of these issues are explained next.

PowerShell Execution Policy

Microsoft has embraced a secure by default mindset, and this is reflected in the *PowerShell Execution Policy*. This policy has several settings that you can modify to allow or disallow the execution of various types of scripts.

If you don't modify the policy, you'll find that each attempt to execute a PowerShell script will result in an error that says "the execution of scripts is disabled on this system." This message is telling you that the execution policy is set to Restricted, the default setting. There are several possible settings for the execution policy:

Restricted The Restricted setting prevents any scripts from being executed and is the default setting. You can still execute individual PowerShell commands.

RemoteSigned It's common to change the execution policy to RemoteSigned. This will let you execute any scripts on your local system but will prevent scripts that don't have a digital signature from being executed remotely, such as over an Internet connection.

Signed scripts have a digital signature added to them that are associated with a code-signing certificate from a trusted publisher. The idea is that if a script is signed with a certificate, you can identify the writer. Since malicious script writers don't want to be known or identified, they won't sign their scripts.

AllSigned This setting is a little more secure than RemoteSigned. Whereas RemoteSigned will allow the execution of unsigned local scripts, AllSigned will not allow the execution of any unsigned scripts. All scripts must be signed.

Unrestricted Just as it sounds, Unrestricted allows the execution of any scripts. This setting will warn you before running scripts that are downloaded from the Internet.

Bypass This is similar to Unrestricted in that it allows the execution of any scripts, but it does not give any warnings. This setting would be used when an application is using scripts and wouldn't be able to respond to any warnings.

You can use the `Get-ExecutionPolicy` cmdlet to determine the current setting for the execution policy. You can change the policy using the `Set-ExecutionPolicy` cmdlet. You must be running Windows PowerShell with administrative permissions to change the execution policy.

Exercise 1.14 shows how to change the execution policy. The exercise assumes you're logged on and the Start screen is showing.

EXERCISE 1.14

Changing the Execution Policy

1. Type **powershell**. Right-click Windows PowerShell and select Run As Administrator. If prompted by User Account Control, click Yes.

2. Enter the following command to identify the current execution policy:

   ```
   Get-ExecutionPolicy
   ```

3. Enter the following command to set the policy:

   ```
   Set-ExecutionPolicy RemoteSigned
   ```

4. When prompted, type **Y** and press Enter.

5. Enter the following command to verify the policy is changed:

```
Get-ExecutionPolicy
```

6. Close the Administrator window.

Path Usage in PowerShell

When you're using the command prompt, it will always recognize the current path and you don't have to specify it. However, if you're using PowerShell, the current path is not recognized and must be specified.

For example, consider a script used to remove multiple Windows Store apps from a user account in Windows 8.1. It is named `RemoveWindowsStoreApps.ps1` and is available for free here:

```
http://gallery.technet.microsoft.com/scriptcenter/Remove-Windows-
Store-Apps-a00ef4a4
```

You could place the script in the `c:\data\scripts` folder and change the path to the `c:\data\scripts` folder with the `cd` command. However, if you tried the `RemoveWindowsStoreApps.ps1` command, it would fail. Instead, you must specify that the script is in the local folder by using this command:

```
.\RemoveWindowsStoreApps.ps1
```

If you were in a different folder, you could use this command:

```
C:\Data\Scripts\RemoveWindowsStoreApps.ps1
```

Just a Glimpse

Remember, this chapter is not intended to make you an expert on the command prompt or PowerShell. There's no way it can in these few pages. Entire books are written on both the command prompt and PowerShell and if you want to dig deeper, we strongly encourage you to do so.

Just as the angel (Don Cheadle) tells Nicholas Cage in *Family Man*, this is "just a glimpse." It provides you with a glimpse of the possibilities. What you do with this glimpse is up to you.

Summary

The Windows 8.1 interface might be a little different than you're used to, but there are simple ways to get to familiar tools. The charms are simply mini-menus that you can access by pressing Windows logo key+C. The Search charm automatically appears if you just start typing from the Start screen. You can access additional commands by right-clicking any tile to see the alternate menu. You can also access a list of useful tools from the preview menu (by pressing Windows logo key+X).

A new type of account supported in Windows 8.1 is the Microsoft Live account. This is simply an email address that is registered with Microsoft, and domain accounts can be used as a Microsoft Live account. When users use a Microsoft Live account, it streamlines the use of many cloud-based services.

This chapter also included information on the command prompt and Windows PowerShell. There are similarities between the two, and both are heavily used by administrators. Even though these tools aren't specifically mentioned in the objectives, you can fully expect to see both types of commands on the job and on the exams.

Exam Essentials

Know the five charms.   Know the five charms: Start, Search, Share, Devices, and Settings. You can access a menu for each by pressing Windows logo key+C. The Search charm appears when you start typing from the Start screen.

Understand the difference between authentication and authorization.   Users prove who they are by authenticating with a username and password or other authentication method. Authenticated users are authorized to access resources based on the permissions they are granted.

Know the different types of accounts.   Local accounts are used in workgroups and domain accounts are used in domains. A Microsoft Live account can be used in a workgroup or a domain. An administrator account is in the Administrators group and has full control on a computer. A standard user account can perform most actions on a computer but does not have administrative permissions.

Understand picture passwords.   Picture passwords allow users to authenticate with gestures instead of typing a password. Picture passwords can be used with touch interfaces or with a mouse.

Know the command prompt.   The command prompt is a separate interface from the typical Windows GUI where commands are typed at the command prompt. Many commands exist that can be used to perform a wide array of tasks.

Understand Windows PowerShell.   Know how to launch and use Windows PowerShell. Windows PowerShell is an extension of the command prompt. It's integrated into the Microsoft .NET Framework and provides access to significantly more capabilities. PowerShell commands take the form of a verb-noun such as Get-Alias that gets (the verb) a listing of each alias command (the noun). Three common verbs are Get, Set, and Test. By entering the verb and a dash (such as Get-), you can tab through all available nouns that can be combined with the verb to form cmdlets.

Review Questions

You can find the answers in Appendix A.

1. What charm can be used to add Administrative Tools items to the Start screen?

    A. Devices

    B. Search

    C. Share

    D. Settings

2. A Windows 8.1 user is pressing Windows logo key+. (period) to snap an app to the screen location, but this is not working. What is the most likely reason?

    A. Apps are snapped to the screen with Windows logo key+S.

    B. Apps are snapped to the screen with Windows logo key+I.

    C. The screen resolution isn't at least 1024×768.

    D. Apps are snapped to the screen with the Windows logo +. and then using the arrow keys to snap the application to a screen location.

3. Of the following choices, what accurately describes the differences between authentication and authorization? (Choose all that apply.)

    A. Users prove an identity with authentication.

    B. Users prove an identity with authorization.

    C. Authorization methods are used to grant users access to resources.

    D. Authentication methods are used to grant users access to resources.

4. You need to ensure that users can access Microsoft resources like Windows Store and SkyDrive with their user account. What type of account should they use?

    A. Local account

    B. Domain account

    C. Microsoft Live account

    D. Administrator account

5. Which of the following methods can you use to create a Microsoft Live account?

    A. Computer Management ➤ System Tools ➤ Local Users and Groups

    B. Settings charm ➤ Change PC Settings ➤ Accounts

    C. Administrative Tools ➤ Users

    D. Control Panel ➤ Users

6. Users are using touch screens with Windows 8.1 devices. Of the following choices, what can they use for authentication rather than typing in a traditional password? (Choose all that apply.)

    A. PIN

    B. Picture password

    C. Gestures

    D. Windows Live ID

7. Which of the following methods can be used for authentication in Windows 8.1? (Choose all that apply.)

    A. Picture passwords

    B. Biometrics

    C. BitLocker

    D. Smartcards

8. Users in a domain currently use domain-based accounts to access domain resources. The company wants users to be able to access Microsoft-based resources with their Windows 8.1 systems. Of the following choices, what is the easiest solution?

    A. Have users create a separate Microsoft Live account.

    B. Have users register their domain account as a Microsoft Live account.

    C. Create a separate domain account for users to use as a Microsoft Live account.

    D. Create a separate local account for users to use as a Microsoft Live account.

9. You need to start the command prompt to run a command. Which of the follow methods will work? (Choose all that apply.)

    A. Access the charms by pressing Windows logo key+C and selecting Command Prompt.

    B. Type **command** at the Start screen and select Command Prompt.

    C. Access the Settings charm by pressing Windows logo key+K and selecting Command Prompt.

    D. Access the preview menu by pressing Windows logo key+X and selecting Command Prompt.

10. When you try to run a command from the command prompt on a Windows 8.1 computer, you see an error indicating it requires elevated permissions. What should you do?

    A. Run the command using PowerShell.

    B. Run the command with administrative permissions.

    C. Run the command from the GUI.

    D. Log on with an administrative account and run the command.

11. You are an administrator in a domain named Success.com and you have an administrator account named ITAdmin. You are helping a user resolve a problem and realize you need to run a program named App.exe from the command prompt with administrative permissions. The program needs access to the ITAdmin account environment. Which of the following commands should you use?

    A. `runas /user:success\itadmin /env app.exe`

    B. `runas /user:success\itadmin /profile app.exe`

    C. `runas /user:success\itadmin /noprofile app.exe`

    D. `runas /user:success\itadmin /netonly app.exe`

12. You are an administrator in a domain named Success.com and you have an administrator account named ITAdmin. You are helping a user resolve a problem and realize you need to run a program named App.exe from the command prompt with administrative permissions. You want to minimize the amount of time the program takes to run. Which of the following commands should you use?

    A. `runas /user:success\itadmin /env app.exe`

    B. `runas /user:success\itadmin /profile app.exe`

    C. `runas /user:success\itadmin /noprofile app.exe`

    D. `runas /user:success\itadmin /netonly app.exe`

13. You are running Windows 8.1 with two monitors. You want to display applications on both monitors. What should you do? (Choose all that apply.)

    A. Select Extend from the Start screen.

    B. Select Extend from the Settings charm.

    C. Select Second Screen ➤ Extend from the Devices charm.

    D. Run the `displayswitch /extend` command.

14. A computer is running Windows 8.1. What command can you use to remove leftover data fragments on a disk drive that is encrypted with BitLocker Drive Encryption?

    A. `manage-bde -w`

    B. `wipefreespace -bde`

    C. `bitlocker -wipe`

    D. `format -bde`

15. Which of the following commands can you use to install a program named success.msi on a Windows 8.1 computer from the command prompt?

    A. `execmsi /i success.msi`

    B. `install /i success.msi`

    C. `installmsi /i success.msi`

    D. `msiexec /i success.msi`

16. You've tried to execute a PowerShell command but get an error indicating that access is denied. What is the most likely solution?

   A. Change the PowerShell Execution Policy.

   B. Run the command from the PowerShell ISE.

   C. Start PowerShell using the `runas` command.

   D. Start PowerShell with administrative permissions.

17. You are trying to get help on a PowerShell command but only see limited help available for a specific command. What command should you use to get full help?

   A. `Update-Help`

   B. `Get-Help` *command* `-Full`

   C. `Help` *command* `-Full`

   D. `Get-Help` *command* `-Update-Help`

18. You need to set the IP address of a network adapter. Which of the following PowerShell commands can be used? (Choose all that apply.)

   A. `Set-NetIPAddress`

   B. `Get-NetIPAddress`

   C. `New-NetIPAddress`

   D. `ipconfig`

19. You are trying to execute a PowerShell script but keep getting an error indicating scripts cannot be executed. What should be done?

   A. Modify the PowerShell Execution Policy to Restricted.

   B. Modify the PowerShell Execution Policy to RemoteSigned.

   C. Run the script using `runas`.

   D. Launch PowerShell with administrative permissions.

20. You are trying to execute a PowerShell script in the current directory but keep getting an error indicating the script cannot be located. What is a likely solution?

   A. Use `.\` before the script name.

   B. Modify the PowerShell Execution Policy.

   C. Run the command from the PowerShell ISE.

   D. Enclose the script name in quotes.

Chapter 2

Planning the Windows 8.1 Installation

70-687 MICROSOFT EXAM OBJECTIVES COVERED IN THIS CHAPTER:

✓ **Evaluate hardware readiness and compatibility**

- Choose between an upgrade and a clean installation
- Determine which SKU to use, including Windows RT
- Determine requirements for particular features, including Hyper-V, Miracast display, pervasive device encryption, virtual smart cards, and Secure Boot

✓ **Install Windows 8.1**

- Install as Windows To Go
- Migrate from previous versions of Windows to Windows 8.1
- Upgrade from Windows 7 or Windows 8 to Windows 8.1
- Install to VHD
- Install additional Windows features
- Configure Windows for additional languages

70-688 MICROSOFT EXAM OBJECTIVES COVERED IN THIS CHAPTER:

✓ **Support operating system installation**

- Support Windows To Go
- Manage boot settings, including native virtual hard disk (VHD) and multiboot
- Manage desktop images
- Customize a Windows installation by using Windows Preinstallation Environment (PE)

Before installing Windows 8.1 on a computer, you need to ensure that it meets the basic hardware requirements. For earlier operating systems, you often needed much more power than current systems had to get acceptable performance. However, if you have a computer running Windows 7, you will get about the same performance from Windows 8.1 on that computer. In other words, if a system meets the hardware requirements for Windows 7, it meets the hardware requirements for Windows 8.1, though there are some minor differences that we will cover in this chapter.

Windows 8.1 comes in only four versions: *Windows 8.1*, *Windows 8.1 Pro*, *Windows 8.1 Enterprise*, and *Windows RT* (for example, Windows Surface tablets that use ARM processors, which are based on RISC technology). This chapter covers the features and target audience of each version. You'll also learn the hardware requirements for each version of Windows 8.1.

As with earlier operating systems, you can upgrade to Windows 8.1 from the previous Windows version (Windows 7) or perform a clean installation. The upgrade paths are limited, though. You can upgrade to Windows 8.1 from Windows 7, but not from Windows XP or Windows Vista systems.

If you're doing a clean installation, the user's settings and data aren't migrated to the new operating system automatically. However, there are tools you can use to migrate these files. The User State Migration Tool (USMT) can simplify this process for you with the use of ScanState and LoadState.

In most cases, larger enterprises take the time to design a strategy for deploying a new operating system. Operating system images are used, so it's important to understand what an image is and how it can be deployed. This chapter introduces the images, and Chapter 3, "Installing Windows 8.1," provides a step-by-step review of the Windows 8.1 installation process.

CERT OBJECTIVE Choosing a Windows 8.1 Edition

When planning a migration or tech refresh, a simple question to ask is which Windows 8.1 edition is needed. Windows 8.1 offers four editions, and it's relatively easy to determine which edition you need once you are familiar with them.

Microsoft identifies the edition as a stock-keeping unit (SKU) in much of its documentation. For example, the "Evaluate hardware readiness and compatibility" objective for the 70-687 exam includes the phrase "determine which SKU to install." The SKU is the number associated with the barcode you see on just about any retail product. You don't need to know the SKU, but you should be able to pick an appropriate edition for a given scenario.

The following is an overview of the Windows 8.1 versions:

Windows 8.1   Typical home users will use the basic edition known as Windows 8.1. It includes features needed by home users but does not include the advanced features businesses require, such as the ability to join a domain.

Windows 8.1 Pro   Additional features needed by small and medium-sized businesses are included in the Pro edition. Home users can also purchase this edition if they want the additional features.

Windows 8.1 Enterprise   The Enterprise edition includes all available Windows 8.1 features included with Windows 8.1 Pro plus many more needed by larger organizations. It is available only to organizations that have a Software Assurance contract with Microsoft and is purchased through a volume license. Home users won't have access to this edition, but businesses with as few as five PCs can purchase Software Assurance.

Windows RT   Tablets and other small ARM-based devices come preloaded with Windows RT. ARM-based processors use a reduced instruction set computing (RISC) architecture, which is optimized for smaller devices. Windows RT was previously known as Windows on ARM (WOA).

Acronyms are hard enough to remember on their own, but when letters aren't acronyms they become even more confusing. For example, neither RT nor ARM is an acronym. RT is sometimes referred to as Windows Runtime, but that isn't accurate because Windows Runtime is on any edition of Windows 8.1. Also, ARM refers to ARM Holdings, the company that designs and licenses ARM-based processors. ARM Holdings was previously named Advanced RISC Machines, so you might occasionally see ARM spelled out as Advanced RISC Machines.

Some of the features available in all versions of Windows 8.1 are listed in Table 2.1. The table also lists the chapter that covers the feature.

TABLE 2.1   Windows 8.1 common features

Feature	Chapter	Comments
File History	12	Automatically creates backups of library files
Microsoft Live account integration	1	Allows users to log on to a system with a Microsoft Live account
Picture password	1	Lets you use gestures to log into your PC
Reset your PC	12	Similar to a clean installation; removes all data, apps, and settings
Refresh your PC	12	Similar to an upgrade; keeps personal data, apps, and settings
Start screen	1	Includes live tiles and semantic zoom
Storage Spaces	9	Alternate method of managing large volumes of physical drives as logical spaces
Windows Defender	5	Antimalware software; replaces Microsoft Security Essentials

Table 2.2 compares many of the features included in Windows 8.1, Windows 8.1 Pro, and Windows 8.1 Enterprise and lists the chapter where those topics are covered.

TABLE 2.2   Windows 8.1 versions and features

Feature	Chapter	Windows 8.1	Windows 8.1 Pro	Windows 8.1 Enterprise
Maximum random access memory (RAM)	2	4 GB (32-bit) 128 GB (64-bit)	4 GB (32-bit) 512 GB (64-bit)	4 GB (32-bit) 512 GB (64-bit)
32-bit and 64-bit versions	2	Yes	Yes	Yes
BitLocker and BitLocker To Go	9	No	Yes	Yes

Feature	Chapter	Windows 8.1	Windows 8.1 Pro	Windows 8.1 Enterprise
Client Hyper-V	14	No	Yes (64-bit versions only)	Yes (64-bit versions only)
Encrypting File System	9	No	Yes	Yes
Join Domain	7	No	Yes	Yes
Manage with Group Policy	7	No	Yes	Yes
Virtual hard disk booting	2, 3	No	Yes	Yes
Remote Desktop	4, 8	As a client	As client or host	As client or host
Side-load apps	4	No	Yes	Yes
AppLocker	5	No	No	Yes
BranchCache	8	No	No	Yes
DirectAccess	8	No	No	Yes
Virtualization with RemoteFX	14	No	Yes	Yes
Windows To Go	2, 3	No	No	Yes

Windows Media Center is not included in desktop versions of Windows 8.1. You can purchase it as an add-in for Windows 8.1 Pro, but it is not supported in other editions. Windows 8.1 will not play DVDs without the Windows Media Center or another third-party app.

Windows RT and the Surface Tablet

Originally Windows RT was available only on the Microsoft Windows Surface tablet. Other manufacturers also released Windows RT tablets, including Acer, Asus, Samsung, and HP. These tablets come with the Windows RT operating system preinstalled. Some of the unique characteristics of Windows RT are:

- Comes preinstalled on ARM devices
- Only available in 32-bit versions
- Includes Windows Media Center
- Includes several Microsoft apps (Microsoft Word, Microsoft Excel, Microsoft Power-Point, and Microsoft OneNote)

As of this writing, Windows Surface tablets are available in 32 GB and 64 GB versions. However, the operating system and included apps take some space. Users end up with about 16 GB of free space on 32 GB systems and 45 GB of free space on 64 GB systems.

> You can also purchase Surface tablets running Windows 8.1 Pro instead of Windows 8.1. These come in either 64 GB or 128 GB versions.

Software Assurance

Windows 8.1 Enterprise is available only to businesses that have purchased the Software Assurance program, so you may be interested in knowing a little about it. It's a Microsoft program offered to organizations that purchase licenses through a volume-licensing program. Volume licensing allows a company to purchase licenses in bulk at a discount instead of purchasing multiple individual copies.

Organizations that can purchase Software Assurance include businesses with as few as five employees, as well as government entities, schools, and campuses. It is purchased through Microsoft partners, and the benefits are coordinated through Microsoft once they are activated. Benefits differ based on how many clients and licenses are purchased.

The benefits include:

- Free upgrades to newer versions of the software during the licensing period
- The option to spread payments over a longer period of time (as opposed to the initial cost of purchasing all the licenses)
- Training vouchers for Microsoft courses taught by Microsoft partners
- Access to e-learning courses
- 24×7 telephone and web support

CERT OBJECTIVE Evaluating Hardware and Compatibility Requirements

An important consideration when evaluating any operating system is ensuring that the hardware supports the operating system requirements. There's some great news here, though. With very few exceptions, you'll find that any hardware running Windows 7 will run Windows 8.1 with comparable performance.

The following list identifies the basic hardware requirements for installing Windows 8.1:

- Processor: 1 GHz or faster processor
- RAM: 1 GB for 32-bit systems or 2 GB for 64-bit systems
- Hard disk space: 16 GB free disk space for 32-bit systems or 20 GB for 64-bit systems
- Graphics card: A Microsoft DirectX 9 graphics device with a Windows Display Driver Model (WDDM) driver

Windows 8.1 supports touch screens, and Surface tablets that come with Windows RT have built-in touch screens. However, a touch screen is not required to run Windows 8.1 on other systems.

Considering x86 and x64 (32-Bit and 64-Bit)

Windows 8.1 comes in both 32-bit (x86) and 64-bit (x64) editions. Although you must have 64-bit hardware in order to install the 64-bit edition, it is possible to install the 32-bit edition on 64-bit hardware.

32-bit processors are based on Intel Architecture – 32-bit (IA-32). These were first implemented on the Intel 80386 processor and have been commonly referred to as x86. In other words, 32-bit processors can be called IA-32 or x86 processors. 64-bit processors are commonly called x64 but are sometimes referred to as x86-64.

The biggest advantage of using a 64-bit edition over a 32-bit edition is the ability to use more RAM. With a 32-bit system, you're limited to addressing and using no more than 4 GB of RAM. But even that is limited. Because of the way that RAM is addressed and used in Windows operating systems, no more than 3.3 GB of RAM is actually available when 4 GB is installed. The rest of the RAM is unused because of how address space is reserved.

The 64-bit version of Windows 8.1 supports as much as 128 GB of RAM, and 64-bit versions of Windows 8.1 Pro and Enterprise both support as much as 512 GB of RAM. This gives you enough RAM to support multiple virtual environments hosted on a single system and also to support even the most demanding applications.

In addition to supporting more RAM, 64-bit versions provide overall better performance and better security. The 64-bit processors are faster, which allows them to process more data even when using the same clock speed of a 32-bit system. Windows 8.1 uses Kernel Patch Protection (KPP, or PatchGuard) which protects key Windows files from being modified by malicious software (malware).

Determining Screen Resolution

As mentioned in Chapter 1, "Introducing Windows 8.1," Windows 8.1 includes a new feature called *snapping apps*. This feature allows you to share the screen with multiple apps by "snapping" one to the screen edge. This feature works best with a screen resolution of at least 1366×768. Both the video card and the monitor need to support this resolution to snap apps. However, Windows 8.1 will still run if the system doesn't support this higher resolution.

Exercise 2.1 shows how to check the screen resolution of a system. This exercise assumes you're logged in and the Start screen is showing.

EXERCISE 2.1

Checking Screen Resolution

1. Move your mouse to the bottom-left corner.

2. When the Start menu appears, right-click over it and select Desktop.

3. Right-click the Desktop and select Screen Resolution.

4. You can click the down arrow next to Resolution to reveal the screen resolution choices available on your system.

5. If desired, select a different screen resolution and click OK. When prompted, click Keep Changes to use the new screen resolution.

✔ Choosing between an Upgrade and a Clean Install

When installing Windows 8.1 on a computer, you can either upgrade a previous installation of Windows or perform a clean install. An upgrade will keep all of the previously installed applications, and as long as they are compatible, they will be available without you having to reinstall them. A clean install does not include any of the previously installed applications.

If the installation program finds a version of Windows on the system, you'll see the following two choices on the installation screen:

Upgrade: Install Windows And Keep Files, Settings, And Applications When you select this option, the files, settings, and applications from the previous installation are moved to the new installation. This option won't be selectable if the installation program didn't locate an upgradable version of Windows.

Custom: Install Windows Only (Advanced) This is a completely clean installation. None of the files, settings, or applications are moved to the new installation. Existing files are not deleted by default, but they might be moved around.

> If you make changes to any of the partitions of a hard drive during the installation, all existing data on the hard drive is lost. In general, you should consider an installation of a new operating system to be a risky operation for existing data and back up all important data before starting.

If you are doing a Custom installation, you can migrate files and settings from the old operating system to the new Windows 8.1 installation. Migration topics are covered later in this chapter.

Windows.old Folder

If you perform a clean install on a computer with an existing version of Windows, the installation creates a folder named `Windows.old`. This folder includes all of the files directly related to the previous installation (later you can use the Disk Cleanup utility's Clean Up System Files option to remove the `Windows.old` folder). For example, the folder will include the `Windows`, `Programs and Files`, and `Users` folders if you installed Windows 8.1 on an existing Windows 7 system. Other folders are not manipulated, though. For example, if you have a folder you've named `MyData` at the root of C:, it will not be modified at all.

Data and settings from the `Windows.old` folder can be retrieved. A simple way to access the data is to use Windows Explorer, browse to where the data is located, and simply copy it. You can copy the data to another location on the disk, a network drive, or any removable media. You can also transfer this data using USMT tools. Chapter 3 covers the steps in more detail.

An important point to remember is that if you modify any partitions during the installation, all existing data on the drive is lost. The `Windows.old` folder will not be available.

Upgrade Paths

You can upgrade some Windows 7 systems to Windows 8.1, but there are limitations. Table 2.3 shows the supported upgrade paths.

TABLE 2.3 Windows 8.1 upgrade paths

Current operating system	Can upgrade to
Windows 7 Starter, Home Basic or Home Premium editions	Windows 8.1, Windows 8.1 Pro, or Windows 8.1 Enterprise
Windows 7 Professional or Ultimate editions	Windows 8.1 Pro or Windows 8.1 Enterprise

TABLE 2.3   Windows 8.1 upgrade paths *(continued)*

Current operating system	Can upgrade to
Windows 8.1	Windows 8.1 Pro or Windows 8.1 Enterprise
Windows 8.1 Pro	Windows 8.1 Enterprise

Upgrades from Windows XP or Windows Vista are not supported. However, you can migrate files and settings from these operating systems after installing Windows 8.1. You will have to reinstall your applications.

Notice that Table 2.3 also shows the upgrade paths to Windows 8.1. You can upgrade to a higher edition but not to a lower edition. For example, you can upgrade Windows 8.1 to Windows 8.1 Pro, but you cannot upgrade Windows 8.1 Pro down to the basic edition of Windows 8.1.

 You can only upgrade to an edition of the same architecture. In other words, a 32-bit version of Windows can only be upgraded to a 32-bit version. Similarly, a 64-bit version can only be upgraded to a 64-bit version. It is not possible to upgrade a 32-bit version to a 64-bit version.

Windows 8.1 Upgrade Assistant

The Windows 8.1 installation DVD includes a setup program that starts the installation of Windows. When you run it, it will perform a compatibility check of the current system to determine whether an upgrade is possible. If the system is not able to be upgraded, the setup program will prevent you from trying an upgrade.

You can also use the Windows 8.1 Upgrade Assistant before starting an installation to determine compatibility. The Windows 8.1 Upgrade Assistant is a free tool you can run on Windows systems. After running it, it provides you with a compatibility report listing all the apps and devices that are compatible and potential items that might not be compatible and need to be reviewed. For example, most Windows 7 computers are running sidebar gadgets and the compatibility report will list them as something to review because Windows 8.1 does not support sidebar gadgets.

In addition to giving you information on compatibility, the tool includes the ability to purchase and install Windows 8.1. It also includes wizards used to capture settings and data and then migrate them to the new installation.

Exercise 2.2 shows the steps to run the Upgrade Assistant. You can read more about the process here: http://windows.microsoft.com/en-US/windows-8/upgrade-to-windows-8.

EXERCISE 2.2

Running the Upgrade Assistant

1. Download the Windows 8.1 Upgrade Assistant from this location: http://go.microsoft.com/fwlink/p/?LinkId=261871.

2. Locate the download and double-click to start it.

3. If a security warning appears, review it and click Run to start it.

4. If User Account Control (UAC) prompts you to continue, click Yes. The Upgrade Assistant will scan your system to identify apps and devices that are currently installed.

    After a moment, the Upgrade Assistant will complete and list the number of apps and devices that are compatible, along with the number of items that need to be reviewed.

5. Click See Compatibility Details. This opens a report listing the items you should review first, and then the items that are compatible. Most of the items to review will have links to get additional information. Many of these items can be resolved after upgrading the system by installing an update.

6. Click Save. Browse to a location where you want to save the report and click Save. Click Close.

7. If you want to install Windows 8.1, click Next. If not, you can close the Upgrade Assistant by clicking the Close icon in the upper right.

8. On the Choose What To Keep page, select Windows Settings, Personal Files, And Apps. Click Next. This is only selectable if you are running Windows 7. If you're running another operating system, select Just Personal Files and click Next.

9. If you click Order, you can order a Windows 8.1 download that you can install on your system. Click Checkout and provide payment information to continue.

You can also check the Windows 8.1 Compatibility Center to identify different hardware and software that is compatible with Windows 8.1. You can access it here: www.microsoft.com/en-us/windows/compatibility/win8/CompatCenter/.

Upgrade vs. Migration

If you are not doing an upgrade, you can migrate user data to the new installation. Chapter 3 covers in more depth the tools you can use to migrate user data. The primary tool you'll use is the *User State Migration Tool (USMT)*, which includes two tools you can execute from the command prompt. The *ScanState* utility is used to capture user data and settings from the original installation, and *LoadState* is used to restore user data and settings on the new installation.

Here are the basic steps involved with migrating user data to a new installation:

1. Run scanstate on the previous edition of Windows to back up the user's settings and data.

2. Complete a clean installation of Windows 8.1 on a computer.

3. Install any desired applications.

4. Run loadstate on the Windows 8.1 computer to restore the user's settings and data.

The user's settings and data are saved in a migration store and can be stored on the same computer, a network share, an external USB drive, or any type of removable media.

When performing a migration, you'll be performing one of these scenarios:

Side-by-Side   In this scenario, you have the old computer next to the new computer. You perform a clean installation on the new computer and then migrate the user's settings and data to the new computer.

In-Place Migration   In this second scenario, you have only one computer. You do not modify any of the partitions during the installation. Files and settings from the previous installation are automatically retained in the Windows.old folder and you can later apply them to the new installation.

Wipe and Load   In this third scenario, you have only one computer and you either plan on modifying existing partitions or plan on deleting existing data. You first capture the user's settings and data and save it in a migration store. You then perform a clean installation of Windows 8.1 by selecting the Custom Advanced installation choice. Afterward, you can apply the user's settings and data to the new installation of Windows 8.1.

⬥CERT OBJECTIVE Designing an Operating System Installation Strategy

A simple installation for Windows 8.1 can start with putting an installation DVD into the system and starting the setup.exe installation program. However, several other methods are available. In addition to installing from a DVD, you can use one of these choices:

Install from a Network Share   You can copy all of the files from the installation DVD onto a network share. Existing computers can connect to the share and run the setup program over the network.

Install from a USB Flash Drive   You can copy all of the files from the installation DVD onto a flash drive and run the setup program from it. It's also possible to create a bootable USB flash drive with the installation files on it.

Although these choices work well for simple installations of one or two systems, they are much too time consuming when you want to install Windows to multiple systems. Instead, you can use one of the many available methods to automate deployments.

Windows 8.1 Images

Images are used to deploy Windows 8.1 to computers. All of the images are derived from the basic Windows Imaging (WIM) file type in Windows 8.1. This is the same WIM file type used in Windows 7, Windows Server 2008, and Windows Server 2012. The two primary image types are:

Boot Images A *boot image* installs the Windows Preinstallation Environment (Windows PE or WinPE). WinPE is used to provide a basic environment where a full installation can start. The Windows 8.1 installation DVD includes a boot image (named boot.wim in the \sources folder).

Install Images An *install image* includes a full operating system. The Windows 8.1 installation DVD includes the Windows 8.1 install images in the install.wim file. You can also create custom install images. A custom install image would include the operating system, additional drivers, applications, settings, and configuration.

WIM files can contain more than one image. For example, the install.wim file could include two images: one for Windows 8.1 and the other for Windows 8.1 Pro.

The *Deployment Image Servicing and Management (DISM)* tool can be used to view and manipulate image files. It is installed by default in a Windows 8.1 installation and is available at the command prompt. It requires elevated permissions, so you must run the command prompt with administrative permissions. One of the things you can do with it is identify the images in an image file. The format is:

```
dism /get-wiminfo /wimfile:filepath
```

For example, if the install.wim file is located in the e:\sources path, you could use this command:

```
dism /get-wiminfo /wimfile:e:\sources\install.wim
```

It's important to realize the distinction between a WIM file and an image. An image is a full image of a bootable operating system, but it must be contained within a WIM file. Any WIM file can contain one or more images.

Images are stored in image files using compression and single-file technologies. Compression is easy enough to understand: The files are zipped or shrunk and can be uncompressed when needed.

Single-file technologies may be new to you. Files that are in more than one image are stored only once in the image file. For example, the Windows folder holds the regedit .exe file. If your WIM file includes four Windows 8.1 images, the regedit.exe file is stored only once as a resource that is available to each of the images. Space is saved by storing it once instead of four times.

Automating Deployments with Images

Automated deployments are commonly used to deploy Windows 8.1. They save a lot of time, and the images can be modified to meet specific needs.

The overall process of deploying images, shown in Figure 2.1, is explained in the following steps:

FIGURE 2.1   Deploying Windows 8.1 with images

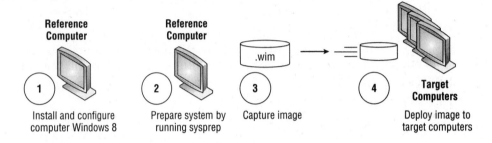

1. Windows 8.1 is installed as a clean installation on a reference computer. This must be a clean installation, not an upgrade. You can then install any desired applications and configure it as desired.

2. The computer is prepared by running the command sysprep. The Sysprep tool removes unique information such as the computer's security identifier (SID). When Sysprep completes, it shuts down the computer.

3. At this point the installation on the reference computer can be captured as an image and stored in a WIM file. This file can be stored on a network computer, an external drive, or a DVD.

4. A single image can be deployed to multiple target computers. Unattended answer files or task sequences can be used to automate these installations so that user interaction is not required. For example, the answer files can automatically enter valid license keys for the target computers.

Several tools are available to assist you with creating and deploying images. These include:

Windows Deployment Services   *Windows Deployment Services (WDS)* is a free server role that is included in Windows Server 2012, and it was also in Windows Server 2008. Administrators can use WDS to capture an image of a Windows 8.1 computer and then deploy the same image to multiple computers.

System Center Configuration Manager   *System Center Configuration Manager (SCCM)* is an add-on product that is a component of the Microsoft System Center product that has many more capabilities than WDS. For example, it has the ability to schedule when Windows 8.1 is deployed to systems, and it is also used to keep systems up-to-date with current patches.

Windows Assessment and Deployment Kit   *Windows Assessment and Deployment Kit (ADK)* is a collection of tools you can use to automate the deployment of Windows 8.1. It includes tools to create unattended installation answer files, Windows Preinstallation Environment (Windows PE) files, and the USMT. You can use these tools by themselves or with WDS and SCCM.

The Windows ADK replaces the Windows Automated Installation Kit (WAIK) used in Windows 7. It includes many of the same tools as the WAIK.

 Real World Scenario

Using Images as Baselines

It's common for many companies to use an image as a baseline. At one organization where this author worked, a single image was created to save time and money and to increase security.

This baseline image included the operating system, several Microsoft Office applications, antimalware software, and some other software programs. The Local Security Policy was modified to ensure that the system met minimal security requirements at the first boot. Other configuration was completed to ensure that it matched the internal environment.

Desktop administrators had this image available on a DVD and could easily apply it to any computer. Two computer resellers also had a copy of this image, and new computers purchased from them included this image when they were received. Once the computer was booted with this image, it was joined to a domain and Group Policy was used to fine-tune the settings.

This approach saved time because the desktop administrators could complete a new installation much more quickly. Most of the time-consuming tasks of a manual installation were already completed. With the same baseline applied to all the systems, they started in a secure state.

This image also reduced the cost of maintenance and troubleshooting. Since all the systems had the same configuration, desktop administrators were able to provide assistance quickly to any user without first trying to learn how the user's system was configured.

Understanding the Different Image Types

You create standard and custom images on reference computers. An organization can have a single standard image used as a baseline for all users. It can also have multiple custom images used for specific needs for different groups of users.

Suppose you work in a large organization with tens of thousands of users. You can create a single standard image and use it to deploy images to computers throughout your organization. Although it can have a significant amount of customization—including additional applications, security, and other settings—it starts as only a baseline. You can then use Group Policy and SCCM to deploy various applications and settings to users within your organization.

The following is a brief overview of the two image types:

Reference Image   A reference image is a single image used as a baseline for all computers. It includes customization such as additional applications, security, and other settings affecting features and components of the operating system. The enterprise then uses Group Policy, SCCM, and other tools to deploy various settings, applications, and updates to systems within the organization.

Custom Image   Instead of a single image for everyone, it's possible for an organization to use different custom images for different target groups. For example, one custom image can be used for users in the Sales department, and the Accounting department can use another custom image. Even when custom images are used, it's common to use Group Policy to enforce settings and to use other tools such as SCCM or Windows Server Update Services (WSUS) to deploy updates.

Online vs. Offline Image Servicing

Images occasionally need to be modified or updated in a process called *servicing*. Images can be serviced either online or offline:

Online Servicing   The image is updated only after booting into the operating system. After the changes are made, the image is recaptured. This is much more time consuming than offline servicing.

Offline Servicing   The image is updated by adding the appropriate files to an image. The image doesn't need to be booted. Additionally, the image doesn't need to be recaptured.

In offline servicing, the image is extracted from the image file in a process referred to as *mounting the image*. Once the image is extracted, files within the image can be modified and packages can be added. DISM, mentioned earlier, is the primary tool used to mount an image and perform offline servicing.

After an offline image is modified, the changes can be saved back as an image contained within the original WIM file or stored in a different WIM file. The image can then be deployed just like any other image.

Creating Images on a Reference Computer

The steps involved in creating a reference computer for imaging begin by first installing the operating system. Next, the system is configured as desired.

1. Install desired applications. You can install any applications you want at this point. Installed applications will be available to users after the image is deployed. These

include full-blown applications such as Microsoft Office, simple applications such as Adobe Reader, Internet Explorer add-ons, and security applications such as antivirus software.

2. **Configure security settings.** Although Windows 8.1 starts in a relatively secure state, it's common to tweak it to meet the needs of the organization. As a few examples, the administrator account is renamed as a best practice, the firewall is configured based on network applications and services, and some services might be disabled or enabled. The Local Security Policy tool (covered in Chapter 8, "Managing Security in Windows 8.1") is the primary tool used to configure security settings.

3. **Configure other desired settings.** You can configure additional settings such as enabling or disabling features and components and modifying the Start screen.

4. **Test, test, test.** Once the system has been configured, it should be well tested to ensure it meets the needs of the organization. Though some modification of the image can be done after it's created, you'll find it much easier to make sure it has everything needed before capturing the image.

5. **Run Sysprep,** which prepares the system for duplication. You use it to remove computer-specific information such as the computer name and the computer security identifier (SID).

After these steps are completed, you can capture the image using tools from the Windows ADK or WDS.

Running Sysprep

The Sysprep (short for system preparation) tool is a very important element of the imaging process. If you deploy an image to multiple computers without running Sysprep, these computers will have problems.

As a simple example, the SID will be the same on these computers if Sysprep isn't run. When more than one computer has the same SID in an environment, you end up troubleshooting a wide assortment of errors, none of which simply states "Duplicate SIDs identified." It's best to avoid these problems completely by running Sysprep.

The sysprep.exe program is located in the Windows\System32\Sysprep folder. You can launch it from the command prompt or by double-clicking it to launch the graphical user interface (GUI).

NOTE   Sysprep cannot be run on an upgraded version of Windows. In other words, if you are running Windows 7 and then upgrade to Windows 8.1, you cannot run Sysprep on the upgraded Windows 8.1 system. If you try, an information dialog box appears, saying, "You can only run Sysprep on a custom (clean) install version of Windows."

Figure 2.2 shows the GUI part of the Sysprep tool.

FIGURE 2.2 Running the Sysprep GUI

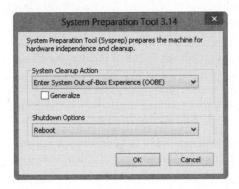

Sysprep includes two System Cleanup Action choices and three Shutdown Options choices. The Generalize option is the most important check box for this GUI. When checked, it will remove system-specific information from the computer, which allows you to reuse the image on different computers.

The two System Cleanup Action choices are Enter System Out-Of-Box Experience (OOBE) and Enter System Audit Mode:

Enter System Out-Of-Box Experience (OOBE)   This option will run and remove all unique settings, and then turn off the system. The image should be captured after selecting this choice. When the system is turned on after using this option, it will mimic the first boot screens from an initial installation. The Windows Welcome program will run when it is booted to reinitialize settings on the computer. It's possible to automate this process with the use of an answer file.

Enter System Audit Mode   The system audit mode can be used by original equipment manufacturers, computer resellers, or enterprises for similar hardware. It allows a custom image to be saved and then booted into audit mode, where additional programs or updates can be added.

You can use audit mode when doing online servicing. It will run many of the initial setup tasks for a normal boot, but it bypasses the Windows Welcome phase, which speeds up the process considerably. After a computer boots to audit mode, it will continue to boot to audit mode until you configure the computer to boot to the Windows Welcome phase by running Sysprep again and selecting Out-Of-Box Experience (OOBE).

The three Shutdown Options are Quit, Reboot, and Shutdown:

Quit   This will exit Sysprep after running it but it won't shut down the system.

Reboot   As you'd guess, this reboots the system. Use it if you plan on either modifying settings in audit mode or immediately capturing the image.

Shutdown   This will power down the system after Sysprep is run.

When running sysprep from the command prompt, you would generally use the following command:

```
C:\windows\system32\sysprep\sysprep /oobe /generalize /shutdown
```

The /oobe switch specifies the Out-Of-Box Experience, the /generalize switch causes unique information to be removed, and the /shutdown switch causes the system to shut down. These command-line switches work the same as the selections in the GUI. After running the command, you should capture the image using one of the available tools. If the system boots normally without capturing the image, you will have to run Sysprep again before the image is captured.

You may want to use two additional switches when running sysprep from the command prompt:

/quiet This switch runs sysprep without displaying any onscreen messages. It would be used if sysprep was automated through a script.

/unattend:answerfile This switch is used to specify the full path and name of an answer file to use when the system is rebooted. Windows 8.1 will use this answer file for an unattended installation. You can use the Windows System Image Manager (part of the Windows ADK) to create an answer file to use with sysprep.

Installing the Windows ADK

The Windows ADK is available as free download. It is relatively small at only 1.2 MB. However, the full installation of the Windows ADK takes up about 5 GB of space. Exercise 2.3 shows the installation steps.

EXERCISE 2.3

Installing the Windows ADK

1. Download the WADK here: www.microsoft.com/en-us/download/details .aspx?id=30652.

2. Locate the download (named adksetup.exe) and double-click it to start it.

3. If a security warning appears, review it and click Run to start it.

4. On the Specified Location page, you can accept the default or browse to a different location. Click Next.

5. Review the information on the Join the Customer Experience Improvement Program (CEIP) page and choose Yes or No. Click Next.

6. Review the License Agreement and click Accept.

7. On the Select Features page, select Application Compatibility Toolkit (ACT), the User State Migration Tool (USMT), and Windows Assessment Services – Client.

8. If your system doesn't have an instance of SQL Server 2005 or newer running on it, select Microsoft SQL Server 2012 Express. Click Install.

9. If UAC prompts you to continue, click Yes. The install program will begin by first downloading the necessary files; this download will take a while.

10. When the installation completes, click Close.

Design Considerations

When identifying a plan to install Windows 8.1 on computers within an organization, you must consider several issues. For example, if you plan on using Windows To Go or Client Hyper-V on the new Windows 8.1 systems, you need to ensure their hardware meets certain requirements.

Windows To Go

Windows To Go is a new capability available only in Windows 8.1 Enterprise that allows you to boot to Windows 8.1 from a USB drive. This can be a USB flash drive or a portable USB hard drive. Users can plug this drive into any system that supports the hardware requirements for Windows 8.1 and can boot to a USB drive and run a Windows 8.1 workspace. The processor and RAM requirements are the same as other Windows 8.1 systems, but the system must also meet the following requirements:

- The system must have a USB 2.0 or 3.0 port.
- The system must be able to boot from a USB drive.
- The BIOS must be configured to boot from a USB drive.

The USB drive holding the Windows To Go workspace should be plugged into a USB port on the computer. Using external hubs for Windows To Go is not supported. Additionally, there are some requirements related to the USB drive:

- The drive must be at least 32 GB. If the drive is smaller, the Windows To Go program won't continue. Also, due to how Windows calculates the space, the Windows To Go program might consider a 32 GB USB drive too small and refuse to install it.
- The drive must be certified for use with Windows To Go. Microsoft does not support drives that do not have this certification.

If you have a 32 GB or larger drive that isn't certified, it might still work. This page has a link to a program you can run to test a drive to see if it will work: http://msdn.microsoft.com/library/windows/hardware/jj123831.aspx.

A Windows To Go drive can be encrypted using BitLocker Drive Encryption. However, a Trusted Platform Module (TPM) is not required or used. A TPM is associated with a specific computer, but a Windows To Go drive can be plugged into any computer. Because of this, BitLocker uses a boot password when configured with a Windows To Go drive.

The Windows recovery environment and push button reset isn't available in a Windows To Go workspace either. If recovery is needed, the drive needs to be re-created from scratch.

Here are some key design considerations related to a Windows To Go deployment:

Data   Consider where the data will be stored and synchronized. Users will be able to access the Windows To Go workspace when away from their normal desktop, but if data is stored on the desktop, it will not be available from the Windows To Go workspace.

Architecture (32-Bit or 64-Bit)   You can create a 32-bit or 64-bit Windows To Go workspace, but there are restrictions. Many newer computers use a Unified Extensible Firmware Interface (UEFI)-based BIOS instead of the traditional BIOS. A 64-bit system using a UEFI-based BIOS can only boot to a 64-bit Windows To Go workspace. In contrast, a 64-bit system using traditional BIOS can boot to either a 32-bit or 64-bit Windows To Go workspace. You cannot boot a 64-bit Windows To Go workspace on any 32-bit system.

Drivers   If you know which systems will be used for the Windows To Go workspace, you should add the drivers to the Windows To Go image before deploying it.

Chapter 3 includes an exercise showing how to install Windows To Go onto a compatible USB drive.

Operating System Virtualization

Client Hyper-V, a new addition in Windows 8.1, is available in 64-bit editions of Windows 8.1 Pro and Windows 8.1 Enterprise. With Hyper-V, you can use a single physical system running Windows 8.1 to host multiple virtual systems. The physical system is called the *host* and the virtual systems are called *guests*. For example, the host system can run Windows 8.1 and you can have a virtual network with a guest virtual server running Windows Server 2012 and two guest virtual workstations running Windows 8.1.

You can configure the virtual network settings within Hyper-V to manipulate how these virtual machines (VMs) are connected. For example, you can configure them to be completely isolated from each other, connected to each other but isolated from the live network, or connected to each other and the live network.

Using a virtual network is an ideal way to learn advanced networking skills within a Microsoft network. You can configure the server as a domain controller and join each of the computers to the domain. You can then manipulate group policy on the domain controller to manage the computers. You can experiment, play, and learn without any risk to a production environment. The worst that can happen is you destroy the entire virtual network and have an opportunity to re-create it.

Users can use Client Hyper-V to create VM environments to test applications or run separate desktops in isolated environments. Client Hyper-V uses the same technologies as Hyper-V uses in Windows Server 2012. In server environments, virtualization is often used to reduce the number of physical servers. For example, a single host server running Hyper-V can support multiple guest servers. This approach reduces the cost of hardware, the amount of space needed, and costs related to power and air conditioning.

A benefit to learning Client Hyper-V is that the knowledge easily transfers to the server version of Hyper-V. There are some differences, but you'll be a step ahead.

The basic requirements to use Hyper-V on a Windows 8.1 system are:

- Only 64-bit editions of Windows 8.1 Pro or Windows 8.1 Enterprise can be used.
- The processor must support hardware-assisted virtualization (this is common in most modern Intel and AMD processors).
- Virtualization must be enabled in the BIOS.
- The system needs a minimum of 4 GB of RAM (more is needed for five or more VMs).

Even though you can install Client Hyper-V only on 64-bit hosts, it supports both 32-bit and 64-bit guest operating systems. You can install almost any version of a Windows desktop operating system in a Hyper-V environment. This includes Windows 95, 98, ME, XP (SP2 or SP3), Windows Vista, Windows 7, and Windows 8.1. Hyper-V supports all Windows desktop operating systems, up to and including Windows 8.1.

 Chapter 4, "Using Virtualization Technologies," Client Hyper-V in more depth, including how to enable it, create and configure VMs, and create and configure other virtual components.

Native VHD Boot

Windows 8.1 supports booting from a virtual hard disk (VHD) file. A VHD-based file includes a fully bootable operating system. Just as with a regular operating system, you can modify it by installing applications, changing settings, and adding files.

If you add the VHD file to a Windows 8.1 computer and configure it properly, it creates a dual-boot environment, allowing you to boot to different operating systems. One of the challenges with traditional dual-boot environments is that you need to ensure each operating system is installed on its own partition. With a VHD file, you can use a single partition and just add the file to the partition.

The VHD file format has been used in Windows 7. Windows 8.1 supports the VHD format and a newer VHDX format. The biggest difference is the maximum size of the files:

- VHD files can be up to 2 TB in size.
- VHDX files can be up to 64 TB in size.

Both file types support either a fixed file size or a dynamically expanding file size. A dynamically expanding file starts at the minimum size and grows as more space is needed. In general, fixed-size files are recommended for the following reasons:

Faster Performance   The process of dynamically expanding a disk slows it down.

Host Space Protection   A dynamically expanding disk can grow so large it consumes the disk space on the host system. A fixed-file size prevents this from happening.

Better Reliability   Dynamically expanding disks can become corrupted if the system suddenly loses power. A fixed-file size uses different write operations and isn't susceptible to the same issue.

Chapter 3 includes an exercise showing how to install Windows 8.1 on a VHD file.

Multiboot Systems

Multiboot systems have more than one operating system (OS) installed. For example, you can have a single system that can boot to Windows XP, Windows 7, Linux, and Windows 8.1.

Older Windows systems used the boot.ini file to identify each OS, including the disk and partition where they were located. In Windows 7 and Windows 8.1, boot.ini has been replaced with a *boot configuration data (BCD)* file. This is commonly called the BCD store, and it includes information on all of the OSs installed on a computer, including Windows recovery partitions. The BCD store can be edited using the *bcdedit* command-line tool.

If you want to boot to a multiboot environment, here are some important considerations:

Separate Partitions   When using multiboot systems, you should always install each OS on a separate partition. For example, you can install one OS on the C: partition and another on the D: partition. If you install more than one OS on any single partition, it may corrupt one or both of the OSs.

Basic Disks Only   Windows operating systems support both basic and dynamic disks. However, only a single OS will recognize dynamic disks. For example, if you have a system running Windows XP and Windows 8.1 and you convert a disk to a dynamic disk, it will be recognized only by the operating system used to convert it. You will no longer be able to boot into the other Windows system.

Installation Order   When you're using multiboot systems, always install the older OS first and the newer OS last. For example, if you want to create a multiboot system running Windows XP and Windows 8.1, install Windows XP first and then Windows 8.1. Windows 8.1 is aware of the settings and requirements for Windows XP and won't corrupt them. However, Windows XP is not aware of the requirements for Windows 8.1 and will corrupt some key files, making Windows 8.1 unbootable.

If you installed an older operating system after installing Windows 8.1, you can recover it. You can use the bcdedit command to modify the boot configuration data (BCD) store to support multiboot systems.

Recovery Partition   The recovery partition will not be available on multiboot systems. The partition is needed for several different recovery options, such as refreshing and resetting a PC. When you perform a clean installation of Windows 8.1, it creates a 350 MB System Reserved partition, but this partition is not created on multiboot systems unless Windows 8.1 is installed first (which is not recommended). Windows 7 uses a similar partition, but it is smaller at only 100 MB.

Multiboot Not Available on Secure Boot Systems   If Secure Boot is enabled on a computer, you will not be able to use it as a multiboot system. Secure Boot is an antimalware feature available in Windows 8.1 that prevents unauthorized software or operating systems from running. It blocks attempts to create a multiboot system.

Secure Boot requires firmware that supports UEFI v2.3.1 and has the Microsoft Windows Certification Authority in the UEFI signature database. UEFI is replacing the traditional BIOS in many computers.

Upgrade vs. Migration

Just because a computer meets one of the upgrade paths, an upgrade isn't necessarily the best choice. There are several reasons why a clean installation along with data migration is a better choice. First, a clean install is the simplest installation method. Fewer things can go wrong, and every system with a clean install will have the same installation. This makes it easier for technicians to troubleshoot.

One of the potential issues is related to applications that run on Windows 7 but have compatibility problems in Windows 8.1. For example, it's possible to disable User Account Control (UAC) in Windows 7 to run an application, but Windows 8.1 apps will not run if UAC is disabled.

Summary

In this chapter, you learned about the various editions of Windows 8.1 that can be used in homes and enterprises. You saw a comparison of the features and capabilities of each. You also learned about the basic hardware requirements, including the differences in requirements for 32-bit and 64-bit systems.

You can upgrade to Windows 8.1 from Windows 7 systems but not Windows XP or Windows Vista. Also, you can upgrade only to editions using the same architecture such as 32-bit to 32-bit editions or 64-bit to 64-bit editions. The setup program will check for basic compatibility issues. The Windows 8.1 Upgrade Assistant is a free download that performs a comprehensive check for compatibility issues.

Even though you can't do a direct upgrade from older operating systems such as Windows XP, you can still migrate data and settings to Windows 8.1 after the upgrade. A key tool used to migrate data is USMT. It includes ScanState, which you use to capture the data and settings from the older Windows system, and LoadState, which you use to restore the data and settings onto Windows 8.1.

Organizations planning on adding Windows 8.1 systems will take the time to design an operating system installation strategy. At the core of any deployment is the use of images, and several tools are available to assist with the creation, modification, and deployment of images. The Windows ADK is the core product, and it includes many additional tools. This chapter also covered issues related to using Windows To Go, implementing virtualization, booting from a VHD file, using multiboot systems, and making a choice between an upgrade and a migration.

Exam Essentials

Know the Windows 8.1 editions and their features.   The three Windows 8.1 editions that can be purchased are Windows 8.1, Windows 8.1 Pro, and Windows 8.1 Enterprise. Windows 8.1 is used by home users. Windows 8.1 Pro has more features needed by businesses. Windows 8.1 Enterprise is available only to organizations that subscribe to the Software Assurance program. Windows RT is preinstalled on tablets and cannot be purchased by itself.

Recognize the features available in different Windows 8.1 editions.   The basic edition of Windows 8.1 has the fewest features and is missing items such as BitLocker, Client Hyper-V, and the ability to join a domain. Windows 8.1 Pro includes these missing features and more, such as the ability to boot from a VHD file. Windows 8.1 Enterprise has the most features, including AppLocker, BranchCache, DirectAccess, and Windows To Go.

Know the hardware requirements to install Windows 8.1.   Windows 8.1 requires only a 1 GHZ or faster processor. 32-bit systems require at least 1 GB of RAM and at least 16 GB of free space. 64-bit systems require at least 2 GB of RAM and at least 20 GB of free space. A minimum resolution of 1366×768 is required to use the new Windows 8.1 feature called snapping apps.

Understand the upgrade paths to Windows 8.1.   You can upgrade Windows 7 to Windows 8.1, but you can't upgrade earlier operating systems such as Windows XP or Windows Vista to Windows 8.1. You can only upgrade to comparable or higher editions. For example, you can upgrade Windows 7 Professional to Windows 8.1 Pro or Windows 8.1 Enterprise, but you cannot upgrade Windows 7 Professional to the basic edition of Windows 8.1. Additionally, upgrades must use the same architecture—32-bit systems can be updated to 32-bit systems, and 64-bit systems can be updated to 64-bit systems, but you cannot upgrade a 32-bit system to a 64-bit system.

Understand user state migration. The User State Migration Tool (USMT) is a part of the Windows Assessment and Deployment Kit (ADK) for Windows 8.1. Two important tools in this kit are ScanState and LoadState. ScanState can collect user state data, including files and settings, and put it in a migration store. LoadState can then read the migration store and apply it to a new installation of Windows 8.1.

Understand images. Know the difference between boot and install images, and how install images can be modified to automate deployments. Be familiar with the process of creating an image, including the use of Sysprep.

Understand Windows To Go requirements. Have a basic understanding of how Windows To Go provides users with a portable Windows 8.1 workspace but can be created only from Windows 8.1 Enterprise systems. It requires a USB drive at least 32 GB in size, and the drive should be certified for Windows To Go.

Know the requirements for Client Hyper-V. Know that Client Hyper-V is only available on Windows 8.1 Pro or Enterprise editions. It will run only on 64-bit systems and requires a minimum of 4 GB of RAM.

Understand the requirements for alternate configurations. Windows 8.1 supports booting from a VHD file, and if used, a fixed size disk provides the best performance. Multiboot systems allow you to boot into more than one operating system but cannot be created on systems with Secure Boot or dynamic disks.

Review Questions

You can find the answers in Appendix A.

1. A home user plans on purchasing a Windows 8.1 computer. He wants to use it to create a virtual network using Client Hyper-V. Which Windows version should he choose?

    A. Windows 8.1 Pro 32-bit

    B. Windows 8.1 Pro 64-bit

    C. Windows 8.1 Enterprise 32-bit

    D. Windows 8.1 Enterprise 64-bit

2. A home user wants to be able to join a new Windows 8.1 computer to a domain. What version of Windows is needed?

    A. Windows 8.1

    B. Windows 8.1 Pro

    C. Windows 8.1 Enterprise

    D. Windows 8.1 RT

3. A business owner uses Microsoft's Software Assurance program and is currently running a Windows domain. He wants to add some Windows 8.1 desktop computers and use Windows To Go. What version of Windows 8.1 is needed?

    A. Windows 8.1

    B. Windows 8.1 Pro

    C. Windows 8.1 Enterprise

    D. Windows 8.1 RT

4. A home user is planning on buying a new Windows 8.1 desktop computer and wants to ensure that she can use BitLocker To Go. What version should she purchase?

    A. Windows 8.1

    B. Windows 8.1 Pro

    C. Windows 8.1 Enterprise

    D. Windows 8.1 RT

5. What is the maximum amount of RAM that can be recognized by Windows 8.1 Pro? (Choose all that apply.)

    A. 4 GB on 32-bit systems

    B. 128 GB on 32-bit systems

    C. 128 GB on 64-bit systems

    D. 512 GB on 64-bit systems

6. A user wants to install a 64-bit edition of Windows 8.1 on an existing Windows 7 system and use it as a dual-boot system. He has two partitions in the system. How much free space is needed?

   A. It needs at least 10 GB of free space.

   B. It needs at least 16 GB of free space.

   C. It needs at least 20 GB of free space.

   D. It needs at least 40 GB of free space.

7. Users can use Client Hyper-V to create VM environments to test applications or run separate desktops in isolated environments. Client Hyper-V uses the same technologies as Hyper-V uses in Windows Server 2012. What are the basic requirements to use Hyper-V on a Windows 8.1 system? (Choose all that apply.)

   A. The OS must be a 64-bit edition of Windows 8.1 Pro or Windows 8.1 Enterprise.

   B. The processor must support hardware-assisted virtualization and virtualization must be enabled in the BIOS.

   C. The system needs a minimum of 4 GB of RAM.

   D. The system needs a minimum of 100 GB of storage space to run.

8. A computer is currently running a 32-bit version of Windows 7 Professional. A user wants to run a 64-bit version of Windows 8.1 Pro on this computer. What type of installation should be selected from the Windows 8.1 installation program?

   A. Upgrade

   B. Clean install

   C. Wipe and Load

   D. Custom

9. A user is planning on converting his Windows XP system to Windows 8.1. He wants to keep as much of his data and settings as possible. Of the following choices, what is the best plan?

   A. Upgrade the computer directly to Windows 8.1.

   B. Run the Windows 8.1 Upgrade Assistant to capture the data and then perform a custom install.

   C. Capture the data and settings, perform an upgrade of Windows 8.1, and then migrate the data to Windows 8.1.

   D. Capture the data and settings, perform a custom install of Windows 8.1, and then migrate the data to Windows 8.1.

10. An organization has multiple computers, including Windows XP, Windows Vista, and Windows 7. Management wants to upgrade any computers that can be upgraded and migrate the data and settings to new installations of Windows 8.1 on the remaining systems. Of the following choices, what should they include in their plan? (Choose all that apply.)

    A. Upgrade Windows Vista and Windows 7 systems to Windows 8.1.

    B. Perform a clean install on all of the systems.

    C. Migrate data from Windows XP and Windows Vista systems.

    D. Perform clean installs on Windows XP and Windows Vista.

11. You are replacing several Windows XP computers with Windows 8.1. You need to ensure that users have as much of their data and settings as possible. What tool can you use to capture these settings from the Windows XP system?

    A. LoadState

    B. ScanState

    C. Sysprep

    D. DISM

12. Of the following choices, what can be used to assist with an automated deployment of Windows 8.1?

    A. Windows Assessment and Deployment Kit

    B. Windows Automated Installation Kit

    C. Windows Software Update Services

    D. Application Compatibility Toolkit

13. You are preparing a computer for imaging. What needs to be done prior to capturing the image?

    A. Run DISM.

    B. Run LoadState.

    C. Run ScanState.

    D. Run Sysprep.

14. You have a Windows 8.1 image that needs additional drivers installed. What tool can you use to add these drivers without booting into the operating system?

    A. Run DISM.

    B. Run LoadState.

    C. Run ScanState.

    D. Run Sysprep.

15. An organization wants employees to have portable workspaces and is considering Windows To Go as a solution. Of the following choices, what is *not* a requirement?

    A. USB drives must be version 3.0.

    B. USB drives must be at least 32 GB in size.

    C. USB drives should be certified for use with Windows To Go.

    D. Computers must be able to boot from a USB drive.

16. Several 32-bit and 64-bit computers used in an organization are using a traditional BIOS. They will be used to boot to Windows To Go workspaces. You are involved in the designing phase of these and need to identify the options you have. Which of the following statements are true? (Choose all that apply.)

    A. Only 32-bit versions of Windows 8.1 can be used with 32-bit computers.

    B. Only 64-bit versions of Windows 8.1 can be used with 64-bit computers.

    C. Both 32-bit and 64-bit versions of Windows 8.1 can be used with 32-bit computers.

    D. Both 32-bit and 64-bit versions of Windows 8.1 can be used with 64-bit computers.

17. A user is planning on running Windows 8.1 and Client Hyper-V. She is trying to determine what types of guest operating systems are supported. Of the following choices, which one is correct?

    A. Client Hyper-V supports only Windows 8.1 guests.

    B. Client Hyper-V supports only Windows 8.1 and Windows Server 2012 guests.

    C. Client Hyper-V supports Windows XP, Windows 7, and Windows 8.1 guests.

    D. Client Hyper-V supports any Windows operating system as long as it is running a 64-bit version of Windows.

18. What is the minimum amount of RAM required for a Windows 8.1 system to use Client Hyper-V?

    A. 2 MB

    B. 2 GB

    C. 4 MB

    D. 4 GB

19. A user wants to create a dual-boot system with a VHD file. What type of file should be created for the best performance?

    A. Fixed size

    B. Dynamically expanding

    C. Encrypted

    D. Compressed

20. A user is running Windows 8.1 on a computer and decides to make it a dual-boot system with another edition of Windows 8.1. However, he is not able to successfully install the second edition of Windows. What is the most likely reason?

    A. He is trying to install the second system on a separate partition.

    B. It is not possible to create a dual-boot system with two Windows 8.1 installations.

    C. The disks are not configured as dynamic disks.

    D. The system has Secure Boot installed and enabled.

Chapter

3

Installing Windows 8.1

70-687 MICROSOFT EXAM OBJECTIVES COVERED IN THIS CHAPTER:

- Install Windows 8.1
- Install as Windows To Go
- Migrate from previous versions of Windows to Windows 8.1
- Upgrade from Windows 7 or Windows 8 to Windows 8.1
- Install to VHD
- Install additional Windows features
- Configure Windows for additional languages

✓ **Migrate and configure user data**

- Migrate user profiles
- Configure folder location
- Configure profiles, including profile version, local, roaming, and mandatory

✓ **Configure remote access and mobility**

- Choose the appropriate remote management tools
- Configure remote management settings
- Modify settings remotely by using MMCs or Windows PowerShell
- Configure Remote Assistance, including Easy Connect

This chapter covers some of the methods of installing Windows 8.1, including Windows To Go, which debuted in Windows 8. It provides exercises to walk you through the steps of performing a single installation of Windows 8.1, installing and configuring Windows To Go on an external USB disk, and creating a virtual hard disk (VHD) for a Windows 8.1 installation.

Profiles include user data and settings, and they are important to understand for two reasons. First, if users log on to different computers, you'll want to design a solution so that they'll have access to their profiles on the different computers. Second, when migrating users to Windows 8.1 systems, you can migrate the profiles so that users have access to the data on their new systems. This chapter includes information on local profiles, roaming profiles, and mandatory profiles. Two additional methods you can use to ensure users have access to their data are folder redirection and a new feature called User Experience Virtualization (UE-V).

The last section in this chapter covers various methods used to migrate user data. The easiest method is the Windows Easy Transfer tool included in Windows 8.1. It is ideal for migrating one or two systems. If you need to migrate several systems, a better choice is the User State Migration Tool (USMT), which includes two tools to capture and load profiles: ScanState and LoadState.

CERT OBJECTIVE Performing a Local Installation

A local installation will install Windows 8.1 on a local computer. If an existing installation supports an upgrade (covered in Chapter 2, "Planning the Windows 8.1 Installation"), you can perform an upgrade. The benefit of an upgrade is that all the existing files, settings, and applications will be included in the new installation. When you do a clean install, the files, settings, and applications aren't moved to Windows 8.1.

During the installation, you'll have the option of modifying the disk partitions. If the partitions aren't modified, existing files on the disk will remain. Files from a previous installation of Windows will be moved to a folder named Windows.old. However, if partitions are modified or formatted, these files will no longer be available.

WARNING If a computer has any important data, ensure you back it up before performing an installation. Although the data should be available if the partitions aren't modified, you should still back up valuable data before starting.

For the most part, the Windows 8.1 installation is straightforward, with few surprises. Installing one or two systems manually is no big deal, but if you have to install 5, 50, or more, you'll want to automate the process.

The biggest challenge may come if you have to change partitions on the hard disk or add additional disk drivers. However, the installation program includes the tools to handle both situations. For example, if your hard drive isn't recognized during the installation, it might be because the installation program doesn't have the required drivers. You can click the Load Driver link shown in Figure 3.1 on the Where Do You Want To Install Windows? page of the Windows Setup wizard. You'll then be prompted to browse to the location where the disk driver is located.

FIGURE 3.1   Selecting the installation partition

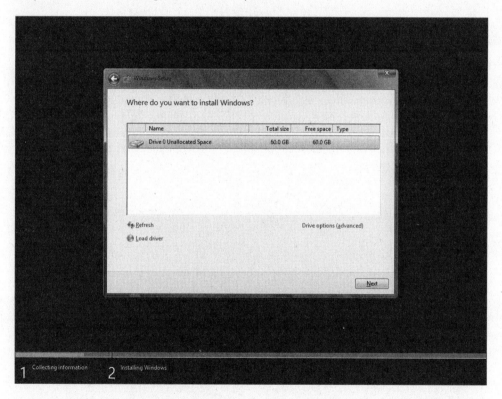

Figure 3.1 shows the initial options if the drive isn't formatted. You can select the Drive Options (Advanced) link to delete, create, or format partitions. If you have a partition and unallocated space on the drive, you can extend the partition to include the unallocated space.

Another important consideration when installing Windows 8.1 locally is the type of account you plan on using. You have two choices:

Microsoft Account   This account can be any email address that either has been or will be registered with Microsoft. It can be used to download apps from the Windows Store, and users can use the same account to log on to different Windows 8.1 devices. This account also allows users to sync settings between different Windows 8.1 devices that they use.

Local Account   This option creates a traditional local account that can be used to log on to the local system only. It doesn't support syncing settings between different systems.

You can install Windows 8.1 directly from the installation DVD by booting to it directly or by running the setup program from within a Windows operating system. You can also copy the contents of the DVD to a network share and run the setup program over the network. Exercise 3.1 walks you through the steps to install Windows 8.1 by booting from the installation DVD.

EXERCISE 3.1

Installing Windows 8.1 from the Installation DVD

1. Place the Windows 8.1 installation DVD in the DVD drive and boot the system. After a moment, the Install Windows screen will appear. The first screen you should pay attention to is the update screen, which prompts you to get any updates that have been made to the operating system since the DVD was released to manufacturing. You might need to modify the basic input/output (BIOS) of the system to ensure it can boot to a DVD drive.

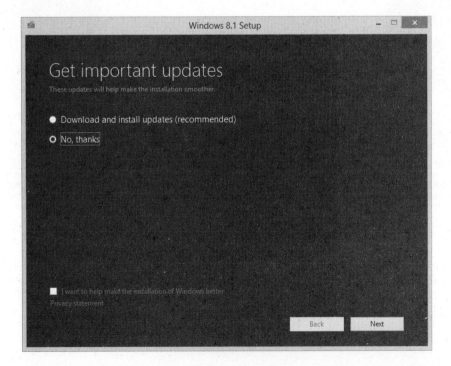

Although it looks like you have few choices here, you can press Shift+F10 to access the command line from this menu. In the "Creating a Bootable VHD" exercises later in this chapter, you'll access the command line to create and configure a VHD file.

2. Make your selections for Language To Install, Time And Currency Format, and Keyboard Or Input Method, and click Next.

3. The Windows 8.1 Install screen appears. Notice that this screen includes a Repair Your Computer link. You can use this option to troubleshoot your installation, and it includes tools to refresh or reset a PC. These tools are explored in more depth in Chapter 12, "Recovery and Backup Options." Click Install Now.

4. Review the license terms, and select I Accept The License Terms. Click Next.

5. Select Custom: Install Windows Only (Advanced) to install a new copy of Windows. If an existing version exists that can be upgraded to Windows 8.1, you can select Upgrade.

6. Select the partition where you want to install Windows. Notice that you can create additional partitions from this screen. However, if you start with anything other than a single existing partition, Windows will create a partition labeled System Reserved that has about 350 MB. For example, we created a single 20 GB partition from a 60 GB disk and Windows also created the 350 GB partition, as shown in the following graphic. This partition includes the Windows Recovery Environment (WinRE) and files needed for both Refresh and Reset features.

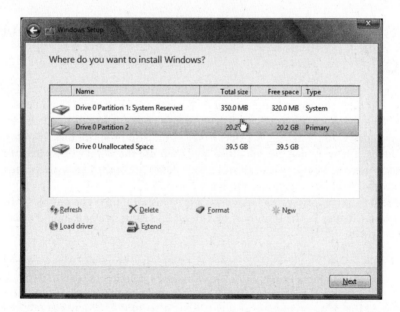

Microsoft recommends that you keep this partition. If you don't want this partition, you must format the entire drive as a single partition before starting the installation. You can do so by accessing the command prompt by pressing Shift+F10 at the Install Now page and using DiskPart. You can later shrink the volume to create additional partitions.

7. The process will take several minutes to install and configure files. When the Personalize page appears, enter a name for the computer. You can also select a different color scheme from this page if desired. Click Next.

8. On the Settings page, click Use Express Settings.

9. The Sign In To Your PC page appears. You can enter an email address you'd like to use as a Microsoft account or create a local account. To create a local account, use these steps:

   a. Click Sign In Without A Microsoft Account.

   b. Click Local Account.

   c. Enter a username, password, and password hint.

   d. Click Finish.

   After a moment the installation will complete and you'll see the Start screen.

Installing and Configuring Windows To Go

Windows To Go is a new feature (introduced in Windows 8 Enterprise) that allows you to boot into a Windows 8.1 workspace on any compatible computer from a USB drive. This workspace includes a full Windows 8.1 operating system and program files. It's portable so that users can use the workspace at the office, and then use the same workspace on a home or mobile computer. Although users can store their data within this workspace, the data isn't easily accessible unless they boot into the workspace.

The first step to get Windows To Go working is to install it on a compatible USB drive. As mentioned in Chapter 2, the USB must be at least 32 GB in size and should be certified for Windows To Go.

If you plug a Windows To Go workspace USB into a system that is already running Windows 8.1, the drive isn't recognized. However, you can use Disk Management to assign a drive letter to the USB disk or mount it to an empty folder. Once the drive letter is assigned or it is mounted, you can browse it with File Explorer.

Installing Windows To Go

Exercise 3.2 leads you through the steps of installing a Windows To Go workspace. This exercise assumes you're logged on to Windows 8.1 with the Start screen showing.

 WARNING Installing Windows To Go on a drive will delete all data on the drive. Make sure you back up any important data before starting.

EXERCISE 3.2

Installing Windows To Go

1. Connect a Windows To Go compatible USB drive to a USB port in the computer.

2. Place a Windows 8.1 installation DVD in your DVD drive. Alternately, you can use any image file with a Windows 8.1 image. For example, if your organization has created a specialized image, you can use it instead of the basic installation file from the DVD.

3. Press Windows logo key+W to open the Search Settings charm.

4. Type **Windows To Go**.

5. When Windows To Go appears, select it. The Create A Windows To Go Workspace windows appears, as shown here:

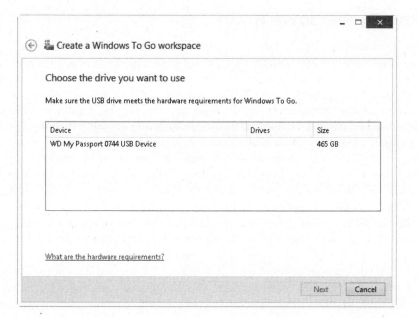

6. Ensure that the Windows To Go–compatible USB drive is selected and click Next.

7. The program searches for the install.wim image file in the sources folder of the DVD. If this is the image you want to use, select it and click Next. If you want to use a different image:

    a. Click Add Search Location.

    b. Browse to the folder where the image is located and click Select Folder.

    c. Select the image file and click Next.

8. On the Set BitLocker Password (Optional) page, you can select Use BitLocker With My Windows To Go Workspace or leave it unchecked. If you select it, enter a BitLocker password in the two text boxes and click Next. Alternately, you can click Skip so that BitLocker is not used.

9. Review the information on the Ready To Create Your Windows To Go Workspace page. Note that this process will reformat the drive and delete all data on the drive. Click Create. The process will take a while.

10. When the installation completes, the Windows To Go Startup Options page will prompt you: Do You Want To Automatically Boot Your PC From A Windows To Go Workspace? If you choose Yes, the setup program will configure the workspace to boot automatically from the USB drive. If you choose No, you'll have to configure the settings manually.

Configuring Windows To Go

When you first start Windows To Go on a computer, Windows 8.1 will detect all the hardware on the computer and automatically install the necessary drivers. This process might take a while the first time Windows 8.1 is started on a computer, but subsequent startups will be quicker. The Windows To Go workspace will identify this computer the next time it's used and automatically use the necessary drivers. The Windows To Go workspace can be used on multiple computers, and it can store and automatically identify the required drivers and settings for each of them.

If you created the drive as a bootable drive during the last step of the installation of Windows To Go, you'll have a bootable USB drive. This step will modify the boot configuration data (BCD) store on the local system. You'll also need to ensure that the computer where it is used is configured to boot to a USB drive. You can do so within the BIOS of the computer; methods of modifying the BIOS vary from computer to computer.

You can modify the Windows To Go startup options on an existing USB drive from within a Windows 8.1 installation. Exercise 3.3 leads you through these steps. These steps will work while you are booted into a normal Windows 8.1 installation, but not if you are booted into a Windows To Go workspace. This exercise assumes you're logged on to Windows 8.1 with the Start screen showing.

EXERCISE 3.3

Configuring Windows To Go

1. Press Windows logo key+W to open the Search Settings screen.

2. Type **Windows To Go** and select Change Windows To Go Startup Options. You'll see a display similar to the following graphic. This is the same display that you'll see when you complete the Windows To Go installation.

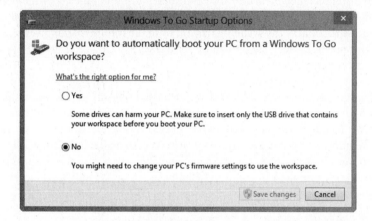

3. Select Yes to configure the system to automatically boot to the Windows To Go workspace. Your computer will now try to boot to the USB drive when it is turned on. If a USB drive is not plugged into the system, it will boot normally.

Using Command-Line Tools

You can also install and configure Windows To Go using a variety of command-line tools, though the process becomes much more complex. For advanced implementations, you can use the following tools:

DISM   The Deployment Image Servicing and Management (DISM) tool is useful in many deployment scenarios. Chapter 2 mentioned it as a method of viewing and manipulating image files. This tool is especially useful for adding drivers and other packages to an image using offline image servicing. You can also use DISM to capture and deploy images, including images used for Windows To Go. You can view the full technical reference, including a listing of How To topics, here: http://technet.microsoft.com/library/hh824821.aspx.

ImageX   While DISM is described as the primary tool used to create and deploy images from the command line for Windows 8.1, ImageX is still mentioned in some documentation. DISM has more capabilities and is a preferred method, but ImageX will still work. You can view the full technical reference for ImageX here: http://technet.microsoft.com/library/cc748966.aspx.

BCDboot You can use the BCDboot tool to configure a Windows To Go drive to be bootable. It configures the BCD store on the system partition so that it is bootable on a BIOS-based system, a Unified Extensible Firmware Interface (UEFI)-based system used as a replacement for BIOS on newer systems, or both.

If you've created a Windows To Go workspace, the USB disk will have two partitions. The system partition includes the BCD store and some additional files, and the boot partition includes the Windows folder and the Windows 8.1 operating system. You can use the bcdboot command to modify the system partition to make it bootable. However, these partitions are not normally accessible to an operating system, so you'll first need to assign a drive letter to the system partition.

Figure 3.2 shows Disk Management, which can be started from the command prompt with the diskmgmt.msc command. Disk 0 is the disk used to boot into Windows 8.1, and it includes the 350 MB System Reserved partition and Windows 8.1 on the C drive. Disk 1 is the Windows To Go workspace USB disk with two similar partitions. By default, neither of the Windows To Go workspace partitions is assigned a drive letter when you are not booted into the Windows To Go workspace, and they are not visible to most operating system tools. For example, you cannot normally see these Windows To Go workspace partitions from File Explorer.

FIGURE 3.2 Viewing a Windows To Go disk in Disk Management

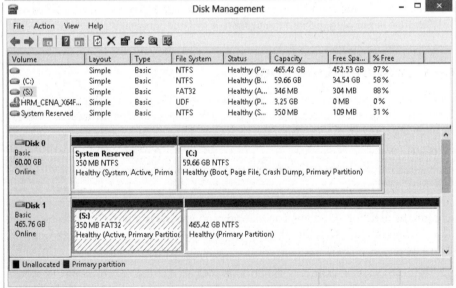

Suppose you have assigned drive letter S to the Windows To Go system partition by right-clicking over it and selecting Change Drive Letter And Paths. After assigning a drive letter to the system partition, you can configure it to be bootable with the following command:

```
bcdboot c:\windows /s s: /f all
```

The following list explains the command elements:

- bcdboot is the name of the command.

- c:\windows identifies the location of the source files that will be written to the system partition.

- The /s s: switch specifies the system partition that will be modified as the S drive.

- The /f all switch specifies that both BIOS and UEFI boot files should be copied to the system partition. This makes it bootable on either BIOS or UEFI systems. You could also use just /f bios or /f uefi to copy just the BIOS boot files or just the UEFI boot files, respectively.

After modifying the partition, you should unassign the drive letter before removing the Windows To Go USB drive. You can read more about BCDboot here: http://technet .microsoft.com/library/hh824874.aspx.

✔ CERT OBJECTIVE Creating and Installing a VHD

A cool feature available with Windows 8.1 is the ability to boot to a virtual hard drive (VHD). As a reminder, you can boot only to a VHD file on Windows 8.1 Pro and Windows 8.1 Enterprise, not to the basic version of Windows 8.1.

The VHD format has been used with Microsoft virtualization products for many years, but the abilities have been expanded. In addition to VHD files, VHDX files are now supported. A VHD file can be up to 2 TB in size and a VHDX file can be up to 64 TB in size. You can create a multiboot environment with one or more systems running from VHD or VHDX files.

One of the challenges with traditional dual-boot environments is that you needed to ensure each operating system was installed on its own partition. If not, one OS could (and usually did) corrupt the other OS. You can get around this problem with a VHD.

You can have several operating systems available on a single machine with a single partition. Each operating system can be contained within VHD or VHDX files. For example, you can create a VHD to test a specific application within Windows 8.1. When you're done testing, you can simply delete the VHD file. There are three overall steps in this process:

1. **Create the file.** When you create the VHD or VHDX file, it starts as a single virtual hard drive. You can configure it to include one or more partitions.

2. **Attach the file.** This activates the VHD or VHDX file so that the host computer views it as a local hard disk drive.

3. **Detach the file.** When the file is detached, the host computer no longer recognizes it. If desired, you can delete it after detaching it.

The following two exercises show the steps used to create a bootable VHD file using DiskPart and Disk Management. They create a VHD file (with an extension of .vhd) at the root of the C drive. You can name the file whatever you want. The size of the file should be at least 16 GB for a 32-bit system and at least 20 GB for a 64-bit system. You can make it larger to accommodate more data and files based on your needs.

You can set the VHD file to be either fixed or expandable. A 20 GB fixed size will always take up 20 GB of space, whereas a 20 GB expandable file will start at less than 100 MB and expand as data is added to the file. The fixed size is quicker since it doesn't need to expand dynamically, and the expandable size consumes only the space needed. If performance is a consideration, you should configure the files with a fixed size.

Exercise 3.4 shows how you can configure a system to create a bootable virtual hard drive from the installation DVD using DiskPart.

EXERCISE 3.4

Creating a Bootable VHD Using DiskPart

1. Turn on the Windows 8.1 system and place the Windows 8.1 installation DVD in the system. When the system starts, select the option to boot from the DVD.

2. When the initial installation screen appears prompting you to select a language, press Shift+F10. This will launch a command window with the prompt X:\Sources>. X: is mapped to the DVD drive, and it is pointed to the sources folder in the drive.

3. At the command prompt, type **diskpart** and press Enter. After a moment, the command prompt will change to DiskPart>.

4. Type the following command, and press Enter to create a 40 GB expandable virtual disk file named Win8.vhd:

   ```
   create vdisk file = c:\win8.vhd maximum=40960 type=expandable
   ```

   You can name the VHD file anything you want, enter a different maximum size, or omit the type=expandable statement to create a fixed-size file. After the file is created, DiskPart will display the message "DiskPart successfully created the virtual disk file."

5. Type the following command to select the virtual disk file and press Enter:

   ```
   select vdisk file=c:\win8.vhd
   ```

   DiskPart will indicate it has successfully selected the virtual disk file.

6. Type the following command to attach the virtual disk file and press Enter:

   ```
   attach vdisk
   ```

DiskPart will indicate it has successfully attached the virtual disk file.

7. Type **exit** and press Enter to exit DiskPart.

8. Type **exit** and press Enter to exit the command prompt window.

9. You will now see the Install Windows screen you saw before pressing Shift+F10. Make sure the correct language, time and currency, and keyboard or input method settings are selected and click Next.

10. Click the Install Now button.

11. Review the license terms, select the I Accept The License Terms check box, and click Next.

12. Select the Custom: Install Windows Only (Advanced) installation type.

13. The Where Do You Want To Install Windows? screen appears. This screen lists all the physical disks and partitions on the system. Below the physical disks and partitions, you will see the virtual disk file identified as a disk labeled as Unallocated Space. It will have a total size of 40 GB and free space of 40 GB (unless you created it as a different size). Select the virtual disk and click Next.

A warning may appear saying "Windows cannot be installed to this disk. (Show Details)," indicating the hardware is not compatible. Don't believe it; just continue. We've seen that message on different systems, but the installation and operation worked without any problems we could identify.

At this point, the Windows installation will progress as would a normal Windows 8.1 installation. You can follow the first exercise in this chapter to complete the installation.

When the installation process completes and reboots, you'll see a dual-boot screen. The new Windows 8.1 choice will be first, and if you don't take any action, it will boot to the Windows 8.1 VHD file in 30 seconds.

You can also put the create, select, and attach diskpart commands into a text file and run them as a script. For example, a text file named createvhd.txt can include the three commands listed in the preceding exercise. You can run the file from the command prompt with the diskpart /s createvhd.txt command. If desired, you can create a log file of the DiskPart session with this command: diskpart /s createvhd.txt > logdiskpart.txt.

If you have Windows 8.1 running on a system, you can create the VHD file using Disk Management, as shown in Exercise 3.5. This exercise assumes you're logged on to Windows 8.1 with the Start screen showing.

EXERCISE 3.5

Creating a Bootable VHD Using Disk Management

1. Move your mouse to the lower-left corner. When the preview menu appears, right-click it and select Computer Management.

2. Select Disk Management from the Storage section.

3. Right-click over Disk Management and select Create VHD.

4. Click Browse and select C:. Enter a filename of **Win8** and click Save.

5. Enter a size of **20** and select GB. Select either VHD or VHDX. Select either Fixed Size (Recommended) or Dynamically Expanding. Click OK. After a few moments, an additional disk will appear in Disk Management.

6. Right-click over the new disk and select Initialize Disk. (If available, select the MBR or GPT partition style before initializing the disk.)

7. Review the information in the Initialize Disk dialog box and click OK. The disk will now appear as a basic disk and online.

8. Right-click over the Unallocated area of the disk and select New Simple Volume.

9. Review the information in the Welcome screen and click Next.

10. Accept the default size and click Next.

11. Accept the default drive letter and click Next.

12. On the Format Partition page, accept the default of NTFS and Perform A Quick Format. If desired, you can rename the volume label. Click Next. Click Finish.

You will now have an attached VHD file that you can use to install Windows 8.1. You can begin the installation from the installation DVD by starting the setup.exe program and then following the steps in this chapter's first exercise.

Designing a Solution for User Settings

When you are deploying Windows 8.1 within an organization where users have existing systems, one of your key considerations is to ensure that users have as much of their original data and settings as possible after the deployment. When performing an upgrade, users automatically have their data and settings transferred. However, when performing a new installation of Windows, you'll need to take some extra steps to migrate users' settings.

The primary location of user data and settings is within their user profiles, and any migration of data and settings will migrate these profiles. With that in mind, you must understand the contents of profiles and how they are used.

User Profiles

A *user profile* is a set of data that is used to re-create the user's environment each time a user logs on. It includes several folders, such as Contacts, Cookies, Desktop, Downloads, Favorites, and more. It also includes user-specific Registry settings.

For example, Bob can use a Windows 8.1 system and have it configured with a left-hand mouse, specific apps on the Start screen, a personal picture on his lock screen, and several drives mapped to network shares he uses regularly. Each time Bob logs on, these settings are re-created from his profile. Sally can use the same computer with a different user account. She can reconfigure all of these settings, and they will be re-created from her profile each time she logs on, without affecting the settings for Bob.

Windows 8.1 profiles are stored in the %systemroot%\Users folder by default. The Users folder includes the standard profiles of any user who has ever logged on to the system. It also includes the *All Users profile* and the *Default User profile*.

All Users   The All Users profile holds settings that affect all users. For example, when you install an application you are often prompted to choose to allow all users access to the program. When you select All Users, the application modifies the All Users profile, ensuring the application is available to any user who logs on to the system.

Default User   This profile is used when a user first logs on to a system. Windows 8.1 will copy the Default User profile to a new folder named with the user's logon name. For example, if a user named Bob logs on, a folder is created that's named Bob and includes all the data from the Default User profile. This new profile is used to re-create the same environment for Bob each time he logs on.

There are many differences between how profiles are implemented in Windows XP and Windows 7. However, the profiles are largely the same in both Windows 7 and Windows 8.1.

If you look in the %systemroot%\Users folder, you won't see the Default User folder, but it's there—it's just hidden. By default, the only folders that a user will see in the %systemroot%\Users\ folder are the Public folder and the profile folders of any users who have logged on.

There are many hidden and system-protected folders that don't show by default. You can follow the steps in Exercise 3.6 to show them. This exercise assumes you're logged on to Windows 8.1 and have the Start screen showing.

Showing Hidden and System-Protected Files

1. Type **explorer**. As you type, the Search screen appears.

2. When File Explorer appears, select it.

3. Click the View menu item to show the View ribbon.

4. Click Options on the far right to open the Folder Options dialog box.

5. Select the View tab.

6. Select the Show Hidden Files, Folders, And Drives check box.

7. Scroll down and deselect the Hide Protected Operating System Files (Recommended) check box. Review the information in the Warning dialog box and click Yes.

8. Click OK.

If you browse to the C:\Users folder, you will now see the Users folder, as shown in Figure 3.3 in the next section.

Local Profiles

Profiles stored in the %systemroot%\Users\username folder are referred to as local user profiles or standard profiles. The profile includes several folders and a Registry hive. The folders hold data and settings needed by the user. The HKEY_CURRENT_USER portion of the Registry holds user-defined settings for the desktop, applications, printers, and more. These are stored in a file named ntuser.dat.

Many of the folders and data are system files and hidden by default. Figure 3.3 shows the user profile with hidden and system files showing. In the figure, the view has been changed to List from the View menu in File Explorer.

Roaming Profiles

Local user profiles work great if a user logs on to the same system all the time. However, in some organizations users frequently log on to different systems. Mapped network drives, apps on the Start screen, and other elements of the user's profile are often useful if they're available to a user no matter where the user logs on. *Roaming profiles* can be implemented to ensure the same profile is available to a user no matter which computer is used.

Figure 3.4 shows how roaming profiles are used. A folder named Profiles is shared on a server named Server1 that is available to the user on the network. The user's account is then configured to use this share for the profile.

FIGURE 3.3   User profile folder

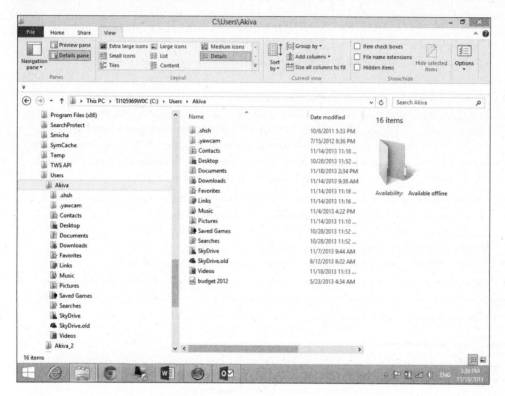

FIGURE 3.4   Using roaming profiles

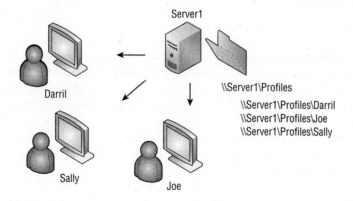

When the user logs on to a computer, the profile is retrieved from the network share and copied to the local computer. If the user makes any changes, these changes are copied up to the roaming profile on the network share. If a user then moves to a different computer and logs on, the profile is copied down to the different computer.

Roaming profiles are typically only implemented in a domain. The two steps used to create a roaming profile are as follows:

1. **Create a share on a server.** This share needs to be accessible to users using the Universal Naming Convention (UNC) path (*servername**sharename*). For example, Figure 3.4 shows a UNC path of \\server1\profiles where server1 is the server and profiles is the share. If more than one user will use this share, the Authenticated Users group should be granted Full Control. It's not necessary to create the folder for each user because it will be created automatically when the user logs on.

2. **Modify the domain user account.** The Profile tab of the user account Properties page includes a Profile Path text box. The UNC path to the share is added here and appended with the %username% variable, giving a full path of \\servername\ sharename\%username%. When the user logs on, a folder will be created within the share with the appropriate permissions for the user to access the folder.

The operating system automatically configures the NTFS permissions for the folder. The user and the system both have full control of the folder, but no other users are granted any access to the data in the folder.

Chapter 7, "Managing Windows 8.1 in a Domain," covers domains in more depth, and Chapter 9, "Managing Files and Disks in Windows 8.1," covers NTFS and share permissions in more depth.

Mandatory Profiles

A *mandatory profile* is a roaming profile that is configured as read-only. Users will use this profile as a roaming profile, but any changes made by the user will not be saved. The primary reason to create mandatory profiles is so that users have a consistent profile.

It is possible for users to modify the standard profile in such a way that it adversely affects the system. This results in a call to the help desk and troubleshooting by a technician. Some companies have had one too many of these calls and have decided to use mandatory profiles to prevent these problems.

Here's how the roaming profile works. The user logs on, the profile is retrieved from the server where it's stored, and then the profile is copied down to the local computer. When the user logs off, any changes to the profile are copied back up to the server where the roaming profile is stored.

The only difference between a roaming profile and a mandatory profile is that the changes are never copied back up to the server when the user logs off. The user can still make changes to the local profile. However, because these changes aren't saved to the server, the next time the user logs on the mandatory profile will be copied from the server down to the client, overwriting any changes the user made.

The three primary steps involved in creating a mandatory user profile are as follows:

1. Create a profile with the desired settings on a Windows 8.1 system. Copy it to a network share.

2. Rename ntuser.dat to **ntuser.man**. This is a hidden system file, so you'll need to modify the File Explorer view to show hidden files and show system files. The steps to do this are listed in Exercise 3.6 earlier in this chapter.

3. Configure accounts to use the mandatory roaming user profile. You use the same steps as you'd use to create a roaming profile except the %username% variable isn't used. Instead, all users will use the UNC path of *servername**sharename* and this share includes the ntuser.man file.

Folder Redirection

Folder redirection is another method that can be used for users who log on to different computers in a network. Instead of including the user's documents in the profile, this method stores the documents on a central server. Users will still have access to these documents no matter which computer they log on to.

The folders that can be redirected include My Documents, My Music, My Pictures, and My Videos. These folders are typically accessed by users through the File Explorer in the Libraries section. By default, they are in the C:\Users*username* folder and the Libraries section provides a shortcut link to each folder named Documents, Music, Pictures, and Videos. If you redirect the folders, the content is moved to the new location, but the Libraries section still provides a shortcut link to its location no matter where it is moved to. From the user's perspective, it works the same way.

You can use folder redirection with or without roaming profiles, but when used with roaming profiles, it will reduce the amount of time it takes for a user to log on. Normally, when a user logs on to a computer using roaming profiles, the entire profile, including all the settings and data, is copied to the computer. Also, the logon process doesn't complete until the data has been copied to the computer. Imagine a user with 1 GB of files in these folders. It can take quite a while for the 1 GB of data to be copied down to the user's system. However, if the data folders are redirected to a central server, they are not copied with the profile.

 Real World Scenario

Using Folder Redirection to Reduce Logon Times

At one organization where this author (Darril) did some consulting work, it took users as long as 20 minutes to complete a logon. Everyone was using roaming profiles, and they commonly stored their files in the My Documents folder. Each time they logged on, all

continues

continued

of their data was copied from a central server to their local system because of the way roaming profiles were used.

Not only was this a ridiculously long time to log on, but their network was often tremendously slow, especially in the morning when users were logging on. All the bandwidth was taken up by copying the data in the profiles.

The company later implemented folder redirection to store users' data on a central server, which separated the data from the profile settings. This significantly reduced the logon times because the data was no longer copied with the rest of the profile. It also improved their overall network performance.

Exercise 3.7 shows how you can redirect user folders on Windows 8.1. This exercise assumes you're logged on to Windows 8.1 and the Start screen is showing.

EXERCISE 3.7

Redirecting Folders to Migrate User Data

1. Type **explorer**. As you type, the Search screen appears.

2. When File Explorer appears, select it.

3. Expand Documents in the Libraries section and select My Documents.

4. Right-click My Documents and select Properties.

5. Select the Location tab. The default location is within C:\Users but you can change it.

6. Enter the path to a different location using the UNC pathname of *servername*\ *sharename*. Click OK.

7. Review the prompt in the Move Folder dialog box and click Yes to move all the files to the new location. If you don't click Yes, the original files will remain in the old location and only new files will be moved to the new location.

8. Connect to the share and verify the files have moved.

You can repeat these steps to redirect the My Music, My Pictures, and My Videos folders. These folders are accessible by expanding the Music, Pictures, and Videos folders within the Libraries section similar to how you can access the My Documents folder by expanding the Documents folder in the Libraries section.

Within a domain, you can use Group Policy to automate this process for multiple users. Chapter 7 covers Group Policy in more depth, but as an introduction, you can configure the settings one time and have it apply to all the users in the domain. You can also configure Group Policy so that it applies the settings to specific groups of users based on how they are organized in the domain.

User Experience Virtualization

User Experience Virtualization (UE-V) is a feature that allows users to experience the same Windows settings even when they roam to different computers. A basic way this has been done in past operating systems is with roaming user profiles, as described earlier. However, UE-V is available in Windows 8.1 with the Microsoft Desktop Optimization Pack (MDOP), and it can be used instead of traditional roaming profiles.

Chapter 16, "Using the Microsoft Desktop Optimization Pack," explores the MDOP in more depth. MDOP provides several tools to help you manage desktops across an enterprise. For example, you can use the Microsoft BitLocker Administration and Monitoring (MBAM) tool to monitor and manage BitLocker disk encryption services on numerous desktop systems throughout an enterprise.

Networks running a Windows Server 2012 domain can create a virtual desktop infrastructure (VDI) so that users have the same interface no matter which computer they use. Microsoft Application Virtualization (App-V) can be used to run applications from a network server while it appears to users as though the applications are running on their computer. UE-V maintains the user settings and data as they roam to different computers.

With MDOP, administrators can identify the specific folders and settings that they want to make available to roaming users Additionally, UE-V synchronizes only the specific settings needed for a user to log on. If a user starts an application, UE-V synchronizes an application's settings only when a user starts or stops an application. This reduces the amount of time necessary for a user to log on.

In contrast, when roaming profiles are used the entire profile is copied to the user's computer when they first log on. When users have large profiles, this can significantly increase the amount of time it takes to log on.

Migrating User Data

If you're installing Windows 8.1 in current systems, you might be replacing Windows XP, Windows Vista, or Windows 7 systems. As mentioned in Chapter 2, the only upgrade path is from Windows 7 or Windows 8 systems. If you're replacing Windows XP or Windows Vista systems, you'll have to use different methods to get the user's data and settings on the new installation other than an upgrade. Even if you're upgrading from Windows 7 systems, Microsoft recommends doing clean installations instead of upgrades. If you follow this recommendation, you'll need to migrate the data after the installation.

> If you do a direct upgrade, you won't need to worry about migration. An upgrade will retain all of the installed applications and all of the user's data will be retained. An upgrade is still considered a risky operation, and it is possible that things can go wrong, so you should always back up the user's data before starting the upgrade.

The two primary tools available for migrations are Windows Easy Transfer and the User State Migration Tool. Both are covered in the following sections.

Windows Easy Transfer

Windows Easy Transfer (WET) provides a simple method to save and transfer user settings. It is useful when transferring data on a single system, but the User State Migration Toolkit provide more capabilities and is used when transferring settings from multiple systems.

The following list identifies some of the data and settings you can transfer from an old PC to a new PC using WET:

- User accounts and their profiles, including documents, Internet favorites, music, videos, and pictures
- Email settings and files
- Any other data files and folders on the system

Windows 7 and Windows 8.1 both include Windows Easy Transfer, and the versions are compatible with each other. You can start the programs from within each operating system without any problem. You can download and copy the program to Windows XP and Windows Vista systems. However, if you're migrating settings from Windows XP, you'll need to ensure Windows XP has Service Pack 3 (SP3) installed. Otherwise, the program won't migrate the data correctly to Windows 8.1.

The only warning is that you must use the program matching the architecture of both systems. In other words, the WET program must be either for 32-bit systems or 64-bit systems. You cannot migrate settings from a 32-bit system to a 64-bit system using WET.

You can capture and transfer data using one of three methods:

Easy Transfer Cable   This is a specially designed USB cable used to connect both systems and is an easy method to transfer files and settings. You start WET on the new system and, when prompted, connect the cable between the two computers.

Network   If both systems are connected to a network, you can transfer the settings from one computer to another over the network. Similarly, if you have a crossover cable, you can connect both of the PCs to each other as if they are connected in full network. A crossover cable is similar to a standard network twisted pair cable, but the main data transmission wires are swapped or crossed over.

External Hard Drive or USB Flash Drive   You can also store the settings and data to an external hard drive or USB flash drive. You first connect this drive to the original PC to capture the data and then connect the drive to the new system to transfer the data. Ensure that the drive is large enough to hold all the data.

When using the network connection, the Windows Firewall will block the connection by default. You'll be prompted to enable an exception to allow the `%systemroot%\system32\migwiz\miwiz.exe` executable file and you should allow this exception. If you're using a third-party firewall, you might need to create the exception manually.

If you use the Easy Transfer cable with a Windows XP or Windows Vista system and Windows 8.1, you'll first start WET on Windows 8.1. WET will prompt you to copy the program to either an external hard disk or USB flash drive. You can use this to install WET on the older system. You can also download the Windows Easy Transfer tool from the Microsoft download site (`http://download.microsoft.com/`) by searching on "Windows Easy Transfer."

WET has easy-to-follow wizards, making it a rather simple process to migrate the data and settings. Figure 3.5 shows the screen that allows you to pick the users you want to migrate, along with the specific type of data you want to migrate. The Shared Items selection allows you to select or deselect any other data on the system that you want to migrate that isn't a part of any specific profile.

FIGURE 3.5   Using WET

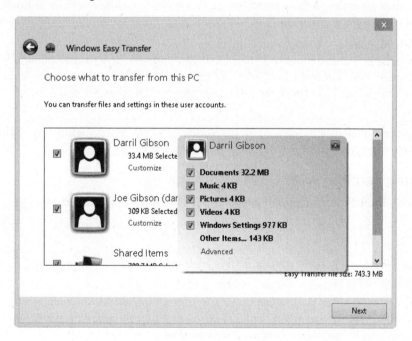

The selections are saved in a single migration store file with an .mig extension. You can then connect the drive to the new PC, run WET on the new PC, and browse to the location of the migration file when prompted.

User State Migration Tool

The User State Migration Tool (USMT) has been updated to version 5.0 in Windows 8.1. It includes the same basic tools as previous editions and can be used in three types of migrations. Each one assumes that you have files and settings from a Windows XP, Windows Vista, Windows 7, or Windows 8.1 installation that you want to restore to a new Windows 8.1 installation.

In-Place Migration   An in-place migration uses the same hardware for the old and new installation of Windows. Hard drive partitions are not modified, and files and settings from the previous installation are automatically retained in the Windows.old folder.

Wipe-and-Load Migration   A wipe-and-load migration uses the same hardware. However, partitions on the hard drive holding the original operating system need to be modified, which will prevent the Windows.old folder from being created during the new installation. Instead, USMT must be used before the installation to save the files and settings to a migration store from the previous installation. This migration store can then be restored to the new Windows 8.1 installation.

Side-by-Side Migration   A side-by-side migration uses two computers. USMT can be used to save the files and settings to a migration store from the original computer before it is decommissioned. The migration store can be copied to a USB disk or network share. USMT can then be used to restore the migration store to Windows 8.1 on the new computer.

The next few sections will focus on in-place migration, the most common type. Then we'll go over scenarios that may require the other types of migration.

Becoming Familiar with USMT Commands

USMT includes the ScanState, LoadState, and USMTutils command-line tools.

ScanState   Run ScanState on the source computer to collect the settings and files and put them in a migration store.

LoadState   Run LoadState on the destination computer to load the settings and files on to the destination computer.

USMTutils   Use USMTutils to determine cryptographic options with the migration. It can be used to remove corrupted hard-link stores that cannot be removed with traditional means. It can also be used to determine data integrity in compressed migration stores.

When the Windows.old folder is no longer needed, you can normally delete it using the Disk Cleanup tool. Open File Explorer and select the Properties of the C: drive. Ensure the General tab is selected and click the Disk Cleanup button. Click the Clean Up System Files button, select the Previous Windows Installation(s) check box, and click OK. In some cases, files and links prevent this method from working, but the USMTutils tool can be used to correct the problems.

When migrating data and settings using ScanState and LoadState, you'll use three basic steps:

1. Run ScanState on the old computer. This captures all the settings and files.

2. Prepare the new computer with the appropriate applications. If the applications are not installed before LoadState is run, the migrated settings will not be applied properly.

3. Run LoadState on the new computer to migrate the data and settings.

We'll get into details of running ScanState and LoadState in a bit, but first let's continue our overview of the USMT tools.

As a reminder, the USMT tools are included in the Window Assessment and Deployment Kit (ADK). Chapter 2 included an exercise to download and install the Windows ADK. When the Windows ADK is installed, it includes two folders for USMT. On 64-bit systems, they are located in the C:\Program Files (x86)\Windows Kits\8.0\Assessment and Deployment Kit\User State Migration Tool folder. On 32-bit systems, they are located in the C:\Program Files\Windows Kits\8.0\Assessment and Deployment Kit\User State Migration Tool folder.

The two USMT folders are:

amd64   This file includes the 64-bit versions of LoadState and ScanState, which should be run on 64-bit systems. Though the folder name implies it's only for AMD 64-bit processors, you also use files within this folder for 64-bit Intel processors.

x86   This file includes the 32-bit versions of LoadState and ScanState, which should be run on 32-bit systems.

A simple way to use these tools is to copy the entire folders to a USB flash drive and carry it with you to systems that need to be migrated. If you are migrating both 32- and 64-bit systems, you can copy both folders. If you are migrating only one or the other, you can just copy the amd64 or x86 folder depending on which one you need.

It's important to realize that you cannot mix 32-bit and 64-bit architectures with either WET or USMT commands. You can migrate only from 32-bit to 32-bit systems or from 64-bit to 64-bit systems. Even though you can't migrate the settings between architectures, you can simply copy the documents from one system to another, such as with a USB flash drive.

Previous editions of toolkits that included ScanState and LoadState also included help files that you could easily browse and search. Unfortunately, the Windows ADK does not include these help files. However, you can find specific topics online.

ScanState topics are here:

`http://technet.microsoft.com/library/hh825093.aspx`

LoadState topics are here:

`http://technet.microsoft.com/library/hh825190.aspx`

USMTutils topics are here:

`http://technet.microsoft.com/library/hh825264.aspx`

Understanding Hard-Link Migration and *Windows.old*

When used for an in-place migration, USMT uses a hard-link migration store when the data is migrated from the `Windows.old` folder. This significantly reduces the time and space required to migrate all this data. Instead of copying the data from one place to another on the hard drive, it just changes the filesystem's links to where the data is located.

This is similar to what happens when you move a file from one location to another using drag and drop in File Explorer within a single volume. For example, imagine a project on which you are working includes several files, so you decide to create a folder named `Project` and drag and drop all the files to that folder. The system doesn't create a brand-new copy of these files and then delete the originals. Instead, it just changes the filesystem links to these files so that they now appear as though they are in the `Project` folder.

Similarly, the hard-link migration feature in `ScanState` and `LoadState` will change the apparent location of these files without having to copy all the data. This can be significant if you're dealing with several gigabytes of data.

It's fairly easy to put the `scanstate` and `loadstate` commands into a batch file that you can use to automate the migration of files and settings for multiple computers in your network. However, before you automate `scanstate` and `loadstate`, it's good to know what the commands are doing.

Running ScanState

The `ScanState` tool is executed first to capture data. You must run `scanstate` from an elevated command prompt with administrative permissions. You'll need to either include the full path of the `scanstate` command or change the directory to the location of the command with the `cd` (change directory) command. This is in the `amd64` or `x86` folder by default, but you can copy the contents of these folders anywhere.

You can use the following command to retrieve the migration data from the `Windows .old` folder. Note that even though it appears on more than one line in this book, it should be entered as a single command without any returns:

```
scanstate.exe c:\store /v:13 /o /c /hardlink /nocompress /efs:hardlink ↵
  /i:migapp.xml /i:migdocs.xml /offlinewindir:c:\windows.old\windows
```

We realize the command is long, but the good news is that you don't need to modify it at all. Just copy if from the book and it'll work for many common migrations. After running the command, you can enter **notepad scanstate.log** to view the log to see all the actions performed by the command. The following list identifies what each of the syntax elements means:

- scanstate.exe is the name of the command.

- c:\store is the location where the migration data will be stored. It will create a USMT folder within the c:\store folder with all of the files and folders of the migration store.

- /v:13 indicates the highest level of verbosity. It will provide a significant amount of output to the log (named ScanState.log) that can be viewed after it completes. The lowest level is 0, which only logs errors and warnings.

- /o causes ScanState to overwrite an existing migration store (if one exists).

- /c tells ScanState to continue to run even if errors are encountered.

- /hardlink is used for in-place migrations to retrieve the data from the Windows.old folder. It requires the use of the /nocompress switch.

- /nocompress specifies that data is not compressed.

- /efs:hardlink specifies that Encrypted Filesystem (EFS) files will be moved using hard-link migration. The /hardlink switch must be used for this to succeed.

- /i:migapp.xml specifies that the migapp.xml file (which is included in the x86 and amd64 folders) will be used to identify application settings to migrate. This switch can be modified to select or deselect application settings.

- /i:migdocs.xml specifies that the migdocs.xml file (which is included in the x86 and amd64 folders) will be used to identify document types to migrate. This switch can also be modified to select or deselect different file types to migrate.

- /offlinewindir:c:\windows.old\windows is used to specify the location of the files from the original installation.

Running LoadState

After the scanstate command is executed to capture the migration data, the loadstate command is executed to restore the migration data to the current installation.

When performing in-place migrations, you can enter the loadstate command with the following switches. Just as the previous scanstate command should be entered as a single line, the following command should be entered as a single line even though it spans more than one line in the book:

```
loadstate.exe c:\store /v:13 /c /lac:P@ssw0rd /lae /i:migapp.xml ⏎
   /i:migdocs.xml /sf /hardlink /nocompress
```

The only item you might want to modify in the command is the password. We used the generic P@ssw0rd, but you can use whatever password you desire. You should use caution if using the password in a batch file because it will be stored in clear text and anyone with access to the batch file can read the password. The following list identifies what each of the syntax elements means:

- `loadstate.exe` is the command.

- `c:\store` is the location of the migration store created by ScanState.

- `/v:13` indicates the highest level of verbosity. It will provide a significant amount of output to the log that can be viewed after the command completes.

- `/c` tells scanstate to continue to run even if errors are encountered.

- `/lac:P@ssw0rd` specifies that local accounts in the migration store should be created if they don't already exist on the new computer. If the `/lac` switch is not used, local accounts will not be migrated. The same password will be used for all migrated accounts. If a password is not specified, the password will be empty. The accounts will not be created if the password doesn't meet the password policy requirements, such as it doesn't contain a minimum number of characters or it is insufficiently complex.

- `/lae` specifies that local accounts should be enabled. The `/lac` switch must have been used to migrate the accounts. When used, all migrated accounts will be enabled.

- `/i:migapp.xml` specifies that the `migapp.xml` file (which is included in the x86 and amd64 folders) will be used to identify application settings to migrate.

- `/i:migdocs.xml` specifies that the `migdocs.xml` file (which is included in the x86 and amd64 folders) will be used to identify document types to migrate.

- `/sf` restores shell folder redirection if a user had previously used folder redirection on any of their local user folders. For example, a user may have redirected the My Documents folder to be stored on a server share or on a different partition.

- `/hardlink` is used for in-place migrations to retrieve the data from the Windows.old folder. It requires the use of the `/nocompress` switch.

- `/nocompress` specifies that data is not compressed.

Creating a Batch File with ScanState and LoadState

If you need to migrate data on multiple systems, an easy way to do so is with a batch file. For example, if you have installed Windows 8.1 on a dozen systems that were previously running Windows XP, you can use a batch file to automate the migrations on these systems. You would put the batch file on a USB flash disk with the appropriate x86 or amd64 folder.

Exercise 3.8 leads you through the process of creating this batch file. This exercise assumes that the Windows ADK for Windows 8.1 has been installed on this system and the Windows 8.1 Start screen is displayed.

EXERCISE 3.8

Running USMT in a Batch File

1. Type File Explorer. When File Explorer appears, click it to select it.

2. Browse to following folder:

    ```
    c:\program files (x86)\windows kits\8.0\assessment ⏎
    and deployment kit\user state migration tool\amd64
    ```

    If using this technique on a 32-bit system, browse to the x86 folder instead.

3. Press Ctrl+A to select all the files and folders in this folder. Press Ctrl+C to copy them.

4. Browse to the root of the C drive. Click Home to display the Home ribbon and then click New Folder.

5. Rename the folder **MyUSMT**.

6. Double-click MyUSMT to open it. Press Ctrl+V to paste all the USMT files into the MyUSMT folder.

7. Right-click within the folder, and select New ➤ Text Document. Press Enter to open the text document.

8. Type the following lines in the text document. Note that the scanstate and load-state commands span two lines in the book, but they should be entered as a single command in the document.

    ```
    cd \myusmt
    rem
    scanstate.exe c:\store /v:13 /o /c /hardlink /nocompress /efs:hardlink ⏎
      /i:migapp.xml /i:migdocs.xml /offlinewindir:c:\windows.old\windows
    rem
    loadstate.exe c:\store /v:13 /c /lac:P@ssw0rd /lae /i:migapp.xml ⏎
      /i:migdocs.xml /sf /hardlink /nocompress
    ```

    The first command ensures the directory is set to the MyUSMT folder. The rem lines are remark or comment lines we added to separate the commands for easier readability.

9. Select File ➤ Save As.

10. Type **usmt.bat** and click Save. By adding the .bat extension, you ensure that Notepad will save the file as a batch file (with a .bat extension) that can be executed instead of a text file (with a .txt extension). Close the file.

11. You can now copy the entire MyUSMT folder to an external USB disk. Take the USB disk to any Windows 8.1 computer that has a Windows.old folder from a previous installation and copy the MyUSMT folder to the root of C.

EXERCISE 3.8 *(continued)*

12. On the new Windows 8.1 computer, with the Start screen showing, type **Command**. When the command prompt appears, right-click it and select Run As Administrator. Click Yes in the User Account Control prompt.

13. Type the following command to change the directory to the c:\myusmt directory you created earlier:

    cd \myusmt

14. Type **usmt** and press Enter to run your batch file. This will take several minutes to complete.

15. Type **notepad loadstate.log** to open the LoadState log file and review it.

16. Type **notepad scanstate.log** to open the ScanState log file and review it.

The scanstate and loadstate commands are long and complex. Don't be surprised if you have a typo and the commands don't work the first time you try them. However, we have copied and pasted them directly into a command prompt and know they work as displayed in the book. If one of the commands is not working, verify there is no typo. A simple trick is to work backward instead of forward. In other words, if the loadstate command isn't working, verify /nocompress is typed correctly and then move backward to the /hardlink switch. Repeat these checks until you get to the beginning of the batch file.

Although the previous exercise copied the contents onto the c:\myusmt folder from the USB flash drive, you can also run the batch file from the flash drive if desired. The only thing you'll need to change is the starting drive. For example, if the USB drive is assigned the letter F, the first command you should enter at the command prompt is **f:** to set F as the current drive. You can then change the directory with the **cd \usmt** command and then start the batch file with the **usmt.bat** command.

Using Wipe-and-Load Migration and Side-by-Side Migration

The previous sections focused on in-place migrations. However, there are some scenarios where the existing system needs to be wiped clean or completely replaced. In these scenarios, you can still use the USMT commands to capture the files and settings and then later restore them, but the process is a little different. The two possible scenarios are a wipe-and-load migration or a side-by-side migration.

Wipe-and-Load Migration

A wipe-and-load migration uses the same hardware but removes all data on the partitions. A simple example may be a system that has multiple partitions that aren't needed in Windows 8.1, so the drive is reconfigured as a single partition. Repartitioning the disk will result in the loss of all the data, so before this is done ScanState is run to capture all the files and settings. The ScanState data can be stored on a server or stored on an external USB drive. After Windows 8.1 and relevant applications are installed, LoadState is executed to restore these settings from the server (or the external USB drive).

Side-by-Side Migration

A side-by-side migration is where a user has an older computer system that will be replaced. ScanState is run on the older system and the data is stored on a network share or on an external USB drive. The user is given a Windows 8.1 system with the applications installed and the older system is decommissioned. LoadState is executed on the new Windows 8.1 system to restore the files and settings.

Wipe-and-Load, Side-by-Side, and ScanState

When you run the ScanState tool for wipe-and-load and side-by-side migrations, you omit the /offlinewindir:c:\windows.old\windows switch. Instead of capturing the files and settings from the Windows.old folder, ScanState will retrieve the migration data from the actual system. Additionally, instead of storing the results in the c:\store folder, you could map a UNC path to a share on a server or connect to an external USB drive.

For example, imagine that you have connected an external USB drive and it is assigned the letter G. The following scanstate command can be used on the older system:

```
scanstate.exe g:\store /v:13 /o /c /hardlink /nocompress /efs:hardlink ↵
   /i:migapp.xml /i:migdocs.xml
```

The captured files and settings can be restored to the Windows 8.1 operating system with the following loadstate command. You might need to change the letter of the drive to reflect the location of the \store folder. For example, the USB drive might have been assigned the letter G on the original computer but it might be assigned E on the newer Windows 8.1 computer. You might also like to change the password. Verify the correct drive letter and then run this command with the correct letter:

```
loadstate.exe e:\store /v:13 /c /lac:P@ssw0rd /lae /i:migapp.xml ↵
   /i:migdocs.xml /sf /hardlink /nocompress
```

Determining Which User Data and Settings to Preserve

When running ScanState, you have some choices for what data and settings to preserve. The easiest choice is to accept the defaults as we've done in this chapter. If your environment is typical and doesn't include any critical one-of-a-kind applications, this choice will meet most, if not all, of your needs. However, you can modify the defaults with the following files:

migdocs.xml   This file includes rules used to find user documents on a computer. Some of the common file types identified in this document are ACCDB, CH3, CSV, DIF, DOC, DOT, DQY, IQY, MCW, MDB, MPP, ONE, OQY, OR6, POT, PPA, PPS, PPT, PRE, PST, PUB, QDF, QEL, QPH, QSD, RQY, RTF, SCD, SH3, SLK, TXT, VL, VSD, WK, WPD,

WPS, WQ1, WRI, XL, XLA, XLB, and XLS. A great online reference for file types is FILExt, located at www.filext.com.

migapp.xml This file includes the rules used to migrate application settings. It will migrate many common applications published by Adobe, Apple, Google, IBM, Intuit, Microsoft, and more.

miguser.xml This file includes rules that can be used to identify different elements of user profiles to include or exclude from the migration. The name implies that you can use this file to include or exclude users, but that isn't true. By default, all users are migrated and this file is *not* used to specify which users to migrate. However, you can use the /ui (user include) and /ue (user exclude) switches with both ScanState and LoadState to include or exclude specific users.

config.xml This file is optional and you create it using the /genconfig switch with scanstate. It can be used specifically to exclude certain components or operating system settings from the migration.

> If you want to limit which users get migrated, you can only do so from the command line. The /ui (user include) and /ue (user exclude) switches can be used to specify local and/or domain accounts with both ScanState and LoadState. You cannot specify which users are migrated using an XML file.

The USMT XML Reference provides more details on all of these XML files. You can access it here: http://technet.microsoft.com/en-us/library/hh824871.aspx.

Considering Local vs. Remote Storage

When creating the migration store, you can use ScanState to store it locally or remotely. *Locally* means you're storing the migration store on a removable USB drive or on an internal drive for a side-by-side migration. *Remotely* means that you're storing the migration data in a shared folder on a server in your network.

Storing data on a network share can be very convenient, but it can also result in a significantly slower migration process. A migration store can hold a large amount of data. With the size of files and the abundance of hard drive space, it would be easy for a user to accumulate 10 GB or more of data. If you're saving this data to a network share over a 100 Mbps network connection, you'll be waiting a while.

Not only will *you* be waiting, but users on the network may also find themselves waiting longer than normal. You should consider how storing the data on network shares affects the rest of the network. If the network is already busy and you begin moving gigabytes of storage over it, things may slow to a crawl and users will start complaining.

If your network infrastructure is reliably running with gigabyte network interface cards, routers, and switches, you will probably be able to use network storage without any problem.

Securing Migrated Data

The amount of data included in a migration store can be considerable, and depending on the user's job responsibilities, the data can be sensitive. Any migration stores with sensitive data should be protected until they are used to restore the user's files and settings. They should be destroyed after the user's files and settings have been restored.

Sensitive data contained in the migration store could include:

- Classified information such as secret data
- Company secrets such as financial data, future product details, or plans for mergers
- Personally identifiable information (PII) on customers and employees, including names, addresses, phone numbers, social security numbers, and credit card information

At the very least, migration stores should be treated with the same level of protection as the original data. For example, if a user has secret data on her system, the migration store obtained from this system should be treated with the same level of protection used to handle secret data anywhere in the organization.

This rule becomes especially important when storing the data on external USB drives. Since these drives are highly portable, it's possible for an administrator to migrate secret data to an external USB drive and then use this migration store to restore the files and settings on a new computer. If the administrator stops there, the USB drive will still hold the secret data. If an educated user later comes across this USB drive and sees the migration store, he could run the loadstate command and restore all the data to his computer.

Destruction of the migration store can take several different forms depending on the type of data used. Some programs will reliably erase the data by overwriting random patterns of 1s and 0s to ensure there isn't any data remaining on the drive that can be recovered.

Testing Your Migration Strategy

Once you've identified what strategy you'll use to migrate the user's data (in-place migration, wipe-and-load migration, or side-by-side migration), you should do some testing.

Except for the wipe-and-load migration, you'll have the original data that can be used to try to save the migration data over and over. The in-place migration retains the original files and settings in the Windows.old folder, so if you're not happy with the results of either ScanState or LoadState, you can simply rerun the tools. Similarly, as long as you keep the original computer in a side-by-side migration, you can rerun both of the tools. However, you only have one chance to run ScanState with a wipe-and-load migration.

After testing and determining the best method, it's worth your time to document the procedure in a batch file. Doing so allows you to easily run the migration commands without struggling to remember the exact syntax of the commands.

Folder Redirection for Migration

As mentioned previously, folder redirection can be used with roaming profiles to reduce logon times. You can also use it as a simple way of migrating user data. The basic steps to do this are as follows:

1. **Redirect folders to a network drive.** Use the same procedure shown in the earlier exercise to redirect the folders. Ensure the user's data has been redirected before proceeding.

2. **Install the user's new computer.** You can use any manual or automated method desired to install the new operating system.

3. **Redirect the folders to the new computer.** This process will copy all of the user's data back to the user's computer.

Although this method can be used to migrate the user's data, it's important to realize that it doesn't copy any of the user's profile information.

Summary

In this chapter you learned some basic methods of installing Windows 8.1 with the installation DVD. A significant feature in Windows 8.1 is Windows To Go, which provides users with a mobile Windows 8.1 workspace. This chapter included exercises to install Windows 8.1 as well as steps for installing and configuring Windows To Go. You learned about some command-line tools (DISM, ImageX, and BCDboot) that can be used to install and configure Windows To Go from the command prompt. You also had an opportunity to create and install a VHD as a separate installation of Windows 8.1.

User settings and data are contained in user profiles. By default, local profiles are stored in the c:\users folder. However, if users log on to different computers in an enterprise, you can implement roaming profiles so that the profiles are stored on a central server in the network. It's also possible to prevent users from modifying their profile by using mandatory profiles. This is a shared roaming profile with the ntuser.dat file changed to ntuser.man.

Folder redirection can be used to separate the user data from the profile. This can be done to improve logon times when users store a lot of data in their profile folders. An advanced method available in Windows 8.1 is User Experience Virtualization (UE-V) when administrators use the Microsoft Desktop Optimization Pack (MDOP).

Windows Easy Transfer (WET) is an easy method of migrating user data and settings between installations. It can be used with an easy transfer cable, over a network, or with an external USB disk.

USMT is more effective when migrating multiple systems. You first run ScanState on the old system to scan it and capture the profile and settings in a migration store. After installing relevant applications on the new computer, you run LoadState on it to migrate the data and settings.

Exam Essentials

Know how to install Windows 8.1.   The installation DVD includes the setup program that starts the installation. You can install from a DVD or copy the contents to a network share and install Windows 8.1 over the network.

Know how to install and configure Windows To Go.   You install Windows To Go onto a USB disk from an image. This can be a standard image from the installation DVD or a custom image. Once you've installed the program, you can configure your PC to boot automatically into Windows To Go using Windows 8.1 or the bcdboot command. You might need to manually configure the BIOS to boot to the USB disk on the system where Windows To Go is used.

Understand profiles.   You should understand differences between local, roaming, and mandatory profiles. Roaming profiles are valuable when users need to log on to different computers but need access to the same profile from any system.

Be familiar with folder redirection.   Folder redirection redirects data folders within the profile such as the My Documents and My Music folders. When used with roaming profiles, folder redirection reduces login times.

Understand UE-V.   Be aware that User Experience Virtualization (UE-V) is a new feature available with the Microsoft Desktop Optimization Pack (MDOP). It can be used instead of roaming profiles and folder redirection but still allows users to have access to their user settings and data when they roam to different systems.

Understand methods used with WET.   The Windows Easy Transfer (WET) tool can be used to migrate user settings and data on a single system. It can be used with an Easy Transfer cable, a network connection, or an external USB drive.

Know the order of migration steps with USMT.   ScanState is used to scan a system and capture migration data and settings from the old system. After applications are installed on the new system, LoadState is used to load the data and settings onto the new system. USMT tools can be used to migrate data using in-place migrations, wipe-and-load migrations, and side-by-side migrations. In-place migrations can be automated with a batch file that will retrieve data from the Windows.old folder created when Windows 8.1 is installed on a computer with a previous version of Windows.

Be familiar with switches used with USMT.   You should be familiar with common load-state and scanstate switches. For example, the /hardlink switch is used for in-place migrations to retrieve data from the Windows.old folder. Users can be included in the migration with the /ui switch or excluded with the /ue switch.

Understand the purpose of the XML files used with USMT.   The migdocs.xml file is used to identify which user documents to migrate based on the file extension. The migapp.xml file is used to identify applications that should have their settings migrated. The miguser.xml file can be used to specify which elements of the user profile are included.

Review Questions

You can find the answers in Appendix A.

1. You need to install a 64-bit edition of Windows 8.1 on a computer currently running a 32-bit edition of Windows 7. You do not want the Windows 7 files on the computer when you complete the installation. What should you do?

   A. Perform an upgrade to Windows 8.1 and do not modify existing partitions.

   B. Perform a custom installation of Windows 8.1 and do not modify existing partitions.

   C. Perform an upgrade to Windows 8.1 and delete existing partitions during the installation.

   D. Perform a custom installation of Windows 8.1 and delete existing partitions during the installation.

2. A computer is currently running Windows 7 Professional. The user wants to upgrade it to Windows 8.1 Pro. Which of the following methods can be used? (Choose all that apply.)

   A. Start the computer from the Windows 8.1 installation DVD.

   B. Start the computer normally, and run the startup program from the installation DVD.

   C. Copy the files on the installation DVD to a network share and run the startup program from the share.

   D. Use the startup program to partition the disk and install Windows 8.1 on the new partition.

3. A user has a Windows To Go workspace on a portable USB system. It automatically boots to Windows To Go on his work computer. His home computer runs Windows 7 by default but does not boot to Windows To Go. What is the most likely solution?

   A. Modify the Windows To Go boot settings in Windows 7.

   B. Modify the Windows To Go boot settings in Windows 8.1.

   C. Modify the BIOS settings on his home computer.

   D. Install Windows 8.1 on his home computer.

4. You are deploying a Windows To Go workspace on a USB disk drive. You want to ensure the drive will boot on a user's home computer. Which of the following tools should you use?

   A. ImageX

   B. DISM

   C. BCDboot

   D. ScanState

5. You are configuring profiles on systems after migrating data to Windows 8.1. You want users to be able to log on to any computer and still have access to their same data and settings. What should you configure?

   A. Local profiles

   B. Mandatory profiles

    C. Roaming profiles

    D. Folder redirection

6. Users in a network regularly roam to different computers. Users need access to their data no matter which computer they log on to, but you want to ensure that the user logon time is minimized. Of the following choices, what is the best solution?

    A. Implement roaming profiles.

    B. Implement folder redirection to a network share.

    C. Implement local profiles.

    D. Modify the Default User profile.

7. Of the following choices, what cannot be redirected using folder redirection?

    A. My Documents

    B. My Music

    C. My Pictures

    D. My Libraries

8. Users in an enterprise regularly log on to different computers using roaming profiles. However, due to the large size of some user profiles, it often takes a long time for them to log on. What can be done to improve this process without losing any capabilities?

    A. Implement local profiles.

    B. Implement mandatory profiles.

    C. Prevent roaming.

    D. Implement UE-V.

9. Your organization has 10 computers running 32-bit editions of Windows XP and you will be swapping them out with 64-bit editions of Windows 8.1. Of the following choices, what is the easiest way to get the user documents from their old system to their new system?

    A. Use the Easy Transfer cable with WET.

    B. Use a crossover cable with WET.

    C. Use a USB flash drive.

    D. Use USMT.

10. Which of the following tools is the easiest to use when migrating data on a single system?

    A. WET

    B. USMT

    C. UE-V

    D. Roaming profiles

11. You want to migrate data between two computers using WET but you don't have an Easy Transfer cable. What can you use instead without storing the data anywhere else?

    A. A crossover cable

    B. A USB cable

    C. A FireWire cable

    D. An RS-232 serial cable

12. You plan on migrating user data and settings after installing Windows 8.1. Where can you get the most current version of USMT to assist with the migration?

    A. Download the Windows AIK.

    B. Download the Windows ADK.

    C. Download the WET tool.

    D. Install it from Programs and Features in Windows 8.1.

13. You are trying to determine what you can use to encrypt a migration store on a computer. What tool can you use to help?

    A. LoadState

    B. ScanState

    C. USMTutils

    D. WET

14. You are migrating data and settings using USMT tools. What is the proper order of steps you should take?

    A. Run LoadState on the old computer, install applications on the new computer, and run ScanState on the new computer.

    B. Run ScanState on the old computer, install applications on the new computer, and run LoadState on the new computer.

    C. Run WET on the old computer, install applications on the new computer, and run WET on the new computer.

    D. Run ScanState on the old computer, run LoadState on the new computer, and install applications on the new computer.

15. A user is running a custom application on Windows 7 and plans on moving the application to a tablet running Windows 8.1 Pro. How can the user migrate the settings and data to the tablet?

    A. Run ScanState on Windows 7 to capture the settings, install the application on the tablet, and run LoadState on the tablet.

    B. Run LoadState on Windows 7 to capture the settings, install the application on the tablet, and run ScanState on the tablet.

    C. Run ScanState on Windows 7 to capture the settings, run LoadState on the tablet, and install the application on the tablet.

    D. Run WET on Windows 7 to capture the settings, install the application on the tablet, and run WET on the tablet.

16. You are planning the deployment of multiple Windows 8.1 computers. Users are currently running Windows 7. You want to capture the user settings from their profiles using tools in the Windows Assessment and Deployment Kit (ADK). What tool should you run on the Windows 7 computers?

A. LoadState

B. ScanState

C. USMTutils

D. WET

17. You are deploying 10 new Windows 8.1 computers for users who are currently running Windows Vista. You have captured profile data for each of the users using tools in the Windows Assessment and Deployment Kit (ADK). What tool should you run on the Windows 8.1 computers to migrate the profiles?

A. ScanState

B. USMT

C. Windows Easy Transfer

D. LoadState

18. You want to migrate user settings with USMT but you do not want to migrate specific accounts. What should you do?

A. Modify the `miguser.xml` file.

B. Modify the `config.xml` file.

C. Use the `/ui` switch with the `loadstate` command.

D. Use the `/ue` switch with the `loadstate` command.

19. You ran LoadState on a computer to restore settings and data on a Windows 8.1 computer. You then installed applications on the computer, but the applications do not have the settings from the LoadState data. What is the most likely cause?

A. The settings were not in the migration store.

B. The application settings were corrupted.

C. The settings are only applied if the applications are installed before the migration.

D. Application settings are applied with ScanState, not LoadState.

20. You are planning on migrating user data and settings using USMT. You want to ensure specific files used by an in-house application are included in the migration. These files have an extension of `.gcga`. What should you do?

A. Modify the `miguser.xml` file.

B. Modify the `migdocs.xml` file.

C. Modify the `config.xml` file.

D. Modify the `migapp.xml` file

Chapter 4

Using Virtualization Technologies

70-687 MICROSOFT EXAM OBJECTIVES COVERED IN THIS CHAPTER:

✓ **Configure Hyper-V**

- Create and configure virtual machines, including integration services

- Create and manage checkpoints

- Create and configure virtual switches

- Create and configure virtual disks

- Move a virtual machine's storage

70-688 MICROSOFT EXAM OBJECTIVES COVERED IN THIS CHAPTER:

✓ **Support desktop apps**

- Desktop app compatibility using Application Compatibility Toolkit (ACT), including shims and compatibility database

- Desktop application co-existence using Hyper-V, RemoteApp, and App-V

- Installation and configuration of User Experience Virtualization (UE-V)

- Deploy desktop apps by using Windows Intune

Windows desktop systems have included virtualization capabilities in several versions, but there are some significant changes in Windows 8.1 and Windows 8.1.1(Windows 8.1 with update 1 applied) capabilities. We're happy to let you know that these changes are overwhelmingly positive. Windows 8.1 includes Hyper-V, which uses the same virtualization technologies as Windows Server products in production environments. A great benefit of learning how this works on Windows 8.1 is that the same knowledge applies to Windows Server products.

Some key testable items with Hyper-V include understanding virtual switches, virtual machines, virtual disks, and snapshots. You can manipulate virtual switches to control connectivity of virtual machines, and use snapshots to capture and restore the state of virtual machines.

This chapter reviews the requirements to use Hyper-V and shows you how to enable it on a compatible Windows 8.1 system. It also includes a wealth of exercises showing you how to create a virtual network. If you complete these exercises, you'll have a virtual machine running Windows Server 2012 as a domain controller and another virtual machine running Windows 8.1 joined to the domain. These exercises will help you gain experience with Hyper-V, and you'll have a virtual environment that you can use to learn more about Windows 8.1 without modifying your primary Windows 8.1 system.

You'll also learn some basics related to designing a virtual application strategy. These can include using Remote Desktop Services to host virtual desktops or RemoteApp applications and using an App-V server.

CERT OBJECTIVE Understanding Virtualization and Hyper-V

Virtualization is a powerful feature used in desktop and server computers. It allows you to run one or more virtual machines (VMs) on a single physical host computer. A *VM* is a fully functioning operating system that is running as a guest on a computer running virtualization software. For example, you can have a single Windows 8.1 computer and run a virtual network that includes one or more Windows Server 2012 systems and one or more Windows 8.1 desktop PCs.

Windows 8.1 supports *Hyper-V for Clients*, which is a fully functioning virtualization application. You can use it to run multiple VMs on a single Windows 8.1 computer. For example, Figure 4.1 shows how a Windows 8.1 physical system can be used with Hyper-V to run two VMs. The physical computer running the virtualization software is called the *host*, and VMs running within the virtual environment are called *guests*.

FIGURE 4.1   Windows 8.1 hosting two VMs

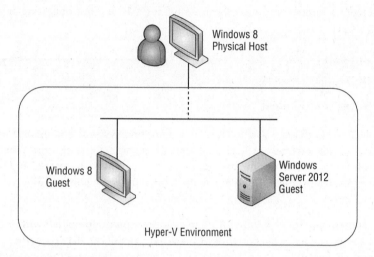

Windows 8
Physical Host

Windows 8
Guest

Windows
Server 2012
Guest

Hyper-V Environment

Many datacenters commonly use virtualization for servers for several reasons. For example, a single physical server hosting four or more virtual server guests provides direct savings. A single physical server costs less than five servers, consumes less power, and requires less heating ventilation and air conditioning. A single physical server that hosts four virtual servers will require serious CPU power and at least 64 GB of RAM—more is always better when it comes to virtualization—but all in all, it will still be a better deal than five stand-alone servers.

Virtualization on desktop PCs isn't new. Microsoft has long had virtual PC products. Early editions were known as Microsoft Virtual PC, and they were renamed to Windows Virtual PC in Windows 7. Windows 7 also included Windows XP Mode, which allows you to run applications from within a virtual Windows XP environment without directly starting the virtual Windows XP machine. Available as free downloads, these products allowed you to run one or more virtual PCs within a single physical host.

Windows XP Mode is available in Windows 7, but it is not available in Windows 8.1. You can still install virtual desktops on Windows 8.1 systems and run applications from within them, but the user must directly start the Windows 8.1 virtual environment first. Also, keep in mind that if you want to run Windows XP in a Windows 8.1 VM, you'll also need to supply a valid Windows XP license.

One of the drawbacks with Windows Virtual PC is that it only supported 32-bit guest operating systems. You could run it on 32-bit or 64-bit host operating systems, but it was unable to run 64-bit VMs. With newer server operating systems such as Windows Server 2008 R2 and server applications such as Microsoft Exchange coming out in only 64-bit editions, this limitation was significant. Many users started moving to alternative solutions such as VMware and VirtualBox to implement virtual environments on desktop systems.

However, Hyper-V supports running both 32-bit and 64-bit guest operating systems and so eliminates this problem.

 Real World Scenario

Using Virtualization to Learn

Using virtual systems is an ideal way to learn new operating systems and applications. You don't need to purchase new hardware but instead can create one or more VMs and play around with them. The worst that can happen is that you make a mistake and the VM no longer boots. No problem. Rebuild it from scratch and gain some additional experience.

For example, if you're learning Windows 8.1 and want to experiment with it within a domain, you can create a simple network with a Windows Server 2012 R2 server running as a domain controller and a Windows 8.1 system running as a member of the domain. This author has re-created this a few times while learning both Windows 8.1 and Windows Server 2012, and I know it's an effective way to learn and gain experience.

With that in mind, we have included the exercises in this chapter that you can use to create your own virtual network with a Windows Server 2012 domain controller and a Windows 8.1 system joined to the domain.

CERT OBJECTIVE Reviewing Requirements for Hyper-V

Chapter 2, "Planning the Windows 8.1 Installation," introduced the requirements for several features, including Hyper-V. As you'll recall, a Windows 8.1 system must meet the following basic requirements to run Hyper-V:

- Must be running either Windows 8.1 Pro or Windows 8.1 Enterprise
- Must be running a 64-bit edition of Windows 8.1
- Must have at least 4 GB of RAM

RAM is an important consideration when using VMs. Each VM requires some physical RAM, so you need to ensure that you have enough RAM for Windows 8.1 and to meet the needs of each VM.

Imagine you want to create a virtual network with two VMs—one running Windows Server 2012 and one running Windows 8.1. The following list identifies the minimum requirements for each:

- 64-bit Windows 8.1 host: minimum of 2 GB
- 64-bit Windows Server 2012 guest: minimum of 512 MB
- 64-bit Windows 8.1 guest: minimum of 2 GB

These requirements indicate that your system must have at least 4.5 GB of RAM installed. However, you might find that using the minimum amount of RAM for each system results in the host system and the guest VMs being too slow. Instead, you might want a minimum of 4 GB for the host Windows 8.1 system, 3 GB for the guest Windows Server 2012 system, and 3 GB for the guest Windows 8.1 system. With these choices, you'll need at least 10 GB of RAM. Of course, when it comes to running VMs more RAM is always better. So, 16 GB would be a more realistic memory allocation for the given configuration.

If you plan on using a Windows 8.1 system with Hyper-V to learn additional operating systems, about 12 to 16 GB of installed RAM is a good target. This allows you to create VMs with enough RAM that they are not running excessively slowly.

A relatively new memory feature in Hyper-V is the use of dynamic memory. It is useful for operating systems that don't require as much memory during normal operation as they do when they are first started. For example, an operating system might only require 312 MB of RAM to run during normal operations but require a minimum of 512 MB of RAM when it initially starts.

Figure 4.2 shows the VM settings for a Window Server 2012 system running the Server Core operating system. Server Core doesn't use a graphical user interface (GUI) but has access only to the command prompt and PowerShell. With the limited interface, it requires less memory to run.

In Figure 4.2 you can see that 512 MB has been set as the Startup RAM and Dynamic Memory has been enabled. The VM will start with 512 MB, and after it has started, Hyper-V will throttle it down to only 312 MB. If the VM needs additional RAM, the Maximum RAM setting allows it to use additional system RAM when it's available. It's worth noting that this setting applies only to the physical RAM assigned to the VM. VMs use paging to gain access to virtual memory in the same way that a physical host uses paging.

FIGURE 4.2 Hyper-V VM settings

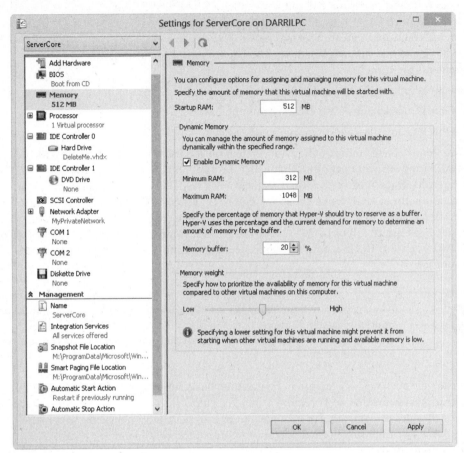

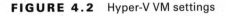 Enabling Hyper-V

If you want to use Hyper-V on a Windows 8.1 system, you'll need to enable it first. You do so by enabling the feature through the Windows 8.1 Programs and Features applet.

Exercise 4.1 shows the steps to enable Hyper-V. This exercise assumes you're logged on to a Windows 8.1 system and the Start screen is showing.

EXERCISE 4.1

Enabling Hyper-V on a Windows 8.1 Computer

1. Right-click on the Start button

2. When the context menu appears, select Programs And Features.

3. Click Turn Windows Features On Or Off.

4. Select the Hyper-V check box. This will enable Hyper-V Management Tools and the Hyper-V Platform.

5. Click OK.

6. Windows 8.1 will install the files necessary for Hyper-V and prompt you to restart your computer. Ensure that you have saved all your work and closed any open applications. Click Restart Now.

7. After a moment, your computer will reboot and prompt you to log on. Log on with an account with administrative permissions. Windows 8.1 will complete the installation of Hyper-V and reboot again.

8. When prompted, log on again. You'll see two new additions to the Start screen: Hyper-V Manager and Hyper-V Virtual Machine Connection. (The aforementioned applets can now also be accessed from Search.) The primary tool used in the following exercises is Hyper-V Manager. When a VM is running, you can select Hyper-V Virtual Machine Connection to connect to the VM.

9. If desired, you can select Hyper-V Manager to start it and take a look. Later exercises in this chapter work primarily within Hyper-V Manager.

Configuring Virtual Switches

Within a network, physical switches are used to connect various network devices. Switches in turn are connected to routers to access other networks, including the Internet. Hyper-V uses virtual switches to provide connectivity between VMs within Hyper-V. A *virtual switch* mimics the functionality of a physical switch, and each VM is associated with a specific virtual switch in order to provide connectivity with other VMs, the physical host, and the physical network.

When you create VMs with Hyper-V Manager, you need to have a virtual switch available in order for the VMs to communicate with each other, the host, or the physical network.

The tool used to create virtual switches is the Virtual Switch Manager, available within Hyper-V Manager. When creating a virtual switch, you have three choices:

External   A physical host is typically connected to a network, and when it is, the guest VMs can share the network connection to also connect to the network. For example, if the physical host has Internet access, the VMs can have Internet access through the physical host. You would create an *external switch* and configure the VMs to use this switch in order to access the external network. An external switch also provides network connectivity to other VMs using the same switch, and network connectivity to the physical host.

Internal   VMs connected to an *internal switch* have network connectivity to each other and network connectivity to the physical host. An internal switch does not provide access to the physical network for the VMs, but the physical host will still have access to the physical network.

Private   VMs connected with a *private switch* have network connectivity to each other only. They do not have network connectivity to the physical host or to the physical network. A private switch is used to keep the VMs isolated from everything else.

The virtual switch only affects network connectivity through the network interface cards used on the client and host systems. It doesn't affect how a host interacts with a guest operating system through Hyper-V Manager.

Figure 4.3 shows the network connectivity for the VMs with each of these virtual switch types. It's important to realize that the virtual switch affects connectivity only for the VMs, not the physical host. In other words, even though Internet connectivity isn't shown in the figure for the internal switch and the private switch, the physical host still has connectivity to the external network and the Internet when these switches are used. Figure 4.3 shows the connectivity for the VMs only when the different types of virtual switches are used.

FIGURE 4.3   Connectivity for different virtual switches

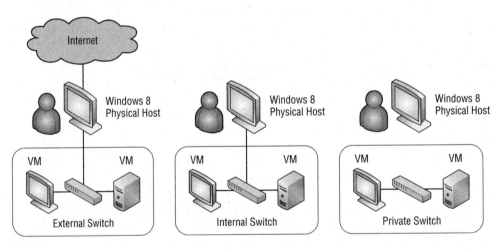

To create a virtual switch, your computer must have a network interface card (NIC) installed and connected to a network. If a NIC isn't installed or it isn't connected, Hyper-V gives errors when you try to create the virtual switch even if you're trying to create a private switch.

Exercise 4.2 leads you through the steps to create a private virtual switch. This exercise assumes you're logged in and the Start screen is showing.

EXERCISE 4.2

Creating a Virtual Switch

1. Select Hyper-V Manager to start it. If it is not selected by default, select the current computer.

2. Select Action ➢ Virtual Switch Manager.

3. Select Private and click Create Virtual Switch.

4. In the Name text box, enter a name such as **MyPrivateNetwork**. Your display will look similar to the following graphic. Click OK. After a moment the virtual switch will be created.

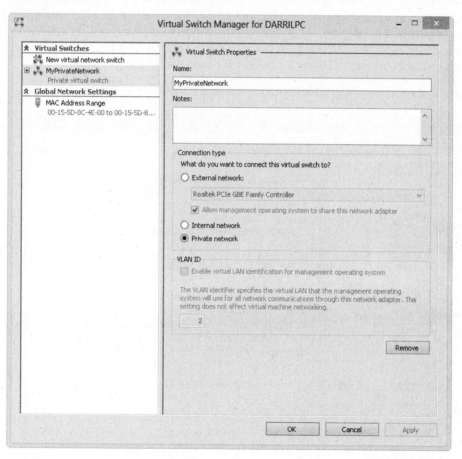

Creating Virtual Machines

Once you've enabled the Hyper-V feature on Windows 8.1 and created a virtual switch, you can start creating VMs. You'll need to have the installation DVD or an ISO image of the DVD.

You can download a free trial evaluation of Windows Server 2012 from here: http://technet.microsoft.com/evalcenter/hh670538.aspx. When you download the ISO file, you can burn it to a DVD if you have a DVD burner. Alternately, you can use the ISO file and load the operating system from it. As an alternative, consider downloading the Windows Server 2012 VHD file. Regardless of the version you choose, you are in for a wait as it downloads. The ISO version is 3.44 GB, whereas the VHD file is 2.47 GB. Depending on your Internet connection speed, your download time could be 30–60 minutes (or longer).

Figure 4.4 shows the Hyper-V settings from a VM. You can see a list of hardware items on the left and IDE Controller 1 is selected. In the middle pane, the Physical CD/DVD Drive has been selected and it has been assigned the drive letter E. When the installation DVD is inserted into the DVD drive, it is available from within the VM.

FIGURE 4.4   Hyper-V VM Settings page showing CD/DVD

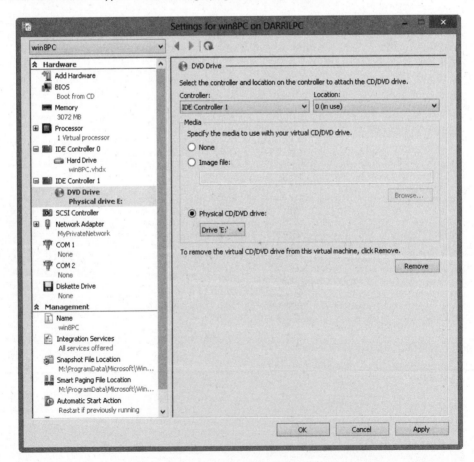

If you're using an ISO file instead of a physical DVD, you would select Image File, browse to the location of the ISO image file, and select it. Within the VM, the ISO image file works as if it is a physical DVD.

 Microsoft has several programs available for IT professionals that allow you to subscribe and get free versions of most of their software. For example, a subscription to Microsoft TechNet will give you access to fully working copies of almost all their desktop and server operating systems. This is one way a regular user can get access to Windows 8.1 Enterprise without being a Software Assurance customer. You can check it out here: http://technet.microsoft.com/subscriptions/.

The remaining exercises in this chapter lead you through the process of creating a virtual network with one VM running Windows Server 2012 configured as a domain controller and another VM running Windows 8.1 as a member of the domain. The exercises are organized as follows:

- Exercise 4.3: Creating a VM for Windows 8.1

- Exercise 4.4: Installing Windows 8.1 in a VM

- Exercise 4.5: Creating a VM for Windows Server 2012

- Exercise 4.6: Installing Windows Server 2012 in a VM

- Exercise 4.7: Configuring Windows Server 2012

- Exercise 4.8: Promoting Windows Server 2012 to a DC

- Exercise 4.9: Joining Windows 8.1 to a Domain

- Exercise 4.10: Logging On to Windows 8.1 with a Domain Account

- Exercise 4.11: Creating Snapshots

When you complete all these exercises, you'll have a virtual network similar to Figure 4.5. As a reminder, the private network will keep your virtual network completely isolated. From a security standpoint, an isolated network is useful because there isn't any chance of these VMs being attacked from malware or other attacks through the network.

FIGURE 4.5   Completed virtual network

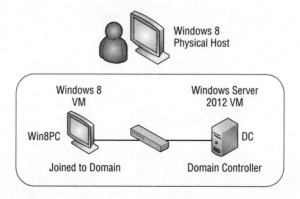

NOTE If desired, you can change the settings on the virtual switch. However, if you decide to connect the VMs to the network you should ensure they are kept up-to-date and are running antivirus software (such as Windows Defender) to help keep them protected.

Creating a VM for Windows 8.1

After you have created a virtual switch, you can begin adding VMs to the virtual network using this switch. When you create a VM, the wizard will lead you through the process of identifying the name of the VM, how much memory you want to assign to it, selecting a preconfigured virtual switch, and where you want to store the VM files.

By default it will store the Hyper-V files in the following two locations:

`C:\Users\Public\Public Documents\Hyper-V` This folder holds the actual virtual hard disks. When you start, this folder will likely consume the most space.

`C:\ProgramData\Microsoft\Windows\Hyper-V` This holds many of the miscellaneous files that support the VMs. It starts out rather small, but if you begin using snapshots it can grow substantially.

If you're concerned you might run out of room on a disk, you can select different locations for these files. Even if you don't select a different location when you create the VM, you can move it later. You simply right-click the existing VM, select Move, and follow the wizard.

You'll also have the option of identifying the installation media you'll use for the VM when you create it. Figure 4.6 shows the Installation Options page where you identify the location of the installation media. However, even if you select one of these options it doesn't install the operating system as a part of VM creation process. You'll still have to start the VM and connect to it.

Exercise 4.3 walks you through the steps to create a VM using Install An Operating System Later as an option. This will give you an opportunity to get into the VM settings page later, which is more directly related to the exam objectives. This exercise assumes you're logged in, the Start screen is showing, Hyper-V has been installed, and a private virtual switch named MyPrivateSwitch has been created.

FIGURE 4.6   Hyper-V installation options

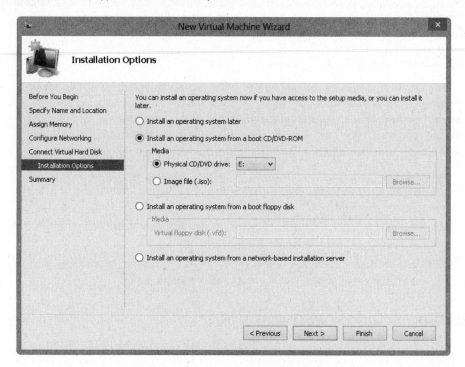

EXERCISE 4.3

Creating a VM for Windows 8.1

1. Select Hyper-V Manager to start it. Ensure the local computer is selected.

2. Select Action ➤ New ➤ Virtual Machine.

3. Review the information on the Before You Begin page and click Next.

4. On the Specify Name and Location page, give your VM a name such as **Win8PC**. If desired, you change the location of the VM. Click Next.

5. On the Assign Memory page, assign the amount of memory you want the VM to have. For example, you can assign it 3 GB by entering **3072**.

EXERCISE 4.3 *(continued)*

6. On the Configure Networking page, select the network you created in the previous exercise from the Connection drop-down box. If you followed the exercise, it is named MyPrivateNetwork. Click Next.

7. On the Create A Virtual Hard Disk page, change the maximum size to 60 GB, accept the defaults for the remaining settings, and click Next. You can give it a different name if desired, choose a different location, or give it a different maximum size. We chose 60 GB so it has a little room to grow but cannot take over the hard drive, and we kept the same name as the VM to avoid any confusion later.

8. Review the information on the Installation Options page. Accept the default option, Install An Operating System Later, and click Next. Review the information on the Summary page and click Finish.

At this point, you have created a VM but it doesn't have anything in it. If you start it, it would be similar to starting a physical computer with a blank disk.

Installing Windows 8.1 in a VM

Once you've created a blank VM, you can install an operating system within it. The primary step you'll need to take before you start the VM is to identify where the installation media is located. You do so by modifying the VM Settings page for the VM.

Exercise 4.4 walks you through the introductory steps to configure the VM and install Windows 8.1 on the VM. This exercise assumes you have completed the previous exercise, Hyper-V Manager is still open, and you have a Windows 8.1 installation DVD or ISO file.

EXERCISE 4.4

Installing Windows 8.1 in a VM

1. With Hyper-V Manager showing, select the VM you created in the previous exercise. If you followed the recommendation, you named it Win8PC.

2. Right-click the VM and select Settings.

3. Select IDE Controller 1 from the hardware list.

   a. If you're using an ISO image, select Image File under Media and click Browse. Browse to the location of the ISO file, select it, and click Open.

   b. If you're using a DVD, ensure the installation DVD is in the DVD drive and select Physical CD/DVD.

4. Click OK to attach the ISO image file or the physical DVD to the VM.

5. Right-click the VM and select Start. Although the VM will start when you do this, it doesn't open. Double-click the VM to open it.

6. The system will automatically boot to the installation DVD and start the setup program to begin installing Windows 8.1.

7. Follow the remaining steps in the installation program to install Windows 8.1. If desired, you can use the steps in Exercise 3.1 in Chapter 3, "Installing Windows 8.1 from the Installation DVD," to complete the installation.

When the personalization page appears, you'll be prompted to name the Windows 8.1 computer. We recommend giving it the same name you gave to the VM. For example, if you named the VM Win8PC, name the computer running within the VM Win8PC. This makes it easier to identify the different computers from within a running VM and when looking at Hyper-V Manager. It also adds consistency when the same name is given to the virtual disk file.

Creating a VM for Windows Server 2012

Just as you created a blank VM for Windows 8.1, you can also create a blank VM for any other operating system. Exercise 4.5 walks you through the steps to create a blank VM for Windows Server 2012. It is similar to Exercise 4.3. This exercise assumes you're logged in, the Start screen is showing, Hyper-V has been installed, a private virtual switch has been created, and Hyper-V Manager is still open.

EXERCISE 4.5

Creating a VM for Windows Server 2012

1. With Hyper-V Manager open, select New ➤ Virtual Machine from the Actions pane on the right. Notice you can select this here or through the Action menu at the top as in the previous exercise.

2. Review the information on the Before You Begin page and click Next.

3. On the Specify Name And Location page, give your VM a name such as **DC** (short for domain controller). If desired, you can change the location of the VM. Click Next.

4. On the Assign Memory page, assign the amount of memory you want the VM to have. For example, you can assign it 3 GB by entering **3072**.

EXERCISE 4.5 *(continued)*

5. On the Configure Networking page, select the network named MyPrivateNetwork you created earlier from the Connection drop-down box. Click Next.

6. On the Create A Virtual Hard Disk page, change the maximum size to 60 GB, accept the defaults for the remaining settings, and click Next. You can change these options, but we chose 60 GB so it has a little room to grow but cannot take over the hard drive.

7. Review the information on the Installation Options page. Accept the default option, Install An Operating System Later, and click Next. Review the information on the Summary page and click Finish.

Just as the Windows 8.1 VM was blank when you first created it, this Windows Server 2012 VM is also blank at this stage. However, it is prepared for you to install Windows Server 2012 onto it.

Installing Windows 2012 in a VM

If you have a regular copy of Windows Server 2012, you can use it in your virtual environment. You can also download the trial version using the web page mentioned earlier in this chapter. The trial version includes all the features of the regular version but expires after a 180-day trial. If the trial version expires, you can re-create another blank VM and repeat the steps. If nothing else, it's good practice.

Exercise 4.6 walks you through the steps to install Windows Server 2012 in this VM. You'll notice that most of the steps are very similar to a Windows 8.1 installation. This exercise assumes you have completed the previous exercise, Hyper-V Manager is still open, and you have a Windows Server 2012 DVD or ISO file.

EXERCISE 4.6

Installing Windows Server 2012 in a VM

1. With Hyper-V Manager showing, select the VM you created in the previous exercise. If you followed the recommendation, you named it DC.

2. Right-click the VM and select Settings.

3. Select IDE Controller 1 from the hardware list.

a. If you're using an ISO image, select Image File under Media and click Browse. Browse to the location of the ISO file, select it, and click Open.

b. If you're using a DVD, select Physical CD/DVD.

4. Click OK to attach the ISO image file or the physical DVD to the VM.

5. Right-click the VM and select Connect. The VM opens within a Virtual Machine Connection window but indicates the VM is turned off.

6. Click the green Start button to start the VM.

7. The system will automatically boot to the installation DVD and start the setup program to begin installing Windows Server 2012.

8. On the initial page, ensure the correct Language To Install, Time and Currency Format, and Keyboard Or Input Method options are selected. Click Next.

9. Click Install Now on the Windows Server 2012 page.

10. Most Windows Server 2012 installation DVDs include multiple images, including both Standard and Datacenter editions, and both Server Core and GUI editions. The Server Core edition only uses a command prompt without a full Windows operating system. If you have multiple choices, select the Standard edition listed as Server With A GUI and click Next.

11. Review the license terms and select I Accept the License Terms. Click Next.

12. Select Custom: Install Windows Only (Advanced).

13. Select Drive 0 Unallocated Space and click Next. The system will configure the drive partitions and start to copy and configure the Windows files. This process will take some time to complete.

14. When the Settings page appears, enter **P@ssw0rd** in the Password and Reenter Password text boxes. This assigns P@ssw0rd as the password for the local administrator account. Click Finish.

Configuring Windows Server 2012

After you install Windows Server 2012, you'll need to complete some basic steps to configure it. Windows Server 2012 includes an updated Server Manager with a dashboard and wizards that can guide you through most tasks. There's a lot more to it than we'll cover in this short section; however, this section will lead you through the steps to configure required settings prior to promoting the server to a domain controller.

Figure 4.7 shows the Server Manager with the Local Server settings modified. After you complete Exercise 4.7, your system should look similar with the Computer Name changed to DC and the Ethernet setting changed to a static IP address of 192.168.1.10.

If you are working exclusively within a single VM, you might want to change it to full-screen mode. You can press Ctrl+Alt+Break to toggle between full screen and a resizable window for any VM. You can also select Full Screen Mode from the View menu to go to full-screen mode. Simply click the minimize button at the top of the screen to return to a normal window.

FIGURE 4.7   Windows Server 2012 Server Manager

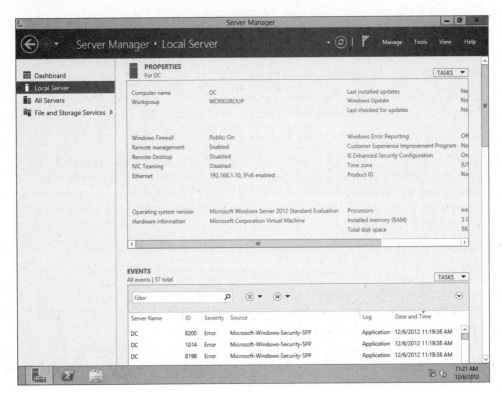

Exercise 4.7 walks you through the steps to configure the Windows Server 2012 server. These steps should be done prior to promoting the server to a domain controller. This process names the server DC so that it is apparent it is a domain controller. This exercise assumes that you have completed the previous exercise, installing Windows Server 2012 in a VM within Hyper-V Manager, and that the Windows Server 2012 VM is running.

EXERCISE 4.7

Configuring Windows Server 2012

1. Click within the Windows Server 2012 VM to ensure it has the focus.

2. Press Ctrl+Alt+End to simulate pressing the Ctrl+Alt+Delete keys to access the logon screen. If desired, you can click the Action menu in the VM instead, and select CTL + ALT + DELETE. Note that if you press Ctrl+Alt+Delete, the host system intercepts the keys and opens the Lock screen.

3. The Administrator account is selected automatically. Enter **P@ssw0rd** as the password and press Enter. You will be logged on to the Windows Server 2012 system with the local Administrator account.

4. The Server Manager opens automatically showing the Dashboard. Click Configure This Local Server.

these steps:

ven a name of WIN followed by a hyphen with some name to open the System Properties page with the

ox, enter **DC** as the computer name.

you must restart the computer and click OK.

Now to restart the server.

elect the local Administrator account, enter
ox, and press Enter. The Server Manager will open
g.

the following steps:

rver.

ddress Assigned By DHCP, IPv6 Enabled.

ace card labeled Ethernet and select Properties.

on 4 (TCP/IPv4) and select Properties.

ddress and enter the following information:

.0

.1

S Server Addresses and enter the following infor-
r: **127.0.0.1**. This causes the computer to use its own
System (DNS) hostname resolution. DNS will be
when the computer is promoted. Your display will
look similar to the following graphic.

g. Click OK. Click Close.

h. Close the Network Connections window by clicking the X in the top-right corner.

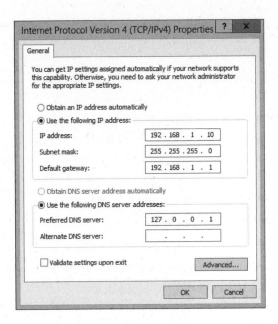

Even though the exercise has you enter an IP address for the default gateway, that IP address is not used. You could leave that field blank and it wouldn't affect the usability of the VMs. If computers in the virtual network had access to computers in another network, the default gateway provides the path to a router leading to the other network. However, the virtual network created in this exercise is isolated. Because the default gateway is commonly configured in a system, we left it in so it didn't look as if something was missing (and so we could include this note!).

Promoting a Server to a DC

When you first install Windows 8.1 and Windows Server 2012, they are a member of a workgroup called Workgroup. Although this is fine for small networks, domains are used in larger networks. A domain has a central server configured as a domain controller (DC) that hosts Active Directory Domain Services (AD DS).

AD DS works as a large database that holds all the objects for a domain, such as user accounts, computer accounts, Group Policy objects (GPOs), and more. Chapter 7, "Managing Windows 8.1 in a Domain," will delve into how a domain and GPOs work to simplify management. While the domain provides some great features for a network, you'll find that it is relatively easy to configure a server as a DC.

Exercise 4.8 walks you through the steps to promote the Windows Server 2012 server to a domain controller. This process creates a domain named GetCertifiedGetAhead.com. This exercise assumes you have completed the previous exercise, "Configuring Windows Server 2012," installing Windows Server 2012 in a VM within Hyper-V Manager, and that Hyper-V Manager is still open.

EXERCISE 4.8

Promoting Windows Server 2012 to a DC

1. If necessary, press Ctrl+Alt+End to log on. Enter **P@ssw0rd** as the password for the administrator account.

2. The Server Manager appears with the Dashboard showing by default. If the Server Manager is open from the previous exercise, select Dashboard.

3. Select Add Roles And Features.

4. Review the information in the Before You Begin page and click Next. Notice that if you ever want to remove a role or feature, you can click the Start The Remove Roles And Features Wizard link on this page.

5. On the Select Installation Type page, ensure that Role-Based Or Feature-Based Installation is selected. Click Next.

6. On the Select Destination Server page, ensure the local server named DC with an IP address of 192.168.1.10 is selected. Click Next.

7. On the Select Server Roles page, select Active Directory Domain Services.

8. A dialog box appears indicating that other features are required for Active Directory Domain Services. Ensure that Include Management Tools (If Applicable) is selected and click Add Features.

9. You'll be returned to the Select Server Roles page with Active Directory Domain Services selected. Your display will look similar to the following graphic. Click Next.

10. On the Select Features page, Group Policy Management and Remote Server Administration Tools are automatically selected. Click Next.

11. Review the information on the Active Directory Domain Services page and click Next.

12. On the Confirm Installation Selections page, select Restart The Destination Server Automatically If Required check box. Review the prompt and click Yes. Click Install.

13. Wait until the wizard completes; when it does, click the Promote This Server To A Domain Controller link. This launches the promotion wizard.

14. Select Add A New Forest.

15. In the Root Domain Name text box, enter **GetCertifiedGetAhead.com**. Click Next.

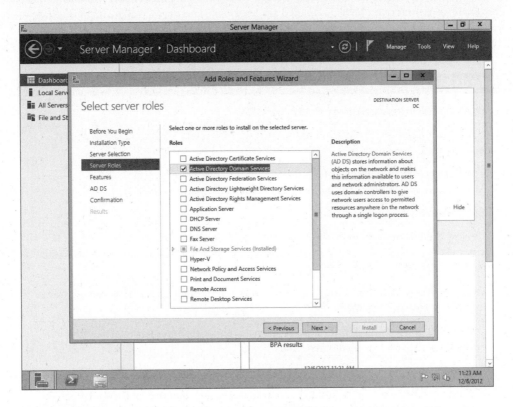

16. In the two Directory Services Restore Mode (DSRM) Password boxes, enter **P@ssw0rd**.

17. Accept the defaults for the remaining items and click Next.

18. Review the information on the DNS Options page. It gives an error, which is normal at this stage. A DNS server role will be added to the server during the promotion. Click Next.

19. On the Additional Options page, you'll see that the NetBIOS Domain Name is truncated to only GETCERTIFIEDGET. This is because NetBIOS is limited to only 15 readable characters, so larger domain names (such as GetCertifiedGetAhead) can cause problems when NetBIOS is used. People sometimes have difficulty understanding this, but seeing how GetCertifiedGetAhead is truncated to GETCERTIFIEDGET provides a good illustration. For a mini–virtual network used for learning, this doesn't cause any problems. However, in a production network using NetBIOS, it's best to limit the domain to 15 characters to avoid problems. Click Next.

20. Review the information on the Paths page and click Next.

21. Review the information on the Review Options page. Notice the DNS Server service will be configured on the computer automatically as part of the process. If desired, you can click the View Script button to see the PowerShell commands used to promote the server. Click Next.

22. The program runs a prerequisite check and enables the Install button when it completes. It might list some warnings in the View Results text box, but it will still run and install. Review the results and click Install.

The promotion wizard will run and the computer will reboot. When it is done, the computer will be configured as follows:

- A domain controller named DC
- Running a domain named GetCertifiedGetAhead.com
- An IP address of 192.168.1.10
- A subnet mask of 255.255.255.0
- A default gateway of 192.168.1.1
- A preferred DNS server using the loopback address of 127.0.01
- DNS is configured and reachable by another client with an IP address of 192.168.1.10

Joining Your Windows 8.1 System to a Domain

Once you have created a domain, you can join your Windows 8.1 computer to the domain. This is a relatively simple process, but it does require you to manually configure the IP address, subnet mask, and DNS settings.

In a production domain, you will often have these settings assigned dynamically with a server running Dynamic Host Configuration Protocol (DHCP). However, for this mininetwork, it's easier to configure the one system manually after you have configured the domain controller. Here are the settings you'll assign to the computer:

- IP address: 192.168.1.50
- Subnet mask: 255.255.255.0
- Default gateway: 192.168.1.1
- DNS server: 192.168.1.10

Exercise 4.9 walks you through the steps to configure the Windows 8.1 computer and join it to the GetCertifiedGetAhead.com domain you created in the previous exercise. This exercise assumes that the VM running the DC is running and configured from the previous exercise. You don't need to log on to the domain controller, but it does need to be running.

The exercise also assumes that the Windows 8.1 VM is running, you're logged on, and the Start screen is showing.

EXERCISE 4.9

Joining Windows 8.1 to a Domain

1. Ensure you are logged on to the Windows 8.1 VM created in a previous exercise.

2. At the Start screen, press Windows logo key+W to open the Search Settings screen.

3. Type **Network and Sharing Center** and select the Network and Sharing Center to start it.

4. Click Change Adapter Settings. Notice that you'll see a display showing a NIC named Ethernet similar to what you saw in Windows Server 2012.

5. Right-click the NIC named Ethernet and select Properties.

6. Scroll down if necessary and select Internet Protocol Version 4 (TCP/IPv4). Select Properties. Notice this also looks just like the interface in Windows Server 2012.

7. Select Use The Following IP Address and enter the following information:

   IP Address: 192.168.1.50

   Subnet Mask: 255.255.255.0

   Default Gateway: 192.168.1.1

8. Select Obtain DNS Server Address Automatically and enter **192.168.1.10** as the address for the Preferred DNS Server. Click OK.

9. Click Close. Close the Network Connections display by clicking the X in the top right. Close the Network and Sharing Center using the same method.

10. Click the folder in the taskbar at the bottom of the Desktop to start File Explorer.

11. Right-click over Computer and select Properties. This opens the System applet. There are multiple ways to get here, including through the Control Panel or by right-clicking the preview menu in the lower-right corner and selecting System.

12. Click Advanced System Settings to open the System Properties page. If necessary, select the Computer Name tab.

13. Click the Change button.

14. Click Domain in the Member Of area. Enter **GetCertifiedGetAhead.com** in the text box and click OK. Your computer will connect with the DC running that domain, and you'll be prompted to enter the name and password of an account with permissions to join the domain.

    If you do not see this prompt but instead you get an error, the most common reason is related to DNS. Either your computer is not configured with the correct IP address of the DNS server (192.168.1.10) or the DNS server is not assigned the correct IP address and subnet mask (192.168.1.10, 255.255.255.0). It's also possible that the DNS server (installed on the server named DC in the previous exercise) is not running. It is easy to make a typo when entering any of these numbers, so a quick double-check is worth your time if you get an error. Verify the DC is operational and has an IP address of 192.168.1.10 with a subnet mask of 255.255.255.0. Verify the local computer has an IP address of 192.168.1.50 with a subnet mask of 255.255.255.0 and has been config-ured to use a DNS server with an IP address of 192.168.1.10.

15. In the Computer Name / Domain Changes text box, enter **Administrator** as the user-name and **P@ssw0rd** as the password. Click OK.

16. After a moment you'll see a message welcoming you to the GetCertifiedGetAhead domain. Click OK.

17. Review the message indicating you need to restart your computer and click OK. Click Close. Click Restart Now to restart your computer.

Logging On to the Domain

After joining your Windows 8.1 computer to a domain, you'll be able to log on locally using a local account or a Microsoft Live account if one has been created, or you can log on to the domain using a domain account. At this point, the only domain account is the Administrator account. For the purposes of these exercises, you can use the domain Administrator account.

When logging on, you can use the NetBIOS name in the format of domain\username or use the User Principal Name (UPN) in the format of username@domain.

The first method uses the NetBIOS name, which is limited to only the first 15 charac-ters. In our domain, you can log on using the Administrator account with **GetCertifiedGet\ Administrator**. The second method uses the full domain name, including the exten-sion, such as .com. In our domain, you can log on as the Administrator account with **Administrator@GetCertifiedGetAhead.com**.

Usernames are not case sensitive. NetBIOS commonly converts everything to uppercase, but you can enter it as lowercase or uppercase and get the same results. Similarly the UPN name is not case sensitive. In contrast, passwords are case sensitive.

Exercise 4.10 walks you through the steps to log on to a Windows 8.1 computer that is joined to the GetCertifiedGetAhead.com domain. This exercise assumes that the VM running the DC is running and configured, but you don't need to log on to the domain controller. The exercise also assumes that the Windows 8.1 VM is running.

EXERCISE 4.10

Logging On to Windows 8.1 with a Domain Account

1. Ensure that Windows 8.1 is started and click on the Welcome screen.

2. By default, the screen shows the last user who was logged on. For example, our computer shows WIN8PC\Darril, indicating the Darril account was logged on using a local account on the computer named WIN8PC. Click the left-facing arrow to the left of the user's image and you'll see a different display.

3. Click Other User. Enter either the NetBIOS logon name of **GetCertifiedGet\Administrator** or the UPN of **Administrator@GetCertifiedGetAhead.com** as the username.

4. Enter **P@ssw0rd** as the password. The first time you log on with this account, it will take some time as the profile is created but subsequent logons will be quicker.

Creating and Manipulating Snapshots

Hyper-V uses snapshots to capture the state of a VM. When you create a *snapshot* of a VM, Hyper-V starts recording all the changes to the VM since the snapshot was created. You can later use this snapshot as a failback to undo all the changes since the snapshot was created. For example, if the VM fails or is misconfigured, you can return the VM to its previous state by reverting the VM using the snapshot.

The following list gives some key points about snapshots:

- You can take a snapshot when a system is running or stopped, but not if it is paused.

- Snapshots don't modify the VM but instead only save the current state.

- The snapshot locks the VM until the snapshot has been completed.

 If you use a snapshot for a VM joined to a domain, it can result in a synchronization problem. Windows 8.1 computers use computer accounts in a domain, and these accounts have passwords that are periodically changed. If you revert the Windows 8.1 PC with a snapshot without reverting the domain controller, these passwords can get out of sync. You will no longer be able to log on to the Windows 8.1 PC until the passwords are synchronized. One way this is done is by joining a workgroup such as Workgroup on the Windows 8.1 PC and then rejoining the domain.

When you create the snapshot, it creates several different files, including:

- Differencing files that record the differences made to the system since the snapshot was created

- Configuration files recording the system's settings

If you've done the previous exercises in this chapter, you now have relatively clean installations of Windows 8.1 and Windows Server 2012. The server is configured as a domain controller and the Windows 8.1 system is joined to the domain. As you work with these VMs, you'll be making many changes and these changes might corrupt these systems. If you create a snapshot of each system now, you'll be to use the snapshots to revert the VMs to their current state.

Be careful, though. If you create snapshots, the size of these snapshots will continue to grow, and if you don't watch them, they can consume all of your disk space.

Exercise 4.11 walks you through the steps to create a snapshot for each of your VMs. This exercise assumes that the two VMs you created earlier are running. It also assumes that you're logged on to Windows 8.1 and that Hyper-V Manager is showing.

EXERCISE 4.11

Creating Snapshots

1. Right-click over the Win8PC VM and select Snapshot. If you look in the Status area of the VM, you'll see the progress as this snapshot is recorded. When it is complete, the Snapshots section of Hyper-V Manager will show the name of the VM along with the date and time when it was captured.

2. Select the DC VM. In the Actions pane on the right, select Snapshot. You'll see the same process repeated for this VM.

Figure 4.8 shows Hyper-V Manager with some VMs and snapshots. In the figure, the Win8PC VM is selected and you can see that it has two snapshots taken and listed in the Snapshots pane. One of the snapshots is selected, and the bottom pane shows the view of the VM when the snapshot was created.

FIGURE 4.8   Hyper-V Manager with VMs and snapshots

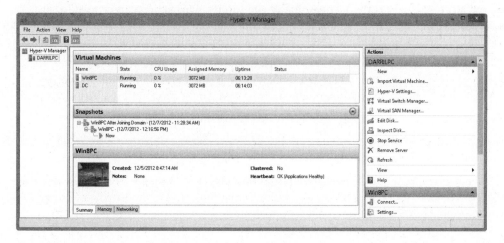

There are several other actions you can take with either the VM or the snapshot:

Revert If you right-click the VM, you can select Revert, which will roll back all changes since the last snapshot.

Apply If you right-click any snapshot, you can select Apply, which rolls back all changes since this snapshot was created. If you do this with only the last snapshot, or there is only one snapshot for the VM, Apply will work the same as Revert.

Delete If you right-click any VM and select Delete, a confirmation screen appears asking if you want to delete it. If you choose Delete, the VM disappears from Hyper-V Manager and all associated snapshots are deleted and removed from the disk.

> Deleting the VM deletes the VM settings and associated snapshots, but it does not delete virtual hard disks. If you want to free up the disk space, you'll need to delete the virtual hard disk files manually. These files are stored in the `Public Documents\Hyper-V\Virtual Hard Disks` folder by default.

Delete Snapshot If you right-click any snapshot and select Delete Snapshot, a confirmation screen appears asking if you want to delete it. If you choose Delete, the changes will be merged with another snapshot if one exists or with the VM the next time the VM is shut down.

Delete Snapshot Subtree If you right-click any snapshot and select Delete Snapshot Subtree, it will merge all the changes to the higher-level snapshot and delete the lower-level snapshots. This frees up disk space from multiple snapshots.

Rename By default a snapshot is labeled with the date and time, but you can rename it and add a comment such as "After joining domain" or "After promoting to DC."

Export You can right-click the VM or a snapshot and select Export when the VM is turned off. It will export the VM to a folder you specify. This action can be used to save a backup copy of the VM to protect against a disk failure. The exported data includes the `Virtual Machines` folder, the `Virtual Hard Disks` folder, and a `Snapshots` folder if snapshots exist.

Pause This action puts the VM into a simulated sleep state. It is not accessible by other VMs, and you cannot do anything within it using VM Connection until the VM is resumed.

Resume You can select Resume for a VM that is paused and it will wake it up.

Reset This action deletes all changes to the VM since the last time they were saved. It then restarts the VM from the last saved state.

If you've exported a VM, you can import it into Hyper-V Manager by right-clicking over the host computer in Hyper-V Manager and selecting Import. An import wizard prompts you to browse to the folder where the VM is located.

VMs and their associated files are identified with a globally unique identifier (GUID). When you export the files, they retain this GUID, and when you import it, you'll be prompted to register the GUID, restore it, or copy the GUID to create a new one. If you try to use two VMs with the same GUID, you'll end up with conflicts and one of the VMs won't work.

Here are the guidelines for each of the three choices:

Register   If you're importing the VM on a different computer than it was exported from, use this option. It will use the same GUID but the GUID doesn't exist on the new system so it doesn't result in a conflict.

Restore   If you copied the VM to a different computer or if you deleted the original VM that was exported, you can use this option to import the VM and restore it with the same GUID. If you use this option without deleting the original VM, it causes a conflict and the import will fail. You also need to ensure the original virtual hard disk file has been deleted from the Public Documents\Hyper-V\Virtual Hard Disks folder.

Copy   If the VM was exported from the same system where you're importing it but you want to have both the current VM and the VM that you exported, you can use Copy. This creates a new GUID used with the copy of the VM. You'll have to store the virtual hard disk in a different location than the original because it will have the same name as the original hard disk.

You can also move a VM to a different location on a single system. For example, if you're running out of disk space you can move the VM to a different partition. If you right-click a VM, you can select Move to open a wizard. You can choose to move only the virtual hard disk, or the virtual hard disk, all the snapshots, and all the other data associated with the VM.

Comparing Test and Production Networks

At this point, it's appropriate to say a few words about security. The VMs created in this chapter are intended to be used as a test environment, but if you were creating VMs to be used within a live production environment you should do things differently. Specifically, there are two important points you should consider.

First, this test environment was created as an isolated network that will not have any access to an outside network. VMs created to be used within a production environment would have access to an outside network and would typically be able to access the Internet. With this in mind, it is important to keep the VMs up-to-date with current patches and install antivirus software on them.

Second, the preceding exercises had you use the domain Administrator account to log on, but you wouldn't do this in a live domain. By default, the Administrator account in the first domain of a forest has omnipotent powers within the forest. It can do anything. It is in the Enterprise Admins group, the Domain Admins group, and the Administrators group. When you log on using this account, you can do anything on any computer in the domain.

If you have multiple domains in your forest, you can do anything on any computer in the forest.

As a best practice for security, it's best to rename the administrator account with another name and rarely use it. Instead, you'd create additional domain accounts, grant them appropriate rights and privileges needed for their needs, and use them. Chapter 5 shows how you can create additional accounts in a domain.

 ## Configuring Virtual Machines

You had an opportunity to configure many of the settings for VMs in previous exercises. You can access them by right-clicking the VM and selecting Settings. Some settings were shown in Figures 4.2 and 4.4 and discussed earlier in this chapter. In addition to some of the items already mentioned, you have other choices.

> You can look at the settings for a VM at any time, but many settings can only be configured when the VM is off. If the setting is dimmed and unchangeable, the most likely reason is that the VM must be turned off before modifying the setting.

Add Hardware   You can add a SCSI controller, additional network adapters, a legacy network adapter, or a Fibre Channel adapter. The legacy network adapter can be used as a preboot execution environment (PXE) NIC to load the operating system from a network-based installation server.

BIOS   You can use this setting to change the boot order for the system. For example, the system would normally be set to boot to CD first, but you can change it to boot from IDE first after the installation is complete. Similarly, you would set it to boot from the legacy network adapter first if you were installing the OS from a network-based installation server. After the installation, you would change it to boot to IDE so that it boots to the virtual hard disk first.

Processor   If your system has multiple cores or multiple processors, you can limit how many cores the system will use. As an example, a four-core Intel processor using hyper-threading appears to the operating system and Hyper-V as eight processors. By default a VM will have access only to a single processor (or a single core), but you can modify this. You can also use Resource Control settings to limit how much processing power the VM can use from the assigned processor.

Figure 4.9 shows the processor settings for a VM. You can set Virtual Machine Reserve (Percentage) to ensure a VM always has at least a certain amount of processing power, or set Virtual Machine Limit (Percentage) to prevent it from taking too much processing power. The Relative Weight setting can also be manipulated to give a VM a higher precedence. By default the setting is 100, but if you change it for a VM, the VM with the higher weight is given precedence if the resources are limited.

FIGURE 4.9   Processor settings

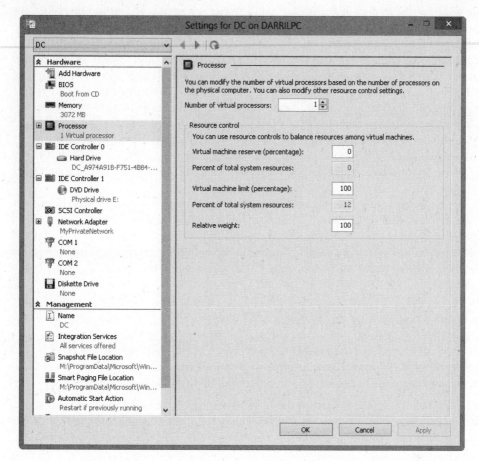

Designing a Virtual Application Strategy

The exercises in this chapter gave you the opportunity to create a virtual network with separate VMs on a Windows 8.1 machine for learning purposes. However, virtualization has much broader uses and is often used in a production environment.

A simple example is when legacy applications are not compatible with newer operating systems. For example, your organization might have one or two older applications that run on Windows XP but will not run on Windows 8.1. One alternative is to install Windows

8.1, add the Hyper-V feature, and then install Windows XP on a VM within Hyper-V. After Windows XP is installed, you can install the legacy application within the VM. This allows the user to have access to the new features in Windows 8.1 without sacrificing the capabilities of the legacy application.

Chapter 3 showed how you can use a VHD to create a dual-boot system. However, the challenge with a dual-boot system is that a user must completely shut down one operating system. With Hyper-V, a user can run Windows 8.1 and run one or more VMs that function as separate applications within Windows 8.1. The user doesn't need to shut down the host operating system as they do with a VHD used for a dual-boot system.

Still, this can be challenging for many users. Most applications can be started with a click or two, but if they are running a legacy application from within a Hyper-V VM, they'll have to start Hyper-V Manager, start the VM, and then start the application from within the VM.

There are some advanced application virtualization options you can use with Windows 8.1 and Windows Server 2012 that simplify the process for end users. These include Remote Desktop Services (RDS), RemoteApp, and App-V. They can be used to run virtual applications from a server in a single window on the user's computer. These look more like typical applications and it's often not apparent to the user that the application is being run remotely.

Remote Desktop Services

A server is configured with *Remote Desktop Services (RDS)* and users connect to the server to run either a desktop or individual applications remotely, depending on how the server is configured. RDS can be used to deliver full desktops or applications to users.

Full Desktops   The user connects to the server from just about any desktop system and can then launch a Windows 8.1 desktop. The Windows 8.1 desktop operates within a window on the client's system but is maintained within the server. If the user disconnects from the session without closing it, it remains on the server. The user can later reconnect to the session and it will look exactly as it was when the user disconnected earlier.

Applications   A single application can be run on the server. RemoteApp applications can be hosted on the RDS server and clients can then start the application from their computer. The application runs in a window on the user's desktop and has the look and feel of a locally run program.

Figure 4.10 shows how RDS can be used in a network. In the figure, three clients are using RDS, which is configured on a server running Windows Server 2012. The clients can be running Windows 7, Windows 8.1, or just about any operating system. They only need network connectivity to the RDS server.

A *virtual desktop infrastructure (VDI)* provides users with an operating system desktop that runs on the remote server. We know of a company that has designed a VDI solution for hospitals and medical centers where doctors regularly roam throughout the organization. Doctors are able to log on to just about any PC within the organization, and when they do,

FIGURE 4.10   RDS used in a network

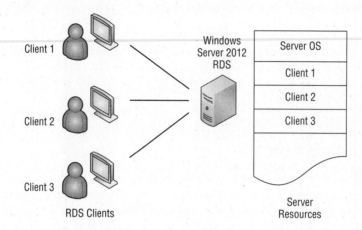

they have the same desktop and access to all the same data. When they're working with a patient, they can see the patient's medical data. When they go back to an office and log on, they can see their schedule and other important data, or even go back to the patient's data and see the same information. These systems are within a domain, so the doctors are able to authenticate with the same account. It's also becoming common for people to connect with mobile devices to the same network, and depending on the capabilities of the mobile device, they might have the same capability from a mobile device as they have with a PC.

This approach works much more effectively for the medical personnel than a disjointed system. If a doctor is forced to use separate devices with different interfaces and passwords depending on where the doctor is accessing the technology, it makes the doctor's job more complicated rather than easier. In this case, the doctors only want to use the technology to provide better patient care but instead they are spending extra energy trying to remember how to use the various devices rather than focusing on patient care.

There are key differences between a Windows server running RDS and one running Hyper-V. RDS is used to host virtual desktops or applications used by end users. In contrast, Hyper-V on a server hosts virtual servers that can be accessed from network users just as if they were physical servers.

Comparing RemoteApp and RemoteFX

RemoteApp is based on the *Remote Desktop Protocol (RDP)* and uses Remote Desktop Services. It allows users to connect to a remote server running RDS to run an application. From the user's perspective, the application looks like it is running on the local system and runs within its own window.

RemoteFX adds additional graphics capabilities providing users with enhanced video. It is especially useful for applications using advanced 3D rendering. RemoteFX can be enabled on the server hosting the RemoteApp application if the server has a dedicated graphics processing unit (GPU) on the graphics card.

> RemoteApp was previously known as Terminal Services Remote App (TSRemoteApp). When Terminal Services (TS) was renamed to Remote Desktop Services (RDS) by Microsoft, TSRemoteApp was renamed to RemoteApp.

Understanding App-V

Microsoft Application Virtualization (App-V) is another method that organizations can use to provide virtual applications to users. With App-V, applications are hosted on an App-V server and streamed to a user's desktop on demand, similar to how audio and video can be streamed to the client. The applications don't make any modifications to the client computer but instead operate in a virtual environment.

The entire application is not downloaded to the client computer when App-V is used. Instead, the App-V server sends only what is needed by the user in streamed chunks. Depending on the activity of the user, different chunks of the application will be sent. Applications can be very large, but most users don't access all their features. For example, Microsoft Word has many different capabilities related to formatting, translating, and more. These capabilities will be streamed to users who need them but not sent to users who don't need them.

App-V can be integrated into System Center Configuration Manager (SCCM) so that applications can be deployed, updated, and managed just as any other application in the enterprise.

Summary

Hyper-V is a significant addition to Windows 8.1, and it can be used for many different purposes. When preparing for the 70-687 (Windows 8.1) or 70-409 Server Virtualization exam, you should have a very good understanding of the requirements to install Hyper-V; how to create and configure virtual switches, virtual machines, and virtual disks; and how to manage snapshots, all of which were covered in this chapter.

Exercises in this chapter gave you the opportunity to enable Hyper-V, create a virtual switch, and create a private network with a domain controller and a member computer running Windows 8.1. A private switch provides connectivity between internal VMs using the private switch but not to any other resources. This effectively keeps the VMs isolated. Other virtual switch types include an internal switch, which provides connectivity to the VMs and the host, and an external switch, which adds connectivity to the external network.

Snapshots are used to capture the state of a VM. You can periodically create snapshots, and if you ever want to return the VM to a previous state, you can apply the snapshot. Snapshots can take up a lot of space on a disk, but you can move them using Hyper-V Manager.

When designing a virtual application strategy, you have several options. If an application is not compatible with Windows 8.1, you can create a Hyper-V VM running an older operating system and the legacy application. Advanced solutions include servers hosting Remote Desktop Services serving either full desktops or individual applications using RemoteApp and RemoteFX. Servers can also be configured with App-V to stream virtual applications to users.

Exam Essentials

Know the requirements for Hyper-V.   Hyper-V runs only on 64-bit editions of Windows 8.1 Pro and Windows 8.1 Enterprise. The system must have at least 4 GB of RAM, but more is generally needed to meet the requirements of the virtual machines. Hyper-V is enabled through the Programs and Features applet.

Understand virtual switches.   Three types of virtual switches are available, and each one is used for specific connectivity requirements. A private switch provides network connectivity only to internal VMs, not the host or the external network. An internal switch includes connectivity to internal VMs and adds network connectivity to the host system. An external VM includes connectivity for internal VMs, the host system, and the external network.

Know how to create and manage snapshots.   Snapshots are used to capture the current state of a VM. They record all the changes to the VM since the snapshot was created. You can select Revert to apply the most recent snapshot or click Apply to apply a specific snapshot.

Be able to create and manage virtual machines.   You should understand how VMs are created and managed within Hyper-V. VMs can be exported from one system and imported into another system. When you delete a VM, the virtual disk is still kept on the system.

Be able to configure virtual machines.   Hyper-V Manager can be used to configure settings for any VM. You can configure how much memory is used, what hardware is available, and what type of connection is used by selecting different virtual switches. You can also specify how many processors a VM can use. Many VM settings cannot be modified while the VM is running.

Know methods used for virtual applications.   RDS can be used to host desktops or applications. RemoteApp and RemoteFX can be hosted on RDS servers to provide users with virtual applications. The applications run on the server but look to the user as though they are running on the user's desktop. App-V streams applications in chunks to the user from an App-V server.

Review Questions

You can find the answers in Appendix A.

1. You are running a 32-bit edition of Windows 8.1 Pro and decide to enable Hyper-V to add some virtual machines. However, you are not able to enable it. What is the most likely reason?

   A. Your computer doesn't have enough RAM.

   B. Hyper-V is not supported on 32-bit systems.

   C. Hyper-V is only supported on server products.

   D. Hyper-V is not supported on Windows 8.1 Pro.

2. You are running a 64-bit edition of Windows 8.1 Pro with 3 GB of RAM and decide to enable Hyper-V to add some virtual machines. What will you need to do first?

   A. Start the Programs and Features applet.

   B. Upgrade to Windows 8.1 Enterprise.

   C. Create a virtual switch.

   D. Add more RAM.

3. You are creating a virtual environment on a Windows 8.1 system and you want to ensure that the client computers can connect with the physical host but not with the network. What should you create?

   A. A virtual switch using the External setting

   B. A virtual switch using the Internal setting

   C. A virtual switch using the Private setting

   D. A virtual switch using the Host setting

4. A user needs to run an application that isn't compatible with Windows 8.1 and the application needs to access a server on the network. You install the application within a Hyper-V VM, but the application fails when it tries to connect to the server. Of the following choices, what is the most likely problem?

   A. The application is not compatible with Windows 8.1.

   B. The application is not compatible with Hyper-V.

   C. The virtual switch is not set to Network.

   D. The virtual switch is not set to External.

5. A user is planning on creating VMs within Windows 8.1 using Hyper-V. The user wants to ensure that the VMs do not have any network connectivity with the host or internal network, but do have network connectivity with each other. What should the user do?

   A. Disable the virtual NIC on each of the VMs.

   B. Configure the virtual switch as an Internal switch.

   C. Configure the virtual switch as a Private switch.

   D. Configure NIC teaming.

6. You have enabled Hyper-V on a Windows 8.1 system that has network access. As you're creating the VMs, you're finding that you cannot configure networking or select any type of connection except Not Connected. What tool should you start to resolve this problem?

A. Virtual Switch Manager

B. Network and Sharing Center

C. Hyper-V Settings for the VM

D. Snapshot properties

7. You are running a Windows 8.1 VM on a Windows 8.1 system with 12 GB of RAM and Hyper-V installed. You want to modify the memory for the Windows 8.1 VM to give it 5 GB of RAM, but you are not able to make the change. What is the most likely reason this is not working?

A. You cannot assign more than 4 GB of RAM to a VM.

B. The physical host doesn't have enough RAM.

C. The physical host is running 32-bit Windows 8.1.

D. The VM is running.

8. You want to transfer a VM from one Windows 8.1 system to another. You want to ensure that all of the same settings are used on the destination system. What should you do?

A. Copy the virtual disk from one system to the other and add it to the destination system.

B. Export it from the original system, copy it, and import it to the destination system.

C. Create a snapshot on the original system, copy it, and import it on the destination system.

D. Detach it from the original system, copy it, and add it to the destination system.

9. You exported a VM on a Windows 8.1 system and later decide you want to import it back into the same system without deleting the original VM. What should you do when importing the VM?

A. Copy the VM and create a new unique ID.

B. Register the VM and use the existing unique ID.

C. Restore the VM and use the existing unique ID.

D. Copy the VM and use the existing unique ID.

10. You are running a Windows 8.1 system with Hyper-V. The hard disk of your primary partition is running out of space, and you suspect it is due to the size of the Hyper-V VMs. What should you do to gain the maximum amount of space for your primary partition without losing any performance capabilities?

A. Move the virtual hard disks to a different partition.

B. Move the virtual hard disks and snapshots to a different partition.

C. Move the Windows operating system folder to a different partition.

D. Compress all of the virtual hard disks.

11. You are running Hyper-V on a Windows 8.1 system. You plan on upgrading an application within a VM, but you want to be able to restore it to its original state if the update causes problems for the VM. Of the following choices, what is the easiest solution?

   A. Run System Restore within the VM prior to doing the update and back up all the data on the VM.

   B. Export the VM and copy it to a network drive.

   C. Create a snapshot before doing the update

   D. Create a snapshot after doing the update.

12. You are running a Windows 7 system within a Hyper-V VM on a Windows 8.1 system. You take snapshots once a week. While using the Windows 7 system you realize it has a problem and you want to restore it to the state it was in two weeks ago. What should you do?

   A. Right-click the desired snapshot and select Apply.

   B. Right-click the desired snapshot and select Revert.

   C. Right-click the VM and select Apply.

   D. Right-click the VM and select Revert.

13. You are running a Windows 8.1 system with Hyper-V installed. You notice that you're running out of disk space, so you have moved the virtual hard disks to a different partition. However, you notice that disk space is still shrinking when you use the VMs. What is the most likely problem?

   A. The virtual hard disks setting files weren't moved.

   B. The virtual hard disks shadow files weren't moved.

   C. Windows 8.1 needs to be restarted.

   D. Snapshots are growing.

14. You are running Windows 8.1 with Hyper-V installed. Your disk is running out of space, so you want to delete all the snapshots captured for a VM and have the changes from these snapshots applied to your VM. What should you do?

   A. Select the newest snapshot and select Delete Subtree.

   B. Select the oldest snapshot and select Delete Subtree.

   C. Select the newest snapshot and select Apply. When this is done, select the newest snapshot and select Delete Subtree.

   D. Turn off the VM and delete the snapshots manually.

15. You use Hyper-V on a Windows 8.1 system and have created several VMs. Your computer is running out of disk space so you decide to delete some old VMs, but you find that the available disk space did not increase. What do you need to do?

   A. Manually delete the snapshots.

   B. Manually delete the virtual hard disk files.

   C. Empty the Recycle Bin.

   D. Restart Hyper-V.

16. You have exported a VM as a backup. Later, you want to use it to view some settings and compare them to the current VM, but you don't want to delete the current VM. You decide to import the exported VM and use Copy to create a new identifier. However, the import fails, giving a conflict error. What is the most likely problem?

A. You need to register the new ID within Hyper-V.

B. The settings files need to be stored in a different location.

C. The snapshots need to be stored in a different location.

D. The virtual hard disk needs to be stored in a different location.

17. You are running Hyper-V on a Windows 8.1 computer with a quad-core processor. You want to be able to have one of the VMs use two processors but another VM only use one processor. What should you do?

A. Configure Virtual Machine Reserve to 25% on the first VM and 12.5% on the second VM.

B. Configure Number Of Virtual Processors to 2 for the first VM and 1 for the second VM.

C. Configure Virtual Machine Limit to 100% on the first VM and 50% on the second VM.

D. Configure Relative Weight to 100% on the first VM and 50% on the second VM.

18. Your organization is migrating systems to Windows 8.1. A legacy application used by the accounting department works in Windows XP but is not compatible with Windows 8.1. What can be done to ensure that all users have Windows 8.1 but the accounting department still has access to their legacy application?

A. Install Microsoft Virtual PC on the Windows 8.1 and run the application from it.

B. Install Windows Virtual PC on the Windows 8.1 and run the application from it.

C. Install Windows XP Mode on the Windows 8.1 and run the application from it.

D. Install Hyper-V on the Windows 8.1 and run the application from a VM.

19. An organization wants to create a solution that will allow users to have the same operating system and desktop no matter which computer they log on to. Of the following choices, what will meet their needs?

A. Client Hyper-V

B. RDS

C. App-V

D. RemoteApp

20. An organization wants to ensure that users have access to a specific application no matter which computer they log on to. Of the following choices, what will meet their needs?

A. App-V

B. Client Hyper-V

C. AppLocker

D. External switch

Chapter

5

Networking

The majority of computers you'll work with are connected to a network. These can be small networks within a home or small business or large networks within an enterprise. Most of the same technologies apply to both types of networks, and you'll need to have a good understanding of how networks are connected and how to configure basic settings within Windows 8.1 when preparing for these exams.

This chapter starts with an overview of networking, IPv4 and IPv6 addresses, and name resolution techniques. It also covers some commands such as ipconfig, ping, and nslookup used to verify network settings and troubleshoot networking issues.

Network locations include three preconfigured profiles you can select based on where your computer is being used. These are private (home or work locations), public (any location with a public IP address), and domain (available only when a computer is joined to a domain). The Network and Sharing Center is a central tool you can use to access and configure many settings, including network locations, wired connections, and wireless connections. Wireless networks are very common today, and this chapter incudes a section on wireless network settings and security. Private networks also support HomeGroups, and this chapter explains how to create, join, and configure HomeGroups.

The final section in this chapter provides basic methods used to resolve connectivity issues. You can use the built-in diagnostics and command-line tools to discover and correct many problems.

Understanding Network Connectivity in an Enterprise

Before digging into the details of Windows 8.1 networking topics, it's worthwhile to review the basics of networking within an enterprise. The Internet is based on TCP/IP, and Windows products all use the TCP/IP suite.

The concepts discussed in this first section work similarly in Windows XP, Windows Vista, Windows 7, Windows 8, and Windows 8.1. If you've been working with networked clients for a while, you can probably skim over the introductory topics. However, this section does lay a foundation for the rest of the chapter.

Figure 5.1 shows several components of a typical network. You should understand the purpose and use of each of these components. They are introduced here and explored in more depth in this chapter and in Chapter 6, "Windows Firewall and Remote Access."

FIGURE 5.1   Components of a typical network

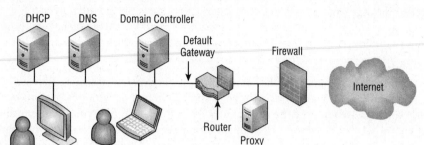

The following are common networking terms you should know to follow along in this chapter:

DNS   The primary purpose of the *Domain Name System (DNS)* server is to resolve hostnames to IP addresses. The client sends the name of a host on the network, and the server responds with the IP address. It can also do reverse lookups (resolving the IP to a name) with pointer (PTR) records and locate domain controllers with server (SRV) records.

DHCP   A *Dynamic Host Configuration Protocol (DHCP)* server will issue TCP/IP configuration information to users. This includes an IP address, subnet mask, address of the DNS server, address of the default gateway, and more.

WINS   A *Windows Internet Name Service (WINS)* server is used to resolve NetBIOS names to IP addresses. The use of NetBIOS names is significantly reduced in current Microsoft networks, but they may still be used by legacy applications requiring the use of a WINS server in a network. One way NetBIOS name resolution is used is when users log on using the NetBIOS name like this: *domain\user*. For example, the users could log on to the domain created in Chapter 4, "Using Virtualization Technologies," with **GetCertifiedGet\ Administrator**.

Domain Controller   A *domain controller (DC)* hosts Active Directory Domain Services (AD DS) in a Microsoft domain. AD DS holds objects (such as users, computers, and groups) that can be centrally managed and administered. Users and computers must have an account in AD DS to be able to log on to the domain and use domain resources. DNS is required for clients to locate DCs on the network.

Default Gateway   A *default gateway* identifies the default path for traffic to any other networks. All of the computers in the drawing to the left of the default gateway are on the same subnet, and their path to the Internet is through the default gateway. The default gateway is also referred to as the near side of a router, and it is specifically identified by the IP address assigned to the network interface connected to the subnet.

A router will often be assigned the first host IP address in a network. This isn't required, but it is a standard that is often followed in many networks. For example, if the network ID is 192.168.1.0 (with a subnet mask of 255.255.255.0), the default gateway is often assigned 192.168.1.1.

Router   A *router* is a hardware device that routes data from one subnet to another. The router in the diagram has two network interfaces: One is the default gateway for the internal network and the other is the connection to the DMZ. Routers have filtering capabilities that allow them to restrict what traffic can be passed through them. These filtering capabilities provide the router with firewall characteristics.

Firewall   A *firewall* is designed to filter traffic so that only specific traffic is allowed into or out of a network. A firewall starts with basic router filtering capabilities but can be much more sophisticated in how the traffic can be examined and filtered. The two firewalls shown in Figure 5.1 (to the left and right of the proxy server) create a perimeter network. This perimeter network is often referred to as a demilitarized zone (DMZ). Firewalls are explored in more depth in Chapter 6.

Proxy Server   A *proxy server* can be used as a central access point for Internet resources. When a proxy server is used in a network, all clients are configured to submit Internet requests to the proxy server, and the proxy server then requests the data from the Internet. Proxies can improve performance of Internet access by caching data requested by users and providing this cached data when it's requested by another user. Proxies can also improve security or enforce business policies by preventing users from going to specific sites.

Unicast, Multicast, and Broadcast

IPv4 traffic travels from host to host in networks using unicast, multicast, or broadcast methods. You'll see these terms throughout this chapter and elsewhere in the book, so it's important to have a clear understanding of them.

Unicast   Data travels from one computer to one other computer. A unicast message will be processed only by the host with the destination IP address.

Multicast   Data travels from one computer to many computers. For example, when you use Windows Deployment Services (WDS) to automate the deployment of Windows 8.1 to multiple computers at the same time, you can use WDS to multicast a single image to multiple computers at the same time. In contrast, if WDS did this as unicast, it would need to send a separate copy of the image over the network for each client.

Broadcast   Data travels from one computer to all computers in the subnet. Each computer that receives the packet will process it and determine if it needs to take action with the packet. Broadcast traffic is not passed through the router.

IPv4 and IPv6 both use unicast and multicast messages. However, instead of broadcast messages, IPv6 uses anycast messages. Broadcast messages are sent to all computers in a subnet. Anycast messages can be sent to all the computers in a subnet but are only sent to one or more of these computers to reduce traffic. IPv6 addresses are explained in more depth later in this chapter.

Understanding IP Addresses

The IPv4 address has two important components: the network ID and the host ID. The network ID identifies the subnet the client is on, and the host ID is a unique address on the subnet. The subnet mask identifies which portion of the IP address is the network ID and which portion is the host ID.

You should easily be able to determine the network ID when you see an IP address and a subnet mask. Moreover, you should be able to determine when they are misconfigured for clients on a network.

Determining the Network ID

Consider the following IP address and subnet mask:

    192.168.1.10

    255.255.255.0

Both the IP address and the subnet mask use dotted decimal format with four decimal numbers separated by dots. To determine the subnet portion of the IP address, look for the 255s in the subnet mask. Since the first three numbers in the subnet mask are 255, the first three numbers in the IP address are the network ID.

    192.168.1.x

    255.255.255.x

The network ID is expressed with all four numbers and the trailing numbers are always set as 0. In other words, the network ID is expressed as 192.168.1.0, not 192.168.1 or 192.168.1.x.

Can you identify the network ID for the following IP address and subnet mask?

    10.80.1.5

    255.0.0.0

Since only the first number in the subnet mask is a 255, only the first number in the IP address is in the network ID. The network ID is 10.0.0.0.

> Subnetting can be more complex than just described, and instead of dealing with just 255 or 0 in the subnet mask, you could have different numbers like 128, 192, and so on. However, for the purpose of the 70-687 exam and this explanation, we're keeping it simple. To learn more about subnetting, read "IP Address Subnetting Tutorial" online at www.ralphb .net/IPSubnet/.

Classful IP Addressing

You may occasionally see IP addresses identified as classful addresses represented without a subnet mask. There are three primary classes you may run across: Class A, Class B, and Class C.

When a classful address is used, you automatically know what the default subnet mask is, and you can then identify the network ID.

Class A   The first number in a Class A address is between 1 and 126 and the subnet mask is 255.0.0.0. For example, an IP address of 10.1.2.3 has a first number of 10, and 10 is between 1 and 126, so the subnet mask is 255.0.0.0 and the network ID is 10.0.0.0.

Class B   The first number is between 128 and 191 and the subnet mask is 255.255.0.0. For example, an IP address of 172.1.2.3 has a first number of 172, which is between 128 and 191, so the subnet mask is 255.255.0.0 and the network ID is 172.1.0.0.

Class C   The first number is between 192 and 223 and the subnet mask is 255.255.255.0. For example, an IP address of 192.1.2.3 has a first number of 192, which is between 192 and 223, so the subnet mask is 255.255.255.0 and the network ID is 192.1.2.0.

 Where's 127? You may have noticed that Class A ends at 126 and Class B starts at 128. Technically, Class A addresses include the 127.x.y.z range, but this entire range is used for testing and so is not considered part of the Class A range.

A benefit of using classful IP addresses is that the subnet mask can be omitted. For example, if you see an address of 10.1.2.3 and classful addresses are used, you automatically know it's a Class A address with a subnet mask of 255.0.0.0 and the network ID is 10.0.0.0. However, it's important to realize that the rules of classful IP addresses can be broken. For example, an administrator can specify an IP address of 10.1.2.3 with a subnet mask of 255.255.255.0. In this case, the network ID is 10.1.2.0.

If you see an IP address that is identified as classful, you can use the first number of the IP address to determine the subnet mask and the network ID. However, if you see an IP address with a subnet mask, use the subnet mask regardless of the first number in the IP address.

Private IP Ranges

IP addresses are either public (on the Internet) or private. Request for Comments (RFC) 1918, published by the Internet Assigned Numbers Authority (IANA), formally designated several IP address ranges as private. (You can find IANA RFCs at http://tools.ietf .org/.) These addresses are never assigned to Internet clients. They are:

- 10.0.0.0 through 10.255.255.255.255
- 172.16.0.0 through 172.31.255.255
- 192.168.0.0 through 192.168.255.255

Public IP addresses must be unique. You will never see two different Internet hosts assigned the same public IP address. However, different private companies can use identical private IP addresses. For example, the Acme Company could use the same private IP address in the 192.168.1.0/24 range as the Get Certified Get Ahead company uses in their private network. Because the addresses are only used privately within each company, they don't conflict with each other.

Network Address Translation (NAT) translates private IP addresses used on an internal network with public IP addresses used on the Internet. Routers or proxy servers at the boundary of a network (between the Internet and the private network) run NAT so that clients with private IP addresses can access Internet resources.

Identifying Misconfigured Clients

All assigned IP addresses within a single subnet must have the same network ID. If not, they will not be able to communicate with other clients on the subnet. Additionally, each client must be configured with the correct default gateway or they will not be able to communicate outside of the network.

Consider Figure 5.2. Each client (numbered 1 through 6) has an assigned IP address (IP), subnet mask (SM), and default gateway (DG). The network interfaces on the router are configured correctly but other settings are incorrect. Can you identify the four clients configured incorrectly?

FIGURE 5.2   A misconfigured network

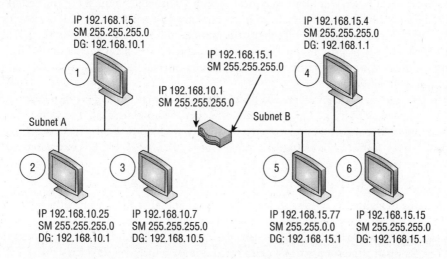

Client 1   This client is configured with an incorrect IP address. The third decimal is 1 but must be a 10 to have the same network ID of 192.168.10.0 as other clients in the subnet, including the default gateway. It currently has a network ID of 192.168.1.0. This client will not be able to communicate with any other clients on Subnet A and will not be able to reach the default gateway to communicate with clients in Subnet B.

Client 2   This client is configured correctly. It has an IP address of of 192.168.10.25 and has the correct default gateway assigned.

Client 3   This client is configured with an incorrect default gateway address. The near side of the router on Subnet A has an IP address of 192.168.10.1, so the default gateway should be 192.168.10.1, not 192.168.10.5. This client will be able to communicate with other clients in Subnet A that have the same network ID of 192.168.10.0 (only client 2 in the figure), but it will not be able to reach the default gateway or communicate with any clients on Subnet B.

Client 4   This client is configured with an incorrect default gateway. The near side of the router on Subnet B has an IP address of 192.168.15.1, so the default gateway should be 192.168.15.1, not 192.168.1.1. This client will be able to communicate with other clients in Subnet B that have the same network ID (only client 5 in the figure), but it will not be able to communicate with any clients on Subnet A.

Client 5   This client is configured with an incorrect subnet mask. The third decimal is 0 but should be 255, resulting in a network ID of 192.168.0.0 instead of 192.168.15.0. This client will not be able to communicate with any other clients on the network.

Client 6   This client is configured correctly. It has an IP address of 192.168.15.15 and has the correct default gateway assigned.

Understanding CIDR Notation

You may occasionally see IP addresses expressed with a slash and a number at the end like this: 192.168.1.5/24. This is referred to as Classless Inter-Domain Routing (CIDR) notation, and the number after the slash (/) represents the number of bits in the subnet mask.

Each IPv4 address and each subnet mask is represented by 32 bits (32 1s and 0s). To simplify the address, you will normally use the decimal format of the IP address instead of listing all the 1s and 0s.

When a subnet mask is represented in dotted decimal format, it has four numbers separated by dots such as 255.255.255.0. If you look under the hood, though, the subnet mask is represented in binary format and each decimal is represented by 8 bits, such as 1 1 1 1 1 1 1 1 or 0 0 0 0 0 0 0 0. For example, a subnet mask of 255.255.255.0 is expressed in binary format as

  1 1 1 1 1 1 1 1 . 1 1 1 1 1 1 1 1 . 1 1 1 1 1 1 1 1 . 0 0 0 0 0 0 0 0

Each string of eight binary 1s represents the decimal number 255. A subnet mask of 255.255.255.0 has three strings of eight binary 1s with a total of 24 1s (3 * 8 = 24). CIDR notation uses the number of 1s in the subnet mask (24 in this example) to express the value. Instead of expressing the subnet mask as 255.255.255.0, you can express it as /24.

Similarly, an address of 10.80.5.2 / 8 would have a subnet mask of 255.0.0.0. The /8 indicates only the first 8 bits of the subnet mask are 1s. In other words, the subnet mask in binary format is:

  1 1 1 1 1 1 1 1 . 0 0 0 0 0 0 0 0 . 0 0 0 0 0 0 0 0 . 0 0 0 0 0 0 0 0

Understanding the DHCP Lease

You'll almost always find at least one DHCP server used within an enterprise. It automates the process of assigning TCP/IP configuration, and once it's configured, it takes very little management to keep it running. A single DHCP server can handle as many as 10,000 clients, though when you have that many clients another DHCP server is usually added for redundancy and fault tolerance.

When a DHCP client turns on, four packets are exchanged over the network between the DHCP client and the DHCP server. This is often referred to as the DORA process because of the name of the IP packets: D for Discover, O for Offer, R for Request, and A for Acknowledge.

Consider Figure 5.3. Here, a single DHCP server is being used on a network. When a DHCP client is powered on, it starts the DHCP process by broadcasting the Discover packet. Routers don't pass broadcast traffic by default, but if the router is RFC 1542 compliant—and most current routers are—it can be configured to pass DHCP broadcast traffic. This allows a single DHCP server within a network to server multiple subnets.

FIGURE 5.3   Using DHCP on a network

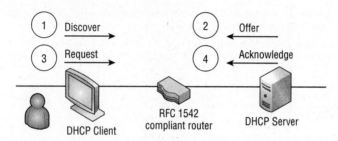

Discover   When the DHCP client turns on, it broadcasts a DHCPDiscover packet. It's similar to asking "Are there any DHCP servers out there?"

Offer   When a DHCP server receives a DHCP Discover packet, it responds by broadcasting a DHCPOffer. This offer is known as the lease offer, and it provides the TCP/IP configuration information for the client. A lease will typically include an IP address, a subnet mask, a default gateway, the address of a DNS server in the network, and the address of a WINS server if it is being used. If multiple DHCP servers are on the network, each one responds to the DHCP Discover request with an offer.

Request   The client sends a DHCP Request in response to the first DHCP Offer it receives. In essence, it says, "Thank you, I'll take that lease." If a second DHCP server sent an offer but did not receive a request in reply, the offer expires without being used.

Acknowledge   When the DHCP server receives the request, it responds with the DHCPACK (Acknowledge) packet. This lets the client know that it has been assigned the lease. The DHCP server also allocates the IP address internally to ensure the IP address is not issued to any other clients.

After 50 percent of the lease length time has expired, clients request a renewal of the lease from the DHCP server. For example, if the lease length is set to 8 days, the client will try to renew the lease after 4 days. If the DHCP server doesn't respond, the client continues to request a renewal until 87.5 percent of the lease length time has expired (after 7 days for an 8-day lease). After 87.5 percent of the time has expired, the client will repeat the DORA process looking for any DHCP server.

DHCP and APIPA

What if the DHCP server doesn't answer, or what if the DHCP lease cannot be renewed and expires? Well, there is an answer for that.

Automatic Private IP Addressing (APIPA) is used to configure clients with addresses in a special range when the DHCP server doesn't respond. The range of addresses is 169.254.0.1 through 169.245.255.254 with a subnet mask of 255.255.0.0.

If a DHCP client doesn't receive a response from a DHCP server, it assigns itself an APIPA address. It will continue to send out DHCP Discover messages in an effort to get a valid lease from a DHCP server.

If you receive an APIPA address starting with 169.254, you know that the DHCP client did not receive a response from a DHCP server but you don't necessarily know why. The DHCP server may be down, the router may be down or misconfigured, or there may be some other network problem.

IPv4 vs. IPv6

Due to the early popularity of the Internet, it became apparent that it would run out of IP addresses if only 32-bit IPv4 addresses were used. As far back as the 1990s, IANA tasked the Internet Engineering Task Force (IETF) to begin looking for alternatives. A 64-bit version was developed and identified as IPv5, but it was rejected when developers realized it didn't provide enough addresses for the future. Ultimately, a 128-bit version was developed and has become the standard known as IPv6.

IPv4 uses 32 bits (232) and it can *only* address about 4 billion clients. However, IPv4 wasted a lot of addresses, so you don't really have 4 billion IP addresses available. For example, the entire range of 127.0.0.0 is reserved for the single loopback address of 127.0.0.1.

IPv6 uses 128 bits (2^{128}), which provides an outrageously large number of IP addresses. Instead of having a total of 4 billion IP addresses on the entire Internet, it allows for as many as 4 billion IP addresses for every person alive today (currently estimated at close to 7 billion people).

An IPv6 address is expressed with hexadecimal characters rather than digital numbers. Hexadecimal characters use the numbers 0 through 9 and the letters A through F, and each character represents four binary bits. For example, binary 0000 is represented as hexadecimal 0, and binary 1111 is represented as hexadecimal F.

An IPv6 address is represented with eight groups of four hexadecimal characters for a total of 128 bits. These groups are separated by colons. For example, here's an IPv6 address:

2000 : 0001 : 4137 : 0000 : 006C : 0000 : 0000 : 01E5

Hexadecimal characters are often identified with a 0x prefix. For example, 0x 123 (pronounced as hex 123) indicates three hexadecimal characters. In contrast, 123 without the hexadecimal notation indicates it is a decimal number.

Displaying IPv6 Addresses

Even though an IPv6 address is 128 bits represented by 32 hexadecimal characters, you won't always see all 32 hexadecimal characters. An IPv6 address can be shortened, as shown in the following three examples representing the same IPv6 address:

2000 : 0021 : 4137 : 0000 : 006C : 0000 : 0000 : 01E5

2000 : 21 : 4137 : 0 : 6C : 0 : 0 : 1E5

2000 : 21 : 4137 : 0 : 6C :: 1E5

The two ways to shorten IPv6 addresses are to remove leading zeroes and to use zero compression:

Removal of Leading Zeroes   Leading zeroes in each group of four can be omitted. For example, 0021 is represented as 21 without the leading zeroes. You can remove leading zeroes within a group, but you would never remove trailing zeroes. In other words, 2000 cannot be shortened to 2. The example IPv6 address looks like this with leading zeroes removed: 2000 : 21 : 4137 : 0 : 6C : 0 : 0 : 1E5.

You can see that the IPv6 address still has eight groups of numbers, with each group separated by a colon. Even though you don't see four characters in each group, the four characters are still implied.

Zero Compression with a Double Colon   Zero compression replaces a long string of zeroes in different groups with a double colon (::). For example, this shows our example address with zero compression: 2000 : 0021 : 4137 : 0000 : 006C :: 01E5. You can see that there are now only six groups of characters, but you know that an IPv6 address has eight groups. The two missing groups represented by the double colon are 0s. You use a double colon no matter how many groups of zeroes are represented.

It's common to omit the leading zeroes when using zero compression. The example would look like this: 2000 : 21 : 4137 : 0 : 6C :: 1E5.

Note that you can use only one double colon. The following address with two double colons is not valid:

2000 : 21 : 4137 :: 6C :: 1E5

You can see that the previous IPv6 address has five groups of characters, so you know that three groups of characters are missing. However, you can't know if the first double colon represents one set of characters or two. If two double colons were used, you wouldn't know which one of the following two IPv6 addresses it was representing:

2000 : 21 : 4137 : 0 : 0 : 6C : 0 : 1E5
2000 : 21 : 4137 : 0 : 6C : 0 : 0 : 1E5

Types of IPv6 Addresses

IPv6 addresses are identified as unicast, multicast, and anycast. You can compare these to the unicast, multicast, and broadcast addresses described earlier for IPv4 addresses. Unicast and multicast addresses are the same for both IPv4 and IPv6, but instead of using the IPv4 broadcast address, IPv6 uses an anycast address.

An anycast address is used by IPv6 to identify services running on nearby systems or on the nearest router. Multiple systems on a network will have the same anycast address, and anycast messages are sent to one (or more) of these systems to get information.

You can think of a unicast message as a one-to-one message. A multicast message is a one-to-many message. Anycast is a one-to-one-of-many message. In other words, a group of systems have the same anycast address, but an anycast message is not sent to all of the systems in this anycast group. Instead, it is sent to one of the systems in the group, and in some cases to more than one of the systems. In contrast, a broadcast message is sent to all the systems in the subnet.

Types of Unicast IPv6 Addresses

IPv6 uses different types of unicast addresses for different purposes. The three types of IPv6 unicast addresses are as follows:

- A *global unicast address* is used on the Internet similar to how a public IPv4 address is used on the Internet.

- A *unique local address* is assigned to a computer in a network, similar to how an IPv4 private address is used in private networks.

- A *link local address* is assigned to a computer using an autoconfiguration method similar to how APIPA is used in IPv4.

 It's common for computers to have more than one IPv6 address assigned. For example, a computer can be assigned a global unicast address that is used for Internet access and a link local address that is used for communicating with internal clients.

A global unicast address is globally routable over the Internet. It uniquely identifies a single host on the Internet and is similar to a public IPv4 address. The address prefix of a global unicast address is 0x 2000::/3. The /3 is CIDR notation and indicates that only the first 3 bits are used in the prefix. In this case, the first character of 0x 2000 is 0x 2, and it is represented by 0010 in binary. The /3 indicates that only the first 3 bits (001) are used to identify the address as a global unicast address.

Although you often see 2000 as the number of a global unicast address, many other numbers are available. For example, 2001::/3 has the same prefix of 001 and is a global unicast address.

Unique local unicast addresses are assigned to clients within an organization, similar to how IPv4 addresses are used. The address prefix is 0x FC00::/7 but is typically displayed as 0x FD00::/8.

The first 7 bits are always 1111 110 (0x FC). The 8th bit is defined as the local flag bit and should be a 1, indicating that the address is a local address. A value of 0 is not defined, so the 8th bit should always be a 1. In other words, the first 8 bits are always 1111 1101 (0xFD).

A link local address is used within a private network and is not recognized outside the enterprise. Link local addresses are assigned using autoconfiguration similar to how IPv4 APIPA assigns addresses starting with 169.254. However, a computer with a link local unicast address assigned can also have global unicast address assigned.

The address prefix of a link local unicast address is 0x FE80::/10. In other words, the first 10 bits are 1111 1110 01 (0x FE8). However, link local unicast addresses are assigned with a 64-bit prefix and all clients in the same subnet will use the same 64-bit prefix. Computers in a different subnet will have a different 64-bit prefix, but they will all start with 0x FE8. This is similar to how IPv4 computers within a subnet will all have the same network ID. For example, all APIPA clients have a network ID of 169.254.0.0.

Site-local addresses (with a prefix of FEC0::/7) were in the original IPv6 documents but were deprecated in September 2004. Unique local unicast addresses are used instead of site-local addresses.

Interface Identifiers

In IPv4, the subnet mask is used to differentiate the network ID portion of an IP address and the host ID. IPv6 doesn't use a subnet mask, but it does use a similar concept of a network ID and a host ID. Specifically, the first 64 bits of an IPv6 address identify the network, and the last 64 bits are used as the interface identifier, similar to a host ID.

Extended Unique Identifier (EUI)-64 addresses are used on many network adapters instead of a 48-bit media access control (MAC) or physical address. Both EUI-64 addresses and MAC addresses are theoretically unique and can be used for the interface identifier portion of the IPv6 address. When the network adapter has a 48-bit MAC address, it is padded with 16 additional random bits to give it 64 bits.

Microsoft recommends using different identifiers to preserve privacy. In other words, Microsoft recommends that instead of using the EUI-64 address or the MAC address, you create different identifiers for the IPv6 computers.

Benefits of IPv6

In addition to providing more than enough IP addresses, IPv6 provides additional benefits. In Windows 8.1, IPv6 is used for remote access and is required to support DirectAccess and VPN Reconnect.

DirectAccess allows users to access an organization's internal network over the Internet without a virtual private network (VPN) connection. DirectAccess requires IPv6. Chapter 6 includes additional information on DirectAccess and VPN Reconnect.

Here are some additional benefits provided by IPv6:

Greater Efficiency   Because of the way in which the addresses are configured, routers are able to process the addresses more efficiently and they don't have to store as much information in internal routing tables.

Stateless Configuration   An IPv6 client can configure its own IPv6 address using a stateless configuration if a DHCP server isn't available to assign an IPv6 address. Clients are able to discover local routers and configure themselves within the network. This is comparable to APIPA used with IPv4, but unlike APIPA, a client with a stateless configuration will be able to communicate with clients on other networks.

Stateful Configuration   IP addresses can be assigned by a DHCPv6-compatible server similar to how IPv4 addresses are assigned by a DHCP server. The DHCPv6 server can provide all the needed TCP/IP settings, including the IP address and other configuration information. It's also possible to configure the DHCPv6 server to provide only the configuration information and allow a client to use a stateless IPv6 address.

Built-in Internet Protocol Security (IPsec) Support   IPv6 natively supports IPsec, which is used to secure traffic. Encapsulating Security Payload (ESP) encrypts traffic, and Authentication Header (AH) is used by clients to authenticate each other and verify the integrity of the traffic.

No NAT Requirement   NAT is required in IPv4 to translate private and public IP addresses, but due to how the global and local addresses are used, NAT is not required.

If you want to read more about IPv6, you'll find a wealth of information on the Microsoft IPv6 page here: http://technet.microsoft.com/en-us/library/hh831730.aspx.

Dual Stack

You don't have to pick either IPv4 or IPv6—you can use both. IPv6 was designed to work in a dual-stack configuration with IPv4. Eventually, IPv6 will replace IPv4 on internal networks and on the Internet, but between now and then, most computers will use a dual stack with both.

IPv6 usage has been steadily growing over the years. On June 8, 2011, thousands of Internet service providers (ISPs) and websites participated in the World IPv6 day. This provided a global trial of IPv6 and showed that the Internet was ready to move to IPv6 permanently. On June 6, 2012, thousands of ISPs, home networking equipment manufacturers, and web companies came together to permanently enable IPv6 on their products and services.

Resolving Names to IP Addresses

People use names and words to communicate, and it's easy to remember a computer or a host with a name. However, computers use numbers such as IP addresses. *Name resolution* is used on networks to resolve these computer names to IP addresses. For example, if you enter bing.com into a web browser's URL line, the computer will perform one or more name resolution queries to identify the IP address.

There are seven methods of resolving names to IP addresses and two types of names. The two types of names are:

Hostnames   A *hostname* can be up to 255 characters in length and is the only type of name used on the Internet. When a hostname is combined with a domain name, it becomes a fully qualified domain name (FQDN) but is still resolved as a hostname. For example, a Windows 8.1 PC named Win8PC in the domain GetCertifiedGetAhead.com has a FQDN of Win8PC.GetCertifiedGetAhead.com. Hostnames and FQDNs are primarily resolved by DNS servers.

NetBIOS Names   A *NetBIOS name* has 15 readable characters, with the 16th byte identifying a service running on the system. NetBIOS names are always single-label names such as Win8PC or DC, and they never include other elements such as .com. NetBIOS names are not used on the Internet, and the use of NetBIOS names has been significantly reduced in networks in favor of hostnames. However, they are still being used by older applications. Since NetBIOS names are not supported in IPv6, their usage will eventually disappear. NetBIOS names are primarily resolved by WINS servers.

Hostname Resolution Methods

DNS is the primary method used to resolve hostnames to IP addresses, but it's not the only method. Three methods are used to resolve hostnames:

DNS   DNS servers will answer queries for name resolution of hostnames. When queried with a name, the DNS server will return the IP address. DNS servers are typically configured with addresses of other DNS servers. If the queried DNS server doesn't know the IP address, it will forward the name resolution request to other DNS servers to get the answer. This forwarding occurs on internal networks and on the Internet.

You can easily check which DNS server is assigned to a client by using the ipconfig /all command.

Hosts File   The *Hosts file* is located in the %windir%\System32\Drivers\etc folder. Entries in the Hosts file are automatically placed into the host cache. Viruses have sometimes modified the Hosts file to prevent a client from accessing specific websites. For example, a known virus placed a bogus entry into this file for Microsoft's update site. This prevented infected clients from getting updates.

Host Cache   Once a name is resolved by DNS, the result is placed in the *host cache*, also called the DNS cache or DNS resolver cache. The DNS cache or DNS resolver cache is a little misleading because this cache also holds entries from the Hosts file. You can view the host cache with the ipconfig /displaydns command.

Host cache entries can be removed from cache using the `ipconfig` `/flushdns` command. This will remove all entries that were cached from previous DNS queries, but it will not remove entries placed in cache from the Hosts file.

NetBIOS Name Resolution Methods

NetBIOS names can be resolved using several methods. These methods are different from the primary methods used to resolve hostnames. However, if a hostname can't be resolved using the primary hostname resolution methods, the NetBIOS name resolution methods can be attempted. The primary methods used to resolve NetBIOS names are:

Link Local Multicast Name Resolution (LLMNR)   Both IPv4 and IPv6 support LLMNR as a method of name resolution for single-label names. LLMNR requests are not passed by routers, so LLMNR name resolution only works for clients on the same link or subnet.

WINS   WINS servers will answer name resolution queries for NetBIOS names. When queried with a name, the WINS server will return the IP address. Although DNS servers can be configured to query other DNS servers to resolve a name, WINS servers cannot query other WINS servers.

GlobalNames Zone   Windows DNS servers support a special GlobalNames Zone for single-label names. If a network doesn't use many NetBIOS names, GlobalNames Zones are sometimes used in place of a WINS server.

Lmhosts File   The Lmhosts file is located in the `%windir%\System32\Drivers\etc` folder. It works similar to the Hosts file except it is only for NetBIOS names.

NetBIOS Cache   Once a NetBIOS name has been resolved to an IP address, the result is placed in the NetBIOS cache. You can view the NetBIOS cache with the `nbtstat /c` command.

Broadcast   A client can also broadcast a single-label name. Broadcast messages do not pass a router, but the broadcast message is sent to all clients on the same subnet. A client with the same single-label name in the broadcast message will respond with its IP address.

Name Resolution Order

Windows 8.1 systems use the following order when they need to resolve a hostname to an IP address:

1. Check to see if the name is the same as the local computer name. If so, the IP address is the same as the local computer.

2. Check the hostname or DNS resolver cache.

3. Check the Hosts file.

4. Query DNS to resolve the name. A computer should be configured with the IP address of a DNS server.

If the name is a single-label name, this indicates it's a NetBIOS name. Windows 8.1 uses the following order to resolve NetBIOS names:

1. Use LLMNR on the local network.

2. Truncate the hostname to the first 15 characters if necessary and check the NetBIOS cache.

3. Query DNS to resolve the name. DNS servers need to be configured with a GlobalNames Zone for this to work.

4. Send a broadcast on the local network.

5. Check the Lmhosts file.

Basic Commands Used with Networking

There are a few commands that you should understand when working with networks and troubleshooting networking issues. This section provides basic information on the ipconfig, ping, and nslookup commands.

Chapter 1, "Introducing Windows 8.1," provides more details on how to launch and use the command prompt.

Using IPconfig

The ipconfig command is a familiar command to many people, but it has some extra capabilities that are sometimes overlooked. Just as with most command prompt commands, ipconfig can be executed alone or with switches that modify what it does.

IPconfig works in Windows 8.1 just as it does in other Windows operating systems such as Windows XP and Windows 7. However, it does show differences in how some naming conventions have been changed in Windows 8.1. For example, in past operating systems the first network interface card (NIC) was always named "Local Area Connection." In Windows 8.1, it is named "Ethernet."

ipconfig and ipconfig /all are two commands commonly used to check the TCP/IP configuration of a system. ipconfig provides the output shown in Listing 5.1 on a Windows 8.1 computer.

Listing 5.1: *ipconfig* output

```
C:\Users\Darril>ipconfig
Ethernet adapter Ethernet:

   Connection-specific DNS Suffix  . :
```

```
     Link local IPv6 Address . . . . . : fe80::8425:9703:4790:4525
     IPv4 Address. . . . . . . . . . . : 192.168.59.130
     Subnet Mask . . . . . . . . . . . : 255.255.255.0
     Default Gateway . . . . . . . . . : 192.168.59.2

Tunnel adapter isatap.{1C690298-4DC7-435F-B4EA-44EF0FA09B98}:

     Media State . . . . . . . . . . . : Media disconnected
     Connection-specific DNS Suffix  . :

Tunnel adapter Teredo Tunneling Pseudo-Interface:

     Connection-specific DNS Suffix  . :
     IPv6 Address. . . . . . . . . . . :
                              2001:0:9d38:953c:3c07:edf:b95f:77f5
     Link local IPv6 Address . . . . . : fe80::3c07:edf:b95f:77f5
     Default Gateway . . . . . . . . . : ::
```

Several items are worth mentioning in this output:

Ethernet adapter Ethernet Ethernet adapter indicates a wired NIC and Ethernet the name of the NIC.

Link local IPv6 Address An IPv6 link local address is assigned with a prefix of 0x FE80.

Connection-specific DNS Suffix This is blank but can be assigned by a DHCP server, entered manually (as shown later this chapter), or listed as localdomain if the computer is not joined to a domain and the address has been entered manually.

Tunnel adapter isatap This is used for DirectAccess. It will normally be followed with a dot (.) and the DNS suffix. When the suffix isn't assigned, it uses a globally unique identifier (GUID). The client isn't connected to a DirectAccess system so this is listed as Media disconnected.

Tunnel adapter Teredo Tunneling Pseudo-Interface You can see the global unicast address starting with 0x 2 and a link local IPv6 address starting with 0x FE8. This information is available only if the computer is able to connect with a router running IPv6.

The ipconfig /all command shows much more information, starting with the hostname. Listing 5.2 shows the partial output of ipconfig /all for a system that is joined to the GetCertifiedGetAhead.com domain. Note that even though the DNS suffix is blank in Listing 5.1 (showing the output of ipconfig), it appears in the output for the ipconfig /all command. In Listing 5.2, the computer is joined to a domain named GetCertifiedGetAhead.com.

Listing 5.2: Partial *ipconfig /all* output (not exhaustive)

```
Windows IP Configuration

    Host Name . . . . . . . . . . . : Win8PC
    Primary Dns Suffix  . . . . . . : GetCertifiedGetAhead.com
    Node Type . . . . . . . . . . . : Hybrid
    IP Routing Enabled. . . . . . . : No
    WINS Proxy Enabled. . . . . . . : No
    DNS Suffix Search List. . . . . : GetCertifiedGetAhead.com

    Physical Address  . . . . . . . : 1C-65-9D-47-29-4E
    DHCP Enabled  . . . . . . . . . : Yes
    DNS Servers . . . . . . . . . . : 192.168.12.56
```

Here's some of the important information in the /all output you will need for troubleshooting:

Physical Address Also known as the media access control (MAC) address.

DHCP Enabled This is Yes or No depending on whether the client has received a DHCP lease. If it is Yes, you'll also see information on when the lease was obtained, when it expires, and the DHCP server's IP address.

DNS Servers This lists the IP addresses of DNS servers used by this system.

Table 5.1 shows the various switches available with the ipconfig command.

TABLE 5.1   ipconfig command switches

Switch	Comments
/?	Displays help.
/all	Displays the full configuration information for the client.
/release	Releases the DHCP-assigned IPv4 address for the adapter, giving it an address of 0.0.0.0. This does not have any effect on adapters with statically assigned addresses.
/release6	Releases the DHCP-assigned IPv6 address for the adapter. This does not have any effect on adapters with statically assigned addresses.
/renew	Requests a new IPv4 DHCP lease for the adapter from a DHCP server. If a DHCP server is not available, an APIPA address (169.254.y.z) will be assigned. This does not have any effect on adapters with statically assigned addresses.

TABLE 5.1   ipconfig command switches *(continued)*

Switch	Comments
/renew6	Requests a new IPv6 DHCP lease for the adapter. If a DHCP server does not respond, a link local address with a prefix of 0x FE80 is assigned. This does not have any effect on adapters with statically assigned addresses.
/displaydns	Displays the contents of the host cache. Each time a name is resolved by DNS, the result is placed in cache.
/flushdns	Purges the contents of the hostname cache. Names in cache from the Hosts file will always remain in cache.

Using Ping

The *ping* tool is a basic but invaluable troubleshooting aid. It sends out echo request packets and returns echo reply packets using the Internet Control Message Protocol (ICMP). If you receive the packets back, you know that the other host is up and operational. You should also know what the ping responses mean when the host is not up and operational.

Ping was invented by Michael Muus, who named it after the sound that sonar makes when it hits another object and is reflected back. Sonar sends sound waves out and measures the sound waves that are reflected back to gather information. Similarly, the ping command sends packets out to a target host, which are then reflected back to the sending host.

ICMP is often used in malicious software (malware) attacks, so it's common for firewalls to block ping messages. In other words, if you don't receive a response from ping, you can't assume the other host is down. In contrast, if you do receive a response you know the host is operational.

You can ping an IP address or a hostname. When a hostname is used in the ping command (as shown in Listing 5.3), the name is first resolved to an IP address. ping normally sends out four echo request packets and receives four echo reply packets in return.

Listing 5.3: Using *ping* to check connectivity

```
C:\>ping blogs.getcertifiedgetahead.com
Pinging blogs.getcertifiedgetahead.com [174.122.52.195] with 32 bytes of data:
Reply from 174.122.52.195: bytes=32 time=17ms TTL=128
Reply from 174.122.52.195: bytes=32 time=17ms TTL=128
Reply from 174.122.52.195: bytes=32 time=19ms TTL=128
Reply from 174.122.52.195: bytes=32 time=17ms TTL=128
Ping statistics for 192.168.1.101:
    Packets: Sent = 4, Received = 4, Lost = 0 (0% loss),
Approximate round trip times in milli-seconds:
    Minimum = 1ms, Maximum = 1ms, Average = 1ms
```

Here are common error messages you'll see when using the ping command:

Request Timed Out   The echo request did not receive an echo reply. This could be because the target was not operational, a firewall on the host blocked the traffic, or network problems between the source and target prevented the ping packets from reaching the target or source. If the network policy of the target is set to Public, the firewall will be configured to block pings and you'll receive this message even though the system is up and operational.

Ping Request Could Not Find Host   The name could not be resolved to an IP address. If you know the IP address and can successfully ping the IP address but not ping the name, it typically indicates something is wrong with DNS. Either the DNS server is not operational or the client is not configured with the correct IP address of the DNS server.

Destination Host Unreachable   This message often indicates TCP/IP is not configured with the proper default gateway on either the source or destination computers. It could also indicate a problem with a router configured as the default gateway for either of the computers. Finally, it could be something as simple as an incorrect IP address or incorrect subnet mask on either end.

Normally, ping will send out only four echo request packets, but you may occasionally want it to continue sending the messages while you troubleshoot. The -t switch is used to start a ping loop as in the following command:

```
Ping -t 192.168.1.1
```

ping will continue sending messages until you press Ctrl+C to interrupt the process.

Using NSlookup

While the ipconfig and ping commands can often be useful when troubleshooting networking issues, there are times when you'll want to query the DNS server directly to get detailed information. The *NSlookup* tool is a command-prompt utility that you can use to get specific information from a DNS server and verify that the DNS server is able to resolve specific names to IP addresses.

DNS has multiple resource records that can be queried. Two important records that you should know about for this topic are:

Host   This includes the name of a host on the network and its IP address. When the DNS server is queried with the name, it returns the IP address. This is referred to as a forward lookup name resolution request. The name is resolved to an IP address. Also, host records are maintained in a forward lookup zone on the DNS server.

PTR   The pointer (PTR) record is used for reverse name resolution. Clients can query the DNS server with an IP address, and the DNS server responds with the computer name that has this IP address. PTR records are maintained in a reverse lookup zone on the DNS server, but these zones are optional and not always used.

For example, you may want to verify that DNS can provide the IP address of a file server named FS1. Listing 5.4 shows how nslookup can be used to verify this. The line numbers are shown for explanation purposes. Line 1 is the command and lines 2–6 show the results.

Listing 5.4: Using *nslookup*

```
1 C:\>nslookup fs1
2 Server:  dc.getcertifiedgetahead.com
3 Address:  192.168.1.10
4
5 Name:     fs1.getcertifiedgetahead.com
6 Address:  192.168.1.21
```

Lines 5 and 6 provide the result of the query and are the most important information from the command. They show definitively that the DNS server (running on the computer named DC) can resolve the server named FS1 to an IP address of 192.168.1.21.

If the DNS server does not have a record for the name and can't resolve it, you'd see something similar to Listing 5.5.

Listing 5.5: Verifying a DNS record doesn't exist with *nslookup*

```
1 C:\>nslookup fs25
2 Server:  dc.getcertifiedgetahead.com
3 Address:  192.168.1.10
4
5 *** dc.getcertifiedgetahead.com can't find fs25: Non-existent domain
```

Lines 2 and 3 identify the DNS server that is answering the query. The client is configured with the DNS server IP address and uses a reverse lookup to determine the DNS server's name.

 Most DNS lookups are forward lookups. You send the name and the DNS server responds with the IP address. In a reverse lookup, you send the IP address and the DNS server responds with the name from a PTR record.

The information provided in lines 2 and 3 is dependent on the DNS server having a reverse lookup zone and a PTR record in the zone for the DNS server. However, reverse lookup zones are optional, so this part of the query will often fail. Even if the reverse lookup fails, though, you can still verify that other records exist by looking at the output on lines 5 and 6, as shown earlier.

Listing 5.6 shows what you'll see if the DNS server doesn't have a PTR record in the DNS server's reverse lookup zone.

Listing 5.6: Using *nslookup* without a PTR record in the DNS server

```
1 C:\>nslookup fs1
2 Server:  Unknown
3 Address:  192.168.1.10
4
5 Name:     fs1.getcertifiedgetahead.com
6 Address:  192.168.1.21
```

Line 2 shows that the DNS server couldn't be identified (since the PTR record doesn't exist) and instead just lists it as Unknown. However, it's important to note that FS1 is still successfully resolved on lines 5 and 6.

If the DNS server doesn't have a reverse lookup zone, it will still work, although the result looks as if something is drastically wrong. Listing 5.7 shows the result when the reverse lookup zone doesn't exist.

Listing 5.7: Using *nslookup* without a reverse lookup zone

```
1 C:\>nslookup fs1
2 DNS request timed out.
3     timeout was 2 seconds.
4 Server:  UnKnown
5 Address:  192.168.1.10
6
7 Name:    fs1. getcertifiedgetahead.com
8 Address:  192.168.1.21
```

When looking at lines 2 and 3, you may think that DNS isn't responding, but all this is saying is that it timed out when it tried to do a reverse lookup of 192.168.1.10 to determine the name.

Note that lines 7 and 8 still provide the result of the name resolution request. In other words, even though you see the message "DNS request timed out," the DNS server still resolved the hostname to an IP address.

What if the DNS server is not responding at all? This could happen if the DNS server is not operational or reachable. Listing 5.8 shows what you'll see if you don't receive a response from DNS.

Listing 5.8: Using *nslookup* with an unreachable DNS server

```
1 C:\>nslookup fs1
2 DNS request timed out.
3     timeout was 2 seconds.
4 Server:  UnKnown
5 Address:  192.168.1.10
6
7 DNS request timed out.
8     timeout was 2 seconds.
9 DNS request timed out.
10     timeout was 2 seconds.
11 *** Request to UnKnown timed-out
```

Line 5 shows the IP address that the client is using as the DNS server. The rest of the information indicates the DNS server is not responding at all. At this point, you should check that the client is configured with the correct address of a DNS server on the network and that the DNS server is operational.

Using the Network and Sharing Center

A user may not be able to access the Internet with their browser and complain that "the Internet is down," but as a technician you know there are many components between the user's system and the Internet. One of those pieces is much more likely to be the problem than the entire Internet.

If a system is not communicating with other hosts, it's important to check the TCP/IP connectivity and configuration information. A primary tool you can use is the *Network and Sharing Center*, shown in Figure 5.4. You can access the Network and Sharing Center from the Windows 8.1 Start screen by pressing Windows logo key+W, typing **Networking and Sharing Center**, and selecting it.

FIGURE 5.4   Network and Sharing Center

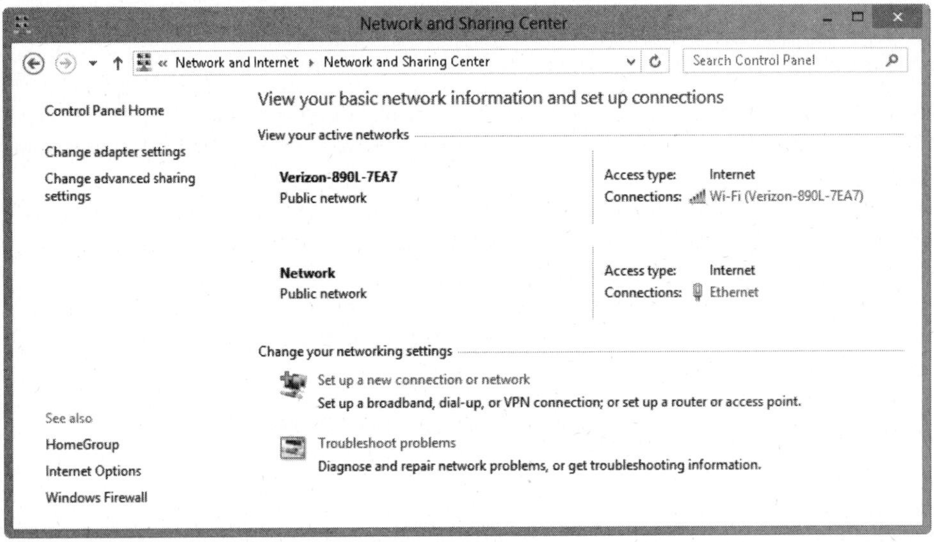

Some of the information that was available in this tool in Windows 7 is no longer available in Windows 8.1, but this tool is still useful. The most important information is in the center pane. It shows that the computer has two connections and each one has access to the Internet. Also, each of these connections is listed as Public, indicating that they are using the Public network location. Public, private, and domain network connections are described in the next section.

The top connection has a signal strength indicator for a wireless connection and also includes a label of Wi-Fi. The network is using a mobile hotspot with a network name of Verizon-890L-7EA7. The network name is also known as the service set identifier (SSID). The next connection is a wired connection named Network using the network interface card named Ethernet.

Figure 5.4 shows how both wired and wireless connections appear in the Networking and Sharing Center. However, using two connections like this will often result in slower performance for each. In practice, you should only use one or the other for a computer.

The left panel includes several links that can be used to configure networking. They include:

Control Panel Home   This will take you to the main page of the Control Panel.

Change Adapter Settings   This link gives access to all of the network adapters and connections on the system. This includes wired adapters, wireless adapters, and virtual private network (VPN) connections if they've been added to the system.

Change Advanced Sharing Settings   Advanced Sharing Settings are used to configure the settings for different profiles such as a public profile (used when connected directly to the Internet) or a private profile (used when connected from a home or work network).

Understanding Network Locations Profiles

Windows 8.1 uses network location profiles to access reconfigured settings for any network. These are similar to how Windows 7 uses network location profiles. These profiles use different firewall and security settings, and you can select these settings by selecting one of the profiles. The three network location profiles in Windows 8.1 are Public, Private, and Domain.

You can access the settings of these profiles by clicking Change Advanced Sharing Settings in the Network and Sharing Center. Figure 5.5 shows this page with the Guest or Public profile open. Notice that this is identified as the Current Profile.

Because this computer is joined to a domain, the Domain profile is also available, but this selection isn't available on all systems. You can expand any of the profiles to view the settings by clicking on them. The primary purposes of each are as follows:

Public   A public (or guest) network is one that is in a public place, such as in an airport or coffee shop. When the network type is identified as Public, the Windows Firewall is configured to protect the client by refusing unsolicited connections. A user can connect to the Internet to retrieve email or Internet pages because these connections are solicited by the user. Any time a computer has a public IP address, Public should be selected as the network type.

Private   A private network is one that is private for the user. For example, a corporate network or a home network is commonly configured with the Private network type. Security on the Windows Firewall is relaxed to improve usability within the network. Private networks are typically protected with a network router and a firewall placed between the user and the Internet.

Domain   A domain network is used when a computer is a member of a domain and authenticates with a domain controller. It will be put into a Domain network location. This is similar to a private network where the Windows Firewall is relaxed to improve usability within the network.

FIGURE 5.5   Public profile settings

The following sections discuss the profile settings in more depth, but as an introduction, Table 5.2 shows the default settings for the different profiles. The domain settings are normally configured by an administrator in the domain using Group Policy.

TABLE 5.2   Default settings

	Public	Private	Domain
Network Discovery		On	Off
File and Printer Sharing	Off	Off	Off
HomeGroups	Not available	Allowed	Not available

The Windows Firewall includes multiple settings for each of these locations that can also be configured. Chapter 6 covers the Windows Firewall in more depth, including how to configure rules to allow or block certain types of traffic and associate the rule with specific network location profiles.

Network Discovery

Network Discovery is used to simplify the process of configuring and connecting network-connected systems and devices. When Network Discovery is enabled, other devices on the network can easily locate the Windows 8.1 computer and the Windows 8.1 computer can easily locate other devices.

For example, Media Center Extender Devices (such as Microsoft's Xbox 360) use the Network Discovery protocol. When the Xbox 360 is on the same subnet and Network Discovery is enabled, clients can easily connect and use all of the features available on the Xbox 360 system. This includes features such as watching movies in one room from the Xbox 360 system located in another room.

Network Discovery is limited to a single subnet. The Network Discovery messages are not passed by routers, so any clients on different subnets will not be located or discovered using Network Discovery.

Network Discovery is enabled by default in private (nondomain) networks and can be enabled in a domain network with Group Policy. Network Discovery should remain disabled in public networks to prevent clients from connecting to the system and accessing resources.

File and Printer Sharing

When file and printer sharing is enabled, the Windows 8.1 computer is able to share folders and printers from the computer. This allows other users to connect to the computer to access the resources.

Chapter 9, "Managing Files and Disks," covers file sharing in more depth, and Chapter 10, "Managing Hardware and Printers," covers printers in more depth.

All Networks

The All Networks section isn't a separate profile. Instead, it shows the settings that apply to all the profiles and includes the following settings:

Public Folder Sharing   This is turned off by default. When enabled, the Public folder on the Windows 8.1 computer is automatically shared. Other users on the network can access files and folders in the Public folder using the Homegroup section within File Explorer. In addition to enabling this setting, you can use it with Password Protected Sharing to restrict access to the Public folder.

Media Streaming   This setting is disabled by default. When enabled, it allows other users to access pictures, music, and videos shared from this computer. Also the user of this computer will be able to access these files on other computers.

File Sharing Connections   By default, this setting is configured to use 128-bit encryption when transferring files. However, if other systems do not support 128-bit encryption you can weaken it to use 40-bit or 56-bit encryption.

Password Protected Sharing   This is enabled by default. When enabled, it restricts access to any shared resources to only users that have a user account on the computer. Users that do not have an account will not be able to access these resources.

Configuring Network Locations

There may be times when you want to change the profile being used by the computer or change some of the settings. Neither is difficult to do, but you can't do so from the same location.

If you want to change the settings within the profile, you can select Advanced Sharing Settings from the Network and Sharing Center. It opens with the currently assigned profile, and you can select any of the settings to turn them on or off. After you've made your changes, click Save Changes. This will modify the underlying settings within the Windows Firewall to allow or block the traffic.

If you want to change which profile is assigned, you need to do so from the Start screen. Exercise 5.1 shows the steps. It assumes you're logged on to Windows 8.1 and the Start screen is showing.

EXERCISE 5.1

Selecting a Network Location Profile

1. Right-click the Quick Access button at the bottom-left corner and select Control Panel from the Quick Access menu. The Network and Sharing Center pane appears.

2. Click the Change Advanced Sharing Settings link in the left side of the pane. You will now see a screen similar to this:

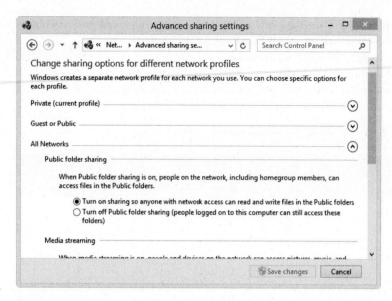

3. Identify the network that you want to modify. Turn Sharing On (or Off) for the network services needed.

4. If you return to the Network and Sharing Center, you'll see the network you selected has been changed.

In some Windows documentation, "network locations" is called "network sharing." This reflects the name used when accessing networks from the Settings charm in the previous exercise. However, in other documentation, including the objectives, the name "network locations" is still used.

Configuring HomeGroup Settings

HomeGroups provide an easy method for users in small home networks to share resources with each other. One user creates the HomeGroup and then all other users can join it and share such resources as files and printers with each other. Each user is able to choose what to share from their computer.

Windows 7, Windows 8, and Windows 8.1 computers support HomeGroups. For example, you can create a HomeGroup on a Windows 7 computer, and all Windows 7, Windows

8, and Windows 8.1 computers can join it, or you can create a HomeGroup on a Windows 8.1 computer for Windows 7 and Windows 8.1 computers.

When you create or join a HomeGroup, you are given a choice of libraries and other resources you want to share. Figure 5.6 shows the screen that you'll see when you join a HomeGroup. In the figure, you can see that most of the selections are being shared but Videos is set to Not Shared. Shared and Not Shared are the only choices.

FIGURE 5.6   Selecting items to share in a HomeGroup

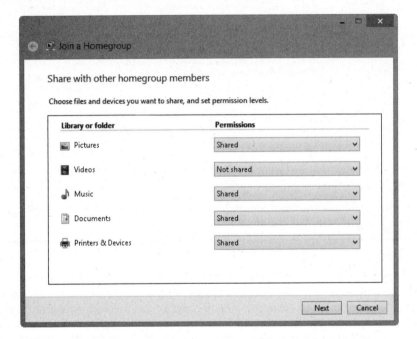

When a HomeGroup is created, the following settings are enabled in the private network location:

- Turn On Network Discovery
- Turn On Automatic Setup Of Network Connected Devices
- Turn On File And Printer Sharing
- Allow Windows To Manage HomeGroup Connections (Recommended)

 You can join or create a HomeGroup only if your computer is using the private network location. If you're using the public network location, you'll be prompted to change the location when you try to use a HomeGroup.

There are two ways you can work with HomeGroups. One method uses the PC Settings applet available from the Start screen. The second uses the HomeGroup applet in the Control Panel, which can also be accessed from the Network and Sharing Center. The following two exercises lead you through steps using each tool. Exercise 5.2 shows how to create a HomeGroup from the PC Settings page, and Exercise 5.3 shows how to join an existing HomeGroup from the Network and Sharing Center.

Exercise 5.2 assumes you're logged on to a Windows 8.1 system with Internet access and the Start screen is showing.

EXERCISE 5.2

Creating a HomeGroup

1. With the Start screen showing, type **HomeGroup**. Select Settings in the Search charm.

2. Select HomeGroup. This opens the PC Settings page with HomeGroup selected. You can also access this page by moving your mouse to the top-right corner, selecting the Settings charm, and clicking Change PC Settings.

3. Click Create.

4. Review the information in the Libraries And Devices page and change any items you want to share from Not Shared to Shared. For example, you can change Media Devices from Off to On. This page also shows the password for the HomeGroup in the Membership section. Share this password with other users who will join the HomeGroup.

5. Press Alt+F4 to close the PC Settings page. Alternatively, you can move your mouse to the top of the screen, click and hold the button, and quickly drag it downward to simulate a downward swipe for a touch screen.

Exercise 5.3 shows how to join a HomeGroup. It assumes you're logged on to a Windows 8.1 system with Internet access and the Start screen is showing.

EXERCISE 5.3

Joining a HomeGroup

1. Press Windows logo key+W to open the Search Settings charm.

2. Enter **Network and Sharing** in the text box and select Network And Sharing Center.

3. Click HomeGroup in the bottom-left corner. If a HomeGroup exists, it will be detected and the name of the computer hosting it will be displayed.

4. Click Join Now. Review the information on the Join A HomeGroup page and click Next.

5. On the Type The HomeGroup Password page, enter the correct password and click Next.

6. Click Finish.

After joining a HomeGroup, you can leave it at any time to stop sharing all resources on the computer. This also prevents users on this computer from accessing any resources on other computers in the HomeGroup. To leave the HomeGroup, start the HomeGroup applet and click Leave The HomeGroup. Then click Leave The HomeGroup on the confirmation page as well.

Configuring a Wired Network Interface Card

You may occasionally need to manually configure the TCP/IP settings on a wired network interface card (NIC). This is a relatively easy process, and exercises in Chapter 4 led you through the process of configuring a NIC for a Windows 8.1 system and a Windows 2012 system.

It's more common to configure NICs to receive their TCP/IP configuration information from a DHCP server. Statically assigning the TCP/IP configuration information requires more administrative effort, which directly translates into costs. However, if you're using a small network, it might be easier to manually assign the IP addresses rather than configure a DHCP server.

Figure 5.7 shows a manually configured NIC. The IP address, subnet mask, default gateway, and DNS server addresses are all entered manually. If your network has a DHCP server that you want to use, you would select the Obtain An IP Address Automatically check box.

If you assign the IP address manually, you might also want to configure the DNS suffix for the computer if the computer is joined to a domain. For example, if your computer is joined to the GetCertifiedGetAhead.com domain, you can set this suffix so that DNS queries use that suffix first. If you enter **ping dc** from the command prompt and the suffix is configured, the computer interprets the command as `ping dc.getcertifiedgetahead.com` and tries to resolve the name to an IP address using this FQDN first.

Exercise 5.4 shows how to configure a wired NIC, including how to configure the DNS suffix. This exercise assumes you're logged on to a Windows 8.1 system and the Start screen is showing.

FIGURE 5.7   Configuring the NIC

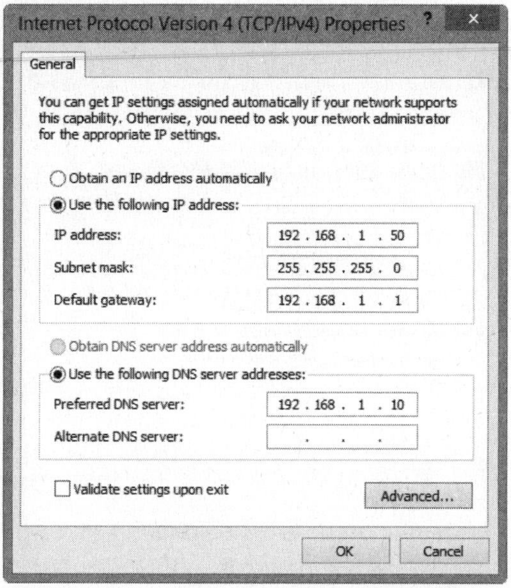

Internet Protocol Version 4 (TCP/IPv4) Properties   ?   ×

General

You can get IP settings assigned automatically if your network supports
this capability. Otherwise, you need to ask your network administrator
for the appropriate IP settings.

○ Obtain an IP address automatically

● Use the following IP address:

IP address: 192 . 168 . 1 . 50

Subnet mask: 255 . 255 . 255 . 0

Default gateway: 192 . 168 . 1 . 1

○ Obtain DNS server address automatically

● Use the following DNS server addresses:

Preferred DNS server: 192 . 168 . 1 . 10

Alternate DNS server: .   .

☐ Validate settings upon exit   Advanced...

OK   Cancel

EXERCISE 5.4

Configuring a Network Interface Card (NIC)

1. Press Windows logo key+W to open the Search Settings charm.

2. Enter **Network and Sharing** in the text box and select Network And Sharing Center.

3. Click Change Adapter Settings in the left panel.

4. Right-click the adapter (named Ethernet by default) and select Properties.

5. If necessary, scroll down to Internet Protocol Version 4 (TCP/IPv4) and select it. Click
    the Properties button. You can use this properties page to manually assign an IP
    address, subnet mask, default gateway, and DNS server address. This will look famil-
    iar if you did Exercise 4.9 in Chapter 4.

6. Click the Advanced button to open the Advanced TCP/IP Settings page.

7. Select the DNS tab.

8. At the bottom of this page is the DNS Suffix For This Connection setting. If your
    computer is joined to a domain but it has not been assigned, you can enter
    it manually here. The following graphic shows it with the DNS suffix set to
    getcertifiedgetahead.com.

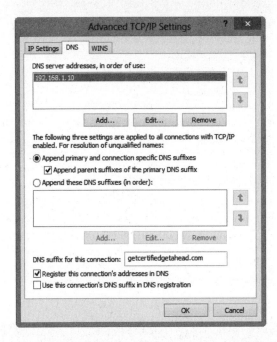

9. Click OK to close the Advanced TCP/IP Settings page. Click OK to close the Internet Protocol Version 4 (TCP/IPv4) Properties page.

10. On the Ethernet Properties page, select Internet Protocol Version 6 (TCP/IPv6) and click Properties.

11. Notice that you can assign an IPv6 address, subnet prefix length, default gateway, and address of a DNS server here.

12. Close all open pages.

Configuring Wireless Network Settings

If your Windows 8.1 computer has wireless capability and a wireless network is available, you'll need to configure the wireless NIC. Before we dig into this too deep, though, it's important to understand some wireless security.

Real World Scenario

Small Wireless Networks

We know many technicians who build up their networking experience by helping friends and associates set up wireless networks. The owner purchases a single wireless router and connects it to the Internet. The wireless router typically has four or more wired connections, which can be used from some systems and devices. Additionally, it has wireless capabilities that can be used with laptops, mobile devices such as smartphones and tablets, and wireless printers.

USB adapters (also called USB dongles) are relatively inexpensive. You can use these for regular PCs instead of using a traditional wired connection.

The biggest benefit of a wireless network is that you don't need to run cables to all the computers. However, security is a major concern, so technicians who set up wireless networks should ensure that they understand wireless security and know how to configure it. This is important when building networking experience and also when taking the Windows 8.1 exams.

Managing Wireless Security

When wireless networks were first designed, the primary goal was ease of use. The designers wanted to make it easy to discover, connect to, and use wireless networks. They did a great job. However, security was more of an afterthought.

They came up with *Wired Equivalent Privacy (WEP)* to provide the same level of privacy for a wireless network as you'd have in a wired network. Unfortunately, WEP had significant problems and was later cracked. Attackers could download software from the Internet and easily crack WEP-protected networks.

Wi-Fi Protected Access (WPA) is the first improvement over WEP. One of the primary benefits of WPA is that it is compatible with most of the same hardware that used WEP. WPA was intended to be an interim fix for WEP until a more permanent solution was identified. Although WPA is more secure than WEP, attackers have cracked it.

Wi-Fi Protected Access 2 (WPA2) is the permanent fix for WEP. It is also known as 802.11i. If you have a choice among WEP, WPA, and WPA2, use WPA2. WPA2 provides the strongest security.

WEP is not recommended for use today. You should use at least WPA, but use WPA2 whenever possible. WEP is easy to crack. Even though WPA has vulnerabilities, it isn't as vulnerable as WEP.

When configuring Windows 8.1 to connect to a wireless network, you should have an understanding of the security types and encryption types available. It's also important to understand what each of these is doing:

Security Type   The security type identifies the type of authentication used. Authentication is used to verify a client's identity prior to allowing access.

Encryption Type   After the client connects, the data can be encrypted. This provides confidentiality by preventing others from being able to read the data. Advanced Encryption Standard (AES) is a strong, efficient encryption algorithm and is used with current wireless networks. WEP can also be selected as an encryption type for some security types. However, WEP is the weakest and is not recommended.

Figure 5.8 shows the security settings for a wireless profile named Verizon-890L-7EA7. As you can see, it is using the WPA2-Personal security type and AES as the encryption type.

FIGURE 5.8   Wireless profile security settings

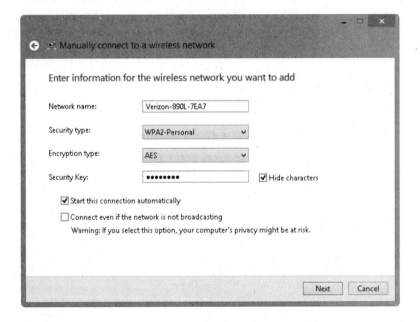

It's important to realize that you must match these settings to the wireless network. In other words, if your network is using a wireless access point with WPA2-Personal you must configure Windows 8.1 to use WPA2-Personal. Otherwise, the system won't connect.

Windows 8.1 supports the following security types:

No Authentication (Open)   This type uses no authentication. It is not recommended for use in a production environment but can be used for testing. You can select either WEP or None for encryption. If you select WEP, you also need to enter a preshared key (PSK).

This is also known as a password or passphrase. You need to enter the same PSK on the Windows 8.1 system as is used on the wireless device.

WPA-Personal *WPA-Personal* uses a preshared key for authentication. This PSK provides limited authentication. You can select either AES or Temporal Key Integrity Protocol (TKIP) for encryption. TKIP is compatible with older hardware, but AES is preferred if your hardware supports it.

WPA2-Personal *WPA2-Personal* is similar to WPA-Personal except it uses the stronger WPA2 authentication instead of WPA. WPA2-Personal uses a PSK. You enter the same PSK on the Windows 8.1 system and the wireless devices and you can select either AES or TKIP for encryption, though AES is preferred.

WPA-Enterprise *WPA-Enterprise* is similar to WPA-Personal except that it uses an additional network authentication method. It is dependent on a preconfigured authentication server on the network generically known as an 802.1x server. The 802.1x server will distribute the keys to each client instead of the clients using a PSK. It can also use smart cards, Protected Extensible Authorization Protocol (PEAP), or other methods of EAP for authentication. Smart cards provide strong security, but they also require more resources on your network. For example, you must have a Public Key Infrastructure (PKI) to issue certificates for the smart cards. You can select either AES or TKIP for encryption. AES is preferred.

WPA2-Enterprise *WPA2-Enterprise* is the strongest security type available with Windows 8.1 wireless networks. It uses an 802.1x server for authentication just as WPA-Enterprise does. It can use smart cards, PEAP, or one of the other EAP methods for authentication. Smart cards provide the best authentication. You can select either AES or TKIP for encryption. AES is preferred.

802.1x The 802.1x security type was intended to provide better protection for WEP by providing a better authentication mechanism when WEP was used. With WEP no longer recommended, this setting is also not recommended. 802.1x uses WEP for encryption.

There's an important distinction when using 802.1x servers. The specific 802.1x security type is not recommended because it uses WEP and WEP is not secure. However, WPA-Enterprise and WPA2-Enterprise both use 802.1x authentication servers with either AES or TKIP for encryption, and these configurations are much stronger than WEP with an 802.1x server. WPA2-Enterprise with AES provides the best security, and it is recommended for use in enterprise environments.

Managing Preferred Wireless Networks

Metered connections, new in Windows 8.1, give you the ability to control and track usage of certain wireless connections. Additionally, when selected, they give preference to unmetered connections to download certain data. They are very useful when you are using a pay-as-you-go data plan.

For example, imagine a user has a mobile hotspot that connects with a cellular network such as Verizon and then broadcasts as a wireless access point. This hotspot uses a pay-as-you-go plan, and if the user exceeds a usage limit such as 2 GB per month, he'll be charged additional fees. The user also has a wireless connection he uses at home connected through a broadband connection that isn't subject to any usage limits.

The user periodically uses the mobile hotspot for connections when outside the home and the home wireless connection when at home. If these two were treated equally, the mobile hotspot might be used to automatically download Windows Updates. Depending on what the updates include, this could consume the user's entire monthly data limit.

However, if the user sets the mobile hotspot connection as a metered connection, Windows 8.1 will not use it for Windows Updates. Instead, Windows 8.1 waits until the nonmetered connection is connected and will use it. Additionally, when the setting is enabled Windows 8.1 will track the usage for it.

Figure 5.9 shows what you'll see when you select a connection configured as a metered connection. The Verizon-890L-7EA7 connection is a mobile hotspot, and it shows that it has transferred about 3.47 MB of data in the past day. The context menu appears when you right-click the connection. If desired, you can select Hide Estimated Data Usage to remove the display.

FIGURE 5.9 Wireless metered connection

Set As Non-Metered Connection is displayed when the connection is set as a metered connection. If you select it, it changes to Set As Metered Connection.

Figure 5.9 also shows the only way you can set a network as a preferred network for connection purposes. When you select Connect Automatically, Windows 8.1 will automatically connect to this network when it is in range. If you have two wireless connections and both are set to connect automatically, Windows 8.1 gives preference to the nonmetered network.

 Windows 7 includes a Manage Wireless Networks link in the Network and Sharing Center when a computer has wireless capabilities. However, this tool is not available in Windows 8.1. Windows 8.1 manages these wireless networks automatically, and you cannot access the wireless profile settings anywhere else. Also, you can access these wireless profiles only when the wireless network is in range.

Connecting to a Wireless Network

If you have a Windows 8.1 system with a wireless NIC, you'll need to configure it before you can connect to a wireless network. It's worth noting that a wireless NIC can come in many different forms. It could be an internal card within a desktop PC or laptop computer. It could also be a USB dongle that plugs into a USB port for connectivity. You should ensure that the computer has up-to-date drivers for the wireless NIC before configuring it.

Once the wireless NIC is recognized by the computer, you can create a wireless profile for it. You'll need to have the following information:

- The name of the wireless network configured on the wireless access point (WAP) or wireless router
- The security type used by the wireless network
- The encryption type used by the wireless network
- The security key if one is used

 The name of the wireless network is also called the Service Set Identifier (SSID). Wireless devices come with default names such as Linksys. However, it's common for administrators to rename the SSID to something else for security reasons.

Exercise 5.5 shows how to configure a wireless NIC profile. This exercise assumes you're logged on to a Windows 8.1 system and the Start screen is showing.

EXERCISE 5.5

Configuring a Wireless NIC

1. Press Windows logo key+W to open the Search Settings charm.
2. Enter **Network and Sharing** in the text box and select Network And Sharing Center.

Exercise 5.5 *(continued)*

3. Click Set Up A New Connection Or Network.

4. Select Manually Connect To A Wireless Network and click Next.

5. In the Network Name text box, enter the SSID or the name of the wireless network.

6. Select the Security Type used by the wireless network device.

7. Enter the security key or passphrase used by the wireless network device.

8. If you always want to use this wireless network when it is available, select Start This Connection Automatically. If the SSID is not broadcasting, you can select Connect Even If The Network Is Not Broadcasting. Your display will look similar to the following graphic. Click Next, and then click Close.

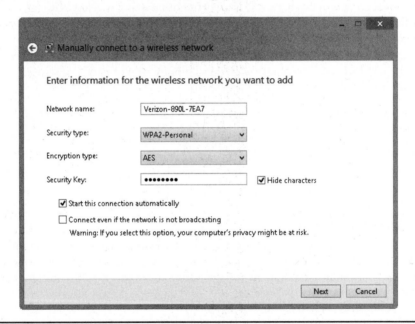

Exercise 5.6 shows how to designate a wireless connection as a metered connection. This exercise assumes you're logged on to a Windows 8.1 system and the Start screen is showing.

EXERCISE 5.6

Creating a Metered Connection

1. Move the mouse to the top-right corner and select Search to open the Search charm. Select Settings from the drop-down menu and search for "Change Wi-Fi settings."

2. Click Change Wi-Fi settings from the search results. The default Wi-Fi pane will appear. You can also open Networks via the PC Settings charm and click on the Wi-Fi setting you want to change.

3. Click Set As Metered Connection. Windows 8.1 will now give a higher preference to other connections not set as metered connections.

4. Click on the connection you just selected as a metered connection. It now displays additional data in this section showing how much data has been downloaded. You can also reset this connection to have it start from 0 again.

Most cellular plans are charged on a monthly basis. When you enable metered connections, you can reset it on the same day that your monthly connection is reset.

Exercise 5.7 shows how to connect to a wireless network using the Network and Sharing Center. This exercise assumes a wireless NIC has been configured, you're logged on to a Windows 8.1 system, and the Start screen is showing.

EXERCISE 5.7

Connecting to a Wireless Network

1. Press Windows logo key+W to open the Search Settings charm.

2. Enter **Network and Sharing** in the text box and select Network And Sharing Center.

3. Click Change Adapter Settings. You will see both wired and wireless NICs similar to what is shown in the following graphic. The graphic shows one wired NIC named Ethernet and one Wireless NIC named Wi-Fi.

4. Right-click the Wi-Fi NIC and select Connect/Disconnect. The Networks window appears along the right pane and shows wired connections under Connections and wireless networks under Wi-Fi.

5.   Select the Wi-Fi network that you want to connect to by clicking it. Click Connect. The system will attempt to make a connection with the WAP, and as long as the settings have been configured correctly, it will connect.

a.   If the network hasn't been configured, you'll be prompted to enter the Network Security Key (also known as the SSID preshared key). Enter the correct key and click Next.

b.   You'll be prompted to turn on sharing between PCs. If this is a public network, select No, Don't Turn On Sharing Or Connect To Devices. If this is a private network, select Yes, Turn On Sharing And Connect To Devices.

c.   If the settings are not configured correctly, you'll see a message indicating that the computer can't connect to the network. Click Close and you'll be returned to the Networks display on the right side of the screen.

d.   Right-click the Wi-Fi connection and select Status. Click the Wireless Properties button.

e.   Select the Security tab. You can select different settings for Security Type, Encryption Type, and Network Security Key. Enter the information used by your wireless network.

f.   Close all open windows.

Resolving Connectivity Issues

The symptoms a user may see and report when a computer has connectivity problems can be wild and varied. You might hear users say "The server is down," "Email doesn't work," or "This program doesn't work." When troubleshooting connectivity, you need go back to basics.

Basic network troubleshooting often starts with using the ipconfig command to check TCP/IP configuration and continues with the ping command to check connectivity. ipconfig (including ipconfig /all), discussed in greater depth earlier in this chapter, is useful in gathering several valuable pieces of information:

IP Address and Subnet Mask   An address of 169.254.y.z. should jump right out at you as an APIPA address. This tells you the client is a DHCP client but cannot reach a DHCP server.

Source of IP Address   If DHCP Enabled is set to Yes, you'll also see the IP address of the DHCP server. If DHCP Enabled is set to No, you won't see a DHCP address.

Default Gateway   The default gateway should be on the same subnet with the same network ID of the client. When TCP/IP is manually configured, the default gateway can sometimes be configured incorrectly through simple typos.

DNS Address   The DNS server is usually on a different subnet. You can use it to check connectivity through a router with ping. If you can ping the DNS server, you know you can get through the router via the default gateway. The DNS server address is also used by nslookup, and you can use nslookup to check for records on the DNS server, as shown earlier.

Armed with the information from ipconfig, you can check connectivity with other systems using basic troubleshooting steps such as these:

- Verify hardware and cabling.
- Use ping to test connectivity and determine the scope of the problem.
- Verify that name resolution is working.

Verifying Hardware and Cabling

If ipconfig doesn't list the network adapter or lists Media State as Media Disconnected, check the hardware. The NIC must be enabled, operating correctly, and connected to the network for normal network connectivity.

You can view the status of the adapter from the Network Connections display. Access this by clicking Change Adapter Settings in the Network and Sharing Center. Figure 5.10 shows the Ethernet display with an X and the message Network Cable Unplugged. The Wi-Fi connection is active without any problems.

FIGURE 5.10   Symptoms when the NIC is disconnected

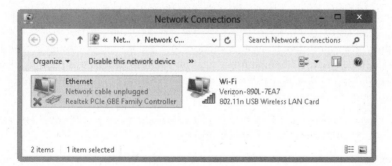

In this case, the cable could be unplugged or faulty at the NIC, at the network device (hub, switch, or router), or at one of the connections between the NIC and the network device, such as at a wall connection. When the cable is plugged in correctly, you should see a link light. However, if other symptoms show it's not connected the link light will be missing.

A quick check to determine whether the problem is internal to the computer (or external) is to swap the cables. Find another computer close by that's working and showing a good link light on the NIC and swap the cables. If the original faulty computer is still faulty, the problem is in the computer. If the original faulty computer now has a link light and shows that the NIC is connected, the problem is in the original cabling or the network device.

If the hardware is not the problem, you can use the built-in diagnostics within Windows 8.1 or use command prompt tools to check connectivity with other devices.

Exercise 5.8 shows how to verify and diagnose the network adapter. You can use these steps to reset the network adapter and can often resolve problems related to the NIC. This exercise assumes you're logged on to a Windows 8.1 system and the Start screen is showing.

EXERCISE 5.8

Verifying and Diagnosing the Network Adapter

1. Press Windows logo key+W to open the Search Settings charm.

2. Enter **Network and Sharing** in the text box and select Network And Sharing Center.

3. Launch the Troubleshoot Problems wizard:

   a. Click the Troubleshoot Problems link in the Change Your Networking Settings section.

   b. Select Network Adapter and follow the wizard to troubleshoot the network adapter(s) in the computer. These diagnostics run several checks and provide various results depending on what the diagnostics determine. If Internet access isn't detected, the adapter is reset, which will often resolve problems. Other times, a specific problem will be detected, and you may be prompted to apply the fix.

4. Troubleshoot a specific adapter with these steps:

   a. In the View Your Active Networks section, locate the adapter connection and click it. By default it is named Ethernet. You can also access this page by clicking Change Adapter Settings in the Network and Sharing Center, right-clicking the adapter, and selecting Status.

   b. Click the Details button. This shows you information you would see if you ran ipconfig /all from the command prompt.

   c. Click the Diagnose button. The Windows Network Diagnostics wizard will run. This runs similar to the wizard in the previous step.

Using Command Prompt Tools for Troubleshooting

If the wizard was unable to identify and resolve the problem, the issue probably isn't within the Windows 8.1 system. However, you can use some of the command prompt tools to check other issues on the network.

From a basic troubleshooting perspective, you should quickly try to determine the scope of the problem. After all, if the problem is affecting the entire network, you don't need to spend much time troubleshooting a single system.

Consider Figure 5.11. Bob normally prints to a shared printer on Sally's computer, but for some reason it isn't working anymore. What should you do?

FIGURE 5.11   Troubleshooting a network problem

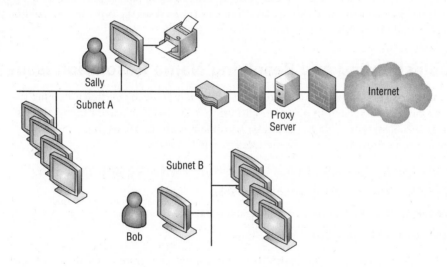

 It's important to remember that the Windows Firewall can block packets. If the ping requests succeed, you have verified connectivity. However, if the ping requests fail, it doesn't necessarily mean the other system is down.

Here are some steps that you can take using ping from Bob's computer to narrow down the scope of the problem:

Use `ipconfig` to check the TCP/IP configuration.   This step verifies that the local computer has a valid assigned IP address, subnet mask, and default gateway. If the IP address, subnet mask, or default gateway is incorrect, fix it and recheck the connection. You can also get the DNS server address by using `ipconfig /all`, and you should verify it has been entered correctly.

Ping Sally's computer by IP address.   You can do this to verify connectivity with Sally's computer.

Ping Sally's computer by name.   If the ping succeeds, it verifies that name resolution is working on the network. When ping is used to check connectivity with a hostname, it first resolves the name to an IP address. If the name can't be resolved, ping will reply, "Ping request could not find host." If name resolution works, the first line of the ping packet identifies the IP address.

Ping the IP address of the default gateway.   This is the near side of the router. If you can't get successful pings to the default gateway, you have either a TCP/IP configuration problem on the local system or a problem with the router. However, if the router has a problem, more than just a single person will be complaining.

Ping the local IP address and the loopback address.   If you can't successfully ping the local IP address or the loopback address (127.0.0.1), it indicates you have a problem with TCP/IP itself or a hardware problem with the NIC. You can try to reset the NIC or do a cold boot by completely shutting down the computer and restarting it.

Troubleshooting and Resolving Name Resolution Issues

If you can successfully ping the IP address of a client but you can't successfully ping the name, the problem is related to name resolution. In a Microsoft network today, this usually indicates a problem with DNS but could be a problem with the Hosts file.

Here are some basic steps you should take:

- Verify that the client is configured with the correct IP address of a DNS server.

- Verify that DNS is operational and reachable.

- Verify that DNS is responding to name requests.

- Verify that DNS has a record for the name.

You can accomplish these steps with the basic command prompt tools of ipconfig, ping, and nslookup, as discussed earlier.

If recent work was accomplished on DNS, the system may have either incorrect TCP/IP configuration information or stale DNS records. You can renew the DHCP lease by using ipconfig /release and ipconfig /renew to verify that the client is configured with current DHCP information.

Use ipconfig /displaydns to view the records currently in cache. If you suspect they are stale records with incorrect IP addresses, you can use ipconfig /flushdns to remove existing records and ensure only new records are used. If records remain after flushing the DNS cache, check the Hosts file at %windir%\System32\Drivers\etc. Malware sometimes modifies this file to prevent access to specific servers.

Exercise 5.9 shows the steps you can use to check name resolution issues. This exercise assumes you're logged on to a Windows 8.1 system with Internet access and the Start screen is showing.

EXERCISE 5.9

Using Hostname Resolution Methods

1. With the Start screen showing, start typing **command**. The Search screen appears as you start typing. When the command prompt appears, select it.

2. Enter the following command to resolve a name using DNS:

    ```
    ping blogs.getcertifiedgetahead.com
    ```

    The first line should be something like this:

    ```
    Pinging msn.com [174.122.52.195] with 32 bytes of data:
    ```

    The IP address verifies that name resolution is working. It's possible that the GetCertifiedGetAhead.com domain will block the ping, so you might see Request Timed Out errors. However, this method still verifies that name resolution using DNS is working.

3. Enter the following command to view the host cache entries:

    ```
    ipconfig /displaydns
    ```

    You'll see that the address of `blogs.getcertifiedgetahead.com` is included in this result with other data from the answering DNS server. The Time To Live line indicates how long (in seconds) the entry will remain in cache.

    ```
    -----------------------------------------
    Record Name . . . . . : blogs.getcertifiedgetahead.com
    Record Type . . . . . : 1
    Time To Live  . . . . : 83132
    Data Length . . . . . : 4
    Section . . . . . . . : Answer
    A (Host) Record . . . : 174.122.52.195
    ```

4. Enter the following command to clear the host cache of all DNS entries:

    ```
    ipconfig /flushdns
    ```

5. Enter the following command to view the host cache entries again:

    ```
    ipconfig /displaydns
    ```

    You'll see that the address of `blogs.getcertifiedgetahead.com` is no longer shown. The only entries showing are those derived from the Hosts file, if any exist.

6. Enter the following command to open the Hosts file:

    ```
    notepad %windir%\System32\Drivers\etc\hosts
    ```

    The Hosts file normally only has comments with every line starting with a # character. These are ignored by the computer. If you see any lines without the # character, it indicates a line has been added and will be recognized by the system.

7. Close all open systems.

Summary

In this chapter you learned about many of the basics of networking with Windows 8.1 clients. TCP/IP is used in Microsoft networks, and for the most part, TCP/IP works the same in Microsoft networks as it does in other networks. The majority of Windows 8.1 clients in an enterprise receive TCP/IP configuration via DHCP. If DHCP isn't working, the client will be assigned an APIPA address starting with 169.254.

Both IPv4 and IPv6 are enabled by default in Windows 8.1. IPv4 uses dotted decimal format to represent 32 bits with four decimals separated by dots. IPv6 has 128 bits and uses eight groups of four hexadecimal characters, each separated by colons. IPv6 addresses are shortened by omitting leading zeroes and with zero compression.

Name resolution resolves computer names to IP addresses. DNS is the primary method used. Three tools that are valuable when troubleshooting DNS and other networking issues are ping, IPconfig, and NSlookup. You learned how to use these tools for basic troubleshooting.

The Network and Sharing Center is a central console that lets you quickly identify connectivity for a Windows 8.1 client and configure various settings. You can use it to determine whether the network type is identified as public or private. When it is configured as public, Network Discovery is disabled, and the Windows Firewall blocks all unsolicited incoming connections.

Wireless is commonly used on many computers today. Security can be implemented with WEP, WPA, or WPA2. WEP is not secure and should not be used. WPA2 is the strongest. WPA and WPA2 support either Personal or Enterprise modes such as WPA2-Personal or WPA2-Enterprise. Personal modes use a preshared key or password. WPA2-Enterprise provides the best security, and it is combined with an authentication server. The Windows 8.1 client must match the settings used on the wireless devices in the network.

Many tools are available to resolving connectivity issues, including built-in diagnostics. If the diagnostics don't resolve the problems, use command-line tools such as ping, IPconfig, and NSlookup.

Exam Essentials

Understand networking basics.   Networks use TCP/IP and traffic is sent over the network using unicast, multicast, or broadcast messages for IPv4. IPv4 addresses use a subnet mask to differentiate the network ID from the host ID, and all systems on the same subnet must have the same network ID. DHCP is commonly used to assign IP addresses, but they can also be manually assigned. You should be able to identify misconfigured clients.

Know the differences between IPv4 and IPv6.   Windows 8.1 supports both IPv4 and IP6, and you should know the differences between them, including how the addresses are used and assigned. You should also be familiar with basic TCP/IP settings, including the IP address, subnet mask, default gateway, and DNS server address, and how to configure these settings.

Understand name resolution.   Names are resolved to IP addresses using several different methods. Hostnames are used on the Internet and primarily resolved with DNS. NetBIOS names (also known as single-label names) are used only in internal networks and are not compatible with IPv6. Other name resolution methods are the DNS resolver cache, the Hosts file, LLMNR, WINS servers, the Lmhosts file, and the NetBIOS cache.

Know how to use command-line tools.   You should be familiar with IPconfig, ping, and NSlookup and how you can use them to verify and troubleshoot network problems. The ipconfig command is useful for verifying and resetting some basic TCP/IP settings. Ping is used to verify connectivity with other systems. NSlookup is used to check DNS and verify that records exist.

Know the capabilities of the Network and Sharing Center.   Know how to access and use the Network and Sharing Center. You should especially be aware of the differences in public and private network location profiles, how to configure these settings, and how to select a network location profile.

Know how to configure wireless connectivity.   Understand that wireless connection settings on the Windows 8.1 computer must match those on the wireless devices. Security is very important with wireless. Windows 8.1 supports WEP, WPA, and WPA2. WEP should be avoided. WPA2 is the strongest. WPA-Personal and WPA2-Personal use a preshared key. WPA-Enterprise and WPA2-Enterprise use an 802.1x server for authentication. WPA2-Enterprise with smart card authentication provides the best protection.

Understand metered connections.   Wireless connections can be set as metered connections so that Windows doesn't use them automatically for some downloads such as Windows Update. When two wireless connections are set to connect automatically and one is a metered connection, the nonmetered connection will be used as the preferred connection.

Review Questions

You can find the answers in Appendix A.

1. You are troubleshooting a computer that is having connectivity issues. You use `ipconfig` and determine that it has an address of 169.254.4.7. What is the problem?

    A. DNS is not working.

    B. DHCP is not working.

    C. The network location is set to private.

    D. The network location is set to public.

2. Your organization is planning on implementing DirectAccess so that users can access the organization's network when working from home. Of the following choices, what must be included in the plan?

    A. IPv6

    B. WINS

    C. HomeGroups

    D. Preferred wireless settings

3. Your network uses IPv6 addresses. Of the following choices, what is a valid IPv6 address?

    A. 2000 : 0021 : 4137 : 0000 : 006C : 0000 : 01E5

    B. 2000 : 0021 : 0 : 4137 : 0 : 6C : 0 : 0 : 1E5

    C. 2000 : 21 : 4137 : 0 : 6C :: 1E5

    D. 2000 : 21 : 4137 :: 6C :: 1E5

4. You are troubleshooting a Windows 8.1 computer. It needs an IPv6 address to connect to an Internet resource, but you're getting an error indicating that it doesn't have an IPv6 address. Using `ipconfig`, you've verified it has an IPv6 of FE8 : 21 : 137 :: 6C : 1E5. What is the most likely problem?

    A. The computer isn't assigned an anycast address.

    B. The computer isn't assigned a global unicast address.

    C. The computer isn't assigned a link local address.

    D. The computer isn't assigned a unique local address.

5. You are troubleshooting a Windows 8.1 client that is unable to connect to most resources on the network. After troubleshooting it you realize you can successfully ping the IP address of some resources but it fails when you try to ping the name. What is the most likely problem?

    A. DHCP

    B. DNS

    C. Default gateway

    D. An APIPA address is assigned.

6. Your organization includes over 100 computers configured in a domain. What would these computers use for name resolution?

   A. DHCP

   B. DNS

   C. Domain controller

   D. WINS

7. Which one of the following commands can you use to see whether a DNS server can resolve a hostname to an IP address?

   A. `ipconfig`

   B. `nslookup`

   C. `ping`

   D. `tracert`

8. You suspect that the DNS resolver cache has incorrect entries. What can you use to remove the entries?

   A. `ipconfig`

   B. `nslookup`

   C. `ping`

   D. Disable DHCP

9. A Windows 8.1 computer has a DHCP lease. The DHCP was recently modified with new information and you want the computer to get a new lease. What should you use?

   A. APIPA

   B. `nslookup`

   C. `ping`

   D. `ipconfig`

10. A user is connecting her home computer directly to the Internet through her ISP. She doesn't have a home network and her computer is assigned an IP address from the ISP. What type of network location profile should she use?

    A. Private

    B. Public

    C. Domain

    D. IPv6

11. Of the following choices, what is the easiest way to disable Network Discovery on a Windows 8.1 system so that other users cannot see it?

    A. Disable the firewall.

    B. Create a rule in the firewall.

    C. Select the private network location.

    D. Select the public network location.

12. A user has configured a home network with a wireless router and three internal computers. Which network location should he choose when setting up networking for a Windows 8.1 computer?

   A. Domain

   B. Internal

   C. Public

   D. Private

13. You are running Windows 8.1 on a public network and want to share some files with a friend running Windows 7. You try to create a HomeGroup but can't get it to work. What is the most likely reason why this is not working?

   A. HomeGroups are not available for Windows 7.

   B. HomeGroups can only be created in a public network.

   C. HomeGroups can only be created in a domain network.

   D. HomeGroups can only be created in a private network.

14. A user has recently joined a HomeGroup and realizes that documents are being shared that she doesn't want shared. What can the user do to stop sharing these documents but access HomeGroup resources from other computers?

   A. Leave the HomeGroup.

   B. Change the Media Device section to Off.

   C. Change the Documents section to Not Shared.

   D. Change the Files section to Not Shared.

15. You are configuring a wireless network for a home network. You want to ensure the strongest possible security is used, but you do not have access to an authentication server. What should you use?

   A. WEP

   B. WPA-Enterprise

   C. WPA2-Personal

   D. WPA2-Enterprise

16. A user has a computer with a wired and a wireless connection. The user wants to ensure that Microsoft Updates are not downloaded on the wireless connection. What should the user do?

   A. Set the wireless connection to metered.

   B. Set the wireless connection to nonmetered.

   C. Set the wired connection to metered.

   D. Set the wired connection to nonmetered.

17. A user has a laptop running Windows 8.1. He connects to a wireless network at home and a wired network at work. He wants to ensure that he can download updates automatically from his home network. What should he do?

    A. Set his work network connection to metered.

    B. Set his work network connection to nonmetered.

    C. Set his home network connection to metered.

    D. Set his home network connection to nonmetered.

18. Of the following choices, what can you use to connect to a wireless network on a Windows 8.1 system?

    A. Access the Control Panel and click on the Wireless applet.

    B. Access the Network selection from the Settings charm.

    C. Access the Network selection from the Devices charm.

    D. Click Manage Wireless Networks in the Network and Sharing Center.

19. Your organization is planning on implementing a wireless network. They want to use the best possible security and ensure that users authenticate before being granted access to the network. What should they use?

    A. WPA2-Enterprise

    B. WPA2-Personal

    C. AES

    D. TKIP

20. You need to manually assign an IP address to a Windows 8.1 computer. What should you access to make this change?

    A. Access the Network page from the Settings charm.

    B. Access the Network Adapters from the PC Settings page.

    C. Access the Ethernet applet in the Control Panel.

    D. Access the Network Connections page from the Network and Sharing Center.

Chapter

6

Windows Firewall and Remote Access

70-687 MICROSOFT EXAM OBJECTIVES COVERED IN THIS CHAPTER:

✓ Configure remote access and mobility

70-688 MICROSOFT EXAM OBJECTIVES COVERED IN THIS CHAPTER:

✓ Maintain resource access

✓ Maintaining and supporting mobile devices

✓ Syncing files between devices

Security is an integral part of any administrator's job. Computers continue to be attacked, and it's only getting worse. Similarly, the amount of money and data lost because of attacks continues to rise. One way to combat attacks on your computer is to use a firewall to ensure the data coming into your computer originates from an authorized source. Windows 8.1 includes Windows Firewall, which has been a key component of the Windows operating system since Windows XP.

This chapter introduces you to Windows Firewall. In Windows 8.1, Windows Firewall is a program that adds a layer of protection to your computer to guard against network attacks, including attacks from the Internet.

Windows Firewall is enabled by default. Depending on your network access needs—or any requirements of the software you use on your computer—you may have to modify the settings. This chapter shows you how to configure Windows Firewall.

This chapter also discusses setting up and using Windows remote access features. With remote access, users can connect to a computer at a remote location and take over that computer as if they are sitting in front it physically. Many times remote access is required to perform technical support on a remote computer, modify settings on a remote server, or perform other tasks while not sitting at a computer.

CERT OBJECTIVE Configuring Windows Firewall

Windows Firewall has been standard since Windows XP. In Windows XP SP2, it was enabled by default, and it has steadily improved over the years. A *firewall* is designed to protect a computer or network by controlling inbound and outbound traffic. Most firewalls operate with an "implicit deny" philosophy. In other words, all traffic is blocked (implicitly denied) unless there is a rule that explicitly allows the traffic.

Windows Firewall on Windows 8.1 uses an implicit deny philosophy. The only traffic that is allowed is the following:

- Traffic that is explicitly allowed by an exception or a rule. Both inbound and outbound rules can be configured.

- Return traffic that has been requested. For example, if a user requests a web page from a website, the web page is allowed as return traffic.

Windows Firewall works as a packet-filtering firewall. Data on a network, such as the Internet, travels via packets. The packets each have a header, which includes information (such as source and destination) about the data within that packet. A *packet-filtering firewall* allows only those packets of data permitted by your firewall policy to pass through the firewall. The packet-filtering firewall inspects every packet and then determines whether or not that packet can pass.

There are two types of packet-filtering firewalls: stateless and stateful. Windows Firewall is a stateful firewall. A stateful firewall, also known as a smart or dynamic firewall, can monitor the state of a connection. Instead of examining each packet individually, it evaluates the packets in the conversation. This enables a stateful firewall to detect and block many attacks. With a stateless firewall, the packets of information that are processed by the firewall are not logged or saved.

A packet-filtering firewall can filter traffic based on IP addresses, ports, and some protocols. Packets can be allowed or blocked based only on what is in each packet. However, unlike a stateful firewall, a stateful firewall cannot evaluate packets based on the entire communication.

As noted earlier, a stateful firewall can monitor the state of a connection established through it. Stateful firewalls can inspect and filter all IPv4 and IPv6 traffic.

The types of packet information analyzed by the firewall are as follows:

Source IP Address of the Packet   The firewall can block or restrict traffic by the source IP address of the packet.

Destination IP Address   The firewall can block, restrict, or redirect traffic by the destination IP address of the packet.

TCP/UDP Port Number   TCP/UDP ports are used in denial-of-service (DoS) attacks. Abnormal traffic on these ports will be picked up by the firewall.

IP Protocol ID   These IDs translate into port numbers; however, some firewalls are able to be configured to monitor according to the detected IP protocol ID.

ICMP Message Type   These types determine what message is returned the client. A firewall can use this information for reporting and detection of attempted DoS through ICMP traffic flooding.

Fragmentation Flags   These determine how fragmented data is reassembled.

Windows Firewall includes a feature called *stealth mode* that is used to combat against attacks that start by trying to determine your computer's operating system (OS). (This is called OS fingerprinting.) In stealth mode, the firewall receives probing packets that hackers use to determine what services and equipment it can target. The firewall simply loses the packets and does not send anything back to the source.

When you configure Windows Firewall, it is important to note that your configuration changes affect only the current Windows profile. If you make several changes to firewall exceptions and other configuration changes, and then log in as a different user, those changes will not be applied.

Exercise 6.1 shows how to configure Windows Firewall on a system. This exercise assumes you're logged into Windows 8.1.

EXERCISE 6.1

Configuring Windows Firewall

1. Right-click the Start button and select Search. In the Search box type **Windows Firewall**.

2. Click the Windows Firewall icon.

3. On the left side of the Windows Firewall window, select Turn Windows Firewall On or off. This opens the Customize settings for each type of network dialog box as shown below.

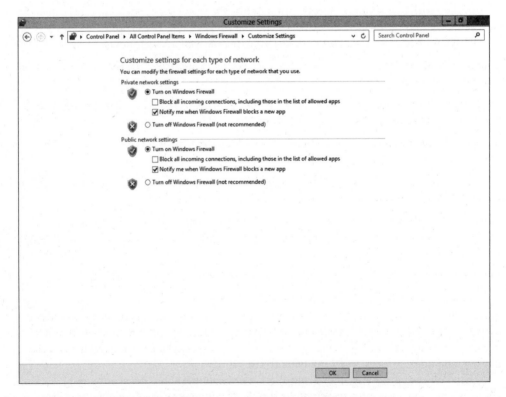

4. In the Private Network Settings area, click Turn On Windows Firewall.

5. In the Public Network Settings area, click Turn On Windows Firewall.

6. Click OK to save your changes.

Firewall Limitations

Firewalls do not protect your computer against viruses. Viruses are malicious forms of software intended to harm your computer, services, and programs or to steal data. Firewalls are not used to protect against these forms of attacks. Rather, antivirus software, such as Windows Defender or similar products, have the capability to track incoming programs and either alert you to possible virus attacks or remove the threat when a virus is on your computer.

Firewalls also do not protect against malware or adware. Again, third-party programs designed to track and eliminate or minimize the attack of malware or adware are necessary to protect your computer.

Another common threat for computer users is email spam. Firewalls do not protect against spam. Your email provider or email server software must be designed to catch spam, or you must use a third-party product to detect, capture, and eliminate email spam.

Windows Firewall Exceptions

Windows Firewall exceptions can be set for several reasons. For example, firewall exceptions allow incoming network connections for certain programs and services that need unrestricted network traffic. Another reason to set up a firewall exception is to allow specific ports from which to allow incoming traffic. For example, a website devoted to providing secure school exams might require a specific port open to ensure secure and confidential test-taking procedures. In this case, a specific port that is not the common port 80 (which is the default port for website access) would need to be configured as an exception in your firewall.

As a general rule, most programs you install on your computer are preconfigured by Windows Firewall to allow incoming and outgoing traffic. However, if an exception is not set, you would need to set that as a manual exception. The top link on the left of the Windows Firewall status screen is labeled Allow A Program Or Feature Through Windows Firewall. Click this link to create an exception for various applications. When an exception is enabled, traffic will be allowed. To create an exception, select the check box for any of the features listed. You can create an exception for an application by clicking the Allow Another Program button. Most installed programs will automatically appear in this list, but you can also click Browse to locate a particular application.

When setting port exceptions, you must specify the port number and set the type of network protocol in use. The port number is obtained from the vendor, software publisher, website, or service for which you are applying the port exception. If you are not sure of this port number, do not guess. Contact technical support or another key contact for that company and ask for the specific port information. If you do not enter the correct port number, the software, website, or service will not communicate properly with your computer.

Similarly, set the network protocol type to TCP or UDP based on information from the software or website company. TCP is used in most cases, but UDP is common for multicasting and broadcasting data.

An optional feature when setting the port exception is to change the scope of a firewall rule. The scope feature enables you to specify the remote computer by its specific IP address, rather than a range.

Exercise 6.2 shows how to configure Windows Firewall exceptions on a system. This exercise assumes you're logged into Windows 8.1 and Windows Firewall is turned on.

EXERCISE 6.2

Configuring Windows Firewall Exceptions

1. Right-click the Start button and select Search. In the Search box type **Windows Firewall**.

2. Click the Windows Firewall icon.

3. On the left side of the Windows Firewall window, select Allow An App Or Feature Through Windows Firewall.

4. On the Allow Apps to Communicate through Windows Firewall window, click the Change Settings button. If you are not logged in as an Administrator, you will be prompted for a password.

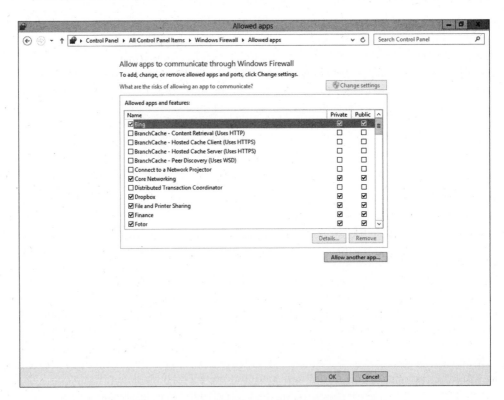

5. Select an app or program from the Allowed Apps And Features list.

6. Click the check box in the Private and Public columns to allow the selected app to communicate through Windows Firewall.

7. Click OK to save your settings.

Windows Firewall with Advanced Security

For most of your general network and Internet traffic, you can use Windows Firewall. In some cases, however, you may need to use Windows Firewall with Advanced Security. Windows Firewall with Advanced Security provides three distinct differences over Windows Firewall:

- You can configure outbound and inbound network traffic using Windows Firewall with Advanced Security. With Windows Firewall, you can configure only inbound traffic.

- With Windows Firewall with Advanced Security, you are not limited to configuring firewall exceptions for only the current profile as you are with Windows Firewall. Instead, you can configure all network profiles at the same time.

- For those instances when you need to specify IPsec traffic rules, you must use Windows Firewall with Advanced Security instead of Windows Firewall.

> **NOTE** IPsec is a network technology that encrypts network traffic so another computer cannot intercept that traffic. IPsec uses digital signatures to help protect network traffic. With Windows Firewall with Advanced Security, you can set the following IPsec parameters: Data Protection, Key Exchange, and Authentication Method. See `http://technet.microsoft.com/en-us/library/cc730833(v=ws.10).aspx`.

For minimum security, a two-way firewall that combines inbound and outbound protection is highly recommended. Inbound protection ensures only allowed connections can access your computer from the Internet or other network. The outbound protection stops spyware from sending your data (which originates from your computer inside the firewall) out to the Internet.

With Windows Firewall with Advanced Security, you can turn Windows Firewall on or off for each network profile, or use the same configuration for all network profiles. For these profiles, you can set inbound and outbound to allow network traffic or to block network traffic. As you work with Windows Firewall with Advanced Security, note that by default the Public network profile is set so all incoming traffic is blocked and all outgoing traffic is allowed. For Private network profiles, however, the default is that both incoming and outgoing traffic is blocked. The Block All Connections option is used to block all incoming traffic. When you set Block All Connections, be advised that this overrides any specific inbound exceptions that you may have previously configured.

Exercise 6.3 shows how to use Windows Firewall with Advanced Security on a system. This exercise assumes you're logged into Windows 8.1.

EXERCISE 6.3

Using Windows Firewall with Advanced Security

1. Right-click the Start button and select Control Panel. Set the Control Panel to use Large icons.

2. Click the Windows Firewall with Advanced Security icon.

3. On the left side of the Windows Firewall with Advanced Security window, click Inbound Rules or Outbound Rules depending on the type of rule you want to create. For this exercise, you're configuring an inbound rule, so select Inbound Rules.

4. Select New Rule.

5. Choose a rule type. If you want to see all the rule options available to you, select Custom and click Next.

6. Select the programs or services affected by this rule. Click Next.

7. Select the protocol type.

8. Select the local and remote port numbers for this rule. Click Next.

9. Select the local and remote IP addresses for this rule. Click Next.

10. Specify one of these connection rules: Allow The Connection, Allow The Connection Only If It Is Secure or Block The Connection. Click Next.

11. Indicate whether you want to allow connections only from specific users. Click Next.

12. Indicate whether you want to allow connections only from specific computers. Click Next.

13. Choose which profile(s) will be affected by this rule. Click Next.

14. Type a name and description for the profile. Click Finish.

The new custom rule appears in the list of Inbound Rules and is enabled by default.

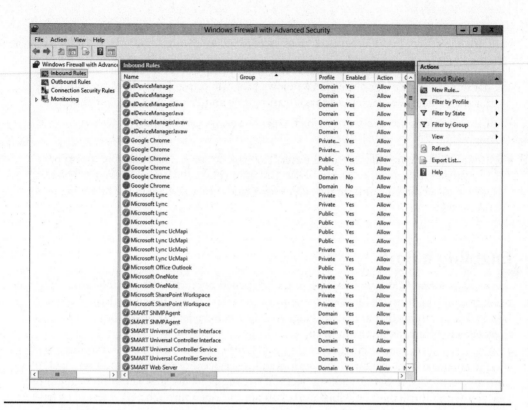

To troubleshoot or allow other computers to communicate with you, use the Incoming Connections troubleshooter. This troubleshooter helps you find and fix problems associated with network traffic and Windows Firewall. When you run the Incoming Connection troubleshooter, you specify one of the following types of networking tasks you want to perform:

- Share Files Or Folders
- Connect To This Computer Using Remote Desktop Connection
- Find This Computer On The Network
- Something Else

The Something Else option (the last item in the previous list) is used when you have issues connecting a specific program to your computer using a network connection.

Setting up inbound and outbound traffic rules requires that you use Windows Firewall with Advanced Security. The types of rules include the following:

- Predefined rules and custom rules. Predefined rules are prepackaged network configuration rules for a specific Windows program or service, such as firewall rules for the Windows Remote Assistance feature, File and Printer Sharing, and more.

- Custom rules provide a way in which you can specify certain network criteria for a rule.

- Connection secure rules are used to set IPsec traffic rules. The following four types of connection security rules can be set: isolation rule, authentication exemption rule, server-to-server rule, and tunnel rule. Those rules are described in the following sections.

Enabling a Port

Some applications require that certain ports be opened or traffic using certain protocols be allowed. If the traffic is blocked, the application won't work. When configuring newly installed applications that aren't working, you should consider the possibility that an exception needs to be created in the firewall.

When you make these changes (opening ports, for example), do so only according to specific and clear documentation for a program or service. For example, you may need to open a port to play an online game or access a streaming media site. Those sites should provide you with information on which ports you need to open through your firewall to have a successful connection. One of the most common ports to have open is port 80, which is for HTTP (web pages) traffic. Unless you or a third-party firewall application has changed the default settings in Windows 8.1, port 80 is open. Before you make any changes, be sure to document on your end which port you opened and which application or service you configured. This way, you can backtrack and close that port in the future should security issues arise.

Some other well-known ports are as follows:

- Port 20—FTP (File Transfer Protocol) data transfer
- Port 23—Telnet
- Port 24—Private mail system
- Port 25—Simple Mail Transport Protocol (SMTP)
- Port 53—Domain Name System (DNS)
- Port 443—Secure Hypertext Transport Protocol (HTTPS)

Exercise 6.4 shows how to enable a port in Windows Firewall. This exercise assumes you're logged into Windows 8.1.

EXERCISE 6.4

Enabling a Port

1. Right-click the Start button and select Control Panel. Set the Control Panel to use Large icons.

2. Click the Windows Firewall with Advanced Security icon.

3. Select Inbound Rules on the left side of the window.

4. Click New Rule on the right side of the window.

5. On the New Inbound Rule Wizard screen, click Port.

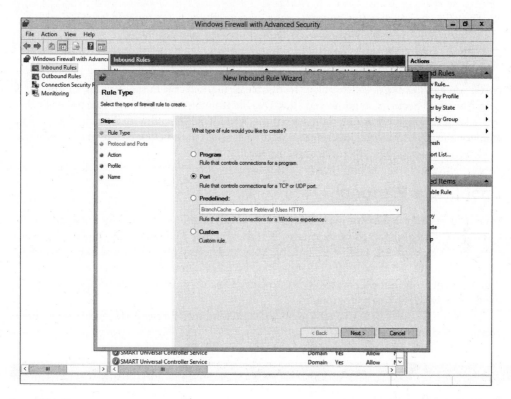

6. Click Next.

7. Select the type of port (TCP or UDP) the rule applies to.

8. In the Specific Local Ports field, type the ports you want to open. If you enter multiple ports, separate each port with a comma.

9. Click Next.

10. Select Allow The Connection To Open The Specified Port Number.

11. Click Next.

12. Specify on which type of network this rule applies. Your choices are Domain, Private, and Public. By default all are selected.

13. Click Next.

14. Type a name for the rule. You also can enter a description for the rule to help you remember why you established it.

15. Click Finish. The new rule appears in the Inbound Rules list in the Windows Firewall with Advanced Security window. By default the new rule is enabled.

If a port rule is no longer needed or if you want to diagnose network issues by closing ports, you can disable or delete rules. To disable a rule, select it in the Windows Firewall with Advanced Security window and click Disable Rule on the right side. Re-enable a rule by clicking Enable Rule on the right side of the Windows Firewall with Advanced Security window. Finally, if you no longer need a port rule, select it and click Delete in that window. Click Yes when prompted to confirm the deletion.

Enabling a Protocol

Similar to opening a port for network traffic, you can enable a protocol for network traffic. Common protocols enabled for normal web traffic include TCP and UDP. You might, however, want to specifically enable a protocol. You can use any protocol listed in the Internet Assigned Numbers Authority (IANA) specified by its number when you use the Custom protocol type in Windows Firewall with Advanced Security. To see a list of the IANA protocols, visit www.iana.org/protocols.

Exercise 6.5 shows how to enable a protocol in Windows Firewall. This exercise assumes you're logged into Windows 8.1.

EXERCISE 6.5

Enabling a Protocol

1. Right-click the Start button and select Control Panel. Set the Control Panel to use Large icons.

2. Click the Windows Firewall with Advanced Security icon.

3. Select Inbound Rules on the left side of the window.

4. Click New Rule on the right side of the window.

5. On the New Inbound Rule Wizard screen, click Custom.

6. Click Next.

7. Specify the type of program that the rule applies to. If it applies to all programs, click All Programs. For a specific program, enter the path to the program name in the This Program Path field, or click Browse to locate it on your system.

8. Click Next.

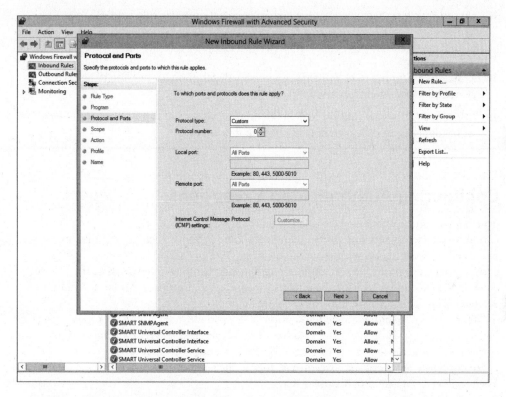

9. On the Protocol And Ports screen, select the type of protocol from the Protocol Type drop-down list. If you want to specify one that's not on the list, select Custom and then enter the protocol number in the Protocol Number field.

10. If available for your selected protocol, specify the local port and remote port options. Some protocols, such as IGMP, do not support modifying the port settings.

11. Click Next.

12. On the Scope screen, specify which local and remote IP addresses are affected by this new rule. You can specify all IP addresses, provide a list of IP addresses, or specify a range of IP addresses.

13. Click Next.

14. On the Action screen, select Allow The Connection option to indicate that network traffic should be allowed when using the specified protocol.

15. Click Next.

16. On the Profile screen, specify on which type of network this rule applies. Your choices are Domain, Private, and Public. By default all are selected.

17. Click Next.

18. Type a name for the rule. You also can enter a description for the rule to help you remember why you established the rule.

19. Click Finish. The new rule appears in the Inbound Rules list in the Windows Firewall with Advanced Security window. By default it is enabled.

Configuring Authenticated Exceptions

You can configure Windows Firewall to exempt computers or IP addresses from authenticating by setting up authentication exceptions. Some systems, such as domain controllers, may need network access without authenticating. You can set up rules specifying that certain ports, programs, or services can receive unauthenticated network traffic. These rules set up exceptions lists for these ports, programs, and services. You use Windows Firewall with Advanced Settings to configure authenticated exceptions.

When you set up authenticated exception rules, you must specify the computers that will be part of the rule by IP address, IP address range, the DNS servers that the computers use, or the role of the computer (such as default gateway and DHCP servers).

To configure authenticated exceptions, follow the steps in Exercise 6.6. This exercise assumes you're logged into Windows 8.1.

Configuring Authenticated Exceptions

1. Right-click the Start button and select Control Panel. Set the Control Panel to use Large icons.

2. Click the Windows Firewall with Advanced Security icon.

3. On the left side of the Windows Firewall with Advanced Security window, click Connection Security Rules.

4. Click New Rule on the right side of the screen.

5. Click Authentication Exemption in the New Connection Security Rule Wizard.

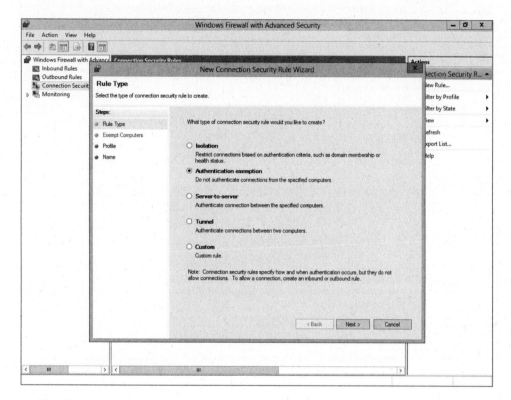

6. Click Next.

7. On the Exempt Computers screen, click Add.

8. On the IP Address screen, type the IP address or IP address range, or select a pre-defined set of computers.

EXERCISE 6.6 *(continued)*

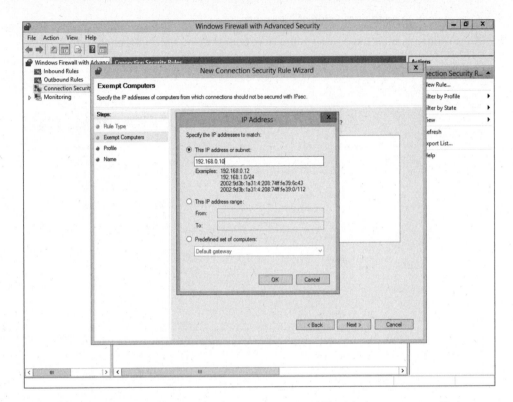

9. Click OK. The computer name, IP address, or range of IP addresses you specify is shown in the Exempt Computer list.

10. Click Next.

11. Specify on which type of network the new rule applies, such as on domain, private, or public networks.

12. Click Next.

13. Enter a name for the new rule. You also can enter a description of the rule.

14. Click Finish.

Configure Connection Security Rules (IPsec)

Windows Firewall with Advanced Security enables you to configure connection security rules, or IPsec rules. Connection security rules are used when you want to authenticate two computers before they can establish a connection. This method is also used to secure information that is transmitted between the two computers. To establish and enforce connection security rules, Window Firewall with Advanced Security uses IPsec. Once you set up the IPsec rule, you may need to also establish a firewall rule that allows network traffic between the computers specified in the IPsec rule.

The previous section showed how to configure authentication exception. You also can create the following types of connection security rules using Windows Firewall with Advanced Security:

Isolation Rule   This type of rule isolates computers by restricting inbound network traffic based on specific credentials. You can specify domain membership, authentication policies (such as computer credentials), or health status.

Server-To-Server Rule   This type of rule protects connections between specified computers, such as between servers. During the configuration process, you must specify the protected endpoints of the network, as well as the authentication types and requirements.

Tunnel Rule   A tunnel rule allows you to configure a secure connection between two computers. One scenario for using a tunnel connection security is when connecting two computers across the Internet between security gateways. When establishing this type of rule, specify the tunnel endpoints by IP address and specify the authentication method, such as a computer certificate.

Custom   Use a custom rule to authenticate connections when the isolation, authentication exemptions, server-to-server, or tunnel methods cannot be used.

The steps in Exercise 6.7 show how to create a connection security rule. This exercise assumes you're logged into Windows 8.1.

EXERCISE 6.7

Configuring Connection Security Rules (IPsec)

1. Right-click the Start button and select Control Panel. Set the Control Panel to use Large icons.

2. Click the Windows Firewall with Advanced Security icon.

3. On the left side of the Windows Firewall with Advanced Security window, click Connection Security Rules.

4. Click New Rule on the right side of the Windows Firewall with Advanced Security window.

5. Select type of connection security rule you want to create, such as Isolation.

EXERCISE 6.7 *(continued)*

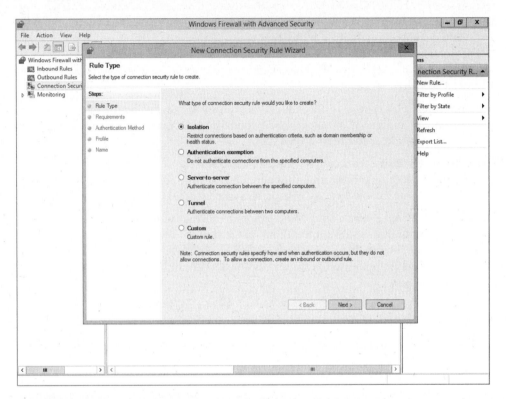

6. Click Next.

7. Specify when you want the authentication to occur. For example, you can specify that authentication is not required, that inbound authentication but not outbound authentication is required, or both inbound and outbound authentication is required.

8. Click Next.

9. Click Default to ensure the IPsec settings are used for authentication.

10. Click Next.

11. Specify on which type of network this rule applies, such as domain, private, or public. By default, all three are selected.

12. Click Next.

13. Enter a name for the new rule. You also can enter a description of the rule.

14. Click Finish.

Configuring Remote Management

The concept of remote management has been around for many years. Usually network administrators, systems administrators, and database administrators use some form of remote management tool to access system servers. Standard users now have many needs to be able to manage remotely, or have their systems managed remotely, using tools available in Windows 8.1.

Remote Access Overview

Remote access allows users to connect to the company's internal network while they are away from the network. They can be traveling, working at a remote customer's site, or working from home. Users can connect with a dial-up connection (albeit less common today) or a virtual private network connection (VPN).

A VPN connection allows a user to connect to a private network over a public network to a VPN server. The majority of the time, the public network is the Internet. Some VPN connections that connect offices use dedicated leased lines instead of the Internet as the public network.

> The terms remote access server and VPN server are sometimes confusing. Remote access server is generic, indicating that it provides remote access. However, VPN server is specific, indicating that remote access is provided using a VPN connection. In other words, a VPN server may also be called a remote access server. However, a remote access server that provides only dial-up access isn't a VPN server.

VPN connections use tunneling protocols. These tunneling protocols include encryption and provide additional protection for the connection. Windows 8.1 supports the following four tunneling protocols:

Internet Key Exchange version 2 (IKEv2)   IKEv2 is the newest tunneling protocol and was introduced with Windows 7 and Windows Server 2008 R2. It can also go through a network address translation (NAT) server and provides an additional choice over PPTP. Windows Vista, Windows Server 2008 servers, or older versions do not support IKEv2.

Secure Shell Tunneling Protocol (SSTP)   SSTP was introduced with Windows Vista and Windows Server 2008. It uses SSL to encrypt the traffic as HTTPS traffic. It can go through a NAT server, providing an additional choice if your VPN server is located behind a NAT server. SSTP provides better security than PPTP and supports both IPv4 and IPv6. You can use SSTP with clients running Windows Vista, Windows Server 2008, or later versions.

Layer 2 Tunneling Protocol (L2TP) L2TP was developed by combining the strengths of Microsoft's PPTP with the strengths of Cisco's Layer 2 Forwarding (L2F) protocol. It encrypts data using IPsec (and is shown as L2TP/IPsec) and supports both IPv4 and IPv6. The only drawback is that IPsec can't go through a NAT server. If the VPN had to go through a NAT, the previous recommendation was to use PPTP. You can use L2TP/IPsec with clients running Windows 2000 or later versions.

Point-to-Point Tunneling Protocol (PPTP) PPTP is the oldest of the four protocols. It encrypts data using Microsoft Point-to-Point Encryption (MPPE). PPTP is not supported on IPv6. While PPTP is still used today, you can expect it to be used less often in the future. You can use PPTP with clients running Windows 2000 or later versions.

> When taking the exams, remember that PPTP does not support IPv6. If your clients must use IPv6, you will not be able to use PPTP. IKEv2 is the most likely choice for Windows 8.1 clients connecting to a Windows Server 2008 R2 server or later.

IKEv2, L2TP/IPsec, and SSTP provide several important security protections:

- Data confidentiality by encrypting the data
- Data integrity (ensures the data hasn't been modified)
- Data authentication (verifies the hosts)

IKEv2 and SSTP both require the use of a public key infrastructure (PKI) to issue certificates. IPsec will work without a certificate using a preshared key, but we highly recommend that you use a certificate.

When you create a VPN connection, it will default to Automatic for the tunneling protocol. In other words, you don't have to choose which tunneling protocol the server is using. Windows 8.1 will attempt to connect to a VPN server using the different tunneling protocols in the following order:

1. IKEv2
2. SSTP
3. PPTP
4. L2TP

Choosing the Appropriate Remote Management Tools

Windows 8.1 offers several remote management tools. While you may already be familiar with some of them, there are others you may not yet have had a chance to use. These tools include the following:

- Remote Assistance
- Remote Desktop Connection

- Virtual Private Networks (VPN)
- Windows PowerShell
- DirectAccess
- BranchCache

The last item in the list, BranchCache, is not a tool that is used for a single computer (such as a client computer). Instead, it provides remote connectivity for remote or branch offices. You'll learn more about it later in this chapter.

Configuring Remote Management Settings

Before accessing a computer remotely, you need to prepare that computer for a remote access or Remote Assistance session. You have the choice of allowing Remote Assistance connections to a computer and to allow or not allow remote connections to a computer.

Remote Assistance is a tool that allows you to connect to a remote computer to provide assistance to another user currently logged into that computer. When you connect via Remote Assistance, you do not have to log into that computer; instead, invitations are sent from the host computer to you so you can take over the computer. You can use the remote computer (the host computer) as if you were sitting in front of it. The user on the other end can watch your activities onscreen. At any time, either user can terminate the session.

Many companies use Remote Assistance in two ways. One way is to use it as a help desk tool to connect to a user's computer while they are using the computer so as to interact with the user to resolve an issue with the computer. Another way is to use Remote Assistance as a distance learning tool to provide training to a user on different Windows or program features. Because the user on the host computer can see all the actions that the remote user performs on the desktop, it makes an excellent teaching tool to show users what menus to click, data to enter, actions to take, and so forth.

The steps shown in Exercise 6.8 show how to set up a computer (the host computer) to allow Remote Assistance. This exercise assumes you're logged into Windows 8.1.

EXERCISE 6.8

Configuring Remote Assistance

1. Right-click the Start button and select Search. In the Search box type **Remote**.

2. Select Allow Remote Assistance Invitations To Be Sent From This Computer. The System Properties dialog box appears, with the Remote tab showing.

3. Click Allow Remote Assistance Connections To This Computer.

EXERCISE 6.8 *(continued)*

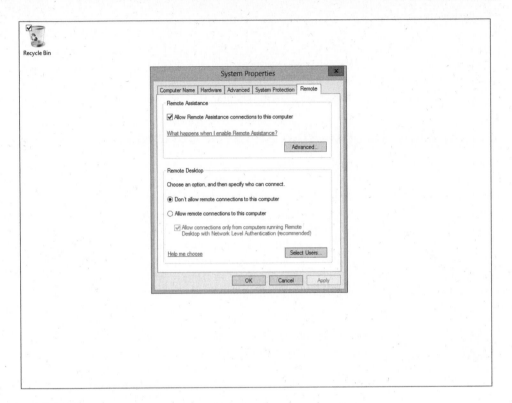

4.   Click OK.

A user on the host computer can now send an invitation to you to allow you to connect to that computer for repair or training purposes. Exercise 6.9 shows how to send an invitation. This exercise assumes you're logged into Windows 8.1.

EXERCISE 6.9

Sending a Remote Assistance Invitation

1.   Right-click the Start button and select Search. In the Search box type **Invite**.

2. Select Invite Someone To Connect To Your PC And Help You, or Offer To Help Someone Else. The Windows Remote Assistance window appears.

3. Click Invite Someone You Trust To Help You.

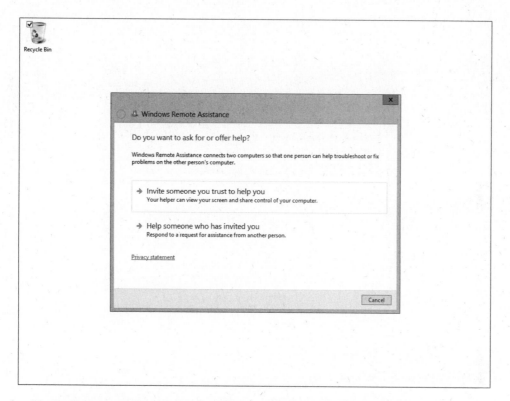

4. The invitation can be sent as a file attachment to an email or as the body of an email. This exercise uses the method of sending the invitation as an email attachment. An RA Invitation file is created, with an extension of .mrscIncident.

5. In the Save As dialog box, specify a location to save the RA Invitation.

6. Click OK. A Windows Remote Assistance dialog box appears, with a password showing.

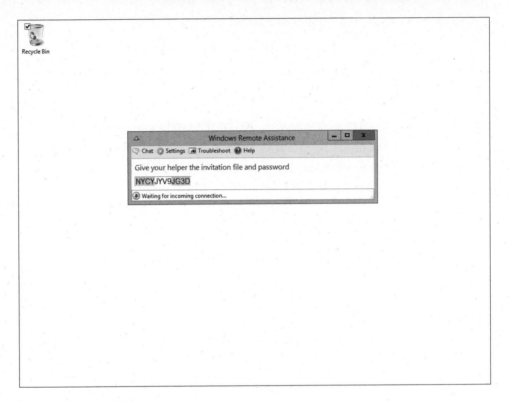

7. Open your email program.

8. Copy the password shown on the screen and paste it as part of your email. Also, attach the RA Invitation file created in step 5 earlier.

9. Send the email and attachment to the user you want to connect to your computer.

10. The trusted helper (which may be you) will need to open the email message, double-click the RA Invitation, enter the password generated in step 7 earlier, and click OK.

12. A message appears on the remote computer (host) that asks the user if they will allow the trusted helper to connect. Click Yes. The helper can now see the host computer desktop, request permission to control it, stop sharing it, send chat messages to the host computer, and end the session.

The Remote Assistance session is halted automatically when the Remote Assistance window is closed.

Configuring Remote Desktop Settings

Another Windows 8.1 remote management tool is Remote Desktop. Remote Desktop is used to access a computer remotely, usually when no one is currently logged into the remote computer. This makes managing a large inventory of computers much easier when you want to simply check the status of a system event, ensure a Group Policy was enabled, or view many other settings without leaving your desk. You might also use Remote Desktop to log into your work computer from home to check the status of a work-related event (such as if a key backup system executed properly).

 You cannot connect remotely to a computer that is asleep or hibernating. Because of this, ensure the remote computer (host) settings for sleep and hibernation are set to Never.

By default, Remote Desktop is not turned on in Windows 8.1. You must manually activate it prior to when you want to access a computer remotely. To activate Remote Desktop, use the steps shown in Exercise 6.10. This exercise assumes you're logged into Windows 8.1.

EXERCISE 6.10

Configuring Remote Desktop

1. Right-click the Start button and select Search. In the Search box type **Remote**.

2. Select Allow Remote Access To Your Computer. The System Properties dialog box appears, with the Remote tab displayed.

3. Click Allow Remote Connections To This Computer.

EXERCISE 6.10 *(continued)*

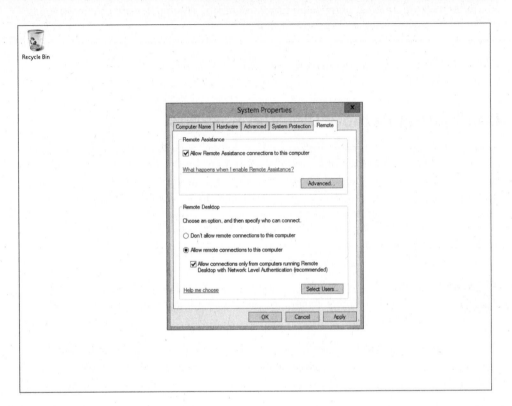

4. Click OK.

Your computer is now configured to allow users to connect to it remotely. You will learn in a later section ("Connecting to a Remote System with Remote Desktop Connection") how to connect to a remote computer.

Configuring Remote Authentication

Once you configure Remote Desktop settings in Windows, you may need to configure remote authentication to allow remote access traffic to your system. You can do this by modifying the Windows Firewall settings.

Another point to remember is that you must specify the users who can authenticate on your system using Remote Desktop. You can specify one or many users. If you are on a network domain, you can use security groups as well as individual user names to specify who can authenticate on your system.

When you set up to allow remote desktop access, you also can choose whether to require Network Level Authentication. Network Level Authentication is the recommended setting if you know that users with Windows 7 or Windows 8.1 will remotely connect to your computer. If other versions of Windows (most versions of Windows Vista will work) need to connect remotely, be sure to turn off the Network Level Authentication setting. With that said, most versions of Windows Vista and Windows XP, SP3 will work with Windows 8.1 Remote Desktop.

A quick way to tell if your version of Windows supports Network Level Authentication is to look at the About window in the Remote Desktop Connection client (which you'll learn about later). If the About window lists "Network Level Authentication supported," then you know it will be able to connect when that feature is turned on.

The way Network Level Authentication works is that it protects the remote computer from hackers and suspicious software (such as malware) by requiring authentication prior to establishing a full connection to the remote computer. This frees the remote computer or remote server from using up resources before an actual authentication occurs, greatly reducing DoS attacks. Network Level Authentication also provides for single sign-on (SSO) to Remote Desktop connections.

 Windows RT and Windows 8.1 (basic edition) can use Remote Desktop as a client only. Computers running those versions cannot be set up as Remote Desktop hosts, meaning you cannot remotely access them from another computer.

Exercise 6.11 shows how to configure Remote Desktop authentication. This exercise assumes you're logged into Windows 8.1.

EXERCISE 6.11

Configuring Remote Desktop Authentication

1. Right-click the Start button and select Search. In the Search box type **Remote**.

2. Select Allow Remote Access To Your Computer. The System Properties dialog box appears, with the Remote tab displayed (see the graphic in Exercise 6.10).

3. Click Add.

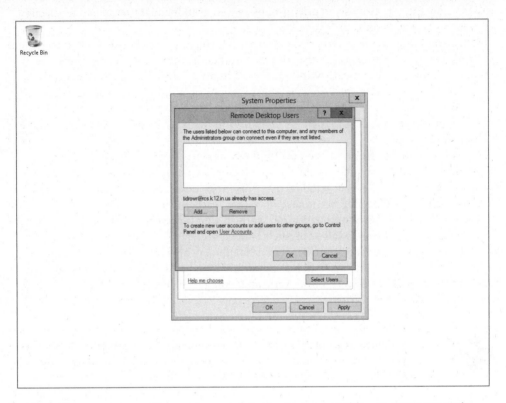

4. Enter the usernames of those who are authorized to access this computer remotely.

5. Click OK after you create your list of authorized users.

6. Click OK again to close the Remote Desktop Users dialog box.

7. Click OK again to close the System Properties dialog box.

Modifying Settings with Windows PowerShell

The Windows PowerShell is a command-line tool that provides a great deal of management power to a systems administrator. With PowerShell you can modify Remote Desktop settings, configure global settings for remote access for your network, disable remote access settings, and more. Over 100 PowerSchool cmdlets are available that are associated with remote access and Remote Desktop.

Connecting to a Remote System with Remote Desktop Connection

Once you have your system configured for Remote Desktop Connection, Windows 8.1 provides two tools to connect to remote computers. You can use the Windows 8.1 Remote Desktop app (new to Windows 8.1) or the Remote Desktop Connection utility that has been part of previous versions of Windows.

The following features are available with the Windows 8.1 Remote Desktop app:

- View remote connections from the home screen.

- Open remote connections.

- Use touch features such as zoom, rotate, the pointer, and the keyboard in your remote session if your local device supports touch capabilities.

- Connect to multiple remote desktops simultaneously.

- Customize remote connection settings.

To use the Windows 8.1 Remote Desktop app, you must first download it from the Windows Store. At the Windows 8.1 Start screen, search using the term **Remote Desktop** and click the Store option below the search box. This connects you to the Windows Store with Remote Desktop displayed in the list of apps. Click its tile and then click the Install link when the Remote Desktop screen appears (see Figure 6.1).

FIGURE 6.1   The Windows 8.1 Remote Desktop app in the Windows Store

After you download the Remote Desktop app, you can use it to connect to a remote computer. Exercise 6.12 shows how to connect to a remote computer using the Remote Desktop app. This exercise assumes you are logged into Windows 8.1 and have downloaded the Remote Desktop app, and that the Start screen is showing. Also, you will need to know the IP address or computer name of the computer to which you want to connect.

EXERCISE 6.12

Connecting to a Remote Computer Using the Remote Desktop App

1. Click the Remote Desktop app tile.

2. At the bottom of the Remote Desktop window, enter the IP address or computer name of the computer to which you want to connect.

3. Click Connect.

4. At the Enter Your Credentials window, enter an authorized username and password.

5. Click OK. If the identity of the remote PC cannot be verified using a security certificate, a window appears asking you to confirm that it is OK to connect to the remote computer.

6. Click Connect Anyway to proceed. The Remote Desktop app shows the desktop of the remote computer.

You can now control the remote computer as if you were sitting in front of it. Once you finish with the remote session, end the session by closing the Remote Desktop app (dragging its top border to the bottom of the Windows screen).

Windows 8.1 also supports the classic Remote Desktop Connection application that many users are familiar with from previous versions of Windows. It can be launched from the Windows Start screen or from the command line using its executable filename, MSTSC.EXE.

Exercise 6.13 shows how to launch and use Remote Desktop Connection. This exercise assumes you're logged into Windows 8.1 and the Start screen is showing. Also, you will need to know the IP address or computer name of the computer to which you want to connect.

EXERCISE 6.13

Connecting to a Remote Computer Using Remote Desktop Connection

1. Click the Remote Desktop Connection tile. If it is not on your Start menu, type **Remote Desktop** and click Remote Desktop Connection.

2. In the Remote Desktop Connection window, enter the IP address or computer name of the computer to which you want to connect. The following graphic shows an example of a computer named roboffice that is used in this exercise example:

3. Click Connect.

4. In the Enter Your Credentials window, enter an authorized username and password.

5. Click OK. If the identity of the remote PC cannot be verified using a security certificate, a window appears asking you to confirm that it is OK to connect to the remote computer.

6. Click Connect Anyway to proceed. The Remote Desktop app shows the desktop of the remote computer.

When you use Remote Desktop Connection, you can click the Show Options button on the main screen before you click Connect to set additional options for your Remote Desktop session. The following are the main tabs you can use to set these options:

General   Provides options for saving your Remote Desktop Connection credentials

Display   Provides options for window size of the Remote Desktop session and the color depth you want to use during the session

Local Resources   Provides options for using remote audio, keyboard combinations, local printers, and Windows Clipboard features during a remote session

Programs   Provides an option to set a program that runs at startup of your remote session

Experience   Provides options for controlling the system performance during the remote session, such as connection speed and bitmap caching for graphics

Advanced   Provides options for controlling authentication alerts and if a Remote Desktop Gateway is to be used for a remote session

Supporting VPNs

Virtual private networks (VPNs) are extensions to a private network over the Internet. VPNs are used by many companies and organizations to allow employees and other users to access private network resources from a remote location. For example, employees from home can connect to their home Internet connection, authenticate into their company's VPN portal (usually a secure website), and access company files, databases, and other secure resources. Originally these Internet connections were accomplished via dial-up connections using a modem and phone line. Due to availability and speed, those dial-up connections have been mostly replaced by broadband connections to the Internet.

The VPN client in Windows 8.1 is optimized for use by the Windows 8.1 touch features. The client is available quickly by searching for it on the Windows 8.1 Start screen.

Establish VPN Connections and Authentication

A VPN connection actually requires two connections. First, you'll need to connect to the Internet, and then you'll connect to the VPN server. It doesn't matter how you connect to the Internet. It can be over a dial-up connection, a DSL line, or a broadband connection, or even through a wireless router.

After creating the connection to the Internet, you can create the VPN connection. Exercise 6.14 shows how to create a VPN connection. This exercise assumes you're logged into Windows 8.1 and the Start screen is showing. Also, you will need to know the IP or Internet address of the computer to which you want to set up a VPN connection.

EXERCISE 6.14

Creating a VPN Connection

1. Right-click the Start button and select Search. In the Search box type Network and Sharing.

2. Click Set up a New connection or network. Then select Connect to a workplace.

3. On the How do you want to connect page, select Use my Internet connection (VPN)

4. Type the IP or Internet address of your VPN host. If you use a workpiece server and enter the name of the VPN server, you'll need to ensure that it is resolvable from the Internet DNS server. If you put in the IP address directly, you'll bypass the DNS name-resolution step.

5. Type a name of the destination computer.

6. Click Remember My Credentials to save this VPN connection for future uses.

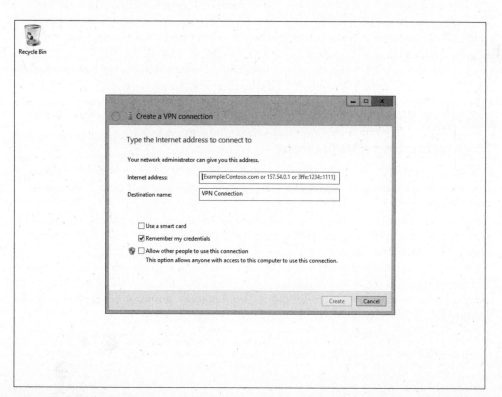

EXERCISE 6.14 *(continued)*

7. Click Create. The new VPN connection is added to your list of available networks on the Charms bar.

8. To connect to the VPN, show the Charms bar and click Settings.

9. Click the network icon (at the top left of the icons on the lower section of the Charms bar).

10. Click the VPN connection to which you want to connect.

11. Click Connect.

12. Type the username and password you use to authenticate to the VPN.

13. Click OK. The connection to the VPN is established.

At this point, the connection is ready to use. Although a lot of the connection activity is automatic, you may need to troubleshoot some connections.

If you do not have a broadband Internet connection, you can set up a dial-up VPN connection instead. In the past, this type of connection was common since home users did not have the capability in many cases to connect to the Internet with a high-speed connection. Nowadays the slower dial-up option is few and far between, but it's a reality in some places.

To set up a dial-up VPN connection, you must have a modem installed in your computer. Open the Network and Sharing Center (type **Sharing** at the home screen, select Settings, and then click Network And Sharing). Click Set Up A New Connection Or Network. Click Connect To A Workplace and click Next. Choose the No, Create A New Connection option, click Next, and then choose Dial Directly. Fill out the telephone number for connecting to the VPN, provide a destination name, and click Next. Enter the VPN credentials (username and password) and click Create. Once created, the connection appears in the Network Connections list and you can use it to access the dial-up VPN.

Troubleshooting a VPN Client

If everything goes well, you'll be able to connect to the VPN server right after you create the connection. However, not everything always goes well—you may need to do a little troubleshooting.

Figure 6.2 shows the error screen you'll probably see if you can't connect. By default, it will try to reconnect three times. However, if it didn't work the first time, it probably won't work the second or third time.

There are a few important steps you can take. First, make sure you have Internet access. Without Internet access, the VPN connection won't work. However, this is the easiest problem to solve because the VPN connection will let you know and prompt you to connect to the Internet.

FIGURE 6.2 VPN connection error

If you have Internet access but still can't connect, you can try these extra steps:

Check the settings The logical first step is to double-check the settings. Often the problem is just a simple issue of entering the wrong IP address. You can do this by checking the properties of the connection. If your VPN server has more specific settings, you'll be able to configure them from these property pages. To see the VPN Connection Properties dialog box, show the VPN connection on the Charms bar, right-click the connection, and choose View Connection Properties. Use the General, Options, Security, Networking, and Sharing tabs to reconfigure your VPN connection.

Enable logging You can enable logging to track VPN events. You can use the netsh command to enable or disable logging. The log files are created in the %windir%\tracing directory. If the tracing directory doesn't exist yet, it will be created when you enable logging. There will also be additional entries enabled in the Security Event log available from the Event Viewer. These commands need to be run from an administrative command prompt to work completely. If you don't run them with administrative permissions, all of the logs won't be enabled. This command will enable logging:

```
netsh ras diag set tracefacilities enable
```

If the VPN is connecting over the Internet, we highly recommended that you use either Require Encryption or Maximum Strength Encryption, which can be found on the Security tab. This ensures that any data transmitted over the VPN tunnel is protected from interception.

DirectAccess

DirectAccess is a feature introduced with Windows 7 and Windows Server 2008 R2, and it is also available with Windows 8.1. It allows clients to access internal resources using Internet access but without creating a VPN. Also, DirectAccess does not require the user to manually create a connection.

You can think of DirectAccess as a virtual tunnel. It uses IPv6 over IPsec to secure the traffic. Once it's configured, remote clients can access servers on the internal network over the Internet, just as if they were on the internal network. In other words, as long as the clients have access to the Internet, they can access servers on the internal network.

To take advantage of DirectAccess, you must meet several requirements:

Clients   Clients must be running Windows 8.1 Enterprise. The clients must also be members of the same domain hosting the DirectAccess servers.

Servers   Servers must be running Windows Server 2008 R2 or later (such as Windows Server 2012). These servers have two NICs: one NIC is connected to the internal network, and the other is connected to the Internet. When used with Windows Server 2012, Windows 8.1 makes DirectAccess easier to deploy and implement with an existing IPv4 corporate infrastructure.

IPv6   Both the client and server must be running IPv6. This includes DNSv6 and DHCPv6 if DHCP is being used.

Network Resources   The servers must be in a Windows domain. Domain controllers and DNS servers must be running at least Windows Server 2008 SP2 or Windows Server 2008 R2. The network must also have a PKI to issue certificates.

BranchCache

BranchCache is another feature that was introduced with Windows 7 and Windows Server 2008 R2 servers, and it's also available with Windows 8.1 and Windows Server 2012. It doesn't apply to mobile computers but instead applies to remote offices. You can use BranchCache to improve performance for users in remote offices.

The primary benefit of BranchCache is that it reduces the amount of traffic over a WAN link. It also improves the response time for users in the remote office because they are able to retrieve data more quickly.

Consider a company with a main office and a branch office. The two offices are connected via a wide area network (WAN). Clients in the branch office have access to servers in the main office. However, because they have to traverse the WAN link, it is slower. Imagine that Sally and Bob both work in the branch office. Sally needs to access a project file in the main office, so she retrieves it over the WAN link. A few minutes later, Bob needs to access the same file. He also retrieves the file over the WAN link.

However, if BranchCache is used, the file is cached on a computer in the branch office. When Bob needs to access the file, his system is able to retrieve the cached file stored in the branch office. The WAN link is used less, and the performance for users is improved.

BranchCache Modes

BranchCache uses two modes. The mode you select largely depends on whether you have a Windows Server 2008 R2 server or later server in the branch office. The two modes are as follows:

Hosted Cache Mode   Files are stored on a Windows Server 2008 R2 server or Windows 2012 Server located in the remote office. The server can be doing other functions, but it needs to have the BranchCache feature enabled.

Distributed Cache Mode   Windows 8.1 clients cache content using a peer-to-peer architecture. Distributed cache mode doesn't require a Windows Server 2008 R2 server or later server in the branch office. The first client that retrieves the file caches it. Other clients in the branch office can then retrieve the file from the first client. Clients can automatically detect the existence of BranchCache files stored on Windows 8.1 computers in the same subnet. If the remote office has more than one subnet, clients on different subnets can cache the same content.

BranchCache Requirements

BranchCache has several requirements that must be met. These primarily focus on ensuring that you have the right operating systems and that they are configured to use BranchCache. The requirements are as follows:

Configuration of Windows 8.1 Clients   Windows 7 and Windows 8.1 clients can cache or access files used with BranchCache. In addition, the clients must be configured using either Group Policy or the netsh command. For example, you can use this command from an administrative command prompt to configure clients to use distributed caching: netsh branchcache set service distributed. This command will configure the firewall and service settings. You can disable it with this command: netsh branchcache set service disabled.

Source Server Requirements   The server hosting content that will be cached must be running Windows Server 2012 R2 (Windows Server 2008 R2 can also be used here) and the BranchCache For Network Files role service must be added as part of the File Services role.

Also, shares must be configured to support BranchCache. Some servers, such as web servers, require additional configuration.

Remote Office Server Requirements   If hosted cache mode is used, you must enable the BranchCache feature on server in the remote office. If you don't have at least a Windows Server 2008 R2, you can use distributed cache mode instead.

Supporting Mobile Devices

With the arrival of Windows 8 and 8.1, your support efforts extend to a variety of new computing devices, not just desktop computers and laptops. Now you also need to support tablets and phones.

The operating system is designed to use live tiles on the phone or tablet Start screen. Figure 6.3 shows an example of live tiles on a Windows tablet. The tiles indicate messages, pictures, and sundry other information for the user. The Windows Phone sports the same interface. You would, however, see phone calls in the UI as well as text messages and so on.

FIGURE 6.3   Windows 8.1 live tiles

Windows 8.1 mobile devices are managed using the System Center Configuration Manager and the Mobile Device Manager. Between the two applets, you can provide management policy and even work with Group Policy Objects (GPOs) for mobile devices.

You also have the option of configuring Near Field Communication (NFC), which enables direct communication between devices such as tablets and printers. A feature called Secure SIM (which will be supported in the near future) allows your devices to securely connect to the network.

To create a compliance policy for your mobile devices, you need access to System Center Configuration on Microsoft Server 2012 or later. The Create Configuration Wizard lets you configure items and settings for password policy, email, security, peak synchronization, roaming, encryption, wireless communication, certificates, and so on.

Remote Wipe is a function of a compliance policy that is set from the System Center Configuration Manager. When a device tries to connect to the network, it will receive the wipe policy and immediately begin wiping the tablet. This action cleans the device and removes all data from it, including email such as an Exchange mailbox.

The next feature you need to know about is ActiveSync. This is the Exchange Synchronization function that it accesses from the Exchange Admin Center (EAC), so you need to have access to these functions as a Microsoft Exchange administrator, which is beyond the scope of this book. EAC lets you create the access and quarantine policies for all manner of Windows 8.1 mobile devices. You should know, however, that the EAC lets you specify whether to allow or block your mobile devices from certain types of access.

Work Folders are new to Windows 8.1 and work with Windows Server 2012 R2 and later. This feature lets remote users synchronize their files with their PCs. To use Work Folders, you must install it as a role service in Windows Server 2012 R2. It will set up a sync share to enable the synchronization. You can also enable synchronization across the Internet, but to do so you need a certificate infrastructure in place.

Keep in mind that a Work Folder is not a huge repository or storage place on the network. Thus, the maximum size of any Work Folder can be 10 GB. If Work Folders are stored on the local machine, they will need an additional 6 GB of space for file storage. The default path for Work Folders is %USERPROFILE%\Work Folders.

The central messaging platform and the management of messaging on all Windows 8.0/ and 8.1 devices is Microsoft Exchange. The management and configuration of user information in Exchange is thus beyond the scope of this book and the domain of Network or Exchange Administrators. System Center and its tools which include Configuration Manager is another key server technology that now contains key support for Windows 8.0 and 8.1 mobile devices.

Sync Center

Sync Center, introduced with Windows 8 and Windows 8.1, lets you sync your various devices. It uses your Microsoft account to connect with your local account so that things like browser history and offline files can be accessible from all your synced devices.

To use Sync Center, type **Sync Center** in Search and then click the icon. This will launch the program, as shown in Figure 6.4. The figure shows the opening screen of Sync Center with various management options presented.

FIGURE 6.4 Sync Center

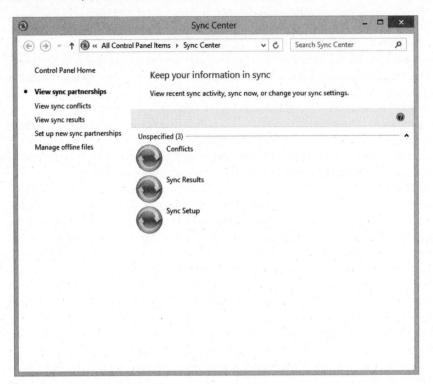

Sync Center lets you resolve sync errors and conflicts. To view these conflicts (if any exist), click the View Sync Conflicts link to access the Conflicts panel, shown in Figure 6.5.

A common conflict you will experience is with offline files where synced files have been changed in numerous places. In this case, Sync Center will allow you to resolve the conflict, such as merging your files manually to the satisfaction of the Sync algorithm.

To create new sync partnerships, click the Set Up New Sync Partnerships link. Windows 8.1 is able to detect what is possible to partner. If a partnership does not exist, it means that some condition is preventing the possible partnership or that the partnership is simply not supported.

The Sync Center wizard lets you configure two options for sync settings:

At A Scheduled Time This lets you set up specific times, such as every day at 4 p.m.

When An Event Occurs This lets you set up syncing when certain events are triggered, such as when you sign into your account.

There are also two types of syncing options on Windows 8.1. A one-way sync can be activated that only transmits data to a device, but not vice versa. A two-way sync enables data to be synced both ways.

FIGURE 6.5   Sync Center's Conflicts panel

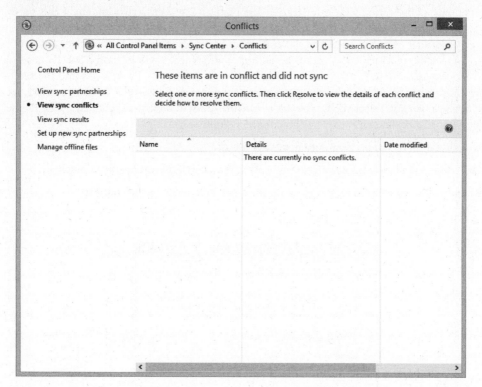

Offline Files

Managing and syncing offline files is one of the main features of Sync Center. To manage offline files, click the Manage Offline Files link to open the dialog box shown in Figure 6.6.

Supporting Broadband

Windows 8.1 expands the support for broadband technologies, making it easier to support and connect mobile devices such as Windows Phone to various networks, especially the Internet.

Windows 8.1 classifies its broadband communications as metered and unmetered connections. Wi-Fi and broadband network would be classified as metered whereas your typical office Ethernet network would not be classified as metered. The features and functions offered in various dialog boxes change according to the choice of metered or unmetered as a connection type.

Metered bandwidth connections, for example, limit updates and synchronization to conserve resources on metered networks. You can also configure group policies for a metered network. To do so, in the Group Policy Management Console (GPMC) navigate to Computer Configuration ➢ Administrative Templates ➢ Network. Two folders in this section are used to manage metered connections, WLAN service and WWAN Service. Both have a subfolder called WLAN and WWAN media cost respectively. If you select either of these, you will see icons in the details pane. For WWAN, they will be called Set 3G cost and Set 4G cost. For WLAN it offers a single one called Set cost. These icons and the settings contained within are used to set the cost of the metered networks. When you click on one of the icons and select the Enable radio button you will have three choices in the Please Select A Cost drop-down box. The choices are as follows:

Unrestricted   The connection does not incur a cost.

Fixed   The connection occurs a cost but only after a certain limit has been reached.

Variable   The connection incurs variable costs per byte used on the connection.

FIGURE 6.6   Offline Files dialog box

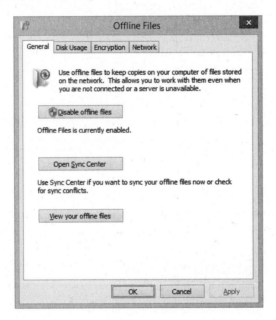

Summary

In this chapter, you learned how to configure and manage Windows Firewall and Windows Firewall with Advanced Security, as well as how to connect to remote computers using Windows 8.1's remote access clients.

As you learned, security is an integral part of any administrator's job. One way to combat attacks on your computer is to use a firewall to ensure the data traffic coming into to your computer is coming from an authorized site. Windows Firewall is designed to work with Windows and has been a key component of the Windows operating system since Windows XP. Windows Firewall adds a layer of protection to your Windows 8.1 computer against network attacks, including attacks from the Internet. Windows Firewall is enabled by default. Depending on your network access needs, or requirements by the software you use on your computer, you may need to modify its settings.

This chapter also discussed setting up and using Windows remote access features. With remote access, users can connect to a computer at a remote location and take over that computer as if they were sitting in front it physically. Many times, remote access is required to perform technical support on a remote computer, modify settings on a remote server, or perform other tasks while not being located at a computer personally.

In this chapter, you also learned about the key management features for mobile devices that can be configured from the device. Windows 8.1's Sync Center lets you manage the synchronization between mobile devices, your network, and your personal computer.

Exam Essentials

Understand firewall basics   You should know that firewalls protect computers by limiting inbound and outbound network traffic. This reduces the chances of your computer being attacked by malicious users and systems. Most firewalls operate with an implicit deny philosophy. In other words, all traffic is blocked (implicit deny) unless there is a rule that explicitly allows the traffic.

Know how to use Windows Firewall   You should know that by default Windows Firewall is configured to allow all outbound traffic. Windows Firewall can be configured to block all traffic inbound and outbound, but it can also be configured to allow exceptions. Exceptions can be created for a single profile or for all users on a computer.

Know how to enable a port and protocol in Windows Firewall   Using Windows Firewall with Advanced Security, you can configure IPsec rules. You can also create connection security rules for these connection types: isolation, authentication exemption, server-to-server, tunnel, and custom.

Understand remote access features   Know that remote access allows users to connect to the company's internal network while they are away from the network. They can be traveling, working at a remote customer's site, or working from home. Users can connect with a dial-up connection or a virtual private network connection.

Know how to configure and use remote access tools   Know that Windows 8.1 includes several tools for connecting to remote computers and managing remote configurations.

These tools include Remote Assistance, the Windows 8.1 Remote Desktop app, Remote Desktop Connection, and PowerShell cmdlets.

Know how to set up VPN connections   VPN connections are a way for users to connect to internal private networks (such as a company file server) over a secure connection. You should know how to set up VPN connections using the Create A VPN Connection wizard and how to set up dial-up VPN connections.

Understand what Sync Center is and how to use it   You should know what you can do with Sync Center, how to synchronize devices, and how to synchronize files.

Review Questions

You can find the answers in Appendix A.

1. You have Windows Firewall set to restrict all incoming traffic except for web traffic. You would like to set up a rule to allow a specific type of network service, such as FTP transfers. Which of the following rules would be recommended for this situation?

   A. Protocol

   B. Program

   C. Port

   D. IPsec

2. Your organization is planning on implementing DirectAccess so users can access the organization's network when working from home. Of the following choices, what must be included in the plan?

   A. IPv6

   B. WINS

   C. Libraries

   D. Preferred wireless settings

3. You are researching to see if Windows Firewall is adequate to protect your computer from attacks. Which of the following are the types of packet information analyzed by Windows Firewall?

   A. Source IP address of the packet

   B. Destination IP address

   C. TCP/UDP port number

   D. All of the above

4. Your company is setting up BranchCache on its enterprise network to allow caching and accessing of file from remote branch offices. Which of the following commands or Windows tools is used to configure BranchCache on the client computers?

   A. netsh command

   B. branchcache command

   C. BranchCache utility

   D. None of the above

5. Your company wants to allow remote users to access the company's internal network in a secure way. Which of the following would allow users to connect to the internal network?

   A. Remote Assistance

   B. AppLocker

   C. PowerShell

   D. VPN

6. You want to restrict the users who can connect to your computer using Remote Desktop Connection. In which dialog box would you find the setting to restrict who can authenticate?

   A. Remote Assistance Settings

   B. Remote Desktop Users

   C. System Properties

   D. Remote Desktop Connection

7. You are using a Windows 8.1 touch-enabled tablet to access your office desktop computer remotely. Which of the following tools is best to take advantage of the Windows 8.1 touch features?

   A. Remote Desktop Connection

   B. Remote Assistance

   C. VPN connection

   D. Remote Desktop app

8. You want to configure Windows Firewall to exempt computers or IP addresses from authenticating to your system. Which of the following methods would you use?

   A. Enabling a port

   B. Authentication exception

   C. Configure remote authentication

   D. All of the above

9. You want to help another user in your office with a computer problem they are experiencing. Which of the following remote tools would be the best tool to use so that they can watch you interact on the screen while you remotely access their computer?

   A. Remote Assistance

   B. Remote Desktop Connection

   C. Remote Desktop app

   D. VPN

10. You have Windows Firewall running with inbound and outbound traffic blocked. You need to provide a way for a program to access the Internet. What would you use to configure this?

   A. Port exception using Windows Firewall with Advanced Security

   B. Protocol exception using Windows Firewall with Advanced Security

   C. Connection blocking with Windows Firewall

   D. Allow an app or feature through Windows Firewall

11. You have a number of users who get permission from time to time to work from home by connecting to their office computers using Remote Desktop. The security officer has asked you to make sure that the home computers that are being used cannot connect to any other corporate network resource. What must you do?

   A. Make a VPN.

   B. Disable the local resource options of the Remote Desktop.

   C. Set up DirectAccess and use it to restrict remote computers.

   D. Configure the Remote Desktop Gateway IP address on the client computer.

12. Hackers like to send communications to your machine in the hope that the replies they get back from the computer will let them know where to attack. How do you prevent your machine from talking back to the hacker?

   A. Remove your machine from the network.

   B. Set up Windows Firewall in stealth mode.

   C. Run `winrs quickconfig hide me`.

   D. Disable return messaging.

13. You have a few hundred computers that have just been upgraded to Windows 8.1 and you need to assign static IPv6 addresses to them using Windows PowerShell. Which cmdlet can you use?

   A. `Set-NetV6IPaddress`

   B. `Set-TCPNetSettng`

   C. `Set-NetIPAddress`

   D. `Set-NetAddressV6`

14. You have 60 Windows 8.1 computers in a new branch office and you find that they are unable to connect to the corporate network via the DirectAccess protocol. After running diagnostics on the client computers, you discover something is missing in the network configuration. What is missing?

   A. The client computers do not have assigned IPv4 addresses.

   B. The client computers do not have IPv6 addresses assigned to the network adapters.

   C. The client computers do not have network adapters.

   D. The gateway address of the branch office switch is missing from the configuration.

15. Your company has several hundred users who telecommute part of the time. These groups need to access files on various devices when they are in the office and in the field, but the files must be synchronized so that changes made on office machines are propagated to laptops, tablets, and so on. What must you do to synchronize the various versions of files?

   A. Enable drive mapping.

   B. Ensure they also have a VPN connection.

   C. Configure Sync Center to sync files on the various devices a user needs to use.

   D. Create a new Remote Desktop connection with new drive settings to allow users to download the latest version.

16. You have been asked to ensure that clients who need to use IPsec tunnels to access sensitive data use the highest encryption available for the service. Which encryption should you use?

    A. AES

    B. RSA

    C. DES

    D. 3DES

17. When setting up a remote office environment, you find that there is no server at the site, only a Windows 8.1 computer used as an administrative machine. What is next best option you have to enable the site for branch computing?

    A. Add a route by using `netsh`.

    B. Download SP1 to enable you to use BranchCache on the workstation.

    C. The site cannot be used as a branch office.

    D. You can use distributed cache mode from the main office.

18. You have a new Window 8.1 client at a remote site who is complaining that it is taking her too long to access a file on the corporate network. What action can you take to help her?

    A. Move the file server closer to her computer.

    B. Configure her machine to use DirectAccess cache by running the DirectAccess cmdlet.

    C. Run the command `netsh branchcache set service distributed` on her computer.

    D. Run the command `netsh branchcache set service enabled` on her computer.

19. Which of the following Windows 8.1 versions can NOT be remote desktop host?

    A. Windows 8.1 Pro

    B. Windows 8.1 Enterprise

    C. Windows RT 8.1

    D. All of them can be

20. You have several hundred computers on the corporate network, all of which are part of a workgroup. You are asked to ensure that remote access uses the most secure network connections on the VPN. What is the most secure tunneling protocol you can use on your Windows 8 and 8.1 computers?

    A. Internet Key Exchange version 2 (IKEv2)

    B. Secure Shell Tunneling Protocol (SSTP)

    C. Layer 2 Tunneling Protocol (L2TP)

    D. Point-to-Point Tunneling Protocol (L2TP)

Chapter

7

Managing Windows 8.1 in a Domain

70-687 MICROSOFT EXAM OBJECTIVES COVERED IN THIS CHAPTER:

✓ **Configure authentication and authorization**

- Configure authentication in workgroups or domains

70-688 MICROSOFT EXAM OBJECTIVES COVERED IN THIS CHAPTER:

✓ **Support authentication and authorization**

- Multi-factor authentication, including certificates, virtual smart cards, and biometrics
- Workgroup versus domain, computer and user authentication, including account policies, and home groups

As you learned in Chapter 5, "Networking with Windows 8.1," the majority of computers you work with will be part of some kind of network. You might have computers connected in workgroups or in domains. Smaller, ad hoc networks are usually workgroups, whereas networks that are stable and have more than 10 network devices (such as computers, printers, and storage devices) are usually in a Windows domain.

It's important to understand the basics of how Windows 8.1 operates in a domain. This chapter provides you with an understanding of differences between workgroups and domains, explains how to manage Windows 8.1 in a domain, and shows you how to set up authentication and authorization in a Windows domain.

This chapter also discusses Group Policies, how to use group policies in a domain to manage computers, and how to use the Group Policy Management Console.

Workgroups vs. Domains

Windows 8.1 can be used in two types of networks: a workgroup or a domain.
When Windows 8.1 is first installed, it is a member of a workgroup by default. Workgroups are used in small offices, home offices, and home networks to allow users to share resources among themselves.

Usually networks of more than 10 users implement domains, although smaller networks set up as domains certainly do exist. There are no hard and fast rules on when a workgroup grows into a domain. One key part is that a domain requires a domain controller, a computer set up with a network operating system (such as Windows Server 2012 R2 or Windows Server 2008 R2). A domain is easier to manage and provides better security than a workgroup. An important benefit of a domain is that it provides single sign-on capabilities. In a domain, each user has one account that they can use to log on to almost any computer in the domain. In a workgroup, users need a separate account for each computer.

Domain Controllers

A Windows domain includes at least one server acting as a domain controller, which hosts Active Directory Domain Services (AD DS). Desktop computers (such as Windows 8.1 computers) are then joined to the domain so that users can access the domain resources. AD DS includes objects such as users, computers, and groups. In order for users to log on to the domain, they need a user account. In addition, users must log on to a computer that is joined to the domain. If the computer is not a member of the domain, users will not be able to log on even if they have a domain account.

This book does not describe how to set up a test or live environment for connecting Windows 8.1 to a domain controller. If you need help in setting up a network with a domain controller, such as creating a virtual test environment, pick up a copy of Windows 7 Desktop Support and Administration by Darril Gibson (Sybex, 2010). It includes a walk-through of setting up a virtual environment that you can use to test Windows 8.1 domain connectivity as well as test Group Policy settings in a networked environment. In addition to the tutorial found in that book, you can download trial editions of Windows Server software, including evaluation VHD (Virtual Hard Disk) that you can use to run in a virtual server environment. Go to www.microsoft .com/en-us/download and search on the Windows Server evaluation files.

A domain controller (DC) hosts AD DS in a Microsoft domain. AD DS holds objects (such as users, computers, and groups) that can be centrally managed and administered. Users and computers must have an account in AD DS to be able to log on to the domain and use domain resources. Further, for client computers to locate domain controllers on a network, a Domain Name Server (DNS) server is required and the Windows 8.1 client must be configured with that DNS configuration.

The DC could be running Microsoft Windows Server 2003, but it's more likely you'll be working with Windows Server 2008 R2 or Windows Server 2012/2012R servers in your domain today. Domain names need to have at least two parts, such as Microsoft.com or Wiley.com. However, they don't need to have a well-known top-level domain name, such as .com, .org, or .net.

Joining a Domain

Once you've created a domain, you can add the Windows 8.1 client to the domain. Adding a Windows 8.1 client will result in the following:

- A computer object will be created in the domain.

- A password will be established for the computer to authenticate in the domain. This password will automatically be changed periodically.

- Users will be able to log on using a domain account and access domain resources.

- Group Policy objects will be applied to the computer and to users logging on to the computer.

Exercise 7.1 shows how to join a Windows 8.1 computer to a domain. This exercise assumes you're logged on to Windows 8.1 with the Start screen showing.

EXERCISE 7.1

Joining Windows 8.1 to a Domain

1. On the Windows 8.1 Start screen, in the Search box, type **computer**.

2. Right-click This PC and choose Properties. The System window appears.

EXERCISE 7.1 *(continued)*

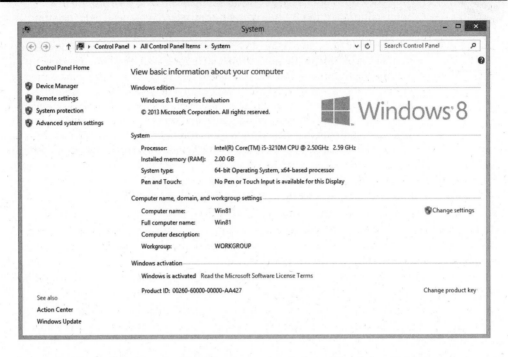

3. Click Advanced System Settings to display the System Properties dialog box.

5. Select the Computer Name tab. Workgroup is the default value for the name of the workgroup.

6. Click Change.

7. In the Computer Name/Domain Changes dialog box, select the Domain radio button and enter the name of the domain.

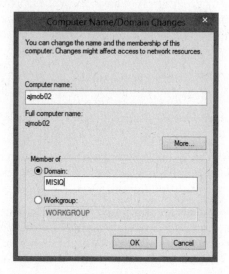

8. Click OK. You'll be prompted to enter the credentials for an account in the domain that has permission to join the domain.

9. Enter the credentials of a user account that has permission to join the domain (such as the Administrator account), and click OK. After a moment, a dialog box will appear welcoming you to the domain. Click OK.

10. You'll be prompted that you must restart the computer to apply the changes. Click OK.

11. Click Close. When prompted to restart the computer, click Restart Now.

You now have joined your Windows 8.1 computer to a Windows domain.

Authentication and Authorization in a Domain

As you learned in Chapter 1, "Introducing Windows 8.1," when accessing resources on a network, including when connecting to a domain, you must be aware of two security principles: authentication and authorization. Authentication is used to identify a user, and authorization is used to control access of the user.

Let's look at an example to help clarify. A user named Sally Smith is given a domain username and password, called her *domain credentials*. When Sally uses those credentials to log into the network domain, she can authenticate onto the domain. Once authenticated, however, she is not necessarily given access to any network resources available on the domain. That is where authorization comes in. Depending on Sally's network permissions, Sally's account is granted authorization to the resources she needs access to, such as printers, storage space, and similar resources.

Authentication

Authentication is used to prove a user's identity. In general, three factors are involved in authentication:

Something You Know   This can be implemented with domain user accounts that have specific user names and passwords. As long as users know their username and password, they are able to use these credentials for authentication.

Something You Have   Smart cards are being used more and more today. A smart card is a credit card–sized card that can be inserted into a reader (often as part of the keyboard). Users insert the card and usually enter a personal identification number (PIN) for authentication. Within a domain, the smart card is associated with a domain user account.

Something You Are   Biometrics can be used to prove a user's identity. Fingerprint readers can be found on more and more mobile computers today. Once the card reader is configured, users authenticate with their finger on the fingerprint reader. Other biometric methods include retinal scanners and hand scanners.

Multifactor authentication involves using more than one authentication factor. For example, a smart card is considered something you have, whereas a PIN or password is something you know, so when a smart card is used with a PIN, it is considered multifactor authentication.

Authorization

Users are granted rights and permissions based on the user accounts that authenticate them. If users log on with the local administrator account, they are able to perform any action and access any of the resources on the system.

Rights and permissions are different but often clumped together. In short, rights identify what a user can *do* on a system and permissions identify the resources a user can *access*.

Figure 7.1 shows the Local Security Policy in the Local Group Policy Editor. It includes several actions that a user can be authorized to perform on a system, such as logging on locally, backing up files and directories, and changing the system time.

FIGURE 7.1 Local Security Policy

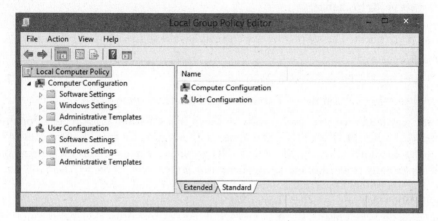

Exercise 7.2 shows how you can access the Local Security Policy on your computer. This exercise assumes you're logged on to Windows 8.1 with the Start screen showing.

EXERCISE 7.2

Accessing Local Security Policy

1. On the Windows 8.1 Start screen, click the icon representing Search (a magnifying glass) and type **policy**. Click the link for Edit Group Policy. This starts the Local Group Policy Editor as shown in Figure 7.1. You can also click Local Security Policy in the Apps area (at the left side of the screen) to open the Local Security Policy window.

2. Click the Local Policies folder under the Security Settings listing on the left side of the window.

3. Click the Security Options subfolder under the Local Policies folder. The local security policies display in the right side of the screen, similar to the display shown in Figure 7.1.

Although rights and permissions can be assigned to individual user accounts, they are much more commonly assigned to groups. If a user is a member of a group, and the group is granted specific rights and permissions, the user also has those rights and permissions.

Many times users are given authorization to resources based on their assignment in the company or corporation. As the base user level, each user can look exactly the same—that is, perhaps a user is given authentication rights to the domain but nothing else. For additional authorization, domain account groups can be created on the Windows Server domain. These account groups can be given the necessary authorization rights for that group. As each user needs a different authorization, that user is copied into the appropriate account group. This helps keep track of which users have which access levels, and it provides a quick way to change authorizations for all users in a group if that group authorization needs to change.

Again, let's look at an example to help clarify. Let's say Sally Smith is assigned to the marketing department. The marketing department has the following network needs:

- Internet access

- Access to three color printers on the third floor

- Shared storage space on the corporate network-attached storage (NAS)

One strategy (and there are several you can use in this situation) is to create a domain account group called MARKETING and assign authorization for the three network needs addressed above. Once the MARKETING group is created, you (as the administrator) can assign Sally (and other marketing department members) to the MARKETING domain account group. Once this is done, Sally (and others) will have her necessary access (Internet, three color printers, and shared NAS space).

Depending on Sally's needs, she may be part of one or more other domain account groups that you've established. In fact, depending on the type of Internet access filtering or monitoring the corporation uses, you may remove the Internet access authorization from the MARKETING group and create a separate group called Internet or even two of them like this:

- NON-MANAGEMENT INTERNET

- MANAGEMENT INTERNET

You can then assign all non-managers in the corporation to the NON-MANAGEMENT INTERNET group and assign managers to the other Internet group. This would put Sally, for example, in two groups: MARKETING and NON-MANAGEMENT INTERNET.

As needs change, you can modify the domain account group and those changes replicate to all members of that group. This makes managing authorization on domains much more efficient than finding all users with a specific authorization and replicating changes one by one.

Windows 8.1 and Windows domains both include many built-in groups. Figure 7.2 shows the built-in groups on a local system, and Figure 7.3 shows some of the built-in groups in a domain. These groups have been assigned specific rights and permissions to perform actions on systems and within domains.

You can access the Computer Management console to view local built-in groups via the Administrative Tools menu or by typing **manage** on the Windows 8.1 Start screen and clicking the Computer Management icon. You view domain built-in groups via the Active Directory Users and Computers console on a domain controller found in the Administrative Tools menu. There is a Builtin container, but additional built-in groups exist in the Users container.

Some of these groups deserve special mention:

Administrators (Local)   Members of the Administrators group on local computers (including Windows 8.1 computers) can do anything on that computer. The local administrator account is a member of this group, and the first account created on a Windows 8.1 computer when it is installed is a member of this group.

FIGURE 7.2   Groups on a Windows 8.1 system

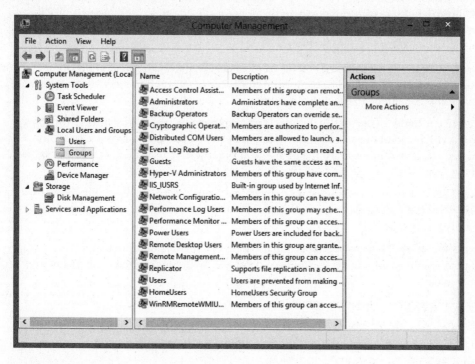

FIGURE 7.3   Built-in groups in a domain

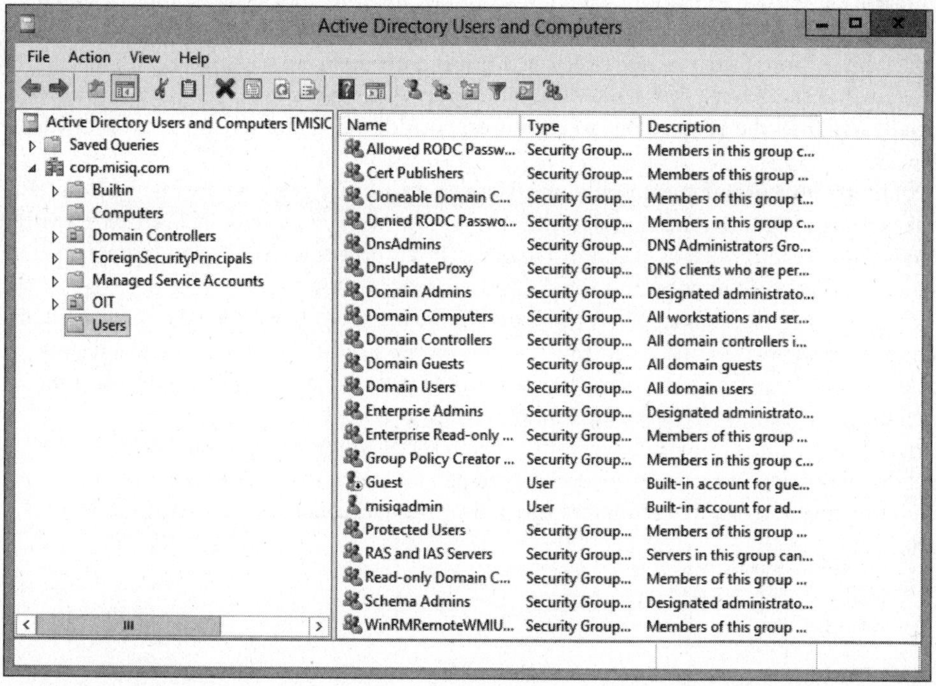

Administrators (Domain)   Members of the domain Administrators group have complete and unrestricted access to computers in the domain. The domain administrator account, the Domain Admins group, and the Enterprise Admins group are all members of the domain Administrators group by default.

Domain Admins   Users in the Domain Admins group can do anything in the domain. This group is automatically added to the local Administrators group for every computer in the domain. It's also added to the domain Administrators group.

Enterprise Admins   Users in the Enterprise Admins group can do anything in the forest. A forest is a group of one or more domains, and users in this group have permissions to add, remove, and administer all the domains in the forest. This group is a member of the domain Administrators group for every domain in the forest.

Power Users   Power Users is a local group added for backward compatibility. It was used on older operating systems to give users additional permissions without putting them in the Administrators group.

Server Operator   This is a special group on domain controllers. It grants members rights and permissions to administer the domain controller without granting them any permission in the domain.

Backup Operators   This group grants members the ability to back up and restore files.

It's also possible to create additional groups to meet specific needs. This is rarely done on local Windows 8.1 systems alone, but it's often done in a domain to organize users and easily grant specific rights and permissions.

Although it takes a little planning initially to design and create groups, it eases the administration burden in the long run. For example, imagine that you originally granted Read permission to a share but later wanted to change this to Modify for all the users in a particular group, such as one called SALES. If a group is created and permissions are assigned to the group, you make the change once and you're done. Conversely, if you originally assigned the permissions to each user, you'd have to modify the permissions for each user.

Groups are also useful even if only one user is a member. For example, imagine that an HR department has only one employee, Maria. On the surface, it may seem easier to assign all the permissions to Maria's account. However, what do you do if Maria is transferred or promoted within the company and someone else needs to take over?

If the permissions are assigned to the individual user, then they all have to be modified to remove Maria's access and grant the new employee's access. However, if a group was created and all the permissions were assigned to the group, you'd simply need to add the new employee's account to the group and remove Maria's account.

Groups created in a domain have both a group scope and a group type. Figure 7.4 shows the dialog box used to create a new group. You can access this dialog box in Active Directory Users and Computers by right-clicking a container and selecting New ➤ Group.

FIGURE 7.4   Creating a new group in a domain

The three group scopes are as follows:

Global   Global groups are commonly used to organize users (such as all the users in the Sales department with a group named G_Sales). Global groups can also contain other global groups.

Domain Local   Domain local groups are sometimes used in administrative models in larger domains. A domain local group commonly identifies assigned permissions to specific resources. As an example, the DL_Print_ClrLaserPrinter group could be used to identify a group that is assigned print permission for a color laser printer. A domain local group typically contains one or more global groups and can also contain universal groups.

Universal   Universal groups are used in multidomain environments. They can contain global groups from any domain and can be added to domain local groups in any domain.

A commonly used naming convention is to begin the group name with the group scope. G_Sales is easily identified as a global group used to organize the users in the Sales group. Similarly, it's common to include the permissions and resources in the domain local group. DL_Print_ClrLaser-Printer identifies it as a domain local group used to grant print permission for a color laser printer.

The two group types are:

Distribution   A distribution group is used for email only. It cannot be assigned permissions.

Security   A security group can be assigned permissions or used as a distribution group.

In larger domains where both global and domain local groups are used, a common strategy known as A G DL P is used. When A G DL P is used, accounts (A) are added to global groups (G). Global groups are added to domain local (DL) groups, and permissions (P) are assigned to domain local groups.

It is important to understand what can be added to a group. For example, accounts can be added to global groups or domain local groups. A global group can be added to a domain local group. However, a global group can't be added to a user, and a local group can't be added to a global group; both of these examples go against the arrow.

Permissions can be assigned to accounts or any type of group, but it's a good practice to assign permissions to groups whenever possible. When you begin assigning permissions directly to users, administration becomes more difficult.

The benefits of using domain local groups are realized only in larger domains where administrators want to manage permissions for some resources more closely. Most organizations use a simpler model of AGP where accounts (A) are placed into global (G) groups and permissions (P) are assigned to the global groups.

Exercise 7.3 walks through the process of creating users and groups in a domain. The exercise assumes you have access to the domain controller computer and have administrator privileges.

EXERCISE 7.3

Creating Users and Groups in a Domain

1. Start the domain controller and log on.

2. Launch Active Directory Users and Computers by clicking Start ➤ Administrative Tools ➤ Active Directory Users And Computers.

3. If necessary, expand the domain to view the Users container. Right-click the Users container and select New ➤ Group.

4. Enter the name of the group in the Group Name text box (such as G_Sales). Global is selected as the Group Scope and Security is selected as the Group Type by default, but you can change these if needed. Click OK.

5. Create a user account in the domain with these steps:

    a. Right-click Users and select New ➤ User.

    b. Enter the First Name, Last Name, and User Logon Name. The User Logon Name must be unique in the domain, and it's common to use a combination of the user's First Name and Last Name. Your display will look similar to the following graphic. Click Next.

c. Enter a password in the Password and Confirm Password text boxes. Click Next and then click Finish.

6. Right-click the user account you just created and select Properties.

7. Select the Member Of tab. You'll see that the user is a member of the Domain Users group. Click Add.

8. Enter **G_Sales** and click OK. (You can also click Advanced and then click Find Now to search or browse for objects in Active Directory.)

9. Click OK on the User Properties dialog box. The user is now a member of the G_Sales group, and any permissions assigned to this group will apply to the user.

Active Directory provides security across multiple domains through interdomain trust relationships. When trust relationships exist between domains, the authentication mechanism for each domain trusts the authentication mechanism for all other trusted domains. If a user or application is authenticated by one domain, its authentication is accepted by all other domains that trust the authenticating domain. Users in a trusted domain have access to resources in the trusting domain, subject to the access controls that are applied in the trusting domain.

Using Group Policy in a Domain

Group Policy is one of the primary tools you have available to manage users and computers within a domain. It doesn't matter how many users or computers you have, you can manage all of them with a single Group Policy object (GPO).

When learning about Group Policy, you must understand how different GPOs are applied. A GPO can be linked to a site, domain, or organizational unit (OU), and where it's linked determines its scope. When multiple GPOs are applied, the settings are merged. To determine what settings apply, you need to understand the order of precedence with multiple GPOs. Because there are too many GPO settings to cover them all in a single chapter, you will learn only a few of them here.

Group Policy and the GPMC

Group Policy is a group of technologies that allows administrators within a domain to configure a setting one time and have it apply to multiple users or computers. Group Policy settings can be configured using the *Local Computer Policy* (using the Group Policy Editor) or the *Group Policy Management Console (GPMC)* in a domain.

Exercise 7.4 walks through the process of starting the Group Policy Editor. The exercise assumes you are at the Windows 8.1 Start screen.

EXERCISE 7.4

Starting the Group Policy Editor

1. Type **Group Policy**.

2. Click Settings below the search field.

3. Click the Edit Group Policy icon. The Group Policy Editor displays.

Figure 7.1 shows the Local Computer Policy for a Windows 8.1 computer, and Figure 7.5 shows the Default Domain Policy for a domain. There are some important differences.

First, the Local Computer Policy affects only the local machine. If only the Local Computer Policy is used, each individual computer must be modified. The Default Domain Policy affects all users and computers in the domain. Other GPOs can be created in a domain that will affect all the user accounts and computer accounts in a site or all the accounts in an OU.

 When you create a reference computer that will be used as an image, you can use the Local Computer Policy to configure settings that will be the same in all deployed images.

Second, domain policy includes policies and preferences. Any settings in the Policies node are enforced and cannot be changed by users once the settings are applied. Settings in the Preferences node are set but aren't enforced. In other words, users can override the settings in the Preferences node.

Group Policy settings are organized in the following nodes:

Software Settings This node can be used to deploy software to clients. Software deployed with Group Policy can be automatically installed on computers or installed based on a user's action. For example, a Group Policy–deployed application can appear on a user's Start menu and be installed when the user first selects it or deployed to a computer and installed the next time the computer restarts.

Windows Settings This node includes Security Settings and Scripts for the computer and also Folder Redirection and Internet Explorer Maintenance for the user. Scripts can be configured to run when the computer starts or stops and when a user logs on or logs off.

Administrative Templates This node includes a large assortment of settings that can be used to modify and manage the user's environment. These settings directly modify the Registry of the client computers.

FIGURE 7.5 Default Domain Policy for the entire domain

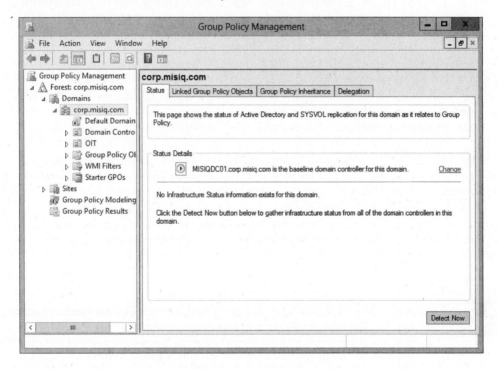

There are literally thousands of Group Policy settings. One of the first things to grasp is that you'll never learn them all. What you should concentrate on first is how Group Policy works. Then, as you work with Group Policy, you'll be exposed to more and more settings. You'll find extensive Group Policy documentation at http://technet.microsoft .com/en-us/windowsserver/bb310732.aspx. The Group Policy Settings Reference is also valuable: http://go.microsoft.com/fwlink/?linkid=54020.

The good news is that most of the settings have built-in documentation. When you find the setting in the GPMC, you also find the documentation. In addition, there's a built-in search feature that makes it easy to find Group Policy settings in the Administrative Templates node. You'll see how to use the search feature later in this chapter.

Group Policy Scope

The GPO scope refers to where it is applied. A Local Computer Policy applies to only a single GPO, but other GPOs can apply to many users and computers in the organization. GPOs can be created and linked to sites, domains, and OUs. Where a GPO is linked determines which users and computers will have the GPO settings applied. Any users or computers within the scope of a GPO will inherit the settings of the GPO. If a user or computer is within the scope of multiple GPOs, it will inherit the settings of all the GPOs.

Even though a user or computer object within the scope of multiple GPOs will inherit the settings of all GPOs, all the settings won't necessarily apply. You'll see later in this chapter how conflicts are handled. In general, if there is a conflict with any settings the last setting applied wins. This default behavior can be modified using different advanced GPO settings, which are also covered later in this chapter.

GPOs linked to the domain apply to all accounts in the domain. When a domain is first created, the Default Domain Policy is also created. It includes some basic settings that apply to all user and computer accounts in the domain.

An Active Directory Users and Computers console in the Sample.com domain, for example, could have multiple OUs (Domain Controllers, Servers, Sales, and IT) and containers within the OUs. You could, for example, have an OU called Sales that includes children OUs called Division 1 and Division 2. All of the other OUs and containers are on the same level and don't have a parent/child relationship with each other.

The Default Domain Policy applies to any accounts that are in any of the OUs or containers in the domain. This includes the Users and Computers container and any accounts in child OUs. Another way of saying this is that GPO settings applied at the domain level are inherited by all the OUs and containers in the domain.

A container looks similar to a folder in Active Directory Users and Computers. The Computers container is the default location for new computers that join the domain, and the Users container holds the Administrator user account and some groups. OUs have an additional icon within the folder, and the only default OU in a domain is the Domain Controllers OU. All other OUs are created by an administrator.

GPOs are not inherited between domains. In other words, if a forest has a root domain of Sample.com and a child domain named Sales.Sample.com, any GPOs applied to the Sample.com domain are not inherited by the Sales.Sample.com domain.

GPOs linked directly to an OU have a scope of that OU. All of the GPO settings apply to accounts in that OU. In addition, any child OUs inherit the settings of GPOs applied to the parent OU.

Within the Group Policy Management console (see Figure 7.6), you can see the hierarchical relationships among the domain, OUs, and child OUs in the GPMC. The OUs and containers are indented to show they are children of the domain. Children OUs, for example ones called Division 1 and Division 2, are indented to show they are children of their parent OU (called Sales, for example). Child OUs inherit GPO settings from the parent.

FIGURE 7.6 Group Policy Management console showing OUs

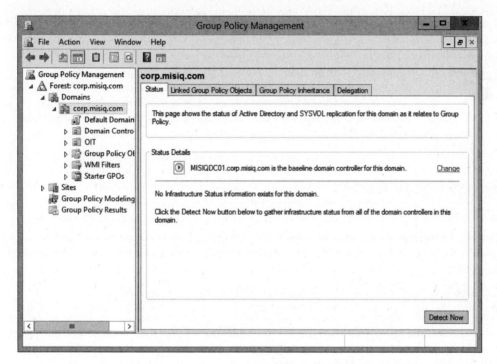

The Default Domain Controllers policy does not apply to any users in the IT, Sales, or Servers OUs because they are all peers. Similarly, the Disable Mandatory Profile GPO applies to accounts in the IT OU but does not apply to accounts in any other OUs or containers.

A site is a group of well-connected computers or subnets used for multiple-location environments. As an example, imagine a company with a main location in one city and a branch office in another city. Individually, each location is well connected using 1 Gbps local area networks (LANs). However, the locations are connected to each other using a T1 line at about 1.544 Mbps. Although a T1 line is not bad for a wide area network (WAN) link, it has only about 1.5 percent of the bandwidth available within the LAN.

Now the organization wants to deploy Microsoft Office to clients using Group Policy. An ineffective method of deploying the application is to use a single GPO linked to a domain. This single GPO would apply to all the accounts in the domain (including all the accounts in both sites).

When a single GPO is used to deploy an application to both sites, it will have to be deployed over the WAN link for some of the clients, which will be a much slower process than if the application was deployed from a server in the same site. If Microsoft Office is deployed from a server in the main office, it will go over the WAN link for clients in the remote office. If it's deployed from a server in the remote office, it'll have to go over the WAN link for users in the main office.

Instead, two separate GPOs (GPO2 and GPO3) can be used. GPO2 can deploy the application from a server in the main office to users in the main office. GPO3 can deploy the application from a server in the remote office to users in the remote office.

> Although it isn't efficient to use a single GPO to deploy applications to multiple sites, it is efficient to deploy settings to multiple sites with a single GPO. For example, if you want to configure computers to use automatic updates, it isn't necessary to create separate GPOs if the organization has multiple sites.

Group Policy Nodes

GPOs have two primary nodes:

Computer Configuration   This node includes settings that apply to computers, no matter which user is logged on. These settings apply only if the computer is in the scope of the GPO.

User Configuration   This node includes settings that apply to a user, no matter which computer the user logs on to. These settings apply only if the user is in the scope of the GPO.

On the surface, the settings that apply are simple to understand. Computer settings apply to computers, and user settings apply to users. However, there are a couple of subtleties that sometimes elude administrators.

It's common for a user object and a computer object to be in the same OU. But if the objects are in different containers, the settings are applied differently. For example, look at Figure 7.7. The User account for Joe is in the IT OU, and he's logging on to a computer in the Sales OU. The Sales OU has a GPO named NoGames that has enabled Remove Games Link From The Start Menu in the User Configuration node. This setting is located in the User Configuration ➢ Policies ➢ Administrative Templates ➢ Start Menu And Taskbar node.

Because Joe's user account is in the IT OU, the User Configuration settings on the Sales OU GPO don't apply to his account. The link to the Games menu will remain on his computer.

On the other hand, if Sally logs on to the same computer, the Games link will be removed because her user account is in the Sales OU.

If there are any conflicting settings between the User Configuration and the Computer Configuration nodes, the User Configuration settings will take precedence. To make this clear, it's important to know when GPOs are applied, and then you can use the simple rule of the last GPO applied wins. The following explains when they are applied:

Computer GPOs Applied When the computer first boots, the computer account retrieves all applied GPOs. If there are any conflicts with any of these settings, the last setting applied wins. The logon screen appears when Group Policy has been applied. In addition, the computer will check for updates or changes to computer Group Policy settings every 90–120 minutes (90 minutes with a random offset of 30 minutes).

FIGURE 7.7   User and Computer objects in different OUs

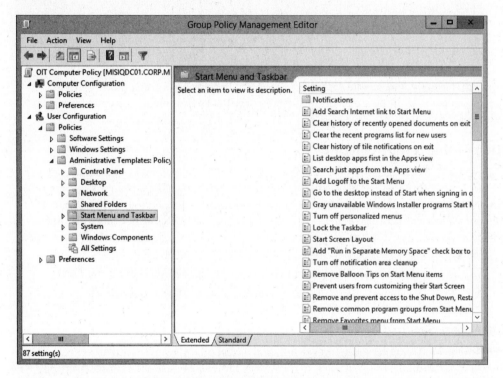

User GPOs Applied When a user first logs on, all the GPO settings that apply to the user are retrieved. If there are any conflicts with any of these settings, the last setting applied wins. If there are any conflicts with the computer settings, the user settings win. The desktop appears when Group Policy has been applied. In addition, a system will check for updates or changes to user Group Policy settings every 90–120 minutes (90 minutes with a random offset of 30 minutes).

You can improve performance of Group Policy by disabling either the User or Computer Configuration setting. For example, if there aren't any computer settings in a GPO, you can right-click over the policy in the Group Policy Editor, select Properties, and then select the Disable Computer Configuration Settings check box.

Group Policy Settings

One thing you will realize quickly about Group Policy is that you will never learn all the settings you can make. Instead, you can learn the process of setting Group Policy options and then use Help or other references to learn about particular Group Policy settings you can make. In this section, we'll look at three key default areas you can modify. Occasionally, you may need to modify the default Group Policy behavior as applied to users and computers within the domain. When necessary, you can use the following three settings for special circumstances:

- Block Inheritance
- Enforced
- Loopback Processing

Use of these settings should be the exception. In other words, their usage should be minimal. Group Policy can be complex on its own, but when you start modifying the default behavior with these exceptions, it can make the environment even more complex and harder to maintain.

Block Inheritance Setting

It's possible to block the inheritance of all GPOs for an OU. For example, you could create an OU for testing purposes and decide that you don't want to allow GPOs from the domain or parent OUs to apply. You can enable *the Block Inheritance* setting on the OU. Enable block inheritance by right-clicking the OU and selecting Block Inheritance. Once this is set, there will be an icon of an exclamation point in a blue circle to indicate block inheritance is enabled.

When using block inheritance, keep in mind these two important points:

- You can block inheritance only at an OU. You can't block inheritance of a GPO.
- All GPOs are blocked. You can't pick and choose which GPO to block.

Enforced Setting

Very often you'll want to configure settings and ensure that they are not overwritten or blocked. Normally, the last GPO applied wins, but you can use the Enforced setting to override this default behavior. In other words, if the *enforced* GPO is the first one applied and other GPOs have conflicting settings, the GPO with the Enforced setting will always win. In addition, if any OUs have the Block Inheritance setting enabled, the GPO configured with the Enforced setting will not be blocked.

As an example, you may have configured different security settings in the Default Domain policy that you want to ensure are applied to all users and computers in the domain. You don't want the settings overwritten by conflicting GPOs or by the Block Inheritance setting on an OU.

The Default Domain Policy GPO can be set to Enforced. This setting is enabled by right-clicking the GPO and selecting Enforced. A GPO that has the Enforced setting will have an icon of a lock to indicate that Enforced is enabled.

Real World Scenario

Configuring Enforced on the Default Domain Policy

The Enforced setting is often configured on the Default Domain policy or another domain policy that administrators want to ensure is applied to all objects in the domain. This prevents administrators who have been delegated permissions at the OU level from blocking the domain-level policy.

In some larger enterprises, rights and permissions are often delegated to administrators to manage different OUs. When this is done, different IT professionals are granted full control at the OU, but they are not granted permissions at the domain level.

For example, an organization could have several departments such as Sales, Marketing, HR, and IT. Full control can be granted to a group of administrators to the Sales OU but no permissions at the domain level or to the other OUs.

Full control also includes the ability to block inheritance. This allows administrators to block domain policies. Although this may be acceptable for some policies, settings enforced on a domain-level policy ensure that the domain-level policy is not blocked.

Loopback Processing Setting

Loopback Processing is a Group Policy setting that will cause the computer Group Policy settings to take precedence over the user settings. Normally, the order in which GPOs are applied is as follows:

1. Computer turns on and computer GPOs are applied.

2. User logs on and user GPOs are applied.

Because the user logs on after the computer starts, the user settings are applied last and the user settings take precedence. However, loopback processing allows this behavior to be reversed. In other words, you can use the Loopback Processing setting to have the computer settings take precedence over the user settings. When configuring loopback processing, there are two approaches you can take:

Replace The computer settings defined in the computer's GPOs completely replace the settings that would normally apply to the user.

Merge The computer settings defined in the computer's GPOs are combined with the user settings that apply to the user. If any conflicts exist, the computer settings in the computer's GPOs take precedence.

Summary

In this chapter you learned about managing Windows 8.1 clients on a domain. As you learned, Windows 8.1 can be used in two different types of networks: a workgroup or a domain. When Windows 8.1 is first installed, it is a member of a workgroup by default. Workgroups are used in small offices, home offices, and home networks to allow users to share resources among themselves.

You also learned about Group Policies, the Group Policy Management Console, and the Group Policy Editor. Group Policy is a group of technologies that allows administrators within a domain to configure a setting one time and have it apply to multiple users or computers. Group Policy settings can be configured by using the Local Computer Policy (using the Group Policy Editor) or by using the Group Policy Management Console (GPMC) in a domain.

Exam Essentials

Understand domain basics.   You should know that usually networks of more than 10 users implement domains, although smaller networks set up as domains certainly do exist. There are no hard and fast rules as to when a workgroup grows into a domain. One key part is that a domain requires a domain controller, a computer set up with a network operating system (such as Windows Server 2012 or Windows Server 2008 R2).

Understand Group Policies.   You should know that the Local Computer Policy affects only the local machine. If only the Local Computer Policy is used, each individual computer must be modified. The Default Domain policy affects all users and computers in the domain. Other Group Policy objects (GPOs) can be created in a domain that will affect all the user accounts and computer accounts in a site or all the accounts in an organizational unit (OU).

Review Questions

You can find the answers in Appendix A.

1. You install Windows 8.1 on a stand-alone computer. You then connect that computer to a network. What is the default network configuration for the new computer on the network?

   A. Domain

   B. Workgroup

   C. Both A and B

   D. Neither A nor B

2. You are tasked with setting up a Windows domain on your network. From the following choices, which constitutes a Windows domain?

   A. One server running Windows Server 2008 or higher

   B. One server running as a domain name server

   C. One server acting as a domain controller and one hosting Active Directory Domain Services (AD DS)

   D. One server acting as the workgroup host

3. You are assigned as the network administrator for your company and you have multiple servers and 100+ client computers running Microsoft Windows 8.1. You want to make a change so that you turn off the Windows Store feature on all client computers. What is the most efficient method for doing so?

   A. Registry Editor

   B. Group Policy Management Console

   C. Domain Control Security Policy

   D. Terminal Servers Configuration tool

4. Which of the following Group Policy nodes lets you deploy applications to clients?

   A. Administrative Settings

   B. Windows Settings

   C. Configuration Settings

   D. Software Settings

5. When accessing resources on a network, including when connecting to a domain, you should be aware of two security principles. One of those principles is authentication; what is the other?

   A. Accessibility

   B. User rights assignments

   C. Authorization

   D. Inheritance

6. You are an administrator of your company network. You use the Computer Management Console to modify authentication groups. Which group provides complete control to all computers in a domain?

    A. Administrators

    B. Domain Admins

    C. Enterprise Admins

    D. Power Users

7. Windows supports two types of networks: domain and workgroup. Which type of network provides single sign-on capabilities so that users can use the same username and password regardless of the computer they use?

    A. Workgroup

    B. Domain

    C. Both A and B

    D. None of the above

8. The GPO scope refers to where it is applied. Which of the following scopes applies only to a single GPO?

    A. Multiple GPOs

    B. Domain OU

    C. Local Computer Policy

    D. Both B and C

9. When Group Policies are used to configure settings in a domain, typically the last GPO applied is the setting that is applied. You can, however, override this behavior using one of the following Group Policy settings—which one?

    A. Block Inheritance

    B. Loopback Processing

    C. Computer GPO

    D. Enforced

10. When referring to authorization, which of the following statements is true?

    A. Users are granted rights and permissions based on the user accounts that authenticate them.

    B. Local administrator accounts are not available in a domain.

    C. Rights identify the resources a user can access.

    D. All of these statements are true.

11. You have a Windows 8.1 user who installed a special printer on his computer. The computer is part of the Accounting group. In order for all members of the Accounting group to print to the printer, what permission must you give to the Accounting group?

    A. Print

    B. Manage Printer

    C. Manage Spooler

    D. Manage Print Queue

12. Which node in the Group Policy Editor would you use to deploy software to users?

    A. Software Settings

    B. Software Deployment

    C. Software Services

    D. Software Distribution

13. Your company upgraded to Windows 8.1 to ensure a more secure computing environment. You must now configure all client computers to require two-factor authentication. One of the authentication factors requires more than four characters or gestures. Which two authentication methods must you choose?

    A. Picture Password

    B. Microsoft account

    C. Biometric authentication

    D. PIN

14. As part of a rollout of Windows 8.1 computers, all users are required to use a new timesheet application that is accessible in Windows Store. To ensure that all users can log in and use the timesheet app, what should you do?

    A. Take a credit card from each user and charge them for using the app.

    B. Install the app on every computer.

    C. Load the app activation key in the GPO for the app.

    D. Create a Microsoft user account to access the app.

15. You received a request from the Director of Operations saying that his Windows 8.1 users are unable to download tools onto their workstations, and he asked you to make the users members of their local Administrators group to do this. However, a new security policy prevents you from making all the users administrators of their machines for the purpose of downloading tools. What should you do?

    A. Install all the tools yourself.

    B. Make all users members of the local Administrator Group, but keep it quiet.

    C. Set the Internet Zone Security to Medium.

    D. Change the setting in Group Policy.

16. You are in charge of 1,000 Windows 8.1 workstations in the main office of your company. Something is causing all the machines to lock out their users with the message that they don't have sufficient rights to log on. To avoid the company shutting down, what should you do?

    A. Disconnect everyone from the network.

    B. Create a GPO to block inheritance to determine if a GPO is causing the problem.

    C. Move everyone to a group not affected by Group Policy.

    D. Link a GPO to the OU that contains the computers you need to manage after hours.

17. The security manager has issued a directive that new users not be allowed to download documents from any corporate machine to a removable storage device, such as a USB "thumb" drive. Existing users should still be able to do so. What's the best way to do this using Group Policy?

    A. Create a GPO and set Allow Save To External Devices to Disabled.

    B. Create a GPO and set Enable External Devices to False.

    C. Create a GPO and set Prevent Installation Of Removable Devices to Enabled.

    D. Create a GPO and set Allow Administrators To Override Device Installation Restrictions Policies to Enabled.

18. What is the default setting for how often a computer checks for Group Policy settings?

    A. Every 90–120 minutes (90 minutes with a random offset of 30 minutes)

    B. Every 60–120 minutes (90 minutes with a random offset of 30 minutes)

    C. Every 60–90 minutes (90 minutes with a random offset of 60 minutes)

    D. None of the statements is true.

19. You created a folder on the corporate file server and shared it for a certain group of users. You have one set of users in the group that need only read permission; a second set needs full access to the files and you need to make sure that no user can delete the folder. How can you configure permissions to protect the share?

    A. Assign a group named Read and give the group Read permissions only and create a group name Owner and assign the Owner group the Full Control permission and use special permission to remove the Delete permission.

    B. Assign the Read group Read permissions and give the latter group Full Control.

    C. Assign the Read group Read And Modify and the latter group the Delete permission.

    D. The folder should be set to Not Shared.

20. You installed and allocated 20 Windows 8.1 tablets to the night nursing staff. You need to force the tablets to sleep when users press the power button. What should you do?

    A. In Power Settings, enable Sleep When Not In Use.

    B. Enable Sleep When Not Active in the tablet's BIOS. Administrator accounts are not available in a domain.

    C. Create a GPO to configure Power Options.

    D. Create a GPO to configure Button Options.

Chapter

8

Users and Groups

70-687 MICROSOFT EXAM OBJECTIVES COVERED IN THIS CHAPTER:

✓ Migrate and configure user data

✓ Migrate user profiles; configure folder location; configure profiles, including profile version, local, roaming, and mandatory

✓ Configure authentication and authorization

✓ Configure authentication in workgroups or domains

✓ Manage Users and Groups

70-688 MICROSOFT EXAM OBJECTIVES COVERED IN THIS CHAPTER:

✓ Manage clients by using Windows Intune

✓ Manage user and computer groups

This may be one of the most important chapters in this study guide. Setting up users, groups, and security are some of the most critical tasks that any IT manager will perform.

One of the most fundamental tasks in network management is creating user and group accounts. Without a user account, a user cannot log on to a computer, server, or network.

When users log on, they supply a username and password. Then their user accounts are validated by a security mechanism. In Windows 8.1, users can log on to a computer locally, or they can log on through Active Directory.

Group accounts are used to ease network administration by grouping users who have similar permission requirements. Groups are an important part of network management. Many administrators are able to accomplish the majority of their management tasks through the use of groups; they rarely assign permissions to individual users that are not part of any group. Windows 8.1 includes built-in local groups, such as Administrators and Backup Operators.

You create and manage local groups through the Local Users and Groups utility. With this utility, you can add groups, change group membership, rename groups, and delete groups.

Windows 8.1 also offers a wide variety of security options. If the Windows 8.1 computer is a part of a domain, you can apply security through a Group Policy object using the Group Policy Management Console. If the Windows 8.1 computer is not a part of a domain, you use Local Group Policy objects to manage local security.

You will learn about the environments in which Windows 8.1 can be installed and the utilities that are used to manage security. You can use policies to help manage user accounts. Account policies control the logon environment for the computer, such as password and logon restrictions. Local policies specify what users can do once they log on and include auditing, user rights, and security options. You can also manage critical security features through the Windows Action Center.

Overview of Windows 8.1 User Accounts

When you install Windows 8.1, several user accounts are created automatically. You can then create new user accounts. As you already know, user accounts allow a user to access resources.

On Windows 8.1 devices, you can create local user accounts. If your network has a Windows Server 2012/2012 R2, Windows Server 2008/2008 R2, Windows Server 2003, or Windows Server 2000 domain controller, your network can have domain user accounts as well.

One of the features included with Windows 8.1 is User Account Control (UAC). UAC provides an additional level of security by limiting the level of access that users have when performing everyday tasks. When needed, users can gain elevated access for specific administrative tasks.

In the following sections, you will learn about the default user accounts that are created by Windows 8.1 and the difference between local and domain user accounts.

Account Types

Windows 8.1 supports two basic types of user accounts: administrator and standard user (see Figure 8.1). Each is used for specific reasons:

FIGURE 8.1   Change Your Account Type screen

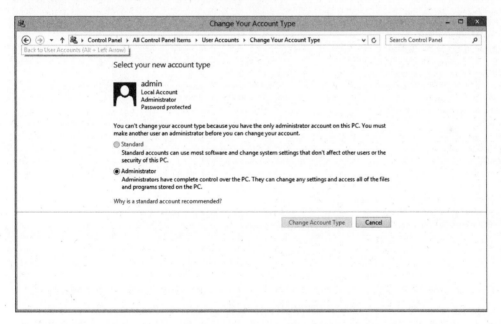

Administrator   The administrator account type provides unrestricted access for performing administrative tasks. As a result, administrator accounts should be used only for performing administrative tasks and should not be used for normal computing tasks.

Only administrator accounts can change the Registry. This is important to know because when most software is installed on a Windows 8.1 machine, the Registry gets changed. This is why you need administrator rights to install most software.

Standard User   The standard user account type should be assigned to every user of the computer. Standard user accounts can perform most day-to-day tasks, such as running Microsoft Word, accessing email, using Internet Explorer, and so on. Running as a standard user increases security by limiting the possibility of a virus or other malicious code from infecting the computer. Standard user accounts are unable to make system-wide changes, which also helps to increase security.

When you install Windows 8.1, by default there are predefined accounts called built-in accounts. Let's take a look at them.

Built-in Accounts

Built-in accounts are accounts that are created at the time you install the Windows 8.1 operating system. Windows 8.1, when installed into a workgroup environment, has four user accounts (see Figure 8.2).

FIGURE 8.2   Four default accounts

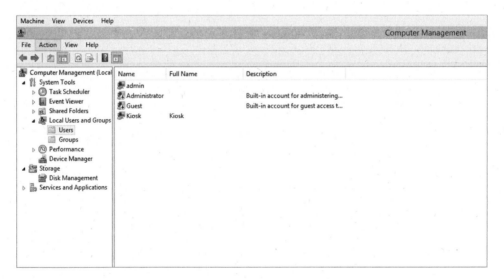

Administrator   The Administrator account is a special account that has full control over the computer. The Administrator account can perform all tasks, such as creating users and groups, managing the filesystem, and setting up printing. Note that the Administrator account is disabled by default.

Guest   The Guest account allows users to access the computer even if they do not have a unique username and password. Because of the inherent security risks associated with this type of user, the Guest account is disabled by default. When this account is enabled, it is usually given very limited privileges.

Initial User   The initial user account uses the name of the registered user. By default, the initial user is a member of the Administrators group.

HomeGroup user   The HomeGroup user is created by default to allow this machine to connect to other machines within the same HomeGroup network. This account is created by default as soon as you set up a HomeGroup.

By default, the name Administrator is given to a user account that is a member of the Administrators group. However, in Windows 8.1, this user account is disabled by default. You can increase the computer's security by leaving this account disabled and assigning other members to the Administrators group. This way, a malicious user will be unable to log on to the computer using the Administrator user account.

These users are considered local users and their permissions are contained to the Windows 8.1 machine. A local user's account is an account that must reside on the Windows 8.1 machine. This account would not let the user access any resources on a networked environment. If you need the user's account to access resources on machines other than their own, you can have users log into the Windows 8.1 computer as remote users and this would be considered a domain or a workgroup user's account. Let's take a look at the difference between these account types.

Local and Domain User Accounts

Windows 8.1 supports two kinds of users: local users and domain users. A computer that is running Windows 8.1 has the ability to store its own user accounts database. The user accounts stored at the local computer are known as local user accounts.

Active Directory is a directory service that is available with the Windows Server 2012/2012 R2, Windows Server 2008 R2, Windows Server 2008, Windows Server 2003, and Windows 2000 Server platforms. It stores information in a central database, called Active Directory, which allows users to have a single user account for the network. The users stored in Active Directory's central database are called domain user accounts.

If you use local user accounts, they must be configured on each computer that the user needs to access within the network. For this reason, domain user accounts are commonly used to manage users on any network larger than 10 users.

On Windows 8.1, Windows Server 2012, Windows Server 2012 R2, Windows Server 2008 R2, Windows Server 2008, Windows Server 2003, Windows Vista, and Windows XP computers, you can create local users through the Local Users and Groups utility, as described in the section "Working with User Accounts" later in this chapter. On all versions of Windows Server domain controllers, you manage users with the Microsoft Active Directory Users and Computers utility.

Active Directory is covered in detail in the *MCSA Windows Server 2012 Complete Study Guide: Exams 70-410, 70-411, 70-412, and 70-417* by William Panek (Sybex, 2013).

Now that we have looked at the different types of users and accounts, it's important to understand how to use accounts to log on and log off the local machine or domain.

Logging On and Logging Off

Users must log on to a Windows 8.1 computer before they can use it. When you create user accounts, you set up the computer to accept the logon information provided by the user. You can log on locally to a Windows 8.1 computer using a local computer account, or you can log on to a domain using an Active Directory account.

When you install the computer, by default it will be a part of a workgroup, which implies a local logon. If the computer is installed into a domain it will require domain logon.

When users are ready to stop working on a Windows 8.1 computer, they should log off. Users can log off through the Windows Security dialog box.

In the following sections, you will learn about local user authentication and how a user logs out of a Windows 8.1 computer.

Using Local User Logon Authentication

Depending on whether you are logging on to a computer locally or are logging into a domain, Windows 8.1 uses two different logon procedures. When you log on to a Windows 8.1 computer locally, you must present a valid username and password (ones that exist within the local accounts database). As part of a successful authentication, the following steps take place:

1. At system startup, users are prompted to click their username in a list of users who have been created locally. This is significantly different from the Ctrl+Alt+Del logon sequence that was used by earlier versions of Windows. The Ctrl+Alt+Del sequence is still used when you log on to a domain environment. You can also use Group Policy to configure the Ctrl+Alt+Del logon sequence as an option in a local environment by using a local Group Policy object (GPO).

2. The local computer compares the user's logon credentials with the information in the local security database.

3. If the information presented matches the account database, an access token is created. Access tokens are used to identify the user and the groups of which that user is a member.

Access tokens are created only when you log on. If you change group memberships, you need to log off and log on again to update the access token.

The following actions also take place as part of the logon process:

- The system reads the part of the Registry that contains user configuration information.

- The user's profile is loaded. (User profiles are discussed in the section "Setting Up User Profiles, Logon Scripts, and Home Folders" later in this chapter.)

- Any policies that have been assigned to the user through a user or Group Policy are enforced. (Policies for users are discussed in Chapter 9 in the section, "Managing Security Configurations.")

- Any logon scripts that have been assigned are executed. (We'll discuss assigning logon scripts to users in the section "Setting Up User Profiles, Logon Scripts, and Home Folders.")

- Persistent network and printer connections are restored.

Now that you have seen how a local logon process works, let's take a look at logging off a Windows 8.1 machine.

Signing Out of Windows 8.1

To sign out of Windows 8.1, you click Start, point to the arrow next to the Shutdown button, and then click Sign Out. Pressing Ctrl+Alt+Del will present you with a screen that will allow you to select whether to lock the computer, switch users, sign out, change the password, or start Task Manager.

Signing Out of Computers

A common problem in many companies is that users come in on Monday, turn on their computers, and then leave them signed on until Friday night. Having users signed in to a local machine or to a network all week long is a dangerous practice. This makes it easy for any other user in the company to sit down at their machine and cause trouble. Have your users get into the practice of signing off at night and locking their keyboard when stepping away for break or lunch.

Now that you understand the different types of accounts on a Windows 8.1 computer, let's take a look at how to manage these accounts.

Working with User Accounts

To set up and manage your local user accounts, you use the Local Users and Groups utility or the User Accounts option in Control Panel. With either option, you can create, disable, delete, and rename user accounts as well as change user passwords.

Using the Local Users and Groups Utility

There are two common methods for accessing the Local Users and Groups utility:

- You can load Local Users and Groups as a Microsoft Management Console (MMC) snap-in.
- You can access the Local Users and Groups utility through the Computer Management utility.

In Exercise 8.1, you will add the Local Users and Groups snap-in MMC to the Desktop. This exercise needs to be completed in order to complete other exercises in this chapter.

EXERCISE 8.1

Adding the Local Users And Groups Snap-In

1. Click the Windows Key and in the Search box, type **MMC** and press Enter.

2. If a warning box appears, click Yes.

3. Select File ➢ Add/Remove Snap-In.

4. Scroll down the list and highlight Local Users And Groups, and then click the Add button.

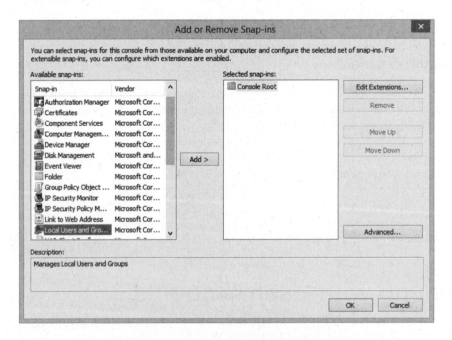

5. In the Choose Target Machine dialog box, click the Finish button to accept the default selection of Local Computer.

6. Click OK in the Add Or Remove Snap-in dialog box.

7. In the MMC window, right-click the Local Users and Groups folder and choose New Window From Here. You will see that Local Users and Groups is now the main window.

8. Click File ➤ Save As. Name the console **Local Users And Groups** and choose Desktop from the Save As drop-down box. Click the Save button.

9. Close the MMC snap-in.

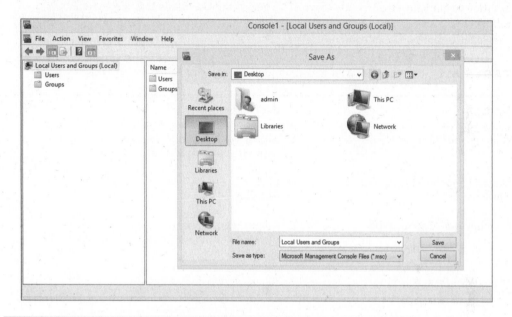

You should now see the Local Users and Groups snap-in on the Desktop. You can also open the Local Users and Groups MMC from the Computer Management utility, which you'll do in Exercise 8.2. Complete this exercise for opening the Local Users and Groups utility from the Computer Management utility.

EXERCISE 8.2

Using the Local Users And Groups Snap-In

1. Right-click on the Quick Access button, and then click Computer Management.

2. In the Computer Management window, expand the System Tools folder and then the Local Users and Groups folder.

If your computer doesn't have the MMC configured, the quickest way to access the Local Users and Groups utility is through the Computer Management utility.

Now let's look at another way to configure users: using the User Accounts option in Control Panel.

Using the User Accounts Option in Control Panel

The *User Accounts* option in Control Panel provides the ability to manage user accounts in addition to configuring parental controls. To access the User Accounts screen, right-click on the Quick Access menu and select Control Panel; then click User Accounts. Table 8.1 shows the options you can configure.

TABLE 8.1   Configurable user account options in Control Panel

Option	Explanation
Change Your Account Name	Allows you to change your account name without changing its GUID.
Make Changes To My Account In PC Settings	Click to access the same settings in PC Settings.
Change Your Account Type	Allows you to change your account type between the standard user and administrator account type.
Manage Another Account	Allows you to configure other accounts on the Windows 8.1 machine.
Change User Account Control Settings	Allows you to set the level of notification of when changes are made to your computer. These notifications can prevent potentially hazardous programs from being loaded onto the operating system.
Manage Your Credentials	Lets you set up credentials that allow you to easily connect to websites that require usernames and passwords or computers that require certificates.
Create A Password Reset Disk	Allows you to create a disk that users can use when they forget their password.
Family Safety	Click to access the Family Safety settings page.
Manage Your File Encryption Certificates	Allows you to manage your file encryption certificates.

Option	Explanation
Configure Advanced User Profile Properties	Brings you directly to the User's Profile dialog box in Control Panel ➤ System ➤ Advanced ➤ System Settings.
Change My Environment Variables	Allows you to access the Environment Variables dialog box directly.

Once Windows 8.1 is installed, you must create user accounts for users who will be accessing the machine. Let's now take a look at how to create new user accounts.

Creating New Users

To create users on a Windows 8.1 computer, you must be logged on as a user with permission to create a new user, or you must be a member of the Administrators group. In the following sections, you will learn about username rules and conventions, usernames, and security identifiers in more detail.

Username Rules and Conventions

The only real requirement for creating a new user is that you must provide a valid username. To be valid, the name must follow the Windows 8.1 rules for usernames. However, it's also a good idea to have your own rules for usernames, which form your *naming convention*.

The following are the Windows 8.1 rules for usernames:

- A username must be from 1 to 20 characters.

- The username must be unique among all the other user and group names stored on the computer.

- The username cannot contain any of the following characters:

    * / \ [ ] : ; | = , + ? < > " @

- A username cannot consist exclusively of periods or spaces.

Keeping these rules in mind, you should choose a naming convention (a consistent naming format). For example, consider a user named Nelson Mandela. One naming convention might be to use the last name and first initial, for the username NelM or NelsonM. Another naming convention might use the first initial and last name, for the username NMandela. This is the naming convention followed by many midsized to larger organizations.

You could base usernames on the naming convention defined for email names so that the logon name and the name in the email address match. You should also provide a mechanism that would accommodate duplicate names. For example, if you had a user named Jane Smith and a user named John Smith, you might use a middle initial for usernames, such as JDSmith and JRSmith.

It is also a good practice to come up with a naming convention for groups, printers, and computers.

Using first name, first initial of last name (NelsonM) as a naming convention may not be the best choice. In a midsized to large company, there is the possibility of having two NelsonMs, but the odds that you will have two NMandelas are rare.

If you choose to use the first name, first initial of last name option, it can be a lot of work to go back and change this format later if the company grows larger. Choose a naming convention that can grow with the company.

Now let's take a look at how usernames get a special ID number associated with the account and how that number affects your accounts.

Usernames and Security Identifiers

When you create a new user, a *security identifier (SID)* is automatically created on the computer for the user account. The username is a property of the SID. For example, a user SID might look like this:

```
S-1-5-21-823518204-746137067-120266-629-500
```

It's apparent that using SIDs for user identification would make administration a nightmare. Fortunately, for your administrative tasks you see and use the username instead of the SID.

SIDs have several advantages. Because Windows 8.1 uses the SID as the user object, you can easily rename a user while still retaining all the user's properties. The reason for this is that all security settings get associated with the SID and not the user account.

SIDs also ensure that if you delete and re-create a user account with the same username, the new user account will not have any of the properties of the old account because it is based on a new, unique SID. Every time you create a new user, a unique SID is associated with it. Even if the username is the same as a previously deleted account, the system still sees the username as a new user.

Because every user account gets a unique SID number, it is a good practice to disable rather than delete accounts for users who leave the company or have an extended absence. If you ever need to access the disabled account again, you have the ability.

When you create a new user, there are many options that you have to configure. Table 8.2 describes all the options available in the New User dialog box.

TABLE 8.2   User account options available in the New User dialog box

Option	Description
User Name	Defines the username for the new account. Choose a name that is consistent with your naming convention (e.g., NMandela). This is the only required field. Usernames are not case sensitive.
Full Name	Allows you to provide more detailed name information. This is typically the user's first and last names. (By default, this field contains the same name as the User Name field.

Option	Description
Description	Typically used to specify a title and/or location (e.g., Sales-Nashville) for the account, but it can be used to provide any additional information about the user.
Password	Assigns the initial password for the user. For security purposes, avoid using readily available information about the user. Passwords are case sensitive.
Confirm Password	Confirms that you typed the password the same way two times to verify that you entered the password correctly.
User Must Change Password At Next Logon	If enabled, forces the user to change the password the first time they log on. This is done to increase security. By default, this option is selected.
User Cannot Change Password	If enabled, prevents a user from changing their password. It is useful for accounts such as Guest and accounts that are shared by more than one user. By default, this option is not selected.
Password Never Expires	If enabled, specifies that the password will never expire, even if a password policy has been specified. For example, you might enable this option if this is a service account and you do not want the administrative overhead of managing password changes. By default, this option is not selected.
Account Is Disabled	If enabled, specifies that this account cannot be used for logon purposes. For example, you might select this option for template accounts or if an account is not currently being used. It helps keep inactive accounts from posing security threats. By default, this option is not selected.

In Exercise 8.3, you will create a new local user account. Before you complete the following steps, make sure you are logged on as a user with permissions to create new users and have already added the Local Users And Groups snap-in to the MMC.

EXERCISE 8.3

Creating New Users

1. Open the Admin Console MMC Desktop shortcut that you created in Exercise 8.1: Adding the Local Users And Groups Snap-In, expand the Local Users and Groups snap-in. If a dialog box appears, click Yes.

2. Highlight the Users folder and select Action ➢ New User. The New User dialog box appears.

3.   In the User Name text box, type **NMandela**.

4.   In the Full Name text box, type **Nelson Mandela**.

5.   In the Description text box, type **Operations Manager**.

6.   Leave the Password and Confirm Password text boxes empty and accept the defaults for the check boxes. Make sure you deselect the User Must Change Password At Next Logon option. Click the Create button to add the user.

7.   Use the New User dialog box to create six more users, filling out the fields as follows:

Name: NMandela; Full Name: Nelson Mandela; Description: IT Admin; Password: (blank)

Name: JDoe; Full Name: John Doe; Description: Cisco Admin; Password: (blank)

Name: GWashington; Full Name: George Washington; Description: President; Password: P@ssw0rD

Name: JAdams; Full Name: John Adams; Description: Vice President; Password: v!$t@

Name: BFranklin; Full Name: Ben Franklin; Description: NH Sales Manager; Password: P3@ch (with an uppercase P)

Name: ALincoln; Full Name: Abe Lincoln; Description: Tech Support; Password: Bearded1 (uppercase B)

8.   After you've finished creating all of the users, click the Close button to exit the New User dialog box.

You can also create users through the command-line utility Net User. For more information, type **NET USER /?** at the command prompt.

As we stated earlier, it's good practice to disable accounts for users who leave the company. Let's take a look at the process of disabling accounts.

Disabling User Accounts

When a user account is no longer needed, the account should be disabled or deleted. After you've disabled an account, you can later enable it again to restore it with all of its associated user properties. An account that is deleted, however, can never be recovered.

You might disable an account because a user will not be using it for a period of time, perhaps because that employee is going on vacation or taking a leave of absence. Another reason to disable an account is that you're planning to put another user in that same function.

For example, suppose that Gary, the engineering manager, quits. If you disable his account, when your company hires a new engineering manager, you can simply rename Gary's user account (to the username for the new manager) and enable it. This ensures that the user who takes over Gary's position will have all the same user properties and own all the same resources.

Disabling accounts also provides a security mechanism for special situations. For example, if your company was laying off a group of people, as a security measure you could disable their accounts at the same time the layoff notices were given out. This prevents those users from inflicting any damage to the company's files after they receive their layoff notice.

In Exercise 8.4, you will disable a user account. Before you complete the following steps, you should have already created new users in Exercise 8.3.

EXERCISE 8.4

Disabling Accounts

1. Open the Admin Console MMC Desktop shortcut and expand the Local Users and Groups snap-in.

2. Open the Users folder. Double-click user NMandela to open his Properties dialog box.

3. In the General tab, check the Account Is Disabled box. Click OK.

4. Close the Local Users and Groups MMC.

5. Log off and attempt to log on as NMandela. This should fail because the account is now disabled.

6. Log back on using your user account.

 You can also access a user's properties by highlighting the user, right-clicking, and selecting Properties.

Now when users have left a company for a long period of time and you know you no longer need the user account, you can delete it. Let's take a look at how to delete user accounts.

Deleting User Accounts

As noted in the preceding section, you should disable a user account if you are not sure if the account will or will not be needed again. But if the account has been disabled and you know that the user account will never need access to it again, you should delete the account.

To delete a user, follow these steps:

1. Swipe in from the right edge of the screen, click Settings, and select Change PC Settings.

2. Click Accounts; then, if there are other accounts on the machine, click Other Accounts.

3. Click the account you want to delete, and then click the Remove option.

Alternatively, open the Local Users and Groups utility, highlight the user account you wish to delete, and click Action to bring up the menu shown in Figure 8.3. Then select Delete. You can also delete an account by clicking on the account and pressing the Delete key on the keyboard.

FIGURE 8.3   Deleting a user account

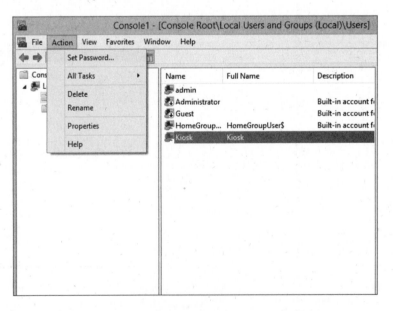

Because deleting an account is a permanent action, you will see the dialog box shown in Figure 8.4, asking you to confirm that you really wish to delete the account. After you click the Yes button, you will not be able to re-create or re-access the account (unless you restore your local user accounts database from a backup).

FIGURE 8.4   Confirming account deletion

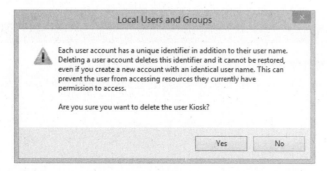

Complete Exercise 8.5 to delete a user account from the MMC. These steps assume you have completed the previous exercises in this chapter.

EXERCISE 8.5

Deleting a User Account

1. Open the Admin Console MMC Desktop shortcut and expand the Local Users and Groups snap-in.

2. Expand the Users folder and single-click on user JAdams to select his user account.

3. Select Action ➤ Delete or right-click the account name and select Delete from the context menu. The dialog box for confirming user deletion appears.

4. Click Yes to confirm that you wish to delete this user.

5. Close the Local Users and Groups MMC.

Now that you have disabled and deleted accounts, let's take a look at how to rename a user's account.

Renaming User Accounts

Once an account has been created, you can rename it at any time. Renaming a user account allows the user to retain all the associated user properties of the previous username. As noted earlier in the chapter, the name is a property of the SID.

You might want to rename a user account because the user's name has changed (for example, the user got married) or because the name was spelled incorrectly. Also, as explained in the section "Disabling User Accounts," you can rename an existing user's account for a new user, such as someone hired to take an ex-employee's position, when you want the new user to have the same properties.

Exercise 8.6 shows you how to rename a user account. These steps assume you have completed all of the previous exercises in this chapter.

EXERCISE 8.6

Renaming a User Account

1. Open the Admin Console MMC Desktop shortcut and expand the Local Users and Groups snap-in.

2. Open the Users folder and highlight user ALincoln.

3. Select Action ➢ Rename.

4. Type the username **RReagan** and press Enter. Notice that the Full Name field retained the original property of Abe Lincoln in the Local Users and Groups utility.

5. Double-click RReagan to open the properties and change the user's full name to Ronald Reagan.

6. Click the User Must Change Password At Next Logon check box.

7. Click OK.

8. Close the Local Users and Groups MMC.

Renaming a user does not change any "hard-coded" names, such as the name of the user's home folder. If you want to change these names as well, you need to modify them manually—for example, through Windows Explorer.

Another common task that we must deal with is resetting the user's password. Let's take a look at how to do that.

Changing a User's Password

What should you do if users forget their password and can't log on? You can't just open a dialog box and see the old password. However, as the administrator, you can change the password, and then the user can use the new one.

It is highly recommended that users create a password reset disk before they encounter password problems. If they have done this, they can use the password reset disk to change their password when they forget it without your help!

It is very important that as IT professionals we teach our users proper security measures that go along with password protection. As you have all probably seen before, the users who tape their password to their monitors or under the keyboards are not using proper security. In Exercise 8.7, you will change a user's password. This exercise assumes you have completed all the previous exercises in this chapter.

EXERCISE 8.7

Changing a User's Password

1. Open the Admin Console MMC Desktop shortcut and expand the Local Users and Groups snap-in.

2. Open the Users folder and highlight user BFranklin.

3. Select Action ➢ Set Password. The Set Password dialog box appears.

4. A warning appears indicating the risks involved in changing the password. This warning relates to the problems that can occur when the account has been used to encrypt data using EFS. The EFS files are encrypted using a certificate that's attached to a specific Windows account, which means that any change to the password or account has the effect that the files cannot be decrypted anymore. Select Proceed.

5. Type the new password and then confirm the password. Click OK.

6. Close the Local Users and Groups MMC.

Now that you have seen how to create users in Windows 8.1, let's see how to configure and manage your users' properties.

Managing User Properties

For more control over user accounts, you can configure user properties. In the user's Properties dialog box, you can change the original password options, add the user to existing groups, and specify user profile information.

To open a user's Properties dialog box, access the Local Users and Groups utility, open the Users folder, and double-click the user account. The user's Properties dialog box has tabs for the three main categories of properties: General, Member Of, and Profile.

The General tab contains the information you supplied when you set up the new user account, including the full name and a description, the password options you selected, and whether the account is disabled. If you want to modify any of these properties after you've created the user, open the user's Properties dialog box and make the changes on the General tab.

You can use the Member Of tab to manage the user's membership in groups. The Profile tab lets you set properties to customize the user's environment. The following sections discuss the Member Of and Profile tabs in detail.

Managing User Group Membership

The Member Of tab of the user's Properties dialog box displays all the groups that the user belongs to, as shown in Figure 8.5. On this tab, you can add the user to an existing group or remove the user from a group. To add a user to a group, click the Add button and select the group that the user should belong to. If you want to remove the user from a group, highlight the group and click the Remove button.

FIGURE 8.5   The Member Of tab of the user's Properties dialog box

Complete Exercise 8.8 to add a user to an existing group. These steps assume you have completed all the previous exercises in this chapter.

EXERCISE 8.8

Changing a User's Properties

1. Open the Local Users and Groups MMC Desktop snap-in that you created previously.

2. Open the Users folder and double-click user Kiosk. The Kiosk Properties dialog box appears.

3. Select the Member Of tab and click the Add button. The Select Groups dialog box appears.

4. Under Enter The Object Names To Select, type **Backup Operators**, and click the Check Names button. After the name is confirmed, click OK.

5. Click OK to close the Kiosk Properties dialog box.

The final tab in the user's properties is called the Profile tab. In the next section, you'll learn about the Profile tab and what options you can configure.

Setting Up User Profiles, Logon Scripts, and Home Folders

The Profile tab of the user's Properties dialog box, shown in Figure 8.6, allows you to customize the user's environment. Here, you can specify the following items for the user:

- User profile path
- Logon script
- Home folder

FIGURE 8.6   The Profile tab of the user's Properties dialog box

The following sections describe how these properties work and when you might want to use them.

Setting a Profile Path

User profiles contain information about the Windows 8.1 environment for a specific user. For example, profile settings include the Desktop arrangement, program groups, and screen colors that users see when they log on.

Each time you log on to a Windows 8.1 computer, the system checks to see if you have a local user profile in the Users folder, which was created on the boot partition when you installed Windows 8.1.

The first time users log on, they receive a default user profile. A folder that matches the user's logon name is created for the user in the Users folder. The user profile folder that is created holds a file called ntuser.dat as well as subfolders that contain directory links to the user's Desktop items.

In Exercise 8.9, you'll create two new users and set up local user profiles.

EXERCISE 8.9

Setting Up User Profiles

1. Using the Local Users and Groups utility, create two new users: BSmith and JJones. Deselect the User Must Change Password At Next Logon option for each user.

2. Select Start ➤ All Programs ➤ Accessories ➤ Windows Explorer. Expand Computer, then Local Disk (C:), and then Users. Notice that the Users folder does not contain user profile folders for the new users.

3. Log off and log on as BSmith.

4. Right-click an open area on the Desktop and select Personalize. In the Personalization dialog box, select a color scheme and click Apply, and then click OK.

5. Right-click an open area on the Desktop and select New ➤ Shortcut. In the Create Shortcut dialog box, type **CALC**. Accept CALC as the name for the shortcut and click Finish.

6. Log off as BSmith and log on as JJones. Notice that user JJones sees the Desktop configuration stored in the default user profile.

7. Log off as JJones and log on as BSmith. Notice that BSmith sees the Desktop configuration you set up in steps 3, 4, and 5.

8. Log off as BSmith and log on as your user account. Select Start ➤ All Programs ➤ Accessories ➤ Windows Explorer. Expand Computer, then Local Disk (C:), and then Users. Notice that this folder now contains user profile folders for BSmith and JJones.

The drawback of local user profiles is that they are available only on the computer where they were created. When computers are part of a domain, local user profiles don't make sense.

User Rick logs on at Computer A and creates a customized user profile. When he logs on to Computer B for the first time, he will receive the default user profile rather than the customized user profile he created on Computer A. For users to access their user profile from any computer they log on to, you need to use roaming profiles; however, these require the use of a network server because they can't be stored on a local Windows 8.1 computer.

In the next sections, you'll learn how roaming and mandatory profiles can be used. To have a roaming or mandatory profile, your computer must be a part of a network with server access.

Using Roaming Profiles

A roaming profile is stored on a network server and allows users to access their user profile regardless of the client computer to which they're logged on. Roaming profiles provide a consistent Desktop for users who move around, no matter which computer they access. Even if the server that stores the roaming profile is unavailable, the user can still log on using a local profile.

If you are using roaming profiles, the contents of the user's systemdrive:\Users\ UserName folder will be copied to the local computer each time the roaming profile is accessed. If you have stored large files in any subfolders of your user profile folder, you may notice a significant delay when accessing your profile remotely as opposed to locally.

If this problem occurs, you can reduce the amount of time the roaming profile takes to load by moving the subfolder to another location, such as the user's home directory, or you can use GPOs within Active Directory to specify that specific folders should be excluded when the roaming profile is loaded.

Using Mandatory Profiles

A *mandatory profile* is a profile that can't be modified by the user. Only members of the Administrators group can manage mandatory profiles. You might consider creating mandatory profiles for users who should maintain consistent Desktops.

For example, suppose you have a group of 20 salespeople who know enough about system configuration to make changes but not enough to fix any problems they create. For ease of support, you could use mandatory profiles. This way, all of the salespeople will always have the same profile, which they will not be able to change.

You can create mandatory profiles for a single user or a group of users. The mandatory profile is stored in a file named ntuser.man. A user with a mandatory profile can set different Desktop preferences while logged on, but those settings will not be saved when the user logs off.

 You can use only roaming profiles as mandatory profiles. Mandatory profiles do not work for local user profiles. User profiles become mandatory profiles when the administrator renames the ntuser.dat file on the server to ntuser.man.

There is a second type of mandatory profile called the super mandatory profile. Let's take a look.

Using Super Mandatory Profiles

A super mandatory profile is a mandatory user profile with an additional layer of security. With mandatory profiles, a temporary profile is created if the mandatory profile is not available when a user logs on. However, when super mandatory profiles are configured, temporary profiles are not created if the mandatory profile is not available over the network and the user is unable to log on to the computer.

Mandatory profiles become super mandatory profiles when stored in a profile path ending in .man—for example, \\server\share\mandatoryprofile.man\.

 Real World Scenario

Copying User Profiles

Within your company you have a user, Paige, who logs in with two different user accounts. One account is a regular user account, and the other is an Administrator account used for administration tasks only.

When Paige established all her Desktop preferences and installed the computer's applications, they were installed with the Administrator account. Now when she logs in with the regular user account, she can't access the Desktop and profile settings that were created for her as an administrative user.

To solve this problem, you can copy a local user profile from one user to another (for example, from Paige's administrative account to her regular user account) by choosing Control Panel ➢ System, clicking Advanced System Settings, and clicking the User Profiles Settings button. When you copy a user profile, the following items are copied: favorites, cookies, documents, Start Menu items, and other unique user Registry settings.

Another configurable item within the Profile tab of the user's properties is using logon scripts. The next section explores logon scripts.

Using Logon Scripts

Logon scripts are files that run every time a user logs on to the network. They are usually batch files, but they can be any type of executable file.

You might use logon scripts to set up drive mappings or to run a specific executable file each time a user logs on to the computer. For example, you could run an inventory management file that collects information about the computer's configuration and sends that data to a central management database. Logon scripts are also useful for compatibility with non–Windows 8.1 clients who want to log on but still maintain consistent settings with their native operating system.

To run a logon script for a user, enter the script name in the Logon Script text box in the Profile tab of the user's Properties dialog box.

Another item that can be configured in the Profile tab is the user's home folder, as we'll see next.

Setting Up Home Folders

Users usually store their personal files and information in a private folder called a home folder. In the Profile tab of the user's Properties dialog box, you can specify the location of a home folder as a local folder or a network folder.

To specify a local path folder, choose the Local Path option and type the path in the text box next to that option. To specify a network path for a folder, choose the Connect option and specify a network path using a Universal Naming Convention (UNC) path.

A UNC consists of the computer name and the share that has been created on the computer. In this case, a network folder should already be created and shared. For example, if you wanted to connect to a folder called \Users\Will on a server called SALES, you'd choose the Connect option, select a drive letter that would be mapped to the home directory, and then type \\SALES\Users\Will in the To box.

If the home folder you are specifying does not exist, Windows 8.1 will attempt to create the folder for you. You can also use the variable %username% in place of a specific user's name.

Exercise 8.10 shows you how to assign a home folder to a user. These steps assume you have completed all the previous exercises in this chapter.

EXERCISE 8.10

Assigning Home Folders

1. Open the Admin Console MMC Desktop shortcut and expand the Local Users and Groups snap-in.

2. Open the Users folder and double-click user NMandela. The NMandela Properties dialog box appears.

3. Select the Profile tab and click the Local Path radio button to select it.

4. Specify the home folder path by typing `C:\HomeFolders\NMandela` in the text box for the Local Path option. Then click OK.

5. Use Windows Explorer to verify that this folder was created.

6. Close the Local Users and Groups MMC.

Using Home Folders

As an administrator for a large network, one of your primary responsibilities is to make sure that all data is backed up daily. This can become difficult because daily backup of each user's local hard drive is impractical. You can also have problems with employees deleting important corporate information when they leave the company.

After examining the contents of a typical user's local drive, you will realize that most of the local disk space is taken by the operating system and the user's stored applications. This information does not change and does not need to be backed up. What you are primarily concerned with is backing up the user's data.

To more effectively manage this data and accommodate the necessary backup, you should create home folders for each user and store them on a network share. This allows the data to be backed up daily, to be readily accessible should a local computer fail and to be easily retrieved if the user leaves the company.

Here are the steps to create a home folder that resides on the network:

1. Decide which server will store the users' home folders, create a directory structure that will store the home folders efficiently (for example, **C:\home**), and create a single share to the home folder.

2. Use NTFS and share permissions to ensure that only the specified user has permissions to their home folder. (Setting permissions is covered later in Chapter 10 in the section "Securing Access to Files and Folders.")

3. After you create the share and assign permissions, you can specify the location of the home folder on the Profile tab of the user's Properties dialog box.

After creating your user accounts, there is a possibility that you can run into errors or issues with the accounts. In the next section, we will look at how to troubleshoot user account issues.

Troubleshooting User Account Authentication

When a user attempts to log on through Windows 8.1 and cannot be authenticated, you will need to track down the reason for the problem.

The following sections offer some suggestions that can help you troubleshoot logon authentication errors for local and domain user accounts.

Troubleshooting Local User Account Authentication

If a local user is having trouble logging on, the problem may be with the username, the password, or the user account itself. The following are some common causes of local logon errors:

Incorrect Username You can verify that the username is correct by checking the Local Users and Groups utility. Verify that the name was spelled correctly.

Incorrect Password Remember that passwords are case sensitive. Is the Caps Lock key on? If you see any messages relating to an expired password or locked-out account, the reason for the problem is obvious. If necessary, you can log on as admin and assign a new password for the locked-out users through the Local Users and Groups utility. As you learned earlier in this chapter, we recommend that each user create a password reset disk. This allows users to solve their own problem.

Prohibitive User Rights　Does the user have permission to log on locally at the computer? By default, the Log On Locally user right is granted to the Users group so that all users can log on to Windows 8.1 computers.

However, if this user right was modified, you will see an error message stating that the local policy of this computer does not allow interactive logon. The terms *interactive logon* and *local logon* are synonymous and mean that the user is logging on at the computer where the user account is stored on the computer's local database.

A Disabled or Deleted Account　You can verify whether an account has been disabled or deleted by checking the account properties through the Local Users and Groups utility.

A Domain Account Logon at the Local Computer　If a computer is a part of a domain, the logon dialog box has options for logging on to the domain or to the local computer. Make sure the user has chosen the correct option.

After creating user accounts, normally we place these user accounts into groups. In the next section, we will discuss groups.

Using, Creating, and Managing Groups

Groups are an important part of network management. Many administrators are able to accomplish the majority of their management tasks through the use of groups; they rarely assign permissions to individual users.

Windows 8.1 includes built-in local groups, such as Administrators and Backup Operators. These groups already have all the permissions needed to accomplish specific tasks. Windows 8.1 also uses default special groups, which are managed by the system. Users become members of special groups based on their requirements for computer and network access.

You can create and manage local groups through the Local Users and Groups utility. With this utility, you can add groups, change group membership, rename groups, and delete groups.

One misconception about groups is that groups have to work with Group Policy objects (GPOs). This is not correct. GPOs are a set of rules that allow you to set computer configuration and user configuration options that apply to users or computers. Group Policies are typically used with Active Directory and are applied as GPOs. GPOs will be discussed in full detail later in this chapter.

In the next sections, you will learn about groups and all the built-in groups. Then you will learn how to create and manage these groups.

Using Built-in Groups

On a Windows 8.1 computer, default local groups have already been created and assigned all necessary permissions to accomplish basic tasks. In addition, there are built-in special groups that the Windows 8.1 system handles automatically. These groups are described in the following sections.

Using Default Local Groups

A local group is a group that is stored in the local computer's accounts database. These are the groups to which you can add users and that you can manage directly on a Windows 8.1 computer. By default, the following local groups are created on Windows 8.1 computers:

- Access Control Assistance Operators
- Administrators
- Backup Operators
- Cryptographic Operators
- Distributed COM Users
- Event Log Readers
- Guests
- Hyper-V Administrators
- IIS_IUSRS
- Network Configuration Operators
- Performance Log Users
- Performance Monitor Users
- Power Users
- Remote Desktop Users
- Remote Management Users
- Replicator
- Users
- HomeUsers (if HomeGroup has been configured)
- WinRMRemoteWMIUsers

We will briefly describe the main groups, their default permissions, and the users assigned to the groups by default.

If possible, you should add users to the built-in local groups rather than creating new groups from scratch. This simplifies administration because the built-in groups already have the appropriate permissions. All you need to do is add the users you want to be members of the group.

Administrators Group The Administrators group has full permissions and privileges. Its members can grant themselves any permissions they do not have by default to manage all the objects on the computer. (Objects include the filesystem, printers, and account management.) By default, the Administrator account, which is disabled by default, and the initial user account are members of the Administrators local group.

> Assign users to the Administrators group with caution since they will have full permissions to manage the computer.

Members of the Administrators group can perform the following tasks:

- Install the operating system.
- Install and configure hardware device drivers.
- Install system services.
- Install service packs, hot fixes, and Windows updates.
- Upgrade the operating system.
- Repair the operating system.
- Install applications that modify the Windows system files.
- Configure password policies.
- Configure audit policies.
- Manage security logs.
- Create administrative shares.
- Create administrative accounts.
- Modify groups and accounts that have been created by other users.
- Remotely access the Registry.
- Stop or start any service.
- Configure services.
- Increase and manage disk quotas.
- Increase and manage execution priorities.
- Remotely shut down the system.
- Assign and manage user rights.
- Re-enable locked-out and disabled accounts.
- Manage disk properties, including formatting hard drives.
- Modify system wide environment variables.
- Access any data on the computer.
- Back up and restore all data.

Backup Operators Group   Members of the Backup Operators group have permissions to back up and restore the filesystem, even if the filesystem is NTFS and they have not been assigned permissions to access it. However, the members of Backup Operators can access the filesystem only through the Backup utility. To access the filesystem directly, Backup Operators must have explicit permissions assigned. There are no default members of the Backup Operators local group.

Cryptographic Operators Group   The Cryptographic Operators group has access to perform cryptographic operations on the computer. There are no default members of the Cryptographic Operators local group.

Distributed COM Users Group   The Distributed COM Users group has the ability to launch and run Distributed COM objects on the computer. There are no default members of the Distributed COM Users local group.

Event Log Readers Group   The Event Log Readers group has access to read the event log on the local computer. There are no default members of the Event Log Readers local group.

Guests Group   The Guests group has limited access to the computer. This group is provided so that you can allow people who are not regular users to access specific network resources. As a general rule, most administrators do not allow Guest access because it poses a potential security risk. By default, the Guest user account is a member of the Guests local group.

IIS_IUSRS Group   The IIS_IUSRS group is used by Internet Information Services (IIS). The NT AUTHORITY\IUSR user account is a member of the IIS_IUSRS group by default.

Network Configuration Operators Group   Members of the Network Configuration Operators group have some administrative rights to manage the computer's network configuration—for example, editing the computer's TCP/IP settings.

Performance Log Users Group   The Performance Log Users group has the ability to access and schedule logging of performance counters and can create and manage trace counters on the computer.

Performance Monitor Users Group   The Performance Monitor Users group has the ability to access and view performance counter information on the computer. Users who are members of this group can access performance counters both locally and remotely.

Power Users Group   The Power Users group is included in Windows 8.1 for backward compatibility. This group is included to ensure that computers upgraded from Windows XP function as before with regard to folders that allow access to members of the group. Otherwise, the Power Users group has limited administrative rights.

Remote Desktop Users Group   Member of the Remote Desktop Users group allows members of the group to log on remotely for the purpose of using the Remote Desktop service.

Replicator Group   The Replicator group is intended to support directory replication, which is a feature used by domain servers. Only domain users who will start the replication service should be assigned to this group. The Replicator local group has no default members.

Users Group   The Users group is intended for end users who should have very limited system access. If you have installed a fresh copy of Windows 8.1, the default settings for the Users group prohibit its members from compromising the operating system or program files. By default, all users who have been created on the computer, except Guest, are members of the Users local group.

Windows 8.1 also uses special groups. In the next section, we will look at special groups and how they work.

Using Special Groups

Special groups can be used by the system or by administrators. Membership in these groups is automatic if certain criteria are met. You cannot manage special groups through the Local Users and Groups utility, but an administrator can add these special groups to resources. Table 8.3 describes several of the special groups that are built into Windows 8.1.

TABLE 8.3   Special groups in Windows 8.1

Group	Description
Creator Owner	This is the account that created or took ownership of an object. This is typically a user account. Each object (files, folders, printers, and print jobs) has an owner. Members of the Creator Owner group have special permissions to resources. For example, if you are a regular user who has submitted 12 print jobs to a printer, you can manipulate your print jobs as Creator Owner, but you can't manage any print jobs submitted by other users.
Everyone	This group includes anyone who could possibly access the computer. The Everyone group includes all users who have been defined on the computer (including Guest), plus (if your computer is a part of a domain) all users within the domain. If the domain has trust relationships with other domains, all users in the trusted domains are part of the Everyone group as well. The exception to automatic group membership with the Everyone group is that members of the Anonymous Logon group are not included as a part of the Everyone group.
Interactive	This group includes all users who use the computer's resources locally. Local users belong to the Interactive group.
Network	This group includes users who access the computer's resources over a network connection. Network users belong to the Network group.
Authenticated Users	This group includes users who access the Windows 8.1 operating system through a valid username and password. Users who can log on belong to the Authenticated Users group.

TABLE 8.3   Special groups in Windows 8.1   *(continued)*

Group	Description
Anonymous Logon	This group includes users who access the computer through anonymous logons. When users gain access through special accounts created for anonymous access to Windows 8.1 services, they become members of the Anonymous Logon group.
Batch	This group includes users who log on as a user account that is used only to run a batch job. Batch job accounts are members of the Batch group.
Dialup	This group includes users who log on to the network from a dial-up connection. Dial-up users are members of the Dialup group.
Service	This group includes users who log on as a user account that is used only to run a service. You can configure the use of user accounts for logon through the Services program, and these accounts become members of the Service group.
System	When the system accesses specific functions as a user, that process becomes a member of the System group.
Terminal Server User	This group includes users who log on through Terminal Services. These users become members of the Terminal Server User group.

Now that we have looked at the different types of groups, in the next section we will discuss how to work with groups. To do so, you can use the Local Users and Groups utility.

Creating Groups

To create a group, you must be logged on as a member of the Administrators group. The Administrators group has full permissions to manage users and groups.

As you do in your choices for usernames, keep your naming conventions in mind when assigning names to groups. When you create a local group, consider the following guidelines:

- The group name should be descriptive (for example, Accounting Data Users).

- The group name must be unique to the computer, different from all other group names and usernames that exist on that computer.

- Group names can be up to 256 characters. It is best to use alphanumeric characters for ease of administration. The backslash (\) character is not allowed.

Creating groups is similar to creating users, and it is a fairly easy process. After you've added the Local Users and Groups MMC or use Local Users and Groups through Computer Management, expand it to see the Users and Groups folders. Right-click the Groups folder and select New Group from the context menu. This brings up the New Group dialog box, shown in Figure 8.7.

FIGURE 8.7 The New Group dialog box

The only required entry in the New Group dialog box is the group name. If appropriate, you can enter a description for the group, and you can add (or remove) group members. When you're ready to create the new group, click the Create button.

Complete Exercise 8.11 to create two new local groups.

EXERCISE 8.11

Creating Groups

1. Open the Admin Console MMC Desktop shortcut you created and expand the Local Users and Groups snap-in.

2. Right-click the Groups folder and select New Group.

3. In the New Group dialog box, type **Data Users** in the Group Name text box. Click the Create button.

4. In the New Group dialog box, type **Application Users** in the Group Name text box. Click the Create button.

After the groups are created, you will have to manage the groups and their membership. The next section explores group management.

Managing Group Membership

After you've created a group, you can add members to it. As mentioned earlier, you can put the same user in multiple groups. You can easily add and remove users through a group's

Properties dialog box, shown in Figure 8.8. To access this dialog box from the Groups folder in the Local Users and Groups utility, double-click the group you want to manage.

FIGURE 8.8 A group's Properties dialog box

From the group's Properties dialog box, you can change the group's description and add or remove group members. When you click the Add button to add members, the Select Users dialog box appears (Figure 8.9).

FIGURE 8.9 The Select Users dialog box

In the Select Users dialog box, you enter the object names of the users you want to add. You can use the Check Names button to validate the users against the database. Select the user accounts you wish to add and click Add. Click the OK button to add the selected users to the group.

> Although the special groups that were covered earlier in the chapter are listed in this dialog box, you cannot manage the membership of these special groups.

To remove a member from the group, select the member in the Members list of the Properties dialog box and click the Remove button.

In Exercise 8.12, you'll create new user accounts and then add these users to one of the groups you created in the previous steps.

EXERCISE 8.12

Adding Accounts to Groups

1. Open the Admin Console MMC shortcut you created and expand the Local Users and Groups snap-in.

2. Create two new users: JDoe and DDoe. Deselect the User Must Change Password At Next Logon option for each user.

3. Expand the Groups folder.

4. Double-click the Data Users group.

5. In the Data Users Properties dialog box, click the Add button.

6. In the Select Users dialog box, type the username **JDoe**; then click OK. Click Add and type the username **DDoe**; then click OK.

7. In the Data Users Properties dialog box, you will see that the users have both been added to the group. Click OK to close the group's Properties dialog box.

There may come a point when a specific group is no longer needed. In the next section, we will look at how to delete a group from the Local Users and Groups utility.

Deleting Groups

If you are sure that you will never again want to use a particular group, you can delete it. Once a group is deleted, you lose all permissions assignments that have been specified for the group.

To delete a group, right-click it and choose Delete from the context menu. You will see a warning that once a group is deleted, it is gone for good. Click the Yes button if you're sure you want to delete the group.

If you delete a group and give another group the same name, the new group won't be created with the same properties as the deleted group because, as with users, groups get unique SIDs assigned at the time of creation.

Creating users and groups is one of the most important tasks that we as IT members can do. On a Windows 8.1 machine, creating users and groups is an easy process.

Now that you understand how to create users and groups, you need to know how to manage security. In the next sections, we will look at how to secure Windows 8.1.

Managing User and Computer Groups in Intune

In today's world, administrators are being asked to manage not only computers but users' mobile devices as well. How do you protect the business data and apps stored on these devices? Moreover, many of these devices are personal devices if your company has adopted a Bring Your own device (BYOD) initiative. In the last section of this chapter, we'll look at how you can use Windows Intune to manage the devices and the user and group accounts that reside on them.

Microsoft Intune

Although Intune can be integrated with a System Center 2012 Configuration Manager infrastructure to encompass managing PCs as well mobile devices, managing mobile devices is one of the more exciting features it provides.

Users register, enroll, and manage their devices as well as install corporate applications from the self-service Company Portal—all from the devices of their choice. From the portal user and computer, accounts and groups can be managed. Among the tasks that can performed are the following:

- Deploy apps.
- Deploy Wi-Fi profiles.
- Deploy virtual private network connect profiles.
- Restrict apps that can run on the device.
- Restrict user experience.
- Remotely wipe devices.

Although a complete overview of the setup of the infrastructure required to use Intune is beyond the scope of this book, a user using a touch screen mobile device would register using the following steps:

1. On the Start screen, tap Settings. The Settings page is displayed.
2. On the Settings page, tap Workplace.
3. On the Workplace page, tap Add Account. The Email Address page is displayed.
4. On the Email Address page, in Email Address, type **account@domain** (where *account* is the name of the user account in the Windows Intune subscription and *domain* is the domain for the Windows Intune subscription), and then tap Sign In.

5. On the Windows Intune sign-in page, in Password, type the password for the user account in the Windows Intune subscription; then tap Sign In. Windows Phone signs in to Windows Intune and downloads settings. The Account Added page is displayed.

6. On the Account Added page, review the information (specifically, that the Install Company App check box is selected), and then tap Done. The Workplace page is displayed. The account is now registered and the app is installed.

Summary

In this chapter you learned about creating, deleting, and managing the properties of local user and group accounts in Windows 8.1. You learned that group accounts are used to ease network administration by grouping users who have similar permission requirements.

You also created and managed local groups through the Local Users and Groups utility. With this utility, you can add groups, change group membership, rename groups, and delete groups.

You also learned how Windows 8.1 accounts can be managed on a domain level through a Group Policy object using the Group Policy Management Console. If the Windows 8.1 computer is not a part of a domain, you use Local Group Policy objects to manage local security.

Finally, you learned how Intune can be integrated with a System Center 2012 Configuration Manager infrastructure to encompass managing PCs as well as mobile devices.

Exam Essentials

Understand the difference between local and domain accounts.   Local accounts are only effective on the computer on which they are created. Domain accounts can be used to log onto the domain from any computer that is member of the domain.

Know how to use the Local user and group's utility.   You can use this to create local user and group accounts and to delete and make changes to those accounts. Moreover, here you can change many properties of the accounts, such as the password. You can also add user accounts to groups and remove users from groups.

Understand Windows Intune.   Although Intune can be integrated with a System Center 2012 Configuration Manager infrastructure to encompass managing PCs as well as mobile devices, managing mobile devices is one of the more exciting features it provides.

Review Questions

You can find the answers in Appendix A.

1. While troubleshooting a client's computer, a company directive requires that you open the Registry and delete a certain key. Which account should you log on with to make the change?

    A. Administrator

    B. Power User

    C. Operator

    D. All of the above

2. Your company has decided to add a 21st machine to the little workgroup you have been managing. When you try to add the new computer to the workgroup, you get a workgroup error. What can you do to add the computer into the group so that it can share network resources?

    A. Decommission one of the other computers first.

    B. Share permissions will need to be redivided between the computers.

    C. Install a domain controller and configure Active Directory.

    D. Buy a new client license for the new computer.

3. In creating a new account name policy for your company, management has decided that for account names the letter a should be replaced with @, the letter e replaced with =, and the letter u replaced with /. The new username you try looks something like @llen but the naming convention is rejected by Active Directory. What is wrong with the name?

    A. The at symbol (@) is illegal.

    B. The name is too short.

    C. The name is too common.

    D. Nothing is wrong. The name is good enough and must be a duplicate.

4. After choosing a naming convention for user accounts that works, based on First Name + Last Name, management decides they want to change the naming convention to Last Name + First Name. Do you have to delete all the user accounts and start again?

    A. Yes, once the accounts are created the name cannot be changed because it is associated with a security identifier (SID).

    B. Yes, usernames are remembered by network resources.

    C. No, but you need to change the security identifier.

    D. No, when you change the username it affects nothing on the network because only the SID is associated with network resources.

5. A user left the company for six months for military service and when she returned found out that she could no longer log onto her computer. You check into the reason and find that her user account was deleted. What is the proper procedure for a user who leaves a company temporarily?

   A. Once an account is deleted, it can be restored if no more than three months have passed. The account's Active Status check box should have been deselected.

   B. The account name can be reassociated with the SID using the SID tool. SIDs are never deleted. You just have to create a new account and replace the SID.

   C. Once an account is deleted, it cannot be restored ever because the SID is deleted. The account should have been disabled. However, you can clone another account with the same resources and rename it.

   D. Once an account is deleted, it cannot be restored because the SID is deleted. The account should have been disabled in AD.

6. Which if the following is not a built-in account in Windows 8.1 with HomeGroups enabled?

   A. Administrator

   B. Guest

   C. Initial user

   D. Power User

7. A user tells you that he forgot his password and after several attempts to log in his account is locked out. He needs his account password reset so he can log back in. What is the procedure if the user does not know his password?

   A. Open the user account and select the option to reset the password. The user must then choose a new password the next time he logs in.

   B. Open the user account within AD DS and select the option to reset the password. Select a temp password for the user. The user must then choose a new password the next time he logs in after he first enters the temporary one. However, you first have to clear the account lockout condition.

   C. Open the user account and select the option to reset the password. The user must then choose a new password the next time he logs in but only after he first answers three security questions correctly.

   D. Open the user account and select the option to reset the password. The user must then choose a new password the next time he logs in without having to know a password.

8. A group of users needs to use several network locations when they log on to their computers. The network locations should be mapped as drive letters when the user chooses to access or save a file. What can you do to create these drive mappings?

   A. Install the drive mappings in a GPO and associate the GPO with the group.

   B. Run a batch file that creates the drive mappings as soon as the user is logged on.

C. Create the drive mappings automatically as soon as the user opens a Save or Open dialog box.

D. Create logon scripts for the user.

9. Shawna works in the IT department, where all of the Windows 8.1 computers have been configured in a workgroup called IT. You want her to be able to create users and groups on the Windows 8.1 computers within the workgroup. To which of the following groups should you add Shawna on each Windows 8.1 computer she will manage?

   A. Administrators

   B. Power Users

   C. Server Operators

   D. Power Operators

10. Rick has been added to the Administrators group, but you suspect that he is abusing his administrative privileges. He only needs permission to view event information and schedule logging of performance counters. To which group or groups should you add Rick so that he can do his job but will have the minimum level of administrative rights? (Choose all that apply.)

    A. Administrators

    B. Power Users

    C. Event Log Readers

    D. Performance Log Users

    E. Performance Monitor Users

11. When are user domain access tokens created?

    A. When the computer starts up

    B. When the user logs in

    C. When the user logs off

    D. When the computer shuts down

12. You are logged on as a member of the Administrators group on a Windows 8.1 computer. You are adding a new user account to the computer. You want to create a temporary password that the user must change, and you want to ensure that the account is enabled. Which of the following options should you configure? (Choose all that apply.)

    A. User Must Change Password At Next Logon

    B. User Cannot Change Password

    C. Password Never Expires

    D. Account Is Disabled

13. Which of the following should guide the creation of usernames?

    A. Naming convention

    B. Naming policy

C. `username.dll`

D. `ntuser.dat`

14. Bette has just installed Windows 8.1. No changes have been made to the default user accounts. She is trying to determine if any of the default account assignments pose a security threat. Which of the following statements are true regarding the built-in accounts? (Choose all that apply.)

A. By default, the Administrator account cannot be deleted.

B. By default, the Guest account cannot be deleted.

C. By default, the Administrator account is enabled.

D. By default, the Guest account is enabled.

15. Rob is the network administrator of a large company. The company requires that all Sales users use a profile that has been specified by the IT department as the corporate standard. Rob has been having problems because users in the Sales group are changing their profiles so that they are no longer using the corporate-defined standard. Which of the following steps should Rob take to create a mandatory profile in Windows 8.1? (Choose all that apply.)

A. In Control Panel, in the User Profiles dialog box, specify that the profile is a mandatory profile.

B. Rename the user profile to `NTUSER.MAN`.

C. Copy the profile to a network share using the User Profiles dialog box accessible from the System Properties dialog box in Control Panel.

D. In the Local Users and Groups utility, on the Profile tab of the user's Properties dialog box, specify a UNC path for the roaming profile.

16. Rob is asked to make sure that all users have the same desktop background, colors, and layout. What is the best way Rob can accomplish this?

A. Rob should buy special third-party software that can do this.

B. Rob can set up user profiles to accomplish this.

C. A logon script needs to be designed to accomplish this.

D. Rob can set this up using a GPO and attaching it to the user's desktop.

17. The following is an example of what?

S-1-5-21-823518204-746137067-120266-629-500

A. MAC address

B. SID

C. IPv6 address

D. Encryption key

18. Jane is trying to connect to a printer and keeps getting an error that says Access Denied. What should Sarah the administrator do to allow Jane to use the network printer without Jane having to try create the connection? (Choose all that apply.)

A. Sarah should make Jane a member of the Print Users group, which has access to the printer Jane needs.

B. Sarah should make Jane a member of the Print Operators group, which has access to the printer Jane needs.

C. Sarah should then give Jane a logon script to automatically create the printer link in Jane's printer folder.

D. None of the above. The error message means that Jane is not logged onto the network.

19. Oscar needs to work from home three days a week and is given an account with telecommuting permission. The CTO asks the network administrator to make sure that Robert can log on from home and work. What's the best approach to accomplish this and set up Oscar's account? (Choose all that apply.)

A. A GPO should be created that provides access to the network resources required to log on remotely.

B. The GPO containing the remote users groups needs to include Oscar's account name.

C. Oscar should be added to a group that is given remote logon privileges.

D. Oscar needs to configure a VPN client so he can access the network from home.

20. You are the Active Directory administrator for your company. A Windows 8.1 computer has been purchased for the finance department, and you want to monitor it for unauthorized access. You configure the Audit Object Access policy to audit both success and failure events. However, when you look at the security event log a few days later, you do not see any entries related to file access. What is the most likely reason for this behavior?

A. Auditing has not been enabled for the appropriate files and folders.

B. A conflicting Group Policy setting is overriding your configuration.

C. Another administrator has disabled your Group Policy setting.

D. Object access events are found in the system event log.

Chapter

9

Managing Security

70-688 MICROSOFT EXAM OBJECTIVES COVERED IN THIS CHAPTER:

✓ **Support authentication and authorization**

- Multi-factor authentication, including certificates, virtual smart cards, picture passwords, and biometrics

- Workgroup versus domain, HomeGroup, computer and user authentication, including secure channel, account policies, credential caching, and Credential Manager

- Local account versus Microsoft account

- Workplace Join

✓ **Support client compliance**

- Manage updates by using Windows Update and Windows Intune, including non-Microsoft updates

- Manage client security by using Windows Defender, Windows Intune Endpoint Protection, or Microsoft System Center 2012 Endpoint Protection

- Manage Internet Explorer 11 security

- Support Group Policy application, including Resultant Set of Policy (RSoP), policy processing, and Group Policy caching

Windows 8.1 offers a wide variety of security options. If the Windows 8.1 computer is a part of a domain, you can apply security through a Group Policy object using the Group Policy Management Console. If the Windows 8.1 computer is not a part of a domain, you use Local Group Policy Objects to manage local security.

In this chapter, you'll learn about the environments in which Windows 8.1 can be installed and the utilities that are used to manage security.

Managing Security

In the following sections, you'll learn about the various environments that Windows 8.1 can be installed in and the utilities that are used to manage security.

You can use policies to help manage user accounts. Account policies control the logon environment for the computer, such as password and logon restrictions. Local policies specify what users can do once they log on and include auditing, user rights, and security options.

Managing Security Configurations

The tools you use to manage Windows 8.1 computer security configurations depend on whether the Windows 8.1 computer is a part of a Windows 2000, Windows 2003, Windows 2003 R2, Windows 2008, Windows 2008 R2, Windows 2012, or Windows 2012 R2 domain environment.

If the Windows 8.1 client is not a part of a domain, you apply security settings through *Local Group Policy objects (LGPOs)*. LGPOs are sets of security configuration settings that are applied to users and computers. LGPOs are created and stored on the Windows 8.1 computer.

If your Windows 8.1 computer is a part of a domain that uses the services of Active Directory, you typically manage and configure security through Group Policy objects (GPOs). Active Directory is the database that contains all your domain user and group accounts along with all other domain objects.

Group Policy objects are policies that can be placed on either users or computers in the domain. The Group Policy Management Console (GPMC) is a Microsoft Management Console (MMC) snap-in that is used to configure and manage GPOs for users and computers via Active Directory.

Windows 8.1 computers that are part of a domain still have LGPOs, and you can use LGPOs in conjunction with the Active Directory GPOs.

Use of Group Policy Objects for domains is covered in greater detail in *MCSA: Windows Server 2012 R2 Complete Study Guide*, by William Panek (Sybex, 2015).

The settings you can apply through the Group Policy utility within Active Directory are more comprehensive than the settings you can apply through LGPOs. Table 9.1 lists some of the options that can be set for GPOs within Active Directory and which of those options can be applied through LGPOs.

TABLE 9.1   Group Policy and LGPO setting options

Group Policy setting	Available for LGPO?
Software installation	No
Remote Installation Services	Yes
Scripts	Yes
Printers	Yes
Security settings	Yes
Policy-based QOS	Yes
Administrative templates	Yes
Folder redirection	No
Internet Explorer configuration	Yes

Now that we've looked at LGPOs, let's explore some of the tools available for creating and managing them.

Group Policy Processing

When a Windows 8.1 computer is a member of a domain, policies are applied to the device when it starts. These polices apply in a default order that will affect which policy is effective when conflicts in the setting occur. The default order is as follows:

1. Local Group Policy object
2. Site policies
3. Domain policies
4. Organizational unit policies

It is important to understand that, in cases where a setting at one level conflicts with the same setting at another level, the *last* setting to be applied is one that is effective.

Using the Group Policy Results Tool

When a user logs on to a computer or domain, a resulting set of policies to be applied is generated based on the LGPOs, site GPOs, domain GPOs, and OU GPOs. The overlapping nature of group policies can make it difficult to determine what group policies will be applied to a computer or user.

To help you determine what policies will be applied, Windows 8.1 includes a tool called the Group Policy Results Tool, also known as the *Resultant Set of Policy (RSoP)*. You can access this tool through the GPResult command-line utility. The gpresult command displays the resulting set of policies that were enforced on the computer and the specified user during the logon process.

Table 9.2 shows the various switches you can use.

TABLE 9.2   gpresult switches

Switch	Explanation
/F	Forces gpresult to override the filename specified in the /X or /H command
/H	Saves the report in an HTML format
/P	Specifies the password for a given user context
/R	Displays RSoP summary data
/S	Specifies the remote system to connect to
/U	Specifies the user context under which the command should be executed
/V	Specifies that verbose information should be displayed
/X	Saves the report in XML format
/Z	Specifies that the super verbose information should be displayed
/?	Shows all the gpresult command switches
/scope	Specifies whether the user or the computer settings need to be displayed
/User	Specifies the username for which the RSoP data is to be displayed

In the next section, we'll look at how to create and apply LGPOs to the Windows 8.1 machine.

Group Policy Caching

Computers in a domain receive policies from domain controllers in two forms. Some policies process in the background, which means they don't affect the performance of the machine for the user while it is occurring. Others apply in the foreground and do have some effect.

The Group Policy caching feature applies only the foreground processing. It works by using a local cache of GPOs rather than pulling them over the network. This process speeds up Group Policy processing and therefore also speeds up actions such as logons. Note that domain controller connectivity is still required, or the policy won't be applied. This cache of policies is updated whenever the background processing of policies takes place.

Managing and Applying LGPOs

As we discussed earlier, policies that have been linked through Active Directory will, by default, take precedence over any established local group policies. Local group policies are typically applied to computers that are not part of a network or are in a network that does not have a domain controller and thus does not use Active Directory.

Previous versions of Windows (before Vista) contained only one LGPO that applied to all of the computer's users unless NTFS permissions were applied to the LGPO. However, Windows Vista changed that with the addition of Multiple Local Group Policy Objects (MLGPOs). Like Active Directory GPOs, MLGPOs are applied in a certain hierarchical order:

1. Local Computer Policy
2. Administrators and Non-Administrators Local Group Policy
3. User-Specific Group Policy

The Local Computer Policy is the only LGPO that includes computer and user settings; the other LGPOs contain only user settings. Settings applied here will apply to all users of the computer.

The Administrators and Non-Administrators LGPOs were new to Windows Vista and are still included with Windows 8.1. The Administrators LGPO is applied to users who are members of the built-in local Administrators group. As you might guess, the Non-Administrators LGPO is applied to users who are not members of the local Administrators group. Because each user of a computer can be classified as an administrator or a nonadministrator, either one policy or the other will apply.

User-Specific LGPOs are also included with Windows 8.1. These LGPOs make it possible for specific policy settings to apply to a single user.

As with Active Directory GPOs, any GPO settings applied lower in the hierarchy will override GPO settings applied higher in the hierarchy by default. For example, any user-specific GPO settings will override any conflicting administrator/nonadministrator GPO settings or Local Computer Policy settings. And, of course, any AD GPO settings will still override any conflicting LGPO settings.

 Domain administrators can disable LGPOs on Windows 8.1 computers by enabling the Turn Off Local Group Policy Objects Processing domain GPO setting, which you can find under Computer Configuration\Administrative Templates\System\Group Policy.

You apply an LGPO to a Windows 8.1 computer through the Group Policy Object Editor snap-in within the MMC. Figure 9.1 shows the Local Computer Policy for a Windows 8.1 computer.

FIGURE 9.1   Local Computer Policy

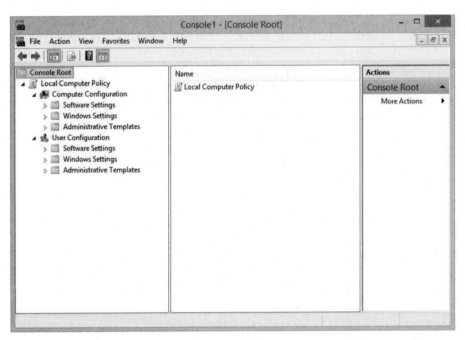

Exercise 9.1 shows you how to add the Local Computer Policy snap-in to the MMC.

EXERCISE 9.1

Adding the Local Computer Policy Snap-In

1. Open the Admin Console MMC shortcut by typing **MMC** in the Search Programs And Files box.

2. A User Account Control dialog box appears. Click Yes.

3. Select File ➤ Add/Remove Snap-In.

4. Highlight the Group Policy Object Editor snap-in and click the Add button.

5. The Group Policy Object specifies Local Computer by default. Click the Finish button.

6. In the Add Or Remove Snap-Ins dialog box, click OK.

7. In the left pane, right-click the Local Computer Policy and choose New Windows From Here.

8. Choose File ➤ Save As and name the console **LGPO**. Make sure you save it to the Desktop. Click Save.

9. Close the MMC Admin console.

Now we'll show you how to open an LGPO for a specific user account on a Windows 8.1 machine. Complete Exercise 9.2 to access the Administrators, Non-Administrators, and User-Specific LGPOs.

EXERCISE 9.2

Accessing the LGPO

1. Open the Admin Console MMC shortcut by typing **MMC** in the Windows 8.1 Search box.

2. Select File ➤ Add/Remove Snap-In.

3. Highlight the Group Policy Object Editor snap-in and click the Add button.

4. Click Browse so that you can browse for a different GPO.

5. Click the Users tab.

6. Select the user you want to access and click OK.

7. In the Select Group Policy Object dialog box, click Finish.

8. In the Add Or Remove Snap-Ins dialog box, click OK. You may close the console when you are done looking at the LGPO settings for the user you chose.

Notice that the Administrators, Non-Administrators, and User-Specific LGPOs contain only User Configuration settings, not Computer Configuration settings.

Now let's take a look at the different security settings that can be configured in the LGPO.

Configuring Local Security Policies

Through the use of the Local Computer Policy, you can set a wide range of security options under Computer Configuration\Windows Settings\Security Settings.

This portion of the Local Computer Policy is also known as the Local Security Policy. The following sections describe in detail how to apply security settings through LGPOs (see Figure 9.2).

FIGURE 9.2   Security settings of the LGPO

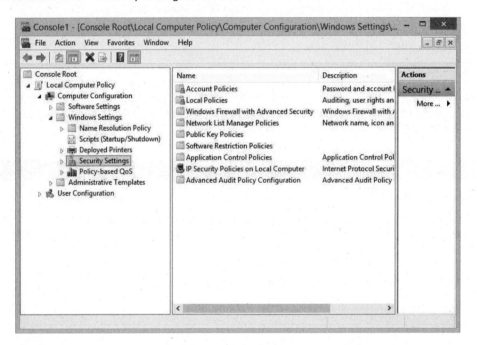

The main areas of security configuration of the LGPO are as follows:

Account Policies   Account policies are used to configure password and account lockout features. Some of these settings include password history, maximum password age, minimum password age, minimum password length, password complexity, account lockout duration, account lockout threshold, and whether to reset the account lockout counter afterward. See the next section, which covers policies in more detail.

Local Policies   Local policies are used to configure auditing, user rights, and security options.

Windows Firewall with Advanced Security   Windows Firewall with Advanced Security provides network security for Windows computers. Through this LGPO you can set domain, private, and public profiles. You can also set this LGPO to authenticate communications between computers and inbound/outbound rules.

Network List Manager Policies   This section allows you to set the network name, icon, and location group policies. Administrators can set Unidentified Networks, Identifying Networks, and All Networks.

Public Key Policies Use the Public Key Policies settings to specify how to manage certificates and certificate life cycles.

Software Restriction Policies The settings under Software Restriction Policies allow you to identify malicious software and control that software's ability to run on the Windows 8.1 machine. These policies allow an administrator to protect the Windows 8.1 operating system against security threats such as viruses and Trojan horse programs.

Application Control Policies This section allows you to set up AppLocker. You can use AppLocker to configure a Denied list and an Accepted list for applications. Applications that are configured on the Denied list will not run on the system, and applications on the Accepted list will operate properly.

IP Security Policies on Local Computer This section allows you to configure the IPsec policies. IPsec is a way to secure data packets at the IP level of the message.

Advanced Audit Policy Configuration Advanced Audit Policy Configuration settings can be used to provide detailed control over audit policies. This section also allows you to configure auditing to help show administrators either successful or unsuccessful attacks on their network.

> You can also access the Local Security Policy by running `secpol.msc` or by opening Control Panel and selecting Administrative Tools ➢ Local Security Policy.

Now that you have seen all the options in the security section of the LGPO, let's take a look at account policies and local policies in more detail.

Support Authentication and Authorization by Using Account Policies

Account policies are used to specify the user account properties that relate to the logon process. They allow you to configure computer security settings for passwords and account lockout specifications.

Local Accounts vs. Microsoft Accounts

When installing Windows 8.1, you'll be presented with a choice between creating a local account or a Microsoft account. Using a Microsoft account (which could be any Microsoft account you have created in the past for services such as Hotmail) does have some advantages. Signing in to Windows 8.1 gives you access to the new Windows Store, where you can go to download modern apps to the Windows 8.1 computer. It also makes it easy to sync data and settings between multiple devices. Finally, it gives free space on OneDrive, a cloud-based storage platform.

If security is not an issue—perhaps because you are using your Windows 8.1 computer at home—then you don't need to bother with account policies. If, on the other hand, security is important—for example, because your computer provides access to payroll information—then you should set very restrictive account policies.

> Account policies at the LGPO level apply only to local user accounts, not domain accounts. To ensure that user account security is configured for domain user accounts, you need to configure these policies at the domain GPO level.

To access the Account Policies folder from the MMC, follow this path: Local Computer Policy\Computer Configuration\Windows Settings\Security Settings\Account Policies. You'll look at all these folders and how to use them throughout the rest of this chapter.

In the following sections you'll learn about the password policies and account lockout policies that define how security is applied to account policies.

Setting Password Policies

Password policies ensure that security requirements are enforced on the computer. It is important to understand that password policies are set on a per-computer basis; they cannot be configured for specific users. Figure 9.3 shows the password policies, which are described in Table 9.3.

FIGURE 9.3   Password policies

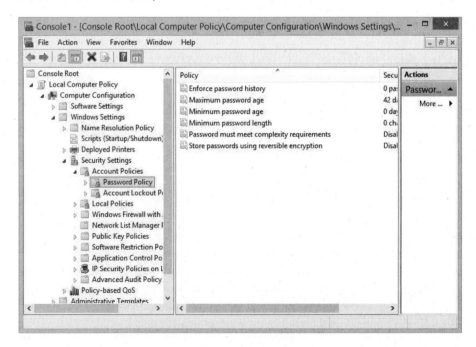

TABLE 9.3 Password policy options

Policy	Description	Default	Minimum	Maximum
Enforce Password History	Keeps track of user's password history	Remember 0 Passwords	Same as default	Remember 24 Passwords
Maximum Password Age	Determines maximum number of days user can keep valid password	Keep Password For 42 Days	Keep Password For 1 Day	Keep Password For Up To 999 Days
Minimum Password Age	Specifies how long password must be kept before it can be changed	0 Days (Password can be changed immediately.)	Same as default	998 Days
Minimum Password Length	Specifies minimum number of characters password must contain	0 Characters (No password required.)	Same as default	14 Characters
Password Must Meet Complexity Requirements	Requires that passwords meet minimum levels of complexity	Disabled		
Store Passwords Using Reversible Encryption	Specifies higher level of encryption for stored user passwords	Disabled		

You can use the password policies in Table 9.3 as follows:

Enforce Password History   Prevents users from repeatedly using the same passwords. Users must create a new password when their password expires or is changed.

Maximum Password Age   Forces users to change their password after the maximum password age is exceeded. Setting this value to 0 will specify that the password will never expire.

Minimum Password Age   Prevents users from changing their password several times in rapid succession in order to defeat the purpose of the Enforce Password History policy.

Minimum Password Length   Ensures that users create a password and specifies the length requirement for that password. If this option isn't set, users are not required to create a password at all.

Password Must Meet Complexity Requirements   Passwords must be six characters or longer and cannot contain the user's account name or any part of the user's full name. In addition, passwords must contain three of the following character types:

- English uppercase characters (A through Z)
- English lowercase characters (a through z)
- Decimal digits (0 through 9)
- Symbols (such as !, @, #, $, and %)

Store Passwords Using Reversible Encryption   This setting should *not* be enabled unless required by an application, and in that case, the benefits of the application should be weighed against the security issues this setting may introduce. This is required for Challenge Handshake Authentication Protocol (CHAP) authentication through remote access or Internet Authentication Services (IAS) and for Digest Authentication with Internet Information Services (IIS).

In Exercise 9.3, you'll configure password policies for your computer. These steps assume that you have added the Local Computer Policy snap-in to the MMC completed in earlier exercises.

EXERCISE 9.3

Configuring Password Policy

1. Open the LGPO MMC shortcut that you created earlier.

2. Expand the Local Computer Policy snap-in.

3. Expand the folders as follows: Computer Configuration\Windows Settings\Security Settings\Account Policies\Password Policy.

4. Open the Enforce Password History policy. On the Local Security Setting tab, specify that five passwords will be remembered. Click OK.

5. Open the Maximum Password Age policy. On the Local Security Setting tab, specify that the password expires in 60 days. Click OK.

Credential Caching and Credential Manager

Credential caching is the saving of passwords and other authentication credentials on a local system so the user does not have to provide the credentials when accessing the site or service for which they are required.

Credential Manager is a graphical tool used in Windows 8.1 to save and store credentials in an encrypted location called the Windows Vault. Figure 9.4 shows the Credential Manager.

FIGURE 9.4 Credential Manager

Workplace Join

Workplace join is a method of enabling a Windows 8.1 device to authenticate as a device to a Windows 2012R2 domain. After the end user downloads and installs the Workplace Join client on a device, the users enters a corporate email and password, which is sent to an Active Directory server to be verified. The server then calls or texts the user at a pre-designated phone number for confirmation that the device should be given "join" rights. Then a new device object is created in Active Directory and a certificate is installed on the device. Once configured, it allows the device to access network resources through single sign-on (SSO).

Let's now take a look at how to set and manage the policies in the Account Lockout Policies section.

Setting Account Lockout Policies

The account lockout policies specify how many invalid logon attempts should be tolerated. You configure the account lockout policies so that after x number of unsuccessful logon attempts within y number of minutes, the account will be locked for a specified amount of time or until the administrator unlocks it.

Account lockout policies are similar to a bank's arrangements for ATM access code security. You have a certain number of chances to enter the correct PIN. That way, anyone who steals your card can't just keep guessing your access code until they get it right. Typically, after three unsuccessful attempts, the ATM takes the card. Then you need to request a new card from the bank. Figure 9.5 shows the account lockout policies, which are described in Table 9.4.

FIGURE 9.5   The account lockout policies

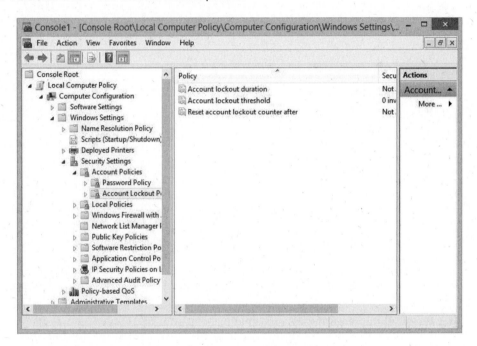

The Account Lockout Duration and Reset Account Lockout Counter After policies will be disabled until a value is specified for the Account Lockout Threshold policy. After the Account Lockout Threshold policy is set, the Account Lockout Duration and Reset Account Lockout Counter After policies will be set to 30 minutes. If you set Account Lockout Duration to 0, the account will remain locked out until an administrator unlocks it.

The Reset Account Lockout Counter After value must be equal to or less than the Account Lockout Duration value.

TABLE 9.4 Account Lockout Policy options

Policy	Description	Default	Minimum	Maximum
Account Lockout Duration	Specifies how long account will remain locked if account lockout threshold is reached	Disabled (If Account Lockout Threshold is enabled, 30 minutes.)	Same as default	99,999 Minutes
Account Lockout Threshold	Specifies number of invalid attempts allowed before account is locked out	0 (Disabled; account will not be locked out.)	Same as default	999 Attempts
Reset Account Lockout Counter After	Specifies how long counter will remember unsuccessful logon attempts	Disabled (If Account Lockout Threshold is enabled, 30 minutes.)	Same as default	99,999 Minutes

Complete Exercise 9.4 to configure account lockout policies and test their effects.

EXERCISE 9.4

Configuring Account Lockout Policies

1. Open the LGPO MMC shortcut.

2. Expand the Local Computer Policy snap-in.

3. Expand the folders as follows: Computer Configuration\Windows Settings\Security Settings\Account Policies\Account Lockout Policy.

4. Open the Account Lockout Threshold policy. On the Local Security Setting tab, specify that the account will lock after three invalid logon attempts. Click OK.

5. Accept the suggested value changes for the Account Lockout Duration and Reset Account Lockout Counter After policies by clicking OK.

6. Open the Account Lockout Duration policy. On the Local Security Setting tab, specify that the account will remain locked for 5 minutes. Click OK.

7. Accept the suggested value changes for the Reset Account Lockout Counter After policy by clicking OK.

8. Log off your Administrator account. Try to log on as one of the accounts that have been created on this Windows 8.1 machine and enter an incorrect password four times.

9. After you see the error message stating that the referenced account has been locked out, log on as an administrator.

10. To unlock the account, open the Local Users And Groups snap-in in the MMC, expand the Users folder, and double-click the user.

11. On the General tab of the user's Properties dialog box, click to remove the check mark from the Account Is Locked Out check box. Then click OK.

In the next section, we'll discuss how to control a user or computer after they have logged into the Windows 8.1 machine.

Device Authentication

Although user authentication may be more common, it is also possible and in some cases desirable to authenticate a device rather than a user. Typically this is done using a certificate. Certificates can be issued to devices as well as users, and once the certificate is issued to the device and is stored on it, the certificate can be used by the devices to authenticate with other devices and services on the network. This requires that the organization have a public key infrastructure (PKI).

Secure Channel

Secure Channel, or Schannel, is a security support provider (SSP) that contains a set of security protocols that provide identity authentication and secure, private communication through encryption.

Schannel is primarily used for Internet applications that require secure HTTP communications. It can be used to authenticate both devices and users, and it uses X.509 certificates. Schannel can support various hashing and encryption mechanisms, and it provides Transport Layer Security (TLS) and Secure Sockets Layer (SSL) support for Windows platforms.

Using Local Policies

As you learned in the previous section, account policies are used to control logon procedures. When you want to control what a user can do after logging on, you use local policies. With local policies, you can implement auditing, specify user rights, and set security options.

To use local policies, first add the Local Computer Policy snap-in to the MMC. Then, from the MMC, follow this path to access the Local Policies folders: Local Computer Policy\Computer Configuration\Windows Settings\Security Settings\Local Policies. Figure 9.6 shows the three Local Policies folders: Audit Policy, User Rights Assignment, and Security Options. You'll look at each of those in the following sections.

FIGURE 9.6   Accessing the Local Policies folders

Setting Audit Policies

Audit policies can be implemented to track the success or failure of specified user actions. You audit events that pertain to user management through the audit policies. By tracking certain events, you can create a history of specific tasks, such as user creation and successful or unsuccessful logon attempts. You can also identify security violations that arise when users attempt to access system management tasks for which they do not have permission.

Auditing Failed Attempts

As an IT manager, you have to make sure that you monitor failed attempts to access resources. A failed attempt to access a resource usually means that someone tried to access the resource and they were denied due to insufficient privileges.

Users who try to go to areas for which they do not have permission usually fall into two categories: hackers and people who are just curious to see what they can get away with. Both are dangerous.

If a user is trying to access an area in which they do not belong, be sure to warn the user about the attacks. This activity is common on a network and needs to be nipped in the bud immediately.

When you define an audit policy, you can choose to audit success or failure of specific events. The success of an event means that the task was successfully accomplished. The failure of an event means that the task was not successfully accomplished.

By default, auditing is not enabled, and it must be manually configured. Once auditing has been configured, you can see the results of the audit in the security log using the Event Viewer utility.

Figure 9.7 shows the audit policies, which are described in Table 9.5.

FIGURE 9.7 The audit policies

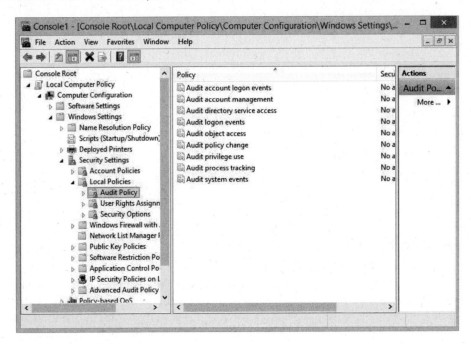

TABLE 9.5 Audit policy options

Policy	Description
Audit Account Logon Events	Tracks when a user logs on or logs off either their local machine or the domain (if domain auditing is enabled)
Audit Account Management	Tracks user and group account creation, deletion, and management actions, such as password changes
Audit Directory Service Access	Tracks directory service accesses

Policy	Description
Audit Logon Events	Audits events related to logon, such as running a logon script, accessing a roaming profile, and accessing a server
Audit Object Access	Enables auditing of access to files, folders, and printers
Audit Policy Change	Tracks any changes to the audit policies, trust policies, or user rights assignment policies
Audit Privilege Use	Tracks users exercising a user right
Audit Process Tracking	Tracks events such as activating a program, accessing an object, and exiting a process
Audit System Events	Tracks system events such as shutting down or restarting the computer as well as events that relate to the security log in Event Viewer

After you set the Audit Object Access policy to enable auditing of object access, you must enable file auditing through NTFS security or print auditing through printer security.

Complete Exercise 9.5 to configure audit policies and view their results.

EXERCISE 9.5

Configuring Audit Policies

1. Open the LGOP MMC shortcut.

2. Expand the Local Computer Policy snap-in.

3. Expand the folders as follows: Computer Configuration\Windows Settings\Security Settings\Local Policies\Audit Policy.

4. Open the Audit Account Logon Events policy. Select the Success and Failure check boxes. Click OK.

5. Open the Audit Account Management policy. Select the Success and Failure check boxes. Click OK.

6. Log off your Administrator account. Attempt to log back on your Administrator account with an incorrect password. The logon should fail (because the password is incorrect).

7. Log on as an administrator.

EXERCISE 9.5 *(continued)*

8. Select Start, right-click Computer, and choose Manage to open Event Viewer.

9. From Event Viewer, open the Security log by selecting Windows Logs ➤ Security. You should see the audited events listed with a Task Category of Credential Validation.

In the next section, we'll look at how to configure user rights on a Windows 8.1 machine.

Assigning User Rights

The user rights policies determine what rights a user or group has on the computer. User rights apply to the system. They are not the same as permissions, which apply to a specific object (permissions are discussed later in this chapter, in "Managing File and Folder Security").

An example of a user right is the Back Up Files And Directories right. This right allows a user to back up files and folders even if the user does not have permissions that have been defined through NTFS filesystem permissions. The other user rights are similar because they deal with system access as opposed to resource access.

Figure 9.8 shows the user rights policies, which are described in Table 9.6.

FIGURE 9.8   The user rights policies

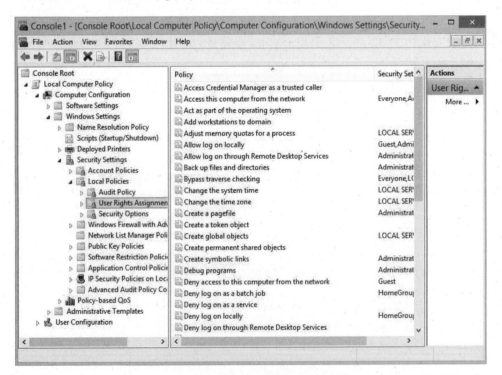

TABLE 9.6   User rights assignment policy options

Right	Description
Access Credential Manager As A Trusted Caller	Used to back up and restore Credential Manager.
Access This Computer From The Network	Allows a user to access the computer from the network.
Act As Part Of The Operating System	Allows low-level authentication services to authenticate as any user.
Add Workstations To Domain	Allows a user to create a computer account on the domain.
Adjust Memory Quotas For A Process	Allows you to configure how much memory can be used by a specific process.
Allow Log On Locally	Allows a user to log on at the physical computer.
Allow Log On Through Terminal Services	Gives a user permission to log on through Terminal Services. Does not affect Windows 2000 computers prior to SP2.
Back Up Files And Directories	Allows a user to back up all files and directories regardless of how the file and directory permissions have been set.
Bypass Traverse Checking	Allows a user to pass through and traverse the directory structure, even if that user does not have permission to list the contents of the directory.
Change The System Time	Allows a user to change the internal time and date on the computer.
Change The Time Zone	Allows a user to change the time zone.
Create A Pagefile	Allows a user to create or change the size of a page file.
Create A Token Object	Allows a process to create a token if the process uses an internal API to create the token.
Create Global Objects	Allows a user to create global objects when connected using Terminal Server.

TABLE 9.6   JUNOS software Preference Values *(continued)*

Right	Description
Create Permanent Shared Objects	Allows a process to create directory objects through Object Manager.
Create Symbolic Links	Allows a user to create a symbolic link.
Debug Programs	Allows a user to attach a debugging program to any process.
Deny Access To This Computer From The Network	Allows you to deny specific users or groups access to this computer from the network. Overrides the Access This Computer From The Network policy for accounts present in both policies.
Deny Log On As A Batch Job	Allows you to prevent specific users or groups from logging on as a batch file. Overrides the Log On As A Batch Job policy for accounts present in both policies.
Deny Log On As A Service	Allows you to prevent specific users or groups from logging on as a service. Overrides the Log On As A Service policy for accounts present in both policies.
Deny Log On Locally	Allows you to deny specific users or groups access to the computer locally. Overrides the Log On Locally policy for accounts present in both policies.
Deny Log On Through Terminal Services	Specifies that a user is not able to log on through Terminal Services. Does not affect Windows 2000 computers prior to SP2.
Enable Computer And User Accounts To Be Trusted For Delegation	Allows a user or group to set the Trusted For Delegation setting for a user or computer object.
Force Shutdown From A Remote System	Allows the system to be shut down by a user at a remote location on the network.
Generate Security Audits	Allows a user, group, or process to make entries in the security log.
Impersonate A Client After Authentication	Enables programs running on behalf of a user to impersonate a client.

Right	Description
Increase A Process Working Set	Allows the size of a process working set to be increased.
Increase Scheduling Priority	Specifies that a process can increase or decrease the priority that is assigned to another process.
Load And Unload Device Drivers	Allows a user to dynamically unload and load device drivers. This right does not apply to Plug and Play drivers.
Lock Pages In Memory	Allows an account to create a process that runs only in physical RAM, preventing it from being paged.
Log On As A Batch Job	Allows a process to log on to the system and run a file that contains one or more operating system commands.
Log On As A Service	Allows a service to log on in order to run.
Manage Auditing And Security Log	Allows a user to enable object access auditing for files and other Active Directory objects. This right does not allow a user to enable general object access auditing in the Local Security Policy.
Modify An Object Label	Allows a user to change the integrity level of files, folders, or other objects.
Modify Firmware Environment Variables	Allows a user to install or upgrade Windows. It also allows a user or process to modify the firmware environment variables stored in NVRAM of non-x86-based computers. This right does not affect the modification of system environment variables or user environment variables.
Perform Volume Maintenance Tasks	Allows a user to perform volume maintenance tasks such as defragmentation and error checking.
Profile Single Process	Allows a user to monitor nonsystem processes through performance-monitoring tools.
Profile System Performance	Allows a user to monitor system processes through performance-monitoring tools.
Remove Computer From Docking Station	Allows a user to undock a laptop through the Windows 8.1 user interface.

TABLE 9.6 JUNOS software Preference Values *(continued)*

Right	Description
Replace a Process Level Token	Allows a process, such as Task Scheduler, to call an API to start another service.
Restore Files And Directories	Allows a user to restore files and directories regardless of file and directory permissions.
Shut Down The System	Allows a user to shut down the Windows 8.1 computer locally.
Synchronize Directory Service Data	Allows a user to synchronize Active Directory data.
Take Ownership Of Files or Other Objects	Allows a user to take ownership of system objects, such as files, folders, printers, and processes.

In Exercise 9.6, you'll apply a user rights policy.

EXERCISE 9.6

Applying User Rights

1. Open the LGOP MMC shortcut.

2. Expand the Local Computer Policy snap-in.

3. Expand the folders as follows: Computer Configuration\Windows Settings\Security Settings\Local Policies\User Rights Assignment.

4. Open the Log On As A Service user right.

5. Click the Add User Or Group button. The Select Users Or Groups dialog box appears.

6. Click the Advanced button, and then select Find Now.

7. Select a user. Click OK.

8. Click OK in the Select Users Or Groups dialog box.

9. In the Log On As A Service Properties dialog box, click OK.

In the next section, we'll look at how users who are not administrators can install resources on Windows 8.1 by using User Account Control.

Configuring User Account Control

Most administrators have had to wrestle with the balance between security and enabling applications to run correctly. In the past, some applications simply would not run correctly under Windows unless the user running the application was a local administrator.

Unfortunately, granting local administrator permissions to a user also allows the user to install software and hardware, change configuration settings, modify local user accounts, and delete critical files. Even more troubling is the fact that malware that infects a computer while an administrator is logged in is also able to perform those same functions.

Limited user accounts in Windows XP were supposed to allow applications to run correctly and allow users to perform necessary tasks. However, in practical application, it did not work as advertised. Many applications require that users have permissions to write to protected folders and to the Registry, and limited user accounts did not allow users to do so.

Windows 8.1's answer to the problem is User Account Control (UAC). UAC enables nonadministrator users to perform standard tasks, such as install a printer, configure a VPN or wireless connection, and install updates, while preventing them from performing tasks that require administrative privileges, such as installing applications.

Managing Privilege Elevation

UAC protects computers by requiring privilege elevation for all users, even users who are members of the local Administrators group. As you have no doubt seen by now, UAC will prompt you for permission when performing a task that requires privilege elevation. This prevents malware from silently launching processes without your knowledge.

Privilege elevation is required for any feature that contains the four-color security shield. For example, the small shield shown on the Change Date and Time button in the Date And Time dialog box in Figure 9.9 indicates an action that requires privilege elevation.

Now let's take a look at how to elevate privileges for users.

Elevated Privileges for Users

By default, local administrators are logged on as standard users. When administrators attempt to perform a task that requires privilege escalation, they are prompted for confirmation by default. This can require administrators to authenticate when performing a task that requires privilege escalation by changing the User Account Control: Behavior Of The Elevation Prompt For Administrators In Admin Approval Mode policy setting to Prompt For Credentials. On the other hand, if you don't want UAC to prompt administrators for confirmation when elevating privileges, you can change the policy setting to Elevate Without Prompting.

Nonadministrator accounts are called standard users. When standard users attempt to perform a task that requires privilege elevation, they are prompted for a password of a user account that has administrative privileges. You cannot configure UAC to automatically

FIGURE 9.9   Date And Time dialog box

allow standard users to perform administrative tasks, nor can you configure UAC to prompt a standard user for confirmation before performing administrative tasks. If you do not want standard users to be prompted for credentials when attempting to perform administrative tasks, you can automatically deny elevation requests by changing the User Account Control: Behavior Of The Elevation Prompt For Standard Users policy setting to Automatically Deny Elevation Requests.

The built-in Administrator account, though disabled by default, is not affected by UAC. UAC will not prompt the Administrator account for elevation of privileges. Thus, it is important to use a normal user account whenever possible and use the built-in Administrator account only when absolutely necessary.

Complete Exercise 9.7 to see how UAC affects administrator and nonadministrator accounts differently.

EXERCISE 9.7

Seeing How UAC Affects Accounts

1.   Log on to Windows 8.1 as a nonadministrator account.

2.   Click either the Windows Key or the Start button ➢ Control Panel ➢ Large Icons View ➢ Windows Firewall.

3.   Click the Turn Windows Firewall On Or Off link on the left side. The UAC box should prompt you for permission to continue. Click Yes. You should not be allowed access to the Windows Firewall Settings dialog box.

4. Log off and log on as the Administrator account.

5. Select Start ➢ Control Panel ➢ Large Icons View ➢ Windows Firewall.

6. Click the Turn Windows Firewall On Or Off link.

7. You should automatically go to the Windows Firewall screen. Close the Windows Firewall screen.

With the Default UAC setting enabled, your Desktop will be dimmed when you are notified of a change to your computer. The administrator or user must either approve or deny the request in the UAC dialog box before you can do anything else on your computer. This action is known as the *secure desktop*. You have the ability to turn off the secure desktop either by modifying the local security policy or by modifying the Registry.

Let's now take a look at elevating privileges for executable applications.

Elevated Privileges for Executables

You can also enable an executable file to run with elevated privileges. To do so, on a one-time basis, you can right-click a shortcut or executable and select Run As Administrator.

But what if you need to configure an application to always run with elevated privileges for a user? To do so, log in as an administrator, right-click a shortcut or executable, and select Properties. On the Compatibility tab, select the Run This Program As An Administrator check box. If the Run This Program As An Administrator check box is unavailable, the program is blocked from permanently running as an administrator, the program doesn't need administrative privileges, or you are not logged on as an administrator.

Many applications that are installed on a Windows 8.1 machine need to have access to the Registry. Windows 8.1 protects the Registry from nonadministrator accounts. Let's take a look at how this works.

Registry and File Virtualization

Windows 8.1 uses a feature called Registry and File Virtualization to enable nonadministrator users to run applications that previously required administrative privileges to run correctly. As discussed earlier, some applications write to the Registry and to protected folders, such as C:\Windows and C:\Program Files. For nonadministrator users, Windows 8.1 redirects any attempts to write to protected locations to a per-user location. By doing so, Windows 8.1 enables users to use the application successfully while it protects critical areas of the system.

Using Advanced Security Options

In the following sections, we'll look at some of the advanced security options that you can configure to protect a Windows 8.1 machine. We'll take a look at the Action Center, shown in Figure 9.10.

FIGURE 9.10   Windows Action Center

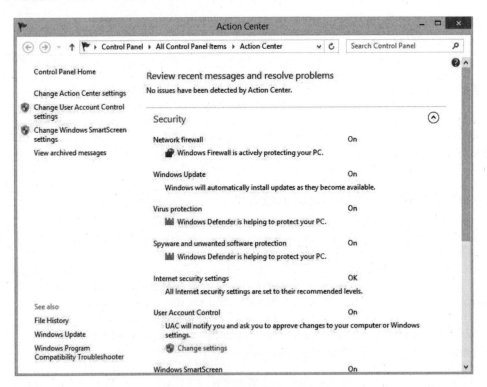

The Action Center is designed to allow you to monitor and configure critical settings through a centralized dialog box. Critical settings include those for automatic updating, malware protection, and other security settings. Malware protection includes virus protection and spyware protection (included through Windows Defender).

Let's start by taking a look at how to configure the Action Center.

Configuring the Action Center

These days, having a firewall just isn't enough. Spyware and viruses are becoming more widespread, more sophisticated, and more dangerous. Users can unintentionally pick up spyware and viruses by visiting websites or by installing an application in which spyware and viruses are bundled.

Even worse, malicious software cannot typically be uninstalled. Thus, antispyware and virus protection applications are also required to ensure that your computer remains protected. Let's take a look at some of the ways you can protect your Windows 8.1 computers using the Action Center.

Using Windows Defender

Windows 8.1 comes with an antispyware application called *Windows Defender*. Windows Defender offers real-time protection from spyware and other unwanted software. You can also configure Windows Defender to scan for spyware on a regular basis.

Like antivirus programs, Windows Defender relies on definitions, which are used to determine whether a file contains spyware. Out-of-date definitions can cause Windows Defender to not detect some spyware. Windows Update is used to regularly update the definitions used by Windows Defender so that the latest spyware can be detected. You can also configure Windows Defender to manually check for updates using Windows Update.

To access Windows Defender (see Figure 9.11), click Start ➢ Control Panel ➢ Large Icons View ➢ Windows Defender. The status appears at the top of the screen and at the bottom is the time of the last scan.

Let's take a look at how you can scan the system for spyware using Windows Defender.

Performing a Manual Scan

You can configure Windows Defender to perform a manual scan of your computer at any time. Three different types of scans can be performed:

- Quick Scan checks only where spyware is most likely to be found.
- Full Scan checks all memory, running processes, and folders.
- Custom Scan checks only the drives and folders that you select.

By default, Windows Defender performs a Quick Scan every morning at 2:00 a.m. You can change this setting by using the Maintenance section of the Action Center as shown in Figure 9.12.

FIGURE 9.11 Windows Defender

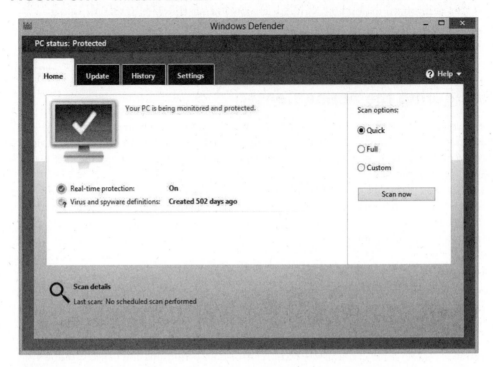

FIGURE 9.12 Setting the maintenance schedule for Windows Defender

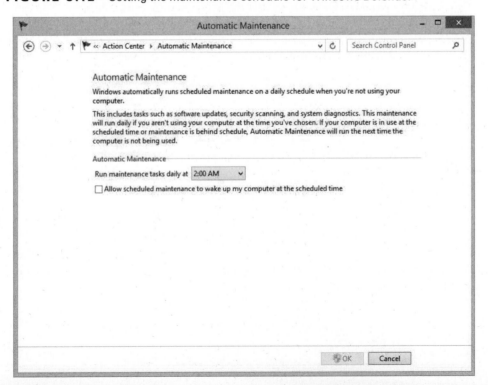

In the next section we'll look at how to configure the many different options of Windows Defender.

Configuring Windows Defender

Windows Defender has been overhauled for Windows 8.1 but for the most part the changes are "under the hood" and you don't need to deal with them or have access to them. Configuring Windows Defender is a lot easier because the software is more automated and thus requires less configuration. The Settings and the History tabs let you fine-tune the service.

Settings Tab

The Settings tab is used to configure Windows Defender. As shown in Figure 9.13, the following items can be accessed through the Settings tab:

Real-Time Protection   This configures whether real-time protection is enabled, which security agents you want to run, how you should be notified about threats, and whether a Windows Defender icon is displayed in the notification area.

Excluded Files and Locations   This allows you to set up files and folders that are to be excluded during a scan.

Excluded File Types   This option lets you configure certain file types that will be excluded from a scan. For example, you can exclude all files with the .doc filename extension if needed.

Excluded Processes   This allows you to list processes to be excluded from a scan. The benefit is a faster scan but the trade-off is less security.

Advanced   The options on the Advanced page configure whether archived files and folders are scanned, whether email is scanned, whether removable drives are scanned, whether heuristics are used to detect unanalyzed software, whether a restore point is created before removing spyware, and which file locations are exempt from scanning.

Microsoft Active Protection Service (MAPS)   This service when enabled allows the system to report malware to Microsoft. It allows for several participation levels from none to providing very detailed information about Malware to Microsoft.

Administrator   The options on the Administrator page configure whether Windows Defender is enabled and whether you display items from all users on this computer.

The next tab we'll look at is History.

History Tab

The History tab is used to view items that have been acted upon by Windows Defender. Three radio buttons allow you to organize your view in various ways. Information is included about each application, the alert level, the action taken, the date, and the status.

FIGURE 9.13 Windows Defender Settings page

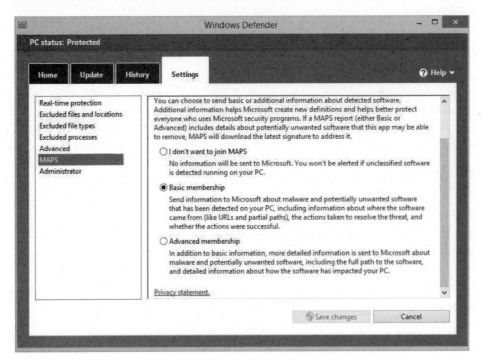

Quarantined Items

Software that has been quarantined by Windows Defender is placed in Quarantined Items. Quarantined software will remain here until you remove it. If you find that a legitimate application is accidentally removed by Windows Defender, you can restore the application from Quarantined Items.

Allowed Items

Software that has been marked as allowed will be added to the Allowed Items list. Only trusted software should be added to this list. Windows Defender will not alert you regarding any software found on the Allowed Items list. If you find that a potentially dangerous application has been added to the Allowed Items list, you can remove it from the list so that Windows Defender can detect it.

All Items

This is a view of both quarantined and allowed items.

Windows Firewall will be covered in detail in Chapter 6, "Windows Firewall and Remote Access."

Later in this chapter, we'll look at using Windows BitLocker Drive Encryption and how it can help you protect your hard drive.

Other Security Options

Windows 8.1 includes some other security options to help make your experience more secure. The following sections take a look at a few extra options you can use to make Windows 8.1 more secure.

Windows 8.1 SmartScreen Filter

Windows SmartScreen is a new security feature in Windows 8.1. SmartScreen allows you to protect your operating system from malware attacks. SmartScreen works when a user downloads a piece of software from the Internet. Once the user tries to run the software, SmartScreen analyzes information about the software and warns the user if the software isn't recognized or may be malicious.

To configure the SmartScreen filter in Windows 8.1, open the Action Center and click the Change Settings button next to the Windows SmartScreen section. Once the Windows SmartScreen window appears, you have three options to choose from:

- Get Administrator Approval Before Running An Unrecognized App From The Internet (Recommended)

- Warn Before Running An Unrecognized App, But Don't Require Administrator Approval

- Don't Do Anything (Turn Off Windows SmartScreen)

Windows 8.1 Secure Boot

Windows 8.1 includes a new configuration called Secure Boot. Once a user enables Secure Boot, the user's computer is protected from booting from illegally copied CDs or DVDs that could cause your system to crash or experience other problems. Secure Boot does not stop a user from using a valid recovery disk or Windows repair disks.

For you to use Secure Boot (which is configured by default on Windows 8.1 devices), your computer must have a Unified Extensible Firmware Interface (UEFI) motherboard. UEFI is an alternative to using BIOS to interface between the software and the firmware of a system. Traditional BIOS does not support Secure Boot.

One issue that you can run into when using Secure Boot is when you are using some older hardware. For example, if you were using an older video card, Secure Boot may not recognize the video card and think that there is an invalid piece of hardware being loaded onto the system.

Managing Internet Explorer 11 Security

Managing the security of the latest version of Internet Explorer (version 11 as of this writing) can be done locally in the Internet Options dialog box, or these settings can be controlled through Group Policy in a domain. Although there are additional tabs on this dialog box, let's take a look at the security-related tabs in Internet Options.

Security Tab

On the Security tab, you can organize specific websites into security zones and then apply various levels of security to these zones. Four default zones are available:

Internet   Will hold all sites not assigned to other zones

Local Internet   Refers to all Internet sites located on the LAN

Trusted Sites   A zone in which you can place sites you trust, which will allow you to lower the required security on this zone

Restricted Sites   A zone in which you can place sites that you do not trust or for which you feel you need to apply stricter security than the default

You can change the default setting of each zone by using the slider on each zone's page or by clicking the Custom Level button. Three preset collections of settings are available on the slider: Medium, Medium High, and High. Clicking the Custom Level button gives you even more granular access to security settings.

Privacy Tab

The Privacy tab is used to control the placement of cookies on the local machine by websites that you visit that are in the Internet zone. It also uses a slider that can be set to five levels: Low, Medium, Medium High, High, and Block All Cookies. At the Low level, all cookies are allowed. At the Block All Cookies level, no cookies are allowed. The other three levels offer compromises between these two extremes.

Advanced Tab

The Advanced tab controls more detailed security settings than are available under any of the zone settings and apply to all zones. Some examples are controlling the uses of certificates and security protocols such as SSL and TLS.

Multifactor Authentication and Biometrics

One security item that you may be seeing a lot more of these days is multifactor authentication and biometrics. Multifactor authentication (explained in greater detail in the "Understanding Smart Cards" section later in this chapter) normally refers to authentication using more than one security check. For example, a smart card is multifactor. You need two items to log onto the system: the smart card and the smart card's PIN number. Three-factor authentication is normally a smart card along with a biometric feature. So you would need the smart card, the PIN number, and some form of biometric entry.

Windows 8.1 also supports what is known as virtual smart cards and picture passwords. Virtual smart cards serve the same purpose as physical smart cards, but they use the Trusted Platform Module (TPM) chip that is available on computers rather than requiring the use of a separate physical smart card and reader. Virtual smart cards are created in the TPM, where the keys that are used for authentication are stored in cryptographically secured hardware.

Picture passwords are a new feature. Using a picture password, users can sign in to their PC with their favorite photo instead of a password. Users choose the picture, and specific gestures—circles, straight lines, or taps—they use, and where on the picture they trace them. They can draw a picture password directly on a touchscreen with their finger, or they can use a mouse to draw the shapes. Everyone who has a Microsoft account on their PC can set up their own picture password.

These authentication add-ons are normally not free. But one of the nice features with this setup is that when you want to log on to the domain, at the logon screen just swipe your finger over the fingerprint reader and it verifies and logs you on to the domain with no other requirements.

When setting up multifactor authentication or biometrics in Windows 8.1, you need to use the software that is included from the maker of the multifactor or biometric readers (to install the proper drivers).

The only downside to multifactor authentication (like a smart card) is that your users tend to lose their smart cards. To avoid losing money, you may have to charge users who lose their smart cards. Multifactor authentication is a great add-on to look into for your organization.

Using BitLocker Drive Encryption

To prevent individuals from stealing your computer and viewing personal and sensitive data found on your hard disk, some editions of Windows 8.1 come with a feature called *BitLocker Drive Encryption*. BitLocker encrypts the entire system drive. New files added to this drive are encrypted automatically, and files moved from this drive to another drive or computer are decrypted automatically.

Only Windows 8.1 Enterprise and Windows 8.1 Pro include BitLocker Drive Encryption, and only the operating system drive (usually C:) or internal hard drives can be encrypted with BitLocker. Files on other types of drives must be encrypted using BitLocker To Go.

BitLocker uses a TPM version 1.2 or higher to store the security key. A TPM is a chip that is found in newer computers. If you do not have a computer with a TPM, you can store the key on a removable USB drive. The USB drive will be required each time you start the computer so that the system drive can be decrypted.

If the TPM discovers a potential security risk, such as a disk error or changes made to BIOS, hardware, system files, or startup components, the system drive will not be unlocked until you enter the 48-digit BitLocker recovery password or use a USB drive with a recovery key as a recovery agent.

The BitLocker recovery password is very important. Do not lose it, or you may not be able to unlock the drive. Even if you do not have a TPM, be sure to keep your recovery password in case your USB drive becomes lost or corrupted.

You must set up BitLocker by using the Local Group Policy editor or by clicking the BitLocker icon in Control Panel. One advantage of using BitLocker is that you can prevent any unencrypted data from being copied onto a removable disk, thus protecting a Windows 8.1 machine.

BitLocker requires that you have a hard disk with at least two partitions, both formatted with NTFS. One partition will be the system partition that will be encrypted. The other partition will be the active partition that is used to start the computer; this partition will remain unencrypted.

Understanding Smart Cards

Another way to help secure Windows 8.1 is by using *smart cards*. *Smart cards* are plastic cards (the size of a credit card) that can be used in combination with other methods of authentication. This process of using a smart card along with another form of authentication is called *multifactor authentication*.

Smart card support allows you to increase the security of many critical functions of your company, including client authentication, interactive logon, and document signing.

Smart cards are now easier to use and deploy due to the new features included with Windows 8.1. The new smart card features are available in all versions of Windows 8.1.

One of the new features of Windows 8.1 allows enhanced support for smart card–related Plug and Play and the Personal Identity Verification (PIV) standard from the National Institute of Standards and Technology (NIST). This allows users of Windows 8.1 to use smart cards from vendors who publish their drivers through Windows Update. This enables Windows 8.1 to use the smart card without needing special middleware. These drivers are downloaded in the same way as drivers for other Windows devices.

When a smart card that is PIV-compliant is placed into a smart card reader, Windows 8.1 will try to download a current driver from Windows Update. If a driver is not available, the PIV-compliant minidriver that is included with Windows 8.1 is used for the smart card. Here are some of the new smart card options in Windows 8.1:

Encrypting Drives with BitLocker   If your users are using Windows 8.1 Enterprise or Ultimate, the users can choose to encrypt their removable media by turning on BitLocker and then choosing the smart card option to unlock the drive. Windows will then retrieve the correct minidriver for the smart card and allows the operation to complete.

Smart Card Domain Logon   When using Windows 8.1, the correct minidriver for a smart card is automatically retrieved. This allows a new smart card to authenticate with the domain controller without requiring the user to install or configure additional middleware.

Document and Email Signing   Windows 8.1 users can use smart cards to sign an email or document. XML Paper Specification (XPS) documents can also be signed without the need for additional software.

Use with Line-of-Business Applications   Using Windows 8.1 smart cards allows applications that use Cryptography Next Generation (CNG) or CryptoAPI to retrieve the correct minidriver at runtime. No additional middleware is needed.

In the next section, we'll look at two of the most important security features available: proper permissions and file- and folder-level security.

Managing File and Folder Security

Setting up proper file and folder security is one of the most important tasks that an IT professional can perform. If permissions and security are not properly configured, users will be able to access resources that they shouldn't.

File and folder security defines what access a user has to local resources. You can limit access by applying security for files and folders. You should know what NTFS security permissions are and how they are applied.

A powerful feature of networking is the ability to allow network access to local folders. In Windows 8.1, it is easy to share folders. You can also apply security to shared folders in a manner that is similar to applying NTFS permissions. Once you share a folder, users with appropriate access rights can access the folders through a variety of methods.

Before diving into the security section of folders, let's first take a look at some folder options.

Folder Options

The Windows 8.1 Folder Options dialog box allows you to configure many properties associated with files and folders, such as what you see when you access folders and how Windows searches through files and folders. You can access Folder Options by choosing Control Panel ➤ Large Icons View ➤ Folder Options. The Folder Options dialog box has three tabs: General, View, and Search. The options on each of these tabs are described in the following sections.

Folder General Options

The General tab of the Folder Options dialog box, shown in Figure 9.14, includes the following options:

- Whether folders are opened all in the same window when a user is browsing folders or each folder is opened in a separate window

- Whether a user opens items with a single mouse click or a double-click

- Whether to have the navigation pane show all folders and automatically expand to the current folder

FIGURE 9.14   The General tab of the Folder Options dialog box

Folder View Options

The options on the View tab of the Folder Options dialog box, shown in Figure 9.15, are used to configure what users see when they open files and folders. For example, you can change the default setting so that hidden files and folders are displayed. Table 9.7 describes the View tab options.

FIGURE 9.15   The View tab of the Folder Options dialog box

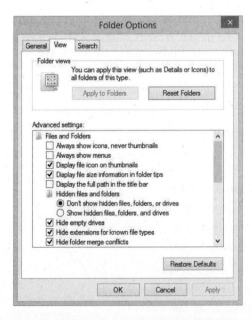

TABLE 9.7   Folder view options

Option	Description	Default value
Always Show Icons, Never Thumbnails	Shows icons for files instead of thumbnail previews.	Not selected
Always Show Menus	Shows the File, Edit, View, Tools, and Help menus when you're browsing for files.	Not selected
Display File Icon On Thumbnails	Displays the file icon on thumbnails.	Enabled
Display File Size Information In Folder Tips	Specifies whether the file size is automatically displayed when you hover your mouse over a folder.	Enabled
Display the Full Path In The Title Bar (Classic Theme Only)	Specifies whether the title bar shows an abbreviated path of your location. Enabling this option displays the full path, such as C:\Word Documents\ Sybex\Windows 8.1 Book\Chapter 9 as opposed to showing an abbreviated path such as Chapter 9.	Not selected
Hidden Files And Folders	Specifies whether files and folders with the Hidden attribute are listed. Choosing Show Hidden Files, Folders, Or Drives displays these items.	Don't Show Hidden Files, Folders, And Drives
Hide Empty Drives In The Computer Folder	This option will prevent drives that are empty in the Computer folder from being displayed.	Enabled
Hide Extensions For Known File Types	By default, filename extensions, which identify known file types (such as .doc for Word files and .xls for Excel files) are not shown. Disabling this option displays all filename extensions.	Enabled
Hide Protected Operating System Files (Recommended)	By default, operating system files are not shown, which protects operating system files from being modified or deleted by a user. Disabling this option displays the operating system files.	Enabled

TABLE 9.7 JUNOS software Preference Values *(continued)*

Option	Description	Default value
Launch Folder Windows In A Separate Process	By default, when you open a folder, it shares memory with the previous folders that were opened. Enabling this option opens folders in separate parts of memory, which increases the stability of Windows 8.1 but can slightly decrease the performance of the computer.	Not selected
Show Drive Letters	Specifies whether drive letters are shown in the Computer folder. When disabled, only the name of the disk or device will be shown.	Enabled
Show Encrypted Or Compressed NTFS Files In Color	Displays encrypted or compressed files in an alternate color when they are displayed in a folder window.	Enabled
Show Pop-Up Description For Folder And Desktop Items	Displays whether a pop-up tooltip is displayed when you hover your mouse over files and folders.	Enabled
Show Preview Handlers In Preview Pane	Shows the contents of files in the pre-view pane.	Enabled
Use Check Boxes To Select Items	Adds a check box next to each file and folder so that one or more of them may be selected. Actions can then be performed on selected items.	Not selected
Use Sharing Wizard (Recommended)	Allows you to share a folder using a simplified sharing method.	Enabled
When Typing Into List View	Selects whether text is automatically typed into the search box or whether the typed item is selected in the view.	Select The Typed Item In The View

Search Options

The Search tab of the Folder Options dialog box, shown in Figure 9.16, is used to configure how Windows 8.1 searches for files. You can choose for Windows 8.1 to search by filename only, by filenames and contents, or by a combination of the two, depending on whether indexing is enabled. You can also select from the following options:

- How To Search, which lets you specify to use or not to use the index when searching the filesystem

- Include System Directories

- Include Compressed Files

- Always Search File Names And Contents

FIGURE 9.16   The Search tab of the Folder Options dialog box

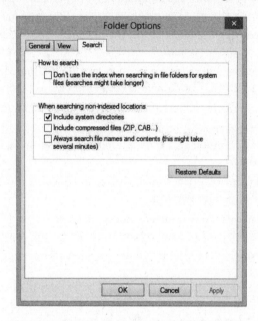

To search for files and folders, click Start ➤ Search and type your query in the search box. In the next section, we'll look at how to secure these folders and files.

Securing Access to Files and Folders

On NTFS partitions, you can specify the access each user has to specific folders or files on the partition based on the user's logon name and group associations. Access control consists of rights and permissions. A right (also referred to as a privilege) is an authorization to perform a specific action.

Permissions are authorizations to perform specific operations on specific objects. The owner of an object or any user who has the necessary rights to modify permissions can apply permissions to NTFS objects. If permissions are not explicitly granted within NTFS, then they are implicitly denied. Permissions can also be explicitly denied, which then overrides explicitly granted permissions.

The following section describes design goals for access control as well as how to apply NTFS permissions and some techniques for optimizing local access. Let's take a look at design goals for setting up security.

Design Goals for Access Control

Before you start applying NTFS permissions to resources, you should develop design goals for access control as a part of your overall security strategy. Basic security strategy suggests that you provide each user and group with the minimum level of permissions needed for job functionality. Some of the considerations when planning access control include the following:

- Defining the resources that are included within your network—in this case, the files and folders residing on the filesystem

- Defining which resources will put your organization at risk, including defining the resources and defining the risk of damage if the resource was compromised

- Developing security strategies that address possible threats and minimize security risks

- Defining groups that security can be applied to, based on users within the group membership who have common access requirements, and applying permissions to groups as opposed to users

- Applying additional security settings through Group Policy if your Windows 8.1 clients are part of an Active Directory network

- Using additional security features, such as Encrypted File System (EFS), to provide additional levels of security or file auditing to track access to critical files and folders

After you have decided what your design goals are, you can start applying your NTFS permissions.

Managing Network Access

In every network, there are resources to which the users need to gain access. As IT professionals, we share these resources so that our users can do their jobs.

Sharing is the process of allowing network users access to a resource located on a computer. A network share provides a single location to manage shared data used by many users. Sharing also allows an administrator to install an application once, as opposed to installing it locally at each computer, and to manage the application from a single location.

The following sections describe how to create and manage shared folders, configure share permissions, and provide access to shared resources.

Creating Shared Folders

You can share a folder in two ways. To use the Sharing Wizard, right-click a folder and select Share. If the Sharing Wizard feature is enabled, you'll see the File Sharing screen. Here, you can add local users.

However, you cannot use the Sharing Wizard to share resources with domain users. To share a folder with domain users, you should right-click the folder, select Properties, and select the Sharing tab, shown in Figure 9.17.

FIGURE 9.17 The Sharing tab of a folder's Properties dialog box

Clicking the Share button will launch the Sharing Wizard. To configure Advanced Sharing, click the Advanced Sharing button, which will open the Advanced Sharing dialog box. When you share a folder, you can configure the options listed in Table 9.8.

TABLE 9.8 Share folder options

Option	Description
Share This Folder	Makes the folder available through local access and network access
Share Name	A descriptive name by which users will access the folder
Comments	Additional descriptive information about the share (optional)
Limit The Number Of Simultaneous Users To	The maximum number of connections to the share at any one time (no more than 10 users can simultaneously access a share on a Windows 8.1 computer)

TABLE 9.8 JUNOS software Preference Values *(continued)*

Option	Description
Permissions	How users will access the folder over the network
Caching	How folders are cached when the folder is offline

If you share a folder and then decide that you do not want to share it, just deselect the Share This Folder check box. You can easily tell that a folder has been shared by the group icon located at the bottom left of the folder icon. The following also holds true:

- Only folders, not files, can be shared.
- Share permissions can be applied only to folders and not to files.
- If a folder is shared over the network and a user is accessing it locally, then share permissions will not apply to the local user; only NTFS permissions will apply.
- If a shared folder is copied, the original folder will still be shared but not the copy.
- If a shared folder is moved, the folder will no longer be shared.
- If the shared folder will be accessed by a mixed environment of clients, including some that do not support long filenames, you should use the 8.3 naming format for files.
- Folders can be shared through the Net Share command-line utility.

Now let's take a look at configuring share permissions for your users.

Configuring Share Permissions

You can control users' access to shared folders by assigning share permissions. Share permissions are less complex than NTFS permissions and can be applied only to folders (unlike NTFS permissions, which can be applied to files and folders).

To assign share permissions, click the Permissions button in the Advanced Sharing dialog box. This brings up the Permissions dialog box, shown in Figure 9.18.

You can assign three types of share permissions:

Full Control Allows full access to the shared folder.

Change Allows users to change data within a file or to delete files.

Read Allows a user to view and execute files in the shared folder. Read is the default permission on shared folders for the Everyone group.

Shared folders do not use the same concept of inheritance as NTFS folders. If you share a folder, there is no way to block access to lower-level resources through share permissions.

When applying conflicting share and NTFS permissions, the most restrictive permissions apply. Remember that share and NTFS permissions are both applied only when a user is accessing a shared resource over a network. Only NTFS permissions apply to a user accessing a resource locally.

FIGURE 9.18   The Permissions dialog box

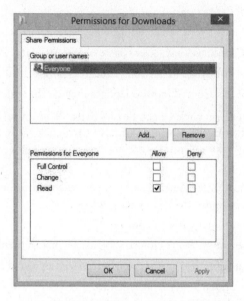

So, for example, if a user's NTFS security settings on a resource were Read and the share permission on the same resource was Full Control, the user would have Read permission only when connecting to that resource. The most restrictive set of permissions wins.

HomeGroup

HomeGroups are groups of computers on a home network that can share files and printers. Pictures, music, videos, documents, and printers can be shared with others in the HomeGroup. HomeGroups are first created and then devices join the group. Resources can be shared at the file, folder or library level. Other people can't change the files that are shared unless given permission to do so. HomeGroups are covered more completely in Chapter 10, "Managing Hardware and Printers."

Using Windows Update

Windows Update is a utility that connects to Microsoft's website and checks to ensure that you have the most up-to-date versions of Microsoft products.

Some of the common update categories associated with Windows Update are as follows:

- Critical updates
- Service packs
- Drivers

Follow these steps to configure Windows Update:

1. Select Start ➤ Control Panel.

   - From Windows Icons View, select Windows Update.

   - From Windows Category View, select System And Security, Windows Update.

2. Configure the options you want to use for Windows Update, and click OK.

   The options you can access from Windows Update include the following:

Check For Updates   When you click Check For Updates, Windows Update will retrieve a list of available updates from the Internet. You can then click View Available Updates to see what updates are available. Updates are marked as Important, Recommended, or Optional.

Change Settings   Clicking Change Settings allows you to customize how Windows can install updates. You can configure the following options:

   - "Install updates automatically (recommended)"

   - "Download updates but let me choose whether to install them"

   - "Check for updates but let me choose whether to download and install them"

   - "Never check for updates (not recommended)"

View Update History   View Update History is used to view a list of all the installations that have been performed on the computer. You can see the following information for each installation:

   - Update Name

   - Status (Successful, Unsuccessful, or Canceled)

   - Importance (Important, Recommended, or Optional)

   - Date Installed

Restore Hidden Updates   With Restore Hidden Updates you can list any updates that you have hidden from the list of available updates. Administrators might hide updates that they do not want users to install.

Sometimes it is important for an administrator to test and verify updates before the users can install them. This area allows you to see hidden updates so that they can be tested before deployment.

Installed Updates   Installed Updates allows you to see the updates that are installed and to uninstall or change them if necessary. The Installed Updates feature is a part of the Programs And Features applet in Control Panel, which allows you to uninstall, change, and repair programs.

Rolling Back Updates

One advantage of Windows 8.1 is the ability to roll back updates if they cause you any problems. When using the Windows Update utility, you can revert any updates that you choose to roll back.

To roll back an update, go to the Installed Updates section and highlight the update, and then choose Uninstall.

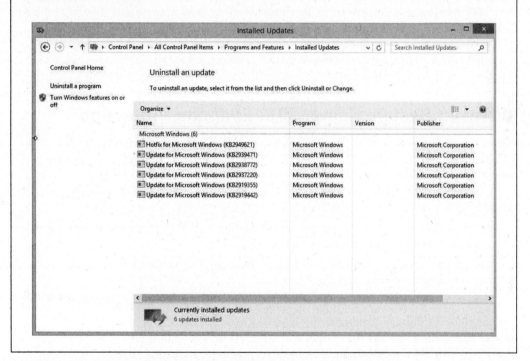

Windows Intune and Intune Endpoint Protection

Windows Intune helps employees with access to corporate applications, data, and resources from virtually anywhere on almost any device while helping to keep information secure. It main benefit is its ability to provide support for the array of mobile devices that users employ to perform work.

Windows Intune supports devices running the Windows desktop operating system, Windows RT, Windows Phone, Mac OS, iOS, or Android—in one unified solution, including the provisioning for updates, even non-Microsoft updates.

It can monitor the devices, track hardware and software inventory, and manage licensing in one solution. Microsoft Intune Endpoint Protection can be used to provide protection from malware and viruses. If this feature discovers protection already present, it doesn't install.

Using System Center 2012

Microsoft System Center 2012 R2 is an integrated management platform that allows administrators to easily and efficiently manage their IT organization using a standard set of included utilities.

Microsoft System Center 2012 R2 is the only platform that gives you the ability to offer comprehensive management of all your Microsoft applications, services, physical resources, hypervisors, software-defined networks, configuration, and automation in a single platform.

Microsoft System Center 2012 Endpoint Protection

One of the utilities that you can use with Windows 8.1 is the Microsoft System Center 2012 R2 Endpoint Protection client. Endpoint Protection allows you to manage and configure antimalware policies and Windows Firewall security settings for client computers.

As an administrator, if you choose to use Endpoint Protection, you get the following benefits:

- You can download the latest antimalware definition files from Microsoft to keep client computers current and protected.

- You can configure antimalware policies and Windows Firewall settings by using custom antimalware policies and client settings.

- You can set up email notifications when malware is detected on client computers.

Endpoint Protection in Configuration Manager allows you to create antimalware policies that contain settings for Endpoint Protection client configurations. You have the ability to deploy the antimalware policies to client computers and then monitor the System Center 2012 R2 Endpoint Protection Status in the Monitoring workspace.

To get more information or get a free trial download of System Center 2012 R2 Endpoint Protection, go to Microsoft's website at www.microsoft.com/en-us/server-cloud/products/system-center-2012-r2/.

Summary

In this chapter, we showed you how to create and manage user and group accounts. We looked at the various tools that you can use to create users in Windows 8.1.

We also looked at Windows 8.1 security. We showed you the difference between LGPOs, which are applied at the local level, and GPOs, which are applied through a Windows 2000, 2003, 2008, Windows Server 2008 R2, Windows Server 2012, or Windows Server 2012 R2 domain, and how they are applied.

We looked at account policies, which control the logon process. The two types of account policies are password and account lockout policies. We also explored local policies, which control what a user can do at the computer. The three types of local policies are audit, user rights, and security options policies.

This chapter discussed some of the advanced security items, such as how to use the Group Policy Results Tool to analyze current configuration settings, how to use User Account Control, and how to use BitLocker Drive Encryption.

You also learned how to configure NTFS and Share permissions. Finally, we discussed Windows Update and the Windows System Center 2012 R2 product.

Exam Essentials

Be able to create and manage user accounts. When creating user accounts, be aware of the requirements for doing so. Understand User Account Control. Know how to rename and delete user accounts. Be able to manage all user properties.

Know how to configure and manage local user authentication. Understand the options that can be configured to manage local user authentication and when these options would be used to create a more secure environment. Be able to specify where local user authentication options are configured.

Know how to manage local groups. Understand the local groups that are created on Windows 8.1 computers by default, and be familiar with the rights each group has. Know how to create and manage new groups.

Know how to set local group policies. Understand the purpose of account policies and local policies. Know the purpose and implementation of account policies for managing password policies and account lockout policies. Understand the purpose and implementation of local policies and how they can be applied to users and groups for audit policies, user rights assignments, and security options.

Understand User Account Control. Understand the purpose and features of User Account Control. Be familiar with Registry and File Virtualization. Understand privilege escalation. Know the basics of the new UAC Group Policy settings.

Know how to use Windows Defender. Be able to configure and use Windows Defender. Understand how quarantine works. Know the purpose of Microsoft MAPS.

Know how to use BitLocker Drive Encryption. Understand the purpose and requirements of BitLocker Drive Encryption. Know which editions of Windows 8.1 (Enterprise and Ultimate) include BitLocker.

Review Questions

You can find the answers in Appendix A.

1. You have a user who has access to the applications folder on your network server. This user belongs to the following groups:

   - NTFS
   - Sales   Read only
   - Marketing   Full Control
   - Shared Permissions
   - Sales   Read only
   - Marketing   Change

   When this user logs into the applications folder from their Windows 8.1 machine, what are their effective permissions?

   A. Full Control

   B. Read only

   C. Change

   D. Read and Write

2. You are setting up a machine for a home user who does not know much about computers. You do not want to make the user a local administrator, but you do want to give this user the right to change Windows Updates manually. How can you configure this?

   A. Modify the LGPO for Windows Update to allow the user to make changes manually.

   B. Explain to the user how to log on as the Administrator account.

   C. Set Windows Update modifications to anyone.

   D. This can't be done. Only administrators can change Windows Update.

3. You are the administrator for a large organization with multiple Windows Server 2012 R2 domain controllers and multiple domains. You have a Windows 8.1 machine that is set up for all users to access. You have an application called StellApp.exe that everyone on this Windows 8.1 computer can use except for the sales group. How do you stop the sales group from accessing this one application?

   A. Deny the Everyone group the rights to the application.

   B. Create an executable rule from the Application Control Policy.

   C. Create a security role from the Application Control Policy.

   D. Give the Everyone group full control to the application.

4. You have a Windows 8.1 machine that multiple users access. All users have the rights to use USB removable devices but you need to deny one user from using USB removable devices. How do you accomplish this?

    A. Deny the one user from using the machine.

    B. Set a USB rule on Hardware Manager.

    C. Deny all users from using USB devices.

    D. Create a removable storage access policy through an LGPO.

5. You are the system administrator for a large organization. You have a Windows 8.1 machine that all users can access. There is a folder on the Windows 8.1 machine called Apps. You need to set up auditing on this folder. How do you accomplish this task?

    A. From the Local Group Policy, enable Directory Service Access.

    B. From the Local Group Policy, enable Audit Object Access.

    C. From the Local Group Policy, enable Account Access.

    D. From the Local Group Policy, enable File And Folder Access.

6. You have a user named Will who has access to the Finance folder on your network server. Will belongs to the following groups:

    - NTFS
    - Admin   Full Control
    - Finance   Modify
    - Shared Permissions
    - Admin   Full Control
    - Finance   Change

    When Will logs into the Finance folder from his Windows 8.1 machine, what are his effective permissions?

    A. Full Control

    B. Read only

    C. Change

    D. Read and Write

7. You are the network administrator for a large organization. You have a Windows 8.1 machine that needs to prevent any user from copying unencrypted files from the Windows 8.1 machine to any removable disk. How do you accomplish this task?

    A. Click the System icon in Control Panel, and set BitLocker Drive Encryption.

    B. Click the Hardware icon in Control Panel, and set BitLocker Drive Encryption.

    C. Click the Device Manager icon in Control Panel, and set BitLocker Drive Encryption.

    D. In a Local Group Policy, set BitLocker Drive Encryption.

8. In which editions of Windows 8.1 can you enable BitLocker? (Choose all that apply.)

    A. Windows 8.1 Home Edition

    B. Windows 8.1 Basic Edition

    C. Windows 8.1 Pro Edition

    D. Windows 8.1 Enterprise Edition

9. Your organization has decided to install Windows Server Update Service (WSUS). You have a Windows 8.1 machine that needs to have the updates done from the WSUS server instead of directly from Microsoft's website. How do you accomplish this?

    A. Modify the Local Group Policy for Windows Update to receive updates from the WSUS server.

    B. Click the Windows Update icon in Control Panel and modify the settings to receive updates from the WSUS server.

    C. Click the System icon in Control Panel and modify the settings to receive updates from the WSUS server.

    D. Modify the WSUS server to force this Windows 8.1 machine to receive updates from the WSUS server.

10. Your network's security has been breached. You are trying to redefine security so that a user cannot repeatedly attempt user logon with different passwords. To accomplish this, which of the following items should you define?

    A. Password Policy

    B. Account Lockout Policy

    C. Audit Policy

    D. Security Options

11. You are the network administrator for a Fortune 500 company. The accounting department has recently purchased a custom application for running financial models. To run properly, the application requires that you make some changes to the computer policy. You decide to deploy the changes through a Local Group Policy setting. You suspect that the policy is not being applied properly because of a conflict somewhere with another Local Group Policy setting. What command-line utility should you run to see a listing of how the group policies have been applied to the computer and the user?

    A. GPResult

    B. GPOResult

    C. GPAudit

    D. GPInfo

12. You have a Windows 8.1 computer that is located in an unsecured area. You want to track usage of the computer by recording user logon and logoff events. To do this, which of the following auditing policies must be enabled?

    A. Audit Account Logon Events

    B. Audit Account Management

    C. Audit Process Tracking

    D. Audit System Events

13. You are the administrator for a printing company. After you configure the Password Must Meet Complexity Requirements policy, several users have problems when changing their passwords. Which of the following passwords meet the minimum complexity requirements? (Choose all that apply.)

A. aBc-1

B. Abcde!

C. 1247445Np

D. !@#$%^&*(-[]

14. You are the system administrator for Stellacon Corp. You have a computer that is shared by many users. You want to ensure that when users press Ctrl+Alt+Del to log on, they do not see the name of the last user. What do you configure?

A. Set the security option Clear User Settings When Users Log Off.

B. Set the security option Interactive Logon: Do Not Display Last User Name In Logon Screen.

C. Set the security option Prevent Users From Seeing Last User Name.

D. Configure nothing; this is the default setting.

15. Mary has access to the R&D folder on your network server. Mary's user belongs to the following groups:

- NTFS
- Sales   Read only
- Marketing Read Only
- Shared Permissions
- Sales   Read only
- Marketing Change

When Mary logs into the R&D folder from her Windows 8.1 machine, what are her effective permissions?

A. Full Control

B. Read only

C. Change

D. Read and Write

16. You have recently hired Will as an assistant for network administration. You have not decided how much responsibility you want him to have. In the meantime, you want him to be able to restore files on Windows 8.1 computers in your network, but you do not want him to be able to run the backups. What is the minimum assignment that will allow Will to complete this task?

A. Add Will to the Administrators group.

B. Grant Will the Read right to the root of each volume he will back up.

C. Add Will to the Backup Operators group.

D. Grant Will the user right Restore Files and Directories.

17. You are the network administrator of a medium-sized company. Your company requires a fair degree of security and you have been tasked with defining and implementing a security policy. You have configured password policies so that users must change their passwords every 30 days. Which password policy would you implement if you want to prevent users from reusing passwords they have used recently?

   A. Passwords Must Be Advanced

   B. Enforce Password History

   C. Passwords Must Be Unique

   D. Passwords Must Meet Complexity Requirements

18. You have a network folder that resides on an NTFS partition on a Windows 8.1 computer. NTFS permissions and share permissions have been applied. Which of the following statements best describes how share permissions and NTFS permissions work together if they have been applied to the same folder?

   A. The NTFS permissions will always take precedence.

   B. The share permissions will always take precedence.

   C. The system will look at the cumulative share permissions and the cumulative NTFS permissions. Whichever set is less restrictive will be applied.

   D. The system will look at the cumulative share permissions and the cumulative NTFS permissions. Whichever set is more restrictive will be applied.

19. You are the network administrator for a bookstore. You install Windows 8.1 on a new computer. Before you connect the computer to the Internet, you want to ensure that the appropriate features are enabled. You open Windows Security Center and notice that there are features that require addressing. Which of the following features must be addressed?

   A. Firewall protection

   B. Spyware and virus protection

   C. Automatic update protection

   D. All of the above

20. You are the Active Directory administrator for your company. A Windows 8.1 computer has been purchased for the finance department, and you want to monitor it for unauthorized access. You configure the Audit Object Access policy to audit both success and failure events. However, when you look at the security event log a few days later, you do not see any entries related to file access. What is the most likely reason for this behavior?

   A. Auditing has not been enabled for the appropriate files and folders.

   B. A conflicting Group Policy setting is overriding your configuration.

   C. Another administrator has disabled your Group Policy setting.

   D. Object access events are found in the system event log.

Chapter

10

Managing Files and Disks on Windows 8.1

70-687 MICROSOFT EXAM OBJECTIVES COVERED IN THIS CHAPTER:

✓ **Manage local storage**

- Manage disk volumes and file systems, manage storage spaces

70-688 MICROSOFT EXAM OBJECTIVES COVERED IN THIS CHAPTER:

✓ **Support data storage**

- Distributed File System (DFS) client, including caching settings

- Storage spaces, including capacity and fault tolerance

✓ **Support data security**

- Permissions, including share, NTFS, and Dynamic Access Control (DAC)

- Encrypting File System (EFS), including Data Recovery Agent

- Access to removable media

- BitLocker and BitLocker To Go, including Data Recovery Agent and Microsoft BitLocker Administration and Monitoring (MBAM)

There has been a huge surge in the number of new file, folder, and storage features that have been added to Windows in the last few years. These features have mainly focused on the areas of securing access and making it easier to get to resources. Windows 8.1 extends the concept of libraries, HomeGroups, and SkyDrive (which is now fully integrated into the operating system as OneDrive). In this chapter, you will learn how to implement best practices for configuring folders, HomeGroups, OneDrive, NTFS permissions, EFS file encryption, auditing, and so on.

Understanding Files and Folders

No matter how advanced the hardware or how powerful the operating system and the software, the one thing that never changes is that files are still the indispensable component in computing. The most logical way to organize files is in folders. Together, these two basic elements comprise the core of information systems.

File Basics

Computer files serve many functions. Users create and use them for documents, drawings, artwork, music and sounds, and so on. The operating system uses files to access functionality in the various OS layers and in utility software that runs on the computer, from Windows programs such as File Explorer to applications like Microsoft Word and Calculator, to mention two out of millions of programs.

The only way to store information on a computer is in files. If you create a drawing it is stored in a file; a document is stored in a file, and all program functionality is contained in files. We know that everything on a computer, a device, or a server is a file, but the operating system sees them as just containers of information and instructions.

Files may also contain sensitive information and functionality, and their access may need to be restricted to a group of users or processes, or a single user or process. Therefore, you need to restrict access to the files and folders with certain access permissions. You can also encrypt files to secure their contents so that even if unauthorized access to the file is achieved by an attacker the contents will be secure. We will discuss permissions and encryption later in this chapter.

Showing or Hiding Filename Extensions

Files are opened by Windows according to the file's extension. Windows associates the file with the program it belongs to. To check the extension of a file, right-click the file's icon and select Properties. The Properties dialog box shows you the type of file to open followed by the extension shown in parentheses. Here's an example. Right-click the icon for a Word file and you will see something like *(docx)*. For example: Type of file: WMV File (.wmv)

You can also look up all the filename extensions for all files shown in File Explorer. Click the View tab at the top of File Explorer and select Options. A dialog box will open that gives you the option to make changes to how File Explorer shows extensions. Click on the View tab and clear the check box next to Hide Extensions For Known File Types. Then click OK.

You can also make filename extensions visible in File Explorer, but this may be confusing to users, and there is the chance they will rename the extension by mistake to something that File Explorer does not recognize. This will prevent the user from opening the file or a program from running.

Changing the Default Program or App to Open a File

You can also configure Windows to change the default program or app that opens when a user clicks an icon or file. This is explained in Exercise 10.1.

EXERCISE 10.1

Changing the Default Program or App

1. In File Explorer, right-click on the file you want to open to display a context menu.

2. Select Open With. The list will now load to display programs and apps that Windows 8.1 knows will open or execute the file (see Figure 10.1).

3. Select the suggested application and then click OK.

There are other options that you can configure (by selecting More options) to provide hints for finding a program or app to open the selected file:

- You can configure Windows 8.1 to browse the Web for an app that will go with the icon or file you are trying to run or load. Select the option Look For An App On The Web, and the File Association web page loads. This page tries to recognize your file and then suggests software you can link to.

- Selecting Look For An App In The Store takes you to the Windows Store, where you can search for an app.

- Selecting Look For Another App On This PC displays the Open With dialog box. From here, you can browse to a location on your computer or device to locate a program that will open the file.

About Folders

Storing all the files in one folder or directory would be chaotic and practically impossible, so we create folders on our computers and network servers where files can be grouped according to usage and users.

To provide access to files and folders and to protect them from unauthorized access, you will need to know how to configure and manage folder and file permissions, share folders, and configure the filesystem for permissions and encryption.

File Explorer is the main application used for managing files. With File Explorer you can move, copy, delete, and manage files and folders. If you are new to the Windows operating system, you should know the following about File Explorer:

- The icon for a folder looks like your typical manila file folder found in your office file cabinet or on your desk (see Figure 10.1). *Folders* and *directories* are the same thing.

- By default, files are represented in folders according to the type of file. For example, a Word document will be identified by the Word icon, and a web file will be identified by the Internet Explorer icon or the icon for another browser. By default, folders are listed before files.

FIGURE 10.1   File Explorer folders

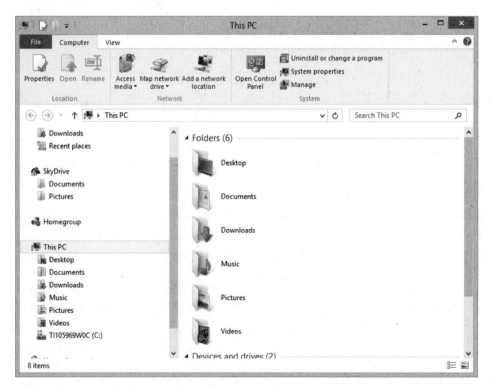

Viewing the Contents of a Folder

Locate the folder in File Explorer and click or double-click the folder's icon. The name of the folder you are looking in will appear at the end of the path in the URL field at the top of File Explorer. The folder's contents will now appear in the main pane. Figure 10.2 shows you the contents of the Documents folder.

FIGURE 10.2   Viewing folder contents in File Explorer

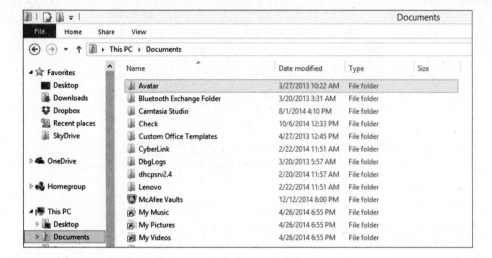

Subfolders

File Explorer also allows you to create folders within folders, or *subfolders*. 10.2 shows the contents of a folder named *Documents*. The folders that you see in the main pane—for example, Avatar and Bluetooth Exchange Folder, are subfolders of the Documents folder.

Subfolders are useful because they allow you to organize your information hierarchically and with some order. It's easier to find your files by traversing a folder hierarchy according to a system you create.

Parent Folders

Above every child folder is a *parent folder*. For example, the parent folder of the Amazon Music folder may be Music. The parent folder of the file hierarchy containing the documents representing the chapters of this book may be Documents. It's easy to navigate through folders using File Explorer. To get to the current folder's parent, click the name in the URL bar. The entire URL is often referred to the as the *breadcrumb trail*.

Managing Favorites

As part of configuring and supporting Windows 8.1 you will configure and set up common locations or favorite places for your users. You can set up a Favorites group to provide one-click access to a drive or folder on the user's computer. You can add shortcuts easily by dragging the icon into the Favorites folder, as shown in Figure 10.3.

FIGURE 10.3   Favorites folder in Explorer

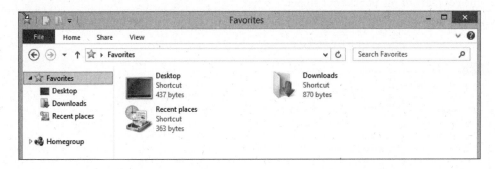

Here are some tips for managing your favorites:

- To rename a shortcut, right-click it, select Rename, type a new name (or edit the current name), and press Enter.

- To list shortcuts alphabetically, right-click Favorites and select Sort By Name.

- To remove a shortcut, right-click the shortcut and select Remove. You will be then asked to confirm; click Yes or No.

Libraries

Libraries were introduced in versions of Windows before Windows 8, but in Windows 8.1 they are hidden by default in File Explorer. However, only the name disappeared—the concept of libraries still exists and will be on the 70-687 exam.

Libraries make it easy to access a common location for documents, photos, music, and your common files. Libraries are the first locations that are searched by the search service, so anything that you have in a library will be first up on the search list.

Although the libraries appear to contain files, those files are still in their folders. The library itself is nothing more than an XML file that contains metadata pointing to the file location. Windows 8/8.1 provides six default folders: Desktop, Documents, Downloads, Music, Pictures, and Videos. Figure 10.4 shows the steps for creating a new library.

You can store several archives of documents in one of your new custom libraries and the contents will be indexed, searchable, and most important, backed up.

Any library can be designated the default location where your program saves changes or new files. To change the location of a folder in the list of library folders, choose the library folder you want to manage, and then click on the Manage tab in the File Explorer ribbon. You will not see the menu option until you actually select the library folder. Select Manage Library and then select Add to add folders to the library list.

FIGURE 10.4   Creating a new library

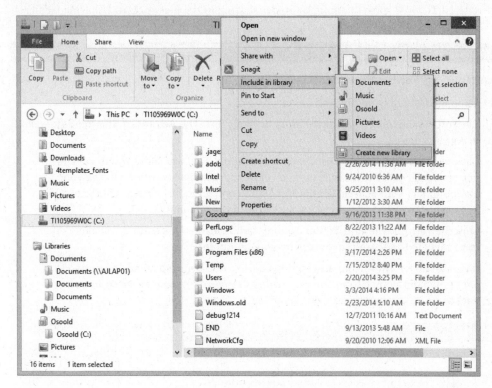

To now change the default save location in your library, right-click the folder in the Manage Library dialog box. Specify the Set Default Save Location option and then click OK. This saves the location and close the dialog box.

Configuring Folder Sharing

Let's now turn to folder sharing configuration. Windows 8.1 gives you substantial options in folder sharing. Shares allow you to share and access devices and file locations on the network. When you share resources, you are letting other users on the network see and access your computer.

There are several ways to share folders. You can use the Network and Sharing Center or share folders from within File Explorer. The Network and Sharing Center is shown in Figure 10.5. Here you can configure computer-wide sharing settings. The Network and Sharing Center, which provides all the required networking and sharing tools in one central location, is covered extensively on the exam.

You can access the Network and Sharing Center by pressing the Windows key and then typing **network**. You can then search for the center. Or you can right-click the network icon and then select Properties, which also opens the Network and Sharing Center. In Exercise 10.2, you'll learn to configure folder sharing in the Network and Sharing Center.

EXERCISE 10.2

Configuring Folder Sharing

1. Open the Network and Sharing Center.

2. Click on the Change Advanced Sharing Settings link. The Advanced Sharing Settings dialog box opens.

3. Click the Turn On Network Discovery radio button. This will allow you to see the network and shared resources that you can access and allow others to see your computer and your shares. (Be careful not to connect to insecure networks to avoid becoming the target of an attack on your devices and shares.)

4. Click the Turn On File And Printer Sharing radio button. This setting will allow others to connect to the shared resources on your computer.

5. If you set up a HomeGroup as described earlier, you can also check the option to either manage HomeGroup computers and devices or to use user accounts and passwords to connect to domain resources.

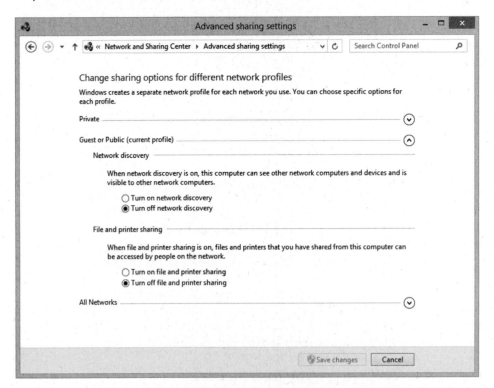

When you share folders in File Explorer, you can also do so by right-clicking a folder and selecting the option Share With from the context menu or ribbon. And then there is the old-fashioned option of right-clicking on the folder, selecting Properties from the context menu, and selecting the Sharing tab in the dialog box that opens. Then select the Share button and the dialog box below appears (see Figure 10.5).

FIGURE 10.5   The Sharing tab in Folder properties

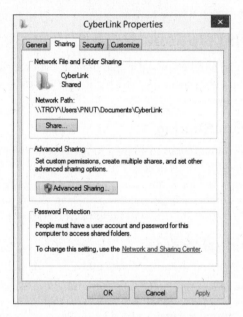

By default, the user account sharing the folder is designated as an owner with full control. That user can give other users access to the folder; those users receive only read access unless you explicitly change the access.

If you are connecting to a computer via the command line, you can share a folder using the net share command. This can be done using the following command:

```
net share sharename = drive:path
```

The full net share option menu is as follows:

```
NET SHARE   sharename
        sharename=drive:path [/GRANT:user,[READ | CHANGE | FULL]]
                             [/USERS:number |  /UNLIMITED]
                             [/REMARK:"text"]
                             [/CACHE:Manual | Documents| Programs | BranchCach
e | None]
        sharename [/USERS:number |  /UNLIMITED]
                  [/REMARK:"text"]
                  [/CACHE:Manual | Documents | Programs | BranchCache | None]
```

```
{sharename | devicename | drive:path} /DELETE
sharename \\computername /DELETE
```

 The Shared Folders snap-in that is opened from within Computer Management is still around and has not changed. Although you may not be asked about it on the exam, it's still a useful tool.

Advanced Sharing Options

While most situations can be handled using simple sharing options, there may be cases where you need to customize the process. In this section we'll look at advanced sharing options that are available to you.

Excluding Items from Sharing

There will be times when you will want to share a folder or a library but restrict or block access to certain folders and files. This is how you do it: Click on the folder you want to exclude. If it's a file you want to block, open the folder containing the file. Click the item you want to exclude, then simply click the link Stop Sharing on the Share tab of the ribbon. What you have now blocked from sharing will no longer be available.

Sharing with Individual Users

There will also be times when you want to share a folder or a file with a particular user. A home user, for example, may want to share a folder or a file with his or her spouse and block access to the kids.

Click on the folder containing the item to be shared. Next, select the Share tab in the ribbon. You can now select Specific People. This will open the File Sharing dialog box. Now choose an account from the drop-down list, and click Add. Then click Share. The dialog box will change and will now indicate that the item has been shared. Click Done and the operation is complete.

Using Public Folders

Windows 7 through 8.1 support a public folder scheme that allows users to share files automatically. Public folders were always accessible from the Libraries node in File Explorer, but unless you updated to Windows 8.1 from a version that placed a public folder in each library, you will no longer find public folders inside each library. In a fresh install of Windows 8.1, allowing public access is a matter of putting all files in a public folder you want to make accessible to all. It is also worth noting that the functionality provided by public folders is also available using HomeGroups.

The public folders are contained in a single folder named Public in the Users folder. (The default path is C:\Users\Public.) The Public folder looks just like your Documents folders. All folders for documents, downloads, music, pictures, photos, and videos are maintained in it. If you have Media Center installed, it adds the Recorded TV folder for storing media files.

To access the folder, open File Explorer and drill down to the public folders, as shown in Figure 10.6.

It is important to understand that the Public folder lets every user on the computer have unrestricted access to its contents. If you have files that you don't want others to have access to, refer to the earlier discussion in the section, "Sharing with Individual Users."

FIGURE 10.6   Public folders

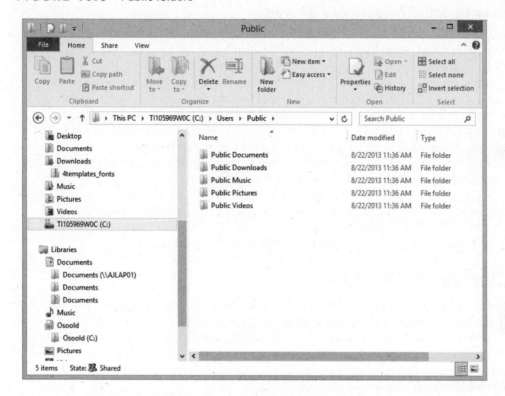

Advanced Sharing

As a user with administrative privileges, you use Advanced Sharing to set custom permissions for multiple users, control the number of simultaneous connections, cache offline files, and set other advanced properties.

Drill down to the folder you want to share, right-click the folder, and select Properties. Next, select the Sharing tab and click Advanced Sharing. You may be asked to provide the credentials of a user possessing the right to perform the operation (but this should not happen if you have the correct rights). Now select Share This Folder and click the Apply button. In Windows 8.1 you can set the number of simultaneous users to a maximum of 20. There is also an option to add a comment.

You may want to change the permissions on the share. Click the Permissions button. This will open the Permissions dialog box for the shared folder. The Permissions dialog box lets you view existing permissions and also add and remove users and groups. There are, however, only three options. You can only specify Full Control, Change, or Read permission for the shares.

In all likelihood, the filesystem supports NTFS permissions, so you can also set NTFS permissions, which are more granular. See the section "Applying NTFS Permissions" later in this chapter for more advanced information.

How to Tell if Folders Are Shared

To determine if a folder is shared, open File Explorer, drill down to that folder, and open it. The words "State: Shared" will appear in the status bar at the bottom of the window if the folder is indeed shared.

We mentioned the Shared Folder snap-in earlier. Well, it comes in handy now because you can use it to see which folders are shared. Open the Computer Management snap-in by right-clicking the Start menu and choosing Computer Management. The Computer Management MMC will open, and you should see the Shared Folders node in the System Tools section of the tree menu on the left. Expand it if necessary and click Shares. The folders that are shared, whether visible or hidden, appear in the right pane. Those that are hidden will have a $ appended to the end of their filename.

Hiding a file makes it invisible when browsing, which means a user must know it is there to access it and must refer to it by its filename with the $ appended. To hide a file, simply append a $ to the end of the filename.

And you can also use the net share command in the command console.

Configuring OneDrive

Although Microsoft rebranded SkyDrive to OneDrive it's important to realize the two Drives refer to the same thing. For a single user, a small office user, or a home user, OneDrive is a sea change in the way you save and protect the files you are working with. Let's face it; no matter how much effort and expense in terms of time and money that you put into backing up and protecting files from unauthorized use, the chore always seems to slip. Backing up is tedious and time consuming.

By configuring Windows 8.1 to save to OneDrive as the default location and with a reasonable always-on Internet connection, you will never again lose files to hostile access or hard and soft computer failure. OneDrive is a Microsoft Cloud service and is accessible from all your Internet-aware devices such as the iPhone and Windows Surface devices.

OneDrive is also a great service for sharing files. The concept is not new. Think of Dropbox or any one of the many online backup services. A caveat, however, is that you need to have a Microsoft online account and password. This can be linked to your local logon accounts. (See Chapters 8 and 9 for more information on this topic.)

When you configure File Explorer or your applications to use OneDrive, any new files or changes made to files will automatically sync to OneDrive. There are two ways to do this—the old way lets you upload files directly to OneDrive folders through Internet Explorer or the online OneDrive application, or you can specify saving to OneDrive as your default location from File Explorer.

To access OneDrive, go to www.onedrive.com (www.skydrive.com will led to the same site). For Windows 8 and earlier, and for other operating systems, you can download several apps that will work with OneDrive. On Windows 8.1, when you log in with your Microsoft account or an account that is linked to your Microsoft account, you will be automatically connected to OneDrive and you can treat it like any other drive, share, or library on your computer.

You can also disconnect from OneDrive at any time by clicking the Unlink option. This disconnects you from OneDrive but leaves it intact on your computer. If your OneDrive is up and running, you will notice that applications that are using it will show two sync arrows on icons of drives in various places in the application. When files are being synced with OneDrive the arrows are spinning. When syncing stops, the arrows stop spinning but remain on the icon to signify that OneDrive is still connected.

To configure OneDrive, open the search box in Windows 8.1 and search for OneDrive. You will be asked to enter your Microsoft credentials to connect to the OneDrive configuration. After you successfully enter your credentials, you have the option of saving documents to OneDrive automatically. You will also have the option to buy more OneDrive space. The default free amount of space is 15 GB. Figure 10.7 shows you the Settings tab of the OneDrive Settings dialog box.

FIGURE 10.7   OneDrive settings

Configuring HomeGroups

HomeGroups are easy to set up and have been designed to be used in home networks for families or very small businesses. The main object of a HomeGroup is to make sharing as hassle free as possible. HomeGroups obviate the need to worry about things like NTFS folder and file access permissions, NTFS, access control lists (ACLs), and so on.

HomeGroups, which run on IPv6, have been around since Windows 7. A HomeGroup is the recommended way for home users to share their music, documents, artwork, photographs, TVs, and game consoles. A HomeGroup allows several devices in the household to share information. HomeGroups are straightforward and easy to configure and use.

Once you have set up a HomeGroup for sharing, you can then specify the folders to share. Folders can be shared with either read or read/write permissions with the other members of the HomeGroup. Permissions are then set on a per-user basis so that access to a folder or file can be restricted.

Any Windows 7, Windows 8, or Windows 8.1 operating system will allow a computer to connect to a Windows 8.1 HomeGroup, but not the reverse. In other words, in a Windows 8.1 HomeGroup only Windows 8.1 can create the HomeGroup.

Although they are mainly for small businesses and home networks, domain-based networks and devices may also connect to them. This is useful, for example, when a third-party vendor needs a HomeGroup for a particular reason and requires a domain-based resource to have access to the HomeGroup.

A HomeGroup is not unlike the old Windows for Workgroups network that became popular in the days before Windows 2000. See Figure 10.8 to see the HomeGroup settings.

FIGURE 10.8   Accessing HomeGroup settings

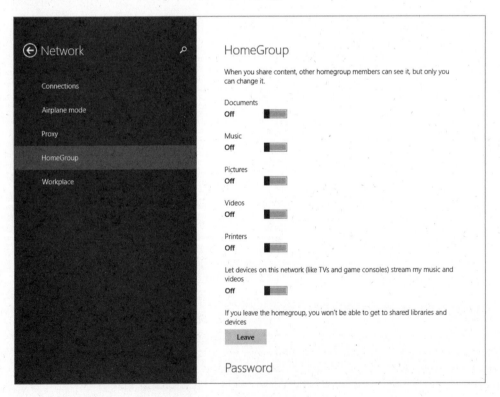

It is important to note that HomeGroups are, as implied by the name, for the home. As soon as you join your computer to external networks, you lose the ability to configure or manage your HomeGroup. Once you create a HomeGroup, you give other Windows 8/8.1 computers access to the HomeGroup (which you do by providing the special system-generated HomeGroup random secure password). You should write down the password so you don't forget it, even though you can regenerate a new password at any time.

You can join a HomeGroup only if you have been given the password to access the HomeGroup. You can also exit a HomeGroup at any time by clicking Leave from the PC Settings ➤ HomeGroup page.

Joining a HomeGroup

To add a computer to the HomeGroup, open Control Panel and then open the HomeGroup applet. Click the Join Now button (see Figure 10.9). In the resulting screen, click Next to choose to view a collection of items you want to share (see Figure 10.10). Click Next and you'll be asked to enter the HomeGroup password. After entering the password, click Finish.

FIGURE 10.9   Click Join Now

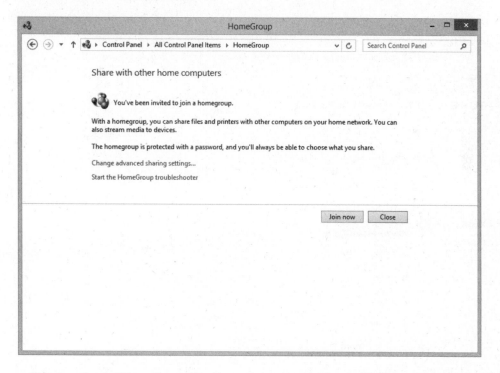

You can change HomeGroup sharing options any time by opening the HomeGroup applet from Control Panel (see Figure 10.11). After selecting Change what you're sharing with the HomeGroup, you can set additional items you want to share by setting them to Shared and set any items you no longer want to share to Not Shared.

FIGURE 10.10 Choosing items to share in Home group

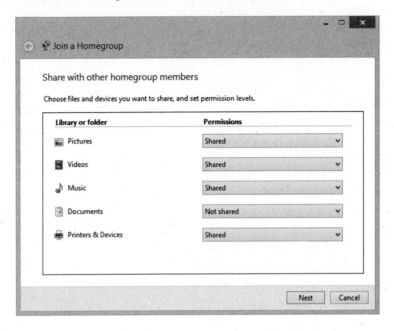

FIGURE 10.11 HomeGroup applet

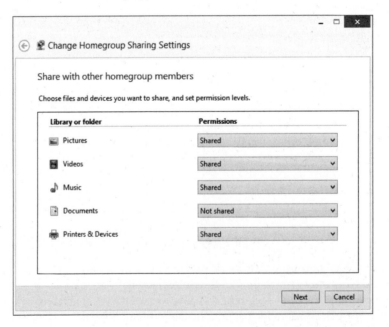

To share items in the HomeGroup, open the folder containing the item you want to share. As shown in the example, click on the Documents folder. The ribbon changes to allow you to select the Share tab. You can now choose HomeGroup (View) and Read and Write options, as shown in Figure 10.12.

FIGURE 10.12   HomeGroup sharing

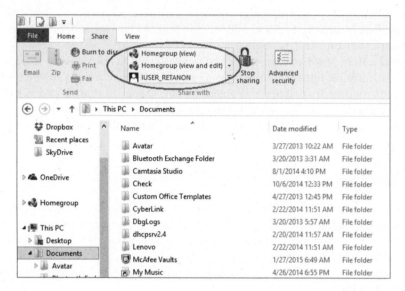

To change the password for the HomeGroup, search for **Change HomeGroup Password** using the Search box. If you regenerate the key, you will need to change the password on the devices in order for them to stay in the network.

Shares and PowerShell

There are several PowerShell cmdlets that you can use to create and manage shares. To create a share, use the following:

```
New-SmbShare –Name ShareName –Path C:\ LocalFolder
```

Other options include:

- `Get-SmbShare`, which gets a list of the existing shares on the computer
- `Set-SmbShare`, which modifies an existing share
- `Remove-SmbShare`, which removes an existing share
- `Get-SmbShareAccess`, which retrieves the share permissions for a share
- `Get-Acl`, which fetches the NTFS ACL Grant-SmbShareAccess that is used for setting share permissions
- `Set-Acl`, which is used to set the NTFS ACL for a specified resource

Managing File and Folder Security

Setting up proper file and folder security is one of the most important tasks that an IT professional can perform. If permissions and security are not properly configured, users will be able to access resources that they shouldn't.

File and folder security defines what access a user has to local resources. You can limit access by applying security to files and folders. You should know what NTFS security permissions are and how they are applied.

A powerful feature of networking is the ability to allow network access to local folders. In Windows 8.1, it is easy to share folders. You can also apply security to shared folders in a manner that is similar to applying NTFS permissions. Once you share a folder, users with appropriate access rights can access the folders through a variety of methods.

Before diving into the security section of folders, let's first take a look at some folder options.

Folder Options

The Windows 8.1 Folder Options dialog box allows you to configure many properties associated with files and folders, such as what you see when you access folders and how Windows searches through files and folders. You can access Folder Options by choosing Control Panel ➤ Large Icons View ➤ Folder Options. The Folder Options dialog box has three tabs: General, View, and Search. The options on each of these tabs are described in the following sections.

Folder General Options

The General tab of the Folder Options dialog box, shown in Figure 10.13, includes the following options:

- Whether folders are opened all in the same window when a user is browsing folders or each folder is opened in a separate window
- Whether a user opens items with a single mouse click or a double-click
- Whether to have the navigation pane show all folders and automatically expand to the current folder and whether to show libraries

Folder View Options

The options on the View tab of the Folder Options dialog box, shown in Figure 10.14, are used to configure what users see when they open files and folders. For example, you can change the default setting so that hidden files and folders are displayed. Table 10.1 describes the View tab options.

FIGURE 10.13   The General tab of the Folder Options dialog box

FIGURE 10.14   The View tab of the Folder Options dialog box

TABLE 10.1 Folder view options

Option	Description	Default Value
Always Show Icons, Never Thumbnails	Shows icons for files instead of thumbnail previews.	Not selected
Always Show Menus	Shows the File, Edit, View, Tools, and Help menus when you're browsing for files.	Not selected
Display File Icon On Thumbnails	Displays the file icon on thumbnails.	Enabled
Display File Size Information In Folder Tips	Specifies whether the file size is automatically displayed when you hover your mouse over a folder.	Enabled
Display The Full Path In The Title Bar (Classic Theme Only)	Specifies whether the title bar shows an abbreviated path of your location. Enabling this option displays the full path, such as `C:\Word Documents\Sybex\Windows 8.1 Book\Chapter 10` as opposed to showing an abbreviated path such as `Chapter 10`.	Not selected
Hidden Files And Folders	Specifies whether files and folders with the Hidden attribute are listed. Choosing Show Hidden Files, Folders, Or Drives displays these items.	Don't Show Hidden Files, Folders, And Drives
Hide Empty Drives	This option will prevent drives that are empty in the Computer folder from being displayed.	Enabled
Hide Extensions For Known File Types	By default, filename extensions, which identify known file types (such as `.doc` for Word files and `.xls` for Excel files) are not shown. Disabling this option displays all filename extensions.	Enabled
Hide Protected Operating System Files (Recommended)	By default, operating system files are not shown, which protects operating system files from being modified or deleted by a user. Disabling this option displays the operating system files.	Enabled

Option	Description	Default Value
Launch Folder Windows In A Separate Process	By default, when you open a folder, it shares memory with the previous folders that were opened. Enabling this option opens folders in separate parts of memory, which increases the stability of Windows 8.1 but can slightly decrease the performance of the computer.	Not selected
Show Drive Letters	Specifies whether drive letters are shown in the Computer folder. When disabled, only the name of the disk or device will be shown.	Enabled
Show Encrypted Or Compressed NTFS Files In Color	Displays encrypted or compressed files in an alternate color when they are displayed in a folder window.	Enabled
Show Pop-Up Description For Folder And Desktop Items	Displays whether a pop-up tooltip is displayed when you hover your mouse over files and folders.	Enabled
Show Preview Handlers In Preview Pane	Shows the contents of files in the preview pane.	Enabled
Show status bar	Shows the status bar at the bottom of File Explorer, which shows you how many items are in an opened folder and how many items are selected.	Enabled
Use Check Boxes To Select Items	Adds a check box next to each file and folder so that one or more of them may be selected. Actions can then be performed on selected items.	Not selected
Use Sharing Wizard (Recommended)	Allows you to share a folder using a simplified sharing method.	Enabled
When Typing Into List View	Selects whether text is automatically typed into the search box or whether the typed item is selected in the view.	Select The Typed Item In The View

Search Options

The Search tab of the Folder Options dialog box, shown in Figure 10.15, is used to configure how Windows 8.1 searches for files. You can choose for Windows 8.1 to search by filename only, by filenames and contents, or by a combination of the two, depending on whether indexing is enabled. You can also select from the following options:

- How To Search, which lets you specify whether you want to use the index when searching the filesystem

- Include System Directories

- Include Compressed

- Always Search File Names And Contents

FIGURE 10.15   The Search tab of the Folder Options dialog box

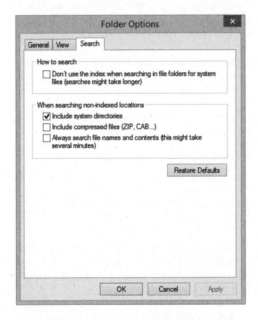

To search for files and folders, click Start ➤ Search and type your query in the search box. In the next section, we will look at how to secure these folders and files.

Securing Access to Files and Folders

On NTFS partitions, you can specify the access each user has to specific folders or files on the partition based on the user's logon name and group associations. Access control consists of rights and permissions. A right (also referred to as a privilege) is an authorization to perform a specific action.

Permissions are authorizations to perform specific operations on specific objects. The owner of an object or any user who has the necessary rights to modify permissions can apply permissions to NTFS objects. If permissions are not explicitly granted within NTFS, then they are implicitly denied. Permissions can also be explicitly denied, which then overrides explicitly granted permissions.

The following section describes design goals for access control as well as how to apply NTFS permissions and some techniques for optimizing local access. Let's take a look at design goals for setting up security.

Design Goals for Access Control

Before you start applying NTFS permissions to resources, you should develop design goals for access control as a part of your overall security strategy. Basic security strategy suggests that you provide each user and group with the minimum level of permissions needed for job functionality. Some of the considerations when planning access control include the following:

- Defining the resources that are included within your network—in this case, the files and folders residing on the filesystem

- Defining which resources will put your organization at risk, including defining the resources and defining the risk of damage if the resource was compromised

- Developing security strategies that address possible threats and minimize security risks

- Defining groups that security can be applied to be based on users within the group membership who have common access requirements, and applying permissions to groups as opposed to users

- Applying additional security settings through Group Policy if your Windows 8.1 clients are part of an Active Directory network

- Using additional security features, such as Encrypted File System (EFS), to provide additional levels of security or file auditing to track access to critical files and folders

After you have decided what your design goals are, you can start applying your NTFS permissions.

Applying NTFS Permissions

NTFS permissions control access to NTFS files and folders. This is based on the technology that was originally developed for Windows NT. Ultimately, the person who owns an object has complete control over the object. You configure access by allowing or denying NTFS permissions to users and groups.

Normally, NTFS permissions are cumulative, based on group memberships if the user has been allowed access. This means that the user gets the highest level of security from all the different groups they belong to. However, if the user had been denied access through user or group membership, those permissions override the allowed permissions. Windows 8.1 offers seven levels of NTFS permissions plus special permissions:

Full Control   This permission allows the following rights:

- Traverse folders and execute files (programs) in the folders. The ability to traverse folders allows you to access files and folders in lower subdirectories, even if you do not have permissions to access specific portions of the directory path.
- List the contents of a folder and read the data in a folder's files.
- See a folder's or file's attributes.
- Change a folder's or file's attributes.
- Create new files and write data to the files.
- Create new folders and append data to the files.
- Delete subfolders and files.
- Delete files.
- Compress files.
- Change permissions for files and folders.
- Take ownership of files and folders.

If you select the Full Control permission, all permissions will be checked by default and can't be unchecked.

Modify   This permission allows the following rights:

- Traverse folders and execute files in the folders.
- List the contents of a folder and read the data in a folder's files.
- See a file's or folder's attributes.
- Change a file's or folder's attributes.
- Create new files and write data to the files.
- Create new folders and append data to the files.
- Delete files.

If you select the Modify permission, the Read & Execute, List Folder Contents, Read, and Write permissions will be checked by default and can't be unchecked.

Read & Execute   This permission allows the following rights:

- Traverse folders and execute files in the folders.
- List the contents of a folder and read the data in a folder's files.
- See a file's or folder's attributes.

If you select the Read & Execute permission, the List Folder Contents and Read permissions will be checked by default and can't be unchecked.

List Folder Contents   This permission allows the following rights:

- Traverse folders.
- List the contents of a folder.
- See a file's or folder's attributes.

Read   This permission allows the following rights:

- List the contents of a folder and read the data in a folder's files.
- See a file's or folder's attributes.
- View ownership.

Write   This permission allows the following rights:

- Overwrite a file.
- View file ownership and permissions.
- Change a file's or folder's attributes.
- Create new files and write data to the files.
- Create new folders and append data to the files.

Special Permissions   This allows you to configure any permissions beyond the normal permissions, like auditing, and take ownership.

Any user with Full Control access can manage the security of a folder. However, to access folders, a user must have physical access to the computer as well as a valid logon name and password. By default, regular users can't access folders over the network unless the folders have been shared. Sharing folders is covered in the section "Creating Shared Folders" later in this chapter.

To apply NTFS permissions, right-click the file or folder to which you want to control access, select Properties from the context menu, and then select the Security tab. The Security tab lists the users and groups that have been assigned permissions to the file or folder. When you click a user or group in the top half of the dialog box, you see the permissions that have been allowed or denied for that user or group in the bottom half.

Complete Exercise 10.3 to manage NTFS security.

EXERCISE 10.3

Managing NTFS Security

1. Right-click the file or folder to which you want to control access, select Properties from the context menu, and click the Security tab.

2. Click the Edit button to modify permissions.

3. Click the Add button to open the Select Users Or Groups dialog box. You can select users from the computer's local database or from the domain you are in (or trusted domains) by typing in the user or group name in the Enter The Object Names To Select portion of the dialog box and clicking OK.

4. You return to the Security tab of the folder Properties dialog box. Highlight a user or group in the top list box, and in the Permissions list, specify the NTFS permissions to be allowed or denied. When you have finished, click OK.

By clicking the Advanced button on the Security tab, you can configure more granular NTFS permissions, such as Traverse Folder and Read Attributes permissions.

To remove the NTFS permissions for a user, computer, or group, highlight that entity in the Security tab and click the Remove button. This will remove their entry in the access control list attached to the object. Be careful when you remove NTFS permissions. You won't be asked to confirm their removal as you are when deleting most other types of items in Windows 8.1.

Controlling Permission Inheritance

Normally, the directory structure is organized in a hierarchical manner. This means you are likely to have subfolders in the folders to which you apply permissions. In Windows 8.1, by default, the parent folder's permissions are applied to any files or subfolders in that folder as well as any subsequently created objects. These are called *inherited permissions*.

You can specify how permissions are inherited by subfolders and files by clicking the Advanced button on the Security tab of a folder's Properties dialog box. This calls up the Permissions tab of the Advanced Security Settings dialog box. To edit these options, click the Disable Inheritance button. You can edit the following options:

- Convert Inherited Permissions Into Explicit Permissions On This Object
- Remove All Inherited Permissions From The Object

If an Allow or a Deny check box in the Permissions list on the Security tab has a shaded check mark, this indicates that the permission was inherited from an upper-level folder.

If the check mark is not shaded, it means the permission was applied at the selected folder. This is known as an explicitly assigned permission. Knowing which permissions are inherited and which are explicitly assigned is useful when you need to troubleshoot permissions.

Understanding Ownership and Security Descriptors

When an object is initially created on an NTFS partition, an associated security descriptor is created. A security descriptor contains the following information:

- The user or group that owns the object
- The users and groups that are allowed or denied access to the object
- The users and groups whose access to the object will be audited

After an object is created, the Creator Owner of the object has full permissions to change the information in the security descriptor, even for members of the Administrators group. You can view the owner of an object from the Security tab of the specified folder's Properties by clicking the Advanced button. At the top of this page the owner will be indicated. You can use this dialog box to change the owner of the object by selecting Change next to the owner name.

Although the owner of an object can set the permissions of an object so that the administrator can't access the object, the administrator or any member of the Administrators group can take ownership of an object and thus manage the object's permissions. When you take ownership of an object, you can specify whether you want to replace the owner on subdirectories and objects of the object. If you would like to see who owns a directory from the command prompt, type **dir /q**.

In the next section, we will discuss how to determine the effective permissions of a file or folder.

Determining Effective Permissions

To determine a user's effective rights (the rights the user has to a file or folder), add all of the permissions that have been allowed through the user's assignments based on that user's username and group associations. After you determine what the user is allowed, you subtract any permissions that have been denied the user through the username or group associations.

As an example, suppose that user Marilyn is a member of both the Accounting and Execs groups. The following assignments have been made to the Accounting group permissions:

Permission	Allow	Deny
Full Control		
Modify	X	
Read & Execute	X	
List Folder Contents		
Read		
Write		

The following assignments have been made to the Execs group permissions:

Permission	Allow	Deny
Full Control		
Modify		
Read & Execute		
List Folder Contents		
Read	X	
Write		

To determine Marilyn's effective rights, you combine the permissions that have been assigned. The result is that Marilyn's effective rights are Modify, Read & Execute, and Read, so she basically has Modify (the highest right).

As another example, suppose that user Dan is a member of both the Sales and Temps groups. The following assignments have been made to the Sales group permissions:

Permission	Allow	Deny
Full Control		
Modify	X	
Read & Execute	X	
List Folder Contents	X	
Read	X	
Write	X	

The following assignments have been made to the Temps group permissions:

Permission	Allow	Deny
Full Control		
Modify		X
Read & Execute		
List Folder Contents		
Read		
Write		X

To determine Dan's effective rights, you start by seeing what Dan has been allowed: Modify, Read & Execute, List Folder Contents, Read, and Write permissions. You then remove anything that he is denied: Modify and Write permissions. In this case, Dan's effective rights are Read & Execute, List Folder Contents, and Read. Now let's take a look at how to see what rights users have.

Viewing Effective Permissions

If permissions have been applied at the user and group levels and inheritance is involved, it can sometimes be confusing to determine what the effective permissions are. To help identify which effective permissions will actually be applied, you can view them from the Effective Access tab of Advanced Security Settings, or you can use the ICACLS command-line utility.

To identify the effective permissions for a user or group, select the Effective Access tab of Advanced Security Settings. Then click Select A User, type the user or group name, and click OK. A list of the effective permissions will be displayed.

The ICACLS command-line utility can also be used to display or modify user access rights. The options associated with the `icacls` command are as follows:

- `/grant` grants permissions.
- `/remove` revokes permissions.
- `/deny` denies permissions.
- `/setintegritylevel` sets an integrity level of Low, Medium, or High.

One issue that IT people run into is what happens to the security when you move or copy a file or folder. Let's take a look at NTFS permissions when they're moved or copied.

Determining NTFS Permissions for Copied or Moved Files

When you copy or move NTFS files, the permissions that have been set for those files might change. The following guidelines can be used to predict what will happen:

- If you move a file from one folder to another folder on the same volume, the file will retain the original NTFS permissions.
- If you move a file from one folder to another folder between different NTFS volumes, the file is treated as a copy and will have the same permissions as the destination folder.
- If you copy a file from one folder to another folder on the same volume or on a different volume, the file will have the same permissions as the destination folder.
- If you copy or move a file or folder to a FAT partition, it will not retain any NTFS permissions.

Now that you have seen how to deal with the NTFS security, you need to understand shared permissions. In the next section, we will look at sharing resources.

Managing Network Access to Folders

In every network, there are resources to which the users need to gain access. As IT professionals, we share these resources so that our users can do their jobs.

Sharing is the process of allowing network users access to a resource located on a computer. A network share provides a single location to manage shared data used by many users.

The following sections describe how to create and manage shared folders, configure share permissions, and provide access to shared resources.

Creating Shared Folders

You can share a folder in two ways. To use the Sharing Wizard, right-click a folder and select Share. If the Sharing Wizard feature is enabled, you will see the File Sharing screen. Here, you can add local users.

However, you cannot use the Sharing Wizard to share resources with domain users. To share a folder with domain users, you should right-click the folder and select Properties, then select the Sharing tab, shown in Figure 10.16.

FIGURE 10.16   The Sharing tab of a folder's Properties dialog box

Click the Share button to launch the Sharing Wizard. To configure Advanced Sharing, click the Advanced Sharing button, which will open the Advanced Sharing dialog box. When you share a folder, you can configure the options listed in Table 10.2.

TABLE 10.2   Share folder options

Option	Description
Share This Folder	Makes the folder available through local access and network access
Share Name	A descriptive name by which users will access the folder

Option	Description
Comments	Additional descriptive information about the share (optional)
Limit The Number Of Simultaneous Users To	The maximum number of connections to the share at any one time (no more than 20 users can simultaneously access a share on a Windows 8.1 computer)
Permissions	How users will access the folder over the network
Caching	How files and programs are cached when the folder is offline

If you share a folder and then decide that you do not want to share it, just deselect the Share This Folder check box. The following also holds true:

- Only folders, not files, can be shared.

- Share permissions can be applied only to folders and not to files.

- If a folder is shared over the network and a user is accessing it locally, then share permissions will not apply to the local user; only NTFS permissions will apply.

- If a shared folder is copied, the original folder will still be shared but not the copy.

- If a shared folder is moved, the folder will no longer be shared.

- If the shared folder will be accessed by a mixed environment of clients, including some that do not support long filenames, you should use the 8.3 naming format for files.

- Folders can be shared through the Net Share command-line utility.

Now let's take a look at configuring share permissions for your users.

Configuring Share Permissions

You can control users' access to shared folders by assigning share permissions. Share permissions are less complex than NTFS permissions and can be applied only to folders (unlike NTFS permissions, which can be applied to files and folders).

To assign share permissions, click the Permissions button in the Advanced Sharing dialog box. This brings up the Permissions dialog box, shown in Figure 10.17.

You can assign three types of share permissions:

Full Control   Allows full access to the shared folder.

Change   Allows users to change data within a file or to delete files.

Read   Allows a user to view and execute files in the shared folder. Read is the default permission on shared folders for the Everyone group.

FIGURE 10.17   The Permissions dialog box

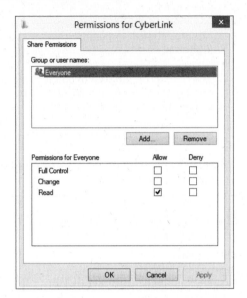

Shared folders do not use the same concept of inheritance as NTFS folders. If you share a folder, there is no way to block access to lower-level resources through share permissions.

When applying conflicting share and NTFS permissions, the most restrictive permissions apply. Remember that share and NTFS permissions are both applied only when a user is accessing a shared resource over a network. Only NTFS permissions apply to a user accessing a resource locally.

So, for example, if a user's NTFS security settings on a resource were Read and the share permission on the same resource was Full Control, the user would have Read permission only when they connect to that resource via the network. The most restrictive set of permissions wins.

Dynamic Access Control

Dynamic Access Control enables administrators to apply access-control permissions and restrictions based on defined rules that can include the sensitivity of the resources, the job or role of the user, and the configuration of the device that is used to access these resources. It was introduced in Windows Server 2012 and Windows 8, and support continues in Windows Server 2012 R2 and Windows 8.1.

For example, users might have different permissions when they access a resource from a desktop computer in the internal network versus when they are using a laptop with a VPN connection. Furthermore, the access could be affected by the security settings of the computer. It may have to meet the security requirements defined by the network administrators. DAC may also alter a user's permissions dynamically without additional administrator intervention if the user's job or role changes.

Although Windows 8.1 computers support the use of DAC, configuring it is done on the domain controller in the domain to which the Windows 8.1 computer belongs. This configuration is beyond the scope of this book.

NTFS Auditing

NTFS Auditing, or Object Access Auditing (OAA) in Windows 8.1, lets you determine which user has accessed a particular object (such as a file, folder, or Registry key). NTFS shares and permissions and EFS can keep a user from accessing an object, but auditing lets you know who tried to do what and when.

Enabling Auditing

To configure NTFS for auditing, follow these steps:

1. Log on with an administrator account.
2. Run gpedit.msc on the Start screen or from the command line and then open Computer Configuration ➤ Windows Settings ➤ Security Settings.
3. Expand Local Policies and open the Audit Policy page. The policy listings are now shown in the right pane.
4. Double-click Audit Object Access and select the Success and Failure check boxes.
5. Click OK to close the Local Group Policy Editor snap-in.

You can now enable the audit policies you need for your audit trail. However, you are not done. Next you have to enable OAA on a folder.

Enabling OAA on a Folder

To enable OAA on a folder, follow these steps:

1. Open File Explorer and select the folder that contains the files that you want to audit.
2. Right-click the folder, select Properties, and then select the Security tab.
3. Click the Advanced button to open the Advanced Security Settings dialog box.
4. Click the Auditing tab, and then click Continue and Allow User Account Control (UAC) Access.
6. Click Select A Principal and type the name of the user or group you want to monitor.
7. Modify the object's Type, Applies To, and Basic Permissions settings, if required, and then click OK. Auditing is now enabled for the selected folder and user.

Reviewing Audit Entries

The Security Event Log keeps track of all audit entries. To view it, open the Computer Management MMC and, in the tree on the left under System Tools, select Event Viewer. With Windows 8.1 you can also audit access to removable storage devices. To use this auditing tool, enable the Audit Removable Storage policy, which generates an event each time there is an attempt to access a removable storage device. The event logs the file-names being moved or copied to the removable drive. You can find this policy under Computer Configuration ➢ Windows Settings ➢ Security Settings ➢ Advanced Audit Policy Configuration ➢ System Audit Policies ➢ Object Access.

Supporting Data Security by Using EFS

Windows 8.1 supports the ability to encrypt files and folders by using the Encrypting File System (EFS). To encrypt a file or folder in Windows 8.1, right-click the file and select Properties. In the Properties dialog box, select the General tab; then click the Advanced button. When the Advanced Attributes dialog box appears, select the Encrypt Contents To Secure Data check box, and then click OK.

The first time you encrypt a file, the system generates an encryption certificate specific to you. You should back up that certificate—if your certificate and key are lost or damaged and you don't have a backup, you won't be able to use the files that you have encrypted. You can locate this file by typing **certmgr.msc** in the Search box and opening a management tool called Cert Manager.

When Cert Manager opens, expand the Personal folder in the tree in the left and click the subfolder Certificates. Personal certificates will appear. Locate the certificate—Encrypting File System should appear in the Intended Purposes column—and right-click it. In the context menu, select All Tasks ➢ Export to launch the Certificate Export Wizard. Follow the steps in the wizard to export both the certificate and the associated private key to removable media so it will be available to you if the hard drive where the key is stored is damaged. It will ask you to create a password to protect the file that it creates, which will be a personal information exchange (PFX) type.

Later if you need to access data that was encrypted with the key, restore the encrypted data to another computer and import the PFX file to the Personal by using the Import Wizard in Cert Manager.

Data Recovery Agent

Although it is possible to back up all certificates and private keys for each user to ensure they can access encrypted data if the certificate is lost on a bad hard drive or by accidental deletion or corruption, there is also another way to mitigate issues with deleted or corrupted EFS certificates and keys. On both the domain level and the local machine level, a user can be designated as a data recovery agent (DRA). By default, this role is assigned to the local administrator at the local machine level.

To add a DRA locally, you must perform two high-level tasks. You must generate a data recovery certificate using cipher.exe/r and then you must add a DRA in a local group policy. To generate the data recovery certificate using cipher.exe/r, follow these steps:

1. Open the command prompt with administrative credentials.

2. Execute the command **cipher.exe/r:*filename***, where *filename* is a name you define. You will be prompted to create a password to protect the file. Type and confirm the password and keep it in a safe place.

3. Open the local group policy by typing **mmc** in the Run box. When a blank MMC opens, select File ➤ Add/Remove Snap-in. In the resulting dialog box, select Group Policy in the list of snap-ins on the left and click Add button to add it to the console. When you do so, accept the default to add it for the local computer.

4. In Local Computer Policy, click Public Key Policies (Local Computer Policy ➤ Computer Configuration ➤ Windows Settings ➤ Security Settings ➤ Public Key Policies).

5. In the details pane, right-click Encrypting File System.

6. Click Add Data Recovery Agent.

7. On the Select Recovery Agent page, select Browse Folders.

8. The system will direct you to the System 32 folder. Scroll until you locate the data recovery agent file created when you were using cipher.exe. It will have the name you gave it. Select that file and click Open.

9. When the system tells you the revocation status cannot be determined, select to install it anyway.

   The certificate will be installed and it will now appear in the Encrypting File System folder in Group Policy as issued to the admin, as shown in Figure 10.18.

FIGURE 10.18   The data recovery agent certificate

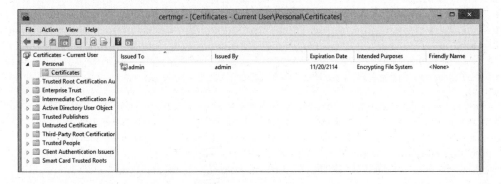

Managing Local Storage

A number of tools are available in Windows 8.1 to manage local storage. These tools can be used to create volumes of various types and to configure the filesystems used to organize and control access to the data residing on these volumes. In the following sections, we'll look at some of these tools. We'll also explore storage features that can provide fault tolerance and more advanced storage concepts such as storage spaces and the Distributed File System.

Managing Disk Volumes and Filesystems

When creating disk volumes in Windows 8.1, you have several options available via a tool called Disk Management. To access this tool, right-click on the Start button in Windows 8.1 and select Disk Management. When the tool opens, it will show the current storage devices attached to the local machine, as you can see in Figure 10.19. Here, we're showing a virtual machine running Windows 8.1 in Oracle VirtualBox, a consumer hypervisor. It has a single disk, Disk 0, and a CD-ROM drive 0, which currently has the VirtualBox Additions CD in the drive.

FIGURE 10.19   Disk Management

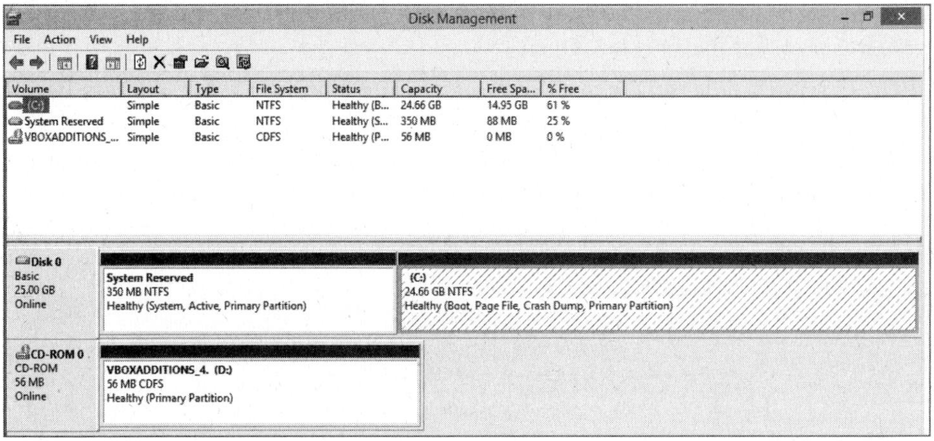

Two types of disks can be created in Windows 8.1: basic and dynamic. By default, Windows 8.1 assigns a type of basic, which is why this machine has a basic disk. Basic disks have been available in Windows systems for many years and are subdivided into primary partitions and logical drives. Basic disks can use a Master Boot Record (MBR) to organize the data on the disk, or they can use a newer concept called the GUID Partition Table (GPT). Most modern systems are moving away from using MBR and are instead using GPT because of longstanding limitations surrounding the use of MBR. For example, using an MBR limits the number of primary partitions to four, meaning if you need more than four partitions on the drive, you must set one of the four to Extended and subdivide it into logical drives. Moreover, if the system is a newer one that uses the Unified Extensible Firmware Interface (UEFI) instead of a BIOS, the use of GPT is required.

Although dynamic disks can also use either MBR or GPT, they offer several advantages over basic disks. All volumes on a dynamic disk are called dynamic volumes; there can be up to 1,000 dynamic volumes per disk group (we'll explain disk groups shortly). Another advantage of dynamic disks is the ability to use them to create volume types that can increase performance or provide fault tolerance. These types of volumes cannot be created in a basic disk. The special volume types include the following:

Simple   This volume uses space on a single dynamic disk.

Spanned   This volume uses space on more than one disk and provides no fault tolerance or increase in performance, but it can be used to extend a volume that has run out of space on one disk.

Striped   This volume uses space on more than one disk and provides no fault tolerance, but it provides an increase in performance because both disks can be read at the same time when reading the data.

Mirrored   This volume uses space on two disks and writes the exact same data to both disks, providing fault tolerance if one of the disks fails.

RAID 5   This requires at least three disks and stripes the data across the disks along with parity information, which can be used to re-create any data lost if a single drive in the RAID array fails. It is important to note that if more than one disk in the array fails, there will be insufficient parity information to re-create the data lost.

In any case where a volume is located on multiple disks, the disks comprise a disk group, as mentioned earlier. Dynamic volumes on a dynamic disk can be extended after they are created, which cannot be done with basic disks.

A basic disk can be converted to a dynamic disk by right-clicking the volume in Disk Management and selecting Convert To Dynamic Disk, as shown in Figure 10.20.

FIGURE 10.20   Converting a disk to dynamic

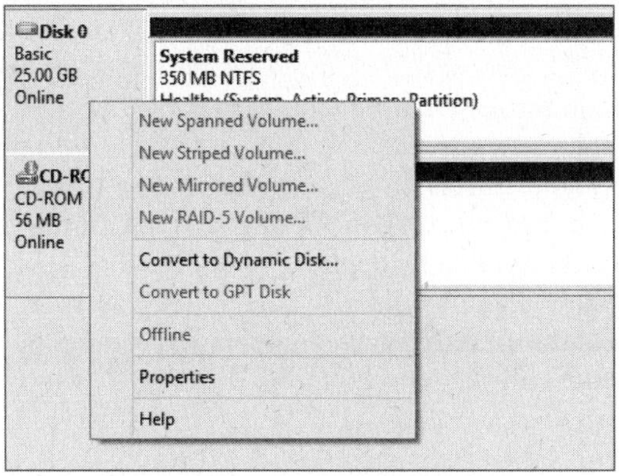

Two filesystems can be applied to volumes in Windows 8.1: NTFS and FAT. NTFS is the preferred system because of the following benefits it provides:

- The capability to recover from some disk-related errors automatically, which FAT32 cannot

- Improved support for larger hard disks

- Better security because you can use permissions and encryption to restrict access to specific files to approved users

NTFS is the preferred system, but there may be cases where you are forced to use FAT. For example, you may have a dual boot with an older operating system that can run only on FAT such as Windows 95, Windows 98, or Windows ME, and you would need to use the FAT system.

You can select the filesystem during the creation of a volume by choosing it from a drop-down box on the Format Partition page, when you create the volume in Disk management. A FAT partition can be converted to an NTFS partition without losing any data using the convert command at the command prompt. The syntax is convert *drive_letter*: / fs:ntfs, where *drive_letter* is the letter of the drive you want to convert. For example, convert E: /fs:ntfs would convert drive E to the NTFS format. This is a one-way operation. It cannot be reversed. Converting a hard disk partition or volume from NTFS to FAT32 requires that you reformat the partition, which deletes any data on it. Be sure to back up any data you want to keep before you begin.

There is also a third filesystem available in Windows 8.1 called the Resilient File System (ReFS). It maximizes data availability, despite errors that would cause data loss or downtime with other filesystems. Data integrity ensures that business-critical data is protected from errors and available when needed. ReFS's architecture is designed to provide scalability and performance in an era of constantly growing data set sizes and dynamic workloads.

Configuring Disk Quotas

Windows 8.1 supports the creation of disk quotas for users. This feature can help to ensure that users are monitored with respect to disk usage or, if desired, prevented from using more space than allowed on the disk. Disk quotas are enabled on a per-volume basis. To enable disk quotes on a volume, right-click the volume and select Properties. Then select the Quota tab, shown in Figure 10.21.

On the Quota tab, click the button Show Quota Settings. In the resulting dialog box, you will see that quotas are disabled by default. To enable them, select the check box Enable Quota Management. If you would also like to deny users from exceeding the limit, select the next check box, Deny Space To Users Exceeding Quota Limit as well. Finally, you set a value for both the limit and a warning level, which when reached will send a message to the user that he is approaching his limit. In Figure 10.22, a limit of 2 MB and a warning level of 1 MB have been set. The traffic light is still red because we have not clicked OK. When we do, the light will turn green to indicate the settings are in force.

FIGURE 10.21   Quota tab

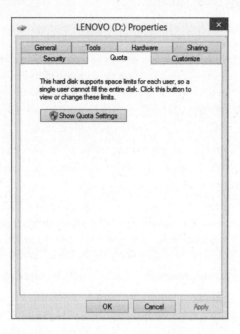

FIGURE 10.22   Setting a quota and a warning level

Managing Storage Spaces

Configuring storage spaces is a fault tolerance and capacity expansion technique that can be used as an alternative to the techniques described in the section "Managing Disk Volumes and Filesystems." This technique enables you to virtualize storage by grouping industry-standard disks into storage pools. You then create virtual disks called storage spaces from the available capacity in the storage pools. This means you must complete three tasks to use storage spaces:

- Create a storage pool, which is a collection of physical disks.
- From the storage pool, create a storage space, which can also be thought of as a virtual disk.
- Create one or more volumes on the storage space.

First let's look at creating the pool from several physical disks. Each of the disks must be at least 4 GB in size and should not have any volumes in them. The number of disks required depends on the type of resiliency you want to provide to the resulting storage space. Resiliency refers to the type of fault tolerance desired. Use the following guidelines:

- For simple resiliency (no fault tolerance), a single disk is required for the pool.
- For mirror resiliency, two drives are required.
- For party resiliency (think RAID 5), three drives are required.

Providing Capacity and Fault Tolerance

To create a pool, open Control Panel and click on the applet Storage Spaces. On the resulting screen, select the option Create A New Pool And Storage Space. On the Select Drives To Create A Storage Pool screen, the drives that are available and supported for storage pools will appear, as shown in Figure 10.23.

FIGURE 10.23   The Select Drives To Create A Storage Pool screen

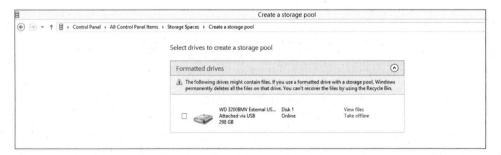

In this example, only one drive is eligible, so we can create only a simple type of pool. Check the drive and click the Create Pool button at the bottom of the page. On the next screen, give the space a name, select a drive letter, choose the filesystem (NTFS or ReFS), the resiliency type (in this case we can only select Simple), and the size of the pool. In Figure 10.24 we have set the pool as Myspace, with a drive letter of F, an NTFS filesystem, simple resiliency, and a maximum size of 100 GB. When we click Create Storage Space, the space will be created. Be aware that any data on the physical drive will be erased in this process!

FIGURE 10.24   Creating a storage space

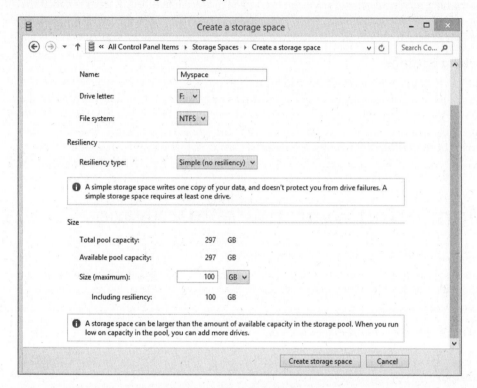

When the process is finished, the new space will appear on the Manage Storage Spaces screen. We now have a pool and a space derived from the pool. The last step is to create a volume in the storage space. If you now access Disk Management you will see a new virtual disk called Myspace. It will be a basic disk, but you can convert it to dynamic by right-clicking it and selecting Convert To Dynamic Disk. This will allow to you shrink or delete the existing volume if you desire.

Supporting Data Storage

Another option for storage is to use the Distributed File System (DFS). Though not a new concept, Windows 8.1 continues to support this feature. DFS allows you to create a virtual file structure that appears to the users to be located on the same server, whereas physically the folders are simply pointers that redirect the user to the physical location of the data in the network. In the next two sections, we'll look at DFS.

Using the DFS Client

Although DFS is a technology that is implemented in Windows Server 2012 R2, a Windows 8.1 computer comes with the DFS client and fully supports it. When DFS has been implemented on a server, the client machines need to have a drive mapped to what is called the root of DFS. When users connect to this location, they will be presented with a folder structure that appear to be physically located in one place although, as we said before, it is not.

Caching Settings

When a client machine accesses the folders in a DFS structure, they are being referred to the physical location of the folder contents. These referrals can be cached. This caching process prevents the client from having to connect to and redownload the list of referrals from the domain controller or namespace server each time the referrals are needed. You can set the amount of time allowed for root referrals as well as for folder referrals. You adjust these caching settings in DFS management on the server; this task is beyond the scope of this book.

Monitoring System Performance

System performance can be monitored in Windows 8.1 by using a tool called Performance Monitor. To access this tool, open Control Panel and choose System and Security ➤ Administrative Tools ➤ Performance Monitor. When the tool opens, it appears as shown in Figure 10.25.

FIGURE 10.25   Performance Monitor

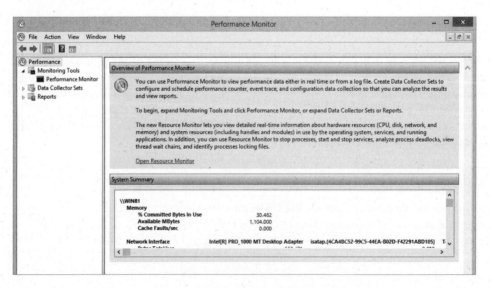

There are several related functions in Performance (as it also known). We are interested in Performance Monitor, so select it. When you do so, a real-time moving graph of the % CPU time will be displayed by default. This tool reports on the use of objects (resources) and uses specific measures of information about the objects called counters to report on the performance of the object. The % CPU time is a counter that describes the time spent by the CPU working on running active programs.

To add additional counters to what is being recorded by Performance, click on the green + at the top of this page. In the dialog box that appears, first select an object from the list on the left and click the arrow next to it to reveal the available counters for that object, as shown in Figure 10.26. In this case we have selected the % Disk Time counter for the Physical disk object.

FIGURE 10.26   Selecting a counter

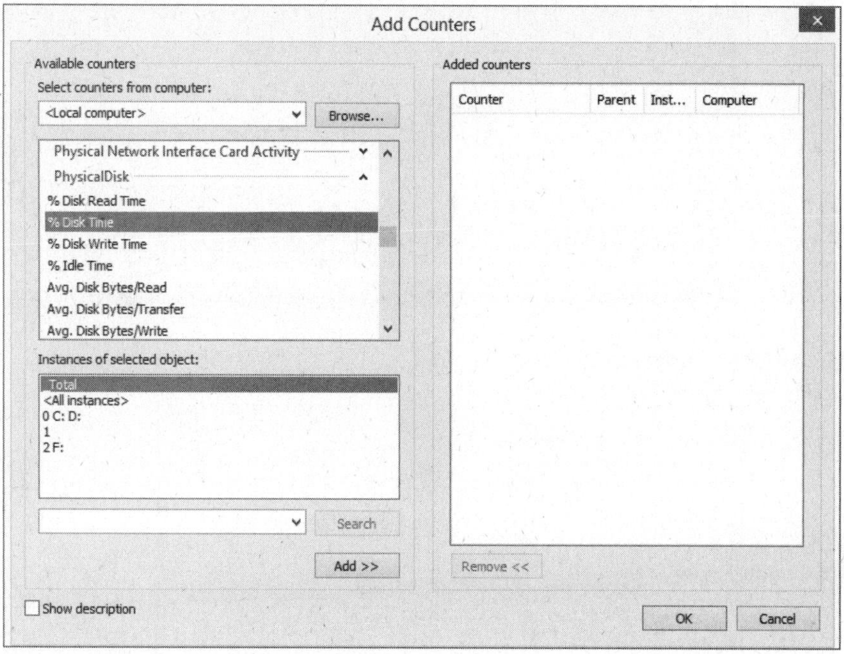

Now click Add in the middle of the two panes to add this counter to the display. Its performance will be represented in real time using a different color than that of the % Processor Time, which was already present in the display. The results are shown in Figure 10.27.

If you need to remove a counter from the display, highlight the counter in the list at the bottom of the page and click the red X next to the green + at the top of the page.

Configuring Indexing Options

Windows uses an index to perform very fast searches on your computer. To manage these indexing operations, use the tool Indexing Options in Control Panel. When the tool opens, it will look like Figure 10.28. A list of currently indexed locations on the computer will appear.

FIGURE 10.27   Two counters in the display

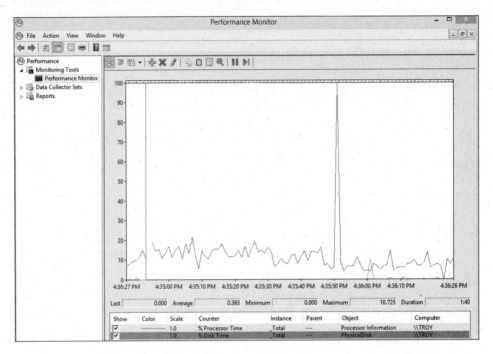

FIGURE 10.28   Indexing Options

To add a location, click the Modify button. In the dialog box that appears, you will be offered additional locations that you have can set to be indexed. Locations that are indexed can be searched more easily by the system. If you are using an unusual file type that may not be recognized by the indexing process, you can add that type by clicking the Advanced button next to the Modify button mentioned earlier. In the Advanced Options dialog box, select the File Types tab and check the box next to the file type you would like to add to the indexing process. If you don't see it, you can type it manually using the Add New Extension To List box at the bottom, as shown in Figure 10.29.

FIGURE 10.29   Adding a file type to the index

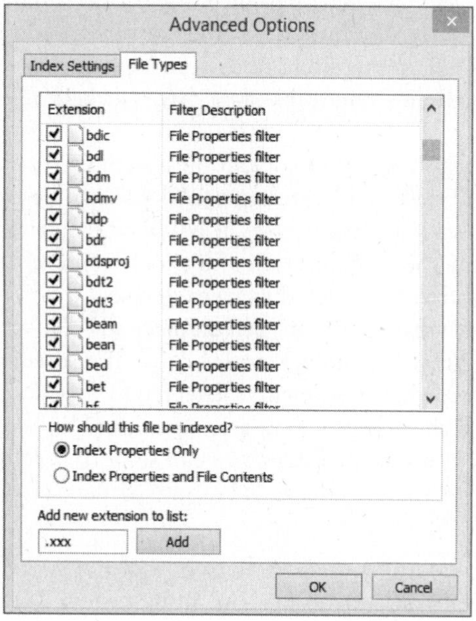

Here are other operations you can perform using the Indexing Options tool:

Rebuild the Index   This may be required after adding a location or a file type to the index. Use the Index Settings tab of the Advanced Options dialog box.

Have Encrypted Files Indexed   This is also done in the Advanced Options dialog box on the Index Settings tab.

Index Words with and without Diacritics   Diacritics are small signs added to letters to change the pronunciation of words. You can configure the index to recognize words with diacritics differently from those without. In the Advanced Options dialog box, select the Index Settings tab and click Treat Similar Words With Diacritics As Different Words.

Change the Location of the Index   You may have to do this when a hard drive where the index is located is running out of space. Again, use the Index Settings tab in the Advanced Options dialog box.

Controlling Access to Removable Media

Windows 8.1 supports securing the data on removable media through the use of encryption. BitLocker and BitLocker To Go are two technologies that can be used to encrypt local drives as well as removable media. In this section, we'll focus on the management of removable media.

BitLocker and BitLocker To Go

Both BitLocker and BitLocker To Go are designed to perform full drive encryption. BitLocker can encrypt the drive Windows is installed on (the operating system drive) as well as fixed data drives (such as internal hard drives). You can also use BitLocker To Go to help protect all files stored on a removable data drive (such as an external hard drive or USB flash drive).

When you use BitLocker to encrypt the operating system drive, it checks the system during startup for any conditions that represent security risks (for example, changes to the BIOS settings). If any issues present themselves, it will lock the drive and the BitLocker recovery key (created during the configuration of BitLocker on the drive) will be required to unlock it. The process required to unlock the drive depends on how you configured it. You can unlock it with a recovery password, or you can place the recovery key on a USB drive that you insert during the process of unlocking the drive. If desired, you can also require a key at every startup, not just when a problem is detected.

When you use BitLocker to encrypt a data drive, you can also require a key to unlock the drive with a password or a smart card, or you can set it to unlock the drive when you unlock the PC.

BitLocker

Bitlocker can be used on both data drives and operating system drives. In the following sections well take a look at the protections these two processes provide and the differences in their configuration.

Operating System Drives

To enable BitLocker on an operating system drive, start by accessing its applet in Control Panel. Then select Turn On Bitlocker. Note that some configurations of BitLocker require that the device have a Trusted Platform Module (TPM) chip on the motherboard. If the device has none, then you will be unable to turn on BitLocker on an operating system drive unless the Require Additional Authentication At Startup policy has been enabled for operating system drives. This policy can be enabled using the Local Group Policy Editor at Computer Configuration ➤ Administrative Templates ➤ Windows Components ➤ BitLocker Drive Encryption ➤ Operating System Drives.

Once you select Turn On BitLocker, the system will scan the computer to see if it has a TPM chip. If it doesn't, it will offer you the unlock option of Insert A USB Flash Drive or Enter A Password, as shown in Figure 10.30.

FIGURE 10.30   Choosing the unlock method

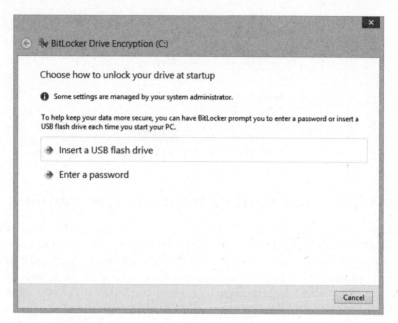

If the computer has a TPM chip, when you choose to enable BitLocker it will initialize the chip and then prompt you to choose how to store the key (either on a USB drive or to a file, or print the key). This key should be stored safely as it will be needed to unlock the drive.

Data Drives

To enable BitLocker on a data drive, start by accessing its applet in Control Panel. Then click Turn On Bitlocker and select the drive of interest. The wizard will offer you two options for unlocking the data drive: a smart card or a password. You can also choose to unlock the drive automatically at startup if the operating system drive is also protected and unlocks successfully.

BitLocker to Go

To enable BitLocker to Go on a removable drive, start by accessing the BitLocker applet in Control Panel. Then click Turn On BitLocker To Go for removable drives and select the drive of interest. Drives on which BitLocker to Go has been enabled will be locked by default, and you must specify how you would like to unlock them. The wizard will offer you two options for unlocking the data drive: a smart card or a password. You can also choose to speed the encryption process by encrypting only used space on the drive. After the drive is encrypted, when you attach it you will be prompted to unlock it with the key, as shown in Figure 10.31.

FIGURE 10.31   Unlocking a removable drive

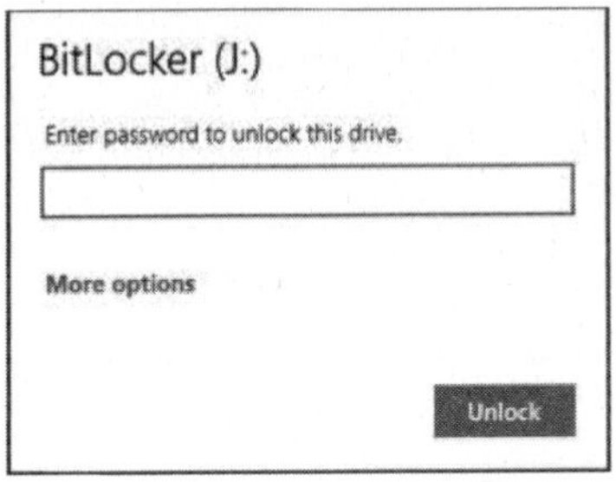

Microsoft BitLocker Administration and Monitoring

Microsoft BitLocker Administration and Monitoring (MBAM) version 2.5, which is included in the Microsoft Desktop Optimization Pack (MDOP) for Microsoft Software Assurance, makes BitLocker implementations easier to deploy and manage and allows you to provision and monitor encryption for operating system and fixed data drives.

A Windows 8.1 computer can participate in this architecture in one of two ways: It can simply be a client with the agent software installed, or it can be used as a management workstation (however, this would preferably be a server operating system) on which new Group Policy templates related to managing MBAM are installed. The MBAM client (agent) is installed on the managed Windows 8.1 device and has the following characteristics:

- Uses Group Policy to enforce the BitLocker encryption of client computers in the enterprise
- Collects the recovery key for the three BitLocker data drive types: operating system drives, fixed data drives, and removable data (USB) drives
- Collects compliance data for the computer and passes the data to the reporting system

The full implementation of all MBAM components uses database servers, domain controllers, and possibly other stand-alone servers and is beyond the scope of this book.

Summary

In this chapter, you learned how files are created and managed on the Windows filesystem using File Explorer. We also looked at folders, and you saw how they are created, managed, secured, and shared. We discussed OneDrive, which is integrated into the Windows 8.1 operating system.

We also looked at Windows 8.1 file and folder permissions using the NTFS permissions system. You learned how to encrypt files and make sure that users have easy access to files they need while unauthorized users are blocked from accessing information they should not see.

You saw how HomeGroups make network computing far easier, and how to create, manage, and join a small home network or a small business network to a HomeGroup.

We discussed auditing and how to choose what to audit and how to review the audit logs to determine who did what and when they did it to a file or a share.

Exam Essentials

Know how to configure and manage File Explorer.   Many features and options are available in File Explorer that make it easier for users to work with their files. These features include making sure that Windows opens the files with the correct applications, showing and hiding filename extensions, setting the default application for a file, and more.

Know how to configure and manage folders.   Users manage their files in folders. You need to know how to manage and secure file and folder access, create and manage shared folders, and configure file and folder compression. You also need to know how to enable and configure OneDrive access, and create and configure shares.

Know how to configure and manage NTFS file and share permissions.   Be able to configure security permissions and know the difference between NTFS and share permissions. You will need to know about NTFS permission inheritance, how to block inheritance, and what happens when you move files from one volume to another.

Know how to configure and manage EFS.   Be able to configure the Encrypting File System. You will need to know how to set up EFS, create and store certificates, manage certificates and user accounts, and make sure users do not lose access to files that have been encrypted when passwords, logons, and computers change.

Know how to set up and manage auditing.   Be able to configure auditing and decide what files and folders are audited, what gets audited, and how to view the results of auditing in Windows log files.

Know how to manage local storage.   Know how to configure disk quotas, manage volumes and their filesystems, use storage spaces, and use disk fault tolerance techniques. Also understand the use of the Distributed File System (DFS).

Know how to monitor system performance.   Know how to use Performance Monitor and how to configure Indexing Options.

Know how to enable BitLocker and BitLocker to Go.   Be able to enable these features on operating system drives, data drives, and removable media. Also understand the role a Windows 8.1 commuter can play when using the Microsoft BitLocker Administration and Monitoring (MBAM) tool.

Review Questions

You can find the answers in Appendix A.

1. You have a user, Alice, who has access to the applications folder on your network server. Alice belongs to the following groups:

    - NTFS
    - Sales   Read only
    - Marketing   Full Control
    - Shared Permissions
    - Sales   Read only
    - Marketing   Change

    When Alice logs into the applications folder from her Windows 8.1 machine, what are her effective permissions?

    A. Full Control

    B. Read only

    C. Change

    D. Read and Write

2. You are the system administrator for a large organization. You have a Windows 8.1 machine that all users can access. There is a folder on the Windows 8.1 machine called Apps. You need to set up auditing on this folder. How do you accomplish this task?

    A. From the Local Group Policy, enable Directory Service Access.

    B. From the Local Group Policy, enable Audit Object Access.

    C. From the Local Group Policy, enable Account Access.

    D. From the Local Group Policy, enable File And Folder Access.

3. You have a user named Will who has access to the Finance folder on your network server. Will belongs to the following groups;

    - NTFS
    - Admin   Full Control
    - Finance   Modify
    - Shared Permissions
    - Admin   Full Control
    - Finance   Change

    When Will logs into the Finance folder from his Windows 8.1 machine, what are his effective permissions?

    A. Full Control

    B. Read only

   C. Change

   D. Read and Write

4. Mary has access to the R&D folder on your network server. Mary's user belongs to the following groups:

- NTFS
- Sales   Read only
- Marketing   Read Only
- Shared Permissions
- Sales   Read only
- Marketing   Change

When Mary logs into the R&D folder from her Windows 8.1 machine, what are her effective permissions?

   A. Full Control

   B. Read only

   C. Change

   D. Read and Write

5. You have a network folder that resides on an NTFS partition on which permissions have been applied. Which of the following statements best describes how share permissions and NTFS permissions work together if they have been applied to the same folder?

   A. The NTFS permissions will always take precedence.

   B. The share permissions will always take precedence.

   C. The system will look at the cumulative share permissions and the cumulative NTFS permissions. Whichever set is less restrictive will be applied.

   D. The system will look at the cumulative share permissions and the cumulative NTFS permissions. Whichever set is more restrictive will be applied.

6. To install a new driver for an unsupported printer, what user account should you use?

   A. Standard user

   B. Power user

   C. Administrator Service account

   D. Built-in administrator

7. Which of the following are characteristics of the HomeGroup feature in Windows 8.1?

   A. Printers are automatically installed.

   B. No networking knowledge is required.

   C. The password must be at least 10 characters in length.

   D. The HomeGroup password must be changed every 90 days.

   E. You must remove all shared folders before configuring HomeGroup.

8. OneDrive users can connect to their files in the cloud through which of the following ways?

    A. OneDrive app Library plug-in

    B. OneDrive desktop app

    C. iPad and iPhone apps

    D. Your credit card

    E. OneDrive is built into Windows 8.1.

9. Which of the following are examples of objects?

    A. File

    B. Partition

    C. Folder

    D. Registry key

10. Security auditing of files can help identify what types of activity on your computer?

    A. Deletion of files

    B. Unauthorized file access

    C. When files are renamed

    D. Files deleted from a FAT drive

11. Which two of the following enables administrators to apply access control permissions and restrictions based on defined rules that can include the sensitivity of the resources, the job or role of the user, and the configuration of the device that is used to access these resources?

    A. DAC

    B. MBAM

    C. EFS

    D. DFS

12. Which of the following isn't a user right?

    A. Log on locally.

    B. Change the time zone.

    C. Manage auditing and security log.

    D. Access this computer from the network.

    E. Edit GPO.

13. You want to give a colleague access to your EFS encrypted files. Which file do you give him?

    A. DOCX

    B. CER

    C. PFX

    D. Certificate

14. In which `certmgr.msc` folder will a user's EFS certificate be located?

  A. Personal

  B. Enterprise Trust

  C. Trusted Publishers

  D. Client Authentication Issuers

15. By default, how is the role of Data Recovery Agent on a local Windows 8.1 computer assigned?

  A. Any member of the Power Users group can take the role.

  B. The local administrator account is assigned the role.

  C. The first user to use EFS is assigned the role.

  D. It must be assigned manually; there are no defaults.

16. When you combine various Allow and Deny permissions, which of following NTFS permissions takes precedence?

  A. Inherited Deny

  B. Inherited Allow

  C. Explicit Deny

  D. Explicit Allow

17. When you move a folder configured with NTFS permissions from one disk to another configured with NTFS permissions, what happens to the original NTFS permissions?

  A. The copied files and folder retain the explicit permissions and also inherit the new folder permissions.

  B. The moved files and folder inherit the permissions of the destination folder.

  C. All permissions are retained.

  D. The moved files and folders lose all permissions.

18. You have a user named Will who has access to the Finance folder on your network server. Will belongs to the following groups;

  - NTFS
  - Admin   Full Control
  - Finance   Modify
  - Shared Permissions
  - Admin   Full Control
  - Finance   Change

When Will logs into the Finance folder from his Windows 8.1 machine, what are his effective permissions?

  A. Full Control

  B. Read only

  C. Change

  D. Read and Write

19. You have a network folder that resides on an NTFS partition on a Windows 8.1 computer. NTFS permissions and share permissions have been applied. Which of the following statements best describes how share permissions and NTFS permissions work together if they have been applied to the same folder?

  A. The NTFS permissions will always take precedence.

  B. The share permissions will always take precedence.

  C. The system will look at the cumulative share permissions and the cumulative NTFS permissions. Whichever set is less restrictive will be applied.

  D. The system will look at the cumulative share permissions and the cumulative NTFS permissions. Whichever set is more restrictive will be applied.

20. Which folder is not part of the default public folder collection on a Windows 8.1 computer?

  A. Desktop

  B. Pictures

  C. Documents

  D. Downloads

Chapter

11

Managing Windows 8.1 Hardware and Printers

70-687 MICROSOFT EXAM OBJECTIVES COVERED IN THIS CHAPTER:

✓ **Configure devices and device drivers**

- Install, update, disable, and roll back drivers
- Resolve driver issues
- Configure driver settings, including signed and unsigned drivers
- Manage driver packages

70-688 MICROSOFT EXAM OBJECTIVES COVERED IN THIS CHAPTER:

- Monitor and manage printers, including NFC Tap-to-Pair and printer sharing

One of the most important roles of an operating system, including Windows 8.1, is to manage computer hardware resources. These resources can include the computer's motherboard, its RAM, USB ports, and other devices. It can also include peripheral devices such as keyboards, mice, monitors, and printers. Software programs designed to communicate between Windows and the hardware are called device drivers. This chapter takes a look at device drivers, how to configure Windows 8.1 with the correct device driver for your devices, and how to manage those drivers in cases where the device or Windows is not behaving properly.

As you learn to manage devices, you will undoubtedly run across setting up, configuring, and (in some cases) troubleshooting printer devices. Although many hard-copy printouts have been replaced by onscreen digital documents, probably the most popular output device is still the laser printer. Windows 8.1 includes many of the most common device drivers for most common printers, but there may be times when you need to update a driver or change one to make a printer work properly. Also, as more and more printers become distributed in networked environments, you will need to know how to configure and manage printer drivers in a network situation. This chapter covers setting up, sharing, and controlling access to printers.

Configuring Devices and Device Drivers

As an operating system, Windows 8.1 relies on some form of hardware to allow users to interact with its feature set. Hardware is any physical device used by the computer, whether internal to the computer or attached externally to the computer. Internal components include the motherboard, memory (RAM), CPU, and expansion cards. Hardware components that perform a given function are generally referred to as hardware devices, or just *devices* for short. You can use numerous types of hardware devices with a computer, such as the following:

- Printers
- Pointing devices, such as mice
- Keyboards

- Monitors
- Disk drives
- Digital cameras

To allow Windows to work with devices and to allow the user to interact with them, a special software program is needed. This special software is called a *device driver*. A device driver is a program that serves as an intermediary between a piece of hardware and an application or the operating system. For example, a display driver enables Windows 8.1 to communicate with and control your computer's display. Likewise, a printer driver enables Windows 8.1 to communicate with and control a printer.

About Firmware

Firmware is also software, in the context that it is program code. The difference is in how the program code is stored. Firmware is stored in a hardware device, typically in read-only memory. For example, the program code that makes your Apple iPad or your digital camera work is firmware. Generally, as a typical Windows 8.1 user you will deal with firmware only when updating firmware on your removable devices, such as MP3 players. You will be adding device drivers and working with Windows updates much more so than you will with firmware.

Device drivers enable the Windows operating system to communicate with and control devices. Although Windows 8.1 comes with a very large number of device drivers for a wide range of devices, most device drivers are written and distributed by the manufacturers of a given device. For example, your video adapter's device driver was written by the company that designed and manufactured the adapter. Device drivers are very much device-specific. That is, a device driver written for one device won't work for a different type of device. For that reason, make sure you have the necessary device driver(s) for a device before you install it. If you have just purchased a new device that requires a device driver not included with Windows, that driver will be included with the new device, typically on a CD or available for download on the manufacturer's website. Because the version of the device driver was developed specifically for the device, you don't have to obtain an updated driver before installing the new device. However, you can visit the manufacturer's website to see if an updated driver is available that adds features or fixes issues with the version you have. We recommend that you first install the device using the driver you have and then check later for an updated driver as needed.

Windows 8.1 has two primary locations where devices are managed. Device Manager is a Control Panel app that has been part of Windows since Windows 95. It provides a hierarchical list of installed devices on a computer (see Figure 11.1), including names of device drivers, settings, and status information. With the introduction of Windows 8.1, a new Devices settings feature is available from the PC Settings charm. The Devices settings feature does not list all of the hardware devices on your computer. Instead, as shown in Figure 11.2, Devices provides management of devices connected to your computer and to devices present on the network.

FIGURE 11.1 You can view hardware devices using Device Manager

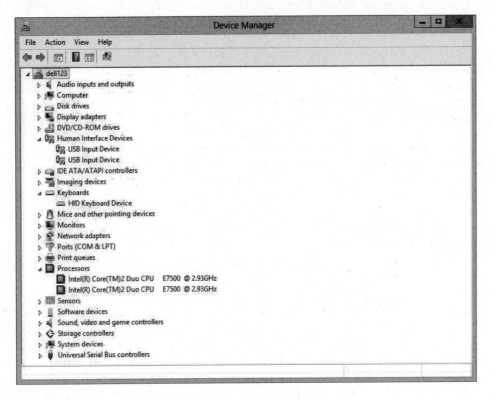

Exercise 11.1 shows how to view the device driver for a specific hardware device in Windows 8.1. This exercise assumes you have Windows 8.1 started and that you have administrative privileges.

FIGURE 11.2 The Devices settings area

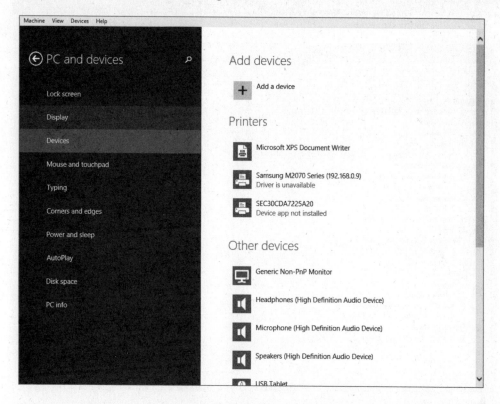

EXERCISE 11.1

Viewing a Device Driver in Device Manager

1. In the Windows 8.1 Search box, type **Device**.

2. Click the Device Manager icon. Device Manager displays.

3. To see details about a hardware device driver, click the arrow to the left of a category in which the hardware you want to inspect resides.

4. Click a device under the hardware category you just expanded.

EXERCISE 11.1 *(continued)*

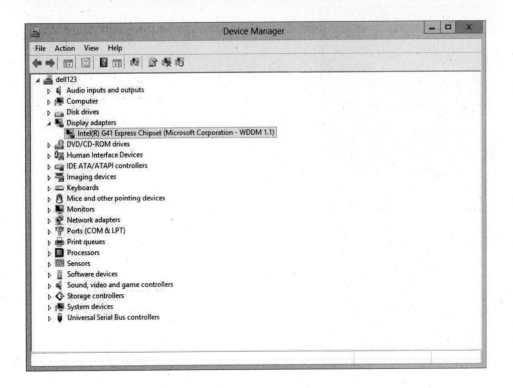

5. Double-click the device to display the properties dialog box.

6. Click the Driver tab.

7. Click the Driver Details button to display the Driver File Details dialog box.

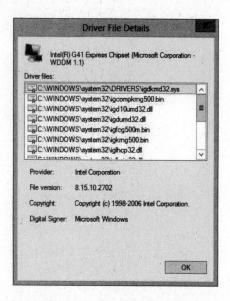

8. Click OK twice to close the dialog boxes when you finish.

To view the Devices setting in the PC Settings charm, see Exercise 11.2. This exercise assumes you have Windows 8.1 started and that you have administrative privileges.

EXERCISE 11.2

Viewing the Devices Setting

1. In the Windows 8.1 Search box, type **Settings**.

2. Click PC Settings to display more Settings options.

3. Click PC Settings And Devices.

4. Click Devices.

5. Click a device name to display a control for removing the device. Or click the Add A Device button for Windows to search for new devices to set up.

EXERCISE 11.2 *(continued)*

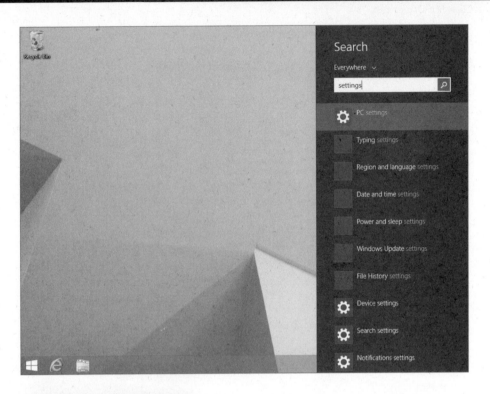

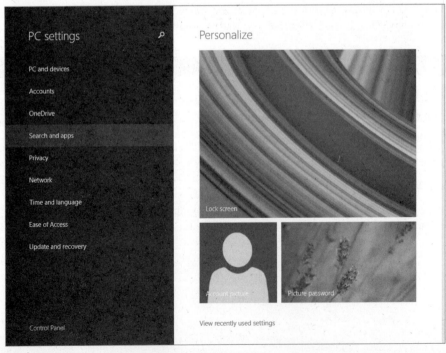

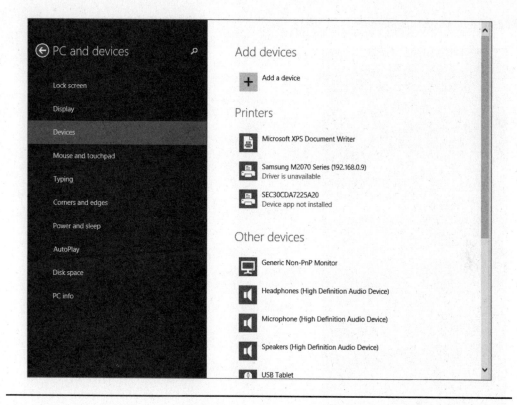

Signed and Unsigned Drivers

A driver that is digitally signed is one that attaches an identifier called a digital signature to the driver. Digital signature is used to verify the integrity of the driver and the vendor (software publisher) who provides the driver. Windows 8.1 supports the ability to control the use of signed and unsigned drivers on both the local computer and domain levels.

Although all of the settings discussed in this section can be adjusted locally, Group Policies are available in Windows Server 2012 R2 that enforce the same settings on a domain of computers. Unlike some earlier editions of Windows, Windows 8.1 does not allow unsigned drivers unless you make some significant changes. The process had been made somewhat complicated to impress upon users the importance of using signed drivers.

To enable the use of unsigned drivers (again, this is not recommended), first access the PC Settings screen as you did in Exercise 11.2. Select Update And Recovery and then click Recovery. The Update And Recovery screen will appear, as shown in Figure 11.3.

On the right side, select Restart Now under Advanced Startup. Once your PC restarts, Windows 8.1 will offer you a new menu called Choose An Option. Select Troubleshoot and then click Advanced Options to open the Advanced Options dialog box shown in Figure 11.4.

FIGURE 11.3 Update And Recovery

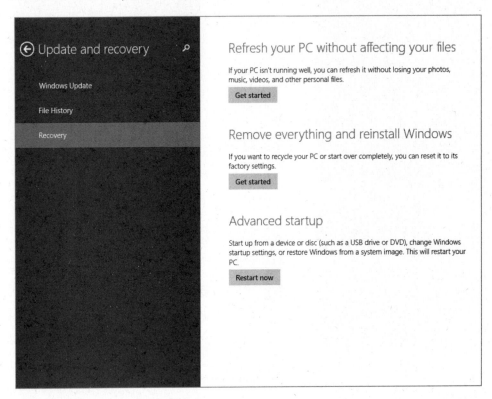

FIGURE 11.4 Advanced Options dialog box

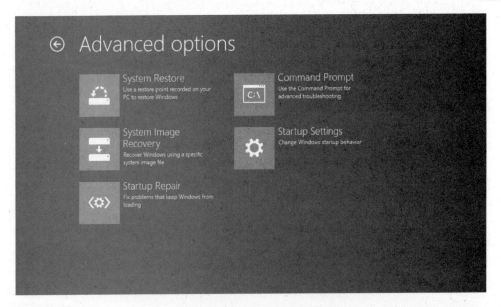

Select Change Windows Startup Behavior under Startup Settings. The Startup Settings dialog box will appear before the computer reboots and will offer the selections shown in Figure 11.5.

FIGURE 11.5   Startup Settings

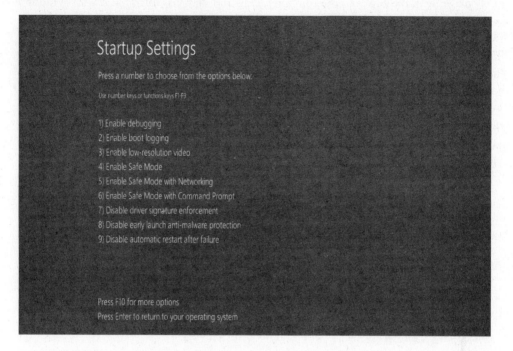

Press the 7 key (which disables driver signature enforcement) and the computer will reboot again. When it is done, you'll be able to install unsigned drivers.

Installing, Updating, and Disabling Drivers

Windows 8.1 includes a number of device drivers as part of its installation package. This makes it fairly easy for the user to install Windows and then have most, if not all, of the user's computer hardware and connected devices recognized and configured automatically by Windows. In addition, as users connect devices or add internal hardware to their computers (such as an additional video card), Windows will search for those devices and set up appropriate drivers for them if they are available.

Sometimes, however, you may need to manually install a device driver for a hardware device that Windows does not recognize. In many cases, this is due to a few occurrences, such as the following:

The hardware device is older than the previous Windows version (such as Windows 7 when upgrading to Windows 8.1).   In some cases, such as a scanning device, if a device driver was not updated for Windows 7, then Windows 8.1 might have trouble finding a driver for your device during the upgrade process.

The device does not support Plug-and-Play.   Plug-and-Play is a hardware specification that permits a hardware device to be readily recognized and configured by Windows 8.1 by simply plugging in the device to the computer. Plug-and-Play was introduced with Windows 95, so most hardware devices introduced after 1995 support the specification. However, you may run across a legacy hardware device that does not support the Plug-and-Play specification, so you will need to manually set up the device.

The hardware device is brand new on the market.   In these cases, the device is so new that Windows 8.1 does not have a set of updated drivers to match the requirements for your new device.

The hardware device has been termed "end of life" or "obsolete" by the hardware manufacturer.   Windows 8.1 may not have an appropriate device driver if even the original manufacturer is not supporting the device any longer.

For these scenarios, try installing a device driver to get your device working. To do so, you would use the Devices And Printers program in Control Panel. You will need to locate a driver that works with your device. Start looking on any discs or flash drive that came bundled with your device. These discs will usually have a specific set of steps to perform to set up the device driver on your system. Be sure to follow these steps so that you get everything installed properly to work with Windows 8.1.

If that search is not successful, turn to the Internet. Many times you will need to look for the driver on the website of the hardware's manufacturer. If your computer monitor, for example, is a ViewSonic, visit the following website and search for a driver for Windows 8.1:

`www.viewsonic.com/us/support/downloads/search_driver`

Another good place to look is the website of the computer firm from which you purchased your computer. For example, Dell Inc. has an excellent resource of device drivers for the hundreds of different hardware devices they sell as part of their computer systems. Visit the following Dell site to start your search:

`www.dell.com/support/drivers`

Many comprehensive device driver sites exist to help you locate drivers. One popular one is Driver Guide at `www.driverguide.com`. These sites provide a one-stop-shopping experience for thousands of devices. Once you locate one of these sites using your favorite search engine, you can search on manufacturer, PC type, or even operating system version. One caveat with sites like these is that they may require you to download a helper application to manage the download process. Many times these downloaders contain links to malware or spyware that can infect your computer. Simply pay attention as you download files and make sure you read everything before advancing through a dialog box or screen.

Exercise 11.3 shows how to use the Devices And Printers tool to install a device driver. The exercise assumes that you have Windows 8.1 started and that you have administrative privileges. It also assumes that you have a hardware device that Windows 8.1 has not automatically identified and configured. Finally, it is assumed you have downloaded a device driver onto your local hard drive so that you can use it during the device driver installation process.

EXERCISE 11.3

Installing a Device Driver

1. Install or plug in the hardware device.

2. In the Windows 8.1 Search box, type **Device**.

3. Click the Devices And Printers icon. The Device And Printers app displays.

4. Click Add A Device.

   Windows 8.1 searches the system and displays a list of found devices.

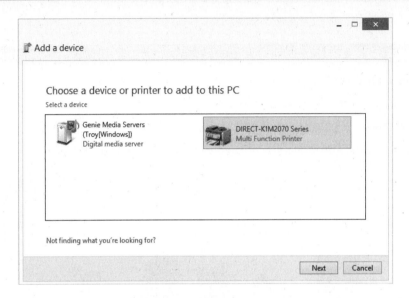

5. Click the device you want to install. Click Next.

6. Browse for the driver software on your system.

7. Select the driver to install.

8. Click Next to install the driver.

9. Click Finish. You may need to shut down and restart your computer based on the driver you installed. In fact, it's a good idea to restart your computer to test your new driver and ensure it's set up correctly.

There are times you may want to update a device's driver. To do so, you can use Device Manager. Exercise 11.4 shows how you how. The exercise assumes that you have Windows 8.1 started and that you have administrative privileges. It is assumed you have downloaded a device driver onto your local hard drive so that you can use it during the device driver update process.

EXERCISE 11.4

Updating a Device Driver

1. Install or plug in the hardware device.

2. In the Windows 8.1 Search box, type **Device**.

3. Click Device Manager.

4. Locate the category in which the hardware device is found. For example, to update a WiFi adapter, expand the Network Adapters category.

5. Right-click the name of the device you want to update.

6. Select Update Driver Software.

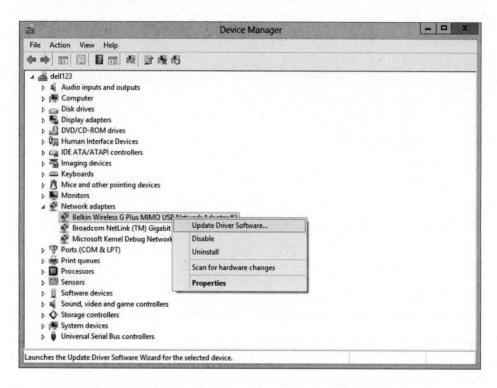

7. Click Browse My Computer For Driver Software in the Update Driver Software dialog box.

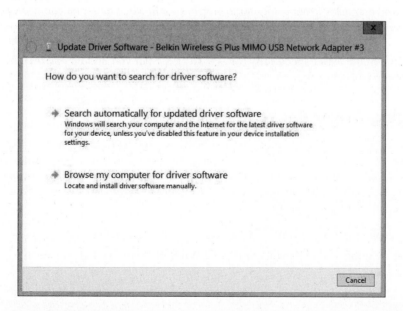

8. In the resulting dialog box, click the Browse button to browse for the device driver on your computer.

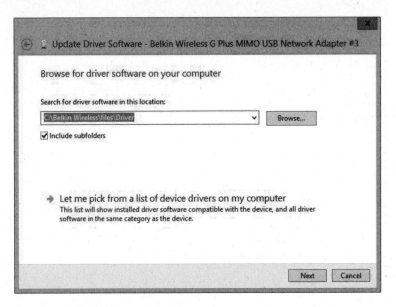

9. Select your new device driver and click OK.

10. Click Next. Windows installs the new updated device driver. A dialog box appears letting you know that Windows has successfully updated your driver software.

11. Click Close.

12. Shut down and restart your computer to ensure your updated driver functions properly.

If you can't find a driver specifically for Windows 8.1 but you do find one for Windows 7, that driver may work.

Managing Driver Packages

In Chapter 2, "Planning the Windows 8.1 Installation," you learned about the process of using images to install Windows 8.1 to multiple computers. You learned that images can be serviced both online and offline. One of the changes we can make is to add driver packages to the image so that when the image is applied all required drivers are present. You can add device drivers to a Windows image:

- Before deployment on an offline Windows image by using DISM
- During an automated deployment by using Windows Setup and an answer file

- After deployment on a running operating system by using PnPUtil or an answer file

For more information on using DISM, see Chapter 2.

Resolving Driver Issues

There may be times when a newly installed hardware device prevents Windows 8.1 from starting properly. In most cases, such devices will be disabled automatically so that Windows 8.1 can start. If it works that way, you can typically follow the steps described in the preceding section to try to get the updated driver online.

If Windows 8.1 cannot disable or work with the new device, you may be able to start in Safe Mode With Networking and either get updated drivers there or disable the device manually. You will need to also log in with the Administrator account.

Before you physically remove a device from the system, first uninstall it through Device Manager by following these steps:

1. Start Device Manager as you did in the previous exercise.

2. Expand the category in which the device is listed. Then right-click the name of the device you intend to remove and choose Uninstall, as in Figure 11.6.

FIGURE 11.6   Uninstall a hardware device

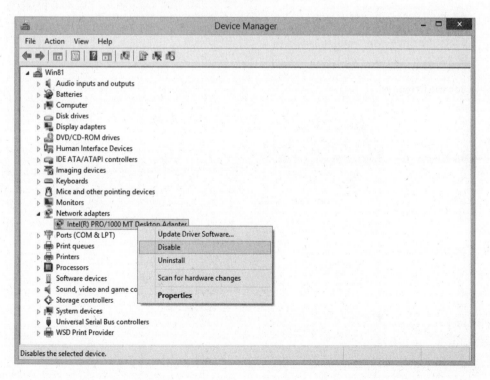

3. Click OK.

4. Shut down the computer, unplug the power cord, and physically remove the device from the system. Then plug the machine back in and start it up, and everything should be back to the way it was before you ever installed the device.

Rolling Back Drivers

Let's say you updated a device driver and the device you updated works. However, it does not work as well as when you had the previous driver installed. Is there a way to return Windows 8.1 so that it uses the previous driver? Yes, there is. You can use the Roll Back Driver feature of Device Manager.

The Roll Back Driver option uninstalls the most recently updated driver and will "roll back" your configuration to its earlier version. Exercise 11.5 shows how to roll back a driver. The exercise assumes that you have Windows 8.1 started, that you're at the Windows Start screen, and that you have administrative privileges.

EXERCISE 11.5

Rolling Back a Device Driver

1. In the Windows 8.1 Search box, type **Device**.

2. Click Device Manager.

3. Locate the driver you want to roll back and right-click it.

4. Click Properties. The properties dialog box for the device displays.

5. Click the Driver tab.

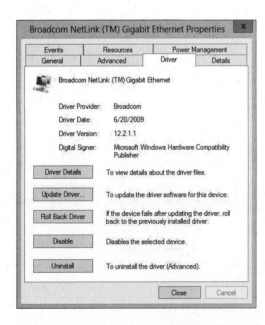

6. Click the Roll Back Driver button. A message appears asking if you are sure you want to roll back the driver

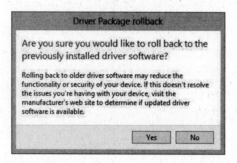

7. Click Yes. Windows 8.1 rolls back the driver to the previous one installed. The Roll Back Driver button is grayed out to indicate that there are no drivers to which you can roll back.

8. Click Close to close the properties dialog box.

When you use the Roll Back Driver feature, the Roll Back Driver button is available only after you have recently updated a driver. Otherwise, the button is grayed out and not available.

Configuring Driver Settings

Device drivers are set with default settings that usually work for many systems. There are times, however, that you may need to change or tweak some driver settings to make a device perform better or with different features. Before you make changes to a device driver, however, you should make note of the current settings so that you can return to those original settings if your changes do not work properly.

The types of changes you can make to a device driver depend on the device driver and device. Some device drivers—for example, the device driver for an Ethernet card—allow you to modify a significant number of settings. On the other hand, the device driver for a keyboard may have only a few settings that can be changed.

To configure driver settings, you use Device Manager. Exercise 11.6 shows how to configure driver settings. The exercise assumes that you have Windows 8.1 started and that you have administrative privileges.

EXERCISE 11.6

Configuring a Device Driver

1. In the Windows 8.1 Search box, type **Device**.

2. Click Device Manager.

3. Locate the driver you want to configure and right-click it.

4. Click Properties. The properties dialog box for the selected driver displays.

5. Click a tab to see if that tab includes user-configurable settings. For example, in the following graphic a Power Management tab is included for this device driver (an Ethernet device). On the Power Management tab, you can set the following items:

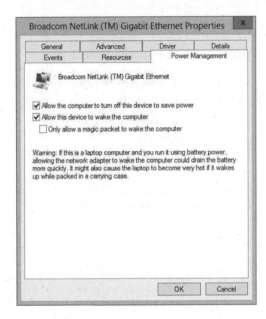

-   Allow the Computer To Turn Off This Device To Save Power

-   Allow This Device To Wake The Computer

-   Only Allow A Magic Packet To Wake The Computer

6. Make the changes you need and click OK to save those configuration changes.

7. Click OK to save your settings.

Installing and Sharing Printers

In theory, using a printer is a fairly simple user process: You prepare a document, send the document to your printer (using File ➤ Print, for example), and wait for the finished product. If everything is installed and configured properly, you get a printed document that looks very similar to what you expect to see. Behind the scenes, however, Windows, device drivers, and your printer are working hard to get your document to print correctly.

Initially a program called a *print spooler* creates a special copy of the document that contains programming codes that tell the printer what to do so that the document it prints looks like the one that you printed. After the spooler creates the printer file, it sends the information to the printer buffer. The buffer is a storage area within the printer that holds the data until it is printed. The amount of data that can reside in the buffer depends on the size of the buffer. In some cases, the buffer will hold a large number of pages. In others, it might hold only a single page, or in the case of a complex document such as a photo, and a relatively small buffer, only part of the page might fit in the buffer at one time.

When the spooler has finished creating the special printer file, there may be another document already printing. There may even be several documents waiting to be printed. So, the spooler has to put all the print jobs into a *queue* (line). All of this activity takes computer time. And because each document has to be fed to the printer in small chunks, there's often time for you to do things like cancel documents you've told Windows to print but that haven't yet been fully printed. To manage those print jobs, you use the *print queue*. If a document is already printing, or waiting to print, you'll see a tiny printer icon in the Notification area. When you point to that icon, the number of documents waiting to be printed appears in a tooltip. Double-click that small icon to open the print queue. As an alternative to using the Notification area, you can get to the print queue from the `Devices and Printers` folder.

Before you can use a new printer, you need to connect it to the computer and install it. Installing printers is one of the most common tasks for Windows 8.1 users. Windows 8.1 has two ways to view and manage your printers. First, the new Windows 8.1 Devices tool lets you view, add, and remove hardware devices, including printers. The `Devices and Printers` folder, which was introduced in Windows 7, is still around as well. It is the place to go to manage hardware devices such as displays, keyboards, input devices, wireless network adapters, and printers.

The Version 4 Architecture

Starting in Windows 8, the printing architecture for Windows changed to Version 4. The end result is that drivers are smaller and faster to install, and there are fewer of them. Beside these improvements, they included:

- Printing from metro-style apps
- Integrating printing into metro-style apps (metro-style apps are designed based on Metro design language, run on Windows Runtime platform and sold, installed, and serviced via Windows Store)
- Printing in Windows RT

This may mean that some of the dialog boxes with which you have interacted in the past may look different, especially if you are printing from a mobile device or from a metro-style app.

Adding and Connecting to Printers

Let's look at adding a printer using the `Devices and Printers` folder. Many printers give you the choice of using the USB port to connect the printer, or a standard printer port. In most cases, USB will work just fine for printing. In fact, most of today's standard computer configurations do not even have a parallel printer port, so USB might be your only option. Likewise, most new printers do not have parallel or serial port connections. Exercise 11.7 shows you how to configure a printer. The exercise assumes that you have Windows 8.1 started, that you're at the Windows Start screen, and you have administrative privileges. Also, this exercise shows installing a standard USB printer. You will see how to share it later.

EXERCISE 11.7

Configuring a Printer

1. Connect your printer according to the instructions provided by the printer manufacturer.

2. When prompted, select the location where the device driver for the printer resides. For example, if the drivers are on a CD or external flash drive, specify the correct drive letter.

3. Walk through the onscreen wizard or instructions to complete the installation.

4. Open the Devices And Printers dialog box to view the installed printer. To do this, display the Start screen and type **printers**. Click Settings beneath the search field, and then choose Devices And Printers.

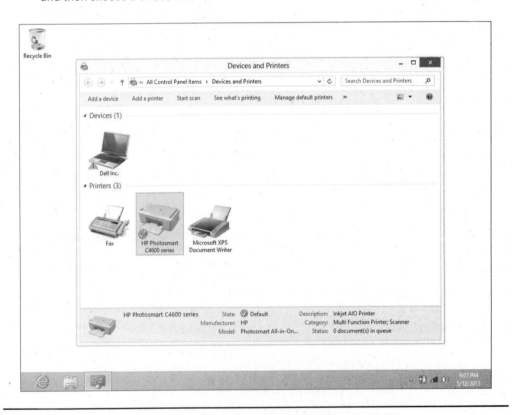

The main rule on installing a printer is to follow the instructions that came with it. Sometimes you need to install drivers first—sometimes you don't. There is no "one rule fits all" when it comes to installing printers, or any other hardware device for that matter. But in a pinch, where there are no instructions, the techniques in the following sections will be your best first guess.

In the print queue, you can change the order in which documents in the queue will print. For example, if you need a printout right now and there's a long line of documents waiting ahead of yours, you can give your document a higher priority so it prints sooner. To change an item in the print queue's priority, right-click the item in the queue and choose Properties. On the General tab of the dialog box that opens, drag the Priority slider, shown in Figure 11.7, to the right. The further you drag, the higher your document's priority. Click OK. Your document won't stop the document that's currently printing, but it may well be the next one to print.

FIGURE 11.7   Priority slider in a print queue item's Properties dialog box

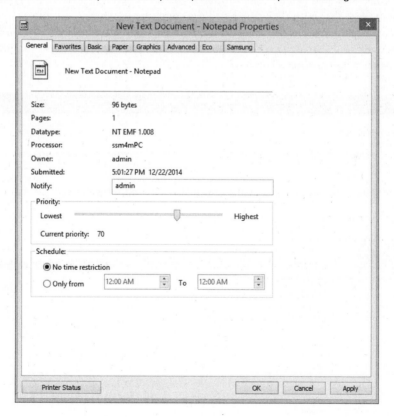

You can close the print queue as you would any other window—by clicking the Close button in its upper-right corner or by choosing Printer ➤ Close from its menu bar. To get help with the print queue while it's open, choose Help from its menu bar.

If your computer is a member of a home or small-business network and you know of a shared printer on another computer in that network, you can use the technique described here to install that printer on your own computer. The same is true of many wireless and Bluetooth printers. But again, this procedure may not be necessary because Windows 8.1 often detects network printers and makes them available automatically. Be sure to check the manual that came with a wireless or Bluetooth printer for an alternative procedure before trying the method described here. Also, be sure to turn the printer on before you try to install it.

Connecting to a Shared Printer

If you're trying to install a printer that's attached to another computer in your private network, make sure that both the printer and the computer to which the printer is physically connected are turned on. Make sure your network is set up and that you've enabled discovery and sharing. Exercise 11.8 shows how to share a printer so that other computers can use it over a network.

EXERCISE 11.8

Sharing a Printer

1. Display Devices And Printers on the computer on which you want to share the printer.

2. Right-click the printer you want to share and choose Printer Properties.

3. Click the Sharing tab.

4. Select Share This Printer.

5. Enter a name for the printer. Use something descriptive so that other users will know which printer this shared one is.

6. Click OK. Windows sets up this printer to be a shared device on the network.

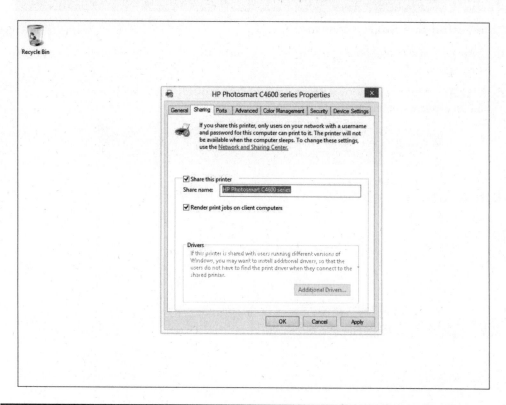

Go to the computer that needs to access the network printer and perform the steps in Exercise 11.9 on that computer. You install a network, wireless, or Bluetooth printer in much the same way you install a local printer. Exercise 11.9 shows how to set up a network shared printer.

EXERCISE 11.9

Connecting to a Shared Printer

1. Display Devices And Printers on the computer on which you want to set up the shared printer.

2. Click Add A Printer. Windows opens the Add Printer dialog box and displays any found printers—in this example, the list is blank.

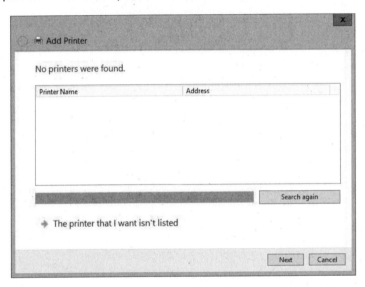

3. Click The Printer That I Want Isn't Listed.

4. In the Select A Shared Printer By Name text box, enter the full UNC path or IP address to the printer if you know it. Otherwise, click Browse to find the printer.

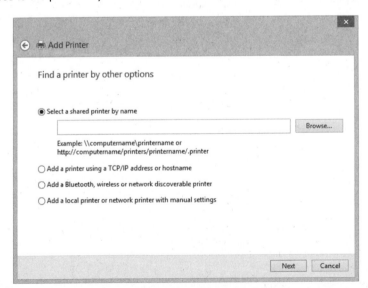

5. Select the computer on which the shared printer resides.

6. If prompted, enter a username and password to gain authorization for the shared printer.

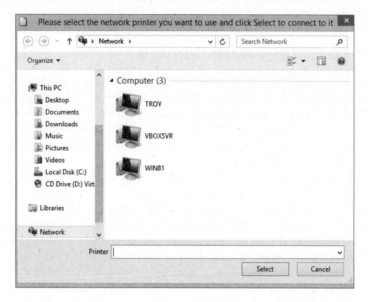

7. Select the shared printer.

8. Click Select. The name of the shared printer appears in the Add Printer dialog box.

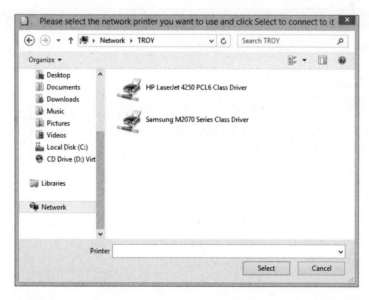

9. Click Next. Windows connects to the computer with the shared printer and sets up a connection to it.

Once installed, the shared printer can be printed to just like any other printer. If you want to make it the default printer, right-click its icon and choose Set As Default Printer (this option is only available while in Devices And Printers). Then, close Devices And Printers and Control Panel.

Configure Location-Aware Printing

Location-Aware Printing is a feature of Windows 8.1 (it was introduced in Windows 7) that enables you to select different default printers for different networks. This is ideal for anyone who has a mobile computing device, such as a Windows laptop, Windows tablet, or Windows Phone. As you connect to a different network, Windows automatically becomes aware of the available printers on that network and selects the current default printer as one of the printers on the available network.

To use location-aware printing, you do have to set up each default printer the first time you connect to that network. After that, Windows automatically establishes the available network printer as the default when you connect to that network. An example is working with a Windows 8.1 tablet at work and at home. When you leave work (and the resources available on the work network) and arrive at home (where you have a home network and a network printer available), Windows changes the default printer from the one you had at work to the one now available on your home network.

Exercise 11.10 shows how to set up a location-aware printer. The exercise assumes that you have access to a shared printer on at least two different networks (such as home and work) and that you have administrator access to your computer.

EXERCISE 11.10

Configuring Location-Aware Printers

1. Display Devices And Printers on the computer that will access multiple network default printers.

2. Select a printer.

3. Click the Manage Default Printers at the top of the Devices And Printers dialog box. The Manage Default Printers dialog box appears.

4. Select Change My Default Printer When I Change Networks.

5. From the Select Network drop-down list, select a network.

6. From the Select Printer drop-down list, select a printer.

7. Click Add.

8. Click OK.

Perform the preceding steps for each network you connect to. Each time you connect to a different network, Windows will know which printer on that network you want to print to as the default printer.

Monitoring and Managing Print Servers

If you share a printer on a Windows 8.1 system, it will behave as a print server and you can manipulate Print Server Properties. Manipulating server properties is commonly done on an actual print server in an enterprise, but if Windows 8.1 is being used in a small office or home office, it can be used to host multiple printers. If a Windows 7 or Windows 8/8.1 computer is used as a print server, it is limited to no more than 20 concurrent connections.

To access the print server features, open the Devices And Printers dialog box, select the shared printer, and then click Print Server Properties. The Printer Server Properties dialog box appears (see Figure 11.8).

FIGURE 11.8   The Print Server Properties dialog box

This dialog box allows you to change settings for all printers on the same computer. It includes five tabs:

Forms   The Forms tab shows the different form sizes (such as letter size or legal size) that are supported by printers on the system. You can also create additional forms from this tab.

Ports   The Ports tab allows you to manipulate the ports such as serial, parallel, or TCP/IP address ports. These are added when a printer is added, but you can also delete ports from this tab.

Drivers   The Drivers tab can be used to add and remove drivers; however, drivers are commonly manipulated using Printer Properties.

Security   Server permissions can be assigned here. By default, administrators are assigned all permissions, and the Everyone group is assigned the Print permission.

Advanced   The most important element here is the location of the Spool folder. By default the Spool folder is located in the C:\Windows\System32\Spool\Printers folder. If the drive is filling up with a high volume of print jobs and/or is causing excessive fragmentation on the drive, you can move the Spool folder to another location by just typing in the new location on this tab.

WARNING   You should ensure the print queue doesn't include any print jobs before moving the Spool folder. Any print jobs held in the queue will be lost when a new path for the Spool folder is entered.

NFC Tap-to-Pair

Near Field Communication (NFC) is a form of contactless communication between devices, almost like a small Wi-Fi network. NFC uses electromagnetic radio fields for communication whereas technologies such as Bluetooth and Wi-Fi focus on radio transmissions. Windows 8.1 introduces NFC tap-to-pair printing for the enterprise. When users locate an NFC-enabled printer in the office, they simply tap their device against the printer and start printing.

There are printers that already have NFC capability built in. You can make any existing non-NFC printer NFC capable by using an NFC tag. NFC tags are like stickers that can be programmed to store the required information.

You can program an NFC tag using a simple PowerShell cmdlet called Write-PrinterNfcTag. Here are the steps to accomplish this:

1. Launch PowerShell as an administrator on a Windows 8.1 system that has NFC hardware capability. You can verify whether the system is NFC capable in Device Manager; if the system has an NFC device, it will be located under Proximity Devices.

2. Type the following command in the PowerShell window:

```
Write-PrinterNfcTag -Sharepath <UNC path of the printer>
```

Here's an example:

```
Write-PrinterNfcTag -Sharepath \\Myprintserver\PrinterX
```

3. You will be prompted to tap the NFC sticker (tag) against the device on which you ran the command. You have to tap it against the NFC radio on the Windows 8.1/2012 R2 system within 30 seconds. Once tapped, the printer share information is written into the NFC tag.

Summary

In this chapter, you learned how to manage, install, and restore device drivers. One of the most important roles of an operating system, including Windows 8.1, is to manage computer hardware resources. These resources can include the computer's motherboard, its RAM, USB ports, and other devices. It can also include peripheral devices such as keyboards, mice, monitors, and printers. Software programs designed to communicate between Windows and the hardware are called device drivers. This chapter showed you how to configure Windows 8.1 with the correct device driver for your devices, and how to manage those drivers in cases where the device or Windows is not behaving properly.

This chapter also examined printers. You learned how to set up printers in a stand-alone computer and how to share that printer with other users on a network. As more and more printers become distributed in networked environments, you will need to know how to configure and manage printer drivers in a network situation. This chapter covered setting up printers, sharing printers, and controlling access to printers.

Exam Essentials

Understand device driver basics. You should know that each hardware device on your computer uses a piece of software called a device driver to allow the device and Windows 8.1 to communicate with each other. Device drivers are available from the hardware manufacturer that made the device. In addition, Windows 8.1 comes with a number of common device drivers to help users quickly set up and configure devices when Windows is initially installed or when a device is plugged into the computer in the future.

Understand where devices are managed. You should know that Windows 8.1 has two primary locations where devices are managed. Device Manager is a Control Panel app that has been part of Windows since Windows 95. It provides a hierarchal list of installed devices on a computer, including names of device drivers, settings, and status information. With the introduction of Windows 8.1, a new Devices Settings feature is available from the PC Settings charm.

Understand the roll-back feature.   You should know that Windows 8.1 includes a feature that enables you to roll back (return to) a previously installed device driver. The Roll Back Driver option uninstalls the most recently updated driver and will "roll back" your configuration to its earlier version.

Understand printer setup basics.   You should know how to set up a printer on a Windows 8.1 computer. Before you can use a new printer, you need to connect it to the computer and install it. Installing printers is one of the most common tasks for Windows 8.1 users. Windows 8.1 has two ways to view and manage your printers. First, the new Windows 8.1 Devices tool lets you view, add, and remove hardware devices, including printers. The Devices and Printers folder, which was introduced in Windows 7, is still around as well. It is the place to go to manage hardware devices such as displays, keyboards, input devices, wireless network adapters, and printers.

Understand printer sharing.   You should know that you can share a printer across a network when you have that printer set up on your computer. You can specify that the printer is shared and even who can have permission to access it. Windows 8.1 also provides support for location-aware printer to enable you to specify different default printers based on the network you are connected to.

Review Questions

You can find the answers in Appendix A.

1. You installed printer on a Windows 8.1 computer. By default, the printer is a member of what type group?

   A. Domain

   B. Workgroup

   C. Both A and B

   D. Neither A nor B

2. Which of the following describes the purpose of a driver signature?

   A. Identify the driver in the driver folder.

   B. Verify the integrity of driver.

   C. Verify the identity of the device.

   D. Prevent software piracy.

3. What is the only place you can obtain a metro-style app?

   A. The vendor of the device

   B. The Windows Store

   C. Directly from the developer

   D. It must be preinstalled on the device by the OEM

4. Which of the following approaches cannot be used to add a driver packages to an image?

   A. On an offline Windows image by using DISM

   B. During an automated deployment by using Windows Setup and an answer file

   C. After deployment on a running operating system by using PnPUtil

   D. On an online Windows image by using DISM

5. Which of the following is *not* an improvement made by the v4 printing architecture?

   A. Printing from metro-style apps

   B. Printing wirelessly

   C. Integrating printing into metro-style apps

   D. Printing in Windows RT

6. You installed a new printer on a Windows 8.1 64-bit computer and configured the settings to allow the printer to be used by a group of users in a department all using Windows 8.1 32-bit. Although everything to share the printer has been done, no one can print to the printer. What steps should you take to make sure the printer can be used by the group?

    A. Get the 32-bit driver and install it on the 64-bit computer.

    B. Change the OS of the print server to 32-bit.

    C. Move the printer to a Windows Server 2012 machine.

    D. Install the 32-bit driver on all 32-bit machines.

7. Many people in your company take one day a week to work from home. After upgrading the users' laptops to Windows 8.1, they all complain that when they try print a document to their default printer the documents instead print to their home computers or they cannot print at all. What's going on here?

    A. Security policy forbids printing from a remote computer.

    B. The printer in the office cannot print to the local computer.

    C. The remote driver for the printer is not installed on the local computer.

    D. You need to set a default printer for each network.

8. You installed a new device driver on a bunch of computers, but it turns out that the driver version was not properly tested on Windows 8 or Windows 8.1 computers and you need to roll back the driver. What should you do?

    A. Restore the computers to the last restore point.

    B. At command prompt, type **/rollback:drv**.

    C. Run Device Manager as an administrator.

    D. Run the Device installation program and choose Uninstall Driver.

9. Which of the following is used to make a printer capable of tap-to-pair?

    A. NFC tag

    B. A special driver

    C. Wi-Fi

    D. Bluetooth

10. Where is firmware stored?

    A. RAM

    B. Hard drive

    C. CPU cache

    D. ROM

11. Which operation requires two reboots?

    A. Updating a driver

    B. Allowing the use of unsigned drivers

    C. Installing a driver

    D. Removing a driver

12. You installed a special printer on a Windows 8.1 workstation computer that is being printed to from a workgroup of 50 computers. Some of the users are reporting problems printing to the printer. What could be the problem?

    A. The network is not fast enough.

    B. The printer driver needs to run at 64-bit.

    C. The users that cannot print do not have permission.

    D. The printer should be installed on a server.

13. A small workgroup of 15 Windows 8.1 computers in a branch office finds that documents queued to the Windows 8.1 client print server are taking forever to print. Users are frustrated, so upon checking the computer, you discover the hard disk drive is highly fragmented and running out of space. What should be done to alleviate the problem?

    A. Clean out the spool folder.

    B. Run **spoolpurge -c** on the spool folder.

    C. Allocate more disk space to the spool folder or relocate it.

    D. Restrict how many documents can be sent to the printer at once.

14. A user has complained to you that her machine is very slow and some applications do not work. Upon inspection, you find that the device driver is the cause of errors that appear in the event log every five seconds. You try to uninstall or roll back the device driver but the machine just hangs. What should you do?

    A. Give the user a new computer.

    B. Open Device Manager, disable the driver, and then restart.

    C. Start the computer in Safe Mode With Networking.

    D. Start the computer in Safe mode Without Networking.

15. Which of the following creates a special copy of a document that contains programming codes that tell the printer what to do so that the document it prints looks like the document that you printed?

    A. Print queue

    B. Print spooler

    C. Print driver

    D. Print port

16. You installed a new printer on the network, connected it to a print server, and set up permissions so that everyone can print. However, for some reason when users try to find the printer they don't see it on the network. What could be the reason the printer is not found?

    A. The users are on another network segment.

    B. The printer has not been shared.

    C. The users are too far away.

    D. The printer has been turned off.

17. For many small workgroup printers, you have several options of networking the printer with various port technologies. Which ones are valid printer ports?

    A. Bluetooth

    B. USB

    C. Ethernet Port

    D. All of the above

18. Which of the following resources on a Windows 8.1 machine would need a device driver to work? (Choose two.)

    A. The Calculator

    B. The mouse

    C. A scanner

    D. A hard disk drive

19. Which of the following is used to manage print jobs?

    A. Print queue

    B. Print spooler

    C. Print driver

    D. Print port

20. Which feature enables you to select different default printers for different networks?

    A. Location-Aware Printing

    B. NFC Tap-to-Pair

    C. v4 architecture

    D. HomeGroups

Chapter

12

Monitoring System Performance and Recovery

70-687 MICROSOFT EXAM OBJECTIVES COVERED IN THIS CHAPTER:

- Monitor system performance
- Configure and analyze event logs, configure event subscriptions, configure Task Manager, monitor system resources, optimize networking performance, configure indexing options
- Configure system recovery
- Configure system restore, perform a refresh or recycle, configure restore points

70-688 MICROSOFT EXAM OBJECTIVES COVERED IN THIS CHAPTER:

- Support operating system and hardware
- Resolve hardware and device issues, including STOP errors and Reliability Monitor
- Optimize performance by using Windows Performance Toolkit (WPT), including Xperf.exe, Xbootmgr.exe, XperfView.exe, and Windows Performance Recorder (WPR)
- Monitor performance by using Data Collector Sets, Task Manager, and Resource Monitor
- Remediate startup issues by using the Diagnostics and Recovery Toolkit (DaRT)

Today's computers need very little maintenance. It was not too long ago that our desktop and server computers contained moving parts or components that deteriorated with use and heat. These included hard disks, floppy disks, fans, and memory chips. Today they have practically no moving parts, but they tend to get bogged down with too much information and data. Disks get fragmented, and it makes access to the data harder for the computer—which means it takes longer to access data or make computations. And with our systems constantly connected to networks, network traffic can have a significant impact on performance.

When you look inside your system, desktop or server, you see your motherboard and the cables that connect the disks to the motherboard; however, the two main components inside the device—desktop, server, or handheld—are your CPU and RAM. These two component systems are responsible for how fast and efficiently your computer runs.

Notice that we talk about component systems here because CPUs and memory components are not necessarily two single components but a collection of memory and processing electronics. CPU speed is as of this edition of Windows still measured in gigahertz (GHz) and billions of instructions per second whereas RAM is still measured in megabytes (MB) or gigabytes (GB).

For a quick glance at what's inside your computer, open File Explorer and right-click on This PC to choose Properties. Alternatively, you can pop up the Charms searcher and type **sys**. In Settings, click System to open the Control Panel applet. In Control Panel, the System applet will tell you some basic things about the computer as well as what version of Windows the computer is running.

To see detailed system information, open the Run dialog box from the Start menu, type **msinfo32**, and press Enter. This will launch the System Information applet. For more detailed and critical use you need to turn to Task Manager, Performance Monitor, and Resource Monitor.

Using Task Manager

Task Manager is used to view and manage the programs that are running on your machine and the processes that are working in the background. With Task Manager you are also able to assess system performance, on both the computer and the network.

Reviewing the Enhancements

If you are familiar with Task Manager, you will notice some changes from previous editions. In Windows 8.1 it is a much improved and updated utility.

Task Manager can be started as follows:

- Press Ctrl+Alt+Del and then click Task Manager. This usually works when a computer has become unresponsive.
- Right-click the Time and Date section in the right corner of the taskbar or any free spot on the taskbar.
- On the Charms bar, click Search, and type **task**. You can then click the Task Manager on the Apps screen.

Any one of these steps will display the new Task Manager and app and programs that are running. Figure 12.1 shows Task Manager with a number of applications running.

FIGURE 12.1   Task Manager

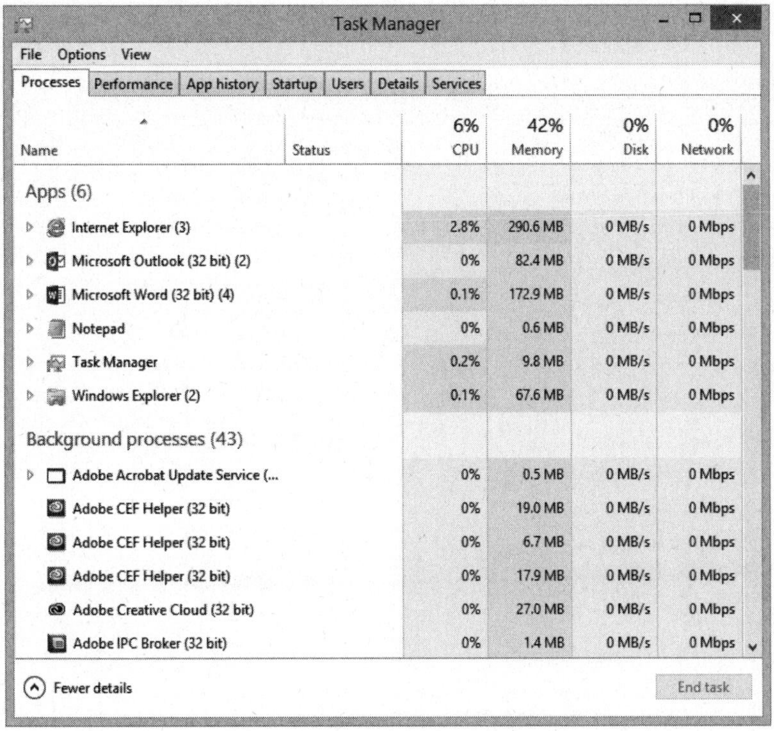

Task Manager

Task Manager works just like any other Windows application or applet. When loaded, it puts an icon on the taskbar. A nice feature of this application is that you can configure it to always stay on top. So if you are busy troubleshooting or managing the computer, Task Manager will not get lost behind other windows.

To configure Task Manager to stay on top, choose select Always On Top from the Options menu.

Task Manager Views

Task Manager gives you the choice of showing only the list of applications that are running (see Figure 12.2). You can also show multiple tabs loaded with all manner of system and application data, as shown in Figure 12.2. You can decide to view more or less data in the views. You can stop an application in either view.

FIGURE 12.2   Task Manager in detailed view

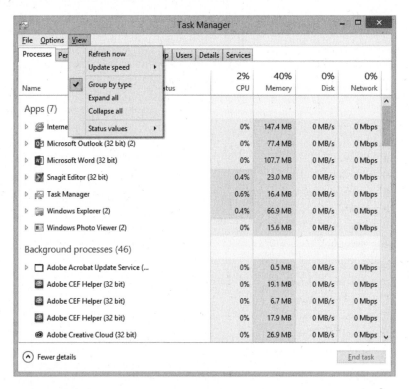

To toggle between the views, click the More Details button at the bottom of Task Manager. You can choose from the following options:

Always On Top   This option makes sure Task Manager is always the top window.

Minimize On Use   This option ensures Task Manager is minimized whenever you switch to another application.

Hide When Minimized   This option hides the button on the taskbar when chosen.

Show Full Account Name   This option shows the full username in the User column.

Show History For All Processes   This option becomes available when you select the App History tab. It displays the history for the past month of a running process.

When Task Manager is up, it puts a box or icon next to the task in the notification area at the bottom right of the bar. When you click on that little box, it will display some critical facts to you about the system, such as CPU, memory, and disk and network usage. This is shown in Figure 12.3.

FIGURE 12.3   Task Manager's notification icon

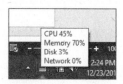

Let's now look at the View menu. You have the following options:

Refresh Now   Refreshes Task Manager data immediately, and ignores the Update Speed setting.

Update Speed   Update Speed tells Task Manger how often to update information to the screen. You have the follow settings:

High   Task Manager updates twice per second.

Normal   Task Manager updates every two seconds.

Low   Task Manager updates every four seconds.

Paused   Task Manager updates when you choose View ➢ Refresh Now.

Group By Type   This option will group all apps, Windows processes, and background processes by type.

Expand All   This option expands the lists of apps and processes so that open documents, open websites (when browsers are running), and other subprocesses are displayed.

Collapse All   This option collapses the list of running apps and processes.

Status Values   This option displays on the Processes tab only and shows the status of suspended processes if set to show these values

Well, that wraps up how you can configure Task Manager. So now what can you really use it for besides just viewing data?

Using Task Manager

When a computer is hanging or not responsive and you cannot switch between applications or get anything to work, pressing Ctrl+Alt+Del and then selecting Task Manager will likely be your only recourse.

Choose the Details tab, as shown in Figure 12.4, and you will be able to see which program is causing problems. A clue will be that the Status column will indicate that the application is hung. The status will be marked as Not Responding.

To close the application, select it in the Name column and then click the End Task button at the bottom right of the window. You may get a chance to recover the application, but if nothing happens you can click the End Process option, which will shut down the application. The application will either restart or shut down completely depending on how it is configured.

FIGURE 12.4   Task Manager's Details tab

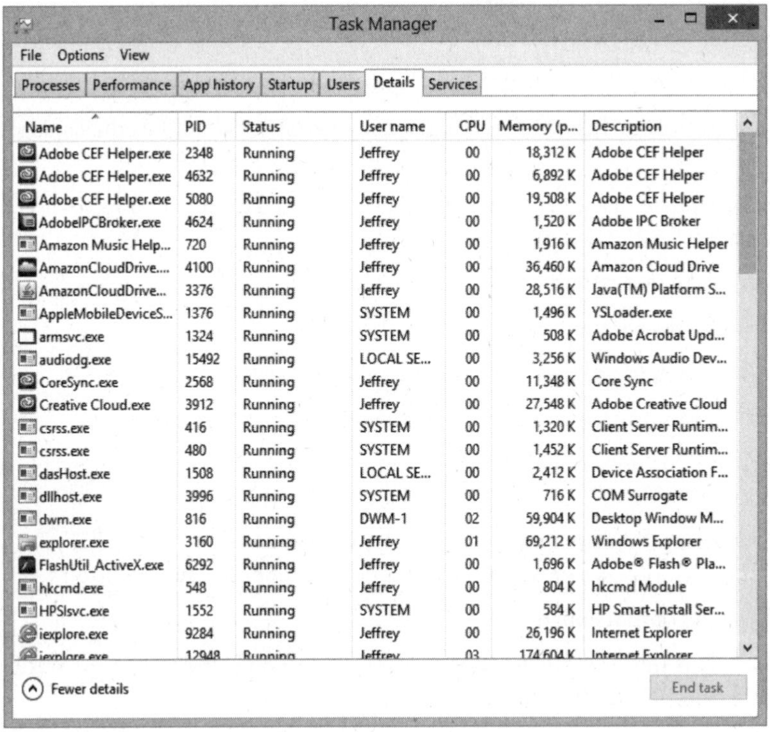

Using Task Manager for Performance Monitoring

Task Manager's Performance tab lets you check how resources on the computer are being used. Figure 12.5 shows you the key resources. You can view the data both as graphical and numeric summaries. The summaries will show CPU, memory, and disk and network usage in detail.

FIGURE 12.5   Task Manager's Performance tab

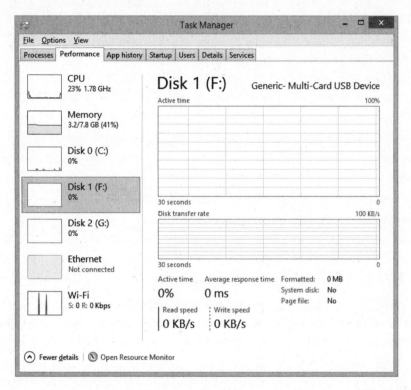

Resources you can monitor include the following:

CPU   Presents you with data about the CPU. This data includes utilization, speed, processes, threads, handles, and uptime. The bar graph also presents you with a 60-second snapshot of CPU usage. See Figure 12.6. Note the initial spike when Task Manager was started.

FIGURE 12.6 Task Manager CPU usage

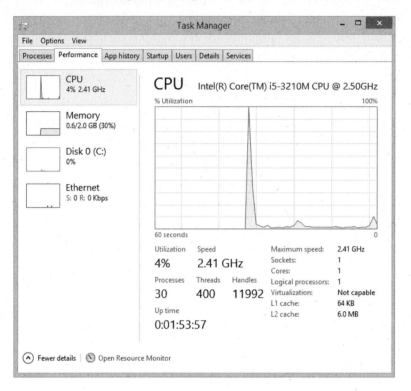

Memory Presents you with data about the RAM in the computer. It shows you the amount of RAM in use, what is committed and to where, the total memory (RAM plus virtual memory), cached memory, the Windows page pool, and the non-page pool. See Figure 12.7.

Disk Displays data about the hard disks on the computer. The information shown includes disk transfer rate, active time in percentage, average response time, disk read speed, and disk write speed. See Figure 12.8. Note the disk is working at 100%.

FIGURE 12.7   Task Manager memory usage

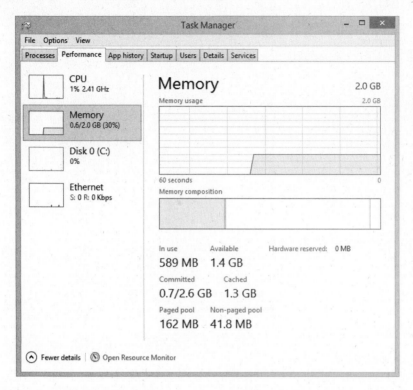

Ethernet   Displays data about any Ethernet interfaces on the computer, shows the adaptor name, confection type, IPv4 and IPv6 addresses, and Kbps sent and received. In Figure 12.9, note that no NIC activity is occurring now but there was activity about 30 seconds ago.

FIGURE 12.8   Task Manager Disk data

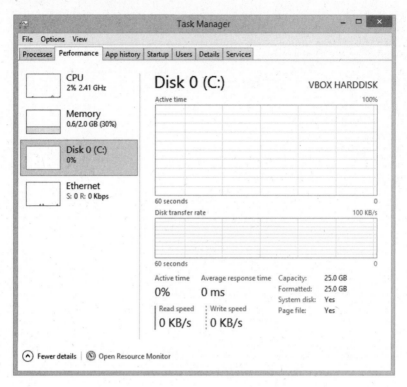

Bluetooth   Displays performance data about your Bluetooth devices.

Wi-Fi   Displays data about the wireless network devices installed on the computer. It shows both send and receive data (see Figure 12.10).

FIGURE 12.9   Task Manager Ethernet data

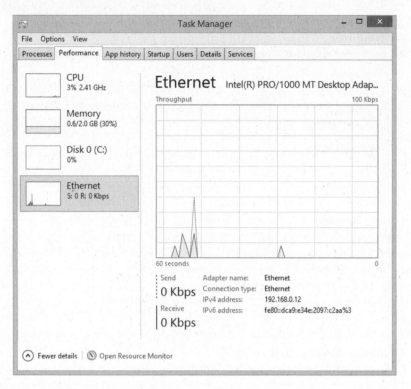

Configuring Startup Options

The Startup tab is new in Task Manager in Windows 8/8.1 and allows you to specify which programs start when the system boots. In earlier versions of Windows you could do this using MSConfig, but you can no longer do that. Figure 12.11 shows the Startup tab and the list of applications that will start at bootup time. The example in Figure 12.11 shows that only one application will start when the operating system boots up.

FIGURE 12.10   Task Manager showing Wi-Fi data

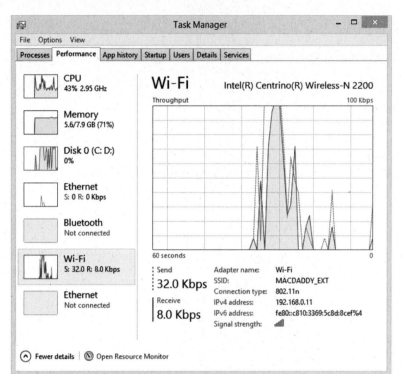

The default columns on this tab are the first four in the following list. The others can be added at any time.

Name   Indicates the name of the program that starts automatically.

Publisher   Displays the name of the company that produces the program.

FIGURE 12.11   Task Manager's Startup tab

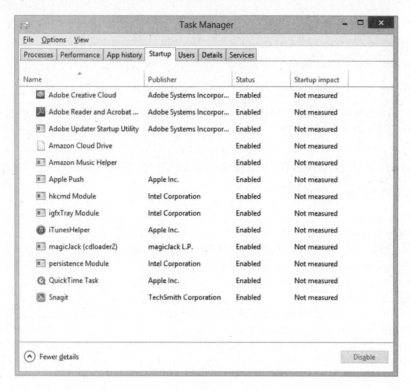

Status   Shows whether the program is enabled or disabled. Enabled means the program or app will start when the OS boots up.

Startup Impact   Indicates the cost on performance the program will have when the OS boots.

Startup Type   Shows the type of app that starts, such as one that is hidden (such as running from a Registry key), or one that launches from the interface.

Disk I/O At Startup   Displays the amount of memory used at startup by the app.

CPU At Startup   Displays the amount of CPU resources used at startup by the app.

Running Now   Lists only those apps currently running under Windows.

Disabled Time   Lists the amount of time the app is disabled.

Command Line   Shows the hard drive path of the listed app.

To prevent the application from starting when the operating system boots up, select it and then click the Disable button.

Remediating Startup Issues by Using the Diagnostics and Recovery Toolkit

Microsoft Diagnostics and Recovery Toolset (DaRT) 8.1 lets you diagnose and repair a computer that cannot be started or that has problems starting as expected. It is a part of the Microsoft Desktop Optimization Pack (MDOP), a dynamic solution that helps reduce software installation costs, enables delivery of applications as services, and helps manage and control enterprise desktop environments.

Although this tool can do many more things, our focus here is that DaRT 8.1 lets you create a recovery image in ISO and WIM file formats and burn the image to a CD, DVD, or USB. You can then use the recovery image files and deploy them locally or to a remote partition or a recovery partition. To download DaRT 8.1 and MDOP, you need a Microsoft account. The details of deploying it, and using it to create recovery images and diagnose startup issues, are beyond the scope of this book. For more information see
https://technet.microsoft.com/en-us/library/hh563900.aspx.

Using Event Viewer

The Windows 8.1 event logs are XML files used to record significant events that are fired on your system. The number of events that can be raised and written to the log files is enormous. From startup to shutdown, just about everything you or a program does on the computer can be logged to the event log. The Event Viewer program lets you view the log and read the event information. Each event logs specific data that can be used for information or troubleshooting system problems.

Event Viewer logs information to a variety of logs. The Windows logs include the following:

Application (Program) Events   Events are classified as Error, Warning, or Information. The more severe the event, the higher the level of concern, with Error the highest and Information the lowest. The Warning event should be taken as an indication that there may be something more serious in the works that will lead to an event. A good example may be a warning that an autosave feature on some program has failed due to a hardware issue, such as network connections or a full hard disk. The Information event typically describes the successful operation of a program, driver, or service.

Security Events   These events are known as audits and are described as successful or failed depending on the event. These are typically configured in Group Policy. A good example of a security event is a user trying to log on to the computer.

System Events   System events are logged by Windows and Windows system services, and are classified as Error, Warning, or Information.

Forwarded Events   These events come from other systems but are written to the local event log.

Application and service logs vary. They include separate logs about the programs that run on your computer, as well as more detailed logs that pertain to specific Windows services.

To view events, open Event Viewer by right-clicking the Start menu and then double-clicking Event Viewer. To see the event list, click an event log in the left pane. The list of events appears in the right pane; you can sort the list by ascending or descending order. Double-click an event to view its details, as shown in Figure 12.12.

FIGURE 12.12   Details of an event

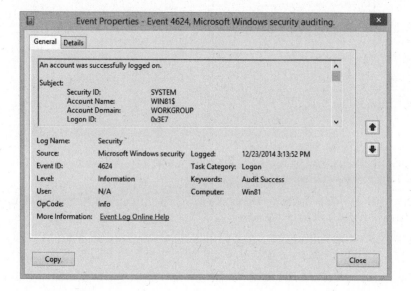

Configuring Event Logs

There are several properties you can set for each event log that you probably will want to address and not leave at the defaults. The two most important things to set are the maximum size allowed for the log and the action you would like the system to take if the log gets full. You can modify both of these settings by right-clicking the log in Event Viewer and selecting Properties from the context menu. The box shown in Figure 12.13 appears.

FIGURE 12.13   Security Log Properties

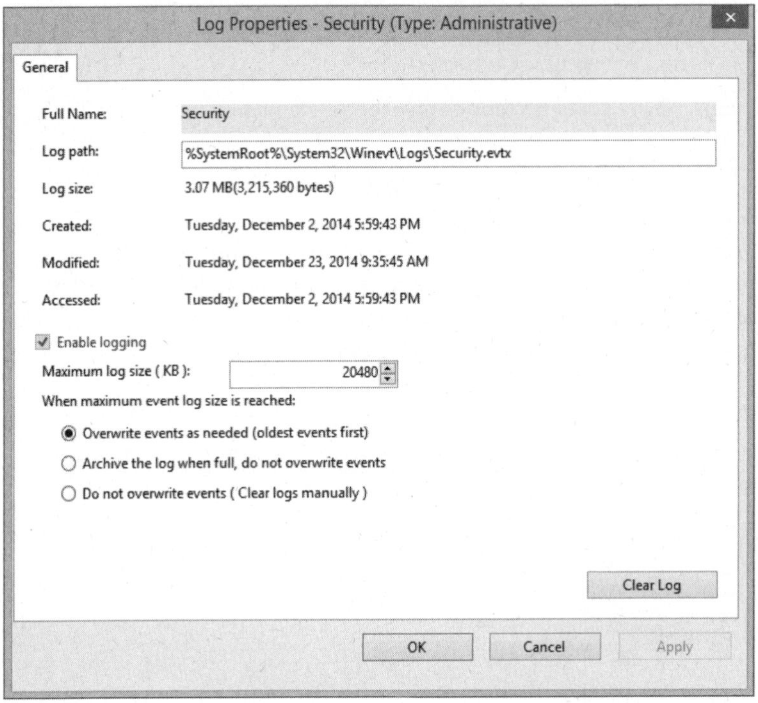

Set the maximum log size by using the Maximum Log Size (KB) spinner box. You have three choices as to how you would like system to react to a full log:

Overwrite Events As Needed (Oldest Events First)   This option will start deleting the oldest events as needed when the log is full.

Archive The Log When Full, Do Not Overwrite Events   This option creates a copy of the current log file as a file and clears the log.

Do Not Overwrite Events (Clear Logs Manually)   This option takes no action and stops collecting events until you delete some events.

Analyzing Event Logs

Understanding how to read the details of an event is an important skill. Let's look at a typical event, shown in Figure 12.14.

FIGURE 12.14   Typical security event

The information concerning this event is organized as follows:

Log Name   This is the log from which the event came; in this case, it's Security.

Source   This is the component that reported the event; in this case, it's Windows Security.

Event ID   All events have an ID that identifies the type of event; in this case, it is 4624.

Level   This indicates the type or severity of the event; our example is an Information event. The five possible event levels are as follows:

Error   An event that indicates a significant problem such as loss of data or loss of functionality. For example, if a service fails to load during startup, an Error event is logged.

Warning   An event that is not necessarily significant but that may indicate a future problem. For example, when disk space is low, a Warning event is logged. If an application can recover from an event without loss of functionality or data, it can generally classify the event as a Warning event.

Information   An event that describes the successful operation of an application, driver, or service. For example, when a network driver loads successfully, it may be appropriate to log an Information event. Note that it is generally inappropriate for a desktop application to log an event each time it starts.

Success Audit   An event that records an audited security access attempt that is successful. For example, a user's successful attempt to log on to the system is logged as a Success Audit event.

Failure Audit   An event that records an audited security access attempt that fails. For example, if a user tries to access a network drive and fails, the attempt is logged as a Failure Audit event.

User   This is the user performing the action (not applicable in our example).

OpCode   Providers use opcodes to logically group events; in this case, it is Info.

Logged   This gives the date and time of the event.

Task Category   This is the category to which the task belongs; in this case, it's the Logon category.

Keywords   Use this to search for all events of this type.

Computer   This identifies the device on which the event occurred; in this case, it was a computer named Win81.

Configuring Event Subscriptions

Troubleshooting an issue might require you to examine a set of events stored in multiple logs on multiple computers. Rather than physically going to each machine and analyzing or copying its log, you can configure what are called *event subscriptions*. The subscription is configured on the computer where you want to collect the events. Exercise 12.1 shows you how to configure a subscription to a log on another computer.

EXERCISE 12.1

Configuring Event Subscriptions

1. On the collector computer, run Event Viewer as an administrator.

2. Click Subscriptions in the console tree. If the Windows Event Collector service is not started, you will be prompted to confirm that you want to start it.

3. On the Actions menu, click Create Subscription.

4. In the Subscription Name box, type a name for the subscription.

5. In the Description box, you can enter a description, although that's optional.

6. In the Destination Log box, select the log file where collected events are to be stored. By default, collected events are stored in the Forwarded Events log.

7. Click Add, and select the computers from which events are to be collected.

8. Click Select Events to display the Query Filter dialog box. Use the controls in the Query Filter dialog box to specify the criteria that events must meet to be collected. Here, we have selected only Critical and Error events from the Application and Security logs.

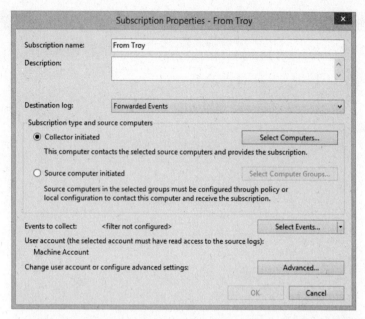

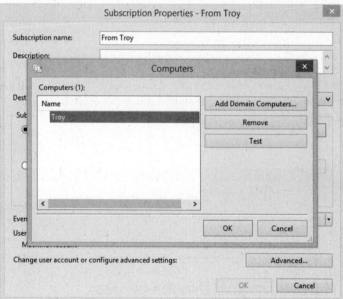

EXERCISE 12.1 *(continued)*

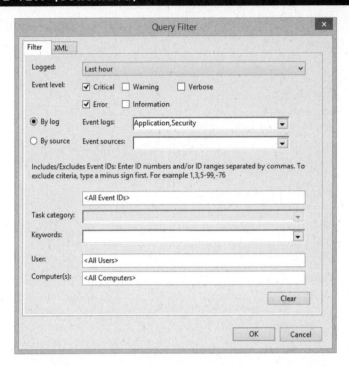

9. Click OK on the Subscription Properties dialog box. The subscription will be added to the Subscriptions pane and, if the operation was successful, the status of the subscription will be Active.

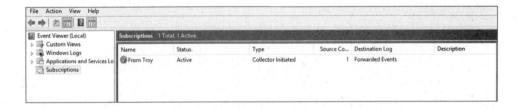

Resolving Hardware and Device Issues

In many cases the system may suffer an issue that causes it to generate a STOP error or "Blue Screen of Death." Although these error messages are certainly scary (if not always as serious as they first appear), there are also many other less serious (and certainly not as dramatic) problems that cause computers to run slow or not as well as they should. In this section, we'll look at those two extremes: resolving STOP error messages and using a tool called Reliability Monitor to troubleshoot less serious issues.

STOP Errors

STOP error messages have been the Windows operating systems method of communicating problems since the days of Windows 95 and can occur if a serious problem causes Windows to shut down or restart unexpectedly. These issues can be rooted in both hardware and software and in many cases resolve themselves during restart.

If you recently added new hardware before the Blue Screen error, shut down, remove the hardware, and try restarting. If restarting is problematic, try to start the computer in Safe Mode, which is one of the startup options (formerly called Advanced Boot options) discussed later in this chapter in the section "Troubleshooting Boot Issues." Finally, when software updates or installations are causing the issue, it may be necessary to "reverse the damage" by using the System Restore utility, discussed in the section "Using System Recovery Options" later in this chapter.

Reliability Monitor

Windows 8.1 supports Reliability Monitor, but you may find that accessing it is a bit different than in earlier versions of Windows. This utility assesses the overall health of the system and arrives at what is called a *stability index*. This value on a scale of 1 to 10 is positively and negatively affected by the events that occur. It charts the movement of the index over time and correlates it to five types of events:

- Informational events
- Warning events
- Miscellaneous errors
- Windows failures
- Application failures

By using the Reliability Monitor dashboard, shown in Figure 12.15, you can see the effect that certain events have on the index value. When you highlight a day in the console (for example, December 27 in Figure 12.15), details about the events that occurred that day are shown the details pane at the bottom of the dashboard (in this case, a successful update of the Windows Defender definitions).

To access Reliability Monitor in Windows 8.1, type **permon /rel** in the Run box and you'll see the screen in Figure 12.15. You can use the Check For Solutions To All Problems option at the bottom of the dashboard to view any solutions that have been found. If there are none, you will see the message shown in Figure 12.16, and you may be alerted later by the Action Center that a solution has been found.

FIGURE 12.15 Reliability Monitor

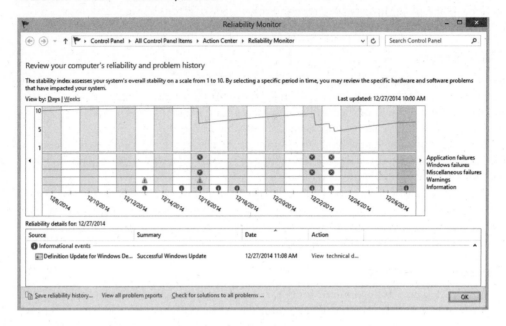

FIGURE 12.16 No new solutions message

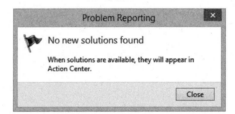

Using Performance Monitor

Task Manager can be used to identify services and applications that may be monopolizing the resources of the computer and can allow you to stop the guilty processes. Windows 8.1 includes other tools to help you monitor and tune your system's performance. Another utility you will also be tested on is one that will help you keep your system running at its optimum level: Performance Monitor.

Performance Monitor, or perfmon as it has been known for more than a decade, provides a way for you to fix and monitor performance counters on your computer. To start

Performance Monitor at the Run box, type **perfmon** and press Enter. Performance Monitor will launch, as you can see in Figure 12.17.

FIGURE 12.17   Performance Monitor

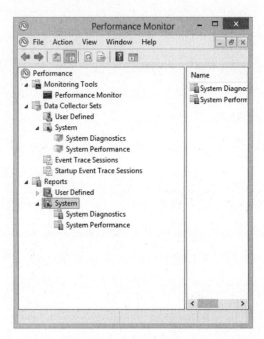

An alternate way of accessing Performance Monitor is to go to Settings Search (Windows Key + W), search for "performance," and select Performance Information And Tools. Under Advanced Tools, select Open Performance Monitor.

When Performance Monitor starts, it shows the Performance branch in the left pane. The pane displays general information about the program, a system summary, and links that can assist you in using Performance Monitor.

System Summary is just a snapshot, albeit a useful one. To see a visual presentation of the snapshot data, click Performance Monitor under the Monitoring Tools branch in the left pane (see Figure 12.18).

The most noticeable feature of Performance Monitor is the graph line that you see traveling across the window as it tracks aspects of your computer's operations. This line tracks your system's CPU activity by default, but it can show activity for a variety of things, such as network usage and memory.

The graph indicates time along its x-axis and percentage on the y-axis. To make decisions about your system's performance, you need to add more counters to the monitor in order to track performance relative to the other components. Exercise 12.2 shows how to add more counters to the graph.

FIGURE 12.18   Performance graphs

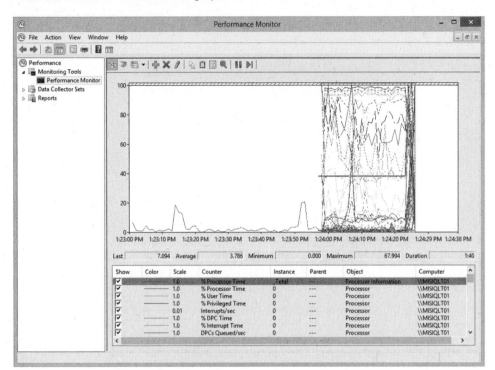

EXERCISE 12.2

Adding Counters to the Performance Monitor Graph

1. Click in the toolbar located just above the monitor window.

2. The Add Counters dialog box pops up and offers the available performance objects you can choose for your system. Click the arrow to the right of the performance objects. This will expand and display the available counters for that object. In the example shown, we selected BitLocker.

   Some options will show more than one instance of the counter depending on the hardware installed. For example, you may have more than one drive on the computer and thus you will get the option to select more than one instance of the counter, one for each drive. The example shows BitLocker selected for All Instances, which means for all drives where it is enabled.

3. Select the Show Description check box in the bottom-left corner of the Add Counters dialog box to view additional information about the counter.

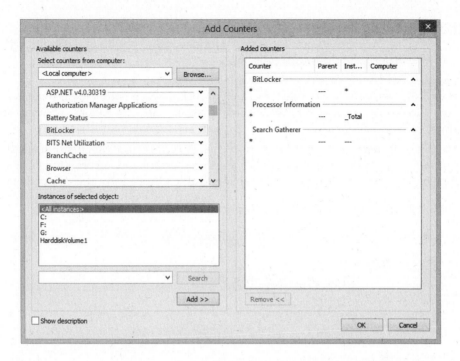

4. To add another counter, select it and click Add to move it to the Added Counters section of the window. Once you have added all the counters you want to monitor, click OK. You will be returned to the monitor pane and the new counters' lines will appear on the graph.

5. The counters are differentiated by color. The counter also appears the bottom of the window. Select the counter in the list and then click the highlighter icon in the toolbar. This will highlight the chosen counter. Once the highlighter is turned on, clicking any counter in the list will highlight the respective counter.

Data Collector Sets

Performance Monitor provides a mechanism for logging the information and events that occur on the system. *Data collector sets* are sets of objects that collect data about your computer. You can create a data collector set to collect data about specific items. For example, a network data collector set can be created to let you collect information about network performance issues. This can be done with a variety of network counters in the set. In another example, you can create a data collector set to analyze drive performance by choosing additional drives for each drive in your system.

The following steps will guide you through the operation of a data collector set:

1. Click the arrow to the left of Data Collector Sets. This expands the tree. Next, expand the System icon beneath Data Collector Sets and click System Performance.

2.   Right-click System Performance and choose Start. You can also click the Start button in the toolbar. As soon as you click Start, Performance Monitor begins collecting data for the components of the started collector.

3.   Give the system some time to gather data and then right-click System Performance again. Now you will choose Stop. You can also click the Stop button in the toolbar. The collector will not stop immediately because of lag time with data in its buffers, so give it a few seconds.

4.   You can now view reports in the Reports section in Performance Monitor. Expand the System branch, as shown in Figure 12.19. Here one performance report is available and the report has been opened so you can see the wealth of troubleshooting information.

FIGURE 12.19   Performance Monitor Reports

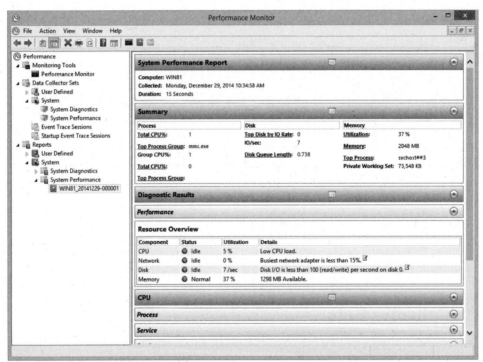

5.   Expand or collapse different parts of the report by clicking the arrows next to each group.

Creating custom data collector sets involves creating your own user-defined data collector sets. This will entail adding data from one of the four categories. To do this, you will open the properties window of the collector and set a collection of properties for each type.

The following four types of data collectors can be added to your custom data collector sets:

Performance Counter Data   The data collected here is the same data that is shown to you by default in Performance Monitor.

Event Trace Data   As certain events are fired in the system, this collector collects them.

Configuration Data   When you modify the system configuration, this collector collects Registry changes.

Performance Counter Alert   You can collect data from a performance counter that reaches a specific point either above or below a value that you define.

To create your data collector set, perform the following steps:

1. Open Performance Monitor and expand the Data Collector Sets branch. Now right-click User Defined and choose New ➤ Data Collector Set. This will start the Create New Data Collector Set wizard (see Figure 12.20).

FIGURE 12.20   The Data Collector Set wizard

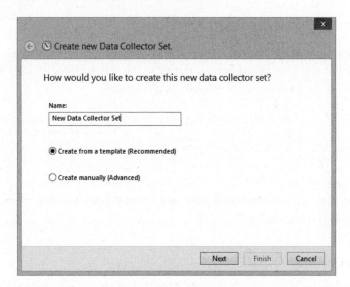

2. Enter a name for the set in the Name text box.

3. At this point you can decide to create the data collector set from a template or manually. Choose Create From A Template so you can add data collectors to the ones already in the template. Click Next.

4. The wizard prompts you to choose a type of data collector. Choose Basic from the list of templates and click Next.

5. Once you provide the location folder where the data will be stored, click Next, and then click Finish.

The new data collector is then added to the User Defined branch in the left pane of the monitor. To add additional collectors to the set, click on the new data collector set's name in the left pane or right-click it in the right pane and choose New ➤ Data Collector. It is important to note that these saved collectors must be started and then stopped to collect any data and generate a report.

It is also possible to set properties of the collector set after creation by right-clicking the set and choosing Properties. Among the options you can set on the tabs provided are the following:

- Set a start day and time (Schedule tab)
- Set a stop day and time (Schedule tab)
- Set a length of time for the collector to run (Stop Condition tab)
- Set a limit to the amount of space used for the data collected (Stop Condition tab)
- Set a task to be performed after the collector set stops (Task tab)

Accessing and Using Reports

With the information logged, you can open reports containing the logged data and use them to help troubleshoot system problems. To open and view reports, follow these steps:

1. Open Performance Monitor using your method of choice.

2. Expand the Reports section.

3. Expand the node under which the report is located. If it is User Defined, expand that node; if it is a default report; expand System.

4. If the set is under User Defined, double-click or right-click it and choose View. If it is under System, expand either System Diagnostics or System Performance, depending on the type it is; right-click the report; and select View. If nothing appears in the right-hand pane, the set needs to be run.

Using Resource Monitor

Resource Monitor is another tool in Windows 8.1 that lets you monitor and troubleshoot your computer system. It also displays real-time information about the CPU, disk, network, and memory.

Resource Monitor (see Figure 12.21) is accessed by selecting Administrative Tools in Control Panel and then selecting Resource Monitor. Resource Monitor can also be launched from the command line by running **resmon** and selecting Open Resource Monitor at the bottom of the Performance tab in Task Manager.

You can view summary information about each of the four performance groups from the Overview tab, as shown in Figure 12.21. To monitor a process, select the check box in the CPU list next to the process's name. Click the category header for a category. This lets you view the data filtered by the selected process.

The other tabs in Resource Monitor show data that is related to the specific category you are monitoring. For example, if you need to see information about memory utilization, then select the Memory tab. The running processes of each category are shown in the top area of Resource Monitor.

FIGURE 12.21   Resource Monitor

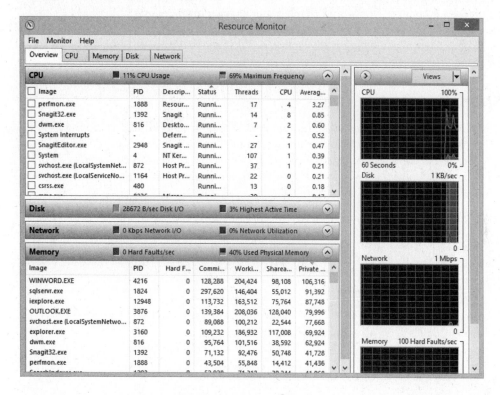

Resources can be filtered to show only what you need to see. You can select and deselect the processes from the list as needed.

Optimizing Performance by Using Windows Performance Toolkit

The Windows Performance Toolkit consists of performance monitoring tools that produce in-depth performance profiles of Windows operating systems and applications. Though not included in Windows 8.1, it is a free download at www.microsoft.com/en-US/download/details.aspx?id=39982. In this section, we'll look at four tools within the WPT.

Xperf.exe

Once the WPT is installed, the Xperf.exe command-line utility will be operational at the administrator Command prompt. This tool can be used to capture and analyze event traces. First, the tool is enabled and then the activity of interest is initiated. For example, if the browser is hanging, you would enable Event Tracing for Windows (ETW) using xperf and then attempt to open the browser. Information would then be gathered that can be analyzed. ETW lets you dynamically enable/disable logging without having to restart the system and/or application.

XperfView.exe

Closely associated with `Xperf.exe`, the `XperView.exe` utility is used to analyze the performance data collection from a previous run of `Xperf.exe`. It is designed to simplify the collection and analysis of performance data. Moreover, it also can collect data from the .NET Garbage Collector (GC) heap. Use of this tool is beyond the scope of this book, but Figure 12.22 shows the tool once installed.

FIGURE 12.22   XperfView tool

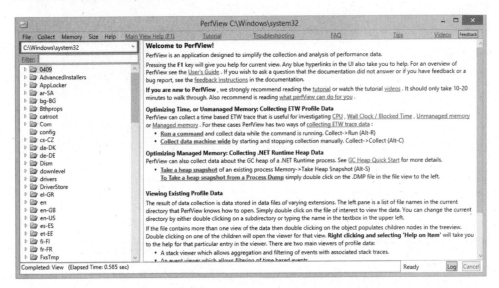

Xbootmgr.exe

Another command-line utility that uses information derived from `Xperf.exe` is `Xbootmgr.exe`. Like Xperf, it will be operational at the administrator Command prompt once the WPT is installed. This tool can be used to analyze startup problems. `Xbootmgr.exe` lets admins gather boot-time statistics and analyze data with Xperf.

From the command prompt, execute the `Xbootmgr.exe` tool to initiate a reboot and collect ETL data for later analysis. For example, the command

```
Xbootmgr -Trace Boot -TraceFlags  DIAG+DRIVERS+POWER+REGISTRY
```

will start a trace and reboot the machine. When it reboots, it will analyze the process and gather information for you about the process after the reboot.

Use the following command to view the data:

```
Xperf Boot_DIAG+DRIVERS+POWER+REGISTRY_1.etl
```

This command will open the trace file using XperfView.exe. Analysis is beyond the scope of this text, but Figure 12.23 shows the events that occurred. In the selected view (which is only one of many), each stage of the boot process is shown along with the time taken for each stage.

FIGURE 12.23   Viewing the trace from Xbootmgr.exe

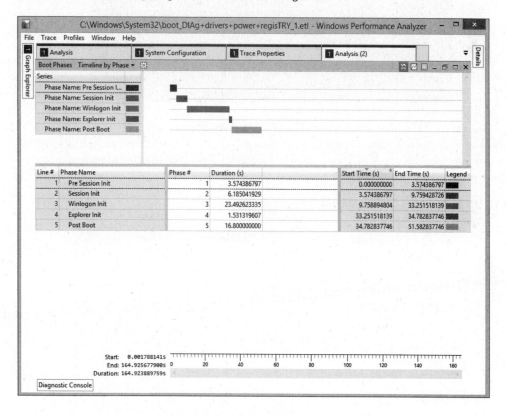

Windows Performance Recorder

The tool Windows Performance Recorder (WPR) can be used to gather information about an error situation that can be viewed and analyzed later using Windows Performance

Analyzer. Once the WPT is installed, WPR will be available as an icon in the Windows Kits section of Apps on the Windows 8.1 Start screen, as shown in Figure 12.24.

FIGURE 12.24 Windows Performance Recorder

Using the tool is quite simple; just click the Windows Performance Recorder icon, and select to start the recording. Then perform the problematic activity. For example, I selected to start my browser and when it was finished opening, I stopped the recording and added a description (Slow Browser) to the generated file, as shown in Figure 12.25.

FIGURE 12.25 Saving the recording file

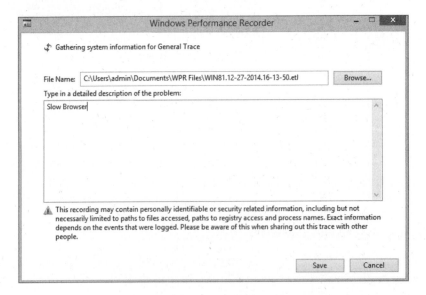

When the file is saved, it will offer me the option of opening it with the Windows Performance Analyzer. The file, opened in WPA, is shown in Figure 12.26.

FIGURE 12.26   Viewing the recording file

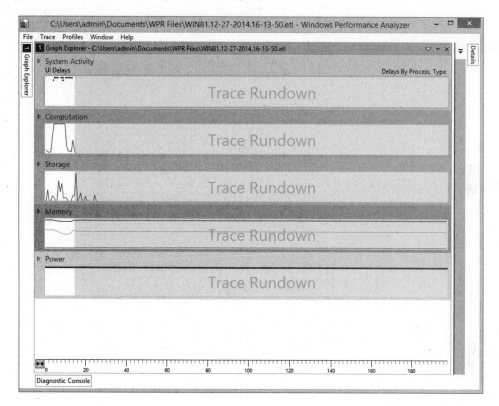

Troubleshooting Boot Issues

Hardware errors are such that even a tiny error can cause a disaster that can have devastating results. They can cause the system to suddenly shut down and make it difficult to get the system started again. Clean booting can also help with software problems that prevent the computer from starting normally or cause frequent errors. However, there will come times when you may have to do a clean boot of your computer.

The procedure for performing a clean boot is as follows:

1. Close all open programs and save any work in progress.

2. At the Windows Desktop, press Windows+X, click Run, and enter **msconfig**.

3. The System Configuration tool opens, as shown in Figure 12.27.

FIGURE 12.27 System Configuration

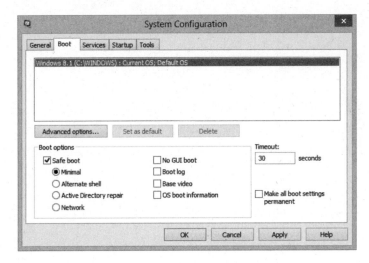

4. On the General tab, choose Selective Startup and make sure the Load Startup Items check box is cleared.

5. Click the Services tab.

6. Select Hide All Microsoft Services and click the Disable All button.

7. Click OK.

8. Click the Restart button.

To return to normal startup after diagnosis, open the System Configuration tool. On the Services tab, click Enable All. On the General tab, choose Normal Startup and click OK.

Using System Recovery Options

In Chapter 11, "Managing Windows 8.1 Hardware and Printers," we took a brief look at the Update And Recovery section of PC Settings when we were setting the system to allow unsigned drivers. As a refresher, the Update And Recovery screen has a selection at the bottom of the list called Recovery. The options when this is highlighted are shown in Figure 12.28.

FIGURE 12.28   Recovery Options

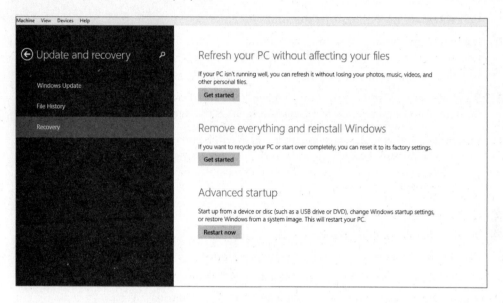

Here you can do three things:

Refresh The PC   This option refreshes all the system files without touching your settings or data. In cases where the system is not running well, this may solve the problem. It may require the installation media that came with the PC. Applications you've installed from websites and DVDs will be removed. Applications that came with your PC and apps you've installed from the Windows Store will be reinstalled. Windows puts a list of removed applications on your Desktop after refreshing your PC.

Reset The PC   This option reinstalls Windows and *deletes* all data.

Restore The PC To An Earlier Point In Time Using Restore Points (not available in Windows RT 8.1)   This option also changes only settings and not data. For example, if it is restored to a time previous to an update, the update will not be present but any data created since the restore point was created will still be there. To perform a system refresh:

1. Under Refresh Your PC Without Affecting Your Files, select Get Started.

2. If any files are missing, Windows will prompt you and you must provide the installation media in the form of a DVD or a USB stick.

    You will be informed what will occur. Then the PC will restart.

3. When the system restarts, it will perform the refresh. When it's done, you can log in and the system will display the browser with a list of any programs that need to be reinstalled.

To perform a system reset:

1. Under Remove Everything And Reinstall Windows, select Get Started.

2. If any files are missing, Windows will prompt you and you must provide the installation media in the form of a DVD or a USB stick.

   Windows will inform you that all data will be removed and the system reinstalled.

3. Windows will ask you if you want to quickly remove the data or thoroughly remove the data. Thorough takes several hours but makes the data very hard to recover.

The system will restart and, when complete, there will be no data present and you'll have a new installation of Windows 8.1 set to factory defaults. You will be required to personalize the system just as you would if it were a new computer. To perform a system restore (to an earlier point in time):

1. Under Advanced Startup, select Get Restart Now.

2. On the Choose An Option screen, select Troubleshoot.

3. On the Troubleshoot screen, select Advanced Options.

4. On the Advanced Options screen, select System Restore.

5. When your username appears, select it and then enter your password.

6. A list of restore points will appear. Select one. The system will restart, and after some time (be patient), you will be presented with a login screen and the computer will be at that state it was when the restore point was taken.

Summary

In this chapter, you learned about the tools available for performance monitoring and troubleshooting in Windows 8.1. Task Manager is used to view and to manage the programs that are running on your machine and the processes that are working in the background.

We looked at Event Viewer, which is used to view the Windows 8.1 event logs. These are special files to which significant events that are fired on your system are written. The operating system, built-in programs, processes, and applications raise events during everyday use. The OS will raise general operating errors and also issue warning and information you can use for troubleshooting. A good example of OS events are security events, such as events when users access certain resources like files in a folder or when they access resources in remote locations, like network file shares.

Performance Monitor was also explored in this chapter. We discussed how it uses special counters to gather information about hardware resources related to CPU, memory, network, and hard disks.

Resource Monitor is part of Performance Monitor, and it lets you monitor and troubleshoot your computer system. It also displays real-time information about the CPU, disk, network, and memory.

We also looked at some system recovery and actions you will take when the computer crashes or you find problems occurring on startup.

Exam Essentials

Understand what Task Manager does and how to use it. You should know what Task Manager does, how to start it up, and how to use it to deal with applications that are not responsive or that processes that need to be stopped. You should know how to use Task Manager to determine which application or processes is causing the computer to become unresponsive.

Understand what the event log is and how to use Event Viewer. Event Viewer is a critical component of the OS, and you should know what information it collects and how applications and processes post events to it. You should also understand what event subscriptions are and how to create them to assist in troubleshooting both the operating system functioning as well as system and independent software vendors' programs.

Understand what Performance Monitor and Resource Monitor are and how to use these tools. Both Performance Monitor and Resource Monitor are essential tools for both troubleshooting and ongoing maintenance of your systems. If you are tasked with supporting a Windows 8.1 machine that is deployed in a mission-critical environment, such as a point-of-sale machine or a workstation that controls machinery, you will need to know how to use these tools to not only keep the machines running at optimum levels but also how to rescue and restore the machine to working condition as soon as possible.

Understand boot options, startup, and System Recovery. You need to know and understand what options you have for bringing back a machine that appears to be dead. Understand the difference between a reset, a refresh, and a restore and how to perform each operation.

Review Questions

You can find the answers in Appendix A.

1. Your computer's application has stopped responding. What should you do?

    A. Run the Event Viewer.

    B. Start backing up like crazy.

    C. Press the Ctrl+Alt+Del key and then click Task Manager.

    D. Restart the computer.

2. Your user tells you that an application is working but the label printer he is using is not working when the application attempts to print labels. What is the first thing you should do to find the problem?

    A. Restart the label printer.

    B. Restart the application.

    C. Buy a new label printer.

    D. Look in the event log for an error.

3. You manage to get Task Manager started, but every time you click on an application Task Manager disappears and you waste time trying to find it under the many applications running. What is the best way to make sure you always have Task Manager in easy reach?

    A. Start a second computer, run Task Manager from it, and connect remotely.

    B. Pin Task Manager to the status bar.

    C. Right-click in any area of Task Manager and select Always On Top.

    D. Simply restart Task Manager.

4. You are tasked with getting a machine up and running as quickly as possible, but it's taking too long for Task Manager to update information and you need instant data after each time you tweak something on the machine. How would you configure Task Manager to give you instant information?

    A. Task Manager updates every 4 seconds and you can't change that.

    B. Click the View tab and select Update Now.

    C. Grab a beer and wait a few more seconds—geez.

    D. On the View tab, choose Manual Update.

5. If a machine is making strange sounds, what areas of hardware performance would Task Manager allow you to assess?

    A. Task Manager gives you critical facts about CPU, memory, disk, and network usage.

    B. Task Manager gives you critical facts about CPU, memory, disks, network usage, and displays.

    C. Task Manager gives you critical facts about CPU, memory, printers, network usage, and displays.

    D. Task Manager gives you critical facts about CPU and memory only.

6. If a machine is making strange sounds, what applications would be best suited to finding out why? (Choose all that apply.)

  A. Task Manager

  B. Event Viewer

  C. Resource Monitor

  D. Paint

7. Which of the following reinstalls Windows and deletes all data?

  A. System Reset

  B. System Restore

  C. System Refresh

  D. System Reimage

8. To see how resources are being used on a machine, which tab in Task Manager should you access?

  A. Performance tab

  B. Hardware tab

  C. Resource Monitor tab

  D. Resources tab

9. How would you configure certain applications to start automatically when the OS boots?

  A. Add the applications startup instructions to the DOS.ini file.

  B. Drag the applications' icons into the startup folder.

  C. Install a batch file and configure it to run when the computer reboots.

  D. Use the Startup tab of Task Manager to enable apps to start when the OS loads.

10. Event Viewer logs information to a variety of logs. These Windows Logs include which of the following?

  A. Application, Security, System

  B. Application, Security, System, Hardware

  C. Application, Security, System, Forwarded

  D. Application, Security, System, User

11. Your user complains that when she comes to work in the morning the applications she left running the night before are closed and it looks like someone was accessing her spreadsheets that keep employee financial data. What would the Security log do for you to try and find out what's going on?

  A. The log would show who was using the system after the rightful owner went home.

  B. The log would show that someone may know the rightful user's password.

  C. The log would show that a remote user may be connecting to the computer illegally.

  D. The log would show that the system was shut down at a certain point in time.

12. To start Performance Monitor from the Run box, what command would you use?

    A. `run pm.msc`

    B. `perfmon`

    C. `monperf`

    D. `monami`

13. What feature of Performance Monitor makes it easy to see at a glance that something is performing very poorly on the computer?

    A. It has a counter that turns red as performance drops.

    B. A bell begins to ring.

    C. The computer calls the service desk.

    D. The main window pane show a graph that represents performance level of a particular domain of hardware.

14. A data collector can be used to gather information about which resources on your computer?

    A. CPU, memory, disk, and network usage

    B. CPU, memory, disk network usage, and application usage

    C. How fast the user can type

    D. The speed of a user-defined stored procedure

15. Which of the following restores the system files to a certain point in time?

    A. System Reset

    B. System Restore

    C. System Refresh

    D. System Reimage

16. A critical program on the workstation seems to act up at different times of the day. How can you use Performance Monitor to gather data without you having to watch the display window 24×7?

    A. Set up a data collector set and start it at 8 a.m. Come back in the afternoon and stop the collecting.

    B. Create a data collector set to begin collecting data as certain events are fired in the system.

    C. Collect data for several days, and then use a report to find the event that can give you clues as to why the machine is acting up.

    D. This feature is only available on Windows Server 2012 R2.

17. To start Resource Monitor from the Run box, what command would you use?

    A. `run rm.msc`

    B. `resmon`

   C. monres

   D. It can only be run from within Performance Monitor.

18. To do a clean reboot of your computer, which app is best suited for this task?

   A. Shutdown

   B. System Configuration

   C. Boot.ini

   D. System Recovery

19. When nothing works to get a machine to restart, what is your last resort to save the image?

   A. Restore the system from the last known good configuration.

   B. Restart the system from the Windows CD and run System Recovery options.

   C. Reinstall the OS.

   D. Run System Restore.

20. System Restore can do a lot to bring back a computer that appears to be dead, but if all else fails what fault or negligent practice during normal operations would kill any chances of ever recovering the system?

   A. You ignore error messages in the event log.

   B. You don't make regular backups.

   C. You ignore daily reports of poor system performance.

   D. You continue operating the machine without creating a restore point.

Chapter

13

Recovery and Backup Options

70-687 MICROSOFT EXAM OBJECTIVES COVERED IN THIS CHAPTER:

✓ **Configure system recovery**

- Configure a recovery drive, configure system restore, perform a driver rollback, perform a refresh or recycle, configure restore points

✓ **Configure file recovery**

- Restore previous versions of files and folders, configure file history, recover files from OneDrive

In the previous chapter, we dealt with booting issues and recovering from a dead system. We touched on the subject of restoring a system image from an image backup. But that is a last-resort option if everything else to restore a system image fails. In this chapter we'll look at a number of options to restore a computer image if you can't boot your computer at all.

We'll also show you how to back up your files to a location away from your computer. That way, if you aren't able to recover from a system image, or if you need to buy a new computer and install the operating system from scratch, you will have access to the files and work that you need.

If you want to back up and restore your personal files using File History, see "Using File History" in the "File Recovery" section of this chapter.

System Protection

With System Protection, you will create a restore point on your system that backs up key Windows system files. Unlike backing up to a remote location or storing an image on remote media, System Protection makes use of your local disks. This means that you will use it to restore a damaged Windows OS or to fix errors on the system to healthy local hard disks. At the most, System Protection will back some key personal files, but you will use it to quickly get back to a stable OS when something gets caught up in the proverbial hard disk meat grinder. If you lose your hard disks, then System Protection will not help you—that is, unless you have made a complete backup of your system drive.

System Protection also works well if you installed something and it either hosed your system or did not work the way it was advertised. With System Protection you can roll back the computer to a time before it choked up, the last known good configuration.

Enabling System Protection

System Protection is enabled by default when you install Windows 8.1. So from the moment you or your user get a new machine, it is already protecting the OS and the key user account folders.

You can also turn this feature off, depending on corporate policy, or decide which volumes on a computer are being protected by it.

To manage System Protection, open your System folder in one of two ways:

- Invoke the Charms bar, select Search, set the focus of the search to Settings, enter **System Protection**, and then click Create A Restore Point in the search results.
- Invoke the Charms bar, choose Search, set the focus of the search to Settings, type **Restore**, and click Create A Restore Point on the Settings page.

In either case the System Properties dialog box will open. By default, the System Protection tab is selected, as shown in Figure 13.1. After setting up the options on the System folder, click OK.

FIGURE 13.1   System Protection tab in the System Properties dialog box

Note that you will need at least 300 MB of free space on each volume for restore points. You can set the amount of disk space you would like to dedicate to restore points as well. On the System Protection tab (see Figure 13.1), click the Configure button. The dialog box shown in Figure 13.2 will appear.

In the Disk Space Usage section, you can move the Max Usage slider to increase or decrease the amount of space for restore points. System Protection does not need a lot of space for future multiple restore points and in fact overwrites the old ones (which you don't need anyway).

It does not make sense to return to a restore point that is, say, older than a month because in a month a system volume can change dramatically and you will lose a lot of healthy configuration by going back too far. For all intents and purposes you only need to go back one or two restore points. At least if the last two did not work, you will be able to recall a day in the last week when everything was working well or just before that new game or app was downloaded that trashed everything. Keep in mind that System Protection is not supported in Windows 8.1 RT.

FIGURE 13.2 The System Protection dialog box

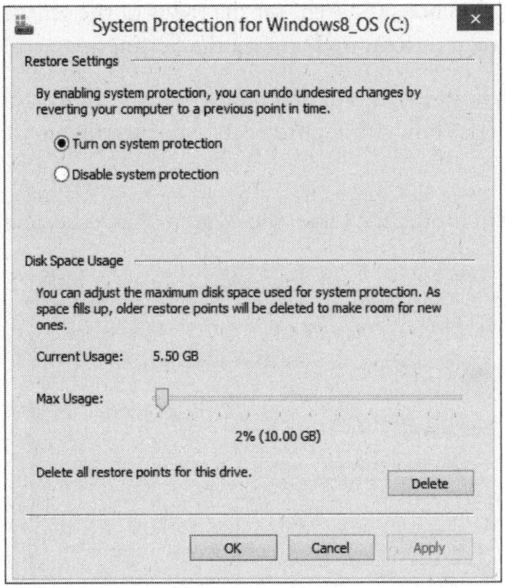

Creating a Restore Point

Windows creates restore points automatically in several situations. Among them are:

- New software installed
- New hardware installed
- Updates applied

You can also create restore points manually. To create a restore point, open the System Protection tab shown in Figure 13.1. Then click the Create button. You have the option to create some annotation about the restore point. Click Create and then click Close. Windows then creates your restore point.

Rolling Back

To restore to the restore point you just created earlier, simply open the System Properties dialog box and click the System Protection tab. This procedure was covered in Chapter 12, "Monitoring System Performance and Recovery," if you need to review it.

Undoing a Restore

If a restore did not work as expected, or if for some reason you need to undo the restore action, do the following:

1. Open System Restore.
2. Select the option Choose A Different Restore Point and click Next.

3. Select the restore point labeled Undo and click Next.

4. Select Finish and follow the onscreen instructions.

You will be prompted to restart the computer. When it has booted up, you will again see a confirmation that the restore has been successful.

File Recovery

If the machine itself is working well and you just need to recover data or files, then File Backup and Restore or File Recovery is your best option. You may also need system files in order for Windows to function properly, and often a file recovery is all you need to get the machine working properly without a refresh, reset, or restore point.

Using File History

File History is not enabled by default. When you enable it, you'll find it is a smart feature for simple backing up of the files on your computer. File History backs up individual files as well as files for all the user accounts on the machine, and it can even encompass the entire filesystem on a computer. When you need your files recovered, simply open File Explorer and drill down into the backup hierarchy.

File History needs external media for the copies. You can use an external hard disk, a USB driver, or a network drive. There is only one place you cannot specify: OneDrive.

To set up File History, you will need administration rights, so before you start make sure you are logged on to the computer with admin rights.

To run File History, on the Charms bar click Search and type **File History**. Click Settings and then click File History on the Settings screen, as shown in Figure 13.3.

FIGURE 13.3   File History main page

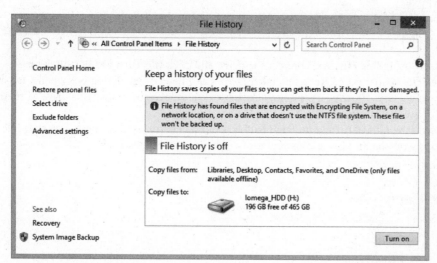

You need to have your media connected before you will be able to turn File History on. Once you connect your media, press F5 or click the Refresh button on the address bar to refresh the screen. To use a network drive, click the Select A Drive option in the middle of the screen and follow the instructions in the next section, "Backing Up to a Network Location." The example in Figure 13.4 uses an external USB drive to back up files. Note that File History is off because the device is disconnected.

FIGURE 13.4   File History screen after connecting a USB drive

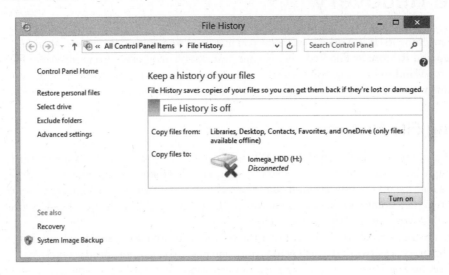

Before turning on File History, note that File History will back up files from the following default locations:

- Libraries
- Desktop
- Contacts
- Favorites

To start using File History, connect the drive and click the Turn On button. This activates File History. The Recommend A Drive For File History dialog box opens. It asks you if you want to allow everyone in your network HomeGroup to use this drive as their backup drive. Select Yes or No.

Now that you have turned on File History, the File History screen alerts you that File History is working and is making copies of your files (see Figure 13.5).

FIGURE 13.5   File History activated

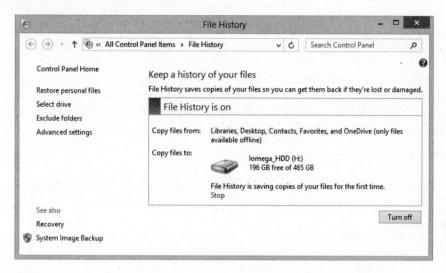

Although File History is very efficient, it takes longer when it first kicks in, because it initially makes a complete backup of all the files and then makes incremental backups only when a file changes. When it is finished, it will appear as shown in Figure 13.6. At this point, you can start a backup manually by clicking the Run Now option.

FIGURE 13.6   The Run Now option

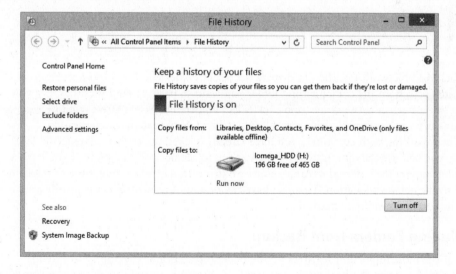

Backing Up to a Network Location

Backing up to a network location is useful because you don't have to worry about a separate device that you have to connect to your computer. The other advantage of network locations is that they tend to have much larger media than locally connected drives such as USB devices.

To enable backing up to a network location, click on the Use Network location when opening the File History screen. You can also choose the Select Drive option on the left of the screen. The Select Drive window will pop up and from there you can choose the network location (see Figure 13.7).

FIGURE 13.7 The Select Drive window

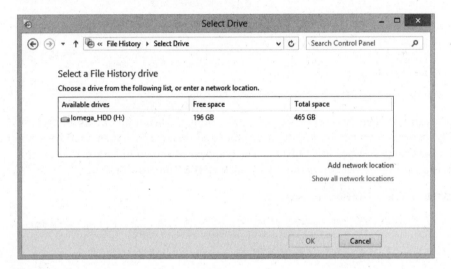

Click Add Network Location to display the Select Folder window (shown in Figure 13.8). Now just search for the computer and folder you want to back up your files to. Once you arrive at the correct network location click Select Folder. The Select Drive window will appear open to the network drive you selected. Click OK to save the configuration.

When working with computers you have already backed up (such as an external USB drive), you can use the option to move the backup to the network location. If you have a large backup on the external hard drive or USB drive, it may take a long time to relocate them to the network location. You also have the option of returning to the locally attached external drive again if you need to.

Excluding Folders from Backup

One of the most important features of any backup program is the ability to exclude certain folders from the backup. For example, you may not need to back up the Windows system folders if you plan to rely on refresh or if you already have an image of the OS.

FIGURE 13.8   Network locations

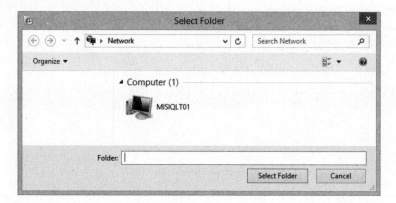

All you need to do to exclude folders is click the Exclude Folders link on the left of the File History window. The Exclude Folders dialog box appears, as shown in Figure 13.9. The default for this feature is that no folders are excluded until you specifically elect to exclude certain folders.

FIGURE 13.9   Exclude Folders window

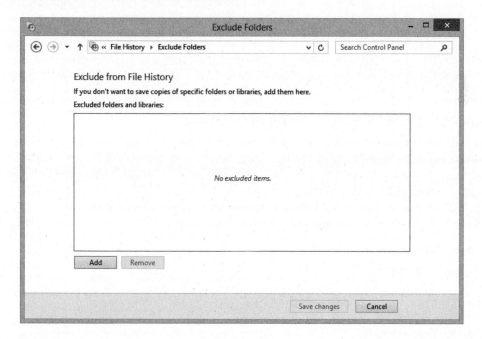

Click the Add button, which opens a Select Folder window from where you can choose the folders you want to exclude (see Figure 13.10). Choose the folders you want to exclude and then click Select Folder. The folders are added to the Excluded Folders collection. When you are done, save the changes.

FIGURE 13.10   The Exclude Folders window

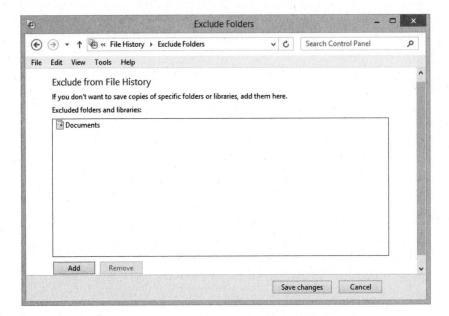

Specifying File History Advanced Settings

You can change how File History works by clicking Advanced Settings on the File History window shown in Figure 13.6. By default, File History checks changes to files that have been backed up every hour. However, if you want checks to occur more often, you can change the intervals between the check times.

Select the desired interval from the Save Copies Of Files drop-down list (see Figure 13.11). The interval choices are as follows:

- Every 10 Minutes
- Every 15 Minutes
- Every 20 Minutes
- Every 30 Minutes
- Every Hour (Default)
- Every 3 Hours
- Every 6 Hours
- Every 12 Hours
- Daily

FIGURE 13.11 Advanced Settings

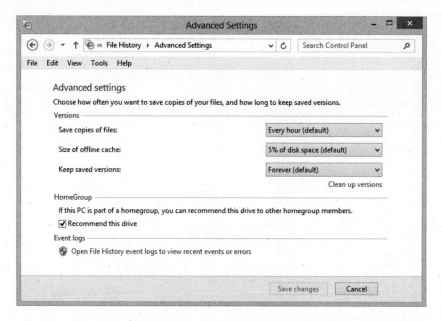

You also have the option to set aside a percentage of disk space for the offline cache. The default is 5%, but you can also choose 2%, 10%, or 20%.

File History copies can start to eat into your available disk space, so you can change how many versions of the saved files are kept. This option is called Keep Saved Versions. The concept is the same as restore point versions explained earlier in the chapter, only here you are dealing with single file versions. If you delete a file by mistake you can at least recover it easily from File History. However, it is a very useful feature if you at any given point need to go back to the way a file "looked" in the not-too-distant past, by date and time. Of course, the more versions you keep, the greater the amount of disk space needed.

The version options are as follows:

- Until Space Is Needed
- 1 Month
- 3 Months
- 6 Months
- 9 Months
- 1 Year
- 2 Years
- Forever (Default)

When you are done with Advanced Settings for File History, click Save Changes to exit.

File History records its activities into log files, which you can access by clicking the Open File History Event Log To View Recent Events Or Errors. Event Viewer is shown in Figure 13.12. See Chapter 12 for information on using Event Viewer.

FIGURE 13.12   File History event log

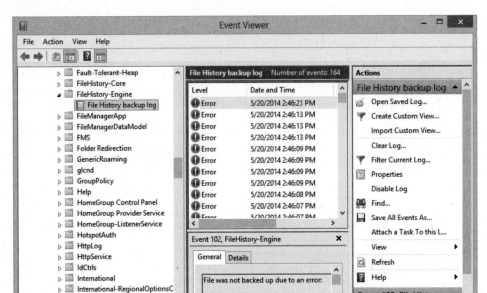

Restoring Files

Restoring files from File History is relatively straightforward. First, if you delete a file check if the deleted file can be restored from the Recycle Bin because this would be a much quicker method to get back the most recent file you deleted. Otherwise, proceed to restore from your backups.

To restore the files, open File History in Control Panel as described earlier in this chapter and click the Restore Personal Files link on the left side of the File History window. Refer back to Figure 13.6 if needed.

You can also access the restore option by selecting the History button on the Home tab of File Explorer. When you are viewing files and folders in File Explorer, selecting the Home tab of File Explorer will bring up a drop-down ribbon, as shown in Figure 13.13. Selecting the History icon (small clock) will allow you to view previous versions of the file. If it is grayed out, it has no history.

FIGURE 13.13   Home tab

Back in the File History dialog box in Control Panel, you can now proceed to find the file or files you need to restore by browsing the folder list. It lets you navigate back in time to previously backed-up versions. If more than one version is available, click on the left and right arrows to scroll through the versions of your files until you find the one you want to restore files from. Select one or more files and/or folders in the version you want to restore from, right-click, and choose either Restore (to the original location) or Restore To (to a different location). In some cases, File History may display a dialog box to give you the following options:

Replace The File In The Destination   This restores the version you selected over a later version.

Skip This File   This ignores the file during the restore phase. The option works when restoring multiple files.

Compare Info For Both Files   This option lets you see file details about the file you selected to restore and the file currently on your hard drive. From the dialog box that loads, you select the file you want to keep or keep both copies. (A sequential number is added to the filename of the restored file.)

After you have made your choices, click Continue to complete the restore process. You can click Preview to preview the file before the restore begins. If you are not sure and do not want to overwrite any copy, you can restore the file to an alternate location. To do so, click Restore To and specify the new location.

Restoring from OneDrive

If you need to recover files you pushed to OneDrive, surf to the OneDrive website. Click the Recycle Bin. Use the check boxes to make your selections, as shown in Figure 13.14. Items in the Recycle Bin are automatically deleted after 30 days. If your Recycle Bin is full, the oldest items will be automatically deleted after three days.

FIGURE 13.14   OneDrive's Recycle Bin

Creating a Recovery Drive

In Chapter 12 you learned how to troubleshoot startup issues. Another option is creating a bootable recovery drive, which is a USB drive that boots right into Recovery Environment (aka Limited Diagnostic Mode) that allows you to repair problems, run System Restore, and refresh or reset your PC.

Note a 32-bit (x86) recovery drive can only be used to fix 32-bit Windows 8.1 editions and a 64-bit (x64) recovery drive works with 64-bit Windows 8.1 editions only. Having said that, you can repair any edition of Windows 8.1 with this drive, as long as it is meant for the same hardware architecture (32-bit or 64-bit). Finally, do not try to use a Windows 8.1 recovery drive to repair Windows 8, and vice versa!

To create a recovery drive, use the following steps:

1. In the Search box, type **recovery drive** and select Create A Recovery Drive.

2. If required, select Yes in the UAC dialog box. In the Create A Recovery Drive dialog box, select Next.

3. If your computer supports a recovery drive, you can choose to copy the contents of this drive to the USB drive. You can do so on the Create A Recovery Drive screen, as shown in Figure 13.15.

FIGURE 13.15   The Create A Recovery Drive screen

4. With the USB drive inserted, choose the drive from the list in the Select The USB Flash Drive dialog box. It appears when you click Next. It will warn you that the drive will be erased.

5. When the operation is complete, you will be informed and the drive is ready to use if you cannot get your system to boot. I recommend that you test its functionality before assuming it will work when the time comes.

Summary

In this chapter you learned about the recovery and backup options you have on Windows 8.1. System Protection lets you create restore points on your system that you can use to back up key Windows system files. System Protection makes use of your local disks to store backup "snapshots" of your system image. We looked at how you can configure System Protection to make restore points and how to use System Protection to revert to the previous version of the image.

You then saw how to use File History to make backups of individual files and folders on your computer. You learned that File History is a convenient backup and restore feature for individual or collections of files and how it makes a nifty version control tool that lets you return to a previous version of a file.

Exam Essentials

Understand what System Protection is and how to use it.   You should know what you can do with System Protection and how to create a restore point of the system image on the computer. You should know how to configure the restore point options and how to return to previous versions of your system files. You should also know how to roll back to the previous version of a device driver.

Understand what File History is and how to use it.   You need to know and understand what options you have for backing up and restoring files using the File History feature. You should understand the various options for looking at file versions, how often File History makes copies, and to which locations the files should be both backed up and restored.

Review Questions

You can find the answers in Appendix A.

1. You are asked to set up System Protection on users' computers; what are the first steps you should take?

    A. Open Control Panel and select System Protection.

    B. Press Ctrl+Alt+Del and select System Protection.

    C. Open the Charms bar, select Search, enter **System Protection**, and click Settings.

    D. Restart the computer and press F8 until System Protection appears.

2. How much space should you reserve on your computer for System Protection to do its work?

    A. None. System Protection saves to network locations.

    B. You need at least a gigabyte on the local hard disk.

    C. System Protection should have 500 MB on a USB hard drive.

    D. You need at least 300 MB for each volume.

3. With System Protection open, how do you create a restore point?

    A. Open the System Restore tab and then click Restore Point.

    B. Select the System Protection tab and then click the Create button.

    C. System Protection does it for you.

    D. Press Ctrl+Alt+R.

4. If a restore point fails to make any difference, what is your next step?

    A. Use the Refresh PC option.

    B. Reinstall Windows 8.1 from installation media.

    C. Use the Choose A Different Restore Point feature.

    D. Try a few more times, and then call technical support.

5. If a sound card was working yesterday and now stopped because of a new driver you loaded, how do you get it working again?

    A. Open Device Manager, right-click the sound card node, and choose the option Repair Driver.

    B. Open Device Manager, click the Driver tab on the sound card that is not working, and select Roll Back Driver.

    C. Open Device Manager, and choose the option "Restore all non-working drivers to their last known good configurations."

    D. Open Device Manager, check the option Roll Back On Start, and reboot the machine.

6. If a machine is not responding to any attempts at System Restore, what is the next option you should attempt to get it back to best working condition as quickly as possible without inconveniencing the user?

    A. Refresh the computer.

    B. Reboot and choose Last Known Good Configuration when it reboots to the recovery console.

    C. Do a system reset.

    D. Copy the user's files and data to a new machine and throw away the old one.

7. You are asked to take a machine from a user who was let go because of Internet usage violation and to assign it to the new employee. What steps should you take to make sure nothing of the terminated user remains on the computer that has to be reassigned?

    A. Replace the hard disk with a new one and reinstall the image.

    B. Reset the PC.

    C. Connect the computer to Microsoft Installation Services and choose the option "Burn old image prior to reinstallation of new image."

    D. Format the hard disk using the "destructive format" option and reinstall the image from an offline restore point.

8. You need to back up a user's files and data at a remote location and have the backups stored at the main datacenter. How would you best set up the process to achieve this?

    A. Buy the user a tape backup system and use Microsoft Backup to make the backups.

    B. Use File History to back up individual files and point the backup to a network location.

    C. Use File History to back up individual files and point the backup to a local external hard disk.

    D. User File History to back up individual files to the local drive; then using the Run Script After Completion option, copy the file to the network.

9. How do you configure File History to back up to the network?

    A. In File History's settings, add the network path in the Network Location text box, and click Test to test the connection.

    B. This option only works in Windows 8.1 Network Edition.

    C. Click the Add Network Location button to display the Select Folder window.

    D. There is nothing to do. When you start File History, it automatically offers you the network connection if it finds it.

10. File History warns you that you don't have enough space on the hard disk to do the backup. How do you configure it to work? (Choose all that apply.)

    A. Delete all previous backups to free up the space.

    B. Install a bigger hard disk and move all the data to the new disk.

    C. Remove the oldest version of File History.

    D. Exclude folders that you don't need to back up.

11. How often does File History check to see if a file has changed by default?

    A. Every hour

    B. Never

    C. As soon as the file has changed

    D. As soon as the app that uses the file starts

12. What is the default percentage of disk space that can be set aside for offline files?

    A. 10

    B. 15

    C. 2

    D. 5

13. To free up disk space for File History to perform new backups, what the best way to remove old backups?

    A. Simply delete the old backups you don't need.

    B. Use the option Purge Old Files No Longer Needed.

    C. Use the backup removal tool.

    D. Use the Keep Saved Versions option.

14. Your user calls you and says she has deleted a very important file. What is the first thing you should instruct her to do?

    A. Ask her to check in the Recycle Bin to see if the deleted file was sent there.

    B. Tell her that you have no option but to report her for violation of the employee handbook.

    C. Tell her that the file is gone forever and that she should start again.

    D. Tell her to wait while you restore the backup file from the backup library.

15. How do you access the Restore option in File History?

    A. Hold down the Windows button and press Ctrl+R.

    B. At the command line, type `filehis.ext` and press Enter.

    C. Open File Explorer and select the Home tab.

    D. Open Help, search for Restore, and click the Open Restore link.

16. What option allows you to restore just the version of the file you need?

    A. Replace The File In The Destination

    B. Replace The File In The Target Folder

    C. There is no option; File Explorer knows where the file needs to go.

    D. Open Destination and choose Restore File.

17. Which Windows 8.1 edition does not support System Restore?

    A. Enterprise

    B. Home

C. RT

D. Pro

18. Which of the following could prevent File History from starting?

   A. The computer is a member of a workgroup.

   B. Encryption is enabled on some files.

   C. Updates are missing.

   D. No external drive is attached.

19. Which of the following is not a default location backed up by File History?

   A. Downloads

   B. Libraries

   C. Contacts

   D. Favorites

20. What is the minimal interval you can choose for File History to check for changes in files that have been backed up?

   A. Every 10 minutes

   B. Once an hour

   C. Every 3 hours

   D. Every 6 hours

Chapter

14

Installing and Configuring Applications

70-687 MICROSOFT EXAM OBJECTIVES COVERED IN THIS CHAPTER:

✓ Configure application restrictions, including Software Restriction Policies and AppLocker

70-688 MICROSOFT EXAM OBJECTIVES COVERED IN THIS CHAPTER:

✓ Manage clients by using Windows Intune

✓ Configure monitoring and alerts

✓ Manage policies

✓ Manage remote computers

✓ Support Windows Store and cloud apps

✓ Sideload apps by using Windows Intune

✓ Deep link apps by using Windows Intune

With the arrival of Windows 8.1, your support efforts now extend to a variety of new computing devices, not just desktop computers and laptops. Now you also need to support tablets and phones. The good news is that the tools you have to manage all the types of apps and applications are easy to use and efficient.

The operating system is designed to use so-called "live" tiles on the phone or tablet Start screen. These tiles are also part and parcel of the desktop operating system running on workstations and laptops. Figure 14.1 shows an example of live tiles on a Windows phone.

FIGURE 14.1   Windows tiles

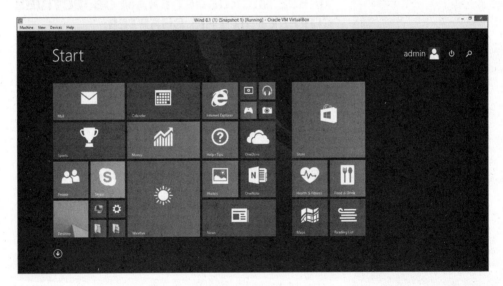

The tiles indicate phone calls, messages, pictures, and sundry other things for the user.

If you don't like using the tile view in Windows 8.1, you can choose to use the legacy desktop view instead. To do so, select the tile that says Desktop and the tile view will be gone. You will see the familiar Windows desktop.

Windows Store

The Windows Store is a place online where you can search for, download, and install all Windows 8.1 apps. You can search for an app in a variety of ways, and once you find what you want, it's easy to install it on the computer so you can start using it immediately. Let's now explore how to access the Windows Store, how to navigate it, how to install apps, how to look for and install app updates, and how to remove apps.

Using the Windows Store

Windows Store is not new to Windows 8.1 and was introduced in Windows 8. It's an online location that allows you to find applications (apps or applets) for any Windows 8 or later device, such as a computer, laptop, tablet or Windows Phone. Although these apps can (and in most cases are) single function, some are multifunction and can be quite complex. Many of the apps in the store provide general services such as text messaging, voice recording, calculations, and so on, whereas others provide specific functionality such as ordering from a pizza shop. These apps are specifically designed for the Windows 8.1 interface. Developers have to adhere to strict application development guidelines in order to get their apps approved and subsequently offered for sale in the Windows Store. Figure 14.2 shows Windows Store in the Windows 8.1 interface.

FIGURE 14.2   The new Windows Store available with Windows 8.1

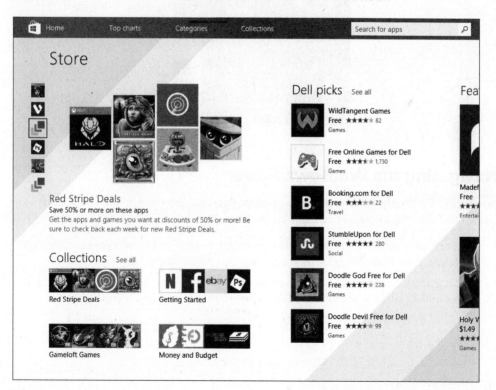

The Windows 8.1 interface is Microsoft's move toward touch-based interaction with the operating system and applications. This is in large part a result of the popularity of handheld device markets, especially phones. But Windows 8.1 also focuses on making applications easy to locate and use and it is not just about touch. Thus much of the focus of the Store is on easy access as well. The Windows Store is an online resource, so you need to ensure the user's computer meets the following requirements:

- High-speed Internet connection
- Screen resolution of at least 1024×768 (or at least 1366×768 for the Snap feature to work)

To use the Windows Store, switch to the Start screen and click the Store app tile (shown in Figure 14.3). The Windows Store page appears.

FIGURE 14.3 The Windows Store tile on the Start screen

Navigating the Windows Store

Navigating the Windows Store is simple. You navigate the Store much like you would a web page. The following list shows you how to get around the store:

- You can use a scroll wheel on a mouse. Scrolling toward you scrolls pages to the right. Scrolling away from you returns you to previous pages on the left.
- You can drag the scroll bar at the bottom of the page to the right to see additional pages to the right. Or scroll to the left to return to previous pages on the left.

- On touch devices, swipe from right to left to see pages on the right. Swipe from left to right to return to previous pages on the left.

  You can navigate back to the main Windows Store page by using the following methods:

- Click the Back button on the top left of the window. You may have to do this several times if you've viewed several pages already.

- Use the three methods listed previously to return to previous pages to the left until you arrive at the main Windows Store page.

- Right-click the top of a page or swipe down from the top edge of the page to show the app menu. From this menu, click Home to return immediately to the Windows Store home page.

Reviewing Windows 8.1 Apps

Upon landing on the site, the Spotlight area highlights the most popular apps. You can find out about your apps and your account by using options available in the Store menu drop down boxes, giving you access to apps, app categories, and your user account. This menu is shown in Figure 14.4.

FIGURE 14.4   The Windows Store menu

Microsoft maintains a very high standard for apps and for the programmers who want to create Windows 8.1 apps. For example, apps cannot contain adult, defamatory, or obscene material. Developers are also not allowed to publish content that encourages irresponsible use of alcohol, tobacco, drugs, or weapons.

It's easy to learn about an app in the Store. Just click its tile. A page will load to display information about the app. You can find out about costs of the apps (many apps are free), ratings, description, and features. Figure 14.5 shows an example of the app page for a free calculator.

You also have access to a review area where you can learn what other users have to say about the app. You can access the review area by clicking on the Ratings and Reviews link (see Figure 14.6). If there are reviews for an app, they show up here. You can also add a review by clicking the Write A Review link on the left side of the screen and filling out the resulting form.

FIGURE 14.5 The details page of a free calculator app

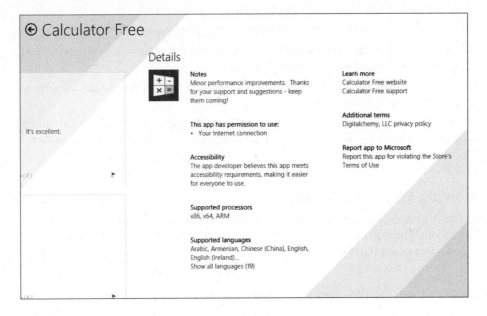

FIGURE 14.6 The review page of a free calculator app

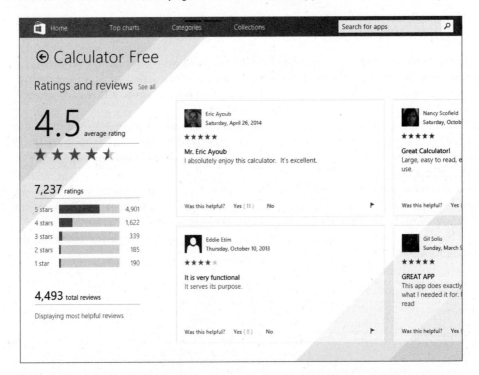

Windows Store Categories

Apps are also displayed in categories to help you locate them more easily. These categories include Games, Social, Entertainment, Photo, Music, and so on.

If you browse each category, you will also notice that certain apps are showcased. They are graded by number of stars for each app. The highest rating is five stars. There is also a New Releases category for apps that have just been released. You can also browse the Top Free category, which offers lists of popular free apps. You can also look for free apps in the Top Free categories.

Costs of Apps

The apps in the Store are not all free and the costs vary. The Store sets up costs as follows:

Free A number of apps are free. However, they will usually have built-in advertisements, which are used to offset the cost of development, support, and upgrades. Sometimes the developers offer the option to upgrade from the free version to a full-featured version. The paid versions usually do not contain ads.

Trial Here you have the features available in a full-paid version, but for a limited time period.

Paid Here you have full access to a full version of the app.

Searching for Apps

The Windows Store is itself a Windows 8.1 app, so you can use the Windows Search tool to find apps. Simply display the Charms bar and click Search. In the Search field, type an app name or a keyword for an app and press Enter. The Windows Store returns a listing of apps that meet your search criteria. Figure 14.7, for example, shows a screen with the Search tool visible with a keyword called calculators and a search results screen from the Windows Store.

FIGURE 14.7   Use the Windows Search tool to locate Windows Store apps

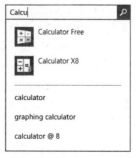

Installing Windows 8.1 Apps

To install an app, click on the app tile to show the app's description page. Next, click the Install button on the left side of the page. The Windows Store now shows a message at the top of the page that the app is installing. After installation is complete, Windows displays a message notifying you of the installation.

Once an app is installed on your computer, the Install button is no longer available when you go to the app's page in the Windows Store. The Store now shows that you own this app. An example is shown in Figure 14.8.

FIGURE 14.8   Your apps page showing that the app is installed

To start using the app, display the Start screen and click the app's tile.

Updating Apps

When updates become available, you will not be informed automatically as in Windows 8. Moreover by default the update must be manually performed in Windows 8.1. However, it is possible to automatically install app updates when they become available. To configure this, follow these steps:

1. On the Start screen, tap or click Store to open the Windows Store.
2. Swipe in from the right edge of the screen, and then tap Settings. (If you're using a mouse, point to the lower-right corner of the screen, move the mouse pointer up, and then click Settings.)
3. Tap or click App Updates.
4. Make sure Automatically Update My Apps is set to Yes.

Removing Apps

If you no longer want an app installed on the computer, just uninstall it. To do this, take the following steps:

1. Display the Start screen.
2. Right-click the app to remove. Windows puts a check mark on the app's tile and displays a menu at the bottom of the screen (see Figure 14.9).
3. Select Uninstall from the menu. A message appears telling you that the app will be removed and any information related to that app will also be removed.

4. Click the Uninstall button to remove the selected app.

FIGURE 14.9   Select Uninstall from this menu

The Windows Store provides access to many different types of apps, including productivity apps, games, news apps, and more.

Sideloading Apps

You can "sideload" line-of-business apps. Sideloading simply means installing a Windows Store app without publishing it and downloading it from the Store. You install it directly, and you cannot sideload an app you purchase from the Windows Store. Although sideloading apps is an advanced topic beyond the scope of this book, you should be aware of this and should know that there are some requirements:

- The computer running Windows 8.1 must be joined to the domain.
- You must enable the "Allow all trusted apps to install" Group Policy setting.
- The app must be signed by a certificate that is chained to a trusted root certificate.

Using Windows Intune

In Chapter 8, "Users and Groups," you were introduced to Windows Intune. Intune can also be used to sideload and manage applications. In this section, we'll look at that functionality of Windows Intune.

Sideloading Apps by Using Windows Intune

Sideloading an app by using Windows Intune is similar to doing so through System Center Configuration Manager. The main advantage to doing so with Intune is that the applications will be available to any device with Internet access. The process looks like this:

Step 1: Uploading the App to Windows Intune

a. Click the Step 1: Add Software link in the Windows Intune Software workspace.

b. On the Software Setup wizard page, select the Windows app package software installer type and the local or Universal Naming Convention (UNC) path to the application.

c. On the Software Description wizard page, specify the publisher, user-friendly name, and description of the app.

Step 2: Deploying the App to Windows Intune Groups

a. Click Manage Deployment in the Managed Software node in the Software workspace.

b. On the Select Groups wizard page, select the Windows Intune groups to which you want to deploy your app.

c. On the Deployment Action wizard page, select the appropriate installation approval for the app. To install the app, you can select Available Install or Required Install from the Approval list. The Available Install option makes the app available to the user, who can then elect to install the app.

When the wizard is complete, the app will be available to users to download.

Deep-Linking Apps by Using Windows Intune

The deep-linking process lets you place apps from the Windows Store in your own company store, or company portal. The users will not be required to possess a code for the app—they can just click the link to the app in Windows Store. The details of this process are beyond the scope of this book, but here are the general steps:

1. Find the app in the Windows Store.

   a. Get a link to the app.

2. Create the app in Windows Intune.

   a. Add the app and choose External link as location of the app.

   b. Deploy the app as in the earlier steps.

   c. Configure Assigned Access.

With the enhanced security of having each Modern App (the Windows term for these applications) sandboxed, there is a new way to provide a single application system (or kiosk computer). Assigned Access allows you to choose any Modern App to be run exclusively and in full screen in a local account. The only Modern Apps that cannot be used are those that would allow a user to make changes to the local system and compromise the kiosk.

With an Assigned Access account, the user will not see any notifications, and the Windows hardware button will be suppressed, as will be many shortcuts and gestures. The steps to set up Assigned Access on a kiosk computer are as follows:

1. Create a local account on the computer to which the app will be assigned.

2. After logging on using the account at least once, locate the Other Accounts section of Accounts under PC Settings on the Start screen.

3. Select the option "Set up an account for assigned access," as shown in Figure 14.10.

FIGURE 14.10   Setting up an account for Assigned Access

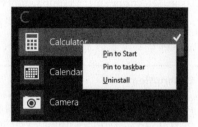

4. On the "Set up an account for assigned access" page, select the Choose An Account button and select the Kiosk account. Notice only local accounts are offered as options.

5. Click the Choose An App button. Choose the app you would like to assign to the user.

To log out of the Assigned Access account so you can log in with another account, thus escaping the limitations imposed by it:

1. Quickly press the Windows logo key five times. This will restart your PC.

2. Sign in with a different account.

Supporting Desktop Apps

We now turn to supporting traditional desktop applications on Windows 8.1. This becomes a critical issue when you are upgrading from a version of Windows prior to Window 8. You now have to test applications to make sure they can be installed and will run on the new OS.

In some cases, the legacy applications will simply run without any need for intervention, but older or poorly written programs will most likely need to be upgraded to versions that are compatible with Windows 8.1.

You can use the Program Compatibility Troubleshooter, which is built into Windows 8.1, to change the compatibility settings of any legacy application. Changing these settings will in most cases resolve the issues. To use the tool:

1. In the Search box on the Start screen, type **run programs**.

2. Tap or click "Run programs made for previous versions of Windows," and then tap or click Next.

3. Either select the program from the presented list or select Not Listed if it is not listed. Click Next and the compatibility wizard will attempt to resolve the problem. In cases where the troubleshooter fails you, it is also possible to change these settings manually. To do so:

   a. In the Search box, type the name of the program and then select Open File Location.

b. Right-click the program file, select Properties, and select the Compatibility tab.

c. Based on the type of issue, select one of the compatibility fixes from Table 14.1

TABLE 14.1   Compatibility fixes

Setting	Description
Compatibility Mode	Runs the program using settings from a previous version of Windows. Try this setting if you know the program is designed for (or worked in) a specific version of Windows.
Reduced Color Mode	Uses a limited set of colors in the program. Some older programs are designed to use fewer colors.
Run In 640 × 480 Screen Resolution	Try this setting if the graphics for the program appear jagged or are rendered improperly.
Disable Display Scaling On High DPI Settings	Turns off automatic resizing of programs if large font sizes are used. Try this setting if large-scale fonts are interfering with the appearance of the program.
Enable This Program To Work With OneDrive Files	Try this setting if the program can't see or open files on OneDrive. Note that when large files are being downloaded, there may be a long delay, with no progress bar reflecting the download.
Run This Program As An Administrator	Some programs require administrator privileges to run properly. If you aren't signed into your PC as an administrator, this option is unavailable.
Change Settings For All Users	Lets you choose settings that will apply to all users on this computer.

Applications that cannot be upgraded or be made to run using compatibility fixes can be made available via technologies such as Client Hyper-V, Remote Desktop, or App-V.

Another option is to set up a shim interface. A shim is software that maps function calls of your legacy application to new function calls on the new operating system. Setting up a shim is not an easy task, but in the Application Compatibility Toolkit (ACT) many prebuilt shims/patches and fixes are available. In cases where no shim is available in the ACT, it may be simpler to set up one of the Remote Desktop or remote application technologies. Nevertheless, if you need to provide shim support, you can start the process by running the sdbins.exe application. This program registers the compatibility fix on the computer so it can function.

Application Updates

You have a number of options at your disposal for providing application updates on Windows 8.1. One of those is App-V5.0 SP2. With App-V 5.0, virtual applications (and updates) work more like traditionally installed applications. This means that users don't have to change the way they use an application just because it's virtual. It also makes it possible to deploy, track, and service virtual applications. App-V lets you deliver application updates without requiring the client machines to reboot. The update is applied to the application on the server, and when the user connects to use the application, the update has already been performed. So these updates can happen without downtime inconvenience to your users.

You can also use System Center 2012 Configuration Manager. The Create Application Wizard provides the utility for this. And there's good old Windows Server Update Services (WSUS), which neatly targets the operating system updates as well as major Microsoft suites of applications like Microsoft Office.

Finally, there's Windows Intune, which also lets you update third-party applications. We discussed Intune earlier in his chapter.

Supporting Legacy Applications with Hyper-V

Hyper-V was introduced to the desktop in Windows 8 and was ported from the server offerings in the virtual machine space. It brings a virtual machine to the desktop and, through interaction with the host operating system (in this case, Windows 8.1), lets you run a legacy operating system (such as Windows 7) on your Windows 8.1 machine. You can then run applications that require Windows 7 in that virtual machine.

Hyper-V requires a supported 64-bit processor that has Second-Level Address Translation (SLAT), and 4 GB of RAM is required. It is only available in the following versions of Windows:

- Windows 8 Pro 64-bit Edition
- Windows 8 Enterprise 64-bit Edition
- Windows 8.1 Pro 64-bit Edition
- Windows 8.1 Enterprise 64-bit Edition

Remote Desktop and RemoteApp

Remote Desktop is an application built into Windows 8.1 that allows you to connect to a remote computer and use it as if you were sitting in front of the devices. It gives the user a similar experience to Hyper-V but you don't need so much RAM and hardware to make good use of it. RemoteApp is an application built into Windows 8.1 that allows you to connect to an application located on a remote server and interact with the application as if it were installed locally. If the remote app is located in an Azure cloud it is referred to an Azure RemoteApp. With Remote Desktop and RemoteApp, your user is actually connecting to a virtual machine sitting on a remote server. This is a good option when you have an application that only a few users need to use. Get it going on the server first, and then you can roll it out in a controlled fashion to just the users who need to use it.

Remote Desktop requires the user to log into the remote server and then run the application from within the remote desktop. RemoteApp takes away the need for the user to login remotely because it runs the remote application through Remote Desktop and the user experiences what appears to be the application running locally.

App-V

The last option you have to consider for supporting legacy applications is App-V, which means application virtualization. It works the same way as RemoteApp, but the server component is designed specifically for serving applications virtually to user desktops.

To use App-V, you need to set up an App-V server. Target applications then need to be prepared for the App-V server through a so-called "sequencing" process. After sequencing, the applications can be published.

Advantages include the following:

- Using App-V removes the need for traditional local installation of the applications.
- The App-V stack sandboxes the execution environment so that an application does not make changes directly to the underlying operating system's filesystem and/or Registry.
- Applications are also sandboxed from each other so that different versions of the same application can be run under App-V concurrently and so that mutually exclusive applications can coexist on the same system.
- Using App-V allows you to centralize installation and management.
- App-V features a tracking interface for tracking the usage of the virtualized application.

    Disadvantages include the following:

- You have an additional component that requires licensing for use.
- Access to the App-V server is required.

Configuring Application Restrictions

It is possible to control a user's ability to run certain types of applications. This can help to prevent malware while also reducing time spent by the IT team supporting the applications and correcting the problems they may cause. Two tools can be used to exercise this control: Software Restriction Policies (SRP) and AppLocker. Although they serve the same purpose, AppLocker is supported on systems running Windows 7 and later and SRP is supported on systems running Windows Vista or earlier. Since this is a book about Windows 8.1, let's take a look at AppLocker.

AppLocker enables you to manage packaged apps and packaged app installers, which are commonly known as Windows 8 apps. Not only can it track the applications that are in use, it can also be used to prevent the use of any applications that you do not want to be used.

As an example of just one of the scenarios this tool can address is the issue of per-user applications, which are those that do not require administrative privilege to install. To do so:

1. Open the Local Security Policy MMC snap-in; in the Search box, type **secpol.msc** and then press Enter.

2. In the console tree, double-click Application Control Policies, and then double-click AppLocker.

3. Right-click Executable Rules, and then click Create Default Rules.

The system will automatically create three default rules:

- Allow All Users To Run Files In The Default Program Files Folder
- Allow All Users To Run Files In The Windows Folder
- Allow Members Of The Built-In Administrators Group To Run All Files

The result of the application of these rules is that you prevent all nonadministrator users from running programs that are installed in their user profile folder.

With only one example of the use of AppLocker, you can see how powerful the tool can be in controlling the installation and use of unapproved applications on both a local machine and a domain. We performed this operation using Local Security, but it can also be done using Group Policy.

Summary

In this chapter you learned about accessing the Windows Store and installing, updating, and removing Windows apps. Windows Store provides access to many thousands of apps that are easy to install and support on the Windows 8.1 operating system.

However, Windows 8.1 is also a standard desktop operating system that runs on laptops and workstations and your users are going to need continuing access to the tens of thousands of standard Windows applications that they have been using for years. This means you need to keep supporting these application regardless of whether they are legacy Windows applications or new versions of software made for previous versions of the operating system.

We looked at using legacy application management services such as Server Updates Services and some of the newer technologies such as Hyper-V and App-V.

Exam Essentials

Understand what Windows Store is.   You should be familiar with the Windows Store and know how to install and manage apps through the Store. You should also know how to support apps that users can download and install on their computers. You should understand that although the Store provides access to thousands of new apps that your users can use, it can present you with a management nightmare.

Know how to install and support both legacy and new traditional Windows applications.   You need to know and understand the options you have for installing and supporting standard Windows applications, such as Microsoft Office. You also need to know how to ensure that users migrating to Windows 8.1 still have access to the legacy applications they were using on previous versions of Windows.

Review Questions

You can find the answers in Appendix A.

1. Your users tell you that they are unable to connect to the Windows Store, and if they do, they find it takes a long time to search for apps. What is the first thing you should be looking at when troubleshooting the reason?

    A. That the users have accounts that allow them access to Windows Store

    B. That users have sufficient memory and CPU on their machines

    C. That users have the latest version of Windows running

    D. That users have high-speed Internet connections

2. How do you find out what an app does?

    A. You need to click on a link to the app's website for this information.

    B. Microsoft publishes a list of all the apps that contains a summary of what each app does.

    C. Clicking an app's tile in Windows Store loads information about the app.

    D. Once you start the app, it tell you what it does.

3. A user has expressed a desire to install an account app she has heard about in the Windows Store. How do you find the app?

    A. Use the Windows Search tool, which also searches the Store.

    B. Search for the application using Bing or Google.

    C. Show the Start screen.

    D. Search for the app at the Microsoft website.

4. What tool is used to control the use of applications in Windows 8.1?

    A. Software Restriction polices

    B. Intune

    C. AppLocker

    D. SCCM

5. A user calls you to remove an app he feels is causing issues. What the best option to remove the app from the user's workstation?

    A. Right-click the app. From the menu you can select to uninstall the app.

    B. Open the Store. Find the app and select Remove from the available options.

    C. The app can only be removed by Windows Server Update Services.

    D. Open Control Panel, click on Programs, and select the Uninstall A Program option.

6. Your company has decided to migrate to Windows 8.1 from Windows 7. You are asked to ensure that all applications needed by the users are migrated to the new operating system. What are your first steps to migrate the applications?

   A. Have every user list the applications they need.

   B. Connect to Microsoft and run the Application Migration Utility.

   C. Remove all the applications before upgrading the machines.

   D. Use the Microsoft Application Compatibility Toolkit (ACT) to check for application compatibility.

7. To use the ACT, what database system does it need access to?

   A. Every user needs a local version of Microsoft Access.

   B. ACT makes flat files so you don't need a database.

   C. ACT needs access to an instance of SQL Server.

   D. When you install ACT, it creates its own database called Act1.

8. You find out that an application running under the old DOS 3.1 operating system is needed by users when they upgrade to Windows 8.1. Microsoft says the only way to provide the support is via a shim interface. How do you explain to your boss what Microsoft is talking about?

   A. Shim is an application that makes very old applications think they are new Windows 8.1 applications.

   B. Shim is software that maps function calls of your legacy application to new function calls on the new operating system.

   C. Shim stands for Sophisticated Holistic Multiple Software System.

   D. Shim is another name for Windows Server Update Services.

9. Your company decides to use a mix of apps and traditional Microsoft applications, and you don't want to support them with multiple software support options. What new service handles both Windows apps support and traditional software installation and upgrading?

   A. System Center 2012

   B. Windows Server Update Services

   C. Microsoft Search

   D. Windows Intune

10. What is Hyper-V and what role does it play in supporting legacy applications on Windows 8.1?

   A. Hyper-V is Microsoft's virtual server technology. It makes it possible to run applications using a VM that runs the operating system supported by the application.

   B. Hyper-V is a software interface that lets legacy applications run faster.

   C. Hyper-V provides an application with as much virtual memory as it needs.

   D. Hyper-V provides an application with additional CPU power.

11. How much memory do you need to run a Hyper-V system on a desktop?

    A. At least 10 GB

    B. At least 4 GB

    C. At least 250 KB

    D. At least 5 GB of unclaimed disk space for virtual memory

12. What is the least attractive aspect of providing Hyper-V to your users?

    A. They need super-fast machines.

    B. They need to operate in very cool rooms.

    C. It takes a lot of work to install and support virtual machines.

    D. Users can delete the machine with the simple click of a button.

13. Why would Remote Desktop be a better alternative than Hyper-V in some situations? (Choose all that apply.)

    A. You don't need so much RAM and hardware to use it.

    B. It's easier to install and maintain software.

    C. The server is more secure.

    D. User are afraid of something that looks very technical running on their machines.

14. When would Hyper-V be a better alternative than Remote Desktop?

    A. When users do not need network access to use the application

    B. When your users have very powerful machines

    C. When your users are technically savvy

    D. When only one or a few users need access to the software and it needs a large amount of memory and CPU to run

15. What is the difference between Remote Desktop and RemoteApp?

    A. Remote Desktop is a service that lets a support technician log in to your machine. RemoteApp is an app running remotely.

    B. RemoteApp lets users run an application from an application server without having to log into a remote system.

    C. Remote Desktop is a mirror of your desktop whereas RemoteApp is a remote version of your app.

    D. Remote Desktop requires you to log into a server to user the app. RemoteApp lets you use the app without the need to log in.

Appendix A

Answers to Review Questions

Chapter 1

1. D. You can add the Administrative Tools items from the Settings charm (after pressing Windows logo key+C). You cannot add these tools from the Devices, Search, or Share charms.

2. D. The shortcut to snap apps is Windows logo key +. (period), not Windows logo key +S or Windows logo key +I. Then you can use an arrow key or your mouse to snap the app.

3. A, C. Users claim an identity with a user account and prove the identity by providing credentials such as a password. If the username credential is accurate, the user is authenticated. Authenticated users are given authorized access to resources by granting them permissions.

4. C. A Microsoft Live account is needed to access the Windows Store. Depending on the environment, the Microsoft Live account might be a local account or a domain account. However, just having a local or a domain account won't ensure they can use it with Windows Store or SkyDrive unless it is created as a Microsoft Live account. An administrator account is not necessary. Both standard and administrator accounts can be used.

5. B. You can create a Microsoft Live account from the Accounts tool available from the Settings charm and the Change PC Settings menu. You can create a local account in the Local Users and Groups tool but not a Microsoft Live account. Administrative Tools does not have a Users tool. The Control Panel does have a Users applet, but you cannot create a Microsoft Live account from this applet.

6. A, B, C. Users can use a personal identification number (PIN) or a picture password instead of a traditional password. A picture password is a group of three gestures such as a tap, drawing a circle, and/or drawing a straight line. It's possible to use a Windows Live ID to log in, but not in place of a password.

7. A, B, D. Picture passwords, biometrics, and smartcards can all be used for authentication in Windows 8.1. Other methods include text passwords and PINs. BitLocker is used to encrypt drives/partitions.

8. C. Domain accounts can be used as a Microsoft Live account by using the UPN format of the account. It is not necessary to have users create a separate Microsoft Live account. It is necessary to create a separate domain account because the existing account can be used. Creating a separate local account is not necessary and would be much more difficult.

9. B, D. You can start the command prompt by typing **command** at the Start screen and selecting Command Prompt from the menu displayed by the Search charm. You can also select it from the Start menu available at the bottom left after pressing Windows logo key+X. The command prompt is not available from the Charms bar or the Settings charm.

10. B. The error indicates that the command needs to be run from a command prompt started with administrative permissions. Running it with PowerShell won't change the permissions. Commands often cannot be executed from the GUI. Even if you logged on with an administrative account, the command prompt doesn't run with administrative permissions by default.

11. B. The runas command can be run with the /profile switch to ensure that the specified user's environment is used for the command. The /env switch uses the current user

environment. The /noprofile switch prevents the user's profile from being loaded and will minimize the amount of time it takes to start the program. The /netonly switch is used for remote access only.

12. C. The runas command can be run with the /noprofile switch to prevent the user's profile from being loaded and minimize the amount of time it takes to start the program. The /profile switch ensures that the specified user's environment is used with the application. The /env switch uses the current user environment. The /netonly switch is used for remote access only.

13. C, D. You can access the Devices charm from the Start screen, select Second Screen, and then select Extend to extend the monitor. You can also use the displayswitch /extend command from the command prompt. The Start screen doesn't include an Extend command. The Settings charm does not include the Extend tile.

14. A. The manage-bde command is used to view and manipulate BitLocker drive encryption drives. The -w switch is short for -wipefreespace and it will remove all data fragments from unused space on a drive. Neither wipefreespace nor bitlocker is a valid command. format is a valid command but it does not have a -bde switch. format will make the data inaccessible to typical users, but forensic experts can often access data on the drive.

15. D. msiexec can be executed from the command prompt to install MSI files. The /i switch specifies that the MSI file will be installed. Other switches are also available. For example, the /qb switch specifies the basic user interface level and will display a progress bar for the user. None of the other answers are valid commands in Windows 8.1.

16. D. An access denied error message indicates that PowerShell needs to be started with administrative permissions. You can do so by right-clicking the tile and selecting Run As Administrator. The PowerShell Execution Policy affects only how scripts are run, not commands. The PowerShell ISE doesn't start with administrative permissions by default, so using it won't change the symptoms. If you use the runas command *and* include credentials for an administrator account this will work, but just by using the runas command.

17. A. The Update-Help command can be used to update help topics for PowerShell commands. The Get-Help and Help cmdlets can be used with the -Full switch to see the full help but not if help hasn't been updated. There is no -Update-Help switch for Get-Help.

18. A, C. The Set-NetIPAddress PowerShell cmdlet can be used to set an IP address if one isn't currently assigned. The New-NetIPAddress can be used to set an IP address if an address is already assigned. The Get-NetIPAddress can be used to retrieve information on a network adapter. ipconfig is not a PowerShell command but is instead executed from the command prompt.

19. B. The default PowerShell Execution Policy is restricted, blocking all scripts, but scripts can be run if the policy is changed to RemoteSigned. Running the script with runas or starting PowerShell with administrative permissions won't affect the PowerShell Execution Policy.

20. A. Scripts can be specified with the full path name or with the .\ prefix if they are in the current directory. The PowerShell Execution Policy doesn't affect the path. Running the command in the ISE won't change the symptoms. Quotes should be used if the script name has spaces, but doing so won't change these symptoms.

Chapter 2

1. B. Client Hyper-V will work only on 64-bit editions of Windows 8.1 and is supported only on Windows 8.1 Pro and Windows 8.1 Enterprise. It will not work on 32-bit editions, and home users cannot purchase Windows 8.1 Enterprise.

2. B. Windows 8.1 Pro and Windows 8.1 Enterprise both support joining the computer to a domain, but only Windows 8.1 Pro is available to home users. The basic version of Windows 8.1 and Windows 8.1 RT do not support joining a computer to a domain.

3. C. Windows 8.1 Enterprise is available for businesses that subscribe to the Software Assurance program and is the only choice that supports Windows To Go.

4. B. Windows 8.1 Pro supports BitLocker To Go and is available to home users. The basic edition of Windows 8.1 does not support BitLocker To Go. Windows 8.1 Enterprise is not available to home users.

5. A, D. Windows 8.1 Pro supports 4 GB on 32-bit systems and 512 GB on 64-bit systems. This is the same for Windows 8.1 Enterprise. None of the 32-bit versions support more than 4 GB. The basic edition of Windows 8.1 supports a maximum of 128 GB on 64-bit systems.

6. C. A 64-bit edition of Windows 8.1 needs at least 20 GB of free space. 32-bit editions need at least 16 GB of free space. None of the Windows 8.1 versions will install with only 10 GB of free space. None of the versions require more than 20 GB of free space.

7. A, B, C. A large amount of storage (D) is not one of the basic requirements to use Hyper-V on a Windows 8.1 Pro or Windows 8.1 Enterprise System. You do, however, need free storage for the VMs.

8. B. Custom: Install Windows Only (Advanced) should be selected to do a clean installation. An upgrade isn't possible between 32-bit versions and 64-bit versions. Neither Wipe and Load nor Custom is an available choice from the Windows 8.1 installation program.

9. D. The data and settings should be captured before performing a custom install (which is a clean install), and the data and settings can then be migrated to Windows 8.1. A Windows XP system cannot be upgraded to Windows 8.1. The Windows 8.1 Upgrade Assistant can evaluate a system to see whether it can be upgraded, but it cannot capture data to be migrated.

10. C, D. Clean installs are needed on the Windows XP and Windows Vista systems after capturing the data on the systems to migrate over to the new installation. While not available as a choice, the Windows 7 systems should be upgraded to Windows 8.1. Windows Vista systems cannot be upgraded to Windows 8.1. One of the goals is to upgrade any computers that can be upgraded, and because the Windows 7 systems can be upgraded clean installs should not be done on all systems.

11. B. ScanState is one of the tools available in USMT and can capture user data and settings from the original installation. LoadState will apply data and settings to a new installation. Sysprep is used to prepare an image. DISM is used to view and manipulate images.

12. A. The Windows Assessment and Deployment Kit includes several tools used to automate deployments of Windows 8.1. It has replaced the Windows Automated Installation Kit used in Windows 7. Windows Software Update Services is used to deploy updates to clients, not the full operating system. The Application Compatibility Toolkit is used to identify compatibility with operating systems; it isn't used to automate a deployment.

13. D. The Sysprep tool is used to prepare a computer imaging. DISM is used to view and manipulate images. ScanState is used to capture user data and settings, and LoadState is used to apply user data and settings.

14. A. DISM is used to view and manipulate images, and it can add drivers in an offline image using a process known as offline image servicing. ScanState is used to capture user data and settings, and LoadState is used to apply user data and settings. The Sysprep tool is used to prepare a computer imaging.

15. A. USB 3.0 performs better, but USB 2.0 drives will work. All of the other statements are valid requirements for Windows To Go.

16. A, D. You can only use 32-bit versions of Windows on 32-bit systems. If a traditional BIOS is used on a computer, both 32-bit and 64-bit versions of Windows To Go are supported. If a UEFI-based BIOS is used, 32-bit versions of Windows 8.1 To Go will not work on a 64-bit system.

17. C. Client Hyper-V can support almost any Windows operating system from Windows 95 to Windows 8.1, including many Windows Server operating systems. The host must be running a 64-bit version of Windows 8.1 Pro or Enterprise, but the guest operating systems can be running 32-bit or 64-bit Windows.

18. D. The minimum amount of RAM required for Client Hyper-V is 4 GB. More is better.

19. A. A fixed-size VHD file is recommended for the best performance. A dynamically expanding disk takes processing power as it expands and slows down the performance. Similarly, encrypted or compressed files take time to unencrypt or uncompress and are rarely used with VHD files.

20. D. If Secure Boot is enabled on a system, it cannot be configured as a dual-boot system. Different operating systems should be installed on separate partitions. It is possible to create dual-boot systems with two Windows 8.1 installations without Secure Boot. Basic disks are required, and if a disk is configured as dynamic in one operating system, the other operating system will no longer be able to boot.

Chapter 3

1. D. You should perform a custom installation, which installs Windows 8.1 by itself, and delete the existing partitions during the installation. You cannot upgrade a 32-bit edition of Windows 7 to a 64-bit edition of Windows 8.1. If you do not modify the existing partitions, the Windows 7 files will remain on the system in a Windows.old folder.

2. A, B, C. Starting the computer from the installation DVD and selecting Upgrade: Install Windows and Keep Files, Settings, And Applications will upgrade Windows 7 Professional to Windows 8.1 Pro. It's also possible to start the startup program from within Windows 7 (either from the installation DVD or a network share) and select Upgrade. If the partitions are modified during the installation, it will delete the data on the disk and only a clean installation is possible.

3. C. The BIOS on his home computer should be modified to boot to the USB drive when it is inserted. Windows 7 doesn't have the option of modifying the Windows To Go boot

settings. Modifying the boot settings in the Windows To Go workspace only affects the computer where it is installed and so cannot be done on the home computer until it can boot into the Windows To Go workspace. It is not necessary to install Windows 8.1 on the home computer.

4. C. The BCDboot tool will prepare the drive to boot on a user's home computer (as long as the user's computer is configured to boot from a USB drive). Both ImageX and DISM can be used to capture and copy a Windows To Go image but not configure it to be bootable. ScanState is used to scan a system and capture user data and settings but cannot configure Windows To Go.

5. C. Roaming profiles allows users to have access to the data and settings no matter which computer they log on to. Local profiles are available only on a single system. Mandatory profiles are not changeable, and users will not have access to their data and settings but instead only the data and settings included in the mandatory profile. Folder redirection gives roaming users access to their data, but not their settings.

6. B. The best solution is to implement folder redirection for the users and redirect the user folders to a network share. This way, the users will have access to their data no matter which computer they log on to. If only roaming profiles are implemented without folder redirection, the user data will be copied to the computer each time the user logs on, which can slow down the logon time. If local profiles are used, the users won't have access to the data on different systems. The Default User profile is used only when the user first logs onto a system and wouldn't help in this situation.

7. D. You cannot use folder redirection for entire libraries, and there is no folder named My Libraries. You can use folder redirection with My Documents, My Music, My Pictures, and My Videos.

8. D. User Experience Virtualization (UE-V) improves logon times by downloading only what a roaming user needs instead of the entire profile. If local profiles are used, the user will not have access to their profile on different systems. If roaming is prevented, users will lose their current abilities to roam. If mandatory profiles are used, users will not be able to modify their profiles.

9. C. The easiest way of the given choices is to copy the user documents to a USB flash drive to move them from the old system to the new system. Although it is easy to use WET with an Easy Transfer cable or a crossover cable, you cannot use WET between a 32-bit and a 64-bit system. USMT takes more time, and you cannot use USMT between a 32-bit and a 64-bit system.

10. A. The Windows Easy Transfer (WET) tool is the easiest to use of the given choices. The User State Migration Tool (USMT) can be used, but it is much more complex. User Experience Virtualization (UE-V) and roaming profiles aren't used for migration.

11. A. One method used with Windows Easy Transfer (WET) is over the network and a crossover cable connecting two systems simulates a network connection. WET does not support using standard USB, FireWire, or serial cables for data transfer.

12. B. The most current version of the User State Migration Tool (USMT) is available in the free download of Windows Assessment and Deployment Kit (ADK). The previous version is in the Windows Automated Installation Kit (AIK). USMT is not included in the Windows Easy Transfer (WET) tool or within a Windows 8.1 installation.

13. C. The USMTutils command-line tool is part of the User State Migration Tool (USMT), and it can be used to determine the cryptographic options available for a migration store. LoadState is used to load migration data and settings onto a computer. ScanState is used to scan a computer and capture migration data and settings. Windows Easy Transfer (WET) is used to transfer the data and settings but doesn't include any encryption capabilities.

14. B. The correct order is to run ScanState on the old computer, install applications on the new computer, and then run LoadState on the new computer. LoadState will not capture data on the old computer. USMT does not include WET. The application settings are not applied if the applications are installed after the settings are migrated.

15. A. The correct order is to run ScanState on the old computer, install the application on the new computer, and then run LoadState on the new computer. The steps are the same no matter which operating system the older computer is running or which platform Windows 8.1 is running on. LoadState will not capture data on the old computer. The application settings are not applied if the applications are installed after the settings are migrated. USMT does not include WET.

16. B. The ScanState tool is used to scan the old computer to capture the settings and data. The LoadState tool is used to load the settings and data onto the new computer. USMTutils provides extra utilities but doesn't capture data. WET is not part of the Windows ADK.

17. D. The LoadState tool is used to load the settings and data onto the new computer. The ScanState tool is used to scan the old computer to capture the settings and data. USMT includes the LoadState and ScanState tools but is not a tool itself. Windows Easy Transfer (WET) is not part of the Windows ADK.

18. D. The user exclude switch (/ue) can be used with the loadstate command to exclude certain accounts from the migration. The miguser.xml file can be used to identify which user components are migrated, but not which users. The config.xml file can be used exclude certain components or settings from the migration, but not users. The user include switch (/ui) is used to include specific users.

19. D. If the applications are installed after LoadState is used to migrate the settings, the settings are not applied. Application settings are typically included in a migration store. There is nothing to indicate that the settings were corrupted. Application settings are captured with ScanState and applied with LoadState.

20. B. You can modify the migdocs.xml file to include files with the .gcga extension. The miguser.xml file is used to identify profile elements to include in the migration. The config.xml file can be used to exclude certain components or settings from the migration, but not user data. The migapp.xml file is used to identify specific application settings to migrate, but not application data.

Chapter 4

1. B. Hyper-V is not supported on 32-bit systems but is supported on 64-bit systems. You need a minimum of 4 GB of RAM, but it's not clear how much RAM the computer in the scenario is using. Client Hyper-V can be installed on 64-bit Windows 8.1 Pro and Windows 8.1 Enterprise editions.

2. D. Hyper-V requires a minimum of 4 GB of RAM, so you'll need to add RAM first. Hyper-V is enabled through the Programs and Features applet, but you won't be able to enable it with only 3 GB of RAM. It is not necessary to upgrade to Windows 8.1 Enterprise because Hyper-V is supported on Windows 8.1 Pro. You can create a virtual switch only after Hyper-V is enabled on a system.

3. B. The Internal type of virtual switch allows the guest operating systems to communicate with each other and the host but not the outside network. An external switch provides access to the outside network. A private switch prevents network access to the host. You cannot create a virtual switch with a Host setting.

4. D. The most likely problem is that the virtual switch for the VM is not set to External. If it is set to Internal or Private, it will not have access to the network and won't be able to connect to the server. An application running within a VM doesn't have to be compatible with Windows 8.1. It only needs to be compatible with the operating system running in the VM. If the operating system is compatible with Hyper-V, the application within the operating system is also compatible with Hyper-V. Virtual switches do not have a Network setting.

5. C. A virtual switch configured with the Private setting allows VMs to communicate with each other but not the host or the external network. If the virtual NIC is disabled, the VMs cannot communicate with each other. If the virtual switch is configured with the Internal setting, VMs can communicate over the network with the host. NIC teaming is used to combine two or more NICs on a single system but is not relevant here.

6. A. The Virtual Switch Manager should be started to create at least one virtual switch. If a virtual switch is not created, you will not be able to configure networking. If the host machine didn't have network access, starting the Network and Sharing Center will resolve the problem for the host, but the host has network access. The Hyper-V settings won't show a connection until a virtual switch has been created with the Virtual Switch Manager. You cannot configure network settings in a snapshot.

7. D. You cannot modify the RAM settings if the VM is running, but you will be able to make this change if you shut down the VM first. You can assign more than 4 GB of RAM if it is available on the physical host, and 12 GB of RAM is more than enough to assign 5 GB to a single VM. If the physical host was running 32-bit Windows 8.1, it could not run Hyper-V.

8. B. You should export the VM from the original system, copy to the destination system, and import it on the destination system. Hyper-V Manager is used to export and import VMs. If you only copy the virtual disk and try to create a VM with it, you will not have all the settings. Snapshots track only the changes to the system.

9. A. You should select Copy The Virtual Machine (Create A New Unique ID) when importing a VM to the same machine. If you are importing it onto a new system, you can select Register. If you are importing it on the original system and you deleted all remnants of the original VM, you can select Restore, but this won't work if the original VM still exists. The Copy option does not use the existing unique ID.

10. B. The best choice is to move the virtual hard disks and snapshots to a different partition. Snapshots can take a lot of space, so if you only move the virtual hard disks you won't gain the maximum amount of space. You can't move the Windows operating system folder. If you compress the virtual hard disks, performance will be slowed down when these VMs are accessed.

11. C. The easiest solution is to create a snapshot before doing the update. If the update fails, you can apply the snapshot to revert the VM to its previous state. System Restore and a full backup will probably work too but would take much more effort. It will also take a lot of effort to export the VM, copy it to a network drive, and then import it if the update fails. Creating a snapshot after the update would capture the VM in its failed state.

12. A. You should right-click the desired snapshot and select Apply to apply its settings. Revert isn't an available option for a snapshot. Apply isn't an available option for a VM. If you select Revert from the VM, it will apply the most recent snapshot, not the snapshot from two weeks ago.

13. D. The most likely problem is that snapshots have been created and are growing. These are separate from the virtual hard disks. The settings files don't take much space. If a VM is using shadow files, these are included within the virtual hard disk of the VM, so moving the VM moved the shadow files. Restarting Windows 8.1 won't affect how snapshot files grow.

14. B. When you select Delete Subtree from the oldest snapshot, it will apply all the changes to the VM since that snapshot was created and then delete all the snapshots. If you select the newest snapshot and select Delete Subtree, only the changes from the most recent snapshot are applied and only the most recent snapshot is deleted. It is not necessary to apply a snapshot before deleting it from Hyper-V Manager. You should not manually delete the snapshot for an existing VM.

15. B. You need to manually delete the virtual hard disk files. When you delete the VMs in Hyper-V Manager, it deletes many of the settings files and the snapshots but it does not delete the virtual hard disk files. These will normally be too large for the Recycle Bin, so you'll be prompted to delete them permanently. Emptying the Recycle Bin might give some extra space if other data has been deleted, but it won't delete the virtual hard disk files from deleted Hyper-V VMs. Restarting Hyper-V will not delete data or free up disk space.

16. D. The most likely reason for the conflict is that the import is trying to copy the virtual hard disk to the same location as the original VM using the same filename. Choosing a different location resolves this problem. When you select Copy, you do not need to register the new ID. The settings files and snapshots are identified with a new ID when you select Copy, so they do not need to be stored in a different location.

17. B. If you want to limit the number of processors used by a VM, set Number Of Virtual Processors to exactly what is desired for each VM. By default a VM is assigned one processor only. The other settings do not specifically limit the processors used by the VM.

18. D. You can add Hyper-V, create a VM on user systems, and install the application into the VM. Microsoft Virtual PC, Windows Virtual PC, and Windows XP Mode are not supported in Windows 8.1.

19. B. Remote Desktop Services (RDS) can be installed on a server and host desktops for users. Roaming users can have the same desktop no matter which computer they log on to. Client Hyper-V can be installed on to a Windows 8.1 system to create virtual machines on a single Windows 8.1 system, but the VMs aren't available for roaming users. App-V and Remote-App can be used to provide applications to roaming users but not desktops.

20. A. App-V can be hosted on a server to stream applications to clients when they log on to different computers. Hyper-V is installed on individual systems and wouldn't help a roaming user. AppLocker is used to restrict which applications can run on different computers and isn't here. An external switch is a choice within Hyper-V for the virtual switch.

Chapter 5

1. B. An address starting with 169.254 is an APIPA address, and a DHCP client assigns itself an APIPA address when it doesn't receive a response from a DHCP server. DNS is used for name resolution and does not assign APIPA addresses. The network location is unrelated to how IP addresses are assigned.

2. A. DirectAccess requires IPv6, so IPv6 must be implemented to support it. WINS is used for NetBIOS name resolution but is not needed for DirectAccess. HomeGroups are used to share information among users within small workgroup but are not related to DirectAccess. Preferred wireless settings are not needed for DirectAccess.

3. C. An IPv6 address includes eight groups of four hexadecimal characters but can be shortened by eliminating leading zeroes and using zero compression with a single set of double colons. Only seven sets of hexadecimal characters without double colons are not valid. Nine sets of characters are not valid. An IPv6 address cannot use two double colons.

4. B. The most likely problem is that the computer isn't assigned a global unicast IPv6 address. The assigned address starts with FE80, indicating it is a link local unicast address. An anycast address is not used for Internet access. Link local and unique local addresses are not used for Internet access.

5. B. The most likely problem is DNS because the symptoms indicate that name resolution is not working when the name is pinged and DNS is the only one of the options provided that performs name resolution. DHCP provides an IP address and other TCP/IP configuration information. The default gateway provides a path to other networks through a router. An APIPA address is used when DHCP cannot be reached.

6. B. DNS is used for hostname resolution in a domain. DHCP is used to assign IP addresses. Domain controllers are needed in a domain and DNS is required within a domain, but domain controllers do not provide name resolution. WINS is used for NetBIOS name resolution, but NetBIOS names are used less and less, so a WINS server might not be needed.

7. B. The `nslookup` command is used to check DNS issues, and it can verify a host record exists on a DNS server. `ipconfig` is used to check TCP/IP configuration on the local computer. `ping` is used to verify connectivity. `tracert` is used to show routers in the path between two systems.

8. A. The `ipconfig /flushdns` command can be used to remove entries from the DNS resolver cache. NSlookup can be used to verify if DNS has the correct entries, but it doesn't affect the DNS resolver cache on the local computer. Ping is used to check connectivity. Disabling DHCP won't affect the DNS resolver cache.

9. D. The `ipconfig /release` and `ipconfig /renew` commands can be used to release and renew a lease from a DHCP server. An APIPA address is assigned when a DHCP client doesn't receive an IP address from DHCP. `nslookup` and `ping` are not used to get DHCP leases.

10. B. The computer is connected directly to the Internet with a public IP address, so it should use the public network location for the best security. The private network location is used for a home or work network when the computer is not connected directly to the Internet. A domain network location is used when the computer is connected to the domain. IPv6 is not a network location.

11. D. Selecting the public network location disables Network Discover and is the easiest way to do so. Disabling the firewall will not disable Network Discovery and is not recommended. It is not necessary to create a rule in the firewall because rules already exist. Network Discovery is enabled by default in the private network location.

12. D. The private network location is used for a home or work network and is appropriate here. A domain network location is used when the computer is connected to the domain. Internal is not a network location choice. Public should be selected if the computer is in a public place such as coffee shop or connected directly to the Internet with a public IP address.

13. D. HomeGroups can only be created when the private network location is used. They are available in for both Windows 7 and Windows 8.1 systems. You cannot create them when a public network or domain network is selected.

14. C. By changing the Documents section to Not Shared, the user ensures that document files in the Documents library will no longer be shared. If the user leaves the HomeGroup, she will not be able to access HomeGroup resources on other computers. Changing the Media Devices section affects streaming media but not document files. HomeGroups do not have a Files section.

15. C. WPA-2 Personal should be selected because it is the strongest when compared with WEP and WPA. WPA2-Enterprise is stronger, but it requires an authentication server.

16. A. Automatic downloads such as Microsoft Updates will not be downloaded on the wireless connection if it is set to metered. If the wireless connection is set to nonmetered, the wireless connection can be used for downloads. You cannot set a wired connection to metered.

17. D. He should set his home network to nonmetered so that automatic updates will download automatically. If the home network is set to metered, the work network will be preferred for these downloads. You cannot set a wired network to metered or nonmetered.

18. B. The Network selection from the Settings charm shows all currently available wireless connections. The Control Panel does not include a Wireless applet. The Devices charm doesn't include a Network selection. Manage Wireless Networks is not available in the Network and Sharing Center in Windows 8.1.

19. A. WPA2-Enterprise uses an authentication server and ensures that users authenticate before being granted access. WPA2-Personal uses a preshared key or password. AES and TKIP are used for encryption of data, not authentication.

20. D. The Network Connections page is accessible from the Network and Sharing Center and shows all adapters on the computer. The Network page from the Settings charm allows you to turn sharing on or off, but it doesn't give direct access to the network adapter. The PC Settings page does not have a Network Adapters page. The Control Panel does not include an Ethernet adapter.

Chapter 6

1. C. A port rule would enable you to specify the specific port number (such as port 20 and port 21 for FTP transfers). To set up the port rule, you use Windows Firewall with Advanced Security and specify that you want to create a new inbound rule.

2. A. DirectAccess requires IPv6, so IPv6 must be implemented to support it. WINS is used for NetBIOS name resolution but is not needed for DirectAccess. Shared libraries are used to share information among users within small workgroup but are not related to DirectAccess.

3. D. Windows Firewall analyzes the source IP of the packet, destination IP address, TCP/UDP port number, and other items.

4. A. The clients must be configured using either Group Policy or the netsh command. For example, you can use this command from an administrative command prompt to configure clients to use distributed caching: netsh branchcache set service distributed.

5. D. VPNs, or virtual private networks, allow users to access private networks while connecting from an outside network, such as the Internet. Remote Assistance is used to allow a user to connect to one client computer. AppLocker is used to restrict which applications can run on different computers and isn't useful here. PowerShell is a Windows scripting language.

6. B. The Remote Desktop Users dialog box is opened by clicking Select Users on the System Properties – Remote tab. Remote Assistance Settings lets you control if a computer can be controlled remotely and how many hours an invitation stays open. The System Properties dialog box has options for enabling Remote Assistance and Remote Desktop connections. The Remote Desktop Connection window does not have options for setting user authentication.

7. D. The Remote Desktop app is designed for Windows 8.1, including touch-enabled devices. Remote Desktop Connection, Remote Assistance, and VPN connections are not touch-enhanced.

8. B. You can configure Windows Firewall to exempt computers or IP addresses from authenticating by setting up authentication exceptions. Enabling a port provides a way for you to allow or block traffic to a specific port or range of ports. You configure remote authentication to allow or restrict users who can remotely access your computer.

9. A. Remote Assistance provides a way for a user who is already logged in to send an invitation for someone else to connect. Remote Desktop Connection and the Remote Desktop app close any current remote session. VPN connections can access other remote network resources, such as files, databases, and so forth.

10. D. The Allow An App Or Feature Through Windows Firewall option provides a way to change allowed apps through Windows Firewall. Port exceptions and protocol exceptions would not necessarily work as those features may allow additional programs to access the Internet. Connection blocking would block all apps and features by default.

11. D. The Remote Desktop Gateway permits a remote computer to make a Remote Desktop connection to a user's computer on the corporate network but blocks the remote computer from accessing anything other than the target computer.

12. B. In stealth mode the firewall receives probing packets that hackers use to determine what services and equipment it can target. The firewall simply loses the packets and does not sending anything back to the source.

13. C. To assign static IP addresses to your client computers, you can use the Windows PowerShell cmdlet Set-NetIPAddress.

14. B. DirectAccess allows clients to access internal resources using Internet access but without creating a VPN. Also, DirectAccess does not require the user to manually create a connection.

15. C. Sync Center was introduced in Windows 8 and Windows 8.1 and lets you sync your various devices. It uses your Microsoft account to connect with your local account so that things like browser history and offline files can be accessible from all your synced devices.

16. A. When using IPsec in the corporate environment where clients access highly sensitive data, it is best to use the highest encryption available.

17. D. If hosted cache mode is used, you must enable the BranchCache feature on the server in the remote office. If you don't have at least Windows Server 2008 R2, you can use distributed cache mode instead.

18. C. Windows 8.1 clients can cache or access files used with BranchCache. In addition, the clients must be configured using either Group Policy or the `netsh` command.

19. D. Windows RT and Windows 8.1 (basic edition) can use Remote Desktop as a client only. Computers running those versions cannot be set up as Remote Desktop hosts, meaning you cannot remotely access them from another computer.

20. A. VPN connections use tunneling protocols. These tunneling protocols include encryption and provide additional protection for the connection.

Chapter 7

1. B. When you first install Windows 8.1 on a computer, it automatically belongs to a workgroup. If you want it to connect to a domain, you must specify the domain name.

2. C. A Windows domain includes at least one server acting as a domain controller and hosting AD DS.

3. B. Group Policy settings can be configured using the Group Policy Management Console in a domain.

4. D. The Software Settings node can be used to deploy software to clients.

5. C. Authentication is used to identify a user, and authorization is used to control access of the user.

6. B. Members of the Domain Administrators group have complete and unrestricted access to computers in the domain. The domain administrator account, the Domain Admins group, and the Enterprise Admins group are all members of the domain Administrators group by default.

7. B. An important benefit of a domain is that it provides single sign-on capabilities. In a domain, each user has one account that they can use to log on to almost any computer in the domain. In a workgroup, users need a separate account for each computer.

8. C. A Local Computer Policy applies to only a single GPO, but other GPOs can apply to many users and computers in the organization.

9. D. Very often you'll want to configure settings and ensure that they are not overwritten or blocked. Normally, the last GPO applied wins, but you can use the Enforced setting to override this default behavior.

10. A. Users are granted rights and permissions based on the user accounts that authenticate them. If users log on with the local administrator account, they are able to perform any action and access any of the resources on the system.

11. A. Groups are granted rights and permissions based on the user needs that are members of the group. All permissions granted to a group are conferred to the members of the group. To allow printing, apply the Print permission.

12. A. The Software Settings node can be used to deploy software to clients. Software deployed with Group Policy can be automatically installed on computers or installed based on a user's action. For example, a Group Policy–deployed application can appear on a user's Start menu and be installed when the user first selects it or deployed to a computer and installed the next time the computer restarts.

13. B and C. Authentication is used to identify a user, and authorization is used to control access of the user. When two authentication factors are required it means that the two methods must be from two of the following categories:

14. D. Users are granted rights and permissions according to their user accounts and the groups of which they are members.

15. D. Group Policy settings can be configured using the Group Policy Management Console in a domain.

16. B. It's possible to block the inheritance of all GPOs for an OU. For example, you could create an OU for testing purposes and decide that you don't want to allow GPOs from the domain or parent OUs to apply. You can enable the Block Inheritance setting on the OU.

17. C. Group Policy settings can be configured using the Group Policy Management Console in a domain. The Prevent Installation Of Removable Devices prevents the use of any new removable devices. It will only affect new devices that are added.

18. A. A computer will check for updates or changes to computer Group Policy settings every 90–120 minutes (90 minutes with a random offset of 30 minutes).

19. A. By using special permissions, you can give the Owner group Full Control except for deleting

20. D. Button options control the action that takes place when you use a particular button, such as the Power button. Using a GPO will allow you to set this for all users

Chapter 8

1. A. Only the Administrator account has the ability to open and manage keys in the Registry.

2. C. If you use local user accounts, they must be configured on each computer that the user needs to access within the network. For this reason, domain user accounts are commonly used to manage users on any network larger than 10 users.

3. A. There are a number rules you have to follow when choosing a naming convention for user account names. The @ symbol is not allowed.

4. D. Windows 8.1 uses the SID as the user object. All security settings get associated with the SID and not the user account.

5. D. When a user account is no longer needed, the account should be disabled or deleted. After you've disabled an account, you can later enable it again to restore it with all of its associated user properties. An account that is deleted can be recovered, but it is not as simple as enabling a disabled account.

   Windows 8.1 uses the SID as the user object. All security settings get associated with the SID and not the user account.

6. D. The four built-in accounts are Administrator, Guest, the initial user, and the Home-Group user.

7. B. When a user locks himself out of an account because the password was entered incorrectly too many times, you first have to unlock the account before the user can do anything.

8. D. Logon scripts are files that run every time a user logs on to the network. They are usually batch files, but they can be any type of executable file.

    You might use logon scripts to set up drive mappings or to run a specific executable file each time a user logs on to the computer.

9. A. A user must be an Administrator to have full control over the computer and thus can create users and groups.

10. C, D. The members of the Event Log Readers group have the ability to read event logs on the local machine. Members of the Performance Log Users group have the ability to schedule logging of performance counters and to enable trace providers.

11. B. Access tokens are created only when you log on. If you change group memberships, you need to log off and log on again to update the access token.

12. A. To configure a temporary password that the user must change, you can select the User Must Change Password At Next Logon option in the New User dialog box. By configuring this option, the user will be required to change his or her password when they first log on to the computer.

13. A. The only real requirement for creating a new user is that you must provide a valid username. It's a good idea to have your own rules for usernames, which form your naming convention.

14. A, B. By default, the Administrator and Guest accounts cannot be deleted, although they can both be renamed. Both the Administrator account and the Guest account are disabled by default.

15. B, C, D. Creating a mandatory profile involves three main steps. First, rename the user profile from NTUSER.DAT to NTUSER.MAN. Second, copy the profile to a network share. Third, in the Local Users and Groups utility, access the properties of the user who will be assigned the roaming profile and specify the location of the mandatory profile. This path must be a UNC path for the mandatory profile to work.

16. B. User profiles contain information about the Windows 8.1 environment for a specific user. For example, profile settings include the Desktop arrangement, program groups, and screen colors that users see when they log on.

17. B. When you create a new user, a security identifier (SID) is automatically created on the computer for the user account. The username is a property of the SID.

18. B, C. When a printer is installed and configured for access via a network port, the administrator needs to give a group permission to access the printer.

19. C, D. One misconception about groups is that groups have to work with Group Policy objects (GPOs). This is not correct. GPOs are a set of rules that allow you to set computer configuration and user configuration options that apply to users or computers.

20. A. The most likely reason there are no file access entries in the security event log is that you did not enable auditing for the appropriate files and folders. This behavior is true of print auditing as well.

Chapter 9

1. C. To figure out a user's rights, you must first add up what their effective NTFS rights are and their effective Shared permissions. Then the most restrictive set takes precedence. So in this example, the user's NTFS rights were Full Control and the Shared permissions were Change, so Change would be the effective permission.

2. A. You do not want this user to have any administrator rights. To allow this user to change Windows Update manually, you must set this in an LGPO.

3. B. Application Control Policy (AppLocker) allows you to configure a Denied list and an Accepted list for applications or users. Applications that are configured on the Denied list will not run on the system or by specific groups and applications on the Accepted list will operate properly.

4. D. LGPOs are policies that you can set on a local Windows 8.1 machine to limit hardware and user usage. You also have the ability to control individual users within the Local Group Policy.

5. B. Audit Object Access enables auditing of access to files, folders, and printers.

6. A. Will's NTFS rights were Full Control and the Shared permissions were Full Control, so Full Control would be the effective permission.

7. D. Windows 8.1 comes with a new feature called BitLocker Drive Encryption. BitLocker encrypts the entire system drive. New files added to this drive are encrypted automatically. To configure BitLocker, you must either use a Local Group Policy or click the BitLocker icon in Control Panel.

8. C, D. BitLocker Drive Encryption is a data protection feature available in Windows Enterprise and Pro editions of Windows 8.1. This feature is not included in Windows 8.1 Home or Basic.

9. A. Within Windows Update, you cannot specify a WSUS server. You need to specify the WSUS server through the use of a Local Group Policy.

10. B. Account Lockout Policy, a subset of Account Policy, is used to specify options that prevent a user from attempting multiple failed logon attempts. If the Account Lockout Threshold value is exceeded, the account will be locked. The account can be reset based on a specified amount of time or through administrator intervention.

11. A. The Group Policy Results Tool is accessed through the GPResult command-line utility. The gpresult command displays the resulting set of policies that were enforced on the computer and the specified user during the logon process.

12. A. Audit Account Logon Events is used to track when a user logs on, logs off, or makes a network connection. You can configure auditing for success or failure, and audited events can be tracked through Event Viewer.

13. B, C. The password Abcde! meets complexity requirements because it is at least six characters long and contains uppercase letters, lowercase letters, and symbols. The password 1247445Np meets complexity requirements because it is at least six characters long and contains uppercase letters, lowercase letters, and numbers. Complex passwords must be at least six characters long and contain three of the four types of characters—uppercase letters, lowercase letters, numbers, and symbols.

14. B. The security option Interactive Logon: Do Not Display Last User Name is used to prevent the last username in the logon screen from being displayed in the logon dialog box. This option is commonly used in environments where computers are used publicly.

15. B. Mary's NTFS rights were Read only and the Shared permissions were Change, so Read only would be the effective permission.

16. D. The Restore Files and Directories user right allows a user to restore files and directories regardless of file and directory permissions. Assigning this user right is an alternative to making a user a member of the Backup Operators group.

17. B. The Enforce Password History policy allows the system to keep track of a user's password history for up to 24 passwords. This prevents a user from using the same password over and over again.

18. D. When both NTFS and share permissions have been applied, the system looks at the effective rights for NTFS and share permissions and then applies the most restrictive of the cumulative permissions. If a resource has been shared, and you access it from the local computer where the resource resides, then you'll be governed only by the NTFS permissions.

19. D. Virus protection is now included with Windows 8.1. Windows Firewall, Windows Defender, and Windows Update are also included with Windows 8.1.

20. A. The most likely reason there are no file access entries in the security event log is that you did not enable auditing for the appropriate files and folders. This behavior is true of print auditing as well.

Chapter 10

1. C. To figure out Alice's rights, you must first add up her effective NTFS rights and her effective Shared permissions. Then the most restrictive set takes precedence. So in this example, Alice's NTFS rights were Full Control and the Shared permissions were Change, so Change would be the effective permission.

2. B. Audit Object Access enables auditing of access to files, folders, and printers.

3. A. Will's NTFS rights were Full Control and the Shared permissions were Full Control, so Full Control would be the effective permission.

4. B. Mary's NTFS rights were Read only and the Shared permissions were Change, so Read would be the only effective permission.

5. D. When both NTFS and share permissions have been applied, the system looks at the effective rights for NTFS and share permissions and then applies the most restrictive of the cumulative permissions. If a resource has been shared, and you access it from the local computer where the resource resides, then you will be governed only by the NTFS permissions.

6. C. Standard users cannot install drivers on their computers. The Power User account is no longer supported on Windows 8.1. Service accounts cannot be used to log on to the computer or used by the user. This also applies to the built-in administrator account, which is usually disabled by default.

7. **A, B.** There is no such rule that the password must be 10 characters or that the password needs to be changed every 90 days. Shared folders are a feature of HomeGroups and option E suggests the opposite.

8. **B, C, E.** Option A is incorrect—there is no such plug-in. Access to OneDrive is possible from multiple apps and utilities. It is designed to be a secure but available anywhere resource in Windows 8.1. As for option D, it may happen one day but OneDrive is not yet connected to your credit card.

9. **A, C, D.** A partition is not considered to be a securable object in Windows 8.1.

10. **A, B, C.** All of these are true as long as the objects reside on an NTFS drive. Auditing is not available on the older FAT file system.

11. **A.** Dynamic Access Control (DAC) was introduced in Windows Server 2012 and Windows 8 and support continues in Windows Server 2012 R2 and Windows 8.1.

12. **E.** Users have no rights or access to the Group Policy Editor (GPE). All others answers are correct. Without the right to log on locally, users would not be able to sign on to their computer.

13. **B.** Although option D might be tempting, the actual file is a CER file, with the `.cer` extension. The DOCX file is Word file and PFX is a graphic file format.

14. **A.** These will be located in the `Personal` folder.

15. **B.** By default, the role of Data Recovery Agent is assigned to the local administrator account.

16. **C.** An explicit permission has precedence over an inherited one and a Deny has precedence over an Allow

17. **D.** When both NTFS and share permissions have been applied, the system looks at the effective rights for NTFS and share permissions and then applies the most restrictive of the cumulative permissions. If a resource has been shared, and you access it from the local computer where the resource resides, then you will be governed only by the NTFS permissions.

18. **A.** Will's NTFS rights were Full Control and the Shared permissions were Full Control, so Full Control would be the effective permission.

19. **D.** When both NTFS and share permissions have been applied, the system looks at the effective rights for NTFS and share permissions and then applies the most restrictive of the cumulative permissions. If a resource has been shared, and you access it from the local computer where the resource resides, then you will be governed only by the NTFS permissions.

20. **C.** The public folders are contained in a single folder named `Public` in the `Users` folder. (The default path is `C:\Users\Public`.) The `Public` folder looks just like your `Documents` folders. All folders for documents, downloads, music, pictures, photos, and videos are maintained in it.

Chapter 11

1. **B.** When you first install Windows 8.1 on a computer, it automatically belongs to a workgroup. If you want it to connect to a domain, you must specify the domain name.

2. B. A driver that is digitally signed has an identifier called a digital signature used to verify the integrity of the driver and to verify the identity of the vendor (software publisher) who provides the driver.

3. B. Metro apps are based on Metro design language, run on WindowsRuntime platform and sold, installed and serviced via Windows Store.

4. D. DISM is used to service offline, not online, images.

5. B. Printing wirelessly was not one of the improvements made by the v4 printing architecture.

6. A. Windows 8.1 Professional can be used as printer server. When a printer is installed on the host computer, make sure that all compatible drivers are also installed.

7. D. When a remote user connects to the office network over a VPN, the default printer will be the printer attached to the local computer. However, you can have more than one default printer when you give it network affinity.

8. C. Device Manager is the central utility in Windows 8/8.1 for the management of devices.

9. A. You can make any existing non-NFC printer NFC capable by using an NFC tag. NFC tags are like stickers that can be programmed to store the required information.

10. A, D. Firmware is also software in that it is program code. The difference is in how the program code is stored. Firmware is stored in a hardware device, typically in read-only memory.

11. B. Unlike some earlier editions of Windows, Windows 8.1 does not allow unsigned drivers without you making some significant changes. The process had been made complicated to impress upon users the importance of using signed drivers. It will require two reboots.

12. D. Windows 8.1 is limited to no more than 20 concurrent connections.

13. C. The spool folder can fill up and cause significant disk fragmentation if disk space is limited. The spool folder should be relocated to a larger hard disk.

14. C. If Windows 8.1 cannot disable or work with the new device, you may be able to start in Safe Mode With Networking and either get updated drivers there or disable the device manually.

15. B. Initially a program called a print spooler creates a special copy of the document that contains programming codes that tell the printer what to do so that the document it prints looks like the document that you printed. After the spooler creates the printer file, it sends the information to the printer buffer.

16. B. While you need to give users permission to use a printer, you also need to explicitly share the printer so that it can be found by browsing for printers on the network.

17. D. Most printers today come with more than one port to connect the printer to a server or the network.

18. B, C. Any external hardware attached to a Windows 8.1 computer is going to need a device driver to work with the computer.

19. A. To manage print jobs, you use the print queue. If a document is already printing, or waiting to print, you'll see a tiny printer icon in the Notification area. When you point to that icon, the number of documents waiting to be printed appears in a tooltip. Double-click that small icon to open the print queue.

20. A. Location-Aware Printing is a feature of Windows 8.1 that enables you to select different default printers for different networks. This is ideal for anyone who has a mobile computing device, such as a Windows laptop, Windows tablet, or Windows Phone. As you connect to a different network, Windows automatically becomes aware of the available printers on that network and selects the current default printer as one of the printers on the available network.

Chapter 12

1. C. When a computer stops responding, the only thing you might still be able to do is start Task Manager. This can best be achieved by pressing Ctrl+Alt+Del to launch the menu option that will allow you to start Task Manager.

2. D. All applications that conform to best practices report errors to the event log. This should be the first place you look to find a possible reason the device is not working. The event may tell you something bad is wrong, or it could be something simple such as "printer out of paper."

3. C. A nice feature of Task Manager is that you can configure it to always stay on top. So if you are busy troubleshooting or managing the computer, Task Manager will not get lost behind other windows. Option D would also work, but it would be a hassle if the machine is slow.

4. B. You have several options to change the speed with which Task Manager updates information. For instant information select update down and you will get a refresh.

5. A. Task Manager can report of a range of hardware components, but it can only monitor hardware that is attached or running on computer's motherboard.

6. A, B, C. Task Manager, Event Viewer, and Resource Monitor are provided to help you troubleshoot a sick computer. Paint is a graphic application that has nothing to do with troubleshooting.

7. A. System Reset reinstalls Windows and deletes all data. The system will be like a new installation when done.

8. A. The Performance tab of Task Manager lets you check how resources on the computer are being used.

9. D. The Startup tab lets you enable a number of apps to start or lets you disable them when Windows 8.1 boots.

10. C. While the other logs reflect information specific to applications, security issues and the operating system, the Forwarded log receives events from remote systems.

11. A. Option A is the most likely answer because the log shows the name of the person who logged on to the system later that night. Option B is unlikely because a hacker would sign back in but be sure to not close any applications left running by the owner. Option C is plausible, but it would not account for the fact that applications are being closed since a network sourced hacker would not want to mess with the desktop. Option D is incorrect because the Security log does not report on system events such as a reboot.

12. B. Perfmon is one of the oldest applications on the Windows OS. To run it, enter **perfmon** in the Run box.

13. D. The higher the graph line in the pane, the more resources are being used.

14. A. You can create a data collector set to collect data about specific hardware resource usage.

15. B. A restore requires a restore point, which is a snapshot of the system files at a point in time. It returns the system files to that state.

16. B. You can create a data collector set to collect data about when certain events are fired in the system.

17. B. Resmon can be run from both the command line and the Run box, and it can be loaded from a menu option in Performance Monitor.

18. B. Run System Configuration. The fast way to load it is by entering **msconfig** in the Run box.

19. B. Reboot to the Windows installation CD and choose to repair your computer when the OS loads from the CD.

20. D. When all attempts to recover a machine fail, if you never created a restore point that can be accessed and used by System Restore to reimage the system quickly, then you cannot use the System Restore tool because it requires a restore point image.

Chapter 13

1. C. System Protection is best accessed from the Search feature of the Charms bar.

2. D. Note that you will need at least 300 MB of free space on each volume for restore points. System Protection does not need a lot of space for future multiple restore points and in fact overwrites the old ones you don't need.

3. B. To create a restore point, select the System Protection tab and click the Create button.

4. C. If the restore does not work, open System Restore, select the option Choose A Different Restore Point, and click Next. Then select the restore point labeled Undo and click Next.

5. B. Open Device Manager and, on the Driver tab for the sound card, select Roll Back Driver.

6. A. The next best step to take is to refresh the computer. This will return it to the state it was when it was first booted up but the user's files and data will be saved. Unfortunately, any applications installed during the life of the machine will have to be reinstalled. System Reset will destroy the user's data, and Last Known Good Configuration is no longer supported.

7. B. Using the PC Reset option, which does a destructive wipe of the computer's hard disk, is the fastest and most secure way of getting a clean machine up and running for a new user.

8. B. File History lets you back up files directly to a network share.

9. C. Search for the computer and folder to back up your files to. Once you arrive at the correct network location, click Select Folder. The Select Drive window will appear, open to the network drive you selected.

10. C, D. Click the Exclude Folders link on the left of the File History window. This will reduce the size of the backup. Option C is also correct because you can remove old versions of File History backups that have been superseded by more recent copies.

11. A. File History by default checks a file for changes every hour.

12. D. The default is 5%, but you can also choose 2%, 10%, or 20%.

13. D. File History copies can eat into your available disk space, so you can change how many versions of the saved files are kept. This option is called Keep Saved Versions.

14. A. The first thing to check is the Recycle Bin. Most deleted files end up in the Recycle Bin, where they can easily be recovered.

15. C. Access the Restore option by selecting the History button on the Home tab of File Explorer.

16. A. The Replace The File In The Destination option restores the version you selected.

17. C. System Protection is not supported in Windows 8.1 RT.

18. D. File History will not be available if the external drive is not attached.

19. A. Before turning on File History, note that File History will back up files from the following default locations:

   - Libraries
   - Desktop
   - Contacts
   - Favorites

20. A. The interval choices are as follows:

   - Every 10 Minutes
   - Every 15 Minutes
   - Every 20 Minutes
   - Every 30 Minutes
   - Every Hour (Default)
   - Every 3 Hours
   - Every 6 Hours
   - Every 12 Hours

Chapter 14

1. D. The Windows Store is an online service, so you need to ensure users have high-speed Internet access.

2. C. It's easy to learn about an app in the Store. Just click its tile. A page will load to display information about the app.

3.   A. The Windows Store is itself a Windows 8.1 app, so you can use the Windows Search tool to find apps. Simply display the Charms bar and click Search. In the Search field, type an app name or a keyword for an app and press Enter.

4.   C. AppLocker is supported on systems running Windows 7 and later and Software Restriction Policies is supported on systems running Windows Vista or earlier.

5.   A. If you no longer want an app installed on the computer, just uninstall it. To do this, right-click the app and choose Uninstall. Windows puts a check mark on the app's tile and displays a menu next to the app that asks you to verify your choice.

6.   D. When you run the toolkit, it makes an inventory of all the applications on the current system and logs all the information into a local database for you to access.

7.   C. ACT stores all user data in SQL Server.

8.   B. Setting up shim is not an easy task. It may be simpler to set up one of the Remote Desktop or remote application technologies. If you need to provide shim support, you can start the process by running the sdbins.exe application.

9.   D. The neat thing about Intune is that it targets both Windows apps (like the ones you get from the Store) as well as traditional software applications. It is also much easier to use than System Center Configuration Manager.

10.   A. Hyper-V brings a virtual machine to the desktop and through interaction with the host operating system lets you run a legacy operating system on your Windows 8.1 machine. You can then run applications that require Windows 7 in that virtual machine.

11.   B. The software needs a lot of memory (at least 4 GB), hard drive space, and CPU power on the host machine to run efficiently.

12.   C. The downside of the client Hyper-V is that it takes some effort to install and run on Windows 8.1 machines, and your users need to be somewhat tech savvy to be comfortable moving in and out of a virtual machine.

13.   A, B. Remote Desktop gives the user a similar experience to Hyper-V but you don't need so much RAM and hardware to make good use of it. With Remote Desktop and RemoteApp your user is actually connecting to a virtual machine sitting on a server somewhere.

14.   D. In some cases the application may run better on a dedicated machine that has the exclusive use of the host operating system and the machine's resources.

15.   D. Remote Desktop requires the user to log into the remote server and then run the application from within the Remote Desktop. RemoteApp takes away the need for the user to log in remotely because it runs the remote application through Remote Desktop and the user experiences what appears to be the application running locally.

Index

Note to the Reader: Throughout this index **boldfaced** page numbers indicate primary discussions of a topic. *Italicized* page numbers indicate illustrations.

X

Z

Free Online Learning Environment

Register on Sybex.com to gain access to the free online interactive learning environment and test bank to help you study for the MCSA exam.

The online test bank includes:

- Assessment Test to help you focus your study to specific objectives
- Chapter Tests to reinforce what you learned
- Practice Exams to test your knowledge of the material
- Electronic Flashcards to reinforce your learning and provide last-minute
- test prep before the exam
- Searchable Glossary gives you instant access to the key terms you'll need
- to know for the exam

Go to http://sybextestbanks.wiley.com to register and gain access to this comprehensive study tool package.